acting on words

an integrated rhetoric, reader, and handbook

david brundage / athabasca university

michael lahey / university of alberta

second edition

PEARSON

Prentice
Hall

Toronto

Library and Archives Canada Cataloguing in Publication

Brundage, David
    Acting on words : an integrated rhetoric, reader and handbook / David Brundage, Michael Lahey.—2nd ed.

Includes bibliographical references and index.
ISBN 978-0-13-243261-0

    1. Exposition (Rhetoric).   2. English language—Rhetoric—Textbooks.
3. College readers.   I. Lahey, Michael, 1954–   II. Title.

PE1408.B78 2008   808'.042   C2008-900175-3

ISBN-13: 978-0-13-243261-0
ISBN-10:   0-13-243261-7

Vice President, Editorial Director: Gary Bennett
Acquisitions Editor: Christopher Helsby
Marketing Manager: Sally Aspinall
Developmental Editor: Jody Yvonne
Production Editor: Avivah Wargon
Copy Editor: Claire Horsnell
Proofreaders: Judith Turnbull, Sharon Kirsch
Senior Production Coordinator: Patricia Ciardullo
Composition: Integra
Permissions Research: Beth McAuley
Art Director: Julia Hall
Cover Design: Jennifer Stimson
Interior Design: Geoff Agnew
Cover Image: © Steve McAlister/Gettyimages

For permission to reproduce copyrighted material, the publisher gratefully acknowledges the copyright holders listed on pages 575–577, which are considered an extension of this copyright page.

2 3 4 5   12 11 10 09 08

Printed and bound in United States of America.

For Professors Faith Guildenhuys, Tom Henighan, Robert Lovejoy, Robin MacDonald and the entire English Faculty of Carleton University, 1969 to 1975. Their commitment to student-centred teaching predated the term.
David Brundage

For Rosemary and Catherine Lahey, "whose lights burn clear."
Michael Lahey

Brief Contents

PART 3 THE HANDBOOK   515

Table of Contents

PART 2 THE READER 371

PART 3 THE HANDBOOK 515
See next page

PART 3 THE HANDBOOK 515

Introduction 516

Preface

TO THE INSTRUCTOR

Since the first edition of this book was published four years ago, we have been able to gather suggestions from dozens of instructors and, through them, thousands of students. We also received evaluations from hundreds more of our own students. Combined with the usual publisher-administered reviews and our own teaching experiences with the first edition, this reflective process helped us to confirm and refine our vision for the second. We dedicated many hours of research and writing toward the enrichments, not least of all a concerted effort to identify new student work that illustrates or responds to important parts of the text. We revised most sections of the book, smoothing readability, inserting many new insights and references that followed publication of the first edition, and generally striving to refresh this resource for us all. We believe the result should be a text that firmly preserves the strengths of the first edition while sharpening, expanding, and updating its methods and content.

As we know, many students enter college and university programs needing to mature in their reading, research, critical thinking, and analytical writing skills. None of these skills can be entirely separated from the others; each plays a crucial role in academic success. Adding support to your encouragement of those skills, we have provided more basic classical theory (especially logos, pathos, ethos) and more illustrations of persuasive appeal; more coverage of critical analysis and argument, with increased models of how the two combine in academic writing; more five-paragraph sample essays and essay outlines; more illustrations of MLA and APA documentation methods; and more consistent demonstration of academic documentation throughout all parts of the text. Many of you may wish to combine this text with Pearson's MyCanadianCompLab, which contains excellent guidance to reinforce Chapters 18 and 19 as well as the Handbook. For grammar quiz support in the "Fifteen Common Errors" section of the Handbook, see the *Acting on Words* Text Enrichment Site at <http://www.pearsoned.ca/brundage>.

In connection with strengthening our focus on *critical* work for this edition, we have increased the proportion of academic sample writing, particularly student writing. As well, many fine additional student essays that we did not have room to include can be easily accessed on the Text Enrichment Site. We now present our Rhetoric *before* the Reader, in recognition that students focus on their post-secondary work through assignment questions calling for various written responses. Based on the nature of the writing assignment called for, students, with your direction, can make their way to the appropriate parts of the Rhetoric and from there to other related sections of the text. We believe that placing the Rhetoric first will appeal to most users by reinforcing the main concern with critical writing. We have also adjusted organization within the three main parts of the text to clarify their presentation of ideas and practice.

While we have increased the focus on critical skills and styles, we have nevertheless continued to give attention to more personal and journalistic forms. Over the years we have come increasingly to believe that for many students, academic writing is best learned through recognizing its location in the family of writing, through exploring personal voice and basic issues inherent in all writing occasions. So we still treat the personal essay and various forms influenced by the creative non-fiction of our time—yet we do so within a clear intent of encouraging students to draw from those experiences, as critical writers.

We like to say that if writing is breathing out, then reading is breathing in. You will find expanded attention to effective reading in this edition of the text. While our first-edition Reader certainly appealed to students and instructors, we have provided updates and made adjustments to maintain a current connection to the issues represented as well as to sharpen attention to critical reading awareness. We believe the Reader continues to offer a valuable range of issues to interest and challenge today's Canadian students. Many of the pieces represent achieved levels of literary craft; others present accomplished student work within reach of diligent, motivated undergrads; still others invite analysis of media purpose, style, and effect. The range of related concerns and styles throughout the Reader should offer much to serve your particular interests and approaches. Those familiar with the first edition will see that a substantial number of pieces have remained. Those pieces have worked well and remain current in their own ways, and we have sharpened their presentation and added student responses to them.

We have continued to focus our address on the needs of Canadian students. However, we have aimed equally to serve those students who come from other countries or who will go on to other countries. Not least, we hope this text serves *you*, the most important resource of all in the work of learning—the instructor.

Supplements

For a wide range of additional support, the following supplements are available for downloading from a password-protected section of Pearson Education Canada's online catalogue (<http://vig.pearsoned.ca>). Navigate to your book's catalogue page to view a list of the supplements available. See your local sales representative for details and access.

Instructor's Manual The Instructor's Manual (978-0-13-239348-5) is an extensive, in-depth guide to teaching with *Acting on Words,* Second Edition. It provides practical guidance to instructors addressing such important concerns as approaches to teaching; creating an effective syllabus; marking and student evaluation; dealing with grammar and mechanics; and English as a foreign language. It offers instructors examples of how to enhance the topics addressed in the text; sample summaries; a rhetorical table of contents for the Reader; and a comprehensive set of overheads, which can be used in the classroom in multiple ways.

Text Enrichment Site The authors have created an integrated Text Enrichment Site to enhance *Acting on Words,* Second Edition. The site provides rich support content, including model documents, supplementary readings, quizzes, sample essays, and language support, which relate directly to the core text. Wherever you see the web icon, you know there is valuable, content-related support material available on the Text Enrichment Site.

TO THE STUDENT

Welcome to *Acting on Words*, a set of guidelines and selected readings aimed at assisting and inspiring your ability to handle the challenges before you as an evolving scholar. The central goal of this book is to increase your success in all courses that require critical reading, research, and writing—probably all of the courses you will take at university.

Over many years of working with student writers—some of whom initially believe, often incorrectly, that they cannot write and do not like writing—we have heard many of the same concerns and questions. What does my instructor mean by "critical thinking"? What does my instructor mean by "employ rhetoric"? Why does your book tell us to place our thesis sentence at the end of the first paragraph when not that many readings in the Reader of this book seem to do that? What's wrong with using Wikipedia? And what's "academic documentation style," anyway? I never learned any grammar terms or how to edit a sentence—how am I going to deliver the correct sentences and punctuation my program says it requires? Suggesting brief answers to these questions may be the best way we can introduce you to this book and its potential to enrich your academic career and, we hope, your life in general.

Let's start with the first question about "critical thinking." Helping you to understand and apply critical thinking within the academy is the central purpose of your first-year writing, business, communications, or English course; it is therefore the main purpose of this text. As we explain in more detail in Chapter 14, the word "critical" in university usage does *not* mean fault-finding or hostile censure. In their trenchant book *They Say, You Say: The Moves That Matter in Academic Writing*, Gerald Graff and Cathy Birkenstein summarize the essence of critical thinking at university: it is a matter of recognizing exactly what is being said on a particular issue of importance and then adding something useful of your own to the discussion. They say . . . and then you say. . . . This basic operation sums up a majority of work at university. Doing it well requires command of the methods covered in this text—how to summarize, how to analyze the language of a text when its main assertions do not appear obvious, how to evaluate the assertions of a text, how to find and evaluate sources of further information on the topic, how to reach your own position—what *you* say—and, finally, how to organize and write an effective, persuasive essay that contributes your views. The various parts of this book, then, all serve this central need to understand and practise critical thinking and writing.

"Rhetoric" in its original, classical sense—as we use it here—does not mean dishonest language but rather *the art of language*. This art functions at the level of words, sentences, paragraphs, and complete structures. If you decide to explain a point by using a comparison, you are applying rhetoric. If you recognize that an essay assignment calls for third-person point of view and a general or even formal level of diction, you are employing rhetorical awareness. As this book and the courses it serves aim ultimately to strengthen your critical thinking and writing, attention to the basic dynamics of writing (covered in Chapters 1 to 7) and to the various patterns of writing (covered in Chapters 8 to 12) should help you sharpen the rhetorical tools you need to inform your analytical (i.e., critical) writing. Increasing your command of rhetoric, therefore, does not consign you to a ship of "phony politicians"; it simply awakens and intensifies your awareness of the nature and effects of language.

As well as encouraging you to think critically, this text will help you to write effective essays for course purposes. Your papers must quickly demonstrate that they have a central point to make and go on to make it. In Chapter 6 we therefore discuss the parts of a complete thesis statement, and we recommend placing that statement at the end of your opening paragraph. This formula helps you to ensure your paper is on track and remains on track; this positioning of your thesis reassures your instructor that you have come to a clear, interesting, critical position, one that will focus your entire essay. Our advice to you concerning thesis elements and location considers the situation you are in as an undergraduate writer. You must write to the occasion, and to your reader, and to your purpose. This restriction doesn't mean that everything you go on to write for all readers under all occasions will need a thesis at the end of the first paragraph (though that technique is surprisingly versatile!).

Nor will you be expected to limit your reading—your search for further sources of information—to other undergraduate essays. While we recommend that you hone complete, precise thesis statements in your own essays, you will surely encounter written and spoken material that does not always present an explicit thesis statement at the end of the first paragraph. You will need to develop your ability to find the main ideas in many different styles of writing. You may well go on to explore philosophers, anthropologists, psychologists, physicists, literary theorists, linguists, and so on. Our Reader therefore reflects a wide range of styles, from classical and highly academic to personal, evocative, and journalistic. Much of the sample writing in the Reader (as opposed to that in the Rhetoric) is not purely academic, and much of it forgoes the formal approach to thesis placement that we recommend in Chapter 6 and that we demonstrate in sample student essays throughout the book. Your awareness of academic style, however, is increased by recognizing its distinctions from other forms. The Reader represents not so much a taste of academic style as a taste of styles, from personal to highly analytical and argumentative. Drawing from those styles, as well as grasping and responding to the important issues presented by the readings, will certainly develop your skills and awareness as a scholar, your growth in critical thinking. You will gain a deeper appreciation of how academic style is based on both carefully assembling and precisely evaluating reliable sources while you contribute your own original critical responses.

We think you will find much in the Reader to capture your interest, but we encourage you to dig into even those pieces that do not seem immediately interesting. Increasing your rhetorical awareness means encouraging yourself to become a more active reader—a reader who questions and probes. Question what a sentence really means—what are the implications of its words but also the effects of their stylistic presentation? Chapters 13, 15, and 16 are specially designed to increase your "higher-level" reading skills. The same degree of questioning that we encourage in those chapters on reading should guide your thinking as you search for additional information on assigned topics.

This questioning, of course, brings us to the subject of research. Is a source of information written by someone who truly understands the subject? Has the information been reviewed and edited by other experts? Has it been properly tested? Wikipedia, for example, is a reader-generated source; its entries are not approved by editors expert in the many fields in question. While studies suggest that Wikipedia may—surprisingly—be more accurate than some critics imagine, it has no guarantee of reliability. Anyone can add to its contents—how do we know that the contributors are experts and have taken care to be completely accurate? As part of your critical thinking at university, you will increase your ability to find and evaluate useful, reliable sources of further information. Various parts of this text, particularly Chapters 18 and 19, present the reasoning behind research methods and how those methods work.

 We can also reassure you that taking control of grammar and punctuation can usually be accomplished by the end of your course through careful, systematic use of the Handbook and associated quizzes at the Text Enrichment Site. Our "Fifteen Common Errors" approach allows you and your instructor to find the main points of grammar that may be most in need of attention in your work. Perhaps just three or four of the common errors will apply in your case; after diagnosing your current knowledge and skills (see quizzes and answer keys at the Text Enrichment Site for the Handbook, Section 3), you can pursue the recommended background information for each specific common correction.

To give the issue of grammar within writing and critical thinking some further special attention, you might also read Rebecca Dickens's speech "Language Arts or Language Departs?" at the Text Enrichment Site, Chapter 16. Do you share her ideas and experiences? Is she right in suggesting that grammar is *language algebra*, and that astrophysics could hardly proceed without precise use of fundamental mathematics? If sciences haven't neglected algebra, why should arts neglect grammar? More discussion of why we make a mistake by marginalizing grammer can be found in "The Five Myths of Grammar" at the Text Enrichment Site for the Handbook. The five myths suggest that grammar is (1) impossible to understand and apply, (2) dry and boring, (3) superficial, (4) limited to "right" and "wrong," and (5) irrelevant to freedom, democracy, and respect for community. Give this essay a chance—go to the Handbook site, read the essay carefully, then decide if these five points are or are not harmful assumptions.

Based on how many former students *have* become interested in the logic of grammar in writing, we expect you will assess your current grammar knowledge and begin to apply our tips for increasing it. We can't provide overnight solutions, but we do offer a system that has been serving well to catch students up to speed (as simply and painlessly as possible) with their grammar and punctuation. To give this aspect of your writing a chance, consider that grammar is simply part of understanding how things work—a core purpose of university thinking.

As you may gather from the tone of these introductory remarks, we don't expect your writing or your English course, or your use of this book, to be immediately easy. We expect, from much experience, that you will need to work on becoming an *active* participant by defining for yourself what university scholarship really entails. It entails active thinking and participation in your learning, an ability to find small important details, understand processes, and see connections to a bigger picture. Your course and this book may be considered analogous to a surfboard. It takes much basic understanding and repeated effort to climb aboard in the right stance, but once you can do that, the experience truly begins.

ACKNOWLEDGMENTS

Many talented and dedicated people have contributed their time and efforts to *Acting on Words*. We would like to thank writing instructor Karen Overbye for material on logos, pathos, and ethos, much of Chapter 15, "Rhetorical Analysis," text site materials, and extensive editorial review. Professor Rebecca Cameron provided major portions of Chapter 11 ("How-to Instructions, Process Description and Definition"), Chapter 18 "Research Methods," and Chapter 19 "Documentation." Joyce Miller wrote Chapter 20, "Oral Presentations," designed and edited "Sample Oral Presentations" (at the text website), contributed several model essays, and wrote "Writing a Film Review," part of "Film and Literary Analysis" at the web site, Chapter 15. Marlene Wurfle, with generous support from the Centre for Language and Literature of Athabasca University, contributed research, editing and writing for the Reader, as did Professor Jolene Armstrong. Veronica Baig contributed important sections of the Handbook and designed our Language Support for the Reader at the text website. Veronica Baig also provided several of the language support entries; Marlene Wurfle provided the majority of language supports accompanying this edition. A number of valuable Reader contributions, retained from the first edition, were made by Lisa Cameron, also with support of the Centre for Language and Literature, Athabasca University. Contributing as well to the Reader, first edition, was Robbie Chernish. Sally Hayward wrote extensive grammar material for the text website, Handbook.

Tasha Ausman wrote much of Chapter 17, "Essays in Examinations," and web support guidelines on "Writing and Revising a Scientific Paper" and "Writing a Case Analysis." Athabasca University editor John Ollerenshaw reviewed our first edition version of, "Documentation" (now Chapter 19). Reference librarians Ione Hooper of the University of Alberta and Pat Wauters of the Lethbridge Public Library provided valuable assistance with research. Theresa Daniels, Shamim Datoo, Carolyn Preshing, and their administrative colleagues with the Department of English at the University of Alberta gave generously of their time in the preparation of the manuscript. Tasha Ausman tracked down a number of copyright holders for the first edition.

Joyce Miller worked extensively on permissions for the first edition. Shari Mitchell contributed manuscript assistance to both editions. We wish to express our deepest thanks to all for these services.

In addition, we wish to thank Marian Allen, co-author of *Forms of Writing*, for having pioneered approaches and standards of great value to this book. Similar recognition is owing to writing course designer and coordinator John Thompson. We thank the fine tutorial staff of Athabasca University's English 255 Introductory Composition as well; their numerous suggestions have made a significant contribution. William Aguiar, Blue Quills First Nations College, offered particularly helpful recommendations for Chapter 14, "Critical Analysis and Evaluation." He also proposed readings that have made an important contribution to this edition. Sharren Patterson of Mount Royal College and Donald McMann of MacEwan College similarly provided valuable manuscript contributions. Peter Roccia, program chair in the MacEwan School of Communications, offered helpful strategies and direction at the outset of the first edition.

Kelly Torrance made this book possible with essential support and understanding in the formative stages. Former Acquisitions Editor Marianne Minaker enabled the next step to reality; she and the entire team at Pearson Education were a pleasure to work with, as have been Jody Yvonne, Avivah Wargon, Beth McAuley, Claire Horsnell, Judith Turnbull, and the entire production team on the second edition. We thank them and especially Vice-President/Editorial Director Michael J. Young and Acquisitions Editor Christopher Helsby for granting us the opportunity to "have at it" under our own lights. Any possible indiscretions that may have resulted from this support and freedom must be considered our doing, not theirs.

On a personal note, we thank the following instructors for their support, guidance, and inspiration, past and present: Professors Lynn Penrod and Mark Simpson of the University of Alberta; Professors Stanley Cowan, John Fraser, Bruce Greenfield, Ron Huebert, and Victoria Rosenberg of Dalhousie University; and Professors Ann J. Abadie, Donald Kartiganer, and Jay Watson of the Center for Southern Culture, University of Mississippi.

It will be clear from some of the readings and other references in this text that we have been readers and admirers of *Reader's Choice* by Kim Flachmann, Michael Flachmann, and Alexandra MacLennan; the *Canadian Writer's Workplace* by Gary Lipschutz, John Roberts, John Scarry, and Sandra Scarry; and *Forms of Writing* by Kay Stewart, Chris Bullock, and Marian Allen. Finally, we are greatly indebted to our many reviewers, including Marc Hewson, Chandra Hodgson, and James Howes, who offered wonderful advice and suggestions at various stages of the manuscript's development.

INTRODUCTION

RHETORIC, in the classic sense, refers to the art of using language: it is the craft of shaping spoken and written persuasions. By "persuasions" we mean to suggest the classical idea that all successful speeches and essays affect us as the writer intended: the works deepen our knowledge and understanding, motivate us to action, and possibly even exert some nurturing magic within. Achieved rhetoric persuades us that the author knows the subject well and has something interesting to add to it. The writer combines knowledge of the subject with logic, feeling, and ethical awareness in proper proportion relative to the purpose and intended audience of the speech or essay.

Based on reader responses to the first edition of this book, we believe our Rhetoric is sufficiently complete to serve all your learning needs as an undergraduate writer and communicator. We have not changed too much from the previous edition, but enough, we hope, to have enhanced the logic, efficiency, thoroughness, and impact of the presentation. Section 1 invites you to enter into the state of mind of a writer and consider what writing *is*. In suggesting important answers to that question, we move on to review basic matters of tone, logic, paragraph skills, and essay outlines. Section 2 takes a close look at different ways you can pattern your writing according to the specific needs raised by the assignment.

Section 3 covers research and citation methods, with enhanced attention to common concerns. Section 4 deals with the special concerns of oral presentations, while Section 5 reinforces that successful writing depends on revision. We have laid out this guidance in a carefully staged progression, yet many readers will find it perfectly manageable to dip into the various self-contained sections without needing to review any or much of the preceding material. The Rhetoric is a reference—a set of guidelines to answer central questions and provide practical direction: it is not something that must be read from start to finish.

A practical approach to using this Rhetoric is to take initial guidance from your essay assignments. What sort of essay is a certain assignment directing you to write? What main terms and concepts surround that type of essay? Go to the relevant part of the Rhetoric for guidance based on the type of essay your assignment requires that you write. If it is a personal essay, see Chapter 8. If it is an analytical essay, see Chapter 14. If it is an argumentative essay, see Chapter 16. Most university essays ask you to perform a combination of analysis and argumentation—so you will likely benefit by giving close attention to sections of the Rhetoric dealing with those important modes.

We have organized our Rhetoric in part to suggest the three stages of writing: pre-writing, drafting, and revising. Even after pre-writing, researching, and outlining, you may find that your first draft is more an exploration of what you want to say than a firm statement. You will need a second draft to sharpen your discoveries, your controlling idea, and your support for that main idea. Finally, you will need to revise to heighten appeals at key locations, to correct grammar, and to perfect style. Successful writers, amateur and professional alike, invariably work through the three basic stages: pre-writing, drafting, and revising. The first and last stages should each represent a substantial proportion of the time dedicated to completing the work. Learning to apply this professional approach and process will make a major contribution to your academic success.

Perhaps the major "change" in this edition of the Rhetoric is our increased effort on almost every page to address the challenge of writing analytical persuasions—essays that convincingly present the findings of your original thinking on assigned topics. Achieving this type of writing requires the ability to summarize as well as research and citation skills. We have provided many new student-length and student-level illustrations of analytical papers using research. We also offer outlining reminders in most chapters along with frequent demonstrations of correct citation methods. In the following pages, from essay writing in general to personal writing, exposition, summaries, evaluations, argument models, research methods, and oral presentations, you should find all you need to hone your writing and communication skills.

THE
RHETORIC

Section 1 Reviewing
the Basics

INTRODUCTION

Your team has gone into an ugly slump. The home reporters wring their hands, calling for trades and benchings, suggesting underlying personal scandals. But the coach has a better idea. He changes practices back to basic skills drills: passing, skating, positional play. He assigns certain players to work on conditioning. By and by the team is playing well again. The same scenario occurs in other professions. Even the most skilled and talented musicians can begin to get lazy, cut corners, stop doing the little things that allow communication of rich thought and feeling. Concert players, as we know, practise hours every day. Asked to play at a party, one might reply, "No, I haven't touched the piano in three days."

The point of these analogies—that dedication and practice are needed in order to improve a particular skill set—applies to writing. People say, "It's hard to write well," with a certain surprise and exasperation, as if it shouldn't be. Yet few would be surprised that athletes and musicians work hard and regularly to stay in the condition required to do their jobs. No one expects a young person to begin solving math problems without practice and training (though exceptions occur). The problem may be a widespread logical fallacy: the over-simplification or false analogy that because we all use words in daily communication (and don't use lots of math, for example), then to handle problem-solving, words must be much easier tools to handle than numbers. But daily conversation *isn't* writing or oral presentation. In fact, in many ways, it is the opposite, with many habits that must be "unlearned," that are actually harmful to achieved communication (since most communication is an outcome of problem-solving). So the best thing you can do as you approach the basics of writing is to empty your mind of any trace of familiarity. Pretend that you don't know anything about words, have never used them before. You are here to learn what words are and how they affect people and therefore the world we live in. Is this hard? The better word is *required*.

Ask a concert player or an athlete if training daily is hard and you will get many different answers. There is no reason at all why practising one's craft should be less than fulfilling and enjoyable. The attitude toward basic practice depends on the individual. A great many people take deep satisfaction in practising a craft and thereby performing it well. Attention to the basics is required in order to write well. Again, it is easy to miss this point because we don't see writers skating laps or playing arpeggios. Much of writerly practice is mental, attitudinal. Some professional musicians will tell you that when they are separated from their instruments, they are able to practise successfully in their imagination. This is how writers practise, much of the time. To do so means gaining a new attitude. That is why we suggest that you enter this section, "Reviewing the Basics," with the attitude of a complete newcomer to the craft of writing, regardless of how much writing you may have done, how much praise you may have received, even how many books you may have read—although if you haven't read many books, get started!

This section does indeed review crucial guidelines in the use of logic, paragraph craft, and essay outlines—basics that should enrich your entire writing future. Before these basics truly sink in, however, you may need an even more important basic comprehension of what writing is—an "attitude adjustment." In our introduction to this text, we suggested that it is not necessary to read *Acting on Words* from cover to cover, that it is primarily a reference tool to be used for various issues as needed, based on assignment specifications. While that is true, we believe that almost everyone should read this section, if nothing else—especially Chapters 1 and 2. The experience is more likely to be rewarding than otherwise—have fun!

Chapter 1

What Is Writing?

Writing is both the act of putting thoughts on paper for purposes of communication and the resulting text that intends to communicate. The key words here are "communication" and "communicate." Effective writing requires the writer to be thoroughly aware of the topic or issue under discussion as well as aware of the intended reader(s) and, by implication, of the reason for the communication.

READER AWARENESS

Effective writers form a strong sense of their intended readers: what do the intended readers know about the subject already? What more should they know? What methods of expressing that information will be most comprehensible for them? The term used again and again by writing instructors is "reader awareness." Unless you consider your intended readers, you may not engage, inform, or persuade them, even though what you have written seems clear and successful to you.

Your Reader

A good person for you to consider as the primary intended reader for many of your university papers is another course student, one who is keenly interested and active in the process of learning. This may simply be an imagined, idealized student, not necessarily one actual person. Let's hope that most or even all of your peers on the course are, like you, interested and active. For this course, however, you and your instructor may wish to set up different writing "occasions" for some of your assignments: that is, you may wish to imagine that you are writing to a particular audience and "market" (perhaps outside the university) for a particular purpose. This increased or specialized attention to reader awareness can be an excellent means of growing as a writer.

Try This Exercise: What Writing Is

To put yourself in the place of a writer, try the following exercise. Your goal is to describe the design in Figure 1.1 to another person in such clear descriptive language that your partner in the exercise is able to draw a close facsimile of the design.

Figure 1.1

PRACTICE
What Writing Is

To gain from this exercise, you must follow certain rules. Your partner must not have seen the design in Figure 1.1. So if your partner is a class member who has already looked at the figure, simply draw or obtain another design of your own. Try to match the irregular nature of Figure 1.1 in your own drawing. Don't make it too complicated or too simple; note that Figure 1.1 is neither too busy nor too regular. It does not contain numerous details, but those it does contain tend to be irregular and abstract. Having decided on the drawing you are to describe, sit back-to-back with your partner. He or she is not allowed to ask any questions whatsoever. Take no more than three minutes to describe your design to your partner. Remind yourself and your partner that there are no questions allowed.

When your three minutes are up, compare your design to the one your partner has drawn according to your verbal directions. If the communication was not entirely successful, discuss why that may have been. Consider and discuss the implications of this exercise for the act of writing. Then see the Text Enrichment Site, Chapter 1, for our further commentary on what this exercise represents about the challenges of effective written communication.

Word Connotations

The problem of words meaning different things to different people can be best appreciated in the case of certain words that tend to be loaded with strong emotional connotations. *The Nelson Canadian Dictionary* defines connotation as "[a]n idea or meaning suggested by or associated with a word." This association need not be the meaning given by the dictionary. To test out this idea, do the following exercise.

PRACTICE
Word Connotations

Draw a line across a piece of paper and mark the left end of the line as minus 5. Mark the right end of the line as plus 5. Place a zero at the middle point of the line. Your line now represents a spectrum, from −5 to +5. Now read the following list of eight words and rate each along the spectrum, according to how you feel about each word. If the word has extremely good connotations for you, give it plus 5. If it has extremely bad connotations for you, give it minus 5. Be as precise as you can in placing each word on the spectrum, but trust your initial emotional response to tell you where the word should be. Here are the exercise words:

Feminist
Politics
Marriage

Homosexual
Occult
Tradition
Peacekeepers
Rhetoric

With classmates and your instructor, explore the range of negative to positive responses that may occur through this exercise. Consider and discuss different writing situations that might present a writer with readers who harbour strong connotative meanings of words that conflict with the denotative meanings. Consider and discuss various strategies the writer might adopt to avoid distancing and possibly losing readers. Then see the Text Enrichment Site, Chapter 1, for our commentary on this exercise.

Since we have been discussing reader awareness, and rhetoric as a response to that awareness, as well as the history of language, now is a good time to introduce a little more formal (and classical) theory on how writing works.

PERSUASIVE APPEALS: LOGOS, PATHOS, AND ETHOS

As you will see from exploring the different sections of our Rhetoric and Reader, writing falls into a wide range of categories—and often one piece of writing stretches across the borders of two or more categories, incorporating certain characteristics of each—but all effective writing shares the characteristic of being *persuasive*. Personal and evocative writing persuades the reader that the writer really lived these experiences, really understands the characters and places being described, really feels the emotions and insights being expressed. Expository writing persuades the reader that there is a valuable and perhaps not so valuable way to understand the topic; effective exposition convinces the reader that the writer truly knows the topic and that the topic has something to offer. Successful argumentation persuades the reader, in spite of recognizing opposing views, to recognize the merits of the author's proposed way of dealing with a certain controversy. In short, all effective writing, in its own ways according to its own special purposes and audiences, is *persuasive*.

Classical rhetoric (the art of composition) refers to persuasive attributes as *appeals*: that is, the writing, in some sense, reaches out and contacts the reader. Despite the numerous ways in which a piece of writing may engage its readers, instructors often agree with Aristotle (the classical rhetorical authority, 384–322 BCE) that the appeals of persuasive writing fall under three main areas. These are *logos* (logical or rational appeal), *pathos* (emotional appeal), and *ethos* (ethical appeal or writer credibility). While the methods of applying these appeals are not completely discrete, each area has some distinctive features. Understanding these appeals and how they are used can benefit both your own writing and your ability to recognize the strengths and weaknesses in the written persuasions of others. You have read enough in this chapter already to be mindful of the logical, emotional, and ethical dynamics that operate when we read or write; the following gives these dynamics a little more traditional, theoretical context.

Logos

Logos literally means "word" and refers to the authority of the word, or logic. All logical arguments depend on the writer's judicious use of logos or logical appeal. This means the development of your argument, your reasoning, must be logical, and you must provide evidence as support for the points you make. For two basic forms of reasoning, see "Induction" and "Deduction" (Chapter 3, "More About Logic"). Stephen Toulmin's argument model (discussed in Chapters 13, 15, and 16) provides a "modern" approach to detecting and applying basic reasoning. All the methods of development that you may look at in Chapters 9 to 12, especially comparison/contrast and cause/effect, can serve as rhetorical strategies whereby you can help convince your readers of the strength of your argument. Note that it is important to balance personal examples with logic, because personal examples may be more emotionally compelling than logically sound, as you will be reminded in Chapter 3 (in reference to various logical fallacies) and in Chapter 4 in a discussion of "warm" and "cool" proofs.

The evidence that you use in your argument must be sound; it must be accessible to testing and verification. Evidence may take the form of facts, statistics (bearing in mind that statistics involve varying levels of interpretation in their presentation), primary sources (eye-witness testimony, legal transcripts, ledgers, and other original pieces of evidence), and secondary sources (such as analysis by experts). Refer to Chapter 18's sections on primary and secondary sources, and especially to the sections on evaluating sources if you need help. And you can also look at the Text Enrichment Site under Chapter 18, "Interviews," for information on a too-often neglected source of new information and insight.

In any logical argument, logos must operate effectively to affirm your appeal. You will notice that the effectiveness of the sample argumentative analysis "Kyoto Discord," in Chapter 14 of the Rhetoric, depends largely on logos. The writer uses facts, statistics, and expert opinions to suggest that the positive effects of accepting the Kyoto Accord outweigh the negative ones. However, as Lee Jennings, who critiques "The Right Stuff" in Chapter 14, points out, Suzuki's essay "The Right Stuff" lacks evidence that would prove the usefulness of his proposal because Suzuki provides only a personal example rather than pointing to any other expert opinions or suggesting any reasonable process by which his method of teaching science could be implemented in high school.

We have discussed logos first not because it is most important (consider Jonathan Swift's famous satirical essay "A Modest Proposal" for an example of mock logos operating without true ethos or pathos). We have discussed logos first because as a college or university student, you will be expected, above all, to handle the logical demands of your assignments. Academic writing—emphasizing analysis and analytical persuasion and often subordinating more personal forms of writing—does place an emphasis on logos. As we explain below, careful attention to logos in academe helps you as a student to gain an increased degree of personal credibility—or ethos—on a topic that may be still relatively new to you.

Pathos

Pathos means "suffering," but in the more modern sense, it refers to appeals that may trigger a variety of emotions: sympathy or empathy, fear, sense of loss or grief, and even anger, to name the most common. An argument that relies mostly on emotional appeal may be persuasive in the short term, but as for those people who are swayed at rallies by emotional appeals alone, the light of day demands logical evidence as well. Ideally, pathos adds to logos so that the audience is "touched" by an argument. For example, an argument made for Canada to send more aid to countries in need might begin with a story of a needy family. As long as that argument is then backed up with other logical appeals, it will garner the interest and immediate sympathy of the readers. Another writer might wish to create anger about an unjust situation, and yet another essay may try to evoke fear so that the audience will be concerned about gang violence, for example.

The main rhetorical methods you will use to create emotional appeal are description (particularly figurative language) and narration, methods that draw the reader in. These are discussed under "The Personal Essay" in Chapter 8, under "Example" in Chapter 10, and again in "Literary and Film Analysis" at the Text Enrichment Site, Chapter 15. Description and narration need not be confined to personal writing or fictional forms. Description and narration can contribute in significant ways to analytical and formal argumentative forms.

Used moderately, emotional appeal is powerful. It represents what we describe in Chapter 4, "Paragraph Skills," as *warm proofs*. If pathos is overdone, however, the appeal can seem insincere and manipulative: readers will feel distracted from the argument itself. You need to be careful, for example, not to use overly emotional language to convey misery, as in the following statement: "In the time that you have taken to read this paragraph, sipping on your three-dollar cup of coffee from the latest trendy outlet, another emaciated, fly-ridden child has died of hunger in abject poverty." Your statement is bound to induce guilt, perhaps even undue guilt, because the causes of gross inequality may well be more complex than your appeal intends to suggest. As mentioned in the previous discussion of word connotations, you need to be sensitive to the "trigger" potential of many words and descriptions. These can result in undesired emotional distraction. The tone recommended for most university analysis and formal argumentation is *moderate*—meaning that your pathos has been subordinated appropriately.

Certain writers may deliberately give pathos rein in the interests of manipulating readers without recourse to complex, balanced thought. Indeed, pathos is a key device in propaganda techniques: methods intended to sway an audience by escaping the notice of logos. Consider the following example: "You can be sure that once the Harper government has been in office for one term, its members will be too used to having their snouts in the troughs to listen to ordinary folk." In this example, the writer has used inflammatory language to convince readers to separate themselves from any connection to the writer's perceived opposition. See the discussion of logical fallacies in Chapter 3, especially fallacies 7 to 10, for problems that occur from the misuse of pathos. One reason that academic writing has traditionally favoured third-person viewpoint is that by removing the "I" from your text, you may be encouraged to shift your perception from personal focus and emotions to the logos required by your topic. Depending on the level of formality of your paper, you should consider using third person. Then, when you do include explicit emotional appeals, your readers will have the choice of involvement and not feel unduly pressured to react in one way.

On the other hand, because traditional rhetoric and the Western academy encourage a respect for logos, let us not succumb to an either/or fallacy (see Chapter 3) by deciding to elevate and perhaps even distort logos at the expense of pathos. Pathos is an essential of all writing, even forms that emphasize logos. A writer needs to feel strongly about the subject, even if that feeling should be explicitly expressed only in certain places. Often, you can gain the reader's attention by using pathos in your introduction, and by using pathos at key moments in the paper. Pathos properly used at the end of your paper can help evoke reader action.

In "Kyoto Discord" (Chapter 14) Gwen Kelley uses an emotional appeal in paragraph 6 when she asks her readers to "imagine that our mother became ill." Here the readers' concern for their own mothers connects to the concern for the earth as figurative "mother." The writer wisely keeps emotional appeal to a minimum on the controversial topic of the acceptance of the Kyoto Accord. Suzuki is more dependent on pathos in "The Right Stuff," where he begins with an anecdote seasoned with a note of nostalgia for his readers—the target audience who would likely be parents concerned about their children's (particularly teenaged children's) education. By referring to his own high school experience, he invites his readers to remember their own. After they have done so, and they remember what they learned in those days, they will be more ready to hear about his proposal. At the end, he returns to having his readers think about how lessons in high school will be recalled "vividly."

Before we leave this brief introduction to pathos, two related points that have run implicitly through the above discussion are worth considering explicitly. The first was mentioned earlier in our discussion of word connotations. As pointed out by

G.I. Gurdjieff (1872–1949) and many other analysts of human nature, emotions are faster and stronger than thoughts. As Sigmund Freud (1856–1939) and other psychoanalysts have observed, if we repress or deny emotions, we will not genuinely control those emotions, but quite the opposite. A veneer of logic may be spread over a repository of unexpressed, unresolved emotions, creating a disturbing parody of balance. In conjunction with this important point—too often neglected in a society that elevates "strong" logic over "weak" emotion— it would be useful for you to read Wayne Booth's essay "The Rhetorical Stance" (Reader, p. 488). There he advocates for reader-writer relationships that balance the needs of the writer, the topic, and the reader. He describes various "corrupt" stances that occur when the desired balance, necessary for a good relationship, is not truly achieved. We might evaluate writing on a similar basis using the litmus test of logos, pathos, and ethos—when looking at a piece of writing, we need to ask if these three have been sufficiently recognized and incorporated in a truly purposeful relationship by the writer.

The second point that must be acknowledged is that in too many cases, the Western academic tendency to elevate logos over pathos (and some critics might even argue over ethos as well) results in what Elizabeth Sargent and Cornelia Paraskevas have described as "horrible writing":

> While we waste our time fighting over ideological conformity in the scholarly world, horrible writing remains a far more important problem. For all their differences, most right-wing scholars and most left-wing scholars share a common allegiance to a cult of obscurity. Left, right, and center all hide behind the idea that unintelligible prose indicates a sophisticated mind. (226)

Odd cultural values and imbalances, some of us would argue, have resulted in the prevalence of academic writing that displays what Booth calls "corrupt stances," especially the "pedant's stance," one that buries pathos in a desire to demonstrate "sophisticated" logos. A good way to avoid following the leader into this trap is to make sure you respect and include pathos along with logos. At times you may feel pressured between the guidelines to balance logos, pathos, and ethos on one hand and the apparent expectations of academic style on the other. It is in just such difficult challenges, however, that you come alive as an independent thinker and writer— doing your best to reconcile the stylistic expectations of some of your courses with your increasing awareness of the needs of considerate writing that truly balances its dimensions, respects its readers, and effectively appeals to all essentials of human experience and understanding.

Ethos

Ethos means, literally, "character." Some texts explain ethos as *ethical appeal*, meaning that the writer must have a demonstrated right to speak on the topic. Often this means finding the right angle from which to view the topic, an angle that does not claim more authority than the writer has, yet one that also brings something informative to the subject. On certain subjects, we simply lack sufficient knowledge and credibility; in such instances, we are best to hold silent, at least until we have "paid our dues" through sufficient learning. Writers sometimes speak of the need to "earn" their material. Certain discussions pose immediate demands for credibility—we need to anticipate those.

For an argument to be accepted, the person making the argument must be seen to share with his or her audience at least a fundamental understanding about what is right and what is wrong on the subject. In a recent article, journalist George Jonas "refutes the popular notions . . . that the Holocaust was a unique event, and that it arose from a peculiarly German kind of anti-Semitism" (47). Many North American readers, hearing this thesis, would be inclined to separate themselves from the writer, on grounds of ethical disconnection. It could sound as if Jonas is out to support those who would deny the Holocaust. But Jonas begins by saying, "I spent the first 10 years of my life in Nazi-occupied Europe. My immediate family and I survived the war by hiding. Since I kept no diary, had the Nazis found me as they had found Anne Frank, I would have disappeared without a trace" (47). The fact that Jonas was among those persecuted in Germany provides a degree of ethos that may encourage otherwise resistant readers to hear what he has to say. The opposing perspectives must be treated fairly: their good points acknowledged, but any logical fallacies also pointed out.

Many students worry, understandably, that because they are taking introductory subjects they are in the position of junior researchers, not "experts." They fear that they therefore have no ethos. You can, however, establish your authority by showing effective use of logos, by showing that you have consulted a variety of sound sources of evidence, especially those of experts, those who have established ethos. In most respects as a student writer, it is your use of logos and pathos (developed through research) that establishes your ethos. You must be seen as knowledgeable. You also must be seen as trustworthy; the audience should not feel manipulated or lied to. That is why it is important that you not use inflammatory language or "low blows." If the writer has known expertise on the subject argued, he or she will have to provide less proof and may even "get away" with some harsher statements about the opposition than you can, since he or she doesn't have to prove lack of bias (for example, see "Canadians: What Do They Want?" Reader, p. 467). The rhetorical stance taken by the writer also says much about his or her credibility. (See Wayne Booth's essay "The Rhetorical Stance," Reader, p. 488). Be aware of the attitude toward your audience, your subject, and even yourself that comes across in your argument. Any hints of boredom, arrogance, or carelessness will undermine your ethos and therefore your argument's success.

One of the other ways that you can build and maintain strong ethos is through correctness. You need to be fair and correct in your use of language and acknowledgment of source material. For example, presenting the ideas of others as your own (i.e., plagiarism) immediately discredits you and therefore your argument. See Chapter 18 on evaluating and using sources and Chapter 19 on documenting them. It's important to choose valid sources and use them correctly, to summarize, paraphrase, and quote accurately. Finally, your ethos may be severely undermined by the appearance of *any* errors: in facts, referencing, grammar, punctuation, spelling, and transcribing (copying names and other words from sources).

Interweaving of Logos, Pathos, and Ethos: Your Essay's Integrity and Tone

The effective interweaving of logos, pathos, and ethos is what gives your essay its integrity. This interweaving occurs as a response to your sense of purpose and to your properly informed awareness of your intended readers. Your specific application of these three fundamental appeals in relation to your purpose and audience, in turn, results in tone—the central concern of the following chapter. As we will see in more detail in the next chapters, you shape tone through various choices and techniques. The words you choose and how you arrange them, for instance, play a major part in your tone, your appeals. In preparation for more on this topic in the next chapter, let us now consider, however summarily, the nature of the resource upon which we all draw as writers in a majority of North American institutions: our English language.

DISTINCTIVE FEATURES AND POTENTIALS OF THE ENGLISH LANGUAGE

English is the remarkable product of many other languages. Although every language has its limits as well as its special glories, English provides an extraordinary range of options, because it contains multiple words for the same referents, offering the particular sensibility of the peoples who provided the root words. Words of Germanic, Latin, Greek, Norse, and French origin have different tones and connotations, in part because of the differing roles played by the various root languages in British history. The Old English–based word "sweat" has coarser associations than the Latin-based word "perspiration," though both name the same thing. Latin and French were used by higher orders of the societies, Old English by the lower. Writing that favours words from Old English over words from Latin and French will have a distinct stylistic effect.

Conversely, within the many varieties of English to have spread around the globe, one finds endless examples of individual words that have acquired multiple meanings. For example, the 2004 CBC documentary *Talking Canadian* points out that the famous Canadian "eh," one single expression, can mean dozens of things according to context and intention, including "like this, see," "you know how it is," "believe me," "I'm not fooling," "you bet," "really," "like that," and "what else?"

As noted by Robert McCrum, William Cran, and Robert MacNeil, the authors of *The Story of English*, ambiguity, innuendo, and wordplay distinguished Anglo-Saxon speech. Hebrew contributed new possibilities for abstract thought, and Old English words gained in sophisticated uses. The legacies of ancient Greece and Rome, imported with Latin, brought not only vocabularies but rhetoric—classical ways of organizing thoughts and shaping appeals.

Anglo-Anxiety

Confronted by this language—its irregularities, idiosyncrasies, and range of vocabulary as well as its formidable tradition of rules (real or imagined), judgements, outlooks, and controls—many of us can feel overwhelmed. English may strike us as the instrument that instills our fears and limitations; we may feel ourselves its victims. Delaware writer and writing teacher Daniel David Moses, Queen's National Scholar, speaks about a sense we can often have of being "bullied by the ghosts" of past writers; bullied by popular ideas of what a writer stands for—"a sort of solitary, spiritual explorer, a pioneer for the empire" (27). These bullying ideas can include the latest "hip" literary prejudices (snobberies) about what writing can and can't be.

Moses also speaks about the profound if still unconscious discomfort he felt during his school years as a result of the rhetorical ideas carried forward by English: form versus content, dichotomy, dialectic, conflict, arguments (30), the "academic conflict model" that imposes "or" rather than "and" (108)—principles inherited from the Greek and Latin past. One doesn't have to be a Native surrounded by the language and carried-over attitudes of British empire as it morphs into American empire to say "I hate English." We hear that confession from students all the time. "I've always hated English!"

But is it really the English language itself that is causing this anxiety? Moses refers to so many of us as "hesitating to act for fear of failure, for fear of playing the fool. 'You Can't Beat City Hall'" would be our banner, he says, if we were "confident enough to organize" (13). Read any of Moses's plays, poems, stories, or essays, and you will see an example of someone taking profound pleasure in the riches of the English language—its sounds, wordplay, concepts, and its personal inner connection: what he calls the language "in the body, of the body" (19). The most important thing about writing, he advises, is to find pleasure in it (29). Writing, he says, is remembering, and "memory work for grown-ups is play" (29). Like many other writers, Moses has shown that the English language *can* be used to "beat City Hall." He was one of a handful of Native students attending universities across the country in the 1980s when he began his undergraduate studies. English is indeed a tool that you can turn to *your* purposes, and you can use it not only to make desired changes but simply to have fun.

We hope that you and your instructor will be open to your taking some adventures in your writing, that you will try connecting with the pleasure of English words and rhythms. We hope that you will explore your own imagination and voice, using English as instrument, guide, and valued assistant.

 See the Text Enrichment Site for this chapter for more on the history of English as well as a timeline of classical rhetoric.

Sentence Structure and Syntax

Sentence structure and syntax (word order) influence style (tone, appeals to logos, ethos, and pathos) through the lengths of thought units and the patterns of grammatical order (e.g., whether subjects lead to verbs or vice versa). Shorter sentences, like shorter words, are generally considered easier to read. Longer sentences tend to occur in more academic literature or that intended for readers with high levels of formal education. It is also worth noting that average sentence lengths in general have diminished over the centuries. In their language workshops, Dr. Eric McLuhan (who worked for many years with his famous father, Marshall, who coined the phrase "The medium is the message") and Roger Davies (three-time winner of the American Business Press Jesse H. Neal Editorial Achievement Award) provide interesting examples on this topic. The following information comes from their 1989 McLuhan and Davies Communications Inc. workshop manual.

> In a typical 300-word passage from Geoffrey Chaucer's translation of *Boethius* (1377–1381), sentences average 68.4 words each.
>
> *The Proem* to *The Canterbury Tales*, printed by William Caxton in 1424, averages 75.3 words per sentence.
>
> A work by Sir Thomas Elyot, 1531, averages 64 words per sentence.
>
> *The Decline and Fall of the Roman Empire* by Edward Gibbon (1776–1788) averages 40.2 words per sentence.
>
> *Kidnapped* by Robert Louis Stevenson (1886) averages 43 words per sentence.
>
> *The Game* by Ken Dryden (1999) averages 21.5 words per sentence.
>
> A typical Harlequin Romance, circa 1990, averages 9 words per sentence.

From the end of the thirteenth century to the beginning of the twenty-first, sentence lengths have declined from as high as 80 words per sentence to as low as 9 words per sentence. Presently, average sentence length is below 18 words per sentence.

Not only are sentences shorter on average, but paragraphs are as well. Mark Twain and Robert Louis Stevenson often used two-page paragraphs in their essays. *The Canadian Press Stylebook* (conscious, as well, of newspaper formatting) advises journalists to begin a new paragraph after 30 words. Today's journalistic paragraph is less than half the length of a sentence from 1400.

For an interesting method of assessing readability of prose (based in part on sentence length), see the Fog Index of Robert Gunning, PhD in mathematics, Professor Emeritus at UCLA, and business consultant. This system pays close attention to the importance of matching sentence length and size of words to the intended audience and purpose. See Chapter 15 of this text for the Fog Index formula and the Chapter 15 Text Enrichment Site material for student uses of the Fog Index.

✒ PRACTICE

Write a one-paragraph summary of the main ideas you find expressed by this chapter in reply to the question "what is writing?" You may wish to look over Chapter 13, "The Summary," before you start.

Works Consulted

Bloom, Harold. *The Best Poems of the English Language from Chaucer Through Frost*. New York: HarperCollins, 2004.

Booth, Wayne. "The Limits and Alternatives to Skepticism: A Dialogue." *College English* 67.4 (March 2005): 378–88.

Chapman, Alan. *Mehrabian Communication Research* (2004). 4 April 2006 <http://www.businessballs.com/mehrabiancommunications.htm>.

Epstein, Norrie. *The Friendly Shakespeare*. New York: Penguin, 1993.

Heller, Louis G., Alexander Humez, and Malcah Dror. *The Private Lives of English Words*. Tarryton, NY: Wynwood, 1991.

Jonas, George. "Why Does the Nazi Holocaust Preoccupy Us More Than Any Other Genocide?" *Maclean's* 12 Sept. 2004: 47–50.

McCrum, Robert, William Cran, and Robert MacNeil. *The Story of English*. London: Faber and Faber, 1986.

Moses, Daniel David. *Pursued by a Bear: Talks, Monologues, and Tales*. Toronto: Exile, 2005.

Sargent, Elizabeth, and Cornelia Paraskevas. *Conversations About Writing*. Toronto: Nelson, 2005.

Slaght, Margaret. Dir. and producer. *Talking Canadian*. Morningstar Entertainment, Inc. CBC home video, 2004.

Speeth, Kathleen Riordan, and Ira Friedlander. *Gurdjieff: Seeker of Truth*. London: Wildwood House, 1980.

Yale University Department of Linguistics <http://sapir.ling.yale.edu/~elf/>.

Chapter 2
Characteristics of Writing Tones

If purpose is *why* you are writing and audience *to whom* you are writing, then tone is *how* you handle your writing. More specifically, tone is the attitude you take to your purpose, topic, and reader—to your interweaving of logos, pathos, and ethos (see Chapter 1). You create that tone through knowing your purpose and refining it while you consider your audience. Tone is the medium through which you engage with your reader, through which you communicate. It is complex, subtle, firm, and distinctive: tone fulfills the work of all the communicative tools traditionally employed in face-to-face address.

A RANGE OF TONES

Depending on your audience and purpose, your tone may range widely from informal to formal: from blue jeans to a business suit or a scholar's hat. A letter to your friend will be informal, friendly, casual, and familiar. Since personal writing emphasizes the writer, your own personal presence—or voice—will be strong, adapted to the particular ideas you are expressing. You might write short sentences and paragraphs and use a quirky style in your letter. In contrast to this informality, a report to the local newspaper editor will use standard language and punctuation. Your personal style and voice will be subordinated to predictable form, and you will pay more attention to the way you organize what you write. In a leaflet promoting your view on a particular cause to members of your community, your tone will be assured and firm, but if you know there might be resistance to your views, you will acknowledge any contrary views (see discussion on consensus-refutation and Rogerian argument, Chapter 16). Your careful organization of the argumentative leaflet will establish your own authority and capture interest as you offer clear, convincing evidence for your opinion before you go on to emphasize that opinion.

Individual words, sentences, paragraphs, and overall construction of these building blocks (some refer to construction as the *architectonics* of writing) all contribute to your tone. This may surprise you, since we often think of tone as primarily auditory, something we hear. When you write, however, you translate the emotion and content of your spoken voice, expressed through sound, into the same values expressed visually in marks on a page. If you do this well, you replicate (insofar as possible) the strengths of oral face-to-face communication in your text.

Graphics as a Part of Tone

Seeking to match the power of oral communication, editors and writers will often add **graphics** to their text, recalling that old cliché that a picture is worth a thousand words. Graphics support advertising, business reports, and technical essays. The colour, size, and layout of a graphic can provide important clues about the content of a piece of writing. Publishers pay careful attention to the illustrations they choose for the covers of paperback novels, for example. First those covers must grab prospective readers' attention; second, the same covers must convey a tone that reflects the content of the book.

Bright, flashy graphics convey a sense of energy and light-heartedness. The yellow covers of the *Computing for Dummies* books demonstrate this well. A Stephen King novel or a Gothic novel, on the other hand, will convey a darker, more sombre mood with its graphics. Even the size of type provides a clue to the character and size of the book's target audience. Large type fonts aim for a wider audience (including perhaps children and senior citizens); smaller type fonts concentrate on a narrower, often more serious reading audience. Journalism that is frequently broken up with graphics may not be taken as seriously as journalism that relies on a written representation of facts and perspectives (the *Toronto Sun* compared to the *Manchester Guardian*, for example). Adapting graphics to purpose and audience is largely a matter of finding the most effective strategy, the suitable tone.

Three Main Levels of Tone Related to Occasion

Notwithstanding infinite variations of tone, three broad categories deserve our recognition: **informal, general,** and **formal.** None of these is "suitable" or "unsuitable," "sincere" or "dishonest" in isolation. The key is whether tone respects the reader and the needs of the occasion while also demonstrating a true connection to the writer. (Establishing a true connection is discussed in Chapter 1 under logos, pathos, and ethos; it is also described in Wayne Booth's essay "The Rhetorical Stance" in the Reader, p. 488). You may say that using formal (or elevated) style (diction and structure) is unnatural to you and therefore insincere; however, as you go on reading and absorbing academic styles, you will become more comfortable with them. Since your academic reader expects academic style, it is respectful on your part to begin to learn that style, without losing touch with your own voice (which we will discuss later in this chapter). You will make academic style a part of your repertoire of words and strategies.

Three Main Features of Tone Related to Purpose

Personal or "creative" writing—sometimes called evocative or expressive—tends to use an informal approach. The tone of such writing is generally considered **evocative** or **expressive**. Its purpose is to connect emotionally with the reader, to effect some change, to stimulate an imaginative experience, perhaps at the unconscious as well as conscious level. Writing that seeks to inform or raise awareness, in the manner of textbooks, for example, uses an **expository** tone. Its purpose is to *inform*. Writing that seeks to change thinking and even incite a call to action is **persuasive** in tone. The purpose of such writing is to change how the reader thinks or acts in relation to a certain issue.

On pages 26–29 of this chapter, we illustrate four somewhat differently shaded writing tones, each resulting from a specific academic occasion and purpose.

TONES CHART—A CRUCIAL REFERENCE

Refer to the following Characteristics of Writing Tones chart (p. 20) with frequency and care: it may well be one of the most useful resources in this text. It will guide you to the characteristics of writing tone suitable to your reader and purpose for everything you write. For handy future reference, this chart is also reproduced on the inside back cover of this text.

DICTION

We invite you to reflect further on the level of individual words, a reflection begun earlier in our discussion of word connotations and triggers (Chapter 1). Imagine you want to persuade a variety of people to re-build a rundown part of town. To a neighbour you could write, "We have to clean up this slum!" To your local politician, you might not want to be that blunt: "We need help to improve the quality of life of this once-vital area of your constituency." To a group of city planners, your tone would probably be more subdued and formal: "We need to raise the living standard in this low-income neighbourhood." All three have the same purpose, but each audience has different requirements, different presumptions, and different communication codes. You'll notice that the "slum" from the first example has become a "once-vital area" in the second and, finally, a "low-income neighbourhood" in the third. All three phrases refer to the same place; the different choice of word establishes a different tone for each piece. Such word choice, or **diction**, is the first element of tone: the words you choose will be your reader's first clue regarding the attitude (emotional point of view) of your piece.

The three phrases given above convey different connotations. Earlier we explained that as opposed to "denotation"—the dictionary definition of words—"connotation" refers to the various unofficial, but no less real, meanings that gather around many words. We have previously considered that certain words are highly charged, particularly for

Characteristics of Writing Tones

Elements	Informal	General	Formal
Diction	Everyday, plain, concrete, colloquial, slang, casual, contractions, shorter words	Assumes a high school education, mixes concrete and abstract, mixes shorter and longer words	Assumes a higher level of education or training, abstract, technical, jargon, longer words
Sentences	Short, simple, some fragments, some comma splices, frequent dashes	Nearly all complete, fragments very carefully controlled, somewhat longer, balances simple and combined structures, fewer dashes, and few (if any) sentence fragments or comma splices	Mostly longer and combined structures, no fragments, few dashes, no comma splices
Paragraphs	Mostly short, casual, no rigorous use of topic sentences, implied rather than explicitly stated transitions	Some longer, more fully developed, more deliberate use of topic sentences and explicit transitions within and between paragraphs	Mostly long, fully developed, consistent use of explicit transitions, complex content organized by clear patterns
Supporting details	"Warm"—anecdotes, personal descriptions, more appeal to emotion than to logic (see Chapter 4)	Includes some "cooler" proofs—data, studies, logical formulations (see Chapter 4)	"Cool"—empirical data and structured logical formulations, academic authorities and references
Organization (or Structure)	Casual, spontaneous, loose, lacking explicit connectors, mainly based on emotion	Deliberate, tighter, using some explicit connectors, reflecting one or more methods, blending emotion and logic, cause and effect	Highly controlled, explicitly connected throughout, tight application of patterns, mostly intellectual
Purposes	More often personal, blending of purposes but often not sustained	Some personal, expository, and argumentative, combined and somewhat controlled	Expository—often analytical, argumentative
Typical uses	Personal letters, diaries, journals, some fiction, much advertising, some newspapers	Many newspapers and magazines, business writing, many expository books and articles, fiction	Academic writing, some textbooks, scientific writing, legal documents

certain groups. Connotations are accumulated meanings that register the socio-political as well as individual attitudes attached to these charged words. In the previous example, you can see how using different words for the same idea significantly alters the connotations of the meaning. English professor Daniel Kies has created a lively webpage on language ("Grammatical Manipulation of the Audience"), with excellent interactive exercises and examples illustrating how various words and other grammatical choices work together to achieve different levels of tone, with varying effects. See our Work Consulted list at the end of this chapter for the web address.

Recognizing Colloquial Language and Jargon

In capturing the best tone for each writing occasion, you may need to treat two types of diction with particular care: **colloquial language** and **jargon**. "Colloquial" means spoken together. Language at this level comprises the informal words we use when speaking or writing to friends or colleagues. In a more formal piece directed at an audience that you do not know well, you would find your readers take you less seriously if you use such language. This impression increases if you use slang (unconventional "in" talk). You probably know far more examples of the latest slang than we do; whatever your example, it may well be replaced in a year or two, although certain slang words do carry on, albeit often changing meaning. Hollywood film-noir classics have frozen in time the American slang of certain eras—words such as "heater" for gun or "dame" for woman. Colloquial language and slang convey vitality; they serve various writing purposes, but not academic writing. Adding to the problems such words create for tone is a tendency of some novice essay writers to spell words as they hear them. You may think that the instructor has said, "I am not bias," but what she really said, intended to say, or should have said, according to standard grammar, is "I am not biased." So words that are too informal are problems, but so are words that sound needlessly formal.

Turning to institutional or professional circles, we might demonstrate jargon by referring to linking words (for example, "and," "so," "but") as "linguistic coherence devices." We might sound much more elevated than a plain writer if we did, and therefore worthy of wealth and status, but alas our editor would not allow it. The editors would accuse us of using needless jargon. Jargon refers to specialized language (professional catchphrases) used by and for a narrow audience of readers who share a great deal of common technical knowledge. Jargon saves time and increases complex knowledge within special fields; it has an important purpose, but you should be careful not to use jargon for more general readers. If you wish to reach a wider audience and the technical phrase seems crucial, then give a clear definition to ensure you include your reader in your discussion. If, on the other hand, you target only that specific, narrow audience, adding such a definition could annoy your readers because you would be telling them something you can presume they know.

Ask yourself seriously, however, if a certain word of jargon (yours or that of another writer) is necessary: too often, academic authors make up jargon for ideas that can be easily and simply expressed by plain, everyday words. Resisting the tendency to show off in this way will gain you considerable respect and gratitude from those readers more interested in the value of what you write than in taking stock of how important and sophisticated you may appear. Since the university is not a perfect place, it contains a good deal of needless jargon. Sifting through needless jargon in pursuit of constructive critical analysis can sometimes be a frustrating effort. For an amusing look at how academic pretension may be manipulated to create an appearance of importance in place of the thing itself, see Daniel Kies's website "Grammatical Manipulation of the Audience."

DEFINING ACADEMIC TONES

Academic tones tend to range between neutral and elevated (formal). Adapting to these levels for your scholarly writing is not pretentious or artificial but simply respectful of the occasion and reader needs. For scholarly audiences, you should avoid not only colloquial words but other colloquial features as well, such as contractions (*can't* instead of *cannot* and so on). If your intended readers have a high level of formal education, they may feel a solid offering of short, concrete words is insufficient to convey nuances of meaning. However, if your audience does not have an education beyond, say, grade 9 or 10, you will need to adapt in the opposite direction. Refer again to the Characteristics of Writing Tones chart. You will notice that informal writing tends to use short, concrete words. For readers lacking university education, avoid too many abstract and polysyllabic words. But even with high levels of formal education, if your audience needs information in a hurry for business decisions, they will appreciate shorter, plain words. In George Orwell's "Politics and the English Language" (Reader, p. 471), the author advises to guard against inflated diction, since it usually obscures your meaning and makes your writing vague. Vagueness, as Orwell points out, makes us vulnerable to manipulation. Orwell recommends never using a long word where a short one will convey the same meaning. His goal with this advice is to keep writing honest. That advice pertains to writing for audiences at any level of education.

CONSIDER WORD ORIGINS: CONSULT YOUR DICTIONARY

We have considered the different effects created by short, concrete words in contrast to longer, abstract ones. **Origin** is another important aspect of words: what are the linguistic roots of the word and what associations do these create? Words of Germanic, Latin, Greek, Norse, and French origin have different tones and connotations, in part because of the differing roles played by the various root languages in British history.

Your dictionary, if you have chosen it carefully for college and university purposes, will tell you the etymology (history) of most words. Some reference books, like the

1998 *Nelson Canadian Dictionary*, provide valuable expanded histories for many entries. English has incorporated words from hundreds of other languages, adding the textures and tones of those cultures. In today's age of information, globalization, and specialist languages, this multilingual nature of English continues to increase— yet its mixed heritage traces back to its earliest years. Gaining a sense of this history will help you to recognize various associations that contribute to the stylistic effects of diction.

SENTENCES AND TONE

We tend to think of long sentences as convoluted and boring and short sentences as abrupt and simplistic. In professional writing, sentence length is more an indication of the reader's available time than it is the complexity of the writer's ideas. Short sentences imply that the reader needs the information in as short a time as possible. Magazine articles use sentences that are a little longer than those in bus advertisements, because a magazine article can usually be read at a more leisurely pace. Sentences in academic articles are even longer because the audience is expected to think hard about the information and construct a reasoned and layered response. So sentence length is often a prime indicator of what you expect your reader to do with your information. Types of sentences—from simple to complex— are explained and illustrated in further detail on the Text Enrichment Site, Chapter 2 and in the Handbook. For now, it is important to recognize that tone and its resultant meanings are heavily influenced by patterns—rhythms, repetitions, variations—and these are embodied in the types of sentences you use. Whether we call patterns and rhythms visceral or paralinguistic or some other term, the important idea to recognize is that style helps to express meaning, and style is much more than the denotative dimension of your words.

Impact Points in Sentences

To reflect a little further on the important contribution of craft to style and tone, consider the shape of the simplest standard sentence in English.

The standard English sentence moves from subject to verb.

In this typical sentence, the subject "sentence" (preceded by two descriptive words) is immediately followed by the verb "moves." The sentence both states and demonstrates a basic fact of English sentence structure. With this pattern in mind, consider the following rhetorical principle: **words at the beginning and ending of the sentence tend to draw the most attention and thus have the most impact.** In their workshops on communication, Eric McLuhan and Roger Davies like to refer to the "Bermuda Triangle" of sentences (based on the popular idea that somewhere over Bermuda is a portal into another dimension, a portal that swallows up passing aircraft and the like).

Figure 2.1
The "Bermuda
Triangle" of
Sentences

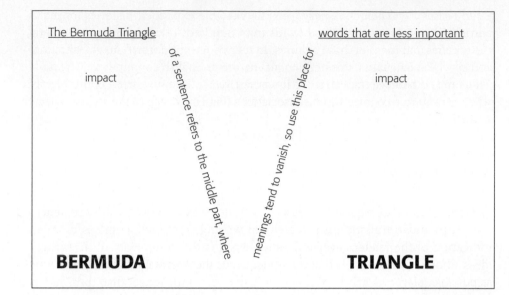

Figure 2.1
The "Bermuda
Triangle" of
Sentences

As you can see in the above example, the underlined words at the beginning and end are the ones that stand out and prove memorable. Guided by this principle, experienced playwrights tend to make sure that important ideas occur at the beginning and ending of speeches, even if some manipulation of usual speaking style is needed to achieve this effect. The same words placed in different locations in your sentences (and paragraphs) will have greater or lesser impact. Remember to use the impact points of sentences and overall structure to maximum effect.

End Terms Qualify Previous Ones: Word Order *Is* Meaning

A closely related principle of word placement is that **final terms qualify or define previous ones**. As an example, the phrase "beggars and kings" suggests that we may be dealing with literal beggars who are metaphorical kings. The last word describes the inner quality of the former word. Reverse the phrase to "kings and beggars," and you reverse the implication: now you appear to be dealing with literal kings who are, at heart, beggars. Word order creates a range of other effects as well, particularly as part of entire sentences and sequences of sentences.

Types of Sentences

Although the most basic sentence pattern in English moves from subject to verb to object or indirect object, numerous variations and combinations exist. For examples of these and how they create larger patterns within a paragraph, see "Sentence Patterns" at the Text Enrichment Site, Chapter 2. Also see "Preparing to Solve the 15 Common Errors" at the website in the Handbook section. The latter discusses common ways in which clauses can be combined into different types of sentences. Your sentence lengths, structures, and patterns all contribute to tone and style.

The wide range of sentence patterns in English means that writers can play with rich formal and rhythmical possibilities. You can have fun manipulating sentence patterns in order to achieve various effects that further your meaning. Sometimes these are best discovered by you in your writing adventures (and pointed out by your instructor), rather than adopted exclusively from a book of guidelines. Even the most thorough rhetoric book is still merely a prompt to get you started; furthermore, the ability to shape sentence patterns resides within you, intuitively. Nevertheless, to inspire your innate ability with sentence lengths and patterns, try the following activity.

PRACTICE
Sentence Patterns, Rhythm, and Tone

Read "Sentence Patterns" at the Text Enrichment Site, Chapter 2. Take note of individual types of sentences as well as how an arrangement of types can create an overall pattern within a paragraph.

Make up a paragraph in which you use at least five of the sentence patterns illustrated in "Sentence Patterns,"

and in "Preparing to Solve the 15 Common Errors" on the text website in the Handbook section. Show your paragraph to your classmates and your instructor and discuss the effects created by sentence patterns.

Paragraphs and Tone

Like sentences, paragraphs also express tone by their length, as well as the pace at which you expect your reader to consider your writing. Tabloid newspapers prefer single-sentence paragraphs. Such writing provides information quickly, but does not encourage the reader to process the information at any complex level. In your academic writing, aim for focused, well-developed paragraphs directed by concise, explicit topic sentences, as discussed in Chapter 4. A typical first-year essay employs paragraphs composed of 6 to 12 sentences.

Most university courses require mastery of third-person expositional, analytical, and argumentative tones. In addition, as you practise these three main tones, your work in university will require increased integration of research sources. Here, then, are brief illustrations of these main academic styles, using suitable sources. See Chapters 18 and 19 for more information about research methods and documentation of sources.

A Pace of Their Own

1   The speed of speech in various parts of Canada reveals a significant range of difference. Parts of Newfoundland and Montreal present two examples of rapid speech. In her essay "Newfoundlandese, If You Please," Diane Mooney observes that "[a]ll Newfoundlanders talk fast; this is just a given" (415). Mooney suggests that certain Irish roots are partly the reason for this. Visitors to Montreal hear a similar quickness of spoken English. This may be due partly to the influence of French, dominant in the city;[1] as well, Yiddish and Mediterranean communities, described by linguist Charles Boberg, have had an influence on the English spoken in the city (Haldane). No doubt the fast city pace of Montreal also influences the speed of speech and vice versa.

2   In contrast to the speech of Newfoundland and Montreal, much slower patterns occur in other parts of the country, for example, in much of Prince Edward Island (PEI), as well as on the prairies. Robert Deal, owner of a small bed and breakfast on the south shore of PEI, says, "On the Island, things are more relaxed: we don't drive so fast as people from away, and we don't rush our conversation." A similar observation is offered by Brenda Mitchell of Carstairs, Alberta, after a holiday in Montreal. "I couldn't get over how much faster people talk in this city," she says. Are ethnic roots as well as lifestyles responsible for the slower pace of speech in these parts of the country? The answer is probably yes.[2] As Boberg states to Maeve Haldane of the *McGill Reporter*, language variation across Canada is a last bastion of cultural separation from the United States.

Notes

1. See the following online article by University of Montreal linguist Professor Blake T. Hanna, published in *Circuit*, March 1990: "Is French Corrupting Montreal English?" (<http://www.iquebec.ifrance.com/names850/anglais.html>). Hanna's question makes one think of "Politics and the English Language," in which George Orwell deplores the influence upon English of foreign words. However, Hanna argues an opposing view: that French (in Montreal) has reinvigorated English to a degree that has not occurred since the eleventh century.

2. As of November 2006, a linguistics course, Ling 790, at the University of New Hampshire, stated the following in its online description: "Canada is a rich environment for socio-linguistic investigation, because there is every possible type of language contact situation imaginable." See <http://www.unh.edu/cie/canada/students.html>.

Works Cited

Deal, Robert. Personal interview. 10 Aug. 2003.

Haldane, Maeve. "Speaking of Montreal." *McGill Reporter* 21 Nov. 2002. 18 pars. 16 Aug. 2003 <http://www.mcgill.ca/reporter/06/boberg/>.

Mitchell, Brenda. Personal interview. 13 June 2003.

Mooney, Diane. "Newfoundlandese, If You Please." *Acting on Words: An Integrated Rhetoric, Reader, and Handbook.* 2nd ed. Ed. David Brundage and Michael Lahey. Toronto: Pearson Prentice Hall, 2008. 110–11.

Sample Writing Academic Analytical Tone—Illustration

Tony and the Bard

1 *The Sopranos*—now entering its final season on HBO—has all the features of a Shakespearean history play, as defined by Norrie Epstein: battlefield heroics, familial relationships, feisty characters, power politics and covert scheming (151). Like Prince Harry overcoming Hotspur in Henry IV, Part 2, Tony prevails over an attempted assassination (season 1, episode 12) as does Chris (season 1, episode 21). Shakespeare's use of domestic scenes is paralleled in *The Sopranos* by similar scenes of family relationships involving Tony, Carmela, Meadow, Anthony Junior, and various other members of the extended crime "family." Feisty Shakespearean characters such as Hotspur, Falstaff, and Mistress Quickly find their modern counterparts in *Sopranos* early-season regulars like Chris, Uncle Junior, and Janice. In particular, Tony resembles Henry IV in his concealing of private anguish beneath a mask of political action. On the matter of power politics, Shakespeare's histories begin with the question of who will succeed to power, who will prevail in the bitter feud between the houses of Lancaster and York. Similarly, *The Sopranos* begins with the death of the local crime boss, Jackie Aprile, Sr., a consequential power vacuum, and problems of how to gain control according to the old code of honour, which means less to certain characters than it does to Tony. Uniting all of these similarities is the strong appeal that both the histories and *The Sopranos* have for their audiences: we envy the rich and the powerful, we experience the vicarious thrill of sin and danger, and we recognize in the ruthless main characters the same moral compromises that govern our own lives.

Work Cited

Epstein, Norrie. *Friendly Shakespeare: A Thoroughly Painless Guide to the Best of the Bard.* New York: Penguin, 1993.

Sample Writing Academic Analytical Tone with Argumentative Edge—Illustration

Publish or Perish

1 In 1990, historian Page Smith published an indictment of higher education in America, condemning, among other things, the publish-or-perish culture. Now fourteen years later, publish-or-perish at Canadian universities is, if anything, worse than ever. No longer is the aspiring academic rightly encouraged to research and publish; he or she must publish as many *separate titles a year* as possible. A recent faculty posting in *University Affairs* reflects this disturbing reality: "Relative to research

funding . . . only Harvard's faculty publish more than UBC's" ("Let's Talk Excellence"). Nothing is said about the quality or value of these publications, or of the compromises made to attain this "distinction." While the UBC ad writer would no doubt reply that quality is assumed, nevertheless, the ad strongly implies that quantity is priority one. Examples abound of how this emphasis on quantity discourages devotion to farsighted works in favour of feeding the KPI mill.[1] Perhaps more disturbingly, this demand for endless short publications undermines teaching. It is generally acknowledged on university campuses that teaching excellence does not play a sufficient part in advancement; introductory and basic skills-related courses—the sorts of courses that often require the utmost teaching diligence—generally repay their instructors with low status. Surely the university's ideal of seeking and teaching truth suffers when the seeking consists of rapid-fire publications and the teaching garners diminishing respect.

Notes

1. "KPI" stands for "Key Performance Indicators," a type of accountability criteria used in business but, according to various critics, unsuitable to the university. See Bruneau, William, and Donald C. Savage. *Counting Out the Scholars: The Case Against Performance Indicators in Higher Education.* Toronto: Lorimer, 2002.

Works Cited

"Let's Talk Excellence." *University Affairs* June/July (2003): 24.
Smith, Page. *Higher Education in America: Killing the Spirit.* New York: Viking, 1990.

Sample Writing Concession-Refutation: Persuasive Tone

Eating Your Cake Before the Icing: Is It True What They Say?

Our last sample of academic tone for this chapter arose from the following fictional scenario. A former business school graduate was asked to write two paragraphs of advice to a graduating class at his alma mater. Here is what he wrote.

1   Five years ago, as I approached my last year of university, my parents and older relatives—with one exception—all advised me to make as much money as I could first, so that I could do what I really wanted to do later, after looking after financial concerns. My parents are practical people; I knew they wanted the best for me. They reminded me that eating the icing after the cake would still be the best plan, even now that I was grown up. The one person who disagreed was my grandmother. Her sister's husband had made his family wait to do the things they wanted—moving to the country—and the year that he finally paid off the mortgage

and said, "Let's move," he died of a heart attack. This story prompted me to do some research.

2   I happened upon an interesting study reported in *Natural Life* magazine, November/December 2002. The study tracked the careers of 1,500 business school graduates from 1960 to 1980. From the beginning, the graduates were grouped into Category A and Category B. Category A was people who wanted to make money first and do what they wanted to do later. Category B pursued their true interests right away, confident that money would follow eventually. Eighty-three percent of the graduates were in Category A. Doing our math, we know that only seventeen percent were in Category B. Probably you are in Category A, right? After twenty years, there were 101 millionaires overall. Just one of those came from Category A. So am I a millionaire now, five years after graduating? No, I'm not even close. But I'm in no financial stress, my young family is happy, and if I died of a heart attack tomorrow, my wife could honestly say that our time together was joyful and rich.

Work Cited

"Designing a Livelihood: Do What You Love & Love What You Do." *Natural Life* magazine. Nov.–Dec. 2002. 10 Dec. 2006 <www.life.ca/nl/88/livelihood.html>.

PRACTICE

See if you can find the features of diction, sentence style, point of view and structure in the sample writing that result in different tones and reflect the purposes connected to those tones. Then consider what the samples have in common from the point of view of purpose and tone. Discuss your findings with your coursemates and your instructor.

For more detailed commentary on individual features of each sample, see "Commentary on Tone: Four Samples of Academic writing" on the Text Enrichment Site, Chapter 2.

COMMON FEATURES OF ACADEMIC TONE

Writing intended to raise awareness is considered expository and is often fairly neutral in tone. Writing intended to change thinking, when it is effective, is persuasive in tone. Writing intended to include a call to action is even more persuasive in tone. The preceding four examples—expository, analytical, analytical-argumentative, and persuasive—have somewhat different shadings of attitude because they have somewhat different intentions; they therefore have somewhat different tones—yet all are within the general spectrum of scholarly style.

Pathos (see Chapter 1) seems least operative in the first example, which is observing language differences. The tone of that first example seems particularly neutral, detached, or "objective." Focus is on the object of discussion. The writer's intention in that sample is to inform or raise awareness. A little more pathos seems to operate in the second example as the writer conveys excitement over the perhaps unexpected connection between Shakespeare's histories and *The Sopranos*. The writer of that sample is intending to raise awareness, but more enthusiasm informs the attempt than is true in the first sample. Still more pathos may be felt in the third example, as the writer clearly deplores and perhaps resents the alleged problem under attack in that piece. All three examples, however, are more similar than different in tone.

All three place emphasis on logos, carefully balanced structure, and proper use of research sources. Note that all of the paragraphs shown in these examples begin with clear, direct topic sentences (sentences that summarize the main focus of the paragraph). These styles and the concomitant tones, resulting from diction, sentence structure, sentence length, standard grammar, and use of sources, represent standards that you will be expected to emulate in your academic writing. The fourth sample, using first person and more informal style, uses careful concession-refutation structure, research, and analysis and evaluation. It includes more pathos than the previous examples in its examples and appeals. This departure from more typical "impersonal" academic style suits the nature of the ceremonial and emotional occasion. Part of the persuasive appeal of the fourth sample is that it uses overt personal voice. Yet it emphasizes logos, as reflected in its use of a secondary source and other analytical attributes.

Organization of Academic Writing—A Feature of Tone

As the four preceding writing samples illustrate, in most academic writing, you need to present your reader with a quickly identifiable structural scheme, a "road map" that will help him or her to travel through your discussion. In the case of an essay, this attention to organization will necessitate a solid **thesis statement** in your introduction and clear **topic sentences** to head your paragraphs. These crucial sentences (thesis statement for the essay and topic sentence for each paragraph) will form the guiding structure of your essay, the spine that holds the body upright. At the very least, your opening should establish the topic and an idea of the general view that the rest of the paper will develop. You will use clear connective language between structural points to help your reader follow your flow of thought. If your academic paper does not convey such purposeful organization, your reader may well decide that its tone is not sufficiently serious, nor the content sufficiently developed. Examples of full five-paragraph essays at the first-year level are provided in many sections of this Rhetoric and others are available on the Text Enrichment Site. How to write topic sentences and handle other skills of paragraphing is covered in Chapter 4. How to write thesis statements and how to structure essays and paragraphs are covered in more detail in Chapter 6 with reference to outlining. As shown in the chart Characteristics of Writing Tones, methods and features of organization play an important role in the overall tone expressed by a piece of writing. Like all features of tone, organization reflects occasion and purpose.

PRACTICE

Choose any two selections from the Reader and describe each according to its diction, sentence structure, paragraphs, point of view, and overall organization. Relate this information to your sense of the main purpose of the writing of each piece, in relation to its intended audience (occasion). Through this analysis, decide on a brief description that best suits the tone—the essayist's attitude toward his or her subject—of each selection. How are the selections essentially similar or different in tone? Explain. Discuss your findings with your coursemates and your instructor.

VOICE

You may hear the term "voice" in discussions of tone. The idea of voice is very close to that of tone, with one useful distinction. As we have seen, tone is an overall attitude expressed by the writer toward himself or herself, the specific subject, and the audience. Your tone may well change quite radically from one piece of writing to another, while your voice will not change, or at least not very much, unless the form requires suppression of it. **Voice** may be closely identified with the character and personality of the writer, with his or her individuality. Some writers and instructors distinguish voice from style and tone as the expression of self, whereas style and tone are expressions of strategy.

Imagine the sort of voice you might expect from a seasoned oil-rig worker and the one you would expect from a career banker. At the risk of stereotyping, we might consider that the oil-rig worker and banker may vary in tone based on attitudes to the world. Both would always retain the essence of their individual voices, however, even when each person is adapting to situations in which expected formality or informality and form would vary. That part of your expression that remains in touch with the values, distinctiveness, and quirks of your own identity is your voice. This essence of you emerges in part through your social and educational background, and ultimately through your personal self. Voice is one of the most difficult qualities of writing to define, yet one of the most indisputable and influential presences on the page. It subtly characterizes both the shape and the content of everything you write.

PRACTICE

Read the essays "A Case for the Demotion of Beauty," Chapter 10 (p. 154), and "Introversion—the Dreaded Other," Chapter 19 (p. 322), both by communications student Colleen Leonard. Describe the tone of each essay and the voice of each essay. If voice and tone seem closely linked in both essays, why might this be? Discuss your findings with your classmates and your instructor.

Now think of one author whose writings you particularly enjoy or admire and a good number of whose works you have read. Pick two works by this writer that differ in tone. Now try to define what is consistent in the writing style and values of both works. You can choose a fiction writer or a poet, but essay writers, politicians, or newspaper columnists are also useful for this exercise. Remember, you are examining the abiding voice in one given writer (or speaker) beneath different stylistic choices and various forms.

FINAL THOUGHTS ON WHAT WRITING IS

Read the sample student essays "In the Words of Stompin' Tom" by Gustavo Miranda (p. 169), and "Canadian Equals Canada" by Brad Henderson (p. 172) in Chapter 11. Note the distinctive voices of these two student writers. Adapting to academic occasion and purpose has not resulted in complete suppression of their personalities. Achieving proper academic tone does not have to mean becoming a stylistic automaton. All writers—even academic ones—share in the universal writer's quest for individual voice. In academic writing, personal voice must remain muted or risk the problem of the Entertainer's Stance (see Wayne Booth's essay "The Rhetorical Stance," Reader, p. 488). Nevertheless, not to develop and use one's own voice (suitably adapted to purpose) is to renounce accountability (and risk boring your readers to tears). Your voice is what infuses your work with its underlying purpose; it is what keeps your reader engaged. Your voice as a writer comes about naturally, by saying things the way you would normally say them—but then by revising, as needed, to meet the standards of academic tone. Finding this balance is a delicate operation, one that much rewriting, along with advice from your classmates and instructor, will help you to accomplish.

Finally, remember that as part of your essential individuality, your voice represents those passions and interests that motivate you; these essentials are what propel researchers to important new insights and revelations. Just as your DNA is entirely your own, no two scholars are alike. If you proceed with genuine commitment, you will offer something new and valuable. This thought, however, leads to a concluding reminder of the true challenge ahead: writing about something entirely familiar is, of course, easier than presenting something new and distinctive, something that may even be initially resisted. The design you were asked to describe at the beginning of the previous chapter is not quite like anything else. That is what makes it particularly hard to describe. Writers so often resort to analogies to familiar items in the effort to make new perception comprehensible, but as Chapter 3 points out, ultimately all analogies fail. It is easier to write clearly about things that have been said again and again than about something new. But what is the purpose in that? Is it not better to try the more difficult task of pursuing new subjects and insights, perhaps to fail at first, but then to try again? Your topics and insights should be as original as the design that you tried to describe early in Chapter 1; therefore, you can expect to struggle to express with confidence and conviction the subjects you come to interpret from your own unique perspective. The key is perseverance.

PRACTICE

Review the paragraph that you wrote as the final prac- tice activity at the end of Chapter 1. With the main points of Chapter 2 now in your mind, what would you add to your original paragraph?

Work Consulted

Kies, Daniel. "Grammatical Manipulation of the Audience." English 1102. Rev. 17 May 2006. College of DuPage. 6 June 2006 <http://papyr.com/hypertextbooks/comp2/manipulation.htm>.

Chapter 3

More About Logic

Chapter 1 introduced the classical idea of a writer's **logos**, or logic. Scholarly experience fundamentally involves the use of logic as you gain, analyze, and contribute to knowledge. But let's say you read an argument on the question of sex education in high school. You know what you think about that, and you're ready to leap in with your answer. Recognizing your immediate response is always valuable, and sometimes your proverbial first thought is the "right answer." But when it comes to developing your thoughts on the topic into a contribution to knowledge, to writing a formal paper presenting your analysis and evaluation, you need to provide more than first thoughts, which are sometimes in the category of "knee-jerk" responses. You need to use logic to make your argument.

THE MAIN CULPRIT IS *HASTY THINKING*

This chapter will go on to describe logical operations and to identify a number of common logical fallacies. But the basic advice that runs through this discussion is simple: *stop and think.*

Really think.

The old advice, "when angered, count to 10," is worth applying to all our writing situations, regardless of what emotions we are experiencing at the time. Our first responses to anything we see or read are invariably emotional. When you find yourself wanting to make initial emotional reactions the basis of your next paper, count to 10 (for the 10 logical fallacies that follow). Consider if you are confusing facts and opinions, relying on inductive thinking without benefit of sufficient testing, or muddling premises as conclusions in deduction. Using Stephen Toulmin's terms, are you assuming, without sufficient investigation, that a proposed element of argument—such as warrant or grounds— is valid? The main weakness behind all unintended logical shortcomings is almost always one shortcoming: *hasty thinking.*

Consider the following statement:

Proper education includes developing and applying skills in citing sources according to the Modern Language Association (MLA), American Psychological Association (APA), or some other approved academic style guide.

Has the writer of this sentence stopped to think that the word "education" in its broadest, most open sense simply means *learning*? The word does not designate where or how one learns. There is so-called informal education—the proverbial university of life—as well as formal education based on institutionalized mechanisms, as well as different cultural forms of institutionalized learning, not all of which practise Western-style citation techniques. Adding the word "post-secondary" in the above statement to describe the word "education" would remove an apparent assumption that all good education occurs in college or university. Before allowing your words to seek the light of day and other readers, be sure your choices of words and the thinking behind your choices have not been too hasty.

FACT AND OPINION: A MATTER OF FACT . . . OR IS IT?

All writing essentially involves articulating an *opinion* on a topic and then providing support based on evidence—various facts and forms of reasoning—to persuade readers that the stated (or sometimes implied) opinion is true or, at least, useful in some important respect. This sounds straightforward enough, so let's move on to the next point—but wait a minute. We just considered the dangers of hasty thinking. Before accepting the previous statement, we should ask, what is an opinion and what is a fact? Try the following quiz, and let's see just how many of us do—or perhaps do not—agree on an answer to these questions.

✏ PRACTICE

Discuss with your classmates and instructor whether the following statements are facts or opinions:

1. Christopher Columbus was the first person to discover North America.
2. Women are physically weaker than men.
3. Alberta has refused to support the Kyoto agreement due to self-interest.
4. Canada's national sport is hockey.
5. The birthplace of hockey was Victoria Rink, Montreal, March 3, 1875.

6. In 1763, under terms of the Treaty of Paris, almost all of New France was ceded to Britain.
7. *Buffy the Vampire Slayer* was the best series on TV during its seven-year run and should have been continued.
8. Oil, a fossil fuel, is a non-renewable resource.

For our thoughts on these statements, see "Commentary on Statements of Fact or Opinion," Text Enrichment Site, Chapter 3.

The advice to draw from the above exercise is that you should support your claims, which you do best in academic discourse by carefully applying inductive and deductive methods and by avoiding logical fallacies.

INDUCTIVE AND DEDUCTIVE FORMS OF REASONING

In the Middle Ages, scholarship, closely tied to the church, was dominated by a type of intellectual reasoning based on traditionally accepted general principles and doctrinal presumptions. This situation prevailed until the Renaissance in Europe, which flourished in the sixteenth century. The study and evolution of empiricism followed: the scientific method of setting up experiments and basing conclusions on rigorous analysis through observation of phenomena and the collection and measurement of data. This "modern" method of reasoning emphasizes **induction**, the use of concrete particulars to derive some larger principles. The much older method of reasoning tends to emphasize **deduction**, which posits (theorizes) a large principle and then looks for supporting examples.

Induction

Inductive conclusions flow from experience and observation. For example, a child touches a red-hot burner. The next time she sees a red-hot burner, she will probably not touch it, because she has formed a conclusion, based on experience: that red-hot burners hurt her when she touches them. Inductive reasoning moves outward from the individual experience; that is, it moves from particular instances to general conclusions.

Deduction

Deductive reasoning, in contrast, moves inward, moves from the concept to the cases. Deduction starts with general principles and applies analysis in order to reach specific conclusions. The popularity of the British literary character Sherlock Holmes has made the process of deduction famous. He would often listen to an account of events and after a survey of the scene suddenly deduce the crime's complete solution by logical guesswork. (For another view of Holmes as informed empiricist rather than deductive genius, see Dr. Penner's essay in Chapter 9, p. 127). Deductive conclusions most often follow from an abstract mental process called the **syllogism**. This construction consists of three steps: a major premise, a minor premise, and a conclusion. A "premise" may be defined as a statement of accepted truth, such as "lawyers work long hours" or "Cathy is a corporate lawyer." The first of these statements expresses a general principle about all lawyers, so this may be considered a major premise. The second statement offers an accepted truth concerning a specific case, so it may be considered a minor premise. Considering the minor premise in relation to the established major premise, we can derive a conclusion:

Major premise: Lawyers work long hours.
Minor premise: Cathy is a corporate lawyer.
Conclusion: Cathy works long hours.

Be aware, however, that the formal reasoning behind a syllogism can sometimes lead to a faulty conclusion, as in the following example:

Major premise: Serious study requires personal discipline.
Minor premise: Andrew, a Dalhousie student, is disciplined.
Faulty conclusion: Andrew studies seriously.

If Andrew is disciplined in other ways (in exercise, diet, money management, confidentiality, dental care, punctuality, and so on) but not in studying, the conclusion does not hold, though the formal logic in the syllogism is technically correct. So be prepared for the possibility that a syllogism may seem structurally sound, yet the conclusion may be wrong when tested against the reality of the specific case.

♪ PRACTICE

Watch the 1941 film *The Maltese Falcon* starring Humphrey Bogart. Early on in the film, private eye Sam Spade (Bogart) concludes, through deduction, that his investigative partner must have been killed by someone his partner knew, because his dead partner's overcoat was still buttoned up and his gun was in his holster. Was Spade lucky to reach this conclusion, or did he make flawless use of the syllogism?

For our thoughts in response to the above practice activity, see "Sam Spade's Use of the Syllogism," on the Text Enrichment Site, Chapter 3.

Deductive Premises Formed by Induction

Most everyday thinking, as well as scholarly work, combines both forms of reasoning, inductive and deductive. Many empirical (inductive) studies, for example, turn to deductive thinking in their conclusions, speculating to some extent on possible broader implications of their specific findings, even setting forth new presumptions or premises to assist future deductions. For an example of this from the Sherlock Holmes stories, see Dr. Penner's essay in Chapter 9 (p. 127).

In many cases, we form or fortify our general principles or presumptions of deduction by inductive observation. We say that all living things die not because we have actually observed every living thing through the course of its own life to death, but because we are generalizing from several observations. We have seen some living things die, have heard of many living things dying, and have not seen or heard of any exceptions to this general belief. Such conclusions are often valid but not always. For just this reason, the "laws" of physics or other sciences are considered right only until they are found (as they periodically are) to be wrong.

In short, deduction often begins and operates on *partial induction*—a generalization derived from a limited range of observed occurrences—for its major premise. Thus, deduction is often an informed estimate rather than a beautifully reliable, self-contained, nearly mathematical derivation, despite what Sherlock Holmes, *Star Trek*'s Mr. Spock, and late-night television detectives would try to lead us to believe. Shakespeare's *Othello* dramatizes flawed deduction abetted by hastily accepted empirical evidence. Consider the play, and then see our further comments at the Text Enrichment Site, Chapter 3.

LOGICAL FALLACIES

Most of us pride ourselves on our command of reason, yet in daily life we frequently stray into illogical conclusions. Acknowledging our biases, seeing issues from unfamiliar points of view, and properly applying the tools of reason may be the greatest task we face in college or university as well as in life. Below, we discuss 10 common forms of logical fallacies. As you will see, the first six of these clearly result from hasty thinking resulting in **oversimplification**: a reduction of complex situations to easy descriptions and one-dimensional conclusions. The last four, while they, too, might be solved by taking more time for complex analysis, are generally considered **fallacies of distortion** in that writers commonly use them on purpose to appeal unfairly to our emotions or prejudices—or even to cut down on the time required to complete a last-minute assignment!

1. Overgeneralization

If you argue that all British people are understated, you are making a hasty generalization (in this case producing a **stereotype**) that can be easily invalidated. All it takes is one counter-example—Mick Jagger, for example, is British *and* flamboyant—to undermine your claim. As our discussion of induction and deduction illustrates, generalizing is an inevitable part of moving from specifics to presumptions, of exploring broader possibilities. But generalize with caution, knowing that your presumption is simply a device in the cause of experimentation, not an absolute certainty. An essayist writes to make a *particular* case about a topic in some defined scope. As Albert Einstein once said, "God is in the details."

2. Either/Or Assumptions

There are many authentic either/or situations. These cases of contrasting choices and fairly certain outcomes are pressing and sometimes dramatic: "Bill Gates either limited Microsoft as a monopolistic company or faced further legal penalties." But in many cases, so-called either/or situations are instances of oversimplification: for example, "Our hockey coach said that if we lose these high school playoffs, we'll never accomplish anything worthwhile in our lives."

Try to think past either/or false opposites toward a range of available, workable alternatives more appropriate to our multi-layered world of complex situations and challenges.

3. False Analogy

Well-chosen analogies make writing vivid, clear, and strong. Consider the following example: "Mr. Cleghorn, our history teacher, talks to his high school students in the same way that Mr. Dress-Up used to talk to his pre-school TV audience." We gain a sure impression of the teacher and how his manner is likely to affect some of the class. Remember, however, that just because two things are alike in some respects, and just because one may illuminate the other on certain points, they will not be alike in all respects. At some point all analogies break down.

A false analogy is a comparison with a faulty basis that detracts from rather than contributes to your point. Consider the following: "Accountants are artists: both are important observers of details." In this analogy, the writer presumes that because both accountants and artists analyze diverse information, they are essentially the same. This overlooks the fundamental distinction that artists—by definition—must use their imaginative powers to create original works of art, whereas accountants use their analytical skills to interpret existing numbers. The analogy invites readers to consider the ways in which accountants are fundamentally unlike Vincent van Gogh, Guy Vanderhaeghe, or the Tragically Hip. Like the either/or fallacy, the false analogy results from oversimplification.

4. Slippery Slope Assumptions

Your car gets chipped; you dream that it is covered in rust. Emotions conspire through hyperbole (extravagant overstatement) to remind you that you should coat the chipped area. However, if you were to believe that your chipped car would soon be covered in rust, you would be committing the fallacy of slippery slope: asserting that a certain event will lead to another event (often an extreme event) along an understood continuum, without considering how. A mother finds some marijuana in her daughter's purse and concludes that the girl will soon be hooked on heroin. The mother has overlooked that a number of significant events along the continuum (or slope) between mild usage and heavy addiction need to occur before the imagined dire outcome.

In this example, clear boundaries between steps along the continuum—from mild usage to heavy addiction—are indeterminate or "slippery" in that they are hard to define, their cause-effect connections uncertain. A conclusion opposite to the mother's but equally hasty would be to assume that because borders and transitions along the continuum are "slippery," therefore no possible connection or relationship exists between one end and the other. Complex study would be needed to appraise the odds for or against the girl's proceeding to addiction.

5. Assumptions Based on Events That Occurred One After the Other or Simultaneously

College tuition fees triple, and six months later, off-street prostitution by college students also triples. You conclude that the one event caused the other. Maybe it did, at least to some extent, but without further study, you have committed the presumption that because A precedes B, therefore A must be the cause of B. The traditional Latin term for this fallacy is *post hoc, ergo propter hoc* (after this, therefore because of this). This is the fallacy of correlation, assuming that two things associated in time (and often space) share a causal or reciprocal relationship. If you always have a headache after drinking coffee and conclude that caffeine (rather than, say, the heat or sugar) causes your ailment, you may also have committed a wrong assumption. The same basic fallacy applies if you assume that two events occurring simultaneously share a causal relationship (*cum hoc, ergo propter hoc*—with this, therefore because of this).

In their most extravagant expressions, these sorts of fallacies are superstitions, the opposite of logic. For example, Wayne Gretzky, the greatest hockey star of his era, reputedly put on his socks, skates, and equipment in exactly the same order before every game of his sports career. If he prepared this way without giving it much notice, dressing in that sequence would have been habit. If, however, he always suited up in the same order because he believed the sequence affected his hockey performance, then his routine would be a personal superstition.

6. Disconnected and Circular Statements

"I feel sad. I guess I'll go drinking." As we know, the inference that drinking will bring happiness is too often false. If there is a logical connection here, the writer has not revealed it to the reader. The following statement illustrates this sort of problem: "After O'Driscoll's arrest, neighbours found it difficult to believe he was a cigarette smuggler. They say he was always friendly, hard-working, and punctual." But isn't smuggling itself hard work? Wouldn't it *help* a smuggler to be punctual and friendly? Such statements that do not follow logically are sometimes known by their classical Latin label, *non-sequiturs* (things that do not follow).

A similar lapse of logic, known as circular reasoning, occurs when premises are stated as conclusions, thereby presuming that what has *yet* to be proven can be treated as a self-evident fact or conclusion. Circular reasoning is sometimes not too hard to spot: "The soap opera is great because it is so exciting." The terms "great" and "so exciting" have virtually the same meaning here, and neither states a reason. In other forms, an initial premise may seem to include an explanation, but on closer inspection, the so-called explanation merely repeats the premise: "God wants you to give me all your money, because an angel told me so in my dream." Why should we accept this dream as the word of God? The claim is still waiting for proof.

7. Red Herring

The red herring uses any number of false appeals—usually highly emotional ones—to lead us away from the real scent. A typical red herring occurs in the following rhetorical question: "Of course Native people were promised certain lands and payments, but wouldn't they like to stand on their own feet?" The writer intends to sweep aside a whole array of complex ethical and legal considerations by this emotional appeal to self-reliance, which draws on the racist stereotype of Native people as dependent and which is irrelevant to the historical and legal matter in question. The following fallacies of bandwagon appeal, motherhood appeal, and character attack all function as forms of red herring, techniques intended to run counter to the spirit of genuine, even-handed argumentation. When used deliberately, as they often are, such logical fallacies are sometimes called **propaganda techniques**.

8. Bandwagon Appeal

Bandwagon appeal is groupthink, calling upon urges toward inclusion but also on fears of exclusion. If we were all honest with ourselves, we might see that we ride various bandwagons at various times in our lives. Bandwagon appeal is the principle upon which so much designer clothing is sold: "Tilo has a pair of Nikes, Mom, so I have to have a pair, too." Here, preference is not really personal expression, only mindless conformity. According to this fallacy, a desire—often a selfish one for a questionable goal—is misrepresented as a need. Like motherhood appeals, which we deal with below, this fallacy preys on an aspect of our emotional nature, the urge to fit in, to join the crowd, to be accepted. At its worst, bandwagon appeal becomes mob mentality.

9. Motherhood Appeals

Also known by the Latin term *ad populum* for "to the people," motherhood appeals seek to manipulate emotional responses to symbols, values, or ideas of particular importance to a particular group. Such appeals make liberal use of *glittering generalities*, words like "country," "family values," "prosperity," "decency," and "freedom," terms that traditionally have positive associations. "Albertans believe in family values, and so they don't follow the stampede to legalize gay rights." The evident note of warning is intended to imply that gays don't live in families and will somehow threaten conventional family life. No definitions are offered, no complexities acknowledged.

Motherhood appeals draw upon other propagandistic strategies such as "plain folks," whereby politicians dress and speak falsely like the "ordinary" people they imagine will support them. Underlying motherhood appeals is the circular argument that we should be (or remain) what we are because this is what we are.

10. Character Attacks

Also known by the Latin term *ad hominem,* Latin for "to the man," character attacks include name-calling, mudslinging, and innuendo. *Ad hominem* attacks the person rather than his or her argument or policy. Although Canadian politics are often described as more "civilized" than those of the United States, the 2000 Canadian federal election demonstrated a great deal of name-calling. Whether or not Jean Chrétien improperly influenced the granting of a bank loan does not logically determine the value of his proposed national budget. Whether or not Stockwell Day libelled the good name of an Alberta lawyer would not determine the value of *his* proposed budget.

Ad hominem attacks serve as a form of red herring (deflecting attention from real issues), and sometimes they include the *straw-man* strategy of deliberately inflating a perceived threat from a certain opponent in order to focus on a supposedly justified counterattack. Prime Minister Pierre Trudeau gained demonic status in Alberta in the late 1970s and 1980s as a supposed enemy of the West; newspaper lampoonists routinely drew him with devil's horns. Alberta's political leaders continually sidestepped complex thoughts and questions merely by invoking the spectre of Trudeau. American political leaders continue to use foreign leaders as embodiments of various evils to deflect the American people's attention away from questioning their own government.

PRACTICE

Try to find at least one instance of each of the above 10 fallacies in various essays in the Reader. Compare your findings with those of your coursemates and your instructor.

TOULMIN'S ARGUMENT MODEL

Modern rhetorician Stephen Toulmin believed that the classical syllogism does not lend itself particularly well to analyzing modern arguments. He advanced his own model, which is described and illustrated in greater detail in Chapter 16, "Argumentation."

Toulmin's model breaks arguments down to a main claim, such as "City Council should enact a bylaw to prevent cats from roaming." Then his model looks for the grounds, consisting of data or other forms of evidence: "Over 500 citizens have signed a petition objecting to roaming cats using neighbourhood gardens as litter boxes." Finally, there must be a warrant expressing common support for the claim and the evidence. In this example, the warrant would be that "citizens in this society don't like their private property to be violated." Toulmin stresses the importance of sufficient backing for the warrant—evidence that the warrant is true.

Chapter 13 demonstrates a summary of "The Right Stuff" (Reader, p. 464) based in part on a Toulmin analysis, and Chapter 15 demonstrates a summary of "College Girl to Call Girl" (Reader, p. 457) based on use of this same model.

PRACTICE

Read "The Right Stuff" (p. 464) and "College Girl to Call Girl" (p. 457). For each essay see if you can identify the claim, the grounds (evidence/support), and the warrant (assumed public attitude). Then look at the Toulmin-style summaries of these two essays given in Chapter 13 ("The Right Stuff," p. 195) and Chapter 15 ("College Girl to Call Girl," p. 241). Discuss your answers and questions with your coursemates and your instructor.

CULTURAL CONSIDERATIONS

Although our discussion of logos, pathos, and ethos, as well as logical forms of reasoning, is intended to inform all types of writing, it particularly applies to analytical persuasion and argumentation, described in Chapters 14, 15, and 16. Before leaving this topic, we should therefore consider, again, the importance of cultural factors in how we respond to rhetorical traditions such as analysis and argumentation. Certain cultures neither engage in nor admire the oppositional, sometimes intensive adversarial approach we discuss in Chapter 16, an approach vigorously taught in North American colleges and universities. For instance, the idea of challenging appeals to social tradition (motherhood appeals) is considered generally unacceptable in many Indigenous communities.

Furthermore, some teachers and writers in mainstream Western culture also regret what they consider the unnecessarily combative spirit our society endorses in critical thinking. In an essay entitled "Burying the Hatchet in Language," McGill University professor David Smith observes how frequently our culture uses military metaphors to discuss verbal engagements—metaphors such as "defend your claims" or be "right on target" (Flachmann 540–44). He refers to linguistic research suggesting that the sort of language we accept can influence our perceptions and therefore our behaviour. He then offers a creative challenge: "Suppose instead of thinking about argument in terms of war, we were to think of argument as a pleasing, graceful dance."

Smith might suggest that our instruction in Chapter 16 on argumentation applying consensus-refutation really is no less biased, after all, than the forms of biased persuasion we have illustrated here. The stressing of contrast—their view versus yours—could be seen as conducive to either/or thinking, promoting an unnecessary opposition of only two considerations. Although we urge "fair play," we also imply that your goal is to "win" over someone else. Certainly the analytical-argumentative essay in Chapter 14 arguing for Canada's support of Kyoto (p. 211), as simply one example, could be accused of skimming over certain points and manipulating others. Smith's longing for a less confrontational approach in language corresponds with an apparently rising discontent with the adversarial political structures in our society.

Focus Question

Does argumentation, as discussed here and in Chapter 16, indeed offer an approach preferable to or even different from those of "biased persuasion"? Explain.

CONCLUSION

Whereas propaganda techniques suggest a coward's avoidance of honest challenge, a fair-minded effort to think from an "opponent's" point of view can be a wonderfully enriching experience. Perhaps it is no coincidence that Shakespeare, widely admired for the balanced representation of multiple viewpoints and characters in his plays, was educated in the classical rhetorical tradition. From a young age, he was obliged by his educators to construct arguments from both sides of a debate and to avoid the use of logical fallacies, regardless of which side he debated. In its best embodiments, rigorous application of logic in constructing arguments encourages understanding and tolerance.

Works Consulted

Honan, Park. *Shakespeare: A Life*. Oxford: Oxford University Press, 1999.

Richardson, Boyce. Dir. *Job's Garden*. National Film Board, 1970.

Shapiro, Howard-Yana, and John Harrisson. *Gardening for the Future of the Earth*. New York: Bantam, 2000.

Smith, David. "Burying the Hatchet in Language." *Reader's Choice*. 3rd ed. Eds. Kim Flachmann, Michael Flachmann, and Alexandra MacLennan. Scarborough: Prentice-Hall, 2000.

Chapter 4
Paragraph Skills: The "4-F Test"

Just as sentences should represent completed thoughts in pieces of writing, paragraphs should represent completed ideas. Here we are using the word "idea" in the sense of an opinion, conviction, or claim. An idea expresses a sense of meaning attached to a certain topic. You may say, "I am going to the lake," and convey a complete thought; you impart awareness of an action or state of being —a **fact** (see Chapter 3 for more on facts and opinions). If you say, "I am going to the lake because it helps me to experience inner peace," then you express what we mean here by an idea. This imbuing of suitable meaning would also occur if you say, "I am going to the life-giving lake." Your discussion would then go on to illustrate the life-giving aspects. The core "idea" often emerges through one word of intensification. This idea—opinion, interpretation, understanding, or claim—then needs further discussion to seem complete. In most academic essays, a paragraph of 6 to 12 sentences affords you the building block needed to complete your idea.

INDENTATION

A new paragraph is signalled by indentation of the first word of the opening sentence. This "small" matter of mechanics makes a major contribution to readability. Remember to indent five spaces when you begin a new paragraph. Your reader can thus easily ascertain the pattern of building blocks with a mere glance at your page.

> For most of your academic writing, especially in the first years of your program, a good rule of thumb is to use paragraphs ranging between 6 and 12 sentences.

WHAT *IS* A PARAGRAPH?

We have suggested thus far that a paragraph is a block of writing of 6 to 12 sentences, and that it expresses a complete idea. The *Canadian Writer's Workplace*—an excellent workbook for those requiring more extensive information on paragraphing than we can provide here—defines a paragraph as follows:

> A paragraph is a group of sentences that develops one main idea. A paragraph may stand by itself as a complete piece of writing, or it may be a section of a longer piece of writing, such as an essay.

Remembering this guideline may be the single most important thing you do to shape your academic essays. Many first-year students, asked to hand in a short essay for their first assignment, will present a paper that looks like one or other of the following:

Sample A

"The Card Cheat" uses an extended metaphor about cards to address questions of human alienation and oppression, two important punk concerns. The melancholy melody of the solo piano at the outset of the song anticipates the opening lyrical emphasis on the loneliness of the song's solitary protagonist. The looming inevitability of his death (whether time moves fast or slow, he does not have long to live) highlights the pathos in his yearning for human contact and consolation. Yet longer life, by itself, would not overcome the futility of his existence: having enough time to reveal all the plans he devised while concealing cards would accomplish nothing, because it holds no meaning. Where a future in narrative—the time needed for storytelling—might ordinarily enable life by organizing teller and listeners into a community, here that possibility is lost, rendered meaningless by the concealing of cards. The card cheat, this opening verse implies, empties hopes and dreams of their meaning. In the second verse, we learn how the card cheat unfolds. Grinning, the gambler plays a card that, we infer, he assumes will win the hand—only to face the dealer's suspicious stare and then to suffer a brutally quick execution. Since the gambler's aim in cheating is to steal time from death, this outcome is cruelly ironic. The verb tense in these lyrics situates the drama of the card cheat in a perpetual present; cutting across differences in social station, it poisons spaces of refined lesiure (signalled by the reference to violin-playing) as well as of debauchery (signalled by the references to gin and opium). As a trick, the card cheat obviously fails, but its failure exposes a fatal logic, one framed by the repetition of the word *lay*, first with respect to the card the gambler plays, then with respect to his floor-prone corpse: the play at bilking chance produces an automatic outcome; the attempt to cheat death makes dying inevitable. And to the extent that this logic has an arc, it reverberates in the song's music, which, ascending in thirds through the first three lines of the verse before falling away, underscores the desperate rise of the grinning gambler's hopes and then their crashing fall as his luck fails. Seemingly, verse three leaves the card metaphor behind. Where verse two introduces us to locales in which card cheating takes place, . . .   **X**

Sample B

The United States perhaps too smugly prides itself on being the "melting pot" of the world, a place where all different races and religions can come together and live peacefully. "E Pluribus Unum": Out of Many, One. This is the motto that the United States is based on, and the people of that nation interpret it to mean: out of many states, one nation, and out of many cultures, unity.

However, there are those who fear that the unity of their country is in jeopardy because of the large groups of non-English-speaking immigrants. They insist that the U.S. needs to establish one official language, English, in order to unify its people, prevent prejudice, and cut government costs associated with its non-English-speaking citizens. Opposition groups believe that Official English is unnecessary and unconstitutional.

They believe that immigrants are assets to the country, and an Official English policy will only create prejudice. Who is right? Although this debate has recently gained strength in the American media, it is not a new issue. Multilingualism has always been a part of the United States. Even before the days of Christopher Columbus, Native American people spoke hundreds of different languages.

As European colonies arrived, they brought with them not only the English language, but also French, German, Dutch, and Spanish.

As the country's population grew, it created new languages: Cajun French, Pennsylvania Dutch, Colorado Spanish, and Hawaiian Pidgin English, to name a few (ACLU). However, with some help from state and federal government legislation, English prevailed and continues to be the dominant language of the United States. In 1879, the state of California took away all Spanish language rights, and in 1897, Pennsylvania established legislation that forced immigrants working in coalfields to learn English (Crawford).

By 1906, multilingualism created enough controversy that the federal government, through the Naturalization Act of June 29, 1906, "made knowledge of the English language a requirement for naturalization" (USCIS). It is the large groups of monolingual immigrants, however, that are at the heart of the controversy. Out of the one million or so immigrants who received permanent citizenship last year, . . .   **X**

Self-test Activity

As the X marks at the end of the sample essays indicate, an instructor or editor would not be pleased with the presentation of either sample A or sample B. The main reason for editorial displeasure would be the lack of demonstrated awareness of where or where not to begin a new paragraph.

Review both samples closely and decide where you would or would not begin a new paragraph and why.

Paragraphing in the preceding samples, by the way, does not portray the wishes of their respective writers. We "messed around" with their originally, carefully paragraphed forms, but what we created is quite typical of early work by students whose paragraph skills have not yet been developed. Once you have made your decisions concerning paragraph breaks in the above samples, look below to see how the two writers concerned actually intended their paragraphs to look on the page. We agree with their paragraph break intentions and have provided marginal notes to explain why.

Sample A Corrected

These are the second and third paragraphs (and partial fourth) from an essay by Mark Simpson called "Betraying the Spirit of Punk? 'The Card Cheat.'"

2 "The Card Cheat" uses an extended metaphor about cards to address questions of human alienation and oppression, two important punk concerns. The melancholy melody of the solo piano at the outset of the song anticipates the opening lyrical emphasis on the loneliness of the song's solitary protagonist. The looming inevitability of his death (whether time moves fast or slow, he does not have long to live) highlights the pathos in his yearning for human contact and consolation. Yet longer life, by itself, would not overcome the futility of his existence: having enough time to reveal all the plans he devised while concealing cards would accomplish nothing, because it holds no meaning. Where a future in narrative—the time needed for storytelling—might ordinarily enable life by organizing teller and listeners into a community, here that possibility is lost, rendered meaningless by the concealing of cards. The card cheat, this opening verse implies, empties hopes and dreams of their meaning.

Focus: The first sentence states a general claim about the song; the second narrows the topic; the sixth ends this focus.

Focus: "Second verse" indicates a new spatial focus: "how the card cheat unfolds." The sixth sentence signals paragraph completion, summing up verse two.

3   In the second verse, we learn how the card cheat unfolds. Grinning, the gambler plays a card that, we infer, he assumes will win the hand—only to face the dealer's suspicious stare and then to suffer a brutally quick execution. Since the gambler's aim in cheating is to steal time from death, this outcome is cruelly ironic. The verb tense in these lyrics situates the drama of the card cheat in a perpetual present; cutting across differences in social station, it poisons spaces of refined leisure (signalled by the reference to violin-playing) as well as of debauchery (signalled by the references to gin and opium). As a trick, the card cheat obviously fails, but its failure exposes a fatal logic, one framed by the repetition of the word *lay*, first with respect to the card the gambler plays, then with respect to his floor-prone corpse: the play at bilking chance produces an automatic outcome; the attempt to cheat death makes dying inevitable. And to the extent that this logic has an arc, it reverberates in the song's music, which, ascending in thirds through the first three lines of the verse before falling away, underscores the desperate rise of the grinning gambler's hopes and then their crashing fall as his luck fails.

Focus: The opening sentence indicates a new topic and thus a new paragraph.

4   Seemingly, verse three leaves the card metaphor behind. Where verse two introduces us to locales in which card cheating takes place, . . .

Sample B Corrected

✓

These are the second and third paragraphs (and partial fourth) from an essay by Andrea Zawaski called " 'E Pluribus Unum': It's All in the Translation.'"

Focus: The writer says the U.S.A. is *not* unified on language issues. After summarizing the positions, she asks an inevitable question to be explored later.

2   The United States perhaps too smugly prides itself on being the "melting pot" of the world, a place where all different races and religions can come together and live peacefully. "E Pluribus Unum": Out of Many, One. This is the motto that the United States is based on, and the people of that nation interpret it to mean out of many states, one nation, and out of many cultures, unity. However, there are those who fear that the unity of their country is in jeopardy because of the large groups of non-English-speaking immigrants. They insist that the U.S. needs to establish one official language, English, in order to unify its people, prevent prejudice, and cut government costs associated with its non-English-speaking citizens. Opposition groups believe that Official English is unnecessary and unconstitutional. They believe that immigrants are assets to the country, and an Official English policy will only create prejudice. Who is right?

3   Although this debate has recently gained strength in the American media, it is not a new issue. Multilingualism has always been a part of the United States. Even before the

days of Christopher Columbus, Native American people spoke hundreds of different languages. As European colonies arrived, they brought with them not only the English language, but also French, German, Dutch, and Spanish. As the country's population grew, it created new languages: Cajun French, Pennsylvania Dutch, Colorado Spanish, and Hawaiian Pidgin English, to name a few (ACLU). However, with some help from state and federal government legislation, English prevailed and continues to be the dominant language of the United States. In 1879, the state of California took away all Spanish language rights, and in 1897, Pennsylvania established legislation that forced immigrants working in coalfields to learn English (Crawford). By 1906, multilingualism created enough controversy that the federal government, through the Naturalization Act of June 29, 1906, "made knowledge of the English language a requirement for naturalization" (USCIS).

Focus: Here the writer narrows the focus to the little-known history of the debate. The main outcome, the Naturalization Act, closes the topic.

4   It is the large groups of monolingual immigrants, however, that are at the heart of the controversy. Out of the one million or so immigrants who received permanent citizenship last year, . . .

Focus: Writer shifts from history to today's mono-lingual residents.

The 4-F Test

Here is a mnemonic device to help you to test your paragraphs:

The 4-F Test.

Make sure every paragraph you write meets the following requirements: focus, fine points, flow, and finality.

FOCUS

Some of us have been taught that the way to focus paragraphs is through the topic sentence. This sentence expresses the controlling idea of the paragraph. A unified purpose emerges: the goal of explaining or otherwise supporting the central assertion. Like the thesis of an essay, the topic sentence sets a track for the elaborating discussion to follow. Thus **focus** refers to unity of idea; but focus also means consistency and purpose of tone, created by point of view, choice of words, and types of details (fine points). Fine points, flow, and finality, in effect, harmonize your paragraph: they work together in fulfillment of one purpose—asserting the controlling idea of the paragraph and, thereby, of the essay.

Topic Sentence

You announce paragraph focus in large part with what writing coaches call a "topic sentence." Usually this is the first sentence of the paragraph. Some paragraphs, however, work well without an explicit topic sentence. The main idea comes across as a result of careful organization and implicit clues. To ensure clarity and control, especially in your academic writing, it's a good idea to shape a topic sentence for every paragraph you write. Placing this sentence first in the paragraph usually serves you well.

The *Canadian Writer's Workplace* uses an engaging metaphor to describe the way in which a paragraph should function: it compares an individual paragraph in a longer piece of writing to a "sequel to a movie" (158). By this, the authors mean that every paragraph should stand on its own, even though it may flow from and possibly into other paragraphs. A paragraph needs its own identity, its own special unity. The topic sentence explicitly defines that identity, that unity or focus. What it says and how it says it establishes a clear sense of where the paragraph is going and why.

Example of Topic Sentence

There is indeed an insistent rhythm to the routine of London.

— Peter Ackroyd, *London*, 457

A topic sentence expresses the most general idea of the paragraph, the main idea. Everything else is a specific form of illustration or support, demonstrating, in some way, the truth of the general idea. But is there a contradiction in the notion of a sentence being focused and also being general? There are two answers to this good question. First, the general idea has its carefully designed limits. In the example above, Ackroyd refers to the daily routine of London—something he feels he can at least suggest in a paragraph of carefully chosen supporting details. He is a Londoner himself, a writer and scholar with enormous ethos on the subject of London. After years of experience and contemplation on the subject, he believes he can distill the essence of London routine into a paragraph. Second, effective topic sentences, in various economic ways, convey a "controlling idea." The controlling idea provides specific intensification, which is what gives the sentence its emotional point of view. What is the "controlling idea" in the topic sentence above?

Yes, it is the single word "insistent." If you look ahead to Chapter 8, to the discussion of "dominant impression," you will gain a better sense of how the concept of the controlling idea adapts to this particular paragraph—which happens to be a description focused on one outstanding aspect or characteristic: the idea of insistency. All good paragraphs convey a clear, committed attitude to their topic. They do not simply point to a topic: they point to it with a specific view, an urgent view—they have something to *say* about the topic. The topic sentence states more than a fact; it states a *claim*, a position, an important point of view.

PRACTICE

Read the four writing samples in Chapter 2, pp. 26–29, entitled "A Pace of Their Own," "Tony and the Bard," "Publish or Perish," and "Eating Your Cake Before the Icing: Is It True What They Say?" For each paragraph, decide which sentence serves as topic sentence. For each topic sentence, identify the main topic and the controlling idea. See the Text Enrichment Site, Chapter 4, for our suggested answers.

Focus Your Point of View: Avoid Unwarranted Shift in Person

Point of view refers to the writer's method of referring to the topic. This reference occurs through the choice of **person**. First person (I, me, we, us) openly refers to the writer(s) as well as to the topic of the writing. When writers use first person, some attention remains directed to them as well as to the topic. This point of view suits informal, personal, expressive, evocative purposes, and often works well for certain types of instruction or persuasion. Second person (you) places emphasis on the reader. The reader becomes a direct participant. This point of view also tends to be informal, and works well for how-to (directional process) writing or certain forms of creative writing. Third person point of view (he, she, him, her, it, they, them) suits many academic purposes, such as expository and analytical reports, essays, and discussions. This point of view reduces attention to the writer and creates more detached, impersonal, or impartial attention to the subject. With this point of view, the writer and reader seem to be observing the people or beings being described. Emphasis in third person is less on an overt emotional dynamic between writer and reader and more on aspects of the topic. As you can see, point of view has a major determining effect. Changing points of view in the middle of a paragraph often causes a serious disruption, an ambiguity of purpose and confused angle of reference.

PRACTICE
Focusing Point of View

Read the following paragraph. Determine if it has lapses in point of view. If you are having trouble recognizing the unwarranted shifts of person, see Common Error 4 in section 3 of the Handbook—Unwarranted Shift—and then try solving the shifts in this paragraph again.

Are you a college student who finds it hard to find time to study? Are you falling behind in your courses? Never fear! We at *Learning A–Z for Youth* have the answer for you. To use our exciting new product, one has only to plug it in, place it under your pillow, and learn while one is sleeping. Yes—it's that easy. We recommend that customers read our online pamphlet before purchasing our product: a machine that reads CDs of school material to them in a gentle, soothing voice while you sleep. By the time you wake up, you will be hours richer in knowledge. *Learning A–Z for Youth* guarantees you will get higher grades, or it will gladly refund the customer's money. Try our QuickLearn today—and get that A tomorrow.

For comments on how to correct the focus of this paragraph, see "Focusing Point of View: Commentary" on the text website for this chapter.

Maintaining one point of view helps you to preserve consistent, unified tone, but you also control tone by appropriate selection and use of supporting details—what we are calling "fine points."

FINE POINTS

How do fine points affect tone? As we will see, supporting details may appeal to personal or impersonal responses—which we have called "warm" and "cool" respectively. The details affect the tone as the fine points go about upholding the topic sentence.

Types of Fine Details

By fine points, we mean the various sorts of **supporting details**, evidence, examples, explanations, justifications, proofs—all offered in support of the claim stated in the topic sentence. These details or proofs may take the form of anecdotes, examples, illustrations, analogies, and other forms of logical reasoning (see Chapter 3), statistics, facts, and other data from first-hand observation or published studies (second-hand sources), and quotations or paraphrases from authorities. In an essay of literary analysis, for instance (see "Literary and Film Analysis" on the text website, Chapter 15), a paragraph must *illustrate* the general position expressed through its topic sentence—for example, "Lois's house in 'Thanks for the Ride' is shown as dismal and depressing." This topic sentence must then be supported by closely observed details, such as the description of "the smell in the house, the smell of stale small rooms, bedclothes, frying, washing, and medicated ointments." A little later in the text, this smell is associated with the grandmother and likened to "a smell of hidden decay, such as there is when some obscure little animal has died under the verandah." Closely observed textual details such as these lend support to the claim in the topic sentence. Without the topic sentence, the paragraph would not be focused. Without the supporting details, the topic sentence would not be sufficiently sustained.

Fine Details Support the Topic Sentence

All paragraph writing, in essence, is a proper balancing of claims and supports, positions and proofs. This balance results from the clarity and commitment of the topic sentence and the validity of the detailed support through the rest of the paragraph.

Fine Details Express Tone: Warm, Neutral, and Cool Appeals

Different types of supporting detail express different tones as a result of presenting different appeals. First-person point of view, personal stories, human subjects, and evocative language tend to appeal to pathos or emotion; these and related techniques create a range of tones that some classify as "warm." So-called "neutral" tones emerge from writing that appeals more directly to logos (logic) than to personal examples, but that does not enter fully into numbers and statistical assessments. So-called "cool" appeals speak primarily to logos, at considerable distance from pathos.

✒ PRACTICE
Fine Details Creating Tone

Read the following three sample paragraphs. For each one, decide what you think is the dominant form of supporting detail and dominant tone (warm, neutral, cool). Explain why you believe the details express the tone you have suggested. The topic sentence of each paragraph has been italicized.

Sample paragraph A: Find the dominant tone

By the encouragement of self-confidence, self-worth and a feeling of pride in their ethnic origin, multiculturalism has helped the immigrants succeed in their social and economic life and has made them feel at home. There is no better indication of how self-image determines the future of the country than when I visited the northern Alberta Arab community of Lac La Biche in the late summer of 1996. "I love it here! In this town we prospered and here we have established our roots." Khalil Abughoush, owner of the IGA supermarket in Lac La Biche, was full of enthusiasm when talking about his small northern city. Like his fellow countrymen—20 percent of the town's 3,000 inhabitants are of Arab-Lebanese origin—he had come to seek his fortune in this northern Alberta resort. In Canada's multicultural society, Abughoush, like the majority of immigrants and their descendants, felt at home. As he prospered he felt no coercion to fit in, no pressure to leave his culture behind.

—Habeeb Salloum, "The Other Canadians and Canada's Future" (Reader, p. 417)

Sample paragraph B: Find the dominant tone

Fundamentally, an understanding of the sacred helps us to acknowledge that there are bounds of balance, order, and harmony in the natural world which set limits to our ambitions and define the parameters of sustainable development. In some cases Nature's limits are well understood at the rational, scientific level. As a simple example, we know that trying to graze too many sheep on a hillside will, sooner or later, be counterproductive for the sheep, the hillside, or both. More wisely, we understand that the overuse of insecticides or antibiotics leads to problems of resistance. And we are beginning to comprehend the full, awful consequences of pumping too much carbon dioxide into the Earth's atmosphere.

—HRH Charles, Prince of Wales, in the Reith lecture broadcast, May 17, 2000

Sample paragraph C: Find the dominant tone

One of the sad consequences of the push towards a hyper-masculine image is that it can rarely be obtained without the use of potentially harmful drugs. A 1993 study conducted for the Canadian Centre for Ethics in Sport concluded that four per cent of males aged 11 to 18—as many as 83,000 young Canadians—used anabolic steroids in 1992 and 1993. In the study, which involved 16,169 high-school and elementary students, one in five reported that they knew someone who was taking anabolic steroids. Among the reasons given for their use, nearly half said it was to change their physical appearance. That contrasted starkly with previously held notions that steroids were used mostly to increase athletic performance, says Paul Melia, the centre's director of education. "The reality is for most of these young men, even if they do get on a regimen of weight training, they are not going to look like these picture boys," said Melia. "And sustaining that look is a full-time job."

—Susan McClelland, "The Lure of the Body Image," *Maclean's*, February 22, 1999 (Reader, p. 449)

 Discuss your findings with your classmates and your instructor. Then have a look at our commentary at the Text Enrichment Site, "Fine Details Creating Tone: Commentary," Chapter 4.

Combining Warm and Cool Supporting Detail: Weaving Tones for Added Strength

Single paragraphs tend to emphasize one form of support over others, which is how they maintain consistency of tone and purpose. Nevertheless, if you read all of Salloum's essay in the Reader (p. 417) in comparison to all of Susan McClelland's article (Reader, p. 447), you will find shifts from warm to cool proofs, or from cool to warm. Each proof has its own particular appeals and persuasive power, and each has its own particular limitations. As a consequence, writers often seek to interweave warm and cool proofs in order to add overall strength to their persuasions. The following paragraph comes from a persuasive essay by student Marylou Orchison in favour of banning smoking in public places. Notice her effective combination of warm, neutral, and cool details, even within the single paragraph.

Sample student paragraph combining warm and cool supporting detail

Up front, I admit it: I used to be one of the many people who indulge everyday in the pleasures of a cigarette. I would light up in public places, without any regard to the fact that over 33,000 Albertans die every year as a result of smoking-related diseases (Health Canada 1997). I was as aware as the next smoker of the arguments against public control: "My dad lived to be 104, and *he* smoked" and "I have my rights—I thought this was supposed to be a free country." I frequently used these very arguments to defend my habit. Then in 1996 my mother became seriously ill. Despite her dry hacking cough, she continued to smoke. She seemed to be suffocating. When she died, I had to face the consequences of smoking, not only for myself but for those around me.

Commentary on Sample Student Paragraph

Orchison's style is relatively informal. This paragraph could almost be the text of a public address, a text intended for the ear. First person gives the paragraph considerable emotional weight, a potential persuasive power. At the same time, too much sentimentality on this topic could have the reverse effect to the one desired, and might seem manipulative. Notice that Orchison guards against the use of loaded adjectives or adverbs (horrifying, terrible, etc.). She speaks personally yet simply, concisely, and declaratively—she simply states the precise personal facts and leaves the emotional reaction to us. This control of tone (keeping the personal aspect constrained) allows her to blend a cool proof (the statistics) into her discussion without creating a jarring sense, a sense that emotional focus has radically altered.

After stating the statistic, she refers to public attitudes, looking outside herself and the personal. This represents a cooler or at least a neutral approach to analysis. But she expresses those attitudes as representative dialogue, a technique from evocative forms, which draws us closer to the personal. Next she says, "I frequently used these very arguments." In other words, she brings the focus back to herself. From there she concludes with the strong emotional appeal related to her mother. The power of the provincial statistics remains, however, and the essay will return from the convincing personal case to its broader relevance. In this paragraph, the writer's inclusion of the general facts adds a reassurance that she is speaking not just from the heart and personal experience but from scientific study and data as well. She implies that the personal realm of knowledge supports and is supported by the empirical realm of studies and analysis. She has managed to combine both warm and cool proofs into one paragraph without compromising consistent tone—but note that achieving this consistency requires care.

Beware of Misuse of Facts and Figures

Use of "cool" appeals is the distinguishing method of much academic research. But remember that statistics and data may be manipulated to reach various faulty conclusions. For example, "Unemployment claims for this year exceed those of 15 years ago by 10 percent. Clearly, abuse is on the increase." This could be a **faulty comparison**, since—for one thing—the number of workers may have significantly increased over 15 years. Other factors could be involved as well. Another misuse of numbers is the following: "Salaries in our company are excellent, averaging over $70,000 per year." This could be a faulty conclusion based on the **myth of the mean.** Perhaps executives make $350,000 each, and a majority of employees earn less than $25,000. (For further discussion of abuses of evidence, proof, and argument, see Chapter 3.)

Abuse of statistics and logic may have serious ethical repercussions. Consider the warning of Jonathan Swift in his classic satirical essay of 1729, "A Modest Proposal" (described by Swift's biographer, A.L. Rowse, as "a lucid nightmare"). In this essay, the writer marshals facts and figures in a seemingly disinterested way, and develops a tone that is highly empirical, unbiased, and above all "civilized." His proposal, however, is that the Irish poor should sell their children as food items. From seemingly logical recourses springs a monstrous idea. As you proceed through academic disciplines, remember Swift's warning that an empirical surface does not guarantee a sound, ethical conclusion. In fact, statistics and detached style may sometimes furnish an ideal mask for unethical intentions. Remember that your supporting details may range from warm to cool, and consider both the advantages of balancing types of proofs and appeals throughout your writing as well as the challenges of integrating differing tones.

FLOW

Flow refers to the way thoughts proceed coherently and purposefully. Within paragraphs, this quality results from two main attributes: (1) purposeful arrangement of supporting ideas (fine points), and (2) transitional words.

Purposeful Order of Points Within a Paragraph

Here is an example from student Lenny Halfe's essay "My Dream Home":

> The internal layout of my dream home is very specific. The east side of the main floor contains a large master bedroom with a walk-in closet, a smaller second bedroom, and a large bathroom. The living room/den is located in the southwest corner, while the kitchen sits in the northwest corner. A large closet greets people as they enter through the back door along with a doorway that leads to the stairs to the basement.

Halfe imagines guiding us in a natural spatial progression. Other principles of coherent order include time, cause-effect relationships, contrasts, and intensification (climactic order). Once you have organized your points, you need to consider firming up the natural flow by use of appropriate transitional words.

Transitional Words and Repetitions

Transitional words organize, guide, and intensify the flow of thought. Here is a sample paragraph by Jacqueline O'Rourke, a writing instructor, in the *English 155 Study Guide: Developing Reading and Writing Skills* (1990), showing transitional words in bold.

A home usually reflects the owner's personality. **First of all**, the furniture one chooses can tell us a lot about that person. **If one chooses** modern, colourful furniture, then we can assume that the person is a modernist, one who appreciates the present. **If one chooses** antiques, then we assume one has a sense of nostalgia for times gone by. The way one decorates the walls and floors **also** tells us a lot. **If** walls are left bare, the person may be a minimalist, **one who** prefers the simple. **If** walls are cluttered, the person may be disorganized and indecisive. **Finally, if** floors match furniture, the person may be organized and may strive to see the patterns in life. **On the other hand**, if floors are in bold contrast to walls and furniture, the person may be slightly eccentric, preferring the unpredictable and chaotic. **Therefore**, by observing someone's choice in home decoration, you can get to know that person without an actual meeting.

We can see two main types of linking devices at work in this paragraph, **transitional terms** and **repetitions**. The transitional phrases include "first of all," "on the other hand," "also," "finally," and "therefore." They reinforce a sense of logical order, reminding the reader that information is presented in a certain patterned manner. The repetition of certain key words may work as a coherence device, or the repetition may use a particular sentence pattern. In this case, the sentence pattern of dependent/independent clauses is repeated through the structure "If . . . then . . ." As well, there is the repetition of relative clauses: "one who appreciates the present," "one who prefers the simple." In your reading of the selections in this text as well as your reading in general, pay close attention to how writers use coherence devices—transitional terms and repetitions—to glue their passages together.

Here is a partial table of **transitional terms** commonly used in connection with the organizing principles outlined earlier in this section. These terms are used within or between sentences and paragraphs.

Standard Transitional Terms

Time:	first, next, then, later, afterwards, presently, by and by, after a while, soon, as soon as, at first
Space:	on, over, under, around, beside, by, from, next, after, across, farther, toward, at, there
Comparison:	like, unlike, in contrast, similarly, on the other hand, conversely
Features:	first, second, third (etc.), another, the last, the final, also, as well, in addition, above all, especially, indeed, more important, particularly, unquestionably
Causes/Effects:	as a result, because, consequently, so, for, therefore, thus, hence

Inserting the Right Transitional Terms

The following paragraph has a clear topic sentence that provides focus at the start, supporting details that elaborate on the topic sentence in a logical, consistent manner, and a concluding sentence that clinches the discussion. But is there a shortcoming in this writing?

Reading is a difficult act. As a writer you should make this act as easy as possible by previewing your points, linking them in logical progression with appropriate transitional terms, and adhering to standard punctuation. There is good reason to preview your points. Doing so is like providing a roadmap to a traveller. The path will be clearer. You should be sure that the path you have charted on the map is efficient, that it leads as logically as it can from point to point. Your points should be in effective order, flowing purposefully one to the other. You should use linking words. This will remove any possible uncertainty about where you are going next and why. Punctuation needs to be considered because lack of correct mechanics can cause readers to wonder where one thought ends and the next begins. An opening overview of points followed by a logical flow of ideas clarified by suitable transitional terms and correct punctuation will earn you grateful readers.

 You have probably observed that this paragraph is choppy. Your task is therefore to insert linking terms, as appropriate, to guide the discussion. Once you have done this, have a look at the Text Enrichment Site under Chapter 4, "Inserting Transitional Terms: Suggested Solutions," for our suggested answers and comments. Your solutions do not have to be exactly the same as those in the suggested answer; the important thing is that you have considered the main ingredients of a paragraph and demonstrated a sense of linkage.

Transitional Paragraphs

In addition to transitional words, **transitional paragraphs** (often just two or three sentences long) are sometimes used in essays to mark major shifts. Typically, such paragraphs summarize the discussion so far and preview the remaining points. As short paragraphs among longer ones, transitional paragraphs stand out as effective markers of division. This effect is lost, however, if they are overused.

Example of Transitional Paragraph

We have just seen how, in essence, Canadians may claim a certain moral superiority over Americans. This advantage pales, however, when we explore each nation on the basis of generosity.

Occasionally, one sentence stands alone as a transitional paragraph between other paragraphs. Usually this denotes a major transition of sections of an essay. Single-sentence paragraphs, even of this nature, are rare in academic writing where style tends toward formality.

FINALITY

Finality reminds you of the principle of clinching or cinching your paragraph: ending with a strong signal that your paragraph is "wrapping up." Concluding your paragraphs with an appropriate final sentence accomplishes two things:

- A concluding sentence fully articulates, or emphasizes, the main point and controlling idea of the paragraph.
- A concluding sentence looks ahead to the topic of the next paragraph.

The following paragraph from an essay by a university student, Jessica Walker, builds to a decisive concluding sentence. This paragraph comes from an essay called "Los Niños de Nicaragua," which describes the author's trip to Managua with the non-profit organization Change for Children Association. In a previous paragraph, she has described how in certain marketplaces "projects" have been set up to offer children a place to meet and play: "Some of the projects are located in small corners of the market, blocked off from the chaos by a few boards nailed together."

Sample paragraph (note the final sentence)

One of the hardest things to face in the projects is the hardship in these children's lives. Most come from large families and are expected to sell goods in the market by day and then come home in the evening to help out with household chores. I met one girl who attended one of the projects for only a couple of hours in the morning because her parents wanted her to resume her sales in the market. She told me she has 10 brothers and sisters, and that after she has sold enough in the market, she must hurry home to start supper for her young brothers and sisters, clean the house, and do laundry. She seemed so much older than she really is. She drew me a colourful picture of a house with a walkway and an abundance of flowers in a front garden—a picture so similar to the ones I used to draw when I was a little girl. She lives in one of the many shacks put together with garbage-bag walls and hard-packed dirt for the floor. The home in her picture is a dream.
      For the kids who live on their own in the market, life is harder still. . . .
[Paragraph continues.]

Walker's terse final sentence—"The home in her picture is a dream"—sums up the details she has provided and drives home the position of her topic sentence. It also prepares us for a transition from children like this young girl to another category of children who are even more unfortunate, the homeless. This worse-off category becomes the focus of the ensuing topic sentence ("For the kids who live on their own in the market, life is harder still"). This transition also demonstrates the effect of climactic organization (building to increasingly powerful points).

Remember that paragraph conclusions, like paragraph topic sentences, frequently assist the important process of linking ideas.

PRACTICE
Finding the 4 Fs

Look closely at Sample A Corrected (p. 47) and Sample B Corrected (p. 48). In as close detail as possible, write down how those two samples apply various methods to achieve the 4 Fs. On the text website, Chapter 4, see our commentary in response to this exercise.

FINAL THOUGHTS

You have now considered the four major attributes of successful paragraphs: focus, fine points, flow, and finality. Certain paragraphs call for additional special awareness. To learn more about these special paragraphs—notably essay introductions and conclusions—and their particular strategies, see Chapter 7, "Introductions and Conclusions."

Essay writing, as we know, involves more than one paragraph. Typical first-year essays are five or six paragraphs long. This is because on complex topics, one focused idea alone will not provide everything you need to say to support the controlling idea of your response. That is why it is useful to think of the paragraph as a building block. It needs to be complete in itself, but the idea it completes may need to be combined with several others to offer proper support for the larger controlling idea expressed by the essay. Your formal organization of these complete ideas, or paragraphs, will provide a staircase for your reader, a logical progression to a new level of awareness and relationship to the topic. Chapter 6 offers guidelines for organizing paragraphs so that they move effectively from one to the next in conjunction with the controlling idea and supporting reasons of an essay.

Writing good paragraphs, and being able to link them effectively to your essay thesis, may indeed prove to be one of the most valuable skills you develop as a writer.

Works Consulted

Ackroyd, Peter. *London: The Biography*. London: Vintage, 2001.

Lipschutz, Gary, John Roberts, John Scarry, and Sandra Scarry. *The Canadian Writer's Workplace*. 5th ed. Toronto: Thomson Nelson, 2004.

O'Rourke, Jacqueline, and David Brundage. *English 155 Study Guide: Developing Reading and Writing Skills*. Athabasca: AU, 1990.

Rowse, A.L. *Jonathan Swift: Major Prophet*. London: Thames and Hudson, 1975.

Chapter 5
Ways of Starting

Training for a marathon, sorting out your work space, establishing a good study routine, organizing for a long trip, or writing an essay—in every case, actually starting the activity will be one of the hardest parts of the process. The prospect of trying to write an effective essay sometimes feels daunting, even paralyzing. Once you begin, however, your efforts can quickly prove rewarding, as you discover ideas, shape a preliminary frame for your discussion, and settle upon a clear point to contend and explore. Working on an essay should increasingly invigorate you as you proceed. Nevertheless, final aspects of any essay seldom come to the writer effortlessly—usually they are the results of a slow process of discovery. So how does an essayist—either novice or experienced—reach that sense of readiness, that sense of having developed sturdy content, that moment of ripeness for producing a formal, organized, analytical college paper? How does one begin?

BEGINNING WITH A TOPIC

As you explore different techniques to help you ease into your essay, you need some idea of your topic. So let's reflect a little more on the matter of a topic.

A topic is a subject: a noun, modified noun, or noun phrase, rather than a complete idea or position. "Athletics" is a topic (a noun). "Women's athletics" is a more specific topic (a noun modified by the possessive noun "women's" serving as an adjective or descriptive word). "Women's athletics at Canadian universities" is more specific still (one modified noun further narrowed by the phrase "at Canadian universities"). If we move beyond nouns or noun phrases to full sentences ("With few exceptions, women's athletics at Canadian universities remain severely underfunded"), we now have a position statement, a possible topic sentence focusing a paragraph or even a thesis sentence focusing a whole essay (see Chapters 4 and 6). That degree of precise comment comes about after much reflection and, usually, considerable drafting. Before reaching that stage, you may well be working with the broadest of possible topics, such as nutrition or music or athletics.

Ideally, you should decide to explore a topic that appeals to you in some important way, one that inspires or compels you to write about it. This will usually mean choosing a topic that you already know something about. An important value in writing is the ethos, or credibility, of the writer. Naturally someone who has completed a marathon has more ethos on the topic of training for long distance than does a non-runner. If the topic you find yourself considering, by scholarly choice or necessity, is one you do not know much about, allow yourself enough time to gain the necessary knowledge you lack, and be sure you can gain access to that knowledge through various sources (see Chapter 18, "Research Methods").

As you know, sometimes you are asked or required to write on a topic that does not immediately interest you. In most cases, with a little patience and flexibility, you can find an interesting dimension to the topic, an angle that engages or motivates you. For example, your instructor might ask you to write a personal essay, but you dislike writing about yourself. Rather than allowing this to intimidate you, you talk with your classmates and your instructor about the assignment, and find out more about the meaning of the key term "personal essay." Once you realize that your instructor requires an essay about some meaningful experience you have undergone or observed (not a revelation of things that you wish to keep private), the topic becomes more inviting. Now you think of the first pet you owned and how it defied many stereotypical ideas about that type of pet. Your essay will be mainly focused on the pet and what you learned from it rather than on you. The topic, initially unappealing, is now of strong interest.

Let's consider another example. Perhaps the assigned topic is politics. You associate politics with legislatures and national relations, matters that may not appeal to you. Your friend, however, explains that politics can refer broadly to member relations within any informal governing body, such as a family. Suddenly you are motivated. You explore the politics of the family through two or three pre-writing activities described in the following pages. These help you to discover a strong interest in the politics of sibling relationships. You then define family politics as the struggles for status and influence in the family. You analyze these issues in terms of sex, age, position, personality type, and relationship to the perceived dominant family members. This leads you to think about the coping strategies that various siblings use. In conclusion, you come to some thoughts about good and bad strategies, and what your ideas mean. You then become curious to know what academic research you can find on the topic, and how that research compares to your personal inferences.

This example suggests how you can use various pre-writing strategies to help you explore and reflect on areas of personal connection; this reflection in turn furthers the important process of narrowing your topic. Consider that essay length (3 pages double-spaced, 12 pages double-spaced, etc.) also dictates how narrow your topic must be. The shorter the paper, the more care you must take to focus on a narrowed topic. In four pages, you will not be able to discuss completely your family, various strategies you have observed for coping with family politics, academic research on the topic, as well as the way your personal perceptions compare to the formal research. All of this would produce three or even four essays of at least four pages each. Your pre-writing reflections will help to provide the topic subdivisions that help you to select what feels right for your preferences, ethos, available sources, and length.

SELECTING A TOPIC FOR PRE-WRITING PRACTICE

Before exploring any pre-writing strategy, choose a topic that interests you and one that you know something about. Consider the value of researching your topic and allow for the time and resources required. Be sure both time and resources are available. Think carefully about the length of the paper requested and recognize the extent to which you will need to narrow your topic. If the topic is one you care about, you will still need to explore the exact aspects of it that suit the assignment. If, on the other hand, the topic seems uninspiring, you will need to search for some interesting aspect and ways to find out more about it. So, in the following practice activities, select one of the suggested topics for each exercise, even if none appeals to you much at first. This practice will help you discover how a seemingly dull topic can develop interesting possibilities. In all cases, you will need to find subdivisions of the topic and consider how these could help narrow and shape your discussion. Pre-writing strategies are enjoyable and effective ways to solve these needs.

PRE-WRITING STRATEGIES

All the completed, published essays we read began as earlier forms, with only loose associations and even random points of interest in their pre-draft and early draft versions. How did these essays develop? You are probably well aware that science has come to associate the left side of our brains with logical, linear, ordered functions, and the right side with intuitive, circular, open functions. While a step-by-step logical approach to essay writing has its value and place, if you become too rigid and "logical" before your ideas are crystallized, you may end up shaping content into material that is not sufficiently interesting, that has not emerged from the intuitive, deeper regions of your mind (those associated with the right brain). Mordecai Richler, the award-winning novelist, worked according to a very disciplined schedule, yet while he was getting started he often listened to music, such as the piano improvisations of jazz musician Oscar Peterson. Paying attention to your surroundings and activities may help *you* with your intuitive and creative ideas. You can employ any number of creative strategies.

In keeping with the mysteries of the right brain—the non-linear conveyer of insights—we also suggest that you not think too rigidly about writing as a series of distinct stages (pre-writing, writing, revising). Consider that writing is recursive, not linear; it involves a back-and-forth motion and a multitude of tiny decisions as we move through the work. Still, it is helpful to think about stages in the production of an essay because it helps us develop ways to deal with challenges that arise. At the so-called pre-writing stage, for example, you are encouraged to indulge in conceptual play. Whatever techniques you find most helpful, pre-writing is a way of talking to yourself that sets in motion some chain of associations that will eventually take shape as the essay's first draft. Here are some common strategies you can use at this pre-writing stage:

- making a collage
- freewriting
- brainstorming
- diagramming
- building a topic-sentence tree
- inkshedding
- keeping a journal

Making a Collage

Let's imagine your assignment is to analyze some aspect of Alice Munro's short story "Thanks for the Ride" (Reader, p. 376). You could begin by exploring your feelings and ideas about this story through a collage. Find images in magazines and elsewhere that express an important element of the story for you. For instance, what image would you choose to portray Lois's dress? How would it contrast to other images expressing her house, her previous relationships, and the town? Assemble these images onto a background, in whatever spatial relationship feels appealing and meaningful to you. A sample collage on "Thanks for the Ride" has been provided by artist Blaise MacMullin (Figure 5.1, p. 65).

The images need not be "realistically representational"; that is, they may be abstract lines, patterns, shapes, or colours. The important thing is that these images speak to you as coming from the heart of the story. Developing this playful, intuitive, tactile relationship may help you grasp your own connections to the story from unconscious, non-verbal sources. Considering your collage, and perhaps discussing it with others, is a good transitional step from free-form communing to translating your ideas into words.

PRACTICE

Make your own collage to express your preliminary responses to one of the three other narrative pieces in the Reader: "The Hockey Sweater" (p. 387), "The Sun Is Your Enemy" (p. 390) or "The King and I" (p. 399).

Freewriting

Freewriting means picking up pen or pencil (or sitting at the keyboard) and simply letting yourself go. You write whatever comes into your head, without stopping, for a designated short period. The continuous nature of freewriting allows for no hesitations in your thinking, diction, syntax, or editing: no second-guessing in any

Figure 5.1
Sample Collage
for "Thanks for
the Ride" by
Blaise MacMullin

way of your thoughts in that moment. Some or even a lot of your freewriting may not even address your topic. The point is not direction or polished content here—only writing in uninterrupted motion, only unfettered thinking as highly personal expression. After all, freewriting is for you only, not for any other audience.

The following sample of freewriting comes from an essay by Peter Elbow. He notes that this is "a fairly coherent" sample; yours may be just as coherent or less so. Whatever works for you is fine.

Freewriting

I think I'll write what's on my mind, but the only thing on my mind right now is what to write for ten minutes. I've never done this before and I'm not prepared in any way—the sky is cloudy today, how's that? Now I'm afraid I won't be able to think of what to write when I get to the end of the sentence—well, here I am at the end of the sentence—here I am again, again, again, at least I am still writing—Now I ask is there some reason to be happy that I am still writing—ah, yes! Here comes the question again—What am I getting out of this? What point is there in it? It's almost obscene to always ask it but I seem to question everything that way and I was gonna say something else pertaining to that but I got so busy writing down the first part that I forgot what I was leading into. This is kind of fun oh don't stop writing—cars and trucks speeding by somewhere out the window, pens clittering across people's papers. The sky is still cloudy—is it symbolic that I should be mentioning it? Huh? I dunno. Maybe I should try colours, blue, red, dirty words—wait a minute—no can't do that, orange, yellow, arm tired, green pink violet magenta lavender red brown black green—now that I can't think of any more colours—just about done—relief? Maybe.

—Peter Elbow, "Freewriting," in *Exploring Language*, 7th ed., ed. Gary Ghoshgarian (New York: HarperCollins, 1995), 19–21.

It may help you to think of this raw prose as a type of play, like making a collage or brainstorming. Freewriting sidesteps your inner critic and releases you from the pressures of "correct" grammar, vocabulary, and structure. As a result, you can have fun. You can enjoy the visceral experience of writing, and contemplate the musical, associative, mysterious dimensions from which you may later draw ideas of potential value.

♪ PRACTICE

Freewrite for one page on one or more of the following topics: an ideal vacation, why you do or do not vote, some good memories, a favourite song.

Brainstorming

When you brainstorm, you jot down spontaneous thoughts, feelings, associations, and notions that are evoked by your topic. As with freewriting, this activity is intuitive and open. But whereas freewriting flows continuously and inkshedding (discussed later) makes considered connections between sentences, brainstorming is more intermittent: a scattering of only possibly related points. It allows you to try out particular hunches, to let your ideas churn. Here, you still conjure rather than edit, writing down single words, phrases, or sentences. You may make lists and draw pictures to represent your conceptualizing. You may lie on the couch listening to music, asking yourself what part of your topic interests you. Trust that answers will come, if you take the activity of reflection seriously. You may wish to try out your initial ideas on a friend or classmate. Some teachers and students encourage group brainstorming as a creative search in which the participants' ideas stimulate further ideas in one another.

You may also want to try talking with only yourself rather than others. Put questions to yourself about your ideas. What is my sense of this? Why do I have this impression? Can I link two of my observations? If I sense some contradictions, can I account for this tension or disjunction?

The important part of brainstorming, whatever techniques you select, is to feel both stimulated and relaxed. Centuries of suddenly revealed solutions, definitions, and intuitions indicate that the results of productive brainstorming often emerge under the influence of other soothing or stimulating activities. Take a bath, listen to music, clean the bathroom, write a letter, or go for a walk—just keep thinking and trying out parts of your ideas.

Brainstorming on the topic of buying a car

Graduation! Time to buy a car??? Cost/features/insurance? Really need a new one or how about second-hand? Student loan still large! One debt after another—just normal life or becoming a consumer drone? What if . . . real life = consumer drone? Worried about all those freeway shootings in L.A.? Road rage increasing in North America? Wow! Feel a car creates a great private space to use to and from work: music, private thoughts. But car as necessary purchase? Perhaps bus not so bad but lots of eccentric commuters who want to talk about the CIA and the X-Files. Car looking good.

🖋 PRACTICE

Brainstorm on one of the following topics: living with a difficult roommate, achieving an interesting look on $30 or less, recognizing four types of customer.

Diagramming

Diagramming draws (pun intended) on the strong link between picturing your ideas and writing about them. Once you have formed some ideas through various intuitive techniques, you visualize, explore, and develop relationships among these ideas through diagramming. The following four figures represent diagramming used to identify and organize ideas in response to essay topics. The first topic is to compare the essays "The Lure of the Body Image" (p. 447) and "Canadians: What Do They Want?" (p. 467). This particular topic is further discussed in Chapter 12. The second topic poses the following question related to "The Rhetorical Stance" (p. 487): what does Wayne Booth mean by "the rhetorical stance" and what current examples can you provide to illustrate the three "corrupt" stances? In other words, the first two topics require critical responses to essays in the Reader of this text. The third and fourth illustrations of diagramming respond to the following two hypothetical questions: discuss the ethics of cloning and discuss social concerns about the internet. Each of these illustrations suggests how you can picture your way toward your position on a particular topic. Diagramming will help you both to develop a thesis—your specific position to be supported—and to consider counter-arguments against your thesis.

Diagramming on the Topics of . . .

Figure 5.2
Comparison Between "The Lure of the Body Image" and "Canadians: What Do They Want?"

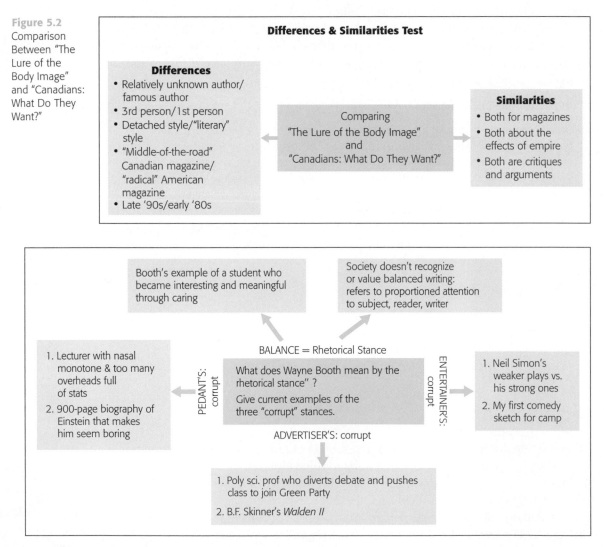

Differences & Similarities Test

Differences
- Relatively unknown author/ famous author
- 3rd person/1st person
- Detached style/"literary" style
- "Middle-of-the-road" Canadian magazine/ "radical" American magazine
- Late '90s/early '80s

Comparing "The Lure of the Body Image" and "Canadians: What Do They Want?"

Similarities
- Both for magazines
- Both about the effects of empire
- Both are critiques and arguments

Booth's example of a student who became interesting and meaningful through caring

Society doesn't recognize or value balanced writing: refers to proportioned attention to subject, reader, writer

BALANCE = Rhetorical Stance

PEDANT'S: corrupt

1. Lecturer with nasal monotone & too many overheads full of stats
2. 900-page biography of Einstein that makes him seem boring

What does Wayne Booth mean by the rhetorical stance" ?

Give current examples of the three "corrupt" stances.

ENTERTAINER'S: corrupt

1. Neil Simon's weaker plays vs. his strong ones
2. My first comedy sketch for camp

ADVERTISER'S: corrupt

1. Poly sci. prof who diverts debate and pushes class to join Green Party
2. B.F. Skinner's *Walden II*

Figure 5.3
What Does Booth Mean by the "Rhetorical Stance"?

Figure 5.4
Ethics of Cloning

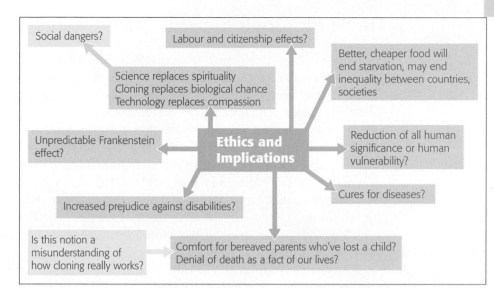

Figure 5.5
Social Concerns
About the Internet

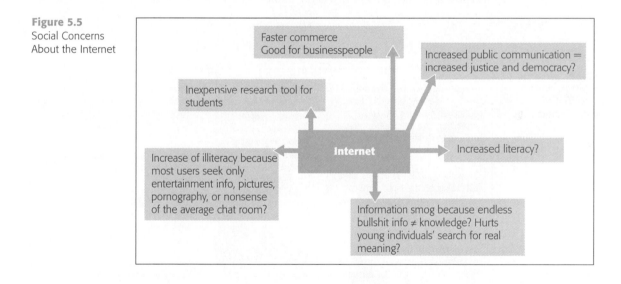

Using these examples for ideas, now try the following exercises.

 PRACTICE

Diagram ideas on two or more of the following topics:

- a comparison of old-car and new-car ownership
- the benefits and/or disadvantages of home learning

- an argument for or against the Kyoto Accord
- a how-to essay sharing your enthusiasm for a favourite activity, such as pool playing

Building a Topic-Sentence Tree

Making a collage, freewriting, brainstorming, and diagramming will lead you to ideas about what you want to say on a topic. A topic-sentence tree helps you develop that sense further, so that you can shape a tentative thesis and overall discussion. Like diagramming, a topic-sentence tree visually represents relationships, examples, assertions, and counterpoints. However, it is a more advanced form of diagramming in that the statements you place in your "tree" may, with a little further consideration and refinement, stand as topic sentences in your essay. You are still at the exploratory stage, still testing—but now with an eye to evolving fully articulated topic sentences in effective relation to the thesis (main trunk) of the whole.

See Figure 5.6 for an example of a topic-sentence tree for an essay on the film *The Blair Witch Project*.

All writing is a form of rewriting, so as you develop your essay from the topic-sentence tree you will probably revise the wording of some sentences, cut certain ones and add new ones. You may wish to explore two or three versions of a topic-sentence tree for your essay.

Figure 5.6
Topic-Sentence Tree: *The Blair Witch Project*

The young characters' helplessness, over such a long period of time, effectively touches the audience more than the antics of a one-dimensional action hero.

Drawing on childhood fears, the film relies on the basic form of a children's ghost story and some fairy tales: a witch in the woods.

The film's raw visual simplicity surprises viewers in an era of Hollywood big egos, big budgets, special effects, complicated plot twists, and complex cinematography.

The film's innovative marketing campaign of pretending the actors were real people who went missing makes the film more terrifying, since we can pretend we are watching documentary footage, not just another scary movie down at the Cineplex.

Tentative Thesis: *The Blair Witch Project* appeals to a wide audience because its simplicity in characterization and presentation easily allows viewers to imagine themselves in the story.

Unlike most horror and thriller films, *The Blair Witch Project* has no resolved ending and, in fact, offers no answers to the nature of its villain.

Like most people, the characters presume to know what they do not.

The characters are average young people with hope and courage, but with weak problem-solving skills, thereby inviting our empathy.

The film relies on amateur, deliberately awkward camera work to make the young filmmakers in the woods seem not only vulnerable, but also like us, the film audience that watches but does not make films.

The Blair Witch Project relies for its terror on three basic childhood fears: fear of the woods (at least, in Euro-American cultures), fear of becoming lost, and fear of the dark.

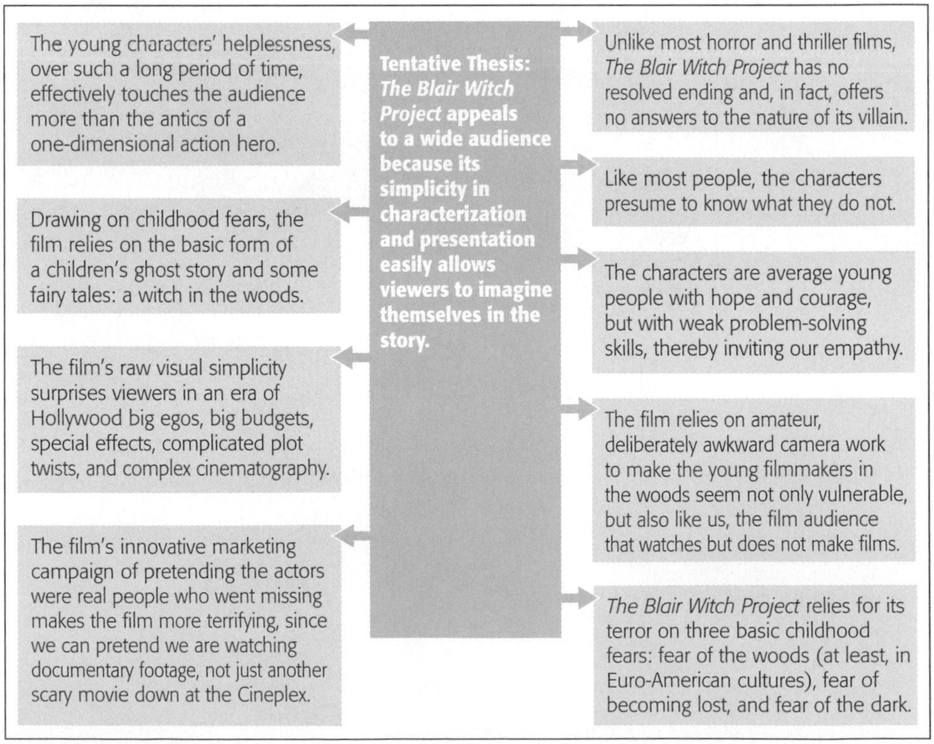

Inkshedding

Inkshedding is really a more focused form of freewriting. Usually, you address a topic in order to express a view or analysis, and the rules of grammar apply. You take more time with your diction and syntax, and you will probably reread your piece of writing to make little adjustments. Though no grade is assigned, the instructor or your classmates will likely read and comment on your short piece of writing, which is less likely with freewriting. Inkshedding is spontaneous writing like freewriting, but not necessarily a continuous motion activity. In some forms of inkshedding, one student can even write after another, as a chain of composition. For one inkshedding exercise, an instructor can usually give students approximately 15 minutes to produce one-half of a page of relatively unified comment on an assigned topic. Many non-fiction prose classes and introductory English and communications classes use inkshedding as a regular writing activity that allows students quick but thorough feedback on their writing skills without undertaking the heavy writing commitment of a formal paper or in-class essay.

Here is what an inkshedding sample might look like. The exercise focuses a student's efforts on taking responsibility for a view that he or she expresses in writing. Inkshedding's spontaneous nature and short duration also encourage students to feel confident and free in their own writing voices.

Inkshedding on the topic of the Kyoto Accord

Should Canada ratify the Kyoto Accord on reducing carbon (greenhouse gas) emissions? I think the agreement is to reduce greenhouse gas emissions by 3.5 percent by 2012. (It was originally to be a 5 percent reduction over current levels by 2010, but it seems to me the latest stories have quoted a smaller objective and an extended time frame. This needs to be checked.) Anyway, the U.S.A., the Alberta government, Australia, and the gas and oil industries in general are opposed to the Kyoto proposal. These parties say they will take action to control or reduce the harmful agents in the emissions, but without guaranteeing reductions in the levels of emissions. This notion, they believe, will take longer than the 10 years required by Kyoto. Given increased climate and health problems, this longer wait for significant improvements may not be a good idea. Kyoto opponents say that evidence of harm is unconvincing; undeveloped countries should be made to comply with Kyoto before the rest of us do; and our economies will suffer. But, on the first point, many scientists support Kyoto. On the second point, undeveloped nations don't produce nearly the levels of emissions that we do. And on the third point, economies are resilient and too complex to be so easily assessed. Privatizing of energy in Alberta has resulted in huge cost increases for low-income consumers. That sort of "economic problem," however, does not seem to have troubled the anti-Kyoto gas and oil cartel. Opponents of Kyoto also demand a "made-by-us" approach. But almost 40 countries agreed on the Kyoto approach. How will we ever reach an agreement if every party reneges on the previous agreement and then demands to create the next one?

PRACTICE

Produce a half-page of inkshedding on one of the following topics: cellphone use, rock concert experiences, standard English versus slang, non-smoking legislation, an essay of your choice from the Reader, violence in sports or in film, tattooing and/or body piercing, true love in the modern world, an enlightening moment.

Keeping a Journal

If you were to poll professional writers on the subject of keeping a journal, you would likely find that the vast majority either keep one or have done so at significant stages in their development. Journals are notebooks in which writers record thoughts, ideas, observations, impressions, descriptions, summaries, quotations, dreams, responses to readings, social and political events, and just about anything else of substance or fleeting impression. The journal can prove a valuable reference source, but even more importantly, the act of keeping it encourages the writer to look intently, to think seriously, to stretch awareness, and most important of all, to keep writing every day ("*jour*" is French for "day"). From this daily exercise, new inspiration and skills will flow. Spending a regular period of 20 minutes or more every day with your journal is an excellent way to discover your own thoughts and to reflect further on them. Keeping a journal can be a form of meditation.

The same benefits apply if you regard yourself more as a student than a writer. The journal provides an excellent forum for thinking before and after classes. Before lectures or workshops you can write down your ideas on the approaching topic. After the class, while the content is still fresh in your mind, you can review your preliminary ideas on the topic and contrast them with what you have learned. You can raise questions and note any points that may remain unclear to you. You may amplify the examples that were given in class and test them. Dating your entries allows you to look back on the unfolding logic of your various subjects.

Journals are private. Like diaries, they represent communications with yourself, though, unlike diaries, they range far beyond straight narrative summaries of daily activities. You can summarize some degree of personal experience in your journal, but your emphasis will be on expanding your knowledge, on reflection, on exploration, and on consciousness of meaning.

Remember that you are writing for yourself in order to produce private expressions that help you think through class texts, discussions, or indirectly related issues. With an academic journal, your instructor may wish to examine your entries and may have some format requests, but otherwise entries can take whatever form works best for you. Many writing instructors find that students produce their best writing in journal entries. This may be because you feel less inhibited when writing to yourself. You can be direct, natural, and honest. These are fundamentals of good writing. So recognize the value of your journal. It can connect you with your own voice, one of the greatest breakthroughs in the growth of any writer.

Here is a brief example of what a journal entry might look like:

Journal entry

– Was given an interesting assignment in my writing class last week (finally!)

– Had to pick a news story from a recent newspaper and look for any social biases in it—in language, the photograph accompanying the article, or the headline. The teacher asked, "<u>How</u> is a meaning or interpretation created?"

– Don't know yet what exactly I'll write my analysis on, but started reading the newspaper a little bit every day now—amazed at how the photos and headlines work as interpretation <u>before</u> I even read the news story.

– Also noticed how different newspapers treat the <u>same</u> story a little differently. (The teacher asked us, "Who is the target audience of different newspapers? And for each news story?")

– Now I'll have to pick a particular story and start a rough draft of my analysis soon.

As we said, keeping a journal allows you to be more regularly productive as a writer. This makes it easier for you to write, in the same way that routine swimming, skating, or stick-handling practice allows swimmers or hockey players to reach and retain their peak form. For this reason, many professional writers keep journals. Following is a sample from the journal of Canadian writer Thomas Wharton, author of two internationally acclaimed novels, *Icefields* and *Salamander*.

Sitting here, nothing by me, rock, and the flutter of the paper in the wind. The barest elements for writing.

I haven't really tried to describe the mountains themselves yet, though. How to do it without lapsing into the easy clichés about their very palpable majesty and fearfulness? Maybe try to think of them as a quantum extrapolation of the ground-up pebbles at my feet. Pick up a single rock and describe it. The cool, pitted, unpretentious, ancient, trustworthy, secretive, implacable feel of a rock in my hand. The delicate, minute surface striations and scoring etchings. Whorls of veins of colour. The globular, unplannable asymmetry that gets recreated in the vast peaks above.

Next try a boulder. Well, it's more an obelisk easily six feet taller than me. That D.H. Lawrence poem about a boy and a horse standing next to each other. The poet says they are in another world. That's what it feels like standing next to this massive rock. We are together, somehow, in another world, where no one speaks.

—Excerpt from journal of Thomas Wharton, spring 1990

Here is what Wharton says about keeping a journal and using it to work out the problem of how to describe the Rocky Mountains:

Early on, I realized that it was healthy to think of what I was doing as a kind of translation. That this place I was trying to write about had a language, so to speak, all its own, a non-verbal language. And that if I was going to go beyond mere postcard clichés about the majesty of the peaks, the pristine beauty, etc., I was going to have to try to carry across to the reader something of that non-verbal world. And that, as I carried my impressions across into words, something of that non-verbal world would be lost.

As I wrote, I kept notebooks of my thoughts, ideas, dreams, alternative story-lines, etc. I saw this series of notebooks as a kind of "dream-version" of the book I was writing, where I allowed myself to write all the immediate, unedited, silly things that might not necessarily be allowed into the novel.

And I find this dream-book fascinating to read through now because it is a raw record of process, in a way that the finished book isn't. I can see the processes of translation at work in my journals. Taking material from my own experiences and memories, from history and literature, from the sheer seductive power of words.

—Commentary by Thomas Wharton, 2002

In Wharton's novel *Icefields*, the author included a passage on pages 77–78 that drew on his previous journal entry. The character Elspeth is sipping tea while watching a distant avalanche:

The morning after the glasshouse party she is in the chalet's front parlour, sipping hot Earl Grey tea from an eggshell china cup.

From her window, she can just make out a climbing team struggling up the glacier against blowing snow. Five tiny figures huddled together, crawling slowly forward up the slope. The alpinists from Zermatt.

Elspeth blows on the surface of the steaming tea, sips from it, raises her head and listens.

Above the sound of the wind, she hears the distant crack and crumple of an avalanche. The thin glass in the windowframe rattles. She glances out. It takes her a moment to find the source, a slender white plume flowing down a dark seam on Mount Arcturus. The avalanche is high on the mountain and the alpinists are in no danger, but they stand motionless, watching as the cascade of snow and ice bursts over a rock ledge.

So graceful and delicate from this distance, as if unconnected to the thunder echoing across the valley. At the glasshouse party, Byrne had told her there could be chunks of ice the size of train cars falling in those powdery veils.

Elspeth takes another sip of tea, pleased with the bitterness of lemon.

Remember, you don't have to be writing a novel to apply the journal-writing process. Journals are the private, emotional, and analytical expressions of your impressions and developing ideas that may, in part, make their way into your essays or exam answers or even questions and answers in class. A journal is a brainstorming form that charts a person's reflections on any number of issues.

PRACTICE

Look in bookstores for a style of blank notebook that suits you. It should be durable, portable, yet large enough to allow fluid writing. Many writers like a notebook that lies open without pressure. Some prefer to use loose-leaf pages or whatever paper is available. Remember to date your entries and to insert them into your journal regularly and in order.

YOUR TOPIC NARROWED

Having explored a topic or topics through one or more pre-writing activities, you have now found an angle of interest and some specific points of relevance. You are now ready to move on to the next stage of more formal drafting, which we will deal with in the next chapter.

Chapter 6
Outlining: Thesis Statements and Topic Sentences

In Chapter 1, we explored what writing is, and identified a crucial tripartite relationship involving writer, topic (or message), and intended reader(s). For every writing occasion you experience, you should visualize your intended readers and anticipate their expectations. In Chapter 1, we suggested that you imagine writing to other course students insofar as shaping a suitable tone (level of language) is concerned. But don't forget that you are also adding to the large store of marking to be handled by your instructor. Consider that person's needs and expectations as well. Your instructor is likely heavily pressed with duties. He or she probably must comment on numerous essays within a limited period of time. Anything you can do to assist this task will help your instructor and consequently assist the quality of comments you receive.

REMEMBER THE PURPOSE OF YOUR UNIVERSITY PAPERS

Perhaps the most important thing you can do for your primary readers is to provide a clear and complete thesis statement at the end of your brief introduction (usually that means at the end of your opening paragraph). This reassures your instructor that you do have a main idea to explain or argue and that you know how you are going to go about the rest of your discussion. A good thesis statement not only keeps you on track as a writer, it also communicates the controlling idea briskly and efficiently to a busy and pressured reader. The occasion of your writing as a university student, in short, favours a highly explicit, direct approach.

WHEN AND WHY TO USE A COMPLETE THESIS STATEMENT AT THE END OF THE OPENING PARAGRAPH

Do all essays use or require a clear, complete thesis statement at the end of the first paragraph? As you will see from a survey of our Reader, they do not. The structure of a piece of writing depends upon the purpose of that writing. The rest of this chapter provides critical guidance to you *as a writer of undergraduate essays,* many of which will involve a combination of analysis and argumentation. Your thesis statement will provide the results of your analysis (your evaluation of the matter) with an indication of your reasons and the methods you will be using to argue those reasons. Like your instructor, you are most likely busy and highly pressured. You need a method that will help you to write up the results of your research and thinking as briskly and efficiently as possible. Before getting started with the actual writing, design an outline that features your tentative thesis statement and the topic sentence of each supporting paragraph. Although you will probably want to revise the wording of these sentences once your first draft is completed, having them in your outline will help to keep you to task as you draft your complete paragraphs.

THESIS STATEMENTS

Nothing contributes so much to the success of your essays as an effective thesis statement. The following advice on this topic will contribute significantly to improved marks in all your liberal arts and sciences courses, provided you apply the guidelines carefully and completely.

All college and university essays attempt to take their readers on a journey looking over the facts, details, assertions, insights, and conclusions provided by the writer. In order to point your reader (and yourself) in the right direction, you need to focus on the issues, interpretations, and content of your discussion.

A **thesis statement** is the one crucial sentence in an essay that focuses you and your readers on your chosen attitude to your topic. You will be most sure of success if your thesis statement, when it first appears, does the following three things:

- occurs as the last sentence of your introduction
- expresses a strong position (a controlling idea)
- expresses the reason(s) for this position and your methods of examination

Making Your Thesis the Last Sentence of Your Introduction

You may not know where you are going until you begin to emerge from pre-writing (see Chapter 5, "Ways of Starting") and finish a spontaneous, exploratory first draft. In your finalized draft, however, you will want to convey the assurance that you knew your destination all along. You can create this impression if you include your thesis statement as the last sentence of your introduction. This location represents a primary point of impact.

Sample Design   Opening Paragraph of Short Essay

Xxxxxxxxxxxxxxxxxxxxxxxxxxxxxxxxxxxxxxxxx. Xxxxxxxxxxxxxxxxxxxxxxxxxxxxxxxxxxxxx xxxxxxxxxxxxxxxxxxxxxxxxxxxxxxxxxxxxxxxxxxxxxxxxxxxxxxxxxxxxxxxxxxxxxxxxxxxxxxxxxxxx xxx. Xxxxxxxxxxxxxxxxxxxxxxxxxxxxxxxxxxxxxxxxxxxxxxxxxxxxxxxxxxxxxxxxxxxxxxxxxxxxxxx xxxxxxxxxxxxxxxxxxxxxxxxxxxxxxxxxxxxxxxx. Xxxxxxxxxxxxxxxxxxxxxxxxxxxxxxxxxxxxxxxxxxxxxx. Xxxxxxxxxxxxxxxxxxxxxxxxxxxxxxxxxxxxxxxxxxxxxxxxxxxxxx. Your thesis sentence goes here, concluding your introductory paragraph.

In longer essays, with introductions of more than one paragraph, the thesis statement should be the last sentence of the introduction.

Providing your thesis statement at the beginning of your essay, as the *last* sentence of the first paragraph(s), makes use of natural impact locations to help ensure that your reader will recognize the importance of this statement and remember it during and after reading the essay. Here, just before launching into the journey proper, your thesis statement clearly notifies the reader of the course you have charted. Both you and your reader should be properly oriented, secure in the direction you intend to pursue as you now begin the first leg of your exploration. While you will not see this pattern in many of the readings in the Reader, or in many writings apart from those found in academic scholarship, you will find it a practical pattern to employ for your student papers, especially if you feel initially uneasy about shaping an essay.

Expressing a Strong Position

The first step in constructing your thesis is to work out your own **opinion** about the topic.

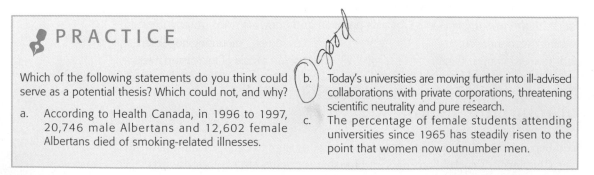

PRACTICE

Which of the following statements do you think could serve as a potential thesis? Which could not, and why?

a.   According to Health Canada, in 1996 to 1997, 20,746 male Albertans and 12,602 female Albertans died of smoking-related illnesses.

b.   Today's universities are moving further into ill-advised collaborations with private corporations, threatening scientific neutrality and pure research.

c.   The percentage of female students attending universities since 1965 has steadily risen to the point that women now outnumber men.

Only statement b above expresses a value-judgement (what some writing coaches might call a **controlling idea**) and could therefore serve as a thesis. Statements a and c set out facts (see Chapter 3, p. 35, for more on distinguishing between fact and opinion). Your thesis should express *pathos*—a strong conviction about your topic, an attitude that you will go on to demonstrate using logos and ethos (Chapter 1 discusses the basic elements of logos, pathos, and ethos). The difference between the pathos of a solid thesis sentence and that of an armchair philosopher is that the former is tested by logos and ethos and adapted to its intended reader.

To shape an effective thesis, you first need to discover and then, in your essay, express a strong position, also known as the controlling idea. Remember that even the most objectively presented expository essay is never completely detached from the writer; it has focused pathos, a core of opinion. For example, on the topic of learning to play guitar, the following thesis statement might be used: "Practising one hour a day, six days of the week, is an excellent way to progress." The words "excellent" and "progress" express a strong position on the approach being recommended—the controlling idea.

🔖 PRACTICE

Do the following proposed thesis sentences express a strong position? If so, what features do you think convey the controlling idea?

1. Roaming cats are susceptible to attack by other animals, to trapping by angry neighbours, and, most of all, to traffic accidents.
2. I begin to realize that my procrastination is caused by distractions, mounting hopelessness, and despair.
3. One of the show's meaningful motifs seems to have been relatively overlooked thus far, food and its relationship to culture, gender, and the violence that underlies the world of the characters (and by extension, our society).

The first thesis sentence above comes from the essay "Should Cats Be Allowed to Roam?" presented on page 83, later in this chapter. The words "susceptible to attack," "angry neighbours," and "traffic accidents" all convey danger and harm. The controlling idea is harm—if cats roam, they risk harm.

The second thesis sentence above comes from the essay "Causes of Procrastination" on the Text Enrichment Site, Chapter 10. The writer expresses a controlling idea concerning procrastination: that it is deeply troubling. "Distractions," "mounting hopelessness," and "despair" express the three reasons for this concern, on a scale of increasing intensity.

The third thesis sentence above comes from the essay "Starving Woman/Stuffed Man in *The Sopranos*" on the website, under "Literary and Film Analysis," Chapter 15. It suggests a controlling idea by telling us that the motif to be examined is not only meaningful but, until now, overlooked. This compounds our sense of how meaningful the insight of the following essay must be. The idea that the motif under consideration throws light on an underpinning of our society reinforces the sense of an important revelation to be gained.

Without overdoing adjectives and adverbs, these three thesis sentences concisely suggest a strong and specific unifying attitude to the subject in question.

Your expressed attitude to the issue under discussion in your essay will shape your presentation of facts as well as increase the reader's interest in your work. So for each assignment, select a topic that interests or concerns you. If the choices do not immediately interest you, approach one of them open-mindedly and ask questions that help you to connect personally with the subject. The more you care about your topic and the more clearly you form your own position on it, the stronger your writing on the topic will be. Research, if you apply proper evaluation of sources, should help you to gain interest as you make new discoveries. Remember that many things that interest you now did not do so initially—you had to learn about and experience them. In addition to hands-on life experience, knowledge comes from informed reading as you use your judgement and imagination to embrace the subject you are researching. So if your first reaction is, "This doesn't interest me," find out more about it before settling on that conclusion.

The following tip may help some new writers of university papers to avoid "deadly dull" regurgitations of research lacking in ethos and pathos. Once you have selected a topic that interests you and have explored some pre-writing activity (see Chapter 5, "Ways of Starting"), write a sentence about the topic that begins, "I believe that . . . " Make sure your opinion takes a stand on an issue related to the topic. You may be choosing between two aspects of it, stating your view of what constitutes the main cause of something, or identifying an overall characteristic that a number of things share. Once you've done this, you will have established the first component of your thesis—a *position*—and one that means something to *you*. If your instructor has assigned an essay that is more suited to third person, you can remove the personal pronoun afterwards. Using the personal pronoun as you develop your controlling idea, however, may help remind you that this paper should include *your* connection to the subject.

Including Reasons for Your Position and Your Methods of Procedure

Finally, you need to come up with reasons *why* you took this position and clarify your way of presenting and explaining them. You don't want your thesis to be purely opinion, because then your readers can dismiss your position as only one person's opinion; someone else could have an entirely different position on the subject. Without reasons, the thesis will focus on you as a person. With reasons, your thesis will focus on your ideas as a reasoned argument. Since most analytical papers discourage first person, this may be the stage at which you drop "I think that . . . ," but your personal connection remains, as it informs the power of your reasons.

Thesis statements with reasons

(I think that) tattoos may represent, at least in part, attainment of warrior status, because that was so for traditional Polynesians and it has been so for me.

(I think that) Alice Munro's stories demonstrate a complex view of humanity because her central characters are ordinary and flawed, her settings contain good and bad aspects, and her endings often feel unresolved.

In the first example, the reasons are the two points that follow the word "because." The essay introduced by this thesis appears to be a hybrid of expositional writing (reporting on research into Polynesian history and culture) and personal writing (reporting on personal experience). In the second example, the reasons are those three items that follow the word "because." Both thesis statements contain a complete map of the essay, which will discuss each of the stated reasons one at a time in the same order as laid out in the thesis statement. Both the reasons and their order of discussion are presented. We refer to this type of complete thesis statement as a **direct list**, because all the reasons for the position are listed directly. After reading a direct-list thesis statement, your audience will have no questions about the content and scope of your essay; each section of your essay body will deal with one of the previewed reasons, in that order.

Here are two more examples of direct-list thesis statements:

(I think) All young people should read a book a month because it promotes intellectual curiosity, a strong vocabulary, and informed opinions.

(I think) Euthanasia is valid for the terminally ill, because it allows them freedom to choose, comfort in their final hours, and peace of mind.

PRACTICE

Read again the three thesis sentences in the previous Practice box. None of those sentences uses the word "because." Does that mean that the sentences present no reasons for their controlling ideas?

Writers often express the word "because" in different ways. In fact, each of the three sentences in the previous Practice box conveys reasons.

The sentence "Roaming cats are susceptible to attack by other animals, to trapping by angry neighbours, and, most of all, to traffic accidents" might be rephrased as follows:

Roaming cats invite danger, because they may fall victim to predators, trapping, or vehicles.

The sentence "I begin to realize that my procrastination is caused by distractions, mounting hopelessness, and despair" might be rephrased as follows:

I begin to realize that I procrastinate because I am distracted and increasingly affected by consequent hopelessness and despair.

The sentence "One of the show's meaningful motifs seems to have been relatively overlooked thus far: food and its relationship to culture, gender, and the violence that underlies the world of the characters (and by extension, our society)" might be rephrased as follows:

The overlooked motif of food is extremely meaningful, because it relates to culture, gender, and the violence that underlies the characters (and by extension, our society).

As you can see, with or without the word "because," complete thesis sentences include the *idea* of "because"; that is, they include reasons why the writer asserts the position that he or she does.

How *Not* to Phrase Your Thesis Statements

Students sometimes have learned, or conclude on their own, that they should state their written thesis in the style of an oral explanation. Here is a typical statement using a style that is often discouraged in university writing:

> In this essay I will argue that *The Sopranos* features the motif of food, and I will show that it relates to culture, to gender, and to the violence that underlies the show and our society.

This sentence *does* express a controlling idea, its reasons, and a planned method (organization) of discussion. However, the oral, explicit style of this sentence sounds too informal for much university writing. Since the purpose of the essay introduced by this sentence is literary analysis, first person is likely not needed and is not suitable for any part of the paper, not least the thesis. During pre-writing it would be fine for the writer to produce the above sentence as a way to connect with the topic and to ensure that he or she find a controlling idea, as we recommended earlier in this chapter. But once the final draft occurs, the writer should revise the thesis something as follows:

> One of the show's meaningful motifs seems to have been relatively overlooked thus far: food and its relationship to culture, gender, and the violence that underlies the world of the characters (and by extension, our society).

 For the complete essay that flows from this thesis, see "Literary and Film Analysis," Chapter 15, on the Text Enrichment Site. Also review the tones chart (inside back cover). You will see that the essay style—thesis included—conforms to the usual level of language for university analysis. So remember, do not announce to your reader what you intend to say and demonstrate in your university essays—simply say it. This advice applies even when you are using first person. Notice that the above writer does not say, "In this essay I will argue that there are three causes of my procrastination." He simply states his realization that there are three causes. The reader understands that he is writing an essay to argue that position. (This advice, however, does not apply to all courses. You must adapt to individual instructor expectations.)

Outlining

Direct lists provide the detailed outline for the body of each essay. Each item (reason) in the list can be adapted to form a topic sentence that directs and shapes a paragraph at the beginning of each section. Here is how this works.

> Outline for "Should Cats Be Allowed to Roam?" by Joyce Miller, with direct-list thesis matched to body

Intro paragraph: Use concession-refutation to establish argumentation tone—end with thesis statement.

Thesis: Roaming cats are susceptible (1) to attack by other animals, (2) to trapping by angry neighbours, and (3) to traffic accidents.

Topic sentence 1: Mauled cats often turn up in veterinarians' offices, demonstrating a high incidence of attacks by predators. [Write 5 to 11 more sentences explaining this and reminding the reader of its connection to the thesis controlling idea that cats should not be allowed to roam. Research SPCA stats.]

Topic sentence 2: A cat is also unequipped to protect itself against traps. [Write 5 to 11 more sentences explaining this, and reminding the reader of its connection to the thesis controlling idea that cats should not be allowed to roam. Balance stats and personal observation. Check on details of city bylaw/procedure.]

Topic sentence 3: The serious injuries seen most often by veterinarians are those caused by cars. [Write 5 to 11 more sentences explaining this, and reminding the reader of its connection to the thesis controlling idea that cats should not be allowed to roam. Balance stats and personal observations.]

Conclusion topic sentence: Although in an ideal world cats should be allowed to roam, our world is not ideal. [Brief, "suggestive" conclusion]. Reinforce thesis.

Joyce Miller used this outline to guide her following essay. (Certain names and details have been fictionalized.)

Sample Essay

Should Cats Be Allowed to Roam?
Joyce Miller

1   Many people believe that because of cats' independent nature, they should be allowed to roam free. This allows them to satisfy their hunting instincts and to function within cat society, one that has its own rules and structure. Some people assert that free-roaming cats are happier cats, living a life closer to that intended by Nature. This is all true, but it is not compatible with modern life in suburban North America. Roaming cats are susceptible to attack by other animals, to trapping by angry neighbours, and most of all, to traffic accidents.

2   [First,] Despite leash laws in most communities, mauled cats often turn up in veterinarians' offices and city pounds. A cat raised with dogs may not recognize a dangerous dog quickly enough. Also, coyotes are a concern in most parts of Canada, including suburban areas, as most domestic cats have lost the degree of wariness they need to protect themselves against wild predators. For the first four months of 2006, as disclosed by Andrea Jensky of the Edmonton SPCA, there were 17 reported coyote attacks on cats living near that city's ravine. Jensky suggests that the risk may be even larger this year with higher numbers of coyotes and shortages of their usual prey. On January 4, 2006, the *Vancouver Province* reported a Vancouver woman

suing the city and the B.C. government for allegedly failing to keep the streets safe after her pet cat was killed by two coyotes (Williams A-7). With all respect for the emotional state of the woman concerned, it isn't realistic to expect Canadian cities to prevent wandering coyotes or ensure that dogs never slip loose with a notion to chase the nearest roaming pet cat.

3   [Second,] A cat is also unequipped to protect itself against traps set out by angry neighbours. As recorded in the Humane Society of Canada Year-End Report for 2003, on March 31 of that year, Edmonton City Council approved a live-capture trapping bylaw to apply from April to September. Citizens may obtain live-capture traps from the city to catch roaming cats on their properties and deliver the animals to Animal Control. Owners must pay a $100 fine and kennel fees (HSCYER). In most other municipalities whose city halls may be less willing to assist, the traps can be rented from private firms. The welfare of the cat is then in the hands of the person who was angry enough to trap it. Cats in the suburbs have to live with other people, not just with other cats, and they cannot be expected to understand the human notion of territory. Do pet owners have the right to make neighbours "share" their animals involuntarily, especially when cats exercise their feline rights to spray, dig gardens, and fight?

4   [Finally,] According to Dr. Ellen Talbot of the Edmonton South-east Veterinary Clinic, studies confirm that the serious cat injuries seen most frequently by veterinarians are those caused by cars (next is injuries from falls). Edmonton SPCA officer Andrea Jensky reinforces this awareness by describing numerous cases of traffic-injured cats that came to her attention in the final months of 2006. Her descriptions should make any cat-owner think twice about allowing their feline pet to roam. According to the American Humane Society, free-roaming cats live lives two or even three times shorter than do indoor cats (AHS). Car accidents are a major contributor to this shorter life expectancy of outdoor cats. Cars are not part of the natural world, but they are an unavoidable part of ours.

5   People in Edmonton, such as the cast of a new Stewart Lemoine play about cat ladies and computer-game addicts, certainly talk about that city's "zany cat laws." People from elsewhere say the same thing. But these laws recognize a large contingent of the public. Perhaps in an ideal world cats should be allowed to roam and live their mysterious, separate lives; our world, as Lemoine and other astute observers of the human condition have noticed, however, is not ideal. So we need to recognize that and prevent our cat pets from becoming victims of our wishful thinking. It doesn't have to be all that bad for our pets as a consequence. We can do our best to accommodate their needs with outdoor enclosures and opportunities for friendship both human and feline (two young, compatible cats will play and sleep together as well as groom each other). For most city-dwellers, the dream of the free-ranging cat must be surrendered as a pastoral myth.

Works Cited

American Humane Society. 24 Jan. 2007 <http://www.americanhumane.org>.

Humane Society of Canada Year-end Report. Humane Society of Canada. 2003. 24 Jan. 2007 <http://www.humanesociety.com/pdfs/YER2003>.

Jensky, Andrea. Personal interview. 13 Jan. 2007.

Talbot, Ellen. Personal interview. 17 Jan. 2007.

Williams, Joan. "Woman Sues over Eaten Tabby." *Vancouver Province* 4 Jan. 2006: A-4.

Note how the conceptual "contact points" (the reasons listed in the direct-list thesis) guide both the writer and her audience through the discussion. Miller might have used the directional words "first," "second," and "third" or "finally" to present her three reasons, both in the thesis and at the start of the body paragraphs. She decided that the structure was clear enough without those additional markers, but we have placed them in editor's square brackets to show you the explicit linkages at work. If the essay were to be read aloud, it would be especially helpful for Miller to include the directional words.

What are some other important features of Miller's outline?

She assigns herself to shape an opening paragraph that sets a suitable tone and observes a suitable pattern for purposes of argumentation. See Chapter 7 on introductions and Chapter 16 on argumentation.

She reminds herself that paragraphs in academic essays generally range between 6 and 12 sentences.

She sets herself the task of balancing "cool" and "warm" proofs (statistics, other researched facts, and personal observations), based on a judgement that this particular method will suit the style of essay called for by her assignment. See Chapter 4 on warm and cool proofs.

She directs herself to suitable sources of information. See Chapters 18 and 19 on research methods and citation of sources.

She advises herself on the type of conclusion she thinks will suit the assignment. See Chapter 7 on introductions and conclusions.

She has cited her sources as they occur in her discussion and listed them at the end of her essay (see Chapter 19 on documentation).

For first-year college and university papers, the direct-list thesis statement is a good idea, since it is the most orderly and exhaustive of the various types of thesis statements: it forces you to consider everything you need to do in the essay, in clear, effective order. Furthermore, it assures your instructor and classmates, upon their first examination of your paper, that it has clear and specific purpose and method.

Choosing Words That Express Your Method

Chapters 8 to 12 as well as 14, 15, and 16 illustrate in detail different points of view and especially different patterns of organization that writers use to strengthen their essays, according to purpose and intended reader. These approaches may be conveyed concisely, often with a single word, for example, "types," "ways," "examples," "kinds," "contrast," "causes," "effects," "process," "define," "analyze," and "argue." Be alert to variations of these core method words (noun forms, verb forms, etc.) and synonyms for them. A writer may say "examine" or "explore" for "analyze," for instance, or "question" for "rebut" or "argue." By using such signal words, however—words keyed to the proposed form of discussion—writers provide valuable focus on method. You will find this illustrated in further detail in the above-mentioned chapters dealing with forms. Without going into such detail at the moment, here are some sample thesis statements employing "form" or "method" signal words:

> Roaming cats are susceptible to attack by other animals, to trapping by angry neighbours, and, most of all, to traffic accidents.

By way of offering a list, Joyce Miller's thesis (illustrated and explored above) implies that her essay organization will concentrate on *classification* and *effects*: she will present three kinds of harmful effects, ordered according to increasing severity. By virtue of their syntactical appearance, direct-list thesis sentences automatically express the idea of classification. But what sort of term is being classified? Is it a cause, an effect, or an element of definition? Miller could have made her intentions even more explicit by a minor rewording to include the signal word "effects":

> Roaming cats are susceptible to three harmful effects: attack by other animals, trapping by angry neighbours, and, most of all, traffic accidents.

The small revision adds explicit precision to the form or pattern of discussion to follow, an attention to harmful effects. At a certain point, adding such words may seem pedantic and artificial; however, keeping these words in mind can help you significantly, especially if you are still gaining assurance as a writer of analytical and persuasive essays.

> Despite the widespread belief that today's young people are ruder than their parents at the same age, examples from numerous sources contradict this stereotype.

Clearly, the essay that flows from this thesis statement will be organized according to a succession of examples, each with its own commentary linking us back to the controlling idea of the thesis. Probably the examples will be organized so that the strongest, most intense, most complete, or most convincing will come last. There is also an implication that some comparison method will be used, if subordinated: today's illustrations will be compared to ones from the parents' generation. An essay on the same topic might take a somewhat different shape and emphasis if the thesis statement were revised as follows:

> Comparing social behaviour 25 years ago with social behaviour today, one might be surprised to find that today's young people are no more rude, on the whole, than were their parents.

The essay linked to this thesis sentence is likely to dedicate as much space to looking at examples from 25 years ago as to examples from today. Would this approach to the topic offer more chance of a balanced and therefore convincing argument than does the first version of this thesis sentence? Your attention to incorporating suitable signal words related to method is a good way to remind yourself to find a method that most serves your intentions—supporting your controlling idea.

> Comparing the generation of Canadians who lived through the Great Depression to that which came of age in the 1960s, one finds three important differences in attitude.

This statement not only conveys a strong position on the topic (the generations are *significantly* different) and suggests the reasons (three specific examples, named together, in general, rather than specifically listed); it also alerts us that the discussion will proceed through the method of *comparison-contrast.* The general (rather than specific) listing illustrates an approach discussed further under "General Thesis Statements" below.

> Lois's character in "Thanks for the Ride" is significantly expressed through four settings: Pop's Café, her house, the bootlegger's farmhouse, and the fields and barn.

This thesis statement alerts us that the writer will be using *description,* or an awareness of descriptive detail, as well as observing the *effects* that various details have upon our understanding of character. We can expect the writer to use verbs such as "express," "show," "indicate," "reveal," "imply," and so on, to reinforce the main purpose of the essay, asserting that setting reveals the character of Lois to us. The writer has used a direct list to name each of the settings rather than compressing them under one general term (four settings).

As you have seen from several examples above, thesis statements may suggest that more than one method of discussion will be employed. Frequently, classification (a direct list) combines with another particular method, such as causes, effects, or contrasts. Here is one more potential thesis statement that clearly conveys a purposeful combination of rhetorical methods:

> Contrary to the common cry, Aboriginal Canadians do not receive preferential treatment; in fact, analysis of their experience with the justice system suggests they are more often the subjects of mistreatment because of cultural imperialism and misunderstanding.

The opening phrase, with its use of "contrary to," signals that the essay to follow will be argumentative; its goal will be to oppose one position with a different position. The word "analysis" alerts us to expect an element of analytical writing: the writer will break a situation into component parts and examine the relationships involved. The words "subjects of" indicate the essay will devote some attention to perceived effects of a certain condition—here, cultural imperialism and misunderstanding. This is a good example to offer as our final one in this section, because a majority of university essays combine analysis (attention to constituent parts and causes and effects) with comparison and contrast of differing interpretations and persuasive presentation of the preferred interpretation.

General Thesis Statements

A disadvantage of the direct-list thesis statement is that it sometimes leaves very little to the reader's imagination. Some writers therefore prefer their thesis statements to refer briefly to all the specific reasons for their position without listing each of these reasons separately. Such thesis statements simply refer to all the reasons in a general way. As we saw above, a direct-list thesis statement might say the following:

> Lois's character in "Thanks for the Ride" is significantly expressed through four settings: Pop's Café, her house, the bootlegger's farmhouse, and the fields and barn.

The general version, cutting to just the controlling idea, might read as follows:

> Alice Munro uses setting effectively to develop the character of Lois.

A statement of this type might be referred to as a **general thesis**. Here is an outline combining a general thesis with the proposed supporting paragraphs.

More Than a Colony: Alberta Must Act Now

Malak Husef

Introduction: Concede arguments for "free trade" but point to recent problems of Alberta's "overheated" economy as example of general problems elsewhere. Research the latest findings/opinions on free trade allowances. Perhaps incorporate brief personal context of having come from Afghanistan and seen what loss of control can do.

Thesis: The time has come for Alberta and Canada to exert stronger controls against the takeover of its economy.

Topic sentence 1: Fatalistic resignation to the forces of demand will see value-added jobs go south and an eventual bust of depleted resources. Use "Peter's Principles" from *Alberta Views*, March 2007; research business reports and journals for a national cross-section suggesting to what extent this applies elsewhere in Canada. Use full twelve sentences to be sure of regional representation. Conclude by showing the common harmful effects of fatalism: loss of jobs, eventual depletion of non-renewable resources. Emphasis here is on criterion of practicality but also ethics: As we get richer, we get poorer (i.e., widening gaps).

Topic sentence 2: The fatalistic approach clearly threatens both the natural and the cultural environments. See Monbiot (*Heat*) and Canadian environmentalists on the natural effects. Find an unexpected source or two expressing concern. Even the oil companies, for example, are proposing imposed carbon reduction controls. Search for latest opinions on state of Canadian and especially Albertan home-grown culture. Noah Richler on home-grown cultural forms as enabling political self-determination and therefore vital to protect. Emphasis here on ethics—we have no right to destroy the planet and deprive future generations. Also emphasize logic: others exert controls for reasonable purposes, so it is only fair that we do the same. Also invoke aesthetics—we can't fit in someone else's clothes. Final point again ethics: we must stand on our own feet to contribute to others and the future. We must be adult and responsible.

Topic sentence 3: We *can* prevent these ongoing problems and make positive change: outline program of reasonably increased natural resources royalties; public ownership of resources; heritage funds—30 percent share for future generations; public diversification leadership; sponsorship of local arts. Research models where these practices have worked.

Conclusion: Use suggestive conclusion. Note the irony of the fact that while Albertans were trained to fear the rest of Canada as an exploiter, the most serious recent exploitation has been occurring from externals and Alberta's own policies; also, reflect upon the extent to which these proposals for Alberta could strengthen Canada as a whole. Final thought—this is not to oppose others but to enable Alberta and Canada to play its part.

What are some important features of Husef's outline?

Like Miller's, Husef's outline provides a combination of ideas for testing, methods to guide the writing, and research directions to refine ideas and gather necessary further detailed support. Husef's topic might be considered more complex and "large" than Miller's, so additional research time may be required. Husef has already identified relevant ideas from a magazine article and two books, but he must look for additional and more specific sources on his topic.

His notes toward the introduction provide a reminder to establish a suitable tone (argumentation) through a concession-refutation approach (see Chapter 15 for more on the value of concession-refutation). He will also think more about the advantages of mentioning his own personal point of view, as a former refugee from a country long troubled by external and internal would-be colonizers. This added element would likely add to the ethos that will increase from further research.

His direct general thesis expresses a strong controlling idea and clearly suggests a problem-solution structure to follow. So while it does not specifically state the reasons to follow, the thesis statement does promise a solid tool (problem-solution structure) with which we will dig for those reasons.

Husef's first topic sentence clearly connects to the thesis by focusing us on two harmful effects of a colonized economy: loss of jobs (quality and quantity) and eventual collapse as natural resources dry up.

His second topic sentence logically connects economic colonization to environmental and cultural implications. This paragraph proposes to show, in turn, how these consequences have further harmful consequences.

Husef's third topic sentence clearly states a proposed program of improvements, with the specifics naturally flowing from there.

His planned suggestive conclusion (see Chapter 7, p. 104) shows continued awareness of possible objections and continues in an effort to refute such objections. He reminds himself that, above all, his conclusion should reinforce his thesis.

With a clear sense of purpose based on a strongly realized controlling idea and with the guidance of a logical outline containing clear support for the thesis, a direct general thesis statement such as Husef's will sometimes serve you well.

Restating Your Thesis Toward the End of Your Essay

Restating your thesis toward the end of your essay will sum up where the journey has taken us, writer and reader, and reinforce your main message in preparation for a concluding thought or challenge. In her survey of English spoken in Newfoundland, "Newfoundlandese, If You Please," Diane Mooney writes, "Taking in only major sections of the province, it is quite easy for any tourist to see clearly that Newfoundland has many different descendants and therefore many different dialects." In her essay "Should Cats Be Allowed to Roam?" Joyce Miller writes, ". . . for most city-dwellers, the dream of the free-ranging cat must be surrendered as a pastoral myth." In both cases, the writers summarize where we have been taken—a destination that had been announced (more or less completely) at the end of the introduction.

Choosing Among Deductive, Inductive, and Implicit Thesis Statements

Although we advise you to place your thesis at the end of your introduction, as you have already gathered, the *location* of a thesis statement may vary from essay to essay. In practice, a thesis statement may be included anywhere in the essay. In general, location of the thesis statement reflects one of three possibilities:

- deductive[1]
- inductive[2]
- implicit

Deductive Placement

In his personal reflective essay "Causes of Procrastination" (text website, Chapter 10), student Willard Dudley ends his first paragraph as follows: "I begin to realize that my procrastination is caused by distractions, mounting hopelessness, and despair." Dudley's essay demonstrates **deductive thesis placement**, because his thesis comes at the beginning of his essay—in this case, as the final sentence of the opening paragraph. His thesis is essentially a direct list ("My procrastination appears caused by three problems: distractions, escalating hopelessness, and despair"). Joyce Miller's essay earlier in this chapter illustrates similar direct-list deductive placement. Malak Husef's outline earlier in this chapter also represents deductive thesis placement, his thesis (general rather than direct-list) coming at the end of his introduction.

---

[1] The term "deductive" has a different meaning in reference to a certain form of reasoning. See "Logic" in Chapter 3.

[2] The term "inductive" also has a different meaning in reference to a certain form of reasoning. See "Logic" in Chapter 3. Since the terms "deductive" and "inductive" are quite commonly used in both senses, we decided to include both usages in this book. Try to keep the two distinct meanings clear. Once you understand what is meant by deductive thinking and inductive thinking, you will probably see how the terms used here refer to the placement of a topic sentence. Inductive conclusions come about *after* an experience, and inductive thesis or topic sentences come *after* the body of the paragraph.

Inductive Placement

For an example of **inductive thesis placement**, read "The Other Canadians and Canada's Future" by Habeeb Salloum (Reader, p. 417). Notice that his introduction comprises the first three paragraphs, and that he begins his third paragraph with the question "How do the Canadian minorities whose origins can be traced to countries over the four corners of the world see the Canada of the future?" He tells us that for the answer, we "must travel back in history." His fourth paragraph begins with information about attitudes at the beginning of this century. He continues to chart the process of history, as it involved and affected minorities, then looks at various different attitudes today—all leading to a final position state- ment. His question in the third paragraph is a clue that he will not state a final position until he has sifted through all the evidence and information he considers important. Finally, in his last paragraph, he states what he believes is the answer to the question he posed at the end of his introduction. Only here, in conclusion, does he come out and state his thesis. This location—at the end of the essay—is inductive.

Using a Question to Anticipate Your Inductive Thesis

If you decide to use inductive structure, placing your thesis at the end, it is a very good idea to focus your discussion, as Salloum has done, with a carefully worded question by the end of your introduction. This question will alert the reader to the central issue you intend to consider and to the specific understanding you are seeking. This focus helps to keep your essay clearly structured and motivated throughout.

Finding an Implicit Thesis

The last type of thesis placement (or, in a sense, non-placement) is **implicit thesis placement**. This type is the most challenging both for you and your readers. It creates an air of mystery, and so invites your readers to participate more in your essay because they have to decipher the position you only suggest. Writing and shaping this kind of thesis statement takes time and thought, but if you want your reader to consider your topic deeply, then an implied or indirect thesis will elevate your essay to a new level of sophistication. Personal essays, which tend toward informal- ity, sometimes leave their thesis unstated. However, if an implied thesis statement takes more time for a reader to recognize, it also takes additional skill and effort for you to handle as a writer.

PRACTICE

Finding an Implicit Thesis

Under the Text Enrichment Site for this chapter, see Tamara Pelletier's personal essay about a car accident, "Suspended in Time." Read her short essay, see if you can identify its implicit thesis, and then read our commentary and suggestions.

Putting It All Together: Introduction, Body, and Conclusion

To consolidate what you have learned in this chapter, read the full text of the 1000-word essay "Betraying the Spirit of Punk? 'The Card Cheat'" and play detective. Recreate the outline and self-directional notes that you imagine writer Mark Simpson wrote as a guide in shaping this essay. Using information from this chapter and Chapter 4, "Paragraph Skills," be as precise as you can in identifying specific principles, methods, and techniques that Simpson has applied. For instance, where is his thesis sentence and what kind of thesis sentence does he use? What principle or strategy of organization does he use to order his paragraphs? How are his paragraphs connected to his thesis, and how do they lead us to increased understanding? Reading Chapter 7 on introductions and conclusions will add to your insights, if you wish to do that first, but it is not necessary at this point.

Simpson's topic assignment was to answer the following question: "Is the Clash song 'The Card Cheat' true to or apart from the spirit of punk?" You do not have to know the song or even punk music in order to infer how Simpson has shaped his answer. In fact, you may gain a heightened appreciation of craft if you know little about this topic or are not interested in it. The primary goal for you in this exercise is not to learn more about punk music but to test your increasing ability to see the structural cohesion and strategies of essays as they are established by thesis statements and outlines.

PRACTICE

Read "Betraying the Spirit of Punk? 'The Card Cheat'" and play detective: write a detailed outline that you believe guided the writer as he shaped his essay.

Betraying the Spirit of Punk? "The Card Cheat"
Mark Simpson

1   "The Card Cheat," track fourteen on the Clash's 1979 masterpiece *London Calling,* is on first listen the album's most improbable song. Combining plaintive piano, surging horns, keening vocals, and cinematic narrative, it recollects a species of pop-rock

anthem—Elton John's "Rocket Man," Billy Joel's "The Piano Man," Kenny Rogers' "The Gambler," even Meat Loaf's "Paradise by the Dashboard Light"—that, epitomizing the bloated excess of popular music in the 1970s, was anathema to punk's buzz-saw sensibility and a ready target for its vitriolic assault. Yet to conclude from this irony in musical style that "The Card Cheat" betrays the spirit of punk would be a mistake. The song's force comes from its ability to transform what punk means.

2   "The Card Cheat" uses an extended metaphor about cards to address questions of human alienation and oppression, two important punk concerns. The melancholy melody of the solo piano at the outset of the song anticipates the opening lyrical emphasis on the loneliness of the song's solitary protagonist. The looming inevitability of his death (whether time moves fast or slow, he does not have long to live) highlights the pathos in his yearning for human contact and consolation. Yet longer life, by itself, would not overcome the futility of his existence: having enough time to reveal all the plans he devised while concealing cards would accomplish nothing, because it holds no meaning. Where a future in narrative—the time needed for storytelling—might ordinarily enable life by organizing teller and listeners into a community, here that possibility is lost, rendered meaningless by the concealing of cards. The card cheat, this verse implies, empties hopes and dreams of their meaning.

3   In the second verse, we learn how the card cheat unfolds. Grinning, the gambler plays a card that, we infer, he assumes will win the hand—only to face the dealer's suspicious stare and then to suffer a brutally quick execution. Since the gambler's aim in cheating is to steal time from death, this outcome is cruelly ironic. The verb tense in these lyrics situates the drama of the card cheat in a perpetual present; cutting across differences in social station, it poisons spaces of refined leisure (signalled by the reference to violin-playing) as well as of debauchery (signalled by the references to gin and opium). As a trick, the card cheat obviously fails, but its failure exposes a fatal logic, one framed by the repetition of the word *lay*, first with respect to the card the gambler plays, then with respect to his floor-prone corpse: the play at bilking chance produces an automatic outcome; the attempt to cheat death makes dying inevitable. And to the extent that this logic has an arc, it reverberates in the song's music, which, ascending in thirds through the first three lines of the verse before falling away, underscores the desperate rise of the grinning gambler's hopes and then their crashing fall as his luck fails.

4   Seemingly, verse three leaves the card metaphor behind. Where verse two introduces us to locales in which card cheating takes place, here we confront scenes and signs of war, not play. Citing diverse times, places, and technologies of combat, the lines intimate a whole history of European warfare. Yet the ensuing lyric recollects, with a difference, the issues of chance and fate raised in the song's earlier verses. Directing his address to those who have fearlessly served the crown, the singer implies that warfare's history ties the fate of courageous men to the chance decisions of royal whim. This king *is* the king of death—in spades—because he cheats his subjects of their lives. Here the metaphor of the card

cheat becomes still grimmer in significance, as its fatal logic takes on more obviously political force. In a world where the fate of common men involves blind, often fatal allegiance to kings, gambling on the cheat is, more than an inevitable temptation, a necessary countermeasure.

5   So conceived, however, the card cheat threatens to displace other forms of human interaction and feeling, as the singer implies in his closing caution. The admonition to guard against forsaking one's lover before facing one's fate recollects the values of contact and consolation first raised in the opening verse, in order to insist on love's power against the card cheat's fatal logic. But the grammatical instability in these lines troubles their import. The use of the past tense makes the advice impossible to follow, since to act on it—to make sure one had not forsaken one's lover—would require undoing a fate already met. The ellipses, meanwhile, ruin the syntax of the concluding pronouncement, isolating (and so forsaking?) the word *lover* within the lyric's meaning. Thus by song's end the difficulties raised within its first two verses have been recast, rather than dispelled. The alternative to the card cheat itself entails risks that seem hard to reckon, let alone embrace.

6   At stake in these lyrics about love, loneliness, chance, and fate is an understanding that even matters of the most personal intimacy are always politically charged. Read this way, "The Card Cheat" belongs to a tradition of popular balladry that envisions and advocates social change through allegories of the everyday. Its significance for—and as—punk involves what literary critics might call defamiliarization: to make strange the familiar, enabling it to register in a new and unforeseen way. In "The Last Testament," the DVD about the making of *London Calling* that accompanies the album's 25th anniversary reissue, Mick Jones talks about how, at a moment when punk's idiom was becomingly increasingly narrow, the members of the Clash felt free to make whatever kind of music they wanted. "The Card Cheat" epitomizes this liberating idea. With its unlikely sound and unsettling message, the song gives us the chance to understand punk expansively, not dogmatically. No longer a prescriptive style, the genre can emerge more emphatically (if also more complexly) as a way of seeing and acting in the world.

For our suggested answers to this activity, see "Commentary on 'Putting It All Together'" on the Text Enrichment Site, Chapter 6.

For study questions on this essay, see the website, Chapter 6.

FINAL THOUGHT

Though it is a cliché, it is also true that the smartest thing a first-year undergraduate can do in pursuit of academic success is to understand how to shape an effective thesis. This advice has been dispensed for years by students and teachers alike; the wisdom of following this advice has been overwhelmingly demonstrated. If you think about it, this advice makes sense, because shaping an effective thesis means that you have applied reading skills, analysis, in many cases research skills, and an understanding of persuasive tone and style. As you become more adept in shaping thesis statements for your essays, you may wish to evolve from the direct-list variety (always deductive) to deductive general ones and even try an inductive one preceded by a rhetorical question at the end of your introduction. In consultation with your instructor or course staff, assess how you are doing with your thesis statements and perhaps experiment with how different kinds may serve expanded purposes.

Chapter 7
Introductions and Conclusions

This chapter covers certain points that closely connect with instruction given in the previous chapter on outlining and thesis statements. Topic sentences respond to the need to set out the main idea of an essay in a flow that works well for its purpose. You have seen in Chapter 6 how the relationship of topic sentences and paragraphs to the thesis and overall outline of order is managed in a way that best serves the thesis. As part of outlining, writers should be mindful of the need to open and close their works effectively. Openings of academic essays are almost always complete paragraphs; closings may be one or two sentences of finality included at the end of a paragraph discussing the last idea in support of the thesis, or alternatively, they may take the form of entire paragraphs. Since this chapter deals with the shaping of paragraphs, you should be aware of the basic information provided in Chapter 4, "Paragraph Skills," and Chapter 6, "Outlining: Thesis Statements and Topic Sentences."

PARAGRAPHS OF ESSAY INTRODUCTION

The introduction of an essay—usually one paragraph—is where you inform readers of your chosen topic. The introduction also allows you to demonstrate you are serious, informed, and qualified to discuss your topic with fairness and insight.

There are many types of essay introductions, but all of them do the following:

- announce the topic
- focus the discussion
- limit the scope of the topic to be examined in the body of the essay

Your commitment to clarity and organization in the introduction will go a long way to earning your audience's attention and good faith for the discussion that unfolds. Introductions frequently **funnel** your readers into your topic. The first sentence addresses the topic in broad terms: "Homelessness is an intolerable situation in a prosperous society." The second sentence begins to narrow the focus of this large topic: "Government subsidies continue to provide inadequate support for Canadian homeless people and for those on the verge of homelessness." A third and perhaps fourth sentence will continue to narrow the introduction's focus on the subject while adding particular information: "Despite the annual increase in national homelessness, politicians' recent proposals to cut taxes for social aid (and 'reward taxpayers') can only signal the continued neglect of society's most helpless citizens." Finally, after setting out and narrowing your field of inquiry, you can announce your **chief assertion** about your selected topic in your thesis statement. The thesis statement provides your **main claim** (or controlling idea) to be established, explained, and/or argued in the essay's body paragraphs. The funnel model is a helpful (and widely used) visual concept that captures the dynamic of the steady narrowing and focusing that a good introduction requires. From the first broad sentence to the specific thesis statement that you will examine in detail, the structure of your introduction should reflect this picture in your mind:

Figure 7.1
The Funnel
Introduction

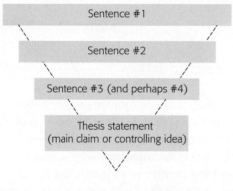

Sentence #1

Sentence #2

Sentence #3 (and perhaps #4)

Thesis statement
(main claim or controlling idea)

Sample Funnel Introduction to Essay Showing Linking Devices

Female action movies appear more **frequently** now since Sigourney Weaver's portrayal of the smart, tough, courageous Ripley in *Alien* and its sequel, *Aliens*. Directors realize audiences are prepared to reject the stereotype of the action movie as an **exclusively** male genre. **In particular**, let us examine how James Cameron's *Terminator II: Judgment Day*, Ridley Scott's *Thelma & Louise*, and Luc Besson's *La Femme Nikita* attempt to redefine the male action genre by depicting independent women capable of defending and asserting themselves **successfully** in moments of danger and crisis. <u>The **significance** of this genre is its examination of everyday social presumptions about female independence, but under extreme conditions.</u>

In this sample, the bolded linking devices serve as transitions between statements while also effectively narrowing the scope of discussion until it eventually culminates in the thesis statement (underlined).

There are several other types of introductions that can work within (or even separate from) the funnel model. As an essayist you should be prepared to work confidently with all of them in order to allow yourself the most flexibility possible in dealing with different types of essays and writing situations over your student years—and after. The method that will work best for you in a given circumstance will depend on your audience and your purpose and so will require your best judgement as an evolving writer.

Seven Types of Commonly Used Introductions

- The head-on account
- The opening definition
- The gesture to authority
- The counter-argument

- The anecdote
- The question
- The unusual or unexpected fact

The Head-on Account

The **head-on account** relies on crisp declarative sentences that simply establish the topic and narrow the focus to the thesis statement. Our example of introduction-building on the topic of homelessness employs this head-on method: you declare your subject and intently press forward with clear, increasingly narrowing statements. You ask no rhetorical questions, present no provisional counter-views (alternative claims), and cite no authority beyond your own writer's voice. The head-on account sets a candid, certain, openly positioned tone for the entire essay.

We strongly recommend this no-nonsense style of introduction for your first essay in a freshman course, unless the instructor has stipulated differently in the assignment.

Sample Head-on Account

'E Pluribus Unum': It's All in the Translation.

Andrea Zawaski
E Pluribus Unum

It has been said that "[l]anguage is the living, breathing expression and essence of a culture" (Pacheco). But what if a nation consists of several cultures, with several languages? Is it, then, a fragmented nation, which can be unified only by one common language, or is a shared set of attitudes strong enough to unify its people? These are questions with which the citizens of the United States struggle.

This type of opening is often ideal when responding to topics in critical analysis for academic purposes. As student Andrea Zawaksi has done, you should open with assertions that are short and to the point—assertions that move your reader as briskly as possible to your main concern, to your thesis statement, or at least to an understanding of the question pointing to your thesis. Consult with your instructor to see if he or she welcomes this approach in general, and especially for certain analytical assignments.

The Opening Definition

The **opening definition** specifies the objective meaning of a term or concept. This technique establishes your sense of fairness and of valid questioning, since you appear to be seeking some neutral middle ground with your audience. Usually the opening-definition method signals that you will carefully and reflectively add to, qualify, or refute this accepted definition in the course of your essay. This type of introduction works best with ambiguous, contested, or emotional terms and concepts, such as "community," "family," "education," "justice," "success," and so on. Always use the opening-definition method sincerely, and not as a convenient way to chew up space.

The Gesture to Authority

The **gesture to authority** is a technique of establishing the importance of your topic beyond the bounds of the essay itself. This method creates initial momentum through your introduction and possibly grounds for debate in your discussion: "Lisa Bugden, a Halifax philosopher, argues that time is a slippery concept, not an empirical fact" or "A recent Canadian survey indicates that more than 65 percent of young adults disapprove of expanded military spending." By citing an authority or a published credible reference, you show that you have marshalled some pertinent facts to support your views. You should make sure, however, that your introduction integrates this reference within your own position. Make sure that outside references serve your own thinking. Also remember that you may cite an authority or reference in order to contend with that view. For instance: "The Manitoban historian Patricia Murphy hastily concludes that Louis Riel was `an outlaw capable only of reckless decisions.' The facts and purpose of defiant uprising invite a far different interpretation, however."

The Counter-Argument

The introduction as **counter-argument** sets a debate in motion. You may cite an authority or reference as in the above example or simply state a commonly held view. This is how George Orwell begins his essay "Politics and the English Language" (Reader, p. 471):

> Most people who bother with the matter at all would admit that the English language is in a bad way, but it is generally assumed that we cannot by conscious action do anything about it.

Orwell elaborates on this typical view in his opening paragraph and then, in his second paragraph, he opposes it by asserting that "the process is reversible."

By starting with a counter-argument, you set your essay's thesis against the assertion of an authority or the commonly held view. This strategy generates a reader's interest immediately because you have energetically engaged in a clearly defined debate—presumably with something important at stake. The counter-argument introduction also confers some solid credit on you as a contentious essayist—a resolved and independent thinker, who is willing to question and redefine accepted notions. Both the opening definition and gesture to authority may adopt the counter-argument strategy of debate and contention.

The Anecdote

The **anecdote** introduction illustrates a point by way of a "language sketch": you spin a brief episode in order to tell by showing. Since this type of introduction draws upon the personal, be sure your audience will appreciate this slightly informal essay opener:

> Two of my Vancouver friends who listen almost entirely to American music tell me that Canadian music no longer exists as a distinct cultural expression. I always quickly remind them of the Tragically Hip's continued references to Canadian history, people, places, habits, and events. I also remind them of The Guess Who's song "American Woman," a 1970s rock 'n' roll expression of the importance of Canadian cultural resistance to Americanization.

The anecdote introduction sets a slightly vulnerable, conversational tone, since it strives to share between writer and reader a vivid personal experience or private observation. Some instructors may prefer that you choose the more formal, traditional approach of beginning your paper with direct exposition or analysis.

The Question

Students often overuse the **question** introduction. If you quickly reel off as many as four consecutive questions in your introduction—not necessarily in logical sequence—in the hope that some focus will magically appear on the page, you undermine the potential benefits of this strategy. Try to resist this tempting late-night writing strategy for your introduction.

You should usually limit your question introduction to a maximum of two carefully considered, genuine inquiries that trigger the reader's immediate interest in the forthcoming discussion. The questions should be sufficiently complex and/or significant to arouse and sustain the reader's interest: "If, as many people claim, capital punishment is legally just in extreme crimes, can anyone ensure that a system of judgement that places people on death row is itself socially just? Why, for instance, are there mostly poor people on death row?"

The Unusual or Unexpected Fact

It wasn't unusual for media reports on amateur hockey in Alberta in the 1990s to open along the following lines:

> The Calgary Cougars bantam hockey team continues to record wins, holding its own in full-contact competition after moving up from the non-contact division where it dominated. By all accounts the best 14-year-old player in Alberta can be found on the Cougars. Like everyone else on the team, she's a girl. Chances are, you'll be hearing a lot more of her—so remember the name Hayley Wickenheiser.

The same technique sometimes serves for critical analysis, where it can be just as effective if somewhat less obvious.

Example of the unusual or unexpected fact applied to critical analysis

Betraying the Spirit of Punk? 'The Card Cheat'

Mark Simpson

"The Card Cheat," track fourteen on the Clash's 1979 masterpiece *London Calling*, is on first listen the album's most improbable song. Combining plaintive piano, surging horns, keening vocals, and cinematic narrative, it recollects a species of pop-rock anthem—Elton John's "Rocket Man," Billy Joel's "The Piano Man," Kenny Rogers' "The Gambler," even Meat Loaf's "Paradise by the Dashboard Light"—that, epitomizing the bloated excess of popular music in the 1970s, was anathema to punk's buzz-saw sensibility and a ready target for its vitriolic assault. Yet to conclude from this irony in musical style that "The Card Cheat" betrays the spirit of punk would be a mistake. The song's force comes from its ability to transform what punk means.

Simpson's basic message, employing the unexpected "fact," is that "The Card Cheat" sounds like anything *but* a punk song, yet on further exploration, it reveals itself to be not only a punk song but one that stretches the genre. We have used quotation marks for "fact" in this instance because the unusual statement turns out to be not a fact but an opinion—the thesis of Simpson's essay, presented with such assurance that it seems to be unusual but true. Starting with the unusual challenges the reader to continue, to see if the unusual claim has merit. For the full essay by Mark Simpson, see Chapter 6 (p. 92).

The following is a less subjective application of this surprise technique used for literary analysis:

> Literary critics generally agree that *The Mystery of Edwin Drood*, Charles Dickens's unfinished final work, maintains his high standards and, in some cases, even surpasses them. These critics are wrong, not because *Edwin Drood* lacks merit, but because it isn't Dickens's last *unfinished* work. It was simply his last work. Three months ago, I discovered the remainder of the work in an old trunk at my uncle's cottage in Portsmouth. Complete scientific tests have now confirmed the authenticity of this claim.

Of course, if this were true, the writer would not need to go on developing her writing skills—at least not for purposes of financial security, since she would be able to hire hacks aplenty to publish her discovery. But the technique does offer itself for more serious uses, on appropriate occasions.

PARAGRAPHS USED TO COMPLETE ESSAYS

An essay conclusion offers you the final chance to reinforce your ideas and move your readers. This is where you want to compress your discussion into one lasting emotional or intellectual package. This package should

- reinforce main ideas
- clinch and cinch your discussion
- raise implications for further consideration

For academic papers of 750 to 1500 words or so, instructors often prefer short, terse conclusions. These tend to suit academic analysis. For example, here is the final paragraph of Valerie Desjardins's critical analysis called "'College Girl to Call Girl': Innocent Victims or Entrants in a Rat Race?" Here we provide just a portion of the preceding paragraph, showing you how the final paragraph flows from the essay body. Desjardins's essay analyzes Sarah Schmidt's essay "College Girl to Call Girl" according to four classical standards, building to the final consideration of style. Having completed her discussion of style, Desjardins is ready to end her argument. For the full essay, see Chapter 16 (p. 257).

Sample paragraph of conclusion

. . . As this paragraph has been pointing out, style, the classical canon dealing with language choices, strongly affects the depiction of Stacy. She "stumbled" (10) and she "scores" (11), words that imply considerable criticism. The word "score," drawn from street vocabulary, implies that Stacy is essentially like any other hooker, except that she's a self-deluding snob.

   Whether this means that she is more to blame for her dilemma than the culture that partly created her is another bigger and more difficult question. But accepting her as an intended embodiment of the endangered, conflicted middle-class today does follow from a careful examination of the classical canons underlying Schmidt's methods. The result is a picture bordering on satire, and as we know, satirists are not known for their moral equivocation.

In the above example, the first sentence of the concluding paragraph speaks to further implications. Up to this point, Desjardins has argued that Sarah Schmidt does *not* present the student prostitute as a helpless victim; here Desjardins recognizes that the essay does not present Stacy as a clear-cut criminal—the ambiguity is acknowledged as raising implications of further complexity, issues taking us beyond the declared scope of the essay. The next sentence reinforces the essay's thesis that Schmidt's goal is to comment on the conflicted middle class, and the final sentence adds finality by firmly upholding the degree to which Schmidt's essay implies a criticism of middle-class life. In this illustration, the implication for further thought comes before the reinforcing and cinching of main ideas, showing the possibility for effective variation of order. The important thing to notice is that Desjardins accounts for all three needs of a closing paragraph, and accomplishes them in just three sentences.

As this example suggests, in order to convey maximum power, **final sentences** of paragraphs and especially of essays are often aphoristic reflections on the thesis. A paper on corporate greed and environmental abuse, for example, might end with the saying of the Cree elder Lone Wolf: "Only when the last tree has died and the last river has been poisoned and the last fish has been caught will we realize we cannot eat money." In some cases, simply one or two final sentences of this nature at the end of your last body paragraph or standing alone as a brief, separate paragraph will be sufficient for your conclusion.

Exhaustive Conclusions

Beginner essayists are often encouraged in their conclusions to repeat their thesis statement as well as the main points of the preceding discussion. This approach, known as the **exhaustive conclusion**, resembles checking off a grocery list (tell 'em what you just told 'em). The following sample exhaustive conclusion ends a paper that has examined the controversy over the Nike company's use of Third World labour to make expensive running shoes.

Sample exhaustive conclusion

Corporate good will cannot be measured directly on a profit sheet. The long-term benefits of the public's perception of corporate responsibility have become a fact in the modern market, however. The controversy over the continuing claims that Nike exploits Third World workers for the construction of a recreational item that promotes the health, appearance, and perhaps hollow vanity of First World joggers may impede the conscientious consumer's willingness to purchase Nike products. Nike should work more on developing a graceful long-season strategy rather than continue to grasp for the quick, questionable win, especially as young consumers become more politically aware on the global level.

Such a conclusion summarizes the essay's previous discussion. The first three sentences do not add anything new; they consolidate the content of the paper, repeating points in the same order as before, but in language slightly different from that used in the discussion itself. The final sentence may also be repeating a point made in the body, or alternatively it might be a considered recommendation of the essayist that has not been previously mentioned (a "suggestive" strategy). Whether the last sentence has an exhaustive or a suggestive aspect, it attempts to impress upon the reader a need for corporate change. An important part of this final sentence's rhetorical strategy is its use of a sports metaphor (the "long season" as opposed to the "questionable win") to drive home an ethical distinction. Your conclusion should represent the completion of the main strategies of your paper: unity of method must be strong at this important, final point.

A weakness of the exhaustive conclusion is that it can seem predictable and tedious; it may also lull you into using too much of your earlier wording. Like a canoe, an essay should try to stay in constant motion. Even in the conclusion, where you must engage in a certain amount of backward reflection, you need to keep moving forward as well.

Suggestive Conclusions

In contrast to the exhaustive approach, the **suggestive conclusion** spends less time revisiting past ground and gives more attention to implications for the reader's further consideration. This strategy assumes that if your discussion has been spirited, then your main points have already been made; it simply remains to gather them briefly together for parting resonance and future consideration. The following suggestive conclusion completes an essay that has discussed three of Wayne Gretzky's contributions to the sport of hockey (as opposed to the business of hockey).

Sample suggestive conclusion

Gretzky's presence in hockey not only introduced more complicated and unpredictable passing strategies, and intensified team play directly in front of the net, but it also reconceptualized the offensive player as a trickster rather than as only a power-skater and power-shooter. His curious habit of suddenly stopping behind the opposing net to survey the scene also proved to be more than a crowd-pleasing showboat gesture. Gretzky in his "office" (behind the opposing net) gave his teammates a sudden wealth of opportunities to evade defenders and position themselves for a pass in front of the net. This recurrent positioning strategy momentarily allowed Gretzky, as a lone player, to set the pace of the entire action at will. Most importantly, Gretzky in his office also demonstrated that hockey can be strategically and psychologically closer to chess than anyone before his appearance was probably willing to believe.

The conclusion's first sentence—its topic sentence—summarizes the three main points of the previous discussion. Now that the entire essay has been cinched, the writer goes on to probe further into those points, thus introducing a fourth point: that Gretzky revolutionized the game with a previously unimagined cerebral style of play. The claim that Gretzky transformed an entire sport is certainly large enough in its suggestive implications to close the whole discussion. The last sentence asserting large psychological implications to Gretzky's style of play will probably continue to resonate with the reader after she or he has finished the essay.

In most cases, your conclusions will draw upon both the exhaustive and the suggestive models. Some instructors prefer very brief conclusions of simply one or two sentences. Others may expect a full exhaustive recapitulation. Ask your instructor about his or her expectations for what a conclusion should or should not attempt.

FINAL WORD

"Specialty" paragraphs respect the same principles of craft required of all effective paragraphs, but with the additional need to serve at key locations. Remember that openings and closings—whether of sentences, paragraphs, or essays—convey heightened impact. Novelist Brian Moore has said that he rewrites his opening pages over a dozen times. If your opening does not work, you risk losing your reader or at least failing to achieve your purpose. If your ending is weak, you dilute your thesis. Take extra care with opening and closing paragraphs, and you will see a difference in your essay grades.

THE

RHETORIC

Section 2   Forms

INTRODUCTION

Many of us know someone who can "play by ear," who can compose or perform songs and other musical compositions without being able to read or write music. If you do not know such persons, a little research will uncover dozens. Their example should remind us that forms can be produced and reproduced without reference to written instructions. Furthermore, it's unlikely that the first music composer found a score and thereby "invented" harmonics, or that the first writer found some equivalent of *Acting on Words* and thereby wrote the world's first essay of argumentation. Documentation of the forms used in composition, musical or literary, comes *after* the appearance of those forms. Information on forms, such as that in the following section of this book, simply records what has already been discovered or created naturally.

This may be well worth remembering as an antidote to the fearful notion that there is a "right" form, and that it is highly unnatural but can be produced by finding the necessary set of instructions. If we had a master blueprint of forms that could lead to another Shakespeare, for instance, we would surely keep the magic formulae all to ourselves. But we write, presumably, because we have something to say. It is our own inner drive to say what we have to say that might put us in the company of Shakespeare and his modern-day heirs. Forms are simply tools we use to give our content impact. We use them as much or as little as we need to serve our particular purpose. If we trust our instincts and use our wits, we will "invent" the forms anew for ourselves. They exist because they are natural and because they make sense— at least, within the culture to which they belong.

A highly deliberate "forms approach" to teaching first-year essay writing was not nearly as common in Canada 30 or more years ago as it is today. Teachers stressed thesis statements and basic essay outlines but did not generally use the fully detailed breakdown of patterns that you will find in the following pages and in numerous other texts on the market. It was assumed that students had absorbed a strong sense of forms from much active reading. Teaching methods, however, follow trends, like the fashion industry, and some would say that the forms approach arose in part because young people read less today than they used to and therefore need more prompting to recognize basic patterns of thought in writing.

Whether this is an unfair stereotype (as it may well be) or whether it really explains the predominance of the forms approach, we suggest that the forms approach has some not-so-good possible side-effects along with some important benefits.

Let's take a moment to consider the not-so-good side-effects, since any method is best applied with your eyes open. The main risk in relying on forms is that your writing could fall into the condition that cultural historian Johan Huizinga believes afflicted literature in the waning Middle Ages. In his view, that literature was "almost exclusively concerned with giving a finished and ornate form to a system of ideas which had long since ceased to grow" (253). According to Huizinga, forms had become "the servants of an expiring mode of thought" (253). Anachronistically speaking, writers of that age were, to Huizinga, on autopilot. They were painting by numbers. This can happen if you are too engrossed by the idea of reproducing a conventional pattern.

Many suggest that we today are overly absorbed with materialism, with things rather than content, with forms rather than ideas. Are we, as a result, turning out the same proportion of "empty rhetoric" that Huizinga finds in the waning Middle Ages? Without taking on that huge question here, we *can* point to small examples of how institutionalized attention to form may, however unintentionally, limit our reasoning. A certain essay-writing text, for instance, will classify a model essay as an example of comparison-contrast; a "rival" text will classify the same essay as an example of definition. By letting the idea of form wag us as the tail is said to wag the proverbial dog, we can end up believing that an essay must be only comparison-contrast or only definition (or worse still, one form for one professor, another for another professor, and good luck guessing which is which); and we can end up concluding that the writer of this "puzzling" essay set out to write an example of comparison or definition (rather than to say something). Our teaching texts do not mean to suggest these conclusions, but student writers might inadvertently come to them, nevertheless. So we wish to make a strong point here, even at the risk of belabouring it: you should remember that consulting forms is not an invitation to produce form for form's sake but a reminder that achieved writing invariably results in effective form.

If you have something to say and are determined to say it, you will find your way, with or without this section, to a successful form. And the chances are that your essay, like everything in nature, will contain a blending of forms, with no straight lines between them.

At the same time, we recommend giving some conscious attention to form, especially at key moments in your essay writing. The notion of opposing individual voice (including inspiration, etc.) to established form, and choosing one or the other, can be a little like separating the individual and God. There is a story from the Hindu tradition of an acolyte whose master taught him that God is not apart from us—God is within, so, in a sense, we are God. The acolyte liked this idea. Soon after his lesson, he was on a jungle trail, feeling godly, when a rogue elephant appeared, heading briskly toward the acolyte. The master happened to be present. Noticing the elephant bearing down on the young man, the master suggested that the acolyte move aside. "But I am God," the young man protested. "Ah," said the master, "that is true. But so is the elephant."

An essay assignment bearing down on you can be something of a rogue elephant. One moral of the story above is that you must grant that elephant its measure of reality. Look the assignment over carefully. What form or forms is the assignment directing you to follow, whether implicitly or explicitly? In almost all cases, the assignment will state a *length* that you must observe, and if this information is not provided you should ask for it. Once you know the *length* of the essay, you will have a basic *size* in your mind—and size represents a basic form. If you think of that basic unit as a suitcase, then you can remind yourself that to fill that suitcase properly you need to select just the right number of clothes and other contents. Next you define the *purpose* of your essay (e.g., personal, expository, analytical, argumentative); then your suitcase has a destination—business, let's say, or a holiday somewhere warm and dry or by the sea, or a combination of business and pleasure. This known destination gives you further important knowledge to guide your packing. Within the established suitcase capacity, you will now be able to place a rain hat, beach towel, dress shoes, business suit, and so on. In this simple way, knowing the form of your essay in terms of size and purpose contributes essentially to your selection and arrangement of its contents.

How exactly you use the following section of this book to arrange the items in your suitcase will depend upon the particular directions accompanying your assignment. If you are asked to write a comparison-contrast essay, then you must, indeed, be careful to follow one of the standard structures illustrated in Chapter 12, and you will most likely gain by that exercise. On the other hand, if you are asked to explain whether one method of government differs from another, then your assignment only implicitly encourages you to apply comparison-contrast structure; you may not wish to consider the standard patterns until after you have one solid draft of your essay. Referring to the pattern choices for comparison as you produce a revised draft will help you to sharpen organizational methods that you have probably already applied instinctively. An exercise for a writing class might require you to follow certain guidelines to the letter, whereas an assignment for a political science course might not require you to be as absolutely attentive to the form.

We do recommend that you carefully read Chapter 9, "Exposition and Expository Patterns," because it defines a broad area of tones and purposes that can be usefully compared and contrasted to those in personal writing on one side and argumentative writing on the other. We suggest that for many university courses, Chapter 13, "The Summary," Chapter 14, "Critical Analysis and Evaluation," Chapter 15, "Rhetorical Analysis," and Chapter 16, "Argumentation," will cover the essence of what university writing comprises. The other chapters, not named here, provide useful detailed support once you have a certain purpose or pattern and would like to refine it. Finally, we wish to repeat our reminder that forms are tools, not absolutes or ends in themselves. You may use comparison structure as a tool for quite different purposes: to express or evoke a personal or fictionalized experience; to help your reader better understand a topic; to analyze and evaluate a subject in reply to difficult critical questions; or to explore two sides of an argument. How you apply a form depends on your purpose. Once you know your purpose, go to the form and the way of using it that most suit your needs. We wish you much satisfaction and many rewards as you negotiate the mysterious relationship between your unique personal being as a writer and the storehouse of existing forms from which to choose.

Work Consulted

Huizinga, Johan. *The Waning of the Middle Ages.* London: Edward Arnold, 1924.

Chapter 8
The Personal Essay

Depending on your field of study, your academic assignments will likely require a *non*-personal style. So why study the personal essay? There are at least three good reasons for giving some attention to first-person voice and reflection on your life as you prepare for your career.

1. Most work on the job entails effective informal communication. The ability to speak and write purposefully in your own natural voice could prove as valuable to your employer as the ability to write a formal report. Well over half of important work-related communication is oral, and much of that is informal.

2. Mastering the personal essay takes you a step closer to becoming a well-rounded writer. Versatility counts as much in writing as it does in other disciplines. As humans we learn and think a great deal through comparisons. We gain a better understanding of light and what it can do by knowing about darkness and what it can do. To better apply *im*personal styles of writing, we benefit from having some experience with personal ones. Furthermore, many writing occasions call upon a combination of approaches, including in some cases a blending of personal and impersonal techniques. "Fusion" occurs as much in writing as it does in music, and we know that musicians playing in fusion groups simply must be adept in the different styles required for the new combination.

3. The personal essay can be an excellent starting point in developing the habit of critical thinking. George Orwell's classic essay "Shooting an Elephant," for example, brings author and reader to grips with colonialism. All of the personal essays in this text contain a certain component of critical thinking. Indeed, there is an old Sufi belief that until you are able to tell the story of your life simply and concisely, you are not ready to progress further in knowledge and understanding. This view holds that life is holistic; therefore the academic and personal sides of existence cannot and should not be totally severed any more than the mind and the body should be. Accordingly, fields such as anthropology, ethology, and women's studies often use the first person as a vehicle for academic and critical expression, although vigorous debate continues over the value of employing this personal perspective. In any case, we suggest that becoming comfortable with your own voice grounds you as a writer and connects you with yourself and your relationship to truth. You can then modify that natural voice to suit the demands of various different writing projects.

PRACTICE

- List what you believe are the arguments against the use of the first person in academic writing.
- List the arguments in favour of using first person as an instrument of personal accountability.

- Discuss the various sides of this debate with your classmates.

DEFINING THE PERSONAL ESSAY

In the personal essay, the thesis, whether explicit or implicit, expresses a point of view on a matter of life experience important to the writer. Usually the personal essay employs narration and description, methods shared with fiction (novels, short stories, and oral stories). Like other forms of artistic storytelling, fiction—at least, effective fiction—engages and somehow changes the whole being of the reader. This "change" may involve a purge, some form of healing, or some form of vicarious visceral understanding. In the classical terms discussed in Chapters 1 and 2, fiction and, to some extent, personal writing emphasize pathos, connecting with the reader on emotional and psychic levels. Personal writing therefore appeals to its readers and "persuades" them in ways that may not appeal as explicitly to logic as those of standard academic analytical writing. This is not to say that logic is absent from personal writing; logic underlies personal writing, but does not always have as direct an influence over tone as we find in much third-person analytical writing.

A wide spectrum of styles can be found in the personal essay, with moods ranging from light and humorous to profoundly solemn. The writer does not necessarily focus directly or at length on the self. A personal essay might concern something observed, with someone other than the writer as the main subject. Usually, however, personal writing expresses an empathetic, close connection between the writer and the subject. Often, the writer narrates or describes something that he or she witnessed if not experienced.

PRACTICE

Arrange with two or more classmates to read and discuss at least two of the following pieces of personal writing from the Reader:

- "Brownie" (p. 375)
- "I Sing the Song of My Condo" (p. 395)

- "The King and I" (p. 399)
- "The Hockey Sweater" (p. 387)

For each piece, discuss the dominant style. Identify examples of organization, paragraphing, sentence structure, and literary technique that convey voice and tone.

The personal essay has **three major impulses**:

- narration
- description
- reflection

NARRATION

Narration simply means telling a story, recounting events, typically in chronological order. There are two important things to consider when telling a story. The first is that it is a fundamental impulse and need of human beings, so primal and important that many scholars as well as elders in traditional societies regard storytelling as a basic aspect of being human. In a recent address to Athabasca University, psychologist and adult learning motivator Raymond Wlodkowski suggested that storytelling is as essential to human existence as food and shelter. When you tell a story, you enter into a natural, life-giving process; you enter into a state as basic and mysterious as sleep.

The second important point to consider is that storytelling arises from and constantly draws upon oral traditions. Delaware author Daniel David Moses says that "the three functions of all stories prehistorically seem to have been: (1) to entertain, (2) to instruct, and (3) to heal" (91).

PRACTICE

Explore oral stories from any of the world's ancient traditions, insofar as we are able to revisit those stories today. Think about old stories you have been told. Talk with family, friends, and classmates to learn about stories they have been told and can share with you. Do you agree that these stories entertain, instruct, and heal? Do you find any common patterns or elements in their structure?

To further your explorations of personal narrative forms, you might wish to consider the following oral-style pattern, which was introduced to us by writing instructor Jannie Edwards.

Short oral story pattern using five steps

Many traditional oral stories reflect the following five steps:

Subject
Background
Problem (conflict or issue)
Climax and resolution
Moral (or thesis)

PRACTICE

Form a story circle within your class. If you have a large class, consider dividing into smaller circles of perhaps seven or eight members each. Try to limit your story to no more than two minutes (using a relaxed, natural pace). Be sure to *tell* the story, using notes or simply memory. If you really wish to read it, use an oral style.

Consider following the above five-step pattern to shape your story. In many traditional societies, storytelling reflects the time of year. Certain stories are to be told only at certain times, for certain purposes connected to that time. In addition, certain stories belong to certain people and must not be re-told without their permission. If you choose a story that you have been told by an elder or someone in the role of guide or teacher, check with that person to see if she or he approves your re-telling it for the purposes of the story circle. If you choose a traditional story that has been handed down in a book, try to determine if the story was published with permission of the person or people to whom the story belongs. Determine to what degree the editor of the story understands and respects the culture to which the story belongs. If you aren't sure that a certain story should be re-told, you can do as student John Roberts did and tell one of your own stories. The subject might be something that happened to you or to someone who would not mind having the experience re-told. If your instructor agrees, you might invent part or all of your story.

Sample Personal Narrative

Title conveys subject and tone; implies goal and thesis.

Step 1: Tell what the story is about.

Step 2: Give enough background to set up the issue, tension, concern, or conflict to follow.

Step 3: Establish the main character's challenge, goal, concern, or issue. In traditional Western terms, this may be the conflict.

Brief narrative summary.

The Time I Nearly Burned Down Northern Quebec

John Roberts

1   This is about the time I nearly burned down northern Quebec.

2   I was a young counsellor in the Laurentians. Camp Napawingue prided itself on being the best boys' camp in Canada, if not the world.[1] Camp Napawingue combined a British boarding school with an RCMP boot camp. Visitors to the white-birch shore of Lake Napawingue breathed in the fresh scent of pine and wood smoke—but we campers breathed in competition. I had to show that I was the best counsellor among the best staff in the best camp.

3   I was assigned to lead a canoe trip through La Vérendrye Park, named for the celebrated explorer. It was important to instill good morale on a canoe trip. The students would write a report afterwards for the canoe trip director, and he must note my impressive teambuilding. I learned how to build team morale from old-time counsellors over an evening beer at Napawingue Hotel (which turned a certain blind eye, Quebec style, to minors). The most impressive counsellor in recent history had been photographed with his campers beside a towering bonfire on a La Vérendrye lake. Everyone referred approvingly to this photo. It was tucked away somewhere in the Administration Building. This added somehow to its mythic power.

4   The canoe trip approached. We packed and packed—and then we set off. After a long truck ride to La Vérendrye Park, we loaded our canoes and paddled: we paddled, portaged, and paddled. The hours slipped by like water alongside our canoes. At last came the first evening. We pitched our tent on a sandy beach, under the

---

[1] The name has been fictionalized.

nodding tops of pine trees. It was time for the Big Event. We leaned the tallest logs we could into a teepee, which we gleefully ignited. We had ourselves a merry inferno, crackling and flaming against the night sky. Then one of the campers started to look anxious. That seemed hardly surprising, since the rest of us considered him a sort of Piglet from the Pooh stories: timid, hesitant, forever anxious. He pointed behind us. "Those sparks are getting kind of close to the trees." Sure enough: a hail of fiery embers was cascading onto the boughs.

A definite plan unfolds, leading to . . .

Step 4: Climax. A final new element in the plot raises the stakes and hastens the conclusion.

5   Did I remember to mention that it had not rained in over a week?

6   I shouted for everyone to grab pots, pans, boots, anything that could hold water.

We doused every side of the roaring teepee, every ember we could find in the bush. But sparks continued to rain from above as if the sky itself were on fire. Then came the distant roar of a motor boat. Everyone knew where it was headed and why. Its mournful motor grew louder and closer. After the park ranger arrested us, I would be fired. I would be as big a disgrace as the famous counsellor was a hero. That is, if the forest didn't burn us, first, to ashes.

7   The last embers were still hissing when the motor backed off and then began to fade into the distance.

8   When I returned to the best camp in the world, with the best staff anywhere, I found a discreet moment to sneak into the Administration Building. There, in a dusty binder, I came upon the famous photo of the heroic counsellor posed with his proud and admiring campers beside their blazing bonfire. It wasn't easy to see who was the famous counsellor and who were the admiring campers. Their eyes were masked by the hoods of their rain slicks. The downpour between camera and subject made it difficult, in fact, to see anything at all.

Step 5: Resolution. Flowing from the climax, the resolution answers the plot question: Will John burn down northern Quebec?

9   And the moral of the story is . . .

Focus Questions

1. Can you think of stories you might tell that would benefit from a little more mingling of the five steps? For instance, what might happen to the reader's interest if the storyteller takes too long with step 2? What other reasons can you think of to alter the steps?
2. What do you think is the moral (thesis) of this story? What, then, is its underlying subject?
3. Can you think of a possible connection between the teaching of this story and Chapters 18 and 19 of this text?
4. In what ways does this story entertain?
5. In what ways does this story heal?

Three Features of Effective Narration

You need not be a professional novelist to benefit from the skills of a storyteller. For example, you may need these skills to begin a speech, an essay, or an article. Narrative techniques are also required in occurrence reports, though often the author uses detached third-person point of view in such cases. Regardless of the viewpoint used to tell a story, good narration relies on three characteristics:

- defining and organizing parts
- proportioning and linking parts
- expressing a sense of causality

Defining and Organizing Parts

Your story should consist of a *manageable* number of discrete sections such as expository subtopics; descriptions; summaries of stages, people, and events; or scenes of action and dialogue (reported speech enclosed within quotation marks). You need to define for yourself exactly what these parts are before you produce a final draft of your essay.

✒ PREPARATION

Read Roch Carrier's "The Hockey Sweater" (Reader, p. 387). Define the separate sections of this fictional memoir and the types of writing techniques used in each section. What principle of organization has been used to structure these sections?

Roch Carrier has clearly conceptualized three main sections for his memoir: (1) an introductory section of background information to "set the stage"; (2) the first half of his story; and (3) the second half and conclusion of his story. These broad sections can in turn be broken down into finer parts.

Part one comprises three paragraphs. The first paragraph tells, in an expository manner, about the "winters of my childhood." They were "long," and they consisted of life at school, the church, and the skating rink. The first two places merely served the third "real" place—the rink. The rink was important above all because that was where the children became Maurice Richard. The second introductory paragraph carries on with the subject of Maurice Richard, supplying details of how the boys emulated their hero. The third paragraph narrows the subject further to describe how the boys pursued this emulation on the rink. Part one, then, works like a funnel, moving from a broad, general orientation to increasingly specific concerns. But even in paragraph 3, Carrier still refers to the way things were in general, not to one particular day.

He takes us into the second part of his memoir with the opening of paragraph 4: "One day." Now we enter the story proper, a story based entirely around the Toronto Maple Leafs sweater. Everything in the narration either will describe why the sweater appeared in his life or what happened as a result. First, he deals with the *whys*. In paragraph 4, he tells us that his Montreal Canadiens sweater was becoming too small and wearing out, and he summarizes the character of his mother. Much humour arises from the discord between the boy's objectives and those of his mother. All he wants is that his old Canadiens sweater last forever. She doesn't want her son to look poor, and she is too proud to buy a new sweater locally. So she orders a new one through the fashionable department store, Eaton's.

Carrier now moves his story along by chronological cause and effect. Because his mother writes to the store, the store, in paragraph 5, responds by sending a sweater. This creates the great crisis of the memoir: the mother, for her own practical reasons, expects her boy to wear the new sweater, even though it bears the notorious Maple Leaf. At this most intense moment, Carrier uses scene, action, and dialogue—a good way to convey crucial material. Not too much speech is recorded, so the lines of dialogue that are reported are very important. In the confrontation with her son, for example, the mother says, "You aren't Maurice Richard." This one line resonates deeply because in its essence the story is concerned with boyhood fantasy and illusion. This scene, bringing part two of the memoir to a climax, concludes with the boy forced to wear the Maple Leafs sweater.

Part three is signalled by the transitional word "so": "So I was obliged to wear the Maple Leafs sweater. When I arrived on the rink . . ." Thus the author leads us into the final extended scene of his memoir. The boy's captain, clearly biased against the detested Toronto sweater, keeps the boy from playing. When the young narrator at last jumps onto the ice, he is penalized for too many men. He breaks his stick in frustration, and ironically the vicar assumes the boy has acted out of the pride of non-conformity. The memoir ends with the amusing tale of the boy sent to church to pray for forgiveness; his actual prayer is for moths to destroy the alien sweater.

In sum, the memoir consists of a three-paragraph introduction, another long paragraph describing the decline of the Canadiens sweater, the character of the mother and her consequent decision (the inciting incident), some 10 paragraphs of action and dialogue when the Leafs sweater arrives, and a final scene of two paragraphs when the boy wears his new sweater to the rink. In each of the two major scenes, the boy's objectives are clear. In the first scene, his objective is to avoid wearing the Leafs sweater. In the second scene, his objective is to get on the ice. Focusing on one main character with one clear objective is a good way to make scenes powerful. Through Carrier's control of specific scenes, we gain a touching portrait of a child's relative powerlessness before time, change, and adults.

Proportioning and Linking Parts

The charm that this memoir holds for so many readers rises in large measure through the author's craft. Carrier knows how long to spend sketching in the background, what to say, and what to leave out. He is careful not to pack in more information than three pages can contain, not to wander into tempting but digressive subplots. For a writer, choosing whether to summarize information or to show it directly through scene and action is a major decision. Balance and variation are key principles. The writer needs to "stay ahead" of the reader—to maintain suspense, yet not to take so long to propel the story forward that the reader loses interest. Like all good narratives, Carrier's memoir consists of a certain amount of summary and a certain amount of direct action. Two scenes, one right after the other, are probably as much direct action as he would present before returning to further summary and exposition.

Links between the sections are simple yet essential—words such as "so," "when," and "one day." In the opening expository section, the image of Maurice Richard ends one paragraph and, logically, becomes the main topic of the next two. Once the story proper begins, the sections are organized according to chronology, one condition occurring *as a result of* a previous action.

Expressing a Sense of Causality

We have already noted how material in "The Hockey Sweater" has been organized according to logical cause-and-effect relationships. The mother orders a new sweater *because* the old one is worn out and *because* she cares what people think. The boy resists wearing the new sweater *because* all the boys idolize the Montreal Canadiens. He feels shame and persecution *because* his mother wins the disagreement over his wearing the sweater. He is treated unfairly by the team captain *because* of bias against the sweater, and so on. The narrative plot's emphasis on causes and effects compels readers to ponder the deeper meaning of the story. Why do certain things happen? What possible social, political, economic, psychological, or spiritual factors are at play? Carrier offers no explicit answers to such questions in his memoir, yet he provokes us to think beyond the issues of one boyhood to the history of Quebec and its unresolved future with English Canada.

DESCRIPTION

Description in all writing means the organized observation of significant detail. In expressive or evocative writing, this detail has two main features:

- appeal to the five senses
- service of a dominant impression

Appeal to the Five Senses

Visual images abound in Carrier's memoir. Let's take the blue-and-white Maple Leafs sweater as an appeal to sight. Sound comes in for the first time with reference to the "tranquility of God," the silence of the church. It occurs again when the referee blows his whistle. Smell and touch are both evoked, if indirectly, by the image of the hair glue. Touch enters again with the detail of the mother smoothing down the creases in the new sweater. Taste is not especially present in this memoir, though we might imagine the enjoyable taste of the blue-and-white sweater for moths, as the sweater likely contained a good portion of wool at that time. Note that all these sensuous details are *precise*. Student writers sometimes think that descriptive writing calls for stock, general phrases such as "a beautiful blanket of snow." But notice how such phrases are not used by Carrier or by any of the descriptive models in this book. Good description puts emphasis on the close observation of unique characteristics. Contrary to common belief, nouns and verbs matter more than adjectives and adverbs. We see this demonstrated in the following example of dominant impression.

PRACTICE

Does Carrier appeal to all five senses in his descriptions? Find five examples of language that evoke sight, sound, smell, taste, and touch.

Service of a Dominant Impression

Dominant impression refers to the central quality or characteristic created by a particular passage of description, or indeed, by an entire work. Here, for example, is a passage from Charles Dickens's *The Mystery of Edwin Drood*:

> Not only is the day waning, but the year. The low sun is fiery and yet cold behind the monastery ruin, and the Virginia creeper on the Cathedral wall has showered half its deep-red leaves down on the pavement. There has been rain this afternoon, and a wintry shudder goes among the little pools on the cracked uneven flagstones, and through the giant elm trees as they shed a gust of tears. Their fallen leaves lie strewn thickly about. Some of these leaves, in a timid rush, seek sanctuary within the low arched Cathedral door; but two men coming out resist them and cast them forth again with their feet; this done, one of the two locks the door with a goodly key, and the other flits away with a folio music book.

At this point in his story, Dickens wishes to convey the suspicion of a murder. The waning of the day and season, the fallen leaves, the reds, the "uneven" flagstones, the ruined monastery, the association of one of the men with a bird (Dickens is continuing a reference to rooks—carrion birds), the rain and the cold gusts of wind that affect the "little" pools as well as the "giant" trees all contribute to a mood that is not only melancholic but, in this context, suggestive of death—the dominant impression that comes through. There are no more than 15 adjectives here, to some 30 nouns. The accuracy and precision of the nouns convey much of the impression: not just a vine but a "Virginia creeper" (with a nuance of untoward activity implied in "creeping"); not just a book but a "folio music book." The verb "flits" describes a birdlike action with no need for adjectives or adverbs.

Regarding structure, we may note how logically organized is the description. Dickens begins with a "wide angle" taking in the full scene of the cathedral, ruined monastery, and horizon. He then moves in to the creepers on the walls and follows these down, echoing the movement of the falling leaves, to the pavement. With the "shudder," he returns us to a wider awareness, encompassing the elms, yet keeps the focus downward, on the fallen leaves. The wind carries some of these leaves toward the opening door of the cathedral, thus connecting his dominant impression with the two men who emerge, one of whom, we suspect, in ironic contrast to the religious setting, is the murderer. Not all of us can animate descriptions with the magic and symbolism of Dickens, yet we can learn from such descriptions the effect of careful order, movement, and attention to specific telling detail.

What might we suggest is the dominant impression of "The Hockey Sweater"? As captured so well in the National Film Board's animated film of this memoir, the dominant impression is one of humorous conformity—all the boys dressing, acting, and thinking the same way, all aspiring to be their idol, Maurice Richard.

As you can see, description and narration are hardly separable. Rarely do we have description without some sense of story or vice versa.

REFLECTION

Similarly, we cannot read a narration or a description without sensing that through these words the writer is reflecting on some larger theme, issue, or concern. Your personal essay, however implicit its meaning, should have a thesis. When the personal essay addresses thematic ideas explicitly, the work becomes more overtly reflective. The following example comes from an essay called "The World Is Flat" by "Poor Will," anonymous contributor to *Countryside: The Magazine of Modern Homesteading*. Since this is from a general readership magazine, paragraphs are shorter than standard in academic or literary essays. The fact that we don't know who the writer is shows that personal writing is not essentially about personality or individual ego.

> When I was just learning how to calculate moonrise and moonset, I discovered that the information printed in my metropolitan daily paper was completely wrong. I called to inform the editor of his error; he apologized, but added that no one had ever complained about the problem before. For as far back as I cared to check in the newspaper archives, moonrise and moonset had been miscalculated. Half a million

readers had never cared enough to match the data with the occurrence. Or maybe if someone had tried, he or she had given up in frustration, attributing the problem to personal incompetence.

It is not enough for me to rationalize that all data is somewhat arbitrary, and that the world spins on assumptions and creeds that may or may not really and truly be valid. Such naiveté is the almanacker's profit. It is the naiveté that embraces size over taste, numbers over experience.

Personal observation and existential fortitude are the only antidotes for such spiritual torpor. And the first step on the journey to intellectual liberation is to have enough courage to say what my senses have told me since I was born: that the world is flat!

Explorers may sail west in order to go east; rockets may shoot to the moon; satellites may send us electrical impulses, which many interpret to be pictures of a "round" earth. I believe their messages at the risk of losing my soul. A healthy skepticism toward vicarious science will keep me away from a cosmos in which the sun and moon rise only on charts, and in which circumference is the equivalent of flavor.

A flat world is accessible to everyone, and it offers challenge enough. After I have walked to its edge, finding my way by the stars I can name from the closed dome above, identifying the plants that grow at my feet, learning the bird songs as I go, then there may be time for more esoteric notions.

—From *Countryside* 87.6 (Nov./Dec. 2003): 91

Note how this reflective approach has a philosophical tone; the essay seems almost *im*personal, akin to a detached essay of analysis.

Here is the opening paragraph of student Mark Radford's personal reflection "Different Worlds":

The world is changing rapidly. When I think about the way my father grew up, compared to the way I grew up and the way my son is growing up now, I'm amazed by the differences. Changes are all around us every day, some seemingly significant and some not, but it isn't until you consciously compare certain things over a number of years that the significance is truly revealed. The differences between my childhood and my son's are not as fundamental as the differences between my father's and mine, but they are still significant.

Radford clearly announces that he will be comparing his three subjects in order to reach a new understanding of the fundamental distinctions between their respective generations. He will be reflecting quite consciously on implications of the differences he examines.

For another example of the reflective personal essay, see Willard Dudley's "Causes of Procrastination" at the Text Enrichment Site under Chapter 10. In that essay, we find a complete, explicit thesis statement, followed by body paragraphs telling us about each cause of his procrastination. The causes, all abstract nouns, stress ideas rather than concrete, sensuous experience. Dudley's short essay, in fact, tells us less about the details of his life and more about his inner contemplation. Because the reflective approach has a philosophical tone, the essay may seem almost *im*personal, akin to a detached essay of analysis.

An Anorexic's Recovery
Leanna Rutherford

As the new millennium rolled in, an estimated 10 million people in the United States had an eating disorder (Gordon 36). Given the similarities between that society and ours, we can expect the problem to be similarly entrenched north of the border. According to Andrea Gordon in Hospital Practice, *research in 2001 suggested that in "developed" countries, one in every 200 young women was affected. An eating disorders recovery program, Milestones in Recovery, defines anorexia nervosa as "a condition in which the sufferer has a fear of weight gain" and experiences loss of appetite along with an aversion to eating. The Milestones online newsletter,* Pale Reflections, *refers to recent research suggesting that one percent of American adolescent women suffer from this particular eating disorder. Like other sources on anorexia nervosa,* Pale Reflections *describes the condition as a "mask" covering various possible causes and suggests that more than 1000 American women die from anorexia nervosa each year. Canadian Leanna Rutherford's personal essay on her own experience with the life-threatening disorder appeared in* Canadian Living Magazine, *1998.*

1   It was March 1995. I was 17 and in my graduating year of high school when I decided that I wanted to lose weight—10 pounds, maybe 15, certainly not more than 20. I was five eight and 155 pounds. I wanted to impress the boys in university, and I thought being thin would help. So I went on a diet.

2   People with eating disorders do not wake up one morning and say to themselves, "I am not going to eat any more" or "I think I will start bingeing and purging." Nobody called me fat or told me life would be perfect if I lost 50 pounds. I can't pinpoint one event that directly led to my disorder. I just needed something to depend on, something to think about and to put all my effort into. I just happened to find dieting at the wrong time. It was comforting to take a break from the changes and worries in my life to concentrate on what I was, or wasn't, going to eat that day. It was also nice to pat myself on the back every time I resisted eating.

3   By June graduation I was down to 130 pounds. I was satisfied but afraid I might regain weight, so I kept dieting. When I entered Bishop's University in Lennoxville, Que., that fall, I weighed 120 pounds. I had heard about the Frosh 15, the 15 pounds on average that university students supposedly gain in first year. I decided that I, dieter extraordinaire, would not become part of that statistic.

4   When I went home to Halifax at Thanksgiving, I weighed myself for the first time in a month and a half. I weighed 115 pounds. I can remember standing on the bathroom scale and saying aloud to myself, "This is a problem. I have got to stop losing weight."

5   But I had lost perspective on what "normal eating" was. I thought that if I ate one piece of pizza or one cookie, I would immediately put on 10 pounds and continue to gain uncontrollably.

6   I returned to school, determined to maintain a weight of at least 112 pounds. I bought a scale and promised myself I would gain five pounds. I increased my daily food intake by one apple and one glass of skim milk.

7   But I weighed myself obsessively—several times a day—to be sure I didn't gain more than five pounds. Within a week I stopped eating the extra food and cut back my intake even further.

8   This is when my mental distortion began. Although I had a scale and knew that 112 pounds at five eight was very thin, I would look in the mirror and see fat everywhere. In reality, though, it was not that any of my body parts were large, but simply out of proportion. My hips looked big because my waist was so thin. My thighs appeared huge to me in comparison to my buttocks and calves. My bones had begun to stick out. I could count every rib and vertebra. But it happened so slowly that I accepted it as normal.

9   My friends eventually begged me to start eating more. But it was too late. I had lost touch with reality. My weight was the only thing that mattered.

10   At Christmas I returned home to a horrified family. I wasn't just thin, I was emaciated. But aside from my looks, I still seemed to have it all together. I was an honours student when I entered university and had an 82 percent average after my first semester. I had made lots of friends and had balanced my social and academic obligations. Except for the state of my health, I was a success story.

11   When I went back to university in January, my life dissolved both emotionally and physically. I cried at least twice a day, although never in public. I couldn't get up for class. I couldn't even walk up the stairs without sitting down to take a rest. Every single moment was a fight between me and every cell in my body—cells that were begging me to give in and nourish them.

12   I yearned to confide in someone but I was convinced that getting help meant getting fat. I carried on in silence.

13   I knew that I could not continue living that way but I saw no alternative. Losing the anorexia nervosa felt like losing everything. I was convinced that it was all I had— my only support, my only true friend.

14   One day in early March, my roommate came home from class to find me curled up, crying and talking about suicide. She walked over and handed me the number for the National Eating Disorder Information Centre Support Line and said, "I'm going to give you 48 hours to phone them. If you don't, then I will." It was a moment for which I will be eternally grateful. She had nagged me in the past about getting help but she had gone easy on me, hoping I would find the help myself. Now she was forceful. She refused to watch me die.

15   I called the support line and said quite simply, "I have a problem. I need help." The counsellor asked me a few questions about my situation and gave me some telephone numbers to call. The closest resource centre was an hour and a half away by car and I had no way to get there.

16   As far as I was concerned, I had made the effort and the medical world had failed me. My roommate did not give up. She told me to go to the medical clinic on campus and again gave me an ultimatum: either I would go myself, or she would go for me. I was not as easily persuaded as I had been before. I made excuses for myself, pretending I'd done all I could.

17   She kept her word. Three days later I was summoned to the doctor's office and asked if I had "lost control." How to answer that question? If I told the doctor I could handle it, maybe she would leave me alone. Only, I knew I had no control. I knew I needed help. And deep down a voice was begging me not to kill myself. So I answered, "No, I don't have control. I can't stop."

18   For the next two and a half months I hated everyone, including friends and family. I was in the hospital and was physically forced to gain weight. I knew I wanted to get better but I didn't believe that that was the doctors' intent. I thought they were my enemies, ruining my life and making me "fat."

19   Legally, anorexia is a mental illness. If you are mentally incapable of eating normally, you can be committed to a hospital and forcibly nourished through the use of restraints and tubal feeding. That may sound extreme, but remember, it is a life or death situation.

20   When I was finally admitted to a voluntary program, I promptly checked myself out. My parents were livid. They kept saying that it was the stupidest thing I had ever done. I told them I was in control again and in fact I believed that I was. I didn't think I needed an in-patient clinic to help me eat. That was the anorexia speaking. It was still very much alive inside my brain.

21   My parents tried everything they could. They begged, made deals, threatened to take away privileges, but finally they gave in. They were my parents, they loved me and ultimately they couldn't bring themselves to refuse to allow me to come home. They did, however, come up with the idea of making me sign a contract. If I lost weight again, or made any decisions they deemed irrational, I would be recommitted to the hospital immediately.

22   With this horrific threat over my head, I went home. It took nine weeks to find an available therapist experienced in counselling patients with eating disorders.

23   Once out of the hospital, I lost all the weight I had gained there and more. Even while seeing my therapist, I managed to drag myself down to a deathly 90 pounds. I hid my weight by wearing baggy clothes and avoiding being weighed.

24   But I finally found the strength to initiate my own battle. The doctors could talk to me, even force-feed me, but until I found my own reasons to be healthy, no one could do more than keep me alive. I had missed a year of university. It took 10 months of boredom, loneliness and tears to realize that anorexia and life are incompatible, that I couldn't weigh 90 pounds and be happy. That is when I began my struggle toward normal eating.

25   Recovery is a long process. I still see both my psychologist and nutritionist monthly and I have 10 more pounds to gain to reach the goal weight I determined with my nutritionist. I'm in my third year of a degree in neuroscience at Dalhousie University in Halifax.

26   Now there is more to my day than what I eat and how much I weigh. I can finally look at a plate of food and see substance and nutrients instead of the number of calories and grams of fat. I can go out to dinner and to parties without being scared by the prospect of unexpected food. And a few months ago, I threw out my bathroom scale.

Focus Questions

1. Does this essay apply the elements of narration, description, and reflection? In what ways and with what degree of success? Discuss your answers with your classmates and your instructor.
2. What do you take to be the controlling idea and supporting reasons (thesis) of this essay? For a summary of this essay, see the Text Enrichment Site under Chapter 13.

FINAL WORD

Personal writing may not be the dominant form you pursue in your academic studies, but gaining confidence with this form will not only be personally rewarding, it will ground your writing approach in general.

Works Consulted

Edwards, Jannie. Personal Interview. 3 Oct. 1992.

Gordon, Andrea. "Eating Disorder: Anorexia Nervosa." *Hospital Practice* 36.2 (2001): 36.

Milestones in Recovery. "Anorexia Nervosa." *Pale Reflections*. 3 Oct. 2006. 21 Oct. 2006 <http://www.pale-reflections.com/anorexia.asp>.

Moses, Daniel David. *Pursued by a Bear: Talks, Monologues, and Tales*. Toronto: Exile, 2005.

Wlodkowski, Raymond. Keynote address, Athabasca University Learning Services Conference. 30 Sept. 2006.

Chapter 9
Exposition and Expository Patterns

Chances are that most of your writing at the secondary level called for **exposition**. You will find that many of your university course textbooks, like those in high school, are expository—that is, they inform you on some topic. While your writing at college or university will increasingly focus on analysis, persuasive discussion, and interpretation of various critical questions, you may well also be called upon by some university assignments to provide expository essays, reports, and oral presentations. Furthermore, the seven patterns presented here as "expository patterns" are, in fact, patterns that writers adapt to many major purposes—analytical, argumentative, and even personal—as well as expository.

Exposition explains, it clarifies—a process that goes on, fundamentally, in *all* writing. This chapter should assist you, then, both by reviewing the nature of expository purpose and tone and by introducing the idea of seven distinctive patterns of organization, which the following three chapters (Chapters 10 to 12) define and illustrate in further detail.

EXPOSITION DEFINED

As the word suggests, expository writing informs. Its *primary* purpose is to clarify a subject rather than express the voice of the writer or build an argument. Traditionally, exposition has been defined as a "neutral," "impartial," or "objective" stance, with emphasis on accurate facts and unbiased observation or an exploration of how those facts relate to each other and an overall meaning. Traditionally, exposition uses third person, especially in academic writing, as a way to place emphasis on the subject.

VARIATIONS AND MIXTURES

On the other hand, expository essays *may* use a personal approach by directly discussing the writer's relationship to the subject. Within non-academic forums, such as newspapers and specialty magazines, a personal approach can help interest the reader in the subject. For instance, travel writing, sometimes viewed as its own genre, reflects a balance of personal and expository writing. With increasing frequency, first-year university assignments ask students to combine expository writing and personal experience, as demonstrated later in this chapter by "Polynesian Maple Leaf" (p. 131) and "Building Blocks: Canada's Chinatowns" (p. 136).

Whether you explore exposition in part through the personal essay or entirely through the more traditional third-person academic approach will be up to you and your instructor. In this chapter and the following three, we include samples of both third-person and first-person approaches to expository writing.

FEATURES OF EXPOSITION

In Chapter 13 we provide instruction on writing the summary, an exercise in observation, accuracy, and concision. Several important features of the summary very much apply to traditional academic expository writing:

- third-person point of view
- impartial tone
- accuracy
- thorough knowledge of the topic
- conciseness
- use of your own words, aside from key technical labels
- attention to a main issue and meaningful connections

Supporting Details as Paramount

Unlike the summary, the expository essay *does* include details; it is imperative, in fact, that all important points or aspects be elaborated through appropriate details, whether data from first- and second-hand studies, statements by reputable sources, or analogies and other necessary descriptive techniques. The type of supporting detail required, and the organization of that detail, will depend on the precise nature of your essay. As with any essay, you will shape a standard opening and thesis statement, a body elaborating upon the thesis, and a conclusion.

METHODS OF EXPOSITION

Within the body you will expand on your thesis according to one or more of seven patterns of organization:

- classification-division
- example
- cause-effect

- directional process (how-to instructions)
- process description (process analysis)
- definition
- comparison-contrast

Chapters 10 to 12 provide illustrations and definitions of these seven common patterns of support. Learning to recognize these patterns will improve your awareness as a reader as well as your organizational and explicative skills as a writer. We have presented comparison-contrast as its own chapter, with special attention, because learning to master comparison-contrast pays major dividends to academic writers. As we noted earlier, these patterns, and the strengths of expository tone, can easily be adapted to serving the complete range of purposes.

Give Your Expository Writing Life

A common problem with expository writing is the writer's failure to imbue the discussion with energy and a sense of purpose. To overcome this problem, you, the writer, must make and express a meaningful connection with your topic. This requires having solid ethos, which you can build through research. But this ethos should also consist of a true interest in the topic. Ideally, you should participate in some aspect of the topic to some extent. You must also ensure that your reader can find a meaningful connection with it. While the subject must matter to you, you should shape your discussion with your readers in mind, and consider how that group of people will be influenced by what you say. Consider the questions they are likely to ask and how best to provide answers in terms they will understand. Above all, ensure that you have a vigorous thesis statement with a committed controlling idea (see Chapter 6, "Outlining: Thesis Statements and Topic Sentences," for the importance of a controlling idea).

The following three sample essays of exposition illustrate controlling ideas, expository tone, and effective short essay structure for this type of writing.

Expository Writing and Research Sources

Remember that quantity is not quality and may even work against quality. In the old days, when instructors were not always trained to be as tactful as they are expected to be today, one of our professors wrote on one of our first-year essays, "You get no extra marks for swallowing the dictionary." The same could be said of sources listed. You get no extra marks for how many sources you list. The important thing is whether your sources are reliable, important, and current, and whether they have helped to shed new light on the topic. Although you should do enough research to be aware of important voices on your topic, more significant than how many sources you list is how meaningfully you connect to the source and how effectively you present it for your reader. The controlling idea of your essay should be strongly shaded by your ethos, pathos, and logos—not simply a re-statement of what someone else says.

Think "Suitcase" and Remember to Outline

As we suggested in our introduction to this section on forms, you can effectively compare your assigned essay to a suitcase. Its required length represents volume or capacity. You can put just so many clothes and other items in there. If you don't pack enough of the right things, on the other hand, then the contents will rattle around. That said, "padding" is not the way to solve a paucity of needed contents. Your goal is to judge how much content you need for the assigned length. You must narrow sufficiently, but not so much that you have content for just one paragraph, instead of the typical five or six. To make these "packing" decisions before your final draft for submission, remember to use an outline. If you are the sort of writer who can get started with an outline, the writing process will likely take less time than it would otherwise. Chapter 6, "Outlining: Thesis Statements and Topic Sentences," provides you with the tools to write effective outlines. As you read the following sample essays, see if you can visualize the outline that led to the finished product.

Sample Essay

Elementary Observations: The Special Skill of Sherlock Holmes
(adapted from a longer essay)
Robert M. Penner, MD

A Fellow of the Royal College of Physicians of Canada, Dr. Penner practises gastro-enterology at Kelowna General Hospital and is assistant clinical professor with the University of British Columbia and the University of Alberta.

1 "You have been in Afghanistan, I perceive," Sherlock Holmes says to Dr. Watson, MD, upon meeting the physician who is to become his junior partner (Doyle 7). Watson thereafter credits Holmes with a power of reasoning unattainable by lesser mortals. These words of greeting, from Arthur Conan Doyle's first Holmes novel, *A Study in Scarlet,* provide a foretaste of many remarkable, yet as Holmes would say, "elementary," observations to follow. Watson, a physician like his creator, might be expected to recognize that reasoning is rarely the step whereby Holmes surpasses those around him. Rather he employs a skill most often associated with physicians: that of looking in the correct direction when all around is distraction.

2 To appreciate the significance of Holmes' first words to Watson, some brief story background is helpful. It is the 1880s. Watson, an army surgeon, has recently returned to London from the British campaign in Afghanistan, weakened from a gunshot wound, the hardships of escape, and a subsequent fever. Pressed for money, he has

met up with an acquaintance, Stamford, who suggests meeting with "a fellow who is working at the chemical laboratory up at the hospital" (3), someone interested in shared lodging. Of course, the "fellow" in the chemical lab is Sherlock Holmes, still a complete stranger to Watson. Surrounded by "retorts, test-tubes, and little Bunsen lamps, with their blue flickering flames" (7), Holmes sees Stamford approaching, informs him of an exciting new discovery, then sees Watson and observes, "You have been in Afghanistan . . . "

3   In explaining *how* he knew that Watson had been in Afghanistan, Holmes states the following:

4   [My] train of reasoning ran, "Here is a gentleman of a medical type, but with the air of a military man. Clearly an army doctor, then. He has just come from the tropics, for his face is dark, and that is not the natural tint of his skin, for his wrists are fair. He has undergone hardship and sickness, as his haggard face says clearly. His left arm has been injured. He holds it in a stiff and unnatural manner. Where in the tropics could an English army doctor have seen much hardship and got his arm wounded? Clearly in Afghanistan." (13)

5   Though this particular example may not seem as remarkable as others involving key plot disclosures, it prepares us for Holmes' famous technique of looking in *unusual* directions (the fair wrists), then drawing confident conclusions. Holmes rarely makes impressive leaps of logic from that which is obvious to all. At the moment of a spectacular revelation, he invariably confides that he has simply been looking in a different direction than have Dr. Watson and the reader. To the disdainful Holmes, all of so-called everyday life is a cheap, transparent card trick able to fool only inferior observers. Ironically, Holmes impresses the physician with a physician's skill of observation that routinely mystifies patients.

6   To better appreciate how this manner of observing is a "physician's skill," one might consider the standard method used to detect endocarditis, an infection of the heart valves. A man suffering from shortness of breath can reason that a physician is applying physical senses towards a diagnosis when the stethoscope is used. The patient does not know exactly for what the doctor is listening, but will draw the conclusion that the sounds of heart and lungs convey information. Imagine the patient's surprise, however, when he goes to the doctor due to shortness of breath and the doctor gives special attention to examining the patient's eyes and fingernails. When the doctor then suspects a diagnosis of endocarditis, the patient might be tempted to suspect magic. It is not unusual, in fact, for patients to credit physicians with supernatural powers of observation. A clean bill of health at an annual physical exam is seen as a promising look into the future. A diagnosis of cancer yields the inevitable question of "How long?" as though the doctor has one's lifeline from birth to death printed out in advance on a mystical chart. What is magic, on the other hand,

if not the ability to reach conclusions by observing that which others do not know they can see? To a doctor who knows that an infected heart valve launches microscopic blood clots into the periphery of the body, there detectable through magnification as tiny spots in the eyes and as hemorrhages under the fingernails, no impressive degree of reasoning is required. The doctor simply applies a specialized—or more focused—awareness to direct his eyes.

7   While it is likely no accident that Doyle selected a physician for Holmes' perennially impressed sidekick, given that Doyle himself was a medical doctor, as previously suggested, it does seem ironic, or at the least "interesting," that a physician should be so surprised by Holmes' powers of observation. Is this a weakness—a lack of verisimilitude—or a strength, a way of conveying the extraordinary powers of Holmes? Certainly Doyle intended to endow Holmes with extraordinary powers. The discovery that Holmes announces in *A Study in Scarlet* before greeting Dr. Watson for the first time is, in fact, within or near the border of science fiction. Practising chemistry, Holmes has found an "infallible test for blood stains" (7), a procedure to replace the guaiac test. The guaiac test, disdained and fictitiously replaced by Holmes, is still used in the twenty-first century on stool as a screening test for colon cancer. Unfortunately its results are no more reliable today than they were a century ago. If only Doyle had elaborated further on his character's discovery, Holmes might have had a chance to mystify a much greater number of doctors, at a benefit far surpassing the several crimes he so brilliantly solved.

Primary Source Consulted

Doyle, Arthur Conan. *A Study in Scarlet.* First published 1887. New York: The Modern Library, 2003.

Connections

Dr. Penner, a doctor himself, makes a strong connection to a character in a novel created by a doctor. But anyone in the medical field or simply with a good knowledge of doctors might have sufficient ethos to make the connection that Dr. Penner has between the main skill of the central character and the characteristic diagnostic methods of doctors. To help his readers make the connections, the writer uses clear, non-technical language and fills in just enough story background to suggest how Holmes applies his "physician's skill" as a detective. A purpose of writing is to shed new light on a subject, and here Dr. Penner has applied knowledge from one field to shed light on another. Notice that he does not need to use first person to convey his ethos; evident enjoyment of Doyle's stories emerges through his tone and potentially inspires his readers to investigate or return to the Holmes books themselves.

An important further connection to the goals of *Acting on Words,* of course, is the example Holmes sets of looking in unusual directions to "observe that which others do not know they can see."

Who is Dr. Penner likely addressing in his essay? This question of intended readers, of course, helps determine *purpose* and therefore how the writer goes about making connections with his readers. If this essay had been written for a university course in literary analysis, the writer likely would have been advised not to recount this much of the plot, to assume that the readers already had a strong knowledge of the story. Dr. Penner's essay, however, refers in detail to the inaugural meeting between Holmes and Watson, suggesting an intention to interest the *general* reader (rather than the literary critic) in the original Sherlock Holmes stories, extremely well known, these days, from second-hand film and television adaptations but perhaps not so widely read as they used to be. It seems that the writer intends to make an interesting connection for those readers who may not know the books, in which case, his presentation of relevant story basics serves his purpose. Note that although the style of writing is expository (explaining and clarifying a subject), a persuasive effect also occurs, namely, an implicit appeal to read these stories, because they offer unexpected connections. Dr. Penner also leaves important critical questions open-ended, so that we will be curious to try answering them for ourselves. A literary analysis assignment—setting up a different purpose—would require more answers from the writer-analyst.

Since Dr. Penner has ample knowledge from professional experience to establish the "physician's skill" that he wishes to discuss, his only required source for this paper is primary: the novel upon which he is casting new light. You might have developed this sort of paper yourself by referring to sources by medical people and perhaps interviewing someone like Dr. Penner. In other words, you would use secondary sources to fill in the necessary missing technical information that Dr. Penner has gained through professional training and practice.

Outline of "Elementary Observations: The Special Skill of Sherlock Holmes"

Controlling idea

Prominently located at the end of his opening paragraph and reinforced in several key positions that follow in the body, the controlling idea seems hard to miss: Sherlock Holmes applies a "physician's skill" (i.e., looks in unexpected but necessary directions).

Introductory paragraph

Establish that Holmes mystifies Watson upon their first meeting, that Watson ever after regards Holmes's skills as almost supernatural, but state the thesis that Holmes simply uses a physician's skill of observation.

First body paragraph

Sketch in the details of the first meeting, interesting the reader in the saga of stories that follows and setting up Holmes's explanation of what he has really done to come to his observation.

Second body paragraph

Provide Holmes's explanation, illustrating his general method of looking in unusual places, and set up the following connection to a physician's typical method.

Third body paragraph

Detecting endocarditis demonstrates the physician's skill. Explain what a patient might expect in contrast to what actually happens and then explain why. An effect is that doctors are considered mystics. Reinforce that in fact they are simply observing that which others do not know they can see.

Concluding paragraph

Return to the point repeated earlier that Watson, a doctor, might be expected to understand Holmes's magic and raise this as an interesting point. It could be a device Doyle wishes to use to heighten Holmes's heroic strengths. This leads to another example of Holmes's superior talents—his improvement of the guaiac test. Conclude with the reflection that if Doyle's creation really had provided a replacement test, a great many more "Watsons" today would be in awe, and maybe more good would be accomplished than the fictional exploits.

Sample Essay

Polynesian Maple Leaf
Danielle Hicks

A junior at the University of Arizona, where she practises gymnastics on an athletic scholarship, Canadian Danielle Hicks wrote a 4000-word essay for her first-year anthropology course Individuals and Societies. The assignment called for her to identify her specific personal and cultural identity in connecting with research into an aspect of another culture. For reasons that will become clear, she chose the topic of tattooing and Polynesian culture. Along with the written assignment, Danielle had to speak to her topic orally, explaining to her primarily American classmates her particular angle on the subject. The following short essay, adapted from the longer paper, reflects the basic goal of expressing to classmates what research sources she used, what relevant knowledge emerged from that reading, and what personal connection linked her to that knowledge.

1   Tattoos in Polynesian culture represented many things—not only beauty, courage, and wealth but also "prowess as warriors" (Gell 1993:57). Polynesians wore minimal clothing so that their tattoos were visible during battle. The tattoos on the Polynesian warriors made them more "impressive to their opponents and their gestures of defiance more horrid" (Gell 1993:57). A Polynesian boy who withstood the unpleasant operation of tattooing at the age of sixteen displayed courage, which meant that his career as a warrior was "committed and voluntary" (Gell 1993:58). Acquiring tattoos not only meant that a boy could now think of marriage, but was automatically considered for wars, in which his tattoos would frighten his enemy, as well as help identify his body if he was killed during

battle. As a young female Canadian of the early twenty-first century, I have done some research into tattoos in traditional Polynesian society, seeking further understanding of what this body art meant to others in different times and places as well as reflecting on the meaning of my own rather special tattoo.

2   The sources I have consulted provide background information on the custom of Polynesian tattooing. Most are ethnographies with detailed descriptions of the Polynesian culture based on fieldwork and history. Turner's fieldwork entailed long-term immersion in a community and involved participant observation. Even though this work is over a hundred and fifty years old and reflects Turner's outside set of values, it describes many interesting aspects of life at that time. *The Works of Ta'Unga* (re-written by Crocombe) also describes life in Polynesia in the 1800s. Caillot's *Histoire de la Polynésie Orientale* provides background information on how Europeans first found the Polynesian Island, including James Cook's descriptions of their people. Fornander provides large amounts of information about marriage and kinships in Polynesia. My knowledge of Polynesian tattooing comes from the works of Gell, who compares and contrasts the differences between tattooing in the West today and Polynesian tattooing in the past. All of the authors have either lived in Polynesia or have done extensive research.

3   According to an ancient Polynesian story, two twins were sent to give the people a message about tattooing. The twins were supposed to say, "Tattoo the women, don't tattoo the men," but as they swam along, they became distracted and got their message mixed up to say, "Tattoo the men, don't tattoo the women" (Gell 1993:66). Further to this story, the Polynesians believe that the natural process of childbirth gives pain to women and joy to men, while the cultural process of tattooing gives pain to the men (who are tattooed) and joy to the women (who aren't but who are attracted by the tattoos) (Hage 1996:343). Childbirth represents the girl's rite of passage into womanhood. Being tattooed represents the boy's rite of passage into manhood. But only the more prosperous Polynesian families today can afford to have their sixteen-year-old sons tattooed. Tattoos today are thus financially painful, but they were also physically so in former times, as they took several months to complete. Before a ban imposed by the French missionaries, bones and mallets were used to tap the ink deep into the skin. Families would celebrate the passage with a great feast of pig, fish, and yams (Turner 1861). Those of us elsewhere in the world with tattoos owe our special marks to the Polynesians: the word "tattoo" is one of only a few words of Polynesian origin to be used internationally (Gell 1993:3). Indeed, the ancient art of tattooing spread around the world from Polynesia, where to this day, a young man's sign of passage, embedded in ink deep beneath the skin, is highly respected as a symbol of everlasting significance.

4   The significance of tattoos was just the opposite in the socially conservative home where I grew up. Although attitudes in the society around us were changing, my family still held to the view that those with tattoos "are involved in criminal activities or involved in some sort of undesirable activity" (Johns 2003:1). My family roots go back to England, Scotland, Ireland, and France. I live in Oshawa, Ontario, which is about an hour east of

Toronto. In the Regional Municipality of Durham, Colonel R.S. McLaughlin enabled the City of Oshawa when he established the General Motors plant. Oshawa is now called the "bedroom" community for Toronto, because most of the population of Oshawa, including my dad and my mom, commute to Toronto everyday for work. Although it is now possible to use lasers to remove or fade tattoos (iEmily 2000), my parents made clear to me their belief that a tattoo was permanent. I understood that if I were ever to have a tattoo, it should represent something extremely important in my life, so that I would never regret having the tattoo. I was brought up to believe that I could do anything that I worked for. Sometimes I would need a little push from my parents, though, and occasionally a bribe to get where I wanted to go in life. My mom and I made a deal: if I was to become the Women's Senior High Performance Champion in gymnastics and go to the 2002 Commonwealth games in Manchester England, I could get a maple leaf tattoo. I won the 2002 Canadian National Championships and was off to England, but of course before I left I went to the tattoo parlour with my mom to get my tattoo.

5   Turner reports that the Polynesian culture taunted and ridiculed untattooed boys (Turner 1861:47). While I was not exactly taunted and ridiculed for the opposite, my entire family including grandparents, aunts, and uncles could not believe that Mom had allowed her sixteen-year-old daughter to get a tattoo. In that respect, it has been something of a military accomplishment, part of an ongoing revolution carrying on from the 1970s when middle-class women in our society seized "increased auton-omy" and, as an expression of their newfound independent identities, wanted to "inscribe a surface of events" (Mascia-Lees & Sharpe 1992:146, 152). It was not a customary family tradition to see a young girl with a tattoo, but my immediate family finally understood that this achievement was very important to me and that I wanted to mark it as such forever.

Works Consulted

Caillot, Eugène
    1910 Histoire de la Polynésie Orientale. Paris: Éditeur Leroux.

Crocombe, Marjorie
    1968 The Works of Ta'Unga, 1833–1896. Canberra: Australia National Press.

Davis, Chris
    2003 French Polynesia. Electronic document, <http://www.polynesianislands.com/fp/>, accessed October 25, 2004.

Fornander, Abraham
    1973 An Account of the Polynesian Race, Its Origin and Migrations. Maui, HI: Charles E. Tuttle Company.

Gell, Alfred
    1993 Wrapping in Images, Tattooing in Polynesia. Oxford: Clarendon Press.

Hage, Per, with Frank Harary and Bojka Milicic
    1996 Tattooing, Gender and Social Stratification in Micro-Polynesia. Journal of the
        Royal Anthropological Institute 2(2):335–351.
iEmily
    2000 A Marked Change: A Girl's Guide to Tattoos. Electronic document,
        <http://www.iemily.com/Article.cfm?ArtID=213>, accessed November 10, 2004.
Johns, Fred
    2004 Sinister Skin Tattoos. Electronic document, <http://portal.citysoup.ca/NR/exeres/
        5775649C-FA70–4286-A8A8-B40EC1010702.htm>, accessed October 11, 2004.
Mascia-Lees, Frances and Patricia Sharpe, eds.
    1993 Tattoo, Torture, Mutilation, and Adornment, The Denaturalization of the Body
        In Culture and Text. Patricia Sharpe, ed. Albany: New York Press.
Shukla, Pravina
    2000 The Human Canvas. Natural History 108(9):80–81.
Turner, the Rev. George, LL.D.
    1861 Nineteen Years in Polynesia: Missionary Life, Travels, and Researches in the
        Islands of the Pacific. London: John Snow, Paternoster Row.

Connections

Danielle's assignment stressed the importance of connecting between self and topic, self and reader, and thereby reader and topic. As directed by assignment guidelines, her first body paragraph summarizes the sources she reviewed, with brief notes on assessment of those sources. She has added a recent general source on Polynesia to the expected "classic" study by the first anthropologist to live among its people, thus aiming to account for observer attitudes of the time. Her main source on the specific subject (tattooing in Polynesia) is relatively recent and nicely supplemented by other more current studies of tattooing in Western societies. Danielle's essay uses the American Anthropological Association style of citation, which is based on the *Chicago Manual of Style*. See <http://aaanet.org>, "Publications," to access information on this widely used system of documentation.

Having summarized her approach to sources, Danielle focuses on the idea of a rite of passage; in her final body paragraph, she expands on her personal background with the intent of demonstrating a rite of passage in how she acquired her own tattoo.

Related Writing

Another component of Danielle's anthropology assignment was to write three pages of creative non-fiction, based on her research, from the viewpoint of a young woman in an earlier Polynesian society. See the Text Enrichment Site, Chapter 9, for Danielle's response to that assignment. Issues surrounding creative non-fiction are discussed in the introduction to Nina Varsava's essay "Non-fiction Isn't Fact—Read with Care" (Reader, p. 485). Writing from the imagined perspective of someone in another culture raises still further questions, some of them heated: is speaking as or for another culture "appropriation"? Some say yes, that speaking for another is an act of disrespect, intrusion, suppression, and distortion (a view perhaps more prevalent in Canada than in the United States). Others say no, that thinking imaginatively from another viewpoint builds bridges to new understanding (a view perhaps more prevalent in the United States than in Canada). The questions may, indeed, be impossible to answer apart from specific contexts.

Outline of "Polynesian Tattoo"

Controlling idea

Prominently located at the end of her opening paragraph, the sentence Danielle provides expresses the purpose, method, and structure of her essay; by mentioning her interest in connections to her "own special tattoo," she not only piques our curiosity but introduces the controlling idea that her tattoo has something important in common with the Polynesian tradition of tattoos. She conveys a note of excitement: exploring tattoos in Polynesia will help illuminate the significance of her tattoo while perhaps the story of her tattoo will help the reader connect to the Polynesian history of tattooing.

Introductory paragraph

Narrow to the role of Polynesian traditional tattoos as marks of the warrior, to set up the inductive thesis that my tattoo also involved a form of battle victory. State the method (outline) and purpose of the essay; create interest and convey my central idea by saying that my tattoo is "special."

First body paragraph

Summarize sources, why I chose them, how I evaluated them.

Second body paragraph

Look at the Polynesian tattoo as, for boys, involving painful rite of passage to becoming a warrior, including family relationships and involvement, and a symbol of everlasting significance.

Third body paragraph

Summarize my social/national background, family relationships, and reason for wanting my own symbol of everlasting significance.

Concluding paragraph

Return to connection to Polynesian young male warriors—the tattoo as symbolizing, for me, a central personal achievement that was enabled by decades of female revolutionary work: one that also reminds the world around me I'm proud of being Canadian (my tribe). Express inductive thesis that even though tattoos may now be removed, mine shares the ethos of celebrating an achievement I value as "everlasting."

Sample Essay

Building Blocks: Canada's Chinatowns
Malissa Phung

Canada boasts an ethnic Chinese population of well over 1 000 000 people, according to Statistics Canada, yet as Malissa Phung, a University of Alberta English major, points out, few Canadians are aware of the Chinese immigrants' contributions and place in modern Canadian history. Phung relies on her own personal experience of growing up in Edmonton's Chinatown and historical research to construct her exposition. Her essay details Chinese immigration history in relation to the geographic phenomenon of Chinatowns that grew out of and transformed the Canadian landscape as Canada began to take shape as a modern nation.

1   An older Chinese man at work once told me that Canada was very young—its history short, nothing compared to China's, and its people naive. At the time, I was at a loss for words. I could not defend the youthful ignorance of Canadians. I, like many other young Canadians, knew more about the birth of America's democracy, the names of more presidents than our prime ministers, and more films, sitcoms, songs, writers, thinkers, actors made and born in the U.S.A.

2   Living in the shadow of her bigger sister in the south, Canada has always been in a state of comparison. It's like hearing your parents asking you in front of their friends: *Why can't you be more like your older sister? Look at what she's accomplished.* Somehow along the way, Canada's past got forgotten. Young Canadians never ask how Canada got here today.

3   As one such young Canadian, I have lived in Edmonton's Chinatown most of my life. I was part of a local generation of Chinese and Vietnamese children who played with each other in the alleyways of Chinatown while their parents ran their businesses for over a decade. Our parents lived and worked in Chinatown, made Chinatown a normal aspect of our everyday lives. But never did I question how and why a town came to be based on China. How almost every major city in North America has a Chinatown instead of a Ukrainiantown, a Germantown, or an Irishtown. For all I know, Chinatowns have always been there. But how did they get there in the first place?

4   In *Chinatowns: Towns Within Cities in Canada,* David Chuenyan Lai provides a historical background on the development of Chinatowns from the late nineteenth century to the 1980s. His overview details the history of Chinese immigration to Canada and the demographic changes resulting from several Canadian immigration policies concerning the Chinese.

5   The first period of migration, in 1858–1884, the period of free entry, allowed Chinese immigrants to enter and leave Canada without restriction (8). During this period, Chinatowns were associated with gold-mining, coal-mining, and fishing and were built only in Vancouver Island and British Columbia (9).

6   In 1885–1923, the period of restricted entry was a response to the alarming rates of Chinese immigration to Canada and to the growing civic discontent with Chinese immigrants taking what was left of the labour pool during economic recessions. To discourage Chinese immigration, the federal government passed the Chinese Immigration Act of 1885, which imposed a head tax of fifty dollars on every new Chinese immigrant for a certificate of entry (52–53). The head tax did not affect Chinese immigration, and the new Chinese influx followed the development of the Canadian Pacific Railway (8–9). So many Chinatowns grew in cities across Canada: Victoria and Vancouver, the largest in the west coast; Calgary, Edmonton, Lethbridge, Saskatoon, Moose Jaw, and Winnipeg, the major ones across the prairies; Ottawa, Hamilton, and Toronto, the largest in Ontario; and Montreal, where ninety percent of Quebec's Chinese lived, and Quebec City (68). Chinatowns were never built in the Atlantic Provinces because the Chinese population in the east had always been so small, consisting mostly of Chinese laundrymen scattered from each other in separate towns, instead of confining themselves to one street in one particular town (68, 101).

7   The head tax, ineffective in curbing the Chinese influx, rose to a hundred dollars in 1901, and then to five hundred dollars in 1903 (54). Although the new head tax had an immediate and noticeable effect, the tax increase was only a temporary deterrent to Chinese immigration. In 1900, 1,325 Chinese arrived in Victoria; in 1904, none; in 1905, twenty-two; and in 1913, 7,078 (54–55). Despite the discrimination and fervent attempts to restrict Chinese immigration, Chinese labourers looked to Canada as hope for a better life (55). In China, they would earn two dollars a month; in Canada, they would earn ten to twenty times more (55). Lai explains the predicament of Chinese immigrants as follows:

8   Since the mid-nineteenth century, China's economy had been deteriorating, affected by wars and revolutions such as the Taiping revolution, the wars against foreign powers, Dr. Sun's revolution, and warfare among the warlords. (55)

Chinese labourers came to Canada to work, to improve their livelihood. However, when the economic conditions deteriorated in Canada, they accepted lower wages and worked even longer hours, threatening the livelihood of white labourers. (27–28)

9   As a result of the ineffective head tax, the Immigration Act of 1923, known as the Exclusion Act, prohibited any Chinese immigrant from entering Canada (8). Since the Chinese population in Canada consisted mostly of males, the new Immigration Act effectively diminished Canada's Chinese population and the vitality of Canada's Chinatowns.

10   Almost every Chinatown built during the late 1800s went through a budding stage (its economy controlled by a few wealthy Chinese merchants) and a blooming stage (its economy boosted by population bursts) (5–7). And when the Exclusion Act was passed, Canada's Chinese population began to decline. Then Chinatowns across

Canada entered the withering stage, which brought a halt to its blooming economies and diminished Chinese ownership of properties, leaving room for non-Chinese businesses to move in, for example, as low-class bars, second-hand shops, and pornographic book-stores (7). When Edmonton's original Chinatown started to depopulate after the Exclusion Act, it diminished into a skid row district, "where there were already many cheap hotels, rooming-houses, shabby theatres, taverns, dance-halls, and second-hand stores" (92). Soon afterwards, middle-class residents moved out of the withering Chinatowns, leaving poor, elderly bachelors behind, weakening community or-ganizations, and declining the level of participation in traditional social activities (7).

11   The Immigration Act of 1967, following the Exclusion Act, which was repealed in 1947, ushered in new types of Chinese immigrants and investors from Hong Kong, Taiwan, and Southeast Asian countries (9). The new wave of Chinese immigrants, its investors and entrepreneurs, played an important role in creating new Chinatowns across Canada, revitalizing and replacing Canada's old Chinatowns or building new Chinatowns in suburban areas, in cities that had never had a Chinatown before (9, 120).

12   Edmonton actually has two Chinatowns—an old Chinatown, partly revitalized through several urban renewal projects since the 1970s, and a new Chinatown, recon-structed since the 1980s. The Chinese Benevolent Association (CBA) attempted to save Edmonton's old Chinatown from government interests that threatened its survival, from federal plans to consolidate its offices in the area, and from a municipal decision to widen its street, which would diminish its remaining commercial strip (139–140). The CBA succeeded only in acquiring government funds for building a senior citizens' home, the Chinese Elders Mansion; and a cultural centre, the Edmonton China Town Multicultural Centre—but at least this provided a focal point for the already widely scattered Chinese community (140). After a public meeting with the CBA decided to relocate Chinatown if efforts to save it failed, the Edmonton Chinese Community Development Committee was formed in 1975 to plan for a new Chinese business strip and a Chinese cultural centre (140). By 1986, the new Chinatown as we know it had already grown to twenty-two Chinese business con-cerns (restaurants, grocery stores, importing companies, bakeries, bookstores) and several Vietnamese stores (156–157), while the old Chinatown became extinct and now is occupied by Canada Place (141).

13   My mother's business is part of this new Chinatown, part of a new local history only two years older than me. And beyond these blocks that have been a part of my young life lies a series of forgotten blocks that have built a part of Canada's history. I remember my mother attempted to reattach me to my roots one summer, ushering me to the Chinese Edmonton China Town Multicultural Centre every day to learn Cantonese—a fruitless attempt as I received only a C average at the end of that summer. But I remem-ber this area of Edmonton well, with its Chinese temple and pagoda-themed buildings jutting across a dry and abandoned landscape of taverns with "No Knives" signs at the

entrance, gravel parking lots, the local XXX pornography store, and bachelor hotels like the Gold Nugget Suite. I also remember this strange area having a street sign that said "Harbin Road," a street sign that confused me and made me wonder why the (new) Chinatown I have always known was only ever called 97 Street.

Work Cited

Lai, David Chuenyan. *Chinatown: Towns Within Cities in Canada.* Vancouver: University of British Columbia Press, 1988.

PRACTICE

Describe Phung's "connections," that is, her relationship to personal experience, her readers, and her research, as discussed in the comments that follow the first two sample essays in this chapter. Describe her controlling idea. Write an outline for the essay, one with directions to the writer, in the style of those that follow the first two essays in this chapter.

For study questions and further sources, which may assist with the above practice activity, see the Text Enrichment Site, Chapter 9.

For another sample student essay of exposition, see Colin Klein's "Math and Philosophy" on the website for this chapter.

Chapter 10
Classification-Division, Example, and Cause-Effect

When writing instructors refer to "forms of writing" or "patterns of exposition," they are signalling how the writing has been organized. Is the material organized according to *time,* as it is in narration, or *space,* as it is in description, or some combination of the two, as in a close reading and interpretation of a song or poem? Other patterns are common as well.

This chapter provides definitions and examples of three such patterns:

Classification-division
Example
Cause-effect

CLASSIFICATION-DIVISION: YOUR BASIC OPERATING SYSTEM

Classification-division affects your writing any time you take pen in hand or turn on the computer to compose. We present classification-division as the first of the expository patterns because, in a sense, it is the operating system needed to enable basic shapes and separations to appear. Things must be categorized according to their fundamental identities before we can think further about their relationships and meanings. Through classification-division, we realize the possibility of deciding how, effectively, to group things together. From tables of elements to orders of life or other schematic overviews of relationships, classification-division underlies the basic content of most academic disciplines. It is, in a sense, the operating system you must have before going any further in your field.

All fields of science depend upon classifications. For example, biology groups plants or animals according to a "family tree" (taxonomy). This hierarchy descends from class to order to family to subfamily to genus and finally to species and even subspecies. Behind such divisions into subordinate groupings stands the idea of identifying meaningful shared elements in order to enable our understanding more about the nature of things. All of the items being subdivided share the same fundamental characteristics as every other member of the overall (or highest) category.

At the level of the largest class, the fundamental characteristics are very basic and broad, for example, communication by vocal signs in language studies or warm-bloodedness in the study of animals. Various members then subdivide further into their own subordinate groupings according to shared differences, such as grammatical patterns or having four legs.

Critics of Western thinking—for example Albert Borgman in his book *Crossing the Postmodern Divide*—maintain that this "pigeonhole" outlook has become too rigid and, in fact, has enslaved us. Whatever you may decide about that critical opinion (*after* reading his book, of course), recognizing our reliance on specific tools does offer us increased opportunity to control them.

Example

The following partial paragraph about Canada's Aboriginal peoples at the time of European contact is taken from Olive Dickason's *Canada's First Nations:*

> These people spoke about fifty languages that have been classified into twelve families, of which six were exclusive to present-day British Columbia. By far the most widespread geographically were those within the Algonkian group, spread from the Rocky Mountains to the Atlantic and along the coast of the Arctic to Cape Fear; Cree and Inuktitut had the widest geographical ranges. This accords with Roger's hypothesis, that by the proto-historical period areas that were once glaciated (most of Canada and a portion of the northern United States) had fewer languages than areas that had been unglaciated. While Canada was completely covered with ice during the last glaciation, except for parts of the Yukon and some adjacent regions, the strip along the Pacific coast was freed very early. According to Roger's calculations, once-glaciated areas averaged eighteen languages per million square miles, and unglaciated regions 52.4 languages per million square miles (2,590,000 square kilometres). . . . (64–66)

✒ PRACTICE

In what ways has this paragraph been organized according to a sense of classifying? Discuss your findings with others.   Then see our "Commentary on Classification Paragraph" at the Text Enrichment Site, Chapter 10.

Terms of Classification

An essay may be organized according to divisions of time or space, according to causes or effects, according to reasons or methods, or according to many other features or attributes occurring within a shared category.

You will certainly find examples of classification in other parts of this text. In Chapter 6, "Outlining: Thesis Statements and Topic Sentences," the essay "Should Cats

Be Allowed to Roam?" illustrates use of a direct-list thesis stating three reasons. In other words, the essay is classified according to three points within the category of why cats should not be allowed to roam. These "reasons," in this case, are effects. Classifying reasons is further demonstrated by the essay "The Causes of Procrastination" at the text website, Chapter 10. In that essay, the terms of classification are causality. Classification-division plays a central role in "Life in the Stopwatch Lane," an analytical essay in the Reader (p. 451), in which Amy Willard Cross discusses the numerous subdivisions of time among the perpetually busy. Her terms of classification are the various subdivisions of time common among the "busy class." Pat Deiter-McArthur's "Saskatchewan's Indian People—Five Generations," in Chapter 11 (p. 166), provides yet another extended example of classification-division. In her essay, the terms of classification are process divisions (stages) of history, closely allied to the chronological stages used in personal narration.

 PRACTICE

Review the Reader for examples of classification-division. Find at least three paragraphs, passages, or complete selections in which this pattern dominates. Describe the pattern in each as precisely as you can. *How* do the examples apply this pattern? Share your findings with your classmates and your instructor to see whether you agree with each other's findings. Ask your instructor to clarify any uncertainties and differing interpretations.

An Aid to Direct-List Thesis Outlining

Classification-division underlies the idea of a controlling idea followed by a carefully controlled number of reasons (often three). The reasons may be thought of as a division of the more general position expressed by the controlling idea. For example, a writer might express the idea that blood clotting, intended by nature as a healthy response to cuts, can have dire consequences, as illustrated by certain problems in the brain, heart, and lungs. In this example, the three areas of the body (divisions of the common organism) will provide specific illustrations of the shared controlling idea. You may think of your three reasons, commonly stated after a controlling idea in your thesis statement at the end of your opening paragraph, as establishing three subtopics (divisions of the main idea), to be covered in body paragraphs according to spatial, temporal, or other taxonomic order. In many cases, classification is the simplest and surest approach to take in your expository essays. But to make this method work, you must be able to identify terms (values, functions, features) that truly share a clear common denominator.

Tips for Using Classification Effectively

1. For an essay of five to seven paragraphs, restrict your categories to three. If you try to cover more categories, you may not have sufficient space to support each

properly. Furthermore, you may be over-complicating your organization. Consider whether certain terms in a lengthy list may in fact be sub-points of other terms in the list. Often a list of six, seven, or even more terms proposed in a rough draft outline can be effectively compressed into simply three terms.

2. Be sure your classified terms or sections are properly matching, that they are genuine subdivisions of a common source or ancestor. Some writing instructors refer to organizing an essay or speech according to "points." This general word implies a wide assortment of possible terms. Remember that if you choose terms that are not commonly considered to fit within the same broad category of phenomena (things of the same family, things of the same subject, things sharing the same function or application), many readers will find your paper or speech somehow illogical or unbalanced. Consider the following draft thesis statement, which presents unmatched terms as though they are matched:

   > Every food server knows the four classes of obnoxious customer: the commander, the mumbler, the sweet talker, and the vanisher.

   The detraction in this scheme is that only the first three are distinguished by speaking style. Presumably the vanisher—who ducks out before paying the bill—could be any of the previous three. Consider the following more careful way of signalling this relationship to your reader:

   > Every food server knows the three obnoxious customer speaking styles and, of course, knows that worst of all customers, the one with no speaking style when it comes to paying the bill.

   The same need to sharpen and clarify your categories occurs if you try to demonstrate the danger of blood clots by organizing a discussion of the veins, brain, heart, and lungs as four completely parallel terms. In this example, blood clots that occur in the veins in various regions of the body could travel to specific critical organs. Such a paper may really be viewing the process in the veins as a cause and that in the other isolated organs as an effect. It would thus make better sense for your reader if you introduced your discussion as dealing with a process that begins in the veins and then affects three key organs in specific ways yet with a shared general effect of serious threat to health. The paper would emphasize a process description starting in the veins, then move to a classification of three impacted organs. In other words, classification would serve in an important way and yet be suitably subordinated to the main concern with process, in this case one involved with causes and serious effects.

3. Remember the principle of building to a climax. To continue using the blood clot example, if you know from research that serious harm from blood clots occurs most often in one of the three regions and least often in another, you would likely build to the area of most serious impact. This pattern would intensify your controlling idea that blood clots can be serious. Your order does not always need to build to the most intense point, but there should be a strategic connection between your order of classified items and your underlying purpose.

Sample Essay   Classification-Division

The Ways of Meeting Oppression

The following is an excerpt from Martin Luther King, Jr.'s book Stride Toward Freedom, *which documents the famous Montgomery bus boycott.*

Martin Luther King, Jr.

1   Oppressed people deal with their oppression in three characteristic ways. One way is acquiescence: the oppressed resign themselves to their doom. They tacitly adjust themselves to oppression and thereby become conditioned to it. In every movement toward freedom some of the oppressed prefer to remain oppressed. Almost 2800 years ago Moses set out to lead the children of Israel from the slavery of Egypt to the freedom of the Promised Land. He soon discovered that slaves do not always welcome their deliverers. They become accustomed to being slaves. They would rather bear those ills they have, as Shakespeare pointed out, than flee to others that they know not of. They prefer the "fleshpots of Egypt" to the ordeals of emancipation.

2   There is such a thing as the freedom of exhaustion. Some people are so worn down by the yoke of oppression that they give up. A few years ago in the slum areas of Atlanta, a Negro guitarist used to sing almost daily: "Been down so long that down don't bother me." This is the type of negative freedom and resignation that often engulfs the life of the oppressed.

3   But this is not the way out. To accept passively an unjust system is to cooperate with that system; thereby the oppressed become as evil as the oppressor. Non-cooperation with evil is as much a moral obligation as is cooperation with good. The oppressed must never allow the conscience of the oppressor to slumber. Religion reminds every man that he is his brother's keeper. To accept injustice or segregation passively is to say to the oppressor that his actions are morally right. It is a way of allowing his conscience to fall asleep. At this moment the oppressed fails to be his brother's keeper. So acquiescence—while often the easier way—is not the moral way. It is the way of the coward. The Negro cannot win the respect of his oppressor by acquiescing; he merely increases the oppressor's arrogance and contempt. Acquiescence is interpreted as proof of the Negro's inferiority. The Negro cannot win the respect of the white people of the South or the peoples of the world if he is willing to sell the future of his children for his personal and immediate comfort and safety.

4   A second way that oppressed people sometimes deal with oppression is to resort to physical violence and corroding hatred. Violence often brings about momentary results. Nations have frequently won their independence in battle. But in spite of temporary victories, violence never brings permanent peace. It solves no social problem; it merely creates new and more complicated ones.

5   Violence as a way of achieving racial justice is both impractical and immoral. It is impractical because it is a descending spiral ending in destruction for all. The old law of an eye for an eye leaves everybody blind. It is immoral because it seeks to humiliate the opponent rather than win his understanding; it seeks to annihilate rather than to convert.

Violence is immoral because it thrives on hatred rather than love. It destroys community and makes brotherhood impossible. It leaves society in monologue rather than dialogue. Violence ends by defeating itself. It creates bitterness in the survivors and brutality in the destroyers. A voice echoes through time saying to every potential Peter, "Put up your sword." History is cluttered with the wreckage of nations that failed to follow this command.

6   If the American Negro and other victims of oppression succumb to the temptation of using violence in the struggle for freedom, future generations will be the recipients of a desolate night of bitterness, and our chief legacy to them will be an endless reign of meaningless chaos. Violence is not the way.

7   The third way open to oppressed people in their quest for freedom is the way of nonviolent resistance. Like the synthesis in Hegelian philosophy, the principle of nonviolent resistance seeks to reconcile the truths of two opposites, acquiescence and violence, while avoiding the extremes and immoralities of both. The nonviolent resister agrees with the person who acquiesces that one should not be physically aggressive toward his opponent; but he balances the equation by agreeing with the person of violence that evil must be resisted. He avoids the nonresistance of the former and the violent resistance of the latter. With nonviolent resistance, no individual or group need submit to any wrong, nor need anyone resort to violence in order to right a wrong.

8   It seems to me that this is the method that must guide the actions of the Negro in the present crisis in race relations. Through nonviolent resistance the Negro will be able to rise to the noble height of opposing the unjust system while loving the perpetrators of the system. The Negro must work passionately and unrelentingly for full stature as a citizen, but he must not use inferior methods to gain it. He must never come to terms with falsehood, malice, hate, or destruction.

9   Nonviolent resistance makes it possible for the Negro to remain in the South and struggle for his rights. The Negro's problem will not be solved by running away. He cannot listen to the glib suggestion of those who would urge him to migrate en masse to other sections of the country. By grasping his great opportunity in the South he can make a lasting contribution to the moral strength of the nation and set a sublime example of courage for generations yet unborn.

10   By nonviolent resistance, the Negro can also enlist all men of good will in his struggle for equality. The problem is not a purely racial one, with Negroes set against whites. In the end, it is not a struggle between people at all, but a tension between justice and injustice. Nonviolent resistance is not aimed against oppressors but against oppression. Under its banner consciences, not racial groups, are enlisted.

Study Questions

For study questions prompting further insight into the ideas and methods of this essay, see the Text Enrichment Site for this chapter.

Essay Topics

For suggested essay topics that invite classification-division structure, see the Text Enrichment Site for Chapter 10.

Final Word on Classification-Division

As we said, classification-division is your basic operating system. It places basic content in logical order. *How* you explore that basic content—whether through close and extended examples, comparisons, discussion of causes and/or effects, or complex definitions—leads us naturally to consider the remaining patterns of organization.

EXAMPLE: YOUR KEY TO BEING VIVID

Perhaps the most familiar comment instructors of writing place on first-year students' essays is "Good point, but now give an effective example." Examples are the bedrock of achieved, sound prose. Sometimes examples enter so significantly into an essay that they may be considered the dominant organizational pattern.

✒ PRACTICE

Read George Orwell's essay "Politics and the English Language" (Reader, p. 471). Document its use of   examples. What purpose do they serve?

As you will have noticed, Orwell runs examples through his essay. He wants to convince us that the language we use is full of "bad habits." His third paragraph, presenting five "representative samples" from published professors and other authors, drives home the point that bad habits *are* the norm. His purpose is persuasive (arguing that despite what most people think, "bad" habits can be changed), but his primary method is expositional—the use of examples, one "piled on" to another, as it were, to wear down the opposition.

Types of Supporting Detail

Supporting detail is discussed (in detail!) in Chapter 4, "Paragraph Skills" (pp. 52–56). In a sense, all forms of supporting detail are examples (justifications, proofs) that help support your claims. Albert Einstein once remarked that "God is in the details." Read our entire discussion of supporting details, paying special attention to the matters of "warm" and "cool" proofs, reliability, suitability, and balance. In expository writing that relies heavily on examples, particularly "warm" ones, these supporting details work together to further the descriptive nature and effect of the prose.

The following essay by a student, Lorena Collins, further illustrates how a number of examples can be linked together to reinforce the writer's main point.

Sample Essay   Use of Examples

Timone
By Lorena Collins

1   I have had several pets share my home throughout my life, but one of the most enjoyable and most entertaining I have ever owned is a little white dog named Timone. Timone is a three-year-old Bichon Frisé I picked up from the city pound last May. As soon as I saw him, I was curious to meet him. Once I met him there was no way I could leave without him. He was so tiny, obviously undernourished, and afraid. When I asked the kennel technician if I could see him in the viewing room, the first thing he did when I squatted down to greet him was curl up between my legs and rest his head on my thigh. He wagged his tail and looked up at me as if to say, "Please take me home." After the paperwork was filled out and he was taken to the vet to get fixed, Timone was mine.

2   Life after I brought him home was not the same. The first thing he did was eat. It was like he had some sort of homing device built in because he knew where his food dish was even though he had never been in my house before. Once he had satisfied his hunger, he claimed a spot on the couch, and then another on my bed. He made himself at home almost instantly, as if he had always lived there. Shortly after I brought him home, however, he developed a bit of an infection from licking his stitches. The vet supplied me with a cone-shaped collar. I waited until I got him home from the vet to put it on him. This cone came from his neck right to the tip of his nose. Once I finally managed to get it on him, he did the funniest thing I have ever seen a dog do. Timone slowly walked up to the kitchen wall and placed the top of the cone against the wall and just stood there, like a pouting child sent to the corner after being naughty. This went on for a few hours. He barely moved. For a while, I thought maybe he wasn't sure if he could move. He eventually accepted it, but it was even more humorous watching him sniff around the floor looking for scraps like a Hoover vacuum.

3   It didn't take long to realize that I would have to start from scratch when it came to training. The only thing he knew how to do was fetch. We started the house-training by keeping him in a medium-sized kennel when we couldn't watch him and allowing him in the kitchen and living room only when we could watch him. I was at wit's end when for weeks he would stand directly in front of me, look me straight in the eye, and proceed to do his business on my cream-coloured plush carpet. But after about four months, he seemed to catch on.

4   Timone was much quicker when it came to learning tricks. Within a few weeks he could sit, lie down, shake a paw, high-five and dance, all for a Milk Bone. In fact, he was so eager to get a treat that sometimes he would stand in front of me and

proceed to do all the tricks in sequence over and over until I gave in and got him a Milk Bone. As part of his trickster side, Timone has proven to be quite an acrobat. When he is in a playful mood, he will sometimes run laps around the living room, leaping from one piece of furniture to the other with the agility and grace of a cat. Other times, if my six-year-old daughter is sitting on the floor watching television, he will run laps around her until she extends both her arms to her sides like an airplane. Timone will then run from one end of the room, jump over one arm, run to the other end of the room, turn around, run back and jump over the other arm. He will do this about three or four times. Sometimes he will even try to jump over her head, notwithstanding the occasional time he misjudges the distance and bounces off the top of her skull. He has the ability to jump straight up in the air to amazing heights from a standing position. Timone has kicked me in the back of the shoulder on occasion in an effort to grab my attention. Sometimes if I go outside without him, he will jump repeatedly at the door, kicking the latch in an attempt to open it. From outside it looks as if he is jumping on a trampoline. The neighbours have been known to remark, "That dog can get some pretty good air!"

5   Timone has proven to be a joy to live with. Whether he is flying around the house, trying to impress with his tricks, or being defiant, he is always loved and appreciated. His intelligence and abilities have often made me wonder what his life was like before he entered mine. He has a unique ability of warming up to anyone he comes in contact with, and I am sure he will continue to win over the hearts of anyone he meets.

Study Questions

 For study questions prompting further insight into the ideas and methods of this essay, see the Text Enrichment Site for this chapter.

Balancing Examples with Logic

As discussed in Chapter 4, examples drawn from personal experience or observation can be more emotionally compelling than logically sound. Using examples can lead to the logical fallacy of overgeneralization. David Suzuki, for instance, uses his own experience of a successful school visit to argue that high schools should teach sex education. However, some readers might argue that one success by one person in anything is not enough proof that an idea should be adopted, and even an essay patterned around several examples will probably still fail to offer conclusive evidence. Some deductive reasoning and other forms of logic may be required to reassure your reader that broader conclusions can be drawn from your examples. On the other hand, the need for other appeals to reasoning does not minimize the value of illustrating your point, and in explaining why you believe something, you will naturally give examples. These represent the inductive side of reasoning, an intrinsic and powerful tool when used with balance and care (see the section on inductive and deductive forms of reasoning in Chapter 3, "More About Logic.")

Description Is at the Heart of Example

In most cases, narration (anecdotes) and description drive example—especially description, since it enables narration to unfold. Descriptions, as explained in Chapter 8 (p. 117), rely on expressing a strong dominant impression and following a logical, purposeful organization suited to serving the central impression. For a good example of a carefully organized description, see the text website for this chapter, where Blue Quills First Nations student Lenny Halfe provides an example of something we can all relate to: a personal vision of something we have wanted for as long as we can remember. In his case, it is a dream home.

Narrative Voice Should Not Be Forgotten

Like description, which may serve personal or expository purposes, narration plays an important role in imbuing various forms with supportive power. Narration imparts voice, shape, and time to example (as opposed to examples that are frozen, timeless), as demonstrated in the following illustration of human response to Hurricane Katrina, which struck New Orleans in August 2005. Vickey Brown, 16, lived in the B.W. Cooper (Calliope) Project in the city centre. This portion of her personal narrative appeared in the online magazine *Slate* under the heading "Hurricane, Remembered: Memoirs by Teenagers Who Survived Hurricane Katrina," <http://slate.com/id/2148125/>, accessed November 2006.

Sample Essay   Narration—Personal Memoir

Hurricane, Remembered
Vickey Brown

1   On August 28, 2005, the day before the storm, I woke up real early to get some last-minute stuff from the store. As I walked to Safeway I started to think about what might happen tomorrow. "What if I don't make it through? Will I survive? Is it the last time I will be able to see the light of day?" When I got home I turned to Channel 6 news to see where they were evacuating to. My mom came over to see if I wanted to come to the Convention Center where she worked.

2   "No, I'm not going, so I'll stay here with my grandma."

3   "Why aren't you coming?"

4   "I don't want to leave my grandma alone. I got to stay. She needs me."

5   I could see in my mama's eyes that she didn't want me to stay there, but she let me because she knew how I felt toward my grandma.

Brown's story focuses our attention on one narrative example. Narrowing your personal writing to one event can be an effective way to achieve an engaging personal work. In this case, a soft personal voice stands against the storm. As we say elsewhere, the range of voice is all but endless. Academic writing usually subordinates personal voice in favour of detached third person, but combining personal voice and example can be effective on suitable occasions. As Vickey Brown's example illustrates, often the power of example is in both its telling images *and* its narrative cadences. For two more essay examples of this—"Where Are You, My Little Village" and "The Tree"— see the text website for this chapter.

Example as Symbol

"Literary and Film Analysis," at the text website, Chapter 15, talks about symbol and metaphor, staples of literature. Resonant examples almost always serve figuratively or symbolically, commenting on deeper or larger conditions, which they merely represent.

PRACTICE

Read "Literary and Film Analysis" at the Text Enrichment Site, Chapter 15, as well as the two student essays for this chapter, "Where Are You, My Little Village" and "The Tree." Based on these guidelines and illustrations, find at least one other piece of writing that you think uses example with such resonance that a metaphoric or symbolic effect clearly emerges. You may find your example in the Reader of this text or elsewhere. Discuss your finding with your classmates and your instructor.

Essay Topics

 For essay topic suggestions using example, see the website for this chapter.

Final Word on Example

Remember, example is the bedrock of your writing. With no examples to support your points, your essays will be deemed insufficient, no matter how promising their ideas may be.

CAUSE-EFFECT: TOWARD CRITICAL ANALYSIS AND EVALUATION

What makes the world around us the way it is? What makes us the way we are? For centuries, religious practitioners, scholars, writers, artists, scientists, and seekers of many stripes have devoted themselves to humanity's eternal quest: a correct understanding of things as they really are. This pursuit of truth, so central to the true mission of the university (sometimes forgotten), involves careful examination of causes and effects. Careful focus on causes and/or effects usually marks the point at which expository tools serve the purposes of analysis, evaluation, and argumentation—the most common forms of thinking and writing at the university. Cause-effect thinking also underscores narration (with its attention to motivation) and process description (e.g., explaining how photosynthesis takes place).

Definition of Cause-Effect

In our pursuit of understanding, much of what we read and write focuses on causes, effects, or some combination of the two. **Cause-effect writing** simply refers to sections of text that are organized according to a concern with causes, effects, or both.

Here are two examples of cause-effect statements taken from "The Lure of the Body Image" by Susan McClelland (Reader, p. 447):

> Statistics on steroid use show an alarming number of male teenagers across the country are using the substance illegally simply to put on muscle.

> One of the sad consequences of the push towards a hyper-masculine image is that it can rarely be obtained without the use of potentially harmful drugs.

The first statement gives a *why*—the desire to look like a beefcake. The second statement gives a *what*—the harm for the steroid user.

✍ PRACTICE

- Find at least one cause-effect statement from each of the four sections of the Reader. Do you find cause-effect writing equally prevalent in personal, expository, and argumentative forms? In response to this question, discuss your impressions and ideas with your classmates.
- Find at least one selection from the Reader that uses a cause-effect pattern as its primary method of organization. Compare your answer with those of your classmates.

- Provide your class discussion group with one example of cause-effect writing taken from a source other than the Reader in this text.

For further examples of cause-effect writing, see "Examples of Cause-effect Writing" at the Text Enrichment Site, Chapter 10.

Signal Words

Certain words help to signal an author's use of cause-effect structure. A complete list of words and phrasing used in this structure would fill many pages; the following is a small sample taken from the above examples. Please note that in many cases words used to signal causes may also be used or adapted to signal effects and vice versa.

Signal words and phrases showing causes

are using the substance illegally [in order] to put on muscle
they can spawn
set the country on the road to
The desire . . . can result in
It is . . . kept hidden
You and I are . . . responsible for
Our affluent lifestyles and preference for ignoring unpleasant things do little
Poverty is . . . very destabilizing
people die because of

Signal words and phrases showing effects

can rarely be obtained without
whole new classes of accidents and abuses
a means of making it through the lean student years
All this changed when
heavily dependent upon
acquires a reputation
The punishment for . . . is swift and harsh.
are the result of
because of its invisibility
This is, in effect,
this does not erase

 PRACTICE

Look over the cause-effect passages and essays you have already identified as part of previous practice work in this chapter. Underline or highlight those words and phrases you feel signal the writers' rhetorical patterns and purposes. Discuss your answers with your classmates and your instructor.

Striving for Sound Conclusions (or Three Parts Superstition, One Part Science)

Those of us with experience as parents or guardians of young children know only too well their questionable sense of causes and effects. "Take your sweater to the picnic," we say, knowing that the warm day will turn into a chilly evening. Unless the child is remarkably obedient, he or she will ignore our suggestion; six hours later we will be treated to bemused observations about the cold. Yet, in our writing, we too can neglect relevant cause-effect considerations. We may have heard the caution that our ancestors based decisions on three parts religion to one part superstition whereas we base decisions on three parts superstition to one part science—but have we considered what that wry comment is trying to suggest? Review our discussion of logical fallacies in Chapter 3, "More About Logic," and the problems of oversimplification and distortion. We humans take great pride in our ability to reason, in our supposed superiority as a species; yet careful analysis of our reasoning, of our tendency to ignore or warp major causal considerations, to bend even the most carefully collected empirical facts and statistics, and to discount personal and cultural bias should remind us that sound thinking—when it does occur—does so only with major effort.

Organizing Cause-Effect Essays

For less confident or experienced writers of university essays, we recommend organizing your cause-effect writing through a deductive, direct-list thesis statement at the end of your opening paragraph—of the kind represented by the following two sample thesis statements. The first sample focuses on causes, the second on effects.

> I have followed all the steps recommended to begin my essay, but I can't seem to start. I begin to realize that my procrastination is caused by distractions, mounting hopelessness, and despair.

> When a beginning rider mounts a horse for the first time, the rider feels awkward, unbalanced, and unsure of what to do. The horse feels exactly the same way. As a result, a horse develops one of three attitudes to beginning riders: playing dead, taking control, and taking off.

The first thesis presents the controlling idea that starting an essay can be hard for three specific reasons. The second thesis presents the controlling idea that a beginning rider can disturb a horse, with three specific results. For the complete essays that go with these thesis statements, see the Text Enrichment Site for this chapter.

Sample Cause-Effect Essay   Focus—Critical Thinking and Argument

The following essay by Ottawa-based arts student Colleen Leonard questions the effects of beauty ideals as purveyed by the media and mainstream Western culture. As part of the discussion, she also ponders reasons why (causes) humans place such emphasis on conventional beauty. You will note in places that Leonard concedes other ideas about the effects of being concerned about conventional beauty, compares those ideas to hers, and decides which ideas make better sense and why. This comparing of contrary interpretations to one's own is covered in more detail in Chapter 14, "Critical Analysis and Evaluation," and Chapter 16, "Argumentation." Notice that she considers possible reasons that she will go on to discount, a method known as "concession-refutation" (Chapter 16).

Comments on the essay appear in black; comments on documentation technique are in green. Note that Leonard uses APA style.

A Case for the Demotion of Beauty

Colleen Leonard

She opens with an anecdote

1   I was enjoying a rare Friday evening alone—which meant having dominion over the television for a change—but then I found out I am suffering from "ptosis." And not only that, I apparently have other "congenital deformities," such as "inframammary asymmetry" for one, which threatens to undermine my "emotional harmony" and "physical balance," apparently. I also found out, before tossing aside the popcorn bowl in order to visit the nearest mirror to check out my freakish deformities, that I can expect to be either a "sinker," or a "sagger," in ten years time. That does not sound good. It seems that I can find out, for certain, by sending in a photo of my face for analysis. I can then take this annotated rendering along for a consultation with a cosmetic surgeon, skilled in surgically reconstructing faces, and thus restoring my "harmony." Fortunately, after leaving the mirror, I consulted my *Woman's Body Encyclopedia* (CMA, 1995). I was relieved to find out that "ptosis" simply means a normal drooping of the breast (inevitable past age fourteen, if the breasts I see at my gym are any indication), and that "inframammary asymmetry" (lopsided breasts) is a fact for almost *all* women. Can *most* of us be deformed? Though I was relieved to conclude that I did not have an actual disease, I *was* left with a sense of shame for caring about such trivialities. Then I recalled a quote, by Eleanor Roosevelt, that Nancy Etcoff provides in *Survival of the Prettiest.* Eleanor's regret was that she had not been prettier. So it seems I am in good company.

APA style includes the date of publication in parentheses. The title is in the usual author position because the entry on "ptosis" does not have a byline.

The quotation refers to actions taken "in the name of beauty." Is the essay, then, partly concerned with a false definition of beauty, thereby inviting us to think of a better definition?

2   To say that our society is preoccupied with physical attractiveness would be a grand understatement. "People do extreme things in the name of beauty . . . In the United States more money is spent on beauty than on education or social services. Tons of makeup— 1,484 tubes of lipstick and 2,055 jars of skin care products—are sold every minute . . ." (Etcoff, 1999, p. 6). She goes on to catalogue further measures being taken today: 696,904 Americans had cosmetic surgery during 1996, and prior to the ban of silicone implants in 1992, hundreds of women were acquiring them daily. Etcoff argues "there is a method in this madness" (p. 6), that it is in our nature to be "susceptible to beauty" (p. 233), and that our relentless quest for beauty "reflects the workings of a basic instinct." Studies do seem to support the idea that beauty matters, and that some of the preoccupation is likely based on ancient "mechanisms" (p. 37) that evolved from a time when it served a purpose for choosing a healthy, young, or strong mate. Maybe so, but our environment is drastically unlike that of most humans throughout history, and therefore the usefulness of such an instinct is questionable in today's world. Some of the other reasons for our relentless pursuit of beauty are similarly debatable, on different grounds. We need to scrutinize these reasons, in order to understand that beauty ought to be put into a perspective that is more sensible and suited to its actual value in today's world. Otherwise, we will continue to be slaves to an archaic instinct, slaves to false assumptions about beauty, or victims to those who benefit from, or discriminate against us, based on our attractiveness.

APA citations include "p." before the page number.

In the text of the essay, article titles are in quotation marks, and initial

3   One of the arguments we often hear, in justification of the "importance" of beauty, is that looks tell us crucial things about the biological "quality" of a potential mate. In a 1996 *Newsweek* article, "The Biology of Beauty," ecologist Randy Thornhill is quoted as saying,

"Throughout the animal world, attractiveness certifies biological quality" (Cowley). This article, and Etcoff's book, describe the entity that biologists call bilateral symmetry, which is the level of match between the right and left sides of an animal. This symmetry is "tied to beauty because it acts as a measure of overall fitness" (Etcoff, 1999, p. 18). Apparently, physical stressors can cause asymmetry in the less resistant, and presumably less appealing, mates. Certainly, this would have mattered to survival in prehistoric times, or perhaps in less developed countries today where parasitic infections, malnutrition, and lack of medicine are typical. This is *not* the situation we have today, in our part of world, so the idea that we need to seek out beautiful people for mate quality is not compelling. Of course biologists are not arguing that we *should* do so, simply that we seem to be programmed to do so, but often these types of findings are used, by society, to justify the notion that beauty should be pursued ferociously. A peahen may have good reason to choose her mate based on his brilliant tail feathers. But perhaps if this peahen had good medical resources at her disposal, ample nutrition, and a knowledge that genetics only play a small part in overall disease patterns, then she might decide, wisely it can be argued, to choose the less brilliant, but more interesting and intelligent peacock, being ignored over by the other tree.

4   Another related reason people feel beauty is very important is that there is a belief that beauty is *necessary* for reproductive success, or for mating in general. While studies (Cowley, 1996) do show that men who are most symmetrical do seem to evoke more orgasms in women, the purpose of which is to possibly increase conception, this finding is not a compelling reason to seek symmetry at all costs. Women may experience more orgasms (for whatever reason) with symmetrical men, but the study also noted that symmetrical males were more likely to be "less attentive to their partners and more likely to cheat on them" (Cowley, 1996). It seems more worthwhile, and certainly less trouble, for asymmetrical males to promote that they may not be perfectly symmetrical, but that they are devoted and monogamous. It is reasonable to think that this might just as easily garner a "response" from women, in today's world. Besides, population control seems more crucial in today's world, and so the idea that abundant reproduction as evolutionary advantage may no longer even be true. For males, symmetry is a key physical indicator, but women often go to great measures in order to achieve the magic waist to hip ratio of .6 to .8, that biologists tell us is irresistible. It is thought that this silhouette was a signal to prehistoric men that women had fertility potential. The *Newsweek* article quotes Devendra Singh, University of Texas psychologist, as saying, "You have to get very close to see the details of a woman's face, but you can see the shape of her body from 500 feet, and it says more about mate value" (Cowley, 1996). Again, as helpful as this indicator might have been to a shortsighted prehistoric man in a hurry, it is reasonable to assume that modern man can use other means for ascertaining this information.

5   In addition, people often claim that they feel compelled to be attractive as a requirement for employment. They point to studies that have shown that attractive people are more highly regarded generally, and by employers specifically. A study of 11,000 people, conducted by London Guildhall University, did demonstrate that physically

letters in words of four letters or more are capitalized. Capitalize the initial letter of all verbs, nouns, adjectives, adverbs, and pronouns. Capitalize the first word after a colon or dash, and the initial letter of a second word in a hyphenated compound.

attractive people earn more than their unattractive colleagues do (Harper, 2000). This study apparently echoed similar findings from North America. These findings do seem to support the hypothesis that physically attractive people are deemed to have more desirable personality traits than those who are less attractive. Nevertheless, this is discrimination because there are no conclusive studies that prove that physically attractive people indeed have these qualities specifically *due* to their appearance. It seems likely that those qualities exist in attractive people, if they do, due to preferential treatment, or perhaps to other extrinsic factors (Kanazawa & Kovar, 2004, p. 229). Which means that beauty *itself* does not imply anything, aside from nice aesthetics, so employers, or anyone else, have no legitimate reason to use this as a criteria. The more sensible solution to this dilemma would be to deflate the "what is beautiful is good" myth and to ensure protective legislation against "looksism," rather than to spend inordinate amounts of time to alter one's appearance to conform. For instance, if an employer would not hire people of a certain skin colour, we would not accept that the solution should be that candidates have surgery to change their skin colour, we would instead expect the employer to change their discriminatory practices. Beauty should not be pursued for this reason.

6   In conclusion, it seems that beauty does matter, though in large part for reasons that are commercial, discriminatory, false, or based on instincts that no longer fit with our reality today. Because beauty does seem to matter so much at present, it is entirely understandable why, as Etcoff says " . . . people have scarred, painted, pierced, padded, stiffened, plucked, and buffed their bodies in the name of beauty" (1999). But none of this justifies that beauty *should* be pursued so fiercely, nor does it prove that beauty has any value whatsoever; aside from being obviously pleasant to look at. It is surely more reasonable to enforce against looks discrimination, and work to detach our tangled-up beliefs that beauty encompasses more than just aesthetics, than to "scar, pierce, pluck, etc." We can also choose not to be exploited by those who stand to profit from our relentless pursuit of beauty. Imagine what medical advances might ensue if funds currently directed at cosmetic and beauty spending would instead be applied to research, as one example. Humans might have been "cast in an ancient mould" (Freedman, 1986), but we can choose how to apply our instinctual, and possibly obsolete, responses in our modern world. Professor Sydney Brenner—Nobel Prize winner who assisted in "cracking" the DNA code—said it well at an International Congress of Genetics: "The brain is more powerful than the genome" (Smith, 2003).

She ends with a carefully chosen "clincher."

References

Canadian Medical Association's The Woman's Body. (1995). Westmount, QC: Reader's
    Digest Association (Canada) Ltd.

In APA, for titles of books and articles in References list, capitalize only the first word, the
first word after a colon or dash, and proper nouns.

Cowley, G. (1996, June 3). The biology of beauty. *Newsweek.* Retrieved March 23, 2006, from http://hss.fullerton.edu/sociology/orleans/symmetry.txt

Titles of articles do not take quotation marks or italics in References list, but do in text. Initial letters of words after first word are not capitalized in References, except word following colon or dash. Titles of periodicals, books, reports, brochures, some monographs, manuals, and audiovisual media take italics.

Etcoff, N. (1999). *Survival of the prettiest.* New York: Random House, Inc.

Freedman, R. (1986). *Beauty bound.* Lexington, MA: Lexington Books.

Harper, B. (2000, November 22). Does appearance matter in the labour market? Retrieved March 21, 2006, from http://www.shortsupport.org/News/0301.html

Hendricks, C., Olson, D., Jennings, S., & Batt, J. (1998). Physical attraction: Attributions. Miami University. Retrieved March 18, 2006, from http://www.units.muohio.edu/psybersite /attraction/attributions.shtml

Kanazawa, S., & Kovar, J. (2004). Why beautiful people are more intelligent. London School of Economics and Political Science. Retrieved March 18, 2006, from http://www.lse.ac .uk/collections/methodologyInstitute/pdf

Smith, D. (2003, July 12). Brain storms. *The Sydney Morning Herald.* Retrieved March 21, 2006, from http://www.smh.com.au/articles/2003/07/11/1057783354656.html

The title of the online periodical is in italics.

Study Questions

For study questions prompting further insight into the ideas and methods of this essay, see the Text Enrichment Site for this chapter.

Final Word

Cause-effect thinking underlies critical analysis and evaluation, which comprises the heart of scholarship. Almost all of your university papers should contain ample amounts of solid cause-effect organization.

Works Consulted

Borgman, Albert. *Crossing the Postmodern Divide.* Chicago: UC, 1992.

Brown, Vickey. "Memoir—Hurricane, Remembered: Memoirs by Teenagers Who Survived Hurricane Katrina." *Slate* 24 Aug. 2006. 12 Nov. 2006 <http://slate.com/id/2148125/>.

Dickason, Olive. *Canada's First Nations: A History of Founding Peoples from Earliest Times.* Toronto: McClelland & Stewart, 1992.

Chapter 11

How-to Instructions, Process Description, and Definition

This chapter provides brief definitions and examples of three expository patterns:

Directional process (how-to instructions)
Process description (process analysis)
Definition

DIRECTIONAL PROCESS: HOW-TO GUIDELINES

Rarely do we come across a piece of writing that can move its readers to tears, rage, or profanity. Instructions have this power. Although they have a more direct impact on the reader than almost any other form of communication, instructions are often overlooked, underestimated, or poorly written.

Instructions are a form of process explanation that assumes that the reader will participate in the process. Instructions aim to teach the reader to replicate a process. Assembly instructions for furniture, operating manuals for cars, the Help function on a word processor, and a college registration pamphlet are all examples of instructive writing. One of the most common texts on the market is a form of directional process: the cookbook—but be aware that it uses note form, not the sentences required of a scholarly essay.

♪ PRACTICE

Think of an activity that you know well enough to describe to a specified reader. Imagine how you would go about describing that activity.

For examples of activities and audiences, see "Directional Process Topics" on the Text Enrichment Site for Chapter 11.

Remember Your Reader and Focus on the Instructions

In many ways, this form of writing is one of the world's most thankless. The writer is much less present than in a persuasive essay or a personal narrative. A good set of instructions simply allows the reader to accomplish the task at hand effectively and to forget the author forever, whether the task is assembling a bookshelf, setting up a VCR, or operating a piece of machinery. Well-written instructions tend not to call attention to themselves except through their absolute clarity, their transparency as pure, practical information. We could say that their aim is the opposite of what we would call establishing or asserting voice in other forms of writing. Although the art of writing instructions is often unappreciated, readers immediately notice poorly written instructions. Of course, poor instructions can cause the reader frustration, despair, or even injury.

Good instructions, like good process descriptions, guide the reader through a process one step at a time, leaving no room for confusion or misunderstanding. The only test of a set of instructions is that a reader can actually follow them. Writing good instructions, however, is not as easy as it may seem. Some instructors like to begin a class on the subject by asking students to write instructions for a seemingly simple task such as tying their shoelaces. Students soon see that this task that they perform automatically on a daily basis is much more complex than they would have thought. Writers find that they know the process so well that they omit important information

Steps to Writing Directional Process (How-to) Guidelines

Process instructions follow a pattern of organization very similar to a process description. The main difference is that instructions address the reader or user directly, usually in the form of short commands.

1. State the goal of the process and its importance (if not obvious from the goal). List any equipment the reader will need to perform the procedure. Is any other preparation necessary or recommended? For complex procedures, you may want to provide an overview of the major steps or tasks involved. Include in your introduction the time, money, and effort that will be required of the reader (when relevant). Establish a tone that encourages your reader. Use of the second person—"you"—helps this friendly, assuring tone.
2. Break the process into ordered steps. You may want to begin with these steps laid out as a series of numbered statements or paragraphs with headings.

For a complex process, divide the instructions into major tasks and subtasks, stating the overall goal as well as the goal of each major task.

and stages. Unfortunately, this is often the case with far more crucial instructions, which are usually written by people with expert knowledge of the process they describe. One of the greatest challenges in writing instructions is putting yourself in the place of the people who will need to follow the instructions, and trying to imagine what they need—and do not need—to know.

Instructive writing can be more than a straightforward sequence of steps. Sometimes you will have to combine descriptive modes (process description) with attention to causes and effects in order to explain a process clearly and effectively. For instance, if your purpose is to explain to a reader how to use a variety of internet search engines for different purposes, you might want to describe generally how each search engine works behind the scenes before you move to step-by-step instructions from a user's perspective.

Consider the following strategies in writing effective instructions:

- Address the reader directly in the form of a command. Avoid the passive voice. (See p. 521 of the Handbook on active and passive voices, and also the section "Fifteen Common Errors," CE 14, p. 563.)

  Poor: Once the coin is inserted, the knob should be turned.
  Better: Insert the coin and turn the knob.

- Use strong, precise verbs to describe the doer's actions: "grasp," "pull," "turn," "stab," "twist," and so on. Stay away from vague terms such as "proper," "correct," "ready," and "right," and so forth. If your readers already know what you mean by "ready" or "correct," chances are they don't need your instructions.

  Poor: Bake the ingredients for 30 minutes, or until they are ready.
  Better: Bake the ingredients for 30 minutes, or until they are golden brown.

- Avoid ambiguous language that could lead to potential misunderstandings.

  Poor: Place the bookshelf on the floor.
  Better: Lay the bookshelf on the floor so that the back faces the ceiling.

- Do not over-instruct. Sometimes you will have to tell your reader exactly how to stand, or which finger to place where, but often this level of detail is unnecessary. Don't make your instructions into a game of Twister for readers trying to follow them.

- State conditions before actions.

  Poor: Press Ctrl-X if you have highlighted the text you want to delete.
  Better: If you have highlighted the text you want to delete, press Ctrl-X.

- State the goal of a particular step before the action.

  Poor: Rub the lens with three or four drops of solution for about 20 seconds to clean it.
  Better: To clean the lens, rub it with three or four drops of solution for about 20 seconds.

- Place warnings and cautions *before* the step to which they apply. There's no use telling your readers the step they've just completed was actually quite dangerous, especially if they're already bruised or bleeding!

• Use illustrations to assist the text by identifying parts and equipment, or demonstrating what specific steps should look like.

Directional Process and Persuasion

Persuasion plays a role in many types of instructions. For instance, a pamphlet in a doctor's office instructing women how to examine themselves for breast cancer also aims to persuade its audience of the importance of stopping breast cancer in its early stages. Self-help and how-to books not only teach their readers about a particular approach to weight loss, relationships, or sales, but also persuade them that the particular method or system described is better than others. Instructions on some commercial products are primarily intended to persuade. For example, one Australian shampoo bottle includes the following instructions under the heading "Salon Directions": "Saturate hair with water. Massage shampoo deeply into scalp and roots. Drench with water to rinse. Repeat." These instructions are clearly not intended to teach the novice user how to use the shampoo, but to persuade him or her to believe in that particular shampoo's luxurious or sensuous effect.

Now here is a sample directional process essay by part-time student Gisela Becker. Notice that while she does use first person to introduce her topic and engage interest, she then switches to the more typical second person ("you"), appropriate for speaking directly in a friendly, informal manner to an involved reader. Note her use of MLA citation.

Sample How-to Essay

Scuba Diving
Gisela Becker

1   It feels strange the first time. The mask. The awkward gear, a bit heavy. You ease into the water and your face slips below the surface. Inhale; the air comes with a reassuring hiss, and for the first time you breathe underwater. In moments, you forget the mask. The equipment transforms itself into something light and agile, and you're free as you've never been before. With that first underwater breath, the door opens to a different world. Not a world apart, but different nonetheless. Go through that door. Your life will never be the same. (IPADI 1)

The writer quotes from a suitable source, with present tense description and second person to draw us in.

2   I had decided that I wanted to learn how to scuba dive. First I read through the *Open Water Diver Manual,* I watched several diving videos, and I received further useful information from my dive instructor. Then I went through several "confined water dives" in the pool. Finally I was ready and prepared for my first open water dive. I had it all in my head about buoyancy and pressure, volume and density underwater, hand signals and emergency procedures. Yes, I was ready for the underwater excitement!

She suggests ways to become informed.

3   Before I could go for my very first sea dive under the watchful eye of my instructor, several preparatory steps had to be completed: finding the right diving location, reviewing and assembling the scuba equipment, gearing up, entering the water, and finally scuba diving.

She summarizes what will be involved.

4   Finding the right dive location is not as easy as it sounds, but do not worry. During your dive course your dive instructor will choose the dive site for you. As you gain more experience in scuba diving, you will also acquire confidence in deciding on an appropriate dive spot. Depths of water, water movement, low or high tide, and easy accessibility are all considerations when choosing the right location. Do not forget about the weather, because changing weather conditions affect the water conditions.

Having previewed the steps, she elaborates on each in order.

5   Now that you have found a nice dive location, you need to get the scuba equipment ready for the dive. First let me say a sentence or two about whether it is better to buy or to rent scuba equipment. Scuba equipment is very expensive! It is probably best to rent your equipment for a starter, until you know how much diving you are going to do. Most dive centres rent the necessary equipment at a reasonable price.

6   Before assembling your scuba equipment, you need to gather all your gear to ensure that nothing is missing. If you thought that you could just jump into the water and enjoy the underwater world, you are wrong there!

7   First you need a mask that covers your eyes and nose, then a snorkel for surface swimming until you reach the dive site, and certainly you need scuba fins to increase your foot power. Your next piece of equipment is a weight belt. If you are like most people, you naturally float in the water. An extra weight system in the form of a belt will help you to sink.

Notice her use of effective transitional words ("now," "before," "first," "next," etc.) to guide us from step to step.

8   Finally your scuba unit consists of three basic components: the buoyancy control device (BCD), the scuba tank, and the regulator.

9   By now you probably think this is pretty complicated stuff, but I can reassure you that between now and a few dives you will have mastered the equipment with no problems at all. Until that mastery becomes second nature, you have your dive instructor at your side for assistance.

10   The BCD is most commonly a jacket style that you inflate or deflate to regulate your buoyancy. "You can do this orally, using air from your lungs, though most of the times you'll use a low pressure inflator, which inflates the BCD with air directly from your tank" (IPADI 38).

11   Your BCD integrates a backpack to hold the scuba tank on your back. The scuba tank itself is a metal container filled with high-pressure oxygen, which allows you to breathe underwater. With your regulator attached to the tank you are able to use the air from your scuba tank. The regulator has two main pieces, the first stage, which connects to the tank valve, and the second stage, which integrates the mouthpiece. The two stages reduce high-pressure air from the scuba tank; this allows comfortable breathing underwater. You may want to consider wearing a wetsuit depending on the water temperature and the climate you are diving in, but this is also a question of personal choice and preference.

She remembers to reassure and motivate her reader.

12   You must be getting tired from all these explanations about scuba equipment! No? Maybe because you dream of that underwater world, where time seems endless and stress does not exist. You will not be that one inexperienced diver who is trying to remain neutrally

buoyant, breathing frantically into his/her mouthpiece. Let me reassure you that with every moment you are getting closer to this extraordinary experience: your first underwater dive.

13   Now that you have had a chance to look at your gear, you want to get ready to assemble your scuba equipment. First you have to put together your tank, regulator, and BCD. You start with sliding the BCD over the standing scuba tank from the top. Then you secure the tank band tightly. You want to avoid a loose tank on your back while you are underwater. As a next step you attach the regulator on the tank valve and also connect the low-pressure hose from the regulator to the BCD low-pressure inflator. Finally turn on the air and confirm that the whole unit is working properly. Take a few breaths from the regulator. Your equipment is ready for your dive.

She maintains her "you" approach from the reader's perspective.

14   Remember I told you that I was about to go for my first sea dive. Take a moment and picture me in all my gear: I put on my mask and snorkel. My instructor had to help me to put on the BCD jacket and the heavy scuba tank filled with air. I still remember wondering why air would be so heavy.

As in her opening, she appeals to the senses, to the reader's imagination.

15   I have a 12-pound heavy weight belt around my hips and smaller weights around each of my ankles, because my feet kept floating on the surface during the training sessions in the pool. As a final step I put on my scuba fins.

She balances opening description of the activity with a concluding image of the activity about to begin.

16   In all my heavy gear I stand at the edge of the pier. My instructor asks me to enter the water with a giant stride entry. "Simply step out with one foot," I hear him say with an encouraging tone. When I finally decide that I have the courage to do it, I enter the water with one big "Splash." And there I am underwater, breathing and experiencing the freedom of "weightlessness" with the most beautiful sights of corals, ferns and underwater creatures.

Her closing shows that this is really about us, not her.

17   Now it is your turn to get ready for your first underwater adventure.

Work Cited

International Professional Association of Diving Instructors. *Open Water Diver Manual.*
    Santa Margarita, CA: IPADI, 1999.

PROCESS DESCRIPTION: EXPLAINING HOW SOMETHING HAPPENS

Process description explains how a particular process works, but unlike directional process does not expect the reader to perform that process. This form is sometimes also known as "process analysis" or "descriptive analysis."

Process descriptions can be used in a wide variety of circumstances, whether you are describing how language develops in a child from gurgles to full sentences, explaining how a pulp-and-paper mill operates, or demonstrating the means by which a piece of writing builds meaning and appeals to its reader. In process description, you present and clarify for your reader a certain operation within a certain system, natural or human made. As the sample essay later in this chapter demonstrates (p. 166), writers who report upon the unfolding events in the history of a certain place or people do so in the manner of a process description. Many of your textbooks, including this one, contain descriptions of a variety of processes. The following brief example represents the spirit of this mode:

> There is no such thing as new water. The Earth is a closed system and the water that quenched the thirst of dinosaurs is the same recycled water we're drinking today. In fact, it's been estimated that eight people before you have consumed every glass of water you drink, so the same molecules of H_2O that passed over the lips of Napoleon, Columbus, Joan of Arc, or Shakespeare could be snaking their way through an underground labyrinth of pipes to a faucet in your home or office.

—Kim Green, "Water, Water Everywhere . . . ," *New Trail*, Spring 2007, 15

Scientific and Technical Writing

Process descriptions are especially common in scientific and technical writing, where they often describe mechanical or natural processes such as combustion, cell division, or oxidation. Many first-year students feel themselves "at sea" when they are asked to write lab reports. For lab-report guidelines and samples, see "Writing a Lab Report" at the Text Enrichment Site for this chapter.

Chronological Order

Process descriptions are organized chronologically most often, moving in sequence from the first stage in a process to the last. We can organize cyclical processes, such as respiration or photosynthesis, in chronological steps, but we have to choose where to begin and end our descriptions.

PRACTICE

Find examples of descriptive process among the selections in the Reader. Compare your findings with those of your classmates.

Reading and Writing Are Processes

You may gain considerable insight and skill as a reader and writer if you realize that these activities are processes, with cause-effect steps along the way. Chapter 15, "Rhetorical Analysis," describes various ways to understand a piece of writing as a process of interacting components. The use of the word "process" in this case refers

Steps to Organizing Process Description

Not every process description will be subjected to intense scrutiny, but you should imagine your readers will all be skeptics anyway and will be looking for holes in your methods. In describing a process, you should find that the following organizational pattern works whether you are providing a brief description of a process within a longer paper or writing a lengthy report describing a more complex process:

1. Explain the purpose of the process by stating its main goal or its end result. You may want to give a general overview of the process by itemizing its main steps in the order you have written them. Besides defining the objective, consider defining how you will measure the results of stages in the process and how you will mark the passage of time.

2. Divide the process into stages or steps, and explain them one at a time. In a process description of several paragraphs, begin each major step with a new paragraph. Steps are often—but not always—arranged in chronological order. A flow-chart diagram may help both you and your reader understand the overall process in its steps. For instance, if you are describing the writing process, the following flow chart may prove useful:

   collage ➡ brainstorm ➡ topic sentence tree ➡ research ➡ revised topic sentence tree ➡ draft ➡ peer edit ➡ draft ➡ peer edit ➡ revision ➡ submission

3. Bring the steps back together. How do all the stages you have described work together? Is the whole as you have outlined it a cyclical process? Is it linear? Is there a predictable or variable end result? You may also want to restate the purpose of the process.

to the text in relationship to the reader, not to the creative process of composition that created the text (also a process, but a relatively separate one). A heightened understanding of rhetoric as a process informs both your reading and your writing.

For examples of texts analyzed as processes, see Chapter 15.

For a process description explaining how one reads an essay under pressure, "Reading an Essay Under Pressure," see the Text Enrichment Site, Chapter 11.

History—A Form of Process Description

We think of process description as a staple of technical and scientific writing, and so it is. Another field that uses process description, however, is history. Think about the history texts and essays you have read—do they not concentrate, primarily, on describing how various historical forces unfold or *proceed?* The following example illustrates a typical style of historical writing, one that describes stages and suggests cause-effect relationships whereby one stage leads to the next.

Saskatchewan's Indian People—Five Generations
Pat Deiter-McArthur

1   It has been about five generations since Saskatchewan Indian people have had significant contact with European settlers. The First Generation strongly influenced by Europeans were the treaty-signers. The key characteristic of this generation was their ability to have some input into their future. They retained their tribal cultures but realized that they had to negotiate with the Europeans for the betterment of future generations. They did not give up their language or religion or the political structures of nationhood. They were perceived by government as an "alien" nation to be dealt with by treaty.

2   The Second Generation (1867–1910) of Indian people was the object of legal oppression by the government. This generation lived under the absolute rule of an Indian agent, a government employee. Through the Indian Act, this generation was denied their religion, political rights, and freedom to travel off their reserves. A pass and permit system was strictly adhered to on the prairies; every Indian person required a pass to leave the reserve and a permit to sell any agricultural produce. All children were required to attend residential schools run by the churches. The goals of their schools were, first, to make Christians out of their students and to rid them of their pagan lifestyles and, second, to provide a vocational education.

3   Tuberculosis was a major killer of Indian people during this time and contributed to decimating their population in Saskatchewan to a low of five thousand in 1910. This generation was treated as wards and aliens of Canada.

4   The laws which served to oppress the second generation were in place until the early 1950s. The Third Generation (1910–1945) was greatly affected by these laws and schooling. This generation can be described as the lost generation. These people were psychologically oppressed. They rejected their Indianness but found that because of the laws for treaty Indians they could not enjoy the privileges accorded to whites. This third generation was our grandfathers' generation. Many Indians at this time could speak their language but would not because of shame of their Indianness. They were still required by law to send their children to residential schools, to send their sick to Indian hospitals, and to abide by the Indian agent. They rarely had a sense of control over their own lives. This generation was considered wards of the government and denied citizenship.

5   Our fathers' time, the Fourth Generation since treaty-signing, can be best described as the generation of an Indian rebirth. This generation (1945–1980) is characterized by a movement of growing awareness—awareness that being Indian is okay and that Indian people from all tribes are united through their aboriginality, historical development, and special status.

6   This generation saw the rise of Indian and Native organizations across Canada, the return of traditional ceremonies, and an acknowledgement of the need to retain traditional languages and cultural ways.

7   Indian people of this generation were given the right to vote in 1960. The pass and permit system was abandoned in the late 1930s. In 1956, Indian children could attend either residential schools or the local public schools. However, the effects of this generation being raised within an institution and their parents being raised in the same way had a severe impact on these individuals. The residential school not only taught them to suppress their language but also to suppress their feelings and sense of individualism. The continued attack on Indian languages by residential schools left this generation with an ability only to understand their language, but many were not sufficiently fluent to call their Native language their first language.

8   During the sixties, there was a rise in Indian urbanization, a trend that continues today. This generation also contributed to an Indian baby boom that is estimated to be eight to ten years behind the non-Indian baby boomers. The federal and provincial vote allowed Indian people to legally consume alcohol. Alcoholism, suicides, and violent deaths were on the rise for this generation.

9   This was a period of experimentation by both the Indian communities and the government. Unfortunately, neither side was ready for each other. The intended government goal of assimilation was besieged with problems of racism, poverty, maladjustment, and cultural shock.

10   Today's Indian people are part of the Fifth Generation. The fifth generation is faced with choices: assimilation, integration, or separation. Indian people are now able to inter-marry or assimilate with non-Indian without the loss of their Indian status. Indian leaders across Canada are seeking a separate and constitutionally recognized Indian government. Indian government is to provide its own services within Indian reserves. Integration allows Indian people to retain a sense of their cultural background while working and living within the larger society.

11   The fifth generation people are the first children since treaty-signing to be raised by their parents. Many of this fifth generation are not able to understand a Native language. Their first and only language is English. This generation is generally comfortable about their Indianness without strong prejudicial feelings to others. However, this generation is challenged to retain the meaning of Indian identity for their children.

Describing Complex Processes

To describe a complex process, such as building a bridge or staging a play, you may have to divide the process into several subprocesses, each of which involves several steps. In these cases, the introduction and conclusion are especially important.

You can use them to help the reader understand how you have broken down the major process into smaller processes, and how these processes work in combination with one another. If you are describing a process unfamiliar to your reader, you may find definitions, comparisons, and analogies helpful.

Process Description Combined with Other Strategies

As we have already seen in this chapter, process description is often used in combination with other rhetorical strategies. For instance, your process description could be one part of a persuasive or analytical essay, report, or letter. To analyze a public relations campaign, write a critical paper on a theory of psychological development, or recommend environmentally friendly changes for a production process, you might provide a brief description of the process before you go on to analyze it or argue for or against it.

DEFINITION: DRAWING ON OTHER PATTERNS TO EXPLAIN COMPLEX TERMS

In the opening of her essay "Global Warming and Population," student Brenda Platt asks two central questions: "Does population growth contribute to global warming? Should population control be a central strategy in stabilizing global environmental change?" Then she says, "In order to answer these questions it is necessary to introduce key concepts . . ."

Definition Used Widely in Introductions

Platt's opening represents a typical start to many academic papers dealing with complex issues: the need to establish the meaning of key terms. One of the terms she goes on to describe is global warming:

> Global warming is the increase in the mean average temperature of the earth's atmosphere. It occurs when the so-called greenhouse gases (carbon dioxide, methane, nitrous oxide, tropospheric ozone) absorb infrared radiation from the planet's surface that would otherwise escape into space. This absorbed radiation is converted to heat and the atmosphere becomes warmer. The predicted consequences include a decline in agricultural productivity, desertification, changes in forestation patterns, more and stronger storms, and flooding of low-lying coastal regions.

Drawing on Other Expository Patterns

Notice that Platt's explanation features descriptive-process writing serving the larger purpose of definition.

PRACTICE

1. Read Wayne C. Booth's essay "The Rhetorical Stance" (Reader, p. 488), an extended attempt to define the ideal position for a writer in any writing occasion. How many different patterns does Booth call on to serve his central purpose in that essay?

2. Go to the Text Enrichment Site, Chapter 11, "Sample Paragraphs of Definition and Commentary." Read the three sample paragraphs provided there. For each sample, determine what concept is being defined and what other patterns of organization are used in the definition. Then read our commentary on each of the three samples.

Sample Student Essay   Definition—Find the Controlling Idea and Organizational Patterns

Note that the writer has chosen to cite sources using MLA style. Marginal notations concerning documentation technique appear in green.

No title page. See p. 330.

In the Words of Stompin' Tom
Gustavo Miranda

1 When one does a quick search on the internet for the phrase "what does it mean to be Canadian" it is very telling that the list of webpage results includes that same question being asked on a multitude of pages by individuals of almost every nationality and cultural background imaginable.

Internet search shows public interest in topic. Caution: sources are not always authoritative.

2   On a variety of forums and websites, Canadians are asking themselves and others this very question. As we progress deeper into the 21st century it is becoming clearer that definitions of Canadian identity need to be reconsidered and reworked to better reflect the realities of the demographic and cultural reality of the country. For too many decades, Canadians have relied on 19th century definitions and institutions as foundations for the creation of a new identity. As communications and information technology expanded in the latter half of the 20th century, coupled with a dramatic increase in non-British immigration into the country, definitions of what it meant to be Canadian were eventually drawn from negative relationships. That is, Canadians defined themselves in terms of what they were not, rather than what they were. It was simple enough to define oneself as "not American" since, given the multicultural makeup of the post-Trudeau Canada, what a Canadian truly was differed greatly between individuals. In the last quarter of the 20th century, the Trudeau-era policy of multiculturalism took root, and the previous stereotypes of English or French Canadians no longer applied. As the 21st century dawned, multiculturalism and demographic diversity seemed to be the driving force behind the construction of a new Canadian identity.

Use title of organization or site if author unknown. Abbreviate if long.

3   The federal government's department of Citizenship and Immigration identifies five values which define a Canadian citizen: equality, respect, freedom, peace and law and order (CIC).

These five values are noble ideals which can easily be adopted as defining characteristics for any modern liberal democratic society. But do they really define what it means to be a Canadian?

4   On the eve of the 1995 sovereignty referendum in Quebec, following nearly two decades of constitutional debates, most Canadians throughout the country paid fairly close attention to this question. Not only did they ask themselves what was so repulsive about Canada that such a large number of its citizens would be willing to abandon it, but they also asked themselves what it meant, then, to be a Quebecker, and how was that different from being a Canadian. Did it truly mean something different than being a Canadian? And if so, what exactly did being a Canadian mean? In 1995, the great entertainer Stompin' Tom Connors offered his answer. After spending the bulk of his life travelling across the country and meeting Canadians of all types, he found that no matter who they were or where they were, they all shared a common set of what he termed "Canadianisms." In his comments, anthologized by Cynthia Good, Connors goes on to say, "Even if our language didn't give us away, our habits, our manner and our behaviour would. No matter how we try to be otherwise, we are Canadians first. And even though we don't recognize it ourselves, the world does" (45).

Citation includes page number "45" in parentheses, with period after.

5   For Stompin' Tom the answer to the question lies in the person's heart. We could create any number of definitions and criteria to suit our needs, but ultimately what makes us Canadian is intangible and indefinable, yet known to all. Stompin' Tom's perception might be the necessary solid foundation for the construction of our identity.

6   Canadian society in the 21st century is perceived as the fulfillment of the vision of a mosaic composed of equal cultural tiles freezing harmoniously together over long winter months. Much of this perception stems from Stompin' Tom's observation that while Canadians are unable to truly define themselves, those from other nations and societies can. And that definition is acceptable and desirable enough that every year more and more of those people choose to come to Canada and join our ranks. With each passing year, the builders of our national identity identify themselves less and less with the traditional symbols and institutions of our brief history. The British legacy which dominates our systems of politics, law, education, language and religion belongs to a shrinking majority who will soon be a minority within this land. For many, the 21st century offers an opportunity to erect a new house employing materials from a multitude of sources. As the First Nations writer and artist Tom Hill notes, "Is it possible that one day 'Canadians' will become Canadians, looking to the land that sustains their lives rather than to Europe for their cultural roots? Is it possible for this young country to look beyond 1867 and the Plains of Abraham to find its history?" (136).

Author (Hill) not in citation because in preceding text. Note question mark precedes parentheses.

7   Tom Hill is speaking in terms of the isolation and discrimination felt by First Nations peoples, but his comment is equally applicable to those of any ethnic or cultural origin beyond the traditional French and English solitudes. It is necessary for all of us to piece together a nation that accepts that our roots lie beyond a limited

colonial history. Our roots and our history lie in Aboriginal societies and in Asia and in Islam and in the Ukraine. In the 21st century Canada needs to recognize the broader history of the nation. A Canadian identity and culture must include a recognition not only of the French and British colonial past, but also of the contributions made by the First Nations as well as other immigrants who have shaped the land in the centuries prior to and since the colonial era. In her diary entries while in low-Earth orbit aboard the space shuttle *Discovery,* Canadian astronaut Roberta Bondar observed that Canada was bigger than its history. She perceived a nation which was united by a greater purpose. From space, the vast geographical distances of our country seem minuscule, and the cultural and political differences seem even smaller. As Bondar observed, "By working to combine all our strengths and vision, we can lift our own spirits to become a greater nation, one poised strategically to set examples to the rest of this small planet" (8).

> Author (Bondar) not included in citation. Here period *follows* parentheses.

8   Moving forward into the future involves acknowledging that demographics have changed. This Canada, the future Canada, is one that is much bigger than the one presented in text books. It reaches out to all corners of the world and draws from the collective global history. With this raw material it builds a home for us and others who likely share the five virtues outlined by the department of Citizenship and Immigration. With unparalleled wisdom, Stompin' Tom Connors provides what is per-haps the most useful definition for Canadians of all walks of life and of all origins for the 21st century: "You are it! And it is you!" (46).

> Author (Connors) not included in citation.

Works Cited

Bondar, Roberta. "Spacelog STS42—Discovery." *If You Love This Country: Fifteen Voices for a Unified Canada.* Ed. Cynthia Good. Toronto: Penguin, 1995. 8–11.

Citizenship and Immigration Canada. "A Look at Canada: What Does Citizenship Mean?" 1 April 2005. 29 March 2006 <http://www.cic.gc.ca/english/citizen/look/look-02e.html>.

> Abbreviated as "CIC," p. 167.

Connors, Tom. "The Liberation of Quebec." *If You Love This Country: Fifteen Voices for a Unified Canada.* Ed. Cynthia Good. Toronto: Penguin, 1995. 45–47.

Hill, Tom. "Kanata: Another Thousand Years." *If You Love This Country: Fifteen Voices for a Unified Canada*. Ed. Cynthia Good. Toronto: Penguin, 1995. 135–37.

Work Consulted

Ferguson, Will, and Ian Ferguson. *How to Be a Canadian (Even if You Already Are One)*. Vancouver, BC: Douglas & McIntyre, 2001.

> Work explored but not cited in essay.

Study Questions

For study questions prompting further insight into the ideas and methods of this essay, see the Text Enrichment Site for this chapter.

Sample Student Essay   Definition—Find the Controlling Idea and Organizational Patterns

Note that the writer has chosen to cite sources using APA style.

Canadian Equals Canada
Brad Henderson

1 What is a Canadian? We know that a Canadian is someone who resides in Canada, we know that Canadians are from diverse cultural backgrounds, each one feeling that they know what it means to them to be Canadian, that they are generally good, environmentally sensitive, peace-loving/promoting and friendly. However, what image do Canadians reflect to the rest of the world? Is it an accurate reflection of what Canadians feel they are as a people? What do Canada's neighbours, trading partners, fellow global citizens think of Canada? Canadians may be hasty in their assumptions about what it means to be a Canadian, and their assumptions that the good-natured ideas they have about themselves are accurately represented by Canada and Canadian companies working abroad. Is Canada as environmentally sensitive as its citizens believe? Is Canada as committed to helping the poorer countries of the world as its citizens would like? Are Canadians "better" than Americans when it comes to foreign policy and their treatment of international business partners? Does Canada represent to the rest of the world what Canadians feel they are inside?

2 Canadians want to save this country from depleting its resources and destroying the environment. A recent study of what Canadians think about sustainability indicates "8 out of 10 Canadians want tougher laws to protect the environment" (Searle, 2006, para. 3), so they must be environmentally sensitive.

3 Nevertheless, what images do other countries have of Canada? Is Canada an environmentally sensitive global citizen? Let's look at some of Canada's mining practices, considering that 60 percent of the mining and exploration companies in the world operate in Canada. How representative are these companies of Canadian ethics? Canada's mining practices are recently controversial, especially in Latin America where Canadian mining companies have outraged citizens and alerted environmentalists because of lax corporate social responsibility. Canada, the country that many Canadians believe is seen as environmentally sensitive and non-aggressive, has fought against citizens of Chile, Mexico, Peru, and Ecuador, to develop mining operations in occupied and environmentally sensitive areas. A research survey by Hassanein, Ludholm, Willis, and Young (2006) for the Canadian Centre for the Study

of Resource Conflict (CCSRC) also concludes that "adoption of voluntary CSR [Corporate Social Responsibility] policies by Canadian oil, gas, mining and exploration companies with international interests is remarkably low" (Executive Summary, para. 3). The authors state that only 5 percent of 202 extractive-sector companies reported subscribing to an "externally formulated and independently accountable set of standards" (p. 30). So persistent are Canada's representative mining companies that in the Huasco Valley in Chile, Toronto-based Barrick Gold plans to relocate three massive glaciers in order to access the gold underneath. The Chilean Environmental Authority and over 18,000 citizens have rejected this proposal because the glaciers are the region's only source of water. Is this representative of the self-image Canadians want to project to the rest of the world?

4   Canadians care about the poor; why else would they support a Live 8 concert in one of their country's fastest-growing cities? Are we an attractive global citizen though? Does Canada succeed in reflecting its citizens' self-image of being helpful or friendly to those countries beckoning for help? What have their inner concentrations done to create a better world or relationship outside of Canada? Lester B. Pearson, Canada's fourteenth prime minister, seems to have had an extremely influential self-image of what it meant to be a Canadian. However, Canada, the representative of its citizens, may be having a hard time echoing some of his strongest beliefs, thoughts and feelings. After Pearson retired from his position as PM of Canada, he headed a UN committee and prepared a report for the World Bank on relations with developing countries. The report established goals for developed countries in terms of a contribution for overseas development assistance (helping developing countries) which set the bar to 0.7% of national GDP by 2015 (Sachs, 2006, p. A23). Canada made the commitment, and today has not even come close to that goal. In fact, Canada is currently contributing around 0.3% of its national GDP, less than half of what it committed to in 1969 and less than it was contributing in 1988 (Sachs, 2006, p. A23).

5   Canadians are kind, aren't they? So is Canada generally nice to its global neighbours? In 2006, during the World Junior Hockey Championship in Vancouver, Canada, and perhaps the world, witnessed a broadcast of Canadian inner feelings. Canadians booed during the American anthem and cheered for the Russians while they played against the Americans. In doing so, Canadians believed they were courageously reminding Americans that their government's global behaviour is unacceptable, that their representatives are not welcome in Canada, and that the American unilateral attitude toward the rest of the world on the environment, trade, the military, wealth, and resources comes at a price. While Canadians may have been successful in reinforcing the Canadian self-image, that they are good, attractive, and improving, they didn't really do a great job of seeing themselves through the eyes of their global neighbours, and neglected to consider what the world might think of

Canada's global behaviour. Canadians should have considered that Canada, its government and therefore the Canadian representative, isn't perfect, and that Canada employs many of the same unilateral principles as America. Oxfam, for example, has recently accused Canada of taxing goods from poor countries at four times the rate of goods from rich countries (Oxfam, 2006, p. 1). As well, Canada's military contribution in Africa, where a presence is obviously needed if Canada expects to adhere to its aging promise of helping to put an end to world poverty, was, and still is, being described as disgraceful by such members of its own political community as Roméo Dallaire, Peter Stollery, and Stephen Lewis.

6   Currently, there seems to be a gap between what Canadians feel they are, and how they may be seen around the world. Canadians have allowed their reputation as a peaceful, helpful and fair country to fade away and are now living on past accomplishments in their current conception of themselves. Canadians should express themselves honestly and consider the world's view of them. It may be attractive for Canadians to believe they are something other than who they are, but it can make their inner goal of being genuinely appreciated difficult and prolonged. Being Canadian means taking on the responsibility to contribute inner thoughts, feelings, and beliefs toward the positive and honest goal of building a nation that supports its citizens literally and metaphorically. Being a Canadian means assuming that the image one has of oneself will be interpreted accurately around the globe, that the world will see Canadians for who they'd like to be. Being Canadian means believing in Canada's ability to present its citizens' self-image to the rest of the world. If Canadians are going to have a country represent their inner thoughts and feelings, they should expect their country to get it right. The feedback they receive internationally and within their own country should complement their struggle to be good, attractive human beings, capable of improving the Canadian ideal and the environment in which Canadians live. Although the image Canadians have of themselves may be inaccurate, it is positive. Perhaps it is enough to help Canadians' self-image improve the way Canada should be seen through the eyes of its neighbours.

References

Hassanein, A., Ludholm, G., Willis, G., & Young, C. (2006). *Corporate social responsibility and the Canadian international extractive sector: A survey*. Canadian Centre for the Study of Resource Conflict, in association with Royal Roads University, Victoria. Retrieved February 14, 2006, from http://www.resourceconflict.org

Lundholm, G. (2006). Corporate social responsibility & the Canadian international extractive sector. *Development in Practice, 23*, 78–81.

Oxfam (2006). Rich country self-interest threatens to stall world trade talks. *Advocacy for Social Justice, 19*, 104–106.

Sachs, J. (2006, April 22). Promises aren't enough. *Globe and Mail,* p. A23.

Searle, S. (2006). What do Canadians think of sustainability? Retrieved December 15, 2006, from http://www.ekostv.com/node/307

Study Questions

For study questions prompting further insight into the ideas and methods of this essay, see the Text Enrichment Site, Chapter 11.

Chapter 12
Comparison-Contrast

We have suggested that classification-division is the operating system beneath expository patterns, because it establishes items and catalogues of items organized in relation to each other. Comparison-contrast, in turn, is surely the tool we human beings use most commonly to make sense of the world around us, and specifically to make sense of those things that we recognize through division to be distinct from each other, yet through classification to share kinship in certain categories. Through comparison-contrast, one thing in a certain category is placed side by side with another in the same category. Suppose you wish to indicate how much your nephew has grown in the past year—you might say, "He comes up to my hip." Our equation of your nephew's new height to the level of your hip gives us a precise understanding. The extent to which we rely on comparison can be found at the heart of our language, specifically in our use of metaphor. Someone asks you how your hockey team did last night. You reply, "We were on fire." The degree of your performance has been compared to the intensity of a fire, even though the comparison was not directly stated by words such as "like" or "as." This natural way of thinking occurs frequently in our use of analogy. For example, tragedy might be likened to being caught on the highway in a passing lane when the line of cars behind you has filled in and suddenly an oncoming car appears. As in a tragic play or story, your choices (to speed up or slow down) appear limited to fatal ones. (You should remember though, as we said in Chapter 3, that any analogy will break down eventually!)

COMPARISON DEFINED

To **compare** means to place two things side by side in order to reach a better understanding of each, and usually, of some third thing. This could result in stressing similarity or difference, advantage or disadvantage. The two things being compared normally share some sort of generic category: two cars, two athletes, two friends, two cities, the country versus the city, etc. A dog is not generally compared to a computer, except for comic purposes. Some people feel that the phrase "compare with" signals the general act of comparing whereas the phrase "compare to" indicates that contrast will be emphasized. "His records are not so impressive compared to those of Crosby." Reference books do not agree on this fine point of distinction.

CONTRAST DEFINED

To **contrast** means to deal with the difference between two things being compared. The study of difference could lead to upholding one thing over the other, or it could simply point out distinctions between them.

Remember, if you are asked to compare two things, you are free to decide whether to stress similarity or difference. If you are asked to *contrast* two things, you must attend to differences.

WIDESPREAD USES OF COMPARE AND CONTRAST

As we said in our opening comments, comparison is the most common and fundamental form of human reasoning. Consider that the binary code (a basic division of two) underlies the complex functions of the computer. The comparative tool is used to serve *all* writing purposes—evocative, analytical, and argumentative as well as expository. (See Chapter 16, "Argumentation," on the crucial importance of comparison in fair and effective debate.) Comparison-contrast is used across all academic disciplines. Students in literature might compare two characters in a play, or compare two novels or two poems. Students in political science might compare two political parties or electoral systems. Students in mechanical engineering might contrast gasoline and electric car engines, concentrating on technical processes and specifications. Ecologists might compare these two while concentrating on environmental effects. Instructors consider comparison-contrast topics an excellent way to test your knowledge and thinking.

TWO MAIN PURPOSES

Dealing with comparison-contrast in an essay involves deft control of breadth and structure; it can sometimes make your head spin. To ward off this kind of vertigo, consider that fundamentally comparison-contrast writing has just two possible *purposes*:

1. To show that one thing is (on specified grounds) to be preferred over another, which guides our thinking of value
2. To demonstrate how both things, in some way, share an important common cause and/or effect or state of being, which points to an interesting broader implication

In a sense, of course, the second purpose is always present, if sometimes subordinated, since the two things must have some purposeful connection in order to stand side by side at all. The first purpose is a specific emphasis derived from the second generic purpose, but defining these two purposes as separate can help you to sharpen your intention and method for specific comparison-contrast assignments. It is possible, of course, to combine and integrate these two purposes. For beginning writers who are developing short essays, however, we believe it will be most helpful to you, for now, to choose one or the other of the two main purposes. Then drive it home.

Most comparison-contrast writing places an emphasis on one or the other of these two basic purposes.

TWO WAYS TO STRUCTURE COMPARISONS

Another helpful consideration, to ward off vertigo, is that in the most general sense, there are just two main *ways* to organize comparison-contrast:

- point by point, and
- subject by subject (sometimes called "block")

A **point** is an observation about an aspect of a subject, while the subject is—well, the subject. Consider two friends who may be very different in some respects, perhaps alike in others. Each friend is a subject: Subject A and Subject B. A "point" would be any broad or specific aspect of their being, for example, gender, age, culture, place of residence, way of life (worker, student, precise job, for instance), personality, values, and so forth. A five-paragraph comparison-contrast would likely mean narrowing the focus of the essay to no more than two or three matching points about Subject A and Subject B. By "matching," we mean within the same category of point—that is, gender and its interesting issues, or employment and its interesting issues, and so on. "Matching" does not mean finding similarity—you could assert a complete contrast on matching points. Also, you could assert similarity on all three points or difference on all three points. If your comparison was of two people rather than two friends (presumably there is something to like about a friend), you could end up deciding that one subject is thoroughly despicable while the other is thoroughly admirable. In that case, you would be demonstrating purpose one (p. 177). If ultimately your controlling idea concerned something in common between the two, then you would be applying purpose two (p.177). In sum, for any short comparison-contrast essay, you need to choose between just two *purposes* and just two *possible ways of organizing* your discussion.

POINT-BY-POINT ORGANIZATION

Let us look at how to organize a point-by-point comparison of two essays. Read Susan McClelland's's essay "The Lure of the Body Image" (p. 447) and Margaret Atwood's essay "Canadians: What Do They Want?" (p. 467). Briefly describe each essay under the following three points:

- tone
- method
- purpose

Here is how a five-paragraph essay comparing these two essays might be laid out according to the point-by-point method. "Points" are the three elements of prose (rhetorical features) you have already identified and described:

Basic pattern for point-by-point comparison

Tone, "Body Image"
Tone, "Canadians"
Method, "Body Image"
Method, "Canadians"
Purpose, "Body Image"
Purpose, "Canadians"

Sample outline for point-by-point comparison of "Body Image" and "Canadians"

Introductory paragraph

Present the topic (beefcake images in advertising) of "Body Image" followed by the topic of "Canadians" (Canadian-American relationships). Note that Susan McClelland, who is not well known, published her essay in *Maclean's*, for Canadians; Atwood, who is famous, published her article, on commission by *Mother Jones*, for Americans. State deductive direct-list thesis: a rhetorical study of tone, method, and purpose in the two essays suggests that different roads can lead to similar destinations.

First body paragraph

Topic sentence: Reading the two essays with attention to tone, one's immediate impression is of the contrast between them: detached, neutral, and reserved language on one hand; witty, ironic, and outspoken on the other. Provide and explain examples from "Body Image," then from "Canadians." Reinforce the contrast in tones with an appropriate concluding sentence.

Second body paragraph

Topic sentence: These notable contrasts, on further investigation, can be identified as outcomes of different rhetorical methods. Look at point of view (third person) in "Body Image"; illustrate and explain. Look at point of view (first person) in "Canadians"; illustrate and explain. Look at use of research in "Body Image." Look at use of analogy and personal reasoning techniques in "Canadians." In conclusion, reinforce that different tones emerge, but—signal shift to next paragraph—does this mean the authors' purposes are different?

Third body paragraph

Topic sentence: In fact, on closer study, the purposes of the two essays appear remarkably similar. "Body Image" looks at the effects of an empire (corporatism); "Canadians" looks at the effects of an empire (that of the United States). Provide and discuss examples from "Body Image"; provide and discuss examples from "Canadians." Note different shadings—the victimization is presented as more entire in "Body Image"; "Canadians" recognizes Canadian complicity in the unhealthy relationship, but ultimately places the problem on the United States as political entity.

Brief conclusion

Use suggestive conclusion. Just as the two essays aim to expose similar problems, both present similar recommendations. "Body Image" recommends critical thinking as a way to deflect pressure "to fall in love with a highly commercialized image." "Canadians" represents critical discernment of the difference between individuals and the collective political will of the nation, and recommends that the reader trust individuals to be innocent till proven guilty, but suspect the nation (on grounds of previous analysis) to be guilty till proven innocent.

See the text website, Chapter 12, for a full version of the essay outlined here.

Basic pattern for subject-by-subject comparison

An essay using the subject-by-subject method (understanding "subjects" to denote the two essays) could be organized from the above outline without significant altering of content, as follows:

> "Body Image"
> Tone
> Method
> Purpose
> "Canadians"
> Tone
> Method
> Purpose

To craft a five-paragraph essay using subject-by-subject structure, you should still use point-by-point for your introductory paragraph. This is because an introduction needs to provide an overview: you need to recognize both subjects equally at that stage. In effect, you would retain the opening paragraph from the above outline for point-by-point structure. Then you would cover two of your points on "Body Image" in one paragraph, and perhaps introduce the third. Since the third point is most important, you could devote a second body paragraph to expanding exclusively on it. You would then do the same concerning "Canadians": including a third body paragraph for points one and two and a fourth body paragraph to expand on the most important third point. That would result in five paragraphs. Would you begin a sixth paragraph for a short conclusion? You might, but you would probably not need to. In wrapping up discussion of the third point as it occurs in "Canadians," you could probably add a sentence or two tying your final thoughts back to include "Body Image." Thus you could deliver five paragraphs as outlined above for the point-by-point approach. Organizing this particular discussion almost entirely by subject-by-subject method may not be the ideal pattern for this essay, but for the purposes of demonstrating the subject-by-subject approach, here is the way your outline for this approach would look:

Sample outline for subject-by-subject comparison of "Body Image" and "Canadians"

Introductory paragraph

Present the topic of "Body Image" followed by the topic of "Canadians." Note that Susan McClelland, not well known, published her essay in *Maclean's*, for

Canadians; Atwood, famous, published her article, on commission by *Mother Jones*, for Americans. State deductive direct-list thesis: a rhetorical study of tone, method, and purpose in the two essays suggests that different roads can lead to similar destinations.

First body paragraph

Topic sentence: The reader's first impression of tone in "Body Image" is one of detachment, and further examination of methods explains how this effect occurs. Provide and discuss examples of tone. Explain that this effect stems from the methods of third person and use of research sources. As a link to the next crucial part of the discussion, note that through these detached methods the writer pursues her purpose. McClelland's purpose in this research-based analysis is to warn readers against the harmful effects of commercialized images dispensed by the advertising empire. Suggest how this is apparent. Link to the next paragraph—to appreciate how pervasive this purpose is, more close, detailed study is needed.

Second body paragraph

Throughout her article, McClelland stresses victimization in her concern to expose the harmful effects of ideas foisted onto people through a form of empire. First explain how she conveys a strong impression of victimization (i.e., she doesn't explicitly concede that those going to extremes might have free will to resist). Then review and reinforce her focus on harmful effects of what she perceives as a form of psychological imperialism. Paragraph finality: she implies this problem is pervasive; surely it is connected to other forces.

Third body paragraph

One might expect Atwood's purpose in "Canadians" to be different from McClelland's, because Atwood's tone and methods indeed present a contrast. Define Atwood's ironic, judgemental tone; provide examples and explain them. This tone results from first person and personal use of analogy and other reasoning techniques rather than formal research and other detached methods used by McClelland. Atwood seeks to advise Americans (and, in effect, Canadians) of the harmful effects Canadians experience as a result of American imperialism. Explain with brief citation of examples. Include the rhetorical question to enable transition—is this purpose significantly different from that of "Body Image"?

Fourth body paragraph ending with brief conclusion

While Atwood concedes a little more to complicity on the part of the "victim" than does McClelland, nevertheless, Atwood, too, drives home an impression of harmful effects of empire. First explain how she concedes that Canadians are somewhat complicit in their dysfunctional relationship with the United States. Then review and reinforce her focus on harmful effects of a situation forced onto Canadians through a form of empire. Resolve with brief conclusion: as different as these two essays may be in tone and method, both lead to similar conclusions. Reflect on these conclusions—do they seem valid? How are the two (corporate advertising on one hand, the United States as political empire on the other) connected? Offer a closing thought on where to go from here.

See the Text Enrichment Site, Chapter 12, for a full version of the essay outlined here.

Effects of These Two Main Methods of Organization

Both methods of comparison, point by point and subject by subject, have at least one main advantage in common: both patterns help the writer, and therefore the reader, to maintain an even-handed attention to both sides of the topic. This can be particularly helpful to ensure complete and fair consideration, for instance, in the case of two opposed critical theories, especially if you (the writer) have an immediate bias toward one side over the other. Concession-refutation pattern, described in Chapter 16, "Argumentation," represents a specific application of comparison-contrast, one that reminds you to give both sides of a debate a fair hearing.

In addition, each method of comparison, point by point and subject by subject, has at least one specific advantage and one specific disadvantage.

Advantage of Point by Point

This method keeps the comparison tight; you maintain awareness of both subjects and how each participates, through comparison, in deepening understanding.

Disadvantage of Point by Point

Because this method involves frequently referring back and forth to both subjects, writing and reading point-by-point essays can begin to feel like following a ping-pong match. The writer is called upon to sprinkle in frequent linking terms suitable for comparison—for example, "on the other hand," "but when we look at the other side," "in contrast to this impression," "in the same manner," and so on. This almost constant back-and-forth, while it keeps the discussion balanced and clear, usually needs some work to ensure smooth, natural flow.

Advantage of Subject by Subject (or Block)

This method allows the reader to process one side of the subject at a time, sometimes a good way to establish and hold interest. If you write a story that tends to jump around, moving to second and third characters before revealing much of the first, there is a risk that some readers will not have time to build up enough interest in the first subject to be curious about the second. The subject-by-subject method allows room and therefore time to develop the reader's interest in one half of the comparison before moving to the second. It also clearly foreshadows the scheme or pattern to be used for the ensuing "block" dealing with the second subject, the second half of the comparison. Subject by subject uses a more gradual and in some ways, for some readers, a more calmly methodical approach than does point by point.

Disadvantage of Subject by Subject (or Block)

By devoting more room and therefore more time to one side of the comparison, this approach risks forgetting the essential comparative purpose of the discussion. Most

Should You Use Disadvantages-Advantages or Similarities-Differences as Blocks?

Some writing instructors recommend using disadvantages-advantages or similarities-differences in block format as a way to organize a comparison. In other words, you might brainstorm on all the advantages of a certain topic and all the disadvantages. You might then select what you consider the three outstanding advantages and discuss them in the first half of your essay body followed by the three outstanding disadvantages in the second half. As an example, a student was asked on an essay exam to compare the advantages and disadvantages of TV and argue which category outweighed the other. The student decided that the disadvantages of TV outweigh the advantages. She therefore discussed disadvantages second, a good way to add emphasis to her position. Here is a brief outline of her essay, with advantages and disadvantages arranged in two blocks:

Title—The Good, the Bad, and the Unplugged

Thesis controlling idea: Although TV does present a number of advantages, after close consideration, the disadvantages outweigh the advantages.

Topic sentence of first body paragraph: TV offers a number of advantages: news and information, some quality programs, and jobs. Discuss each advantage. [This may run into two paragraphs]

Topic sentence of second body paragraph: These advantages rather pale, however, when weighed against the disadvantages: household disruption and alienation, addiction, and manipulation of children. [This may run into two paragraphs]

Short conclusion: Recommend that after sampling the good and anticipating the bad, one's best move is to unplug (which also eliminates a drain on energy).

This essay could be interesting and quite effective, but look closely at the subtopics in the first block and those in the second: they do not match. This may seem to some readers a little like a comparison of apples and oranges. Thinking of the first block as the land of advantages may encourage the writer not to consider anything negative about news or jobs in the TV industry. Similarly, thinking of the second block as the land of disadvantages might discourage the writer from conceding possible value surrounding certain of her points. In discussing TV's harmful effects on children, for instance, it would be best to concede that a number of stations provide good quality programming for children. The advantages-disadvantages approach used here as a structure rather than simply as a brainstorming test could result in the aforementioned oversights. Nevertheless, it is a pattern to consider for certain topics, as is the similarities-differences approach. An essay asking you to compare Vancouver and Seattle, or Calgary and Edmonton, or Ottawa and Quebec City might work well with one half of the body dealing with similarity and the second with difference (or vice versa, depending on your controlling idea and purpose).

PRACTICE

If you were to compare two cities with an intention of showing that the two are fundamentally more similar than different, would you place similarities first or second. Why? If you were to compare the same two cities with an intention of showing that fundamentally the two are more different than similar, would you place similarities first or second and why? To help you to think further about this question, here are some choices for comparison: Halifax and Ottawa, Ottawa and Quebec City, Toronto and New York, Montreal and Winnipeg, Regina and Edmonton, Edmonton and Calgary, Vancouver and Victoria, Victoria and Seattle. Clearly, there are different ways to explore topics, to use different tests of meaning, and to shape patterns of discussion that elaborate a controlling idea. The final determinant is *you* and your powers of analysis and persuasion.

Avoiding Problems in Comparison-Contrast

Comparison-contrast is one of the most challenging patterns to use effectively. In the preceding discussion, we referred to a number of potential problems. To help you ensure that none of these has slipped into your essay, the following checklist may be of use. Try to avoid these problems:

- failing to balance the discussion, so that one subject predominates
- creating a ping-pong effect by using too much point-by-point without due care
- dwelling on one subject for so long that the reader begins to forget the essay's underlying comparative purpose
- applying a structure that revisits rather than advances the main points of discussion
- forgetting that comparison-contrast is a tool for focusing on a controlling idea, not an end in itself

The final problem is especially common. You may be tempted to cover all parts of your plan, noting, for example, similarities and differences, but then fail to conclude your essay with any useful meaning or insight that flows from this comparison. Simply observing that subjects are equally weighted in their similarities and differences or advantages and disadvantages can lead to an essay that lacks any point or clear value. Your comparisons will have a stronger edge if your thesis sentences suggest strong subordination and emphasis, or assign specific value.

 For sample thesis statements that set up clearly purposeful comparisons, see the Text Enrichment Site, Chapter 12, "Sample Thesis Statements for Comparison."

PRACTICE

1. Read "I Am Half-Canadian" by Pamela Swanigan (Reader, p. 411). Which of the two main purposes of comparison-contrast does she appear to use? Explain. Does she appear to have used the differences-similarities test to prepare her controlling idea, or the disadvantages-advantages test, or both? Explain. What would you say is her controlling idea?

2. Read "The Rhetorical Stance" by Wayne C. Booth (Reader, p. 488). In that essay, along with other expository patterns, the author employs comparison-contrast. He uses this pattern to contrast corrupt writing stances to the ideal writer's stance. Which of the two main purposes of comparison-contrast does Booth appear to have in mind? How do you know?

3. Outline an essay of 1000 to 1500 words in which you compare two films that you have seen recently or recall well. Decide on which purpose to argue. Apply point-by-point, subject-by-subject, or a hybrid of the two. Then visit the Text Enrichment Site, Chapter 12, and read the essays by Joyce Miller ("Venus and the Devil") and Stephen Kuntz ("Possibilities of Redemption"). Answer the questions that follow each of those essays and discuss your findings with your classmates and instructor. Then revisit your own essay outline and consider if you would make any changes to it and why. If you decide to pursue this outline as a class assignment, try to watch the two films again in order to test your conclusions and to take down specific supporting details.

FINAL WORD

This is a highly detailed chapter with meticulous attention to "fine" points of purpose and organization. Concentration and sustained thinking are needed to craft a successful comparison essay. But the rewards exceed the investment. Skills honed through comparison writing will make all your other writing easier and more effective than it used to be. Choose comparison topics, when you can, as an ideal way to stretch your thinking and compositional abilities. If you follow the advice in this chapter, you should have the precise guidelines you need to succeed with each new effort.

Chapter 13
The Summary

The ability to write a summary confirms that you are a good reader. This ability is of considerable importance since reading skills contribute to writing skills in general. More specifically, you will often be called upon to apply the skills of summary in your academic and vocational writing.

SUMMARIZATION AND ACADEMIC WORK

In any academic field you will be required to perform research. You will be expected to report to your instructor and classmates on the contents of various books, articles, studies, and so on. Since the goal of research is not simply to repeat what has already been said but to add to that work, you will need to identify the main points of existing work as briefly as you can, leaving time and space for your own critical response to it.

A **summary** concisely re-states the central ideas of a reading, using different words to express the writer's meaning accurately and without judgement. Most summaries also mention the kinds of rhetorical methods used in the material being summarized.

WRITING THE SUMMARY

The summary calls on you to exercise *two* main skills:

1. *First, separate the thesis, related ideas, and general rhetorical methods of the material to be summarized from the supporting details.*

   You may adapt this guideline somewhat on different occasions. Some instructors may want you to include supporting details, depending on the nature of the assignment. Some may request more or less attention to the rhetorical mechanics of the writing. However, for the purposes of learning to separate ideas from details, it is a good practice for you to learn how to write summaries that omit any detail that is not crucial to expressing a central point.

   How long should a summary be? Again, you will want to satisfy different expectations for different assignments. Since good writing expresses one main idea per paragraph, follow the rule of thumb of trying to use no more than one sentence for each paragraph of the original. In most cases, your summary should be less than one-quarter the length of the original.

2. *The second main skill required for a summary is to express ideas in your own words without altering the original meaning.*

   Finding your own words to re-present the writer's ideas helps you to understand those ideas. It also develops your ability to avoid stating other people's words as your own, which is plagiarism.

   You may quote one or two key words or phrases to convey the essence of an idea, but use quotation sparingly. Summarizing is almost always combined with analysis, critical response, and other types of writing. Yet the summary in itself should not express any of your own personal responses to what you are summarizing. Whether you strongly approve or reject what a writer is saying, your summary should simply convey the writer's ideas accurately and impartially. Using the third-person voice for your summaries helps to keep you from stating your own response.

FINDING THE CONTROLLING IDEAS AND SUPPORTING REASONS (THE THESIS)

Bear in mind that almost all writing aims to persuade us of something. As rhetoricians like Stephen Toulmin remind us, most persuasions involve a central claim or assertion (controlling idea), grounds to support that idea (various reasons, proofs, evidence), and awareness of a general attitude toward the topic among the reading public (what Toulmin calls a **warrant**).

Three Tips for Finding the Thesis

Here are three tips to help you identify the controlling idea and supporting reasons in an essay:

1. Determine who the author is and where the reading was published, which may help you to imagine the intended audience. Knowing the background of the author and his or her intended audience may help you to infer what public attitude, attitudes, and assumptions preceded and perhaps precipitated the essay you are to summarize.

2. Scan and skim, concentrating on the title, the opening and closing paragraphs, and the topic and closing sentences of each paragraph. From these key locations, you should be able to infer the main topic (and probably much more). Turn the title[1] of the essay into a question, and read the text seeking an answer to that question: what is this and why is it important? Remember

---

[1] Use the title tip with caution when summarizing from a newspaper or magazine. Titles of media articles are usually decided upon by an editor (headline writer) working hastily and sometimes from the "Entertainer's Stance." (See "The Rhetorical Stance," Reader, p. 488.)

Toulmin's argument model of main assertion, grounds, and warrant as you seek answers.

3. Skim through paragraphs looking for rhetorical methods: stylistic features of point of view and language that contribute to a dominant tone, and patterns of organization—a purposeful structure that helps you understand the relationship between ideas and sections of the reading.

✦ PRACTICE

Read David Suzuki's essay "The Right Stuff" (Reader, p. 488) below. Use a combination of highlighting or underlining along with marginal notes to apply the above tips. With this preparation, write a short summary of no more than 10 sentences. Then look at the following pages of this chapter, which provide suggested highlights and marginal notes, a nine-sentence summary, and a commentary on how we applied the above reading tips to construct our summary.

Sample Essay Finding the Thesis and Central Ideas

What is meant by "The Right Stuff"?

The Right Stuff
David Suzuki

1 Years ago I read a marvellous book entitled *Is There Life After High School?* In spite of the title, it was a serious comparison of human relationships at different stages in life. The study revealed that <u>impressions formed in high school are more vivid</u> and indelible than those formed at any other time in life. The author described how people in their seventies and eighties who had difficulty remembering most of their associates in university and at work would instantly recall most of their classmates by name while leafing through their high school yearbooks. In the analysis of the author, high school society is divided into two broad categories, the innies and the outies. The innies were football and basketball players and cheerleaders who set the whole social climate of the school. The outies were all the rest, the majority of the student body, most of whom lusted to be innies. I sure hope it's different today because that description fits my recollection of high school and it was awful. <u>But I'm getting off the point</u>.

Are "innies" and "outies" really important?
Is high school a time of intense experience?

Cause-effect.

2 <u>Those high school memories are so intense because that is the time when puberty occurs.</u> The enormous <u>physiological changes</u> that take place in response to the surge of <u>new hormones</u> through the body completely <u>transform both anatomy and mind.</u> I always feel kids lose about half their intelligence for a few years in response to that blast of hormones. Relationships change radically. Suddenly parents change from protective, loving gods to dictatorial wardens incessantly imposing restrictions and criticizing everything. A pubescent teenager perceives adults and members of their own age group with totally new eyes. It's not surprising then that <u>attitudes</u> to school, courses, and studying also <u>change dramatically</u>.

A personal anecdote/example.

3 In the early 1970s, <u>I visited</u> a small northern town to judge a science fair. Back then, it was a tough town with a transient population of men working in the oil fields and a high proportion of Native people. The night I arrived, I dropped in to the bar of the motel and a man came over and said, "I hear you're going to talk to the students

at the high school tomorrow." When I affirmed it, he shocked me by adding, "They'll kill you. I'm the science teacher there and I can tell you that all they think about is sex, drugs, and cars. They'll tear you apart."

4   Well, he really scared me. I immediately formed images of a blackboard jungle, filled with switchblades and drug-crazed hoods. The next day when I walked into that auditorium, it was with great trepidation. There were 400 teenagers in the gym, about a third of them Indians. They looked pretty normal, but I had been warned and knew they were just biding their time before turning into raving animals.

5   So I began by saying, "I'm a geneticist. I know that you're basically walking gonads, so I'm going to talk about sex." That opener caught their attention. I started with the beginning of human life by describing eggs and sperm, talked about chromosomes and the X and Y basis for sex determination and went on from there. The kids were dead silent and attentive. I talked for about an hour and then opened it up for questions. I was astounded at the range of topics we covered. We discussed drugs and chromosomes, test-tube babies, amniocentesis, and cloning. The principal finally had to step in to dismiss the group an hour and a half later.

[margin notes: Is this the thesis (the Right Stuff)?]
[margin notes: End of anecdote. Know your audience. Controlling idea?]

6   <u>Science education in high school should be designed around sex and human biology</u>. It's a shock every time I hear that a school board has caved in to pressure and kept sex ed out of schools. I am sure <u>opponents of sex education have no intention of providing that information to their own children.</u> In a time of <u>easy access to the most explicit films, videos, magazines, and books,</u> who can believe it's better to keep youngsters ignorant by denying them some accurate facts? <u>They're going to get all kinds of anecdotal, apocryphal stuff about sex from their peer group, anyway.</u>

[margin notes: Major recommendation. Controlling idea?]
[margin notes: Reasons.]

7   <u>By starting</u> their instruction with human sexuality and reproduction, <u>teachers will be able to go on to practically every other subject in science.</u> It just takes a hard look from a different perspective. After all, we are not trying to train future scientists <u>(only a small percentage of high school graduates will go on in science),</u> yet all of them will be able to use information that science can provide for the rest of their lives. <u>And you can bet they will remember those lessons vividly in their life after high school.</u>

[margin notes: "By" signals cause-effect. First sentence of last paragraph often re-states main idea; concluding sentence links to opening paragraph.]

The above underlining and marginal notes reflect an effort to apply the three tips for finding the thesis. Here is how you might think further about this and other information that you have gathered.

1.   ***Determine who the author is and where the reading was published.***

You'll find this information in the Reader on page 464, as an introduction to the article. This essay, from a collection entitled *Inventing the Future,* first appeared as a newspaper column. David Suzuki, former host of the CBC radio program *Quirks & Quarks* and current host of the CBC television program *The Nature of Things*, trained as a geneticist and has taught zoology at the University of British Columbia. His David Suzuki Foundation enlists volunteer support for environmental causes. From this information, one can anticipate that Suzuki will be a supporter of change and what might be regarded as "liberal" reform. As a humanistic scientist, he will be concerned about "that nature of things" in the sense of the welfare of things—but he will also be a promoter of scientific understanding and probably uncomfortable with religious resistance to knowledge. His intended audience appears to be business people, middle-class parents, and readers of the *Globe and Mail.* They likely share parental hopes and fears concerning their adolescent children whose coming of age could be fraught with "problems." They may well share a common belief, mentioned in the essay: the idea that adolescent years are specially charged, a storm that may bring great joy afterwards but also potential misfortune.

2. *Scan and skim, concentrating on the title, the opening and closing paragraphs, and the topic and closing sentences of each paragraph.*

The title suggests that the essay will recommend a way to do something, but the reader must read on to find out what it is and why it is important. Some essay titles tell you much about the topic and controlling idea. This one provides only a hint, for reasons that may become clear as you continue to search for the main purpose. In this case, however, readers familiar with Tom Wolfe's book and film *The Right Stuff,* about astronauts overcoming adversity, will recognize that Suzuki is reflecting on the viewpoint of that story. Is he endorsing it or asking us to redefine it?

Suzuki's first paragraph still remains guarded. He talks about high school as a time of intense experience and learning, a time that is often remembered long after later experiences are forgotten. The reader isn't sure from this what the essay will deal with specifically, but clearly it will have something to do with high school. His final paragraph, however, begins as follows: "By starting their instruction with human sexuality and reproduction, teachers will be able to go on to practically every other subject in science." This throws considerable light on the somewhat vague beginning. If the reader considers attitudes surrounding the topic of sex education in the schools, the indirect opening becomes more understandable: Suzuki wants to establish common ground and good will before developing more explicit reasons to support the controversial topic of sex education.

We next look at topic and closing sentences of body paragraphs. Suzuki's second paragraph begins by asserting that high school memories are intense because of puberty, an idea reinforced by the closing sentence of the paragraph. His third paragraph topic sentence introduces a personal story about visiting a school. The fourth topic sentence asserts that a school teacher had scared Suzuki with an idea that the pupils were wild and violent. The fifth topic sentence reveals that he began his presentation to the students by saying, "I'm going to talk about sex." The fifth paragraph completion sentence reveals that the students were so interested that it was hard to dismiss them. A skim of the fifth paragraph reveals that Suzuki covered scientific topics. His sixth topic sentence states, "Science education in high schools should be designed around sex and human biology." His sixth paragraph concluding sentence asserts that today's high school students are going to find out about sex, regardless. Skimming the short paragraph reveals a doubt that opponents of sex education will offer their children the necessary instruction; Suzuki also points out that easy access to explicit material is not a healthy substitute for "accurate facts."

3. ***Look for rhetorical methods, a purposeful structure that helps you understand the relationship between ideas and sections of the reading.***

The opening cites a book and elaborates on its point that the teenage years are intense and involve extreme (sometimes cruel) social awareness.

Paragraph 2 goes into cause-effect relationships: hormones cause this intensity and result in a personal revolution of outlook.

Paragraphs 3, 4, and 5 use narration to recount an anecdote offering the moral that you should know your audience in order to capture and hold their attention.

Paragraph 6 states personal opinion and response ("It's a shock every time . . . "). Further opinion and some examples are offered to back up the opinion that high schools should teach sex education.

Paragraph 7 returns to cause-effect relationship, emphasizing the main educational benefit the author foresees for his recommendation.

It appears that Suzuki's structure has been to work indirectly and gradually toward his real topic and recommendation, suggesting that he is aware that some readers might be strongly or at least initially resistant.

Reviewing What You Have Found

Now it is time to go back over what you have found through your marginal notes and preliminary gathering of clues and information according to the three tips. At this stage, read over all your notes and try to pick out just those parts of the essay that seem to be making an assertion. We can find a number in "The Right Stuff":

- Impressions formed in high school are uniquely intense, vivid, and long-lasting.
- High school appears to be a time of dramatic division ("innies" and "outies"); things might go strongly one way or strongly another.
- High school memories are strong because of hormonal changes, which result in new attitudes to everything (presumably including sex).
- Students respond to what interests them, and sex interests them.
- Science education in high school should be designed around sex and human biology.

- Teenagers get sex information in corrupted, undesirable forms.
- Most parents who oppose sex education in schools would not teach it to their children themselves.
- High school science should be geared to generalist, humanistic learning rather than aspire to advanced specialization: it's more important to educate people than to create future scientific world-beaters (for example, heroic astronauts).

Choosing the Controlling Idea

All of the above assertions could be safely considered an opinion, a possible controlling idea of a paragraph or essay—ideas in need of explanation and support. Which, then, represents the core of Suzuki's essay?

The rhetorical structure provides an important clue, even if the summary itself will say little in detail about rhetorical methods. As noted, almost half of the essay presents an extended example, an anecdote with a clear "moral," like that of a parable. Suzuki's approach is contrasted to that of the disaffected teacher, and clearly Suzuki's approach works. Which of the above statements emerges as the moral or lesson of the story? It is the statement that introduces paragraph 6, immediately after the story has concluded: "Science education in high school should be designed around sex and human biology."

We can now return to the title and ask, what *is* this?—that is, what is "The Right Stuff"? The answer seems to be that the right stuff is sex education in the high schools. Knowing that this was also the title of a film about intrepid explorers in space reinforces that Suzuki wishes to suggest an action that will take courage and resolve. The other question we want to ask of the title is *why is this important?* Answering that question will provide the reasons in support of the main assertion.

Looking over the above list of assertions taken from different places in the essay, it seems that all of those that are not the controlling idea itself could be used to support that idea. Going back to Toulmin's idea that arguments depend on a "warrant"—a common value in society to which the writer appeals—could it be that Suzuki spends so much time talking about the adolescent state of being to reinforce a general view of this time as one of critical cause-effect relationships, of volatile possibilities, and things with the potential to fly off one way or another. He suggests that impressions made at this time are critical, and better be the right ones. This appeals to the general sense parents have of a need to take special care with adolescents, the sense of anxiety concerning "those" difficult years, and it also appeals to a suppressed sense of helplessness, an idea that it is increasingly hard to communicate with teenage children.

Using this general attitude to adolescence—this warrant—as a base, Suzuki can suggest that wrong forms of information at this time are especially wrong, that right ones are especially right. It's not a time for procrastination if one wants to make the right impression. Those parents afraid that mentioning sex might be wrong because it will let a monster out of a box may be reassured by Suzuki's parable, which seems to teach that if a scientifically knowledgeable person confronts the monster straight on and uses it, suddenly the energy will be purposefully redirected to personal and mental growth. All of the other assertions identified above lend support to this idea and to a related general assumption of secondary education existing to encourage broad human values and understanding. If adolescence is a time when one's children will inevitably discover all sorts of things about sex, why allow that learning to be detached from a broader sense of caring relationships? The various appeals trigger parental fears attached to a warrant, but then provide reassurances.

From this it seems that the main assertion is the need to place sex education in the high schools; the reasons are that puberty demands the topic be addressed, that proper sex education will lead to other learning and counteract manipulative "explicit" media, and (appealing to the parents' belief in potential teenage "problems") that proper sex education will ensure well-being during the most volatile time of one's life

Following is a summary constructed from the above reading analysis:

Summary of "The Right Stuff"

In his essay "The Right Stuff," David Suzuki argues that high school science courses should begin with sex education. He believes that human sexuality is unavoidable in today's society, yet poorly explained by parents, media, and peers. Most of all, Suzuki believes high school students will find human sexuality a relevant point of departure to other topics.

Suzuki introduces his discussion by emphasizing the intensity of the teenage years, an intensity caused by hormonal change. Using a personal anecdote, he demonstrates how teenage outlook can seem threatening to teachers faced by seemingly uninterested, even hostile students. The anecdote concludes by showing, however, that high school students *will* gain interest if the teacher begins with human sexuality.

Suzuki concludes his essay by briefly defending his proposal. He states that parents opposed to sex education in high school do not offer the necessary education at home. Students are then left to learn from sexually explicit media treatments and the distorted stories of classmates—both poor sources, especially, he implies, at a time of life when a caring introduction to sexuality is so important. Not many students, he points out, go on to careers in science, so high school science need not be in-depth. It is more important that high school science be relevant, interesting, and thus truly educational.

Note what has been omitted:

- any reference to the book *Is There Life After High School?*
- Suzuki's personal memories of high school and the "innies" and "outies"
- the various examples of different changes of attitude toward relationships, parents, and adults in general
- most of the narrative descriptive details concerning the trip to the northern high school (an extended example), such as how many students there

were, what segments of society they represented, what topics they asked questions about

- the different forms of sexually explicit material (videos, films, magazines)

It is often difficult to understand the distinction between a point (an idea, an opinion, or a claim) and a supporting detail. The above summary of "The Right Stuff" should help illustrate the difference. Supporting details can include any of the following:

- authorities cited or quoted
- research findings, data
- examples, whether brief or extended (including anecdotes)
- logical illustrations such as analogies (see Chapter 3, "More About Logic")
- literary devices such as metaphors, imagery, etc.

Three paragraphs of "The Right Stuff" constitute one extended example, so almost all of this was omitted. We chose to include the bare bones of this example because Suzuki pins so much of his argument on it. Notice that we have not offered judgements of the author's ideas or methods. We have tried to be objective and impartial, and the wording is, as much as possible, our own. We began our summary by identifying the title and the author and giving the controlling idea (sex education in high school is

Ten Steps to a Successful Summary

1. Begin by smoothly identifying the author and title of the reading.
2. In your first sentence or short paragraph, re-state the complete thesis (controlling idea and supporting reasons).
3. Include all significant points (ideas) and only inseparable details (for example, Suzuki's "parable").
4. Re-present content in the same order that the author does (but place the thesis at the start, no matter where it occurs).
5. Make each part of your summary directly proportional to the part it summarizes (e.g., three sentences to compress three paragraphs).
6. Use a neutral (impartial/objective) tone—third-person point of view. Avoid using your own metaphors or other literary figures of speech, which convey personal voice and a possible tone of critical evaluation.
7. Exclude any of your own critical response.
8. Be brief—try to summarize each paragraph in no more than a sentence.
9. Use almost entirely your own language—select only key words for quotation.
10. Enclose any of the author's words in quotation marks.

important) and the basic reasons (because high school students need correct, relevant information about human sexuality, and because the subject can be used as a springboard for other science education). Our opening sentence uses the verb "argues" to convey the purpose of the essay (argumentation). After that, we summarized the central points in the same order they occur in the essay. To help you remember and apply this advice, we have consolidated it into 10 steps.

Summary writing is not an absolute science; no two summaries will be exactly alike. As we have noted, different writing requirements affect the final form of any summary. Nevertheless, you and your instructor can review your summaries according to the recommended 10 steps.

✎ PRACTICE

Write as many summaries as you can until you have internalized these skills. Discuss with others your sense of controlling idea and reasons in the essays you examine.

PREPARING TO SUMMARIZE ESSAYS WITH IMPLICIT THESES

There are times when rhetorical analysis additional to the 10 steps in this chapter is necessary to identify an essay's thesis. You may have already read student Tamara Pelletier's essay "Suspended in Time," on the Text Enrichment Site, Chapter 6, and looked for its implicit thesis. We provide commentary at that website on how readers might draw inferences from rhetorical clues to find a thesis in essays that are, for various reasons, more indirect than others. For further help with summarization, it is a good idea to read Chapter 15 of this text. But the most important thing you can do is to practise. Write brief summaries of all the essays and book chapters you read, and compare your findings with those of others.

Warming Up for Summarization

We suggest that you warm up your summarizing skills by reading the following items: "Anorexic's Recovery" (p. 120), "The Rhetorical Stance" (Reader, p. 488), and "Politics and the English Language" (Reader, p. 471). Take them one at a time, allowing yourself sufficient opportunity to apply the three tips (described earlier in this chapter) and the 10 steps as you draft up a preliminary summary for each. Then look at our suggested summaries for these readings at the Text Enrichment Site for this chapter, "Sample Summaries and Commentaries," and our commentary there on decisions that went into the summaries. All three of these suggested readings will present challenges. We hope that warming up on "tougher" essays will help you to summarize the "easier" ones, just as throwing an extra-weight ball in practice helps the football quarterback to achieve greater confidence and control when using the regulation ball during a game.

FINAL WORD

Research papers depend on your ability to summarize and paraphrase (to convert other ideas into your own words without shortening what the original author said). The skill of summarizing essays, books, and public, professional, or scholarly issues is no less critical to the success of a student than is skating to the success of a hockey player. Work on this skill as seriously as players with big league aspirations work on their skating.

Works Consulted

Toulmin's Analysis. 20 Aug. 2006 <http://owlet.letu/contenthtml/research/toulmin.html>.

Toulmin's Argument Model. 20 Aug. 2006 <http://changingminds.org/disciplines/argument/making_argument/toul>.

Chapter 14
Critical Analysis and Evaluation

Figure 14.1

As we suggested in our preface, university success depends upon capability in three related core areas: analysis, evaluation (assessment), and persuasion. At pre-university levels, students are expected primarily to demonstrate knowledge of foundational material in standard fields of learning. This necessitates an emphasis on the skills of exposition (show-and-tell): pre-university students need to demonstrate that they know the main facts and theories associated with the various fields on the curriculum. At university, however, the primary demand is for independent thinking, demonstrated by effective analysis, evaluation, and persuasion. Inquiry becomes probing at college or university, as one not only researches to find what is said, but breaks that information down into

201

parts and appraises the nature of those parts and their relationships. The persuasive element occurs as one describes and supports one's thinking on a specific topic.

CRITICAL ANALYSIS DEFINED

Critical analysis may refer both to the process of analyzing and evaluating and to the subsequent written report, essay, or oral presentation that argues a point of view based upon the results of that process. The word "critical" in university usage does not have the commonly assumed meaning of belabouring faults. As Richard Paul and Linda Elder point out in their booklet *Critical and Creative Thinking* (3), the common representation of a critical person "as skeptical, negative, captious, severe, and hypercritical" is an unfortunate cultural stereotype (see the section on stereotyping as a form of overgeneralization, in Chapter 3). Paul and Elder make the further important point that critical thinking (which assesses) and creative thinking (which originates) are interwoven: neither can be truly separated from the other (3). "Critical" thinking refers to seeking and expressing a deeply informed understanding of a subject. You must employ appropriate logical thinking, research methods, and due impartiality in this pursuit. You should remember, as well, to account for the appeals of pathos and ethos, remembering to distinguish ethics (consideration for others) from other prescribed systems (e.g., theology, social conventions, or law). When you present the results of your evaluation, you should apply the usual attributes of essay writing with an emphasis on clarifying the analytical process you followed and on giving your interpretation a vigorous emphasis (for more on persuasion, see Chapter 16). Your interpretation will contain a strong measure of creative thinking as well; that is, your own original ideas will come into play as you synthesize from the analysis you have performed.

Instructors commonly refer to critical analytical writing as either "analysis" or "argumentation," since this wide-ranging form really combines analysis, evaluation, and the persuasive component of arguing an interpretation. Regardless of what term is used, instructors are looking to see that you are progressing from "subjective" responses in your thinking to so-called more "objective" ones.

Prevalence and Importance of Critical ("Objective") Thinking

One of the central goals of university education is to develop a manner of objective thinking. In contrast to subjective thinking (personal response), objective thinking entails a thorough survey of the "object" of study, using various systems and methods that allow one to diminish personal bias, increase perspectives, test data, and thereby reach toward new and potentially beneficial understanding. On the problem of knowing, you probably recall the old example of the blind men and the elephant. Several blind men fixed at different points of the elephant will imagine themselves touching extremely different objects. A trunk will suggest a much different reality from a tail, a tusk, or a leg. Circling the animal to form an inventory of its different parts and its dimensions, on the other hand, will help the blind men increase their knowledge of the whole. Critical thinking employs various tools to help us circle and thus better know the elephant.

Examples of critical thinking may include scientific methods of experimentation and statistical assessment, film and book reviews (those that stress evaluation over simple description), business case reports, testing of mathematical formulae, delving for causes of an historical event, anticipating possible effects of a new economic policy, comparing the implications of two different models of family organization, examining a theory of criminal behaviour, searching for safeguards against a particular illness, and designing a cost-effective, energy-efficient home. All of these processes—and thousands more that typify university work—demand two main stages of critical thinking—*analysis* and *evaluation.*

TWO MAIN STAGES OF CRITICAL THINKING

For purposes of helping you to write effective essays in response to a critical topic question, we recommend you work through two basic stages of preliminary critical thinking:

- analysis
- evaluation (assessment)

Each of these is broken down and illustrated further for you below.

Analysis

As with most steps related to writing, the two critical thinking stages of analysis and evaluation (assessment) are not mutually exclusive. Nevertheless, to sharpen your own critical thinking, it should prove helpful to concentrate on these two stages one at a time, beginning with **analysis.**

Clarify, Explore, and Focus the Question

The first step in analyzing your subject is to question and refine your assignment. As with any writing assignment, if the initial question seems too vague, your thinking will lack clarity and distinctness. Determine if the topic question is clear and what other important questions may be embedded in it. Decide what type(s) of considerations the question may be addressing, for example, political, legal, social, historical, ethical, aesthetic, and practical. The question "What Do You Think of the Kyoto Accord—Explain in 2000 Words" could be much too broad and vague. Narrowing that general topic to something more specific—for instance, "Has Canada made the right choice in supporting the Kyoto Accord?"—could help you to proceed more purposefully. You would likely consider the arguments for and against environmental effects (containing both practical and ethical issues), economic effects, and political effects. Chapter 12, "Comparison-Contrast," offers two "tests," the disadvantages-advantages test and the differences-similarities test. Those often play a part in your handling of analysis. After amassing a number of considerations in the Kyoto Accord example presented here, you would narrow things down to focus on just one or two.

Examine the Subject in Its Context, Parts, Stages, and Processes

Regardless of your field of study, when you are tasked with forming a critical response, you must first use analysis. This means examining a subject in its context, parts, stages, and processes. Cause-effect relationships are especially important to consider. Your analysis really begins when you examine the initial topic question (discussed above) and consider ways to narrow, focus, and explore it.

You distinguish the key relationships between your subject and its surroundings; you identify your subject's main parts, stages, processes, causes and effects. You should also consider your own point of view. What biases do you bring to the study? Are there ways in which you could broaden your perspective, explore alternative viewpoints? If you were responding to the Kyoto Accord question, you would research the history that resulted in the accord; its stated principles, specifications, and procedures; purported impact on environment, economy, and political affairs; and various theories and arguments surrounding its alleged benefits and deficiencies. You would also consider and assess your own thinking about environment, the influences that caused that thinking, and the possibilities for stretching or reconfiguring your understanding.

 PRACTICE

Without looking at the brainstorming notes in Figure 14.2 (Jenna Benko's analysis of the Irish pub photo), look back at the photograph (Figure 14.1, p. 201) and answer the following question: what elements and relationships do you find in this photograph? Be as detailed as you can in your recording and organizing of the various elements and relationships. Include attention to elements that you believe are implicitly part of the picture, though not shown, and relationships the photograph may have to outside parties and realities.

Once you have recorded the elements and relationships that you see in this picture, review Jenna

Benko's analysis of the Irish pub photograph. By "analysis," in this case, we simply mean her identification of the discrete items and relations that she sees in the photo. You will explore what these items and relations *mean* by using the steps that follow as part of the stage of evaluation or assessment. This next stage involves answering a second question: what are the *effects* of these elements and relationships? You may wish to review causes and effects (see Chapter 10, p. 150). How do the elements and relationships you have identified and that Jenna Benko has identified function to create meaning?

Figure 14.2 reflects the thinking and exploring Jenna Benko did as she identified (analyzed) the elements and relationships in the photograph.

Evaluation (Assessment)

As pointed out by the authors of *Essay Writing for Canadian Students* (113–21), **evaluation** means considering standards by which subjects are judged to have

Figure 14.2
Jenna Benko's
Evaluation of the
Irish Pub Photo
(Figure 14.1):
Analysis

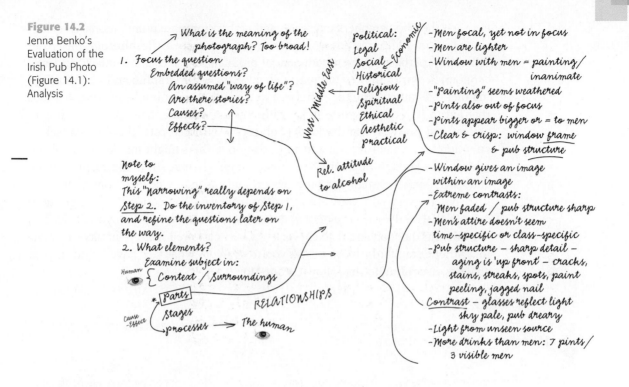

merit, value, efficacy, meaning, and the like. Common standards, as described in the above source, help us measure the degree to which a subject is, for example,

- logical
- practical
- ethical
- aesthetic (pertaining to beauty, art)

In exploring opinions surrounding your topic, you may find certain people upholding a position according to one standard while others denounce the same position according to another standard. Some might reject the Kyoto Accord on practical grounds of economic disruption to certain constituencies while others might defend the accord on ethical grounds of respecting the environment as a living being. On the Kyoto Accord question, you would likely consider logical, practical, and ethical standards related to assessing political, social, economic, and environmental relationships. Your task might then involve determining which set of standards deserves precedence and why, or reconciling seemingly opposed views and standards in some creative way.

In the case of the Irish pub photograph that you have already analyzed for its elements and their relationships, most likely you responded to the picture according to established *aesthetic* standards, those commonly taught and used in the study of art. Your evaluation would then take those identified aesthetic elements and relationships and pursue them for their effects—you would seek to interpret the photographer's intentions and perhaps propose unintentional meanings as well. Some of our readers, however, may have seen the photograph rather differently, perhaps as an embodiment of products, chemicals, manufacturing, and economics. For example, you may recognize the photographic and film developing methods underlying the picture as well as the current book-printing methods that led to its present state. Those with environmental concerns, responding to ethical and practical standards, may object to reliance on textbooks as a lack of attention to the environment and conservation. Others might invoke practical and ethical standards in objecting to our economy's reliance on constant production and consumption, resulting in pressures on students to buy new editions of the same text. But to steer you away from that last awkward reflection, we are going to assume that in the early stage of your analysis, as recommended, you decided to narrow your question and that, conveniently, you narrowed it to an inquiry according to aesthetic standards. Now we ask you to evaluate what you have found in your analysis, according to the following question.

PRACTICE

What might the photographer of the Irish pub photo be attempting to say or suggest through the elements of the photo and their relationships? To answer this question, consider the effect created by these elements and relationships.

To assist your thinking in response to this question, you might find it helpful to review our discussion of "dominant impression" in Chapter 8, "The Personal Essay" (look under "Description"). Reference to narration in the same chapter may suggest further ideas: do the static elements of the picture and their relationships in any way suggest stories and themes of stories? "Literary and Film Analysis," on the Text Enrichment Site, Chapter 15, contains further points that might contribute to this exercise in aesthetic interpretation.

In searching to answer the above questions, you may wish to explore some of the intuitive techniques described in Chapter 5, "Ways of Starting." Once you have done that, turn the page and you will see an example of how Jenna Benko brainstormed on this question. When you have considered her outlined evaluations and completed your own thinking in response to the above question, imagine how you might outline an essay of five or six paragraphs to present the meanings (central and related) that you have found through your evaluation of the parts of the photograph. Then read Benko's essay, which follows. Has she covered some of the same points that you have? Has she overlooked any issues in the usual canon of aesthetic principles and effects?

The Local Pub
Jenna Benko

1   In consuming art, the human eye instinctively draws toward people in a photograph. In the photo of the three Irish men enjoying their beer, the focal point initially seems to be the beer drinkers, yet the men are not in focus and are much lighter than the composition of the photograph. The window and the men look like a weathered painting hanging on the wall: not live images captured on film. The foreground pints of porter on the table appear as out of focus as the men. The beer's placement creates the illusion that the pints are equal in size or larger than the men. The only clear and crisp aspect of the photo is the window frame: the structural element of the pub. The photo is composed in a manner that develops the pub's permanent and timeless nature and is contrasted by the underlying sense that the viewer is not a part of this world.

2   The window presents an image within an image. The light and faded portrayal of the drinkers is in extreme contrast to the shadowy pub. The weathered and cracked window is superimposed on the men, creating an ancient, established feeling. The drinkers appear as archetypal pub frequenting figures. The men are timeless; their attire could be worn by any man, of any class, at any time.

3   The pub's structure, the clear and focused aspect of this photograph, is the scene's foundation; the meditated portrayal of every scratch, stain, and piece of decay demonstrates the cherished, not neglected aspects of the pub. No pretentious attempts seek to hide or cover up the decay: the table's cracks and stains, the window's streaks and spots, the frame's peelings, and the wall's jagged nail. The pub's disrepair and the revelation of this state supply evidence of the life of every man who ever enjoyed a pint of beer in its arms.

4   The illumination and sheer quantity of pint glasses are evidence of the importance of the drink. The glass of the pints reflects light from an unknown source; the sky is pale and the pub is dreary, yet the glasses, and the beer, glow. The importance of the drink permeates the inner and outer world of the pub as men bring their drinks into the yard while, inside, half finished pints await patrons. The drink is always in a position of importance, whether cradled in a drinker's hand or placed on a table with a view of the outside world. Drinks outnumber men. Beer is the cohesive element; there are at least two beers per person and a playful element suggests the seventh pint may belong to the photographer or the audience. However, the action of the photo is disconnected from the audience and the photographer. The patrons are outside—the photographer and audience are inside. The audience is welcome to consume a pint at this sacred place, but this does not inherently make them a part of the pub. The three men in the yard are the symbolic in-crowd.

5   The photograph expresses more than just the essence of a pub and its social climate. One's narrative imagination can form a story of the photographer, a newcomer, amongst pub-men on hallowed drinking ground. Perhaps the drinkers allow the photographer to sit at their table, to enjoy a beer and a laugh, but, eventually, the men take their pint glasses and resume a more personal conversation in the yard. The photographer is left, alone, in the dank pub with a table of half drunk pints and his camera.

6   The image's focus on the structural elements of the pub ensures the pub is a permanent place; the drinkers and their beer may fade away, but the pub will exist, will have patrons: will have beer. There is something comforting in knowing that the pub remains in some context; drinkers and drink change, but social elements prevail. Yet, the permanence compounded with the established sense of otherness also supplies an eerie aura of continued disjunction between photographer and photograph, audience and photograph, and photographer and audience. Photographs allow one to view anything but not necessarily to be a part of it.

Focus Questions

1. Has the writer focused the reader on one clear set of evaluative standards, and, if so, which of the four previously listed main categories of standards is represented?
2. Has she given sufficient attention to the elements and relationships suggested by the composition to support her conclusions? In other words, has she provided adequate supporting detail and explanation? If not, what else might be included?
3. Does her interpretation match yours? What are significant points of agreement and possible disagreement with your evaluation? Explain.
4. Look up the definitions of the terms "synecdoche" and "metaphor." Are there possible examples in the picture? Explain.
5. The writer refers to foreground, middle ground, and background—to different levels of perspective. Are there other levels of planes that could be examined?
6. Are there rhythms created by certain enticements of our eye? What might these be and what meanings might arise as a result?
7. Do you agree that the men's attire is timeless and placeless?

Figure 14.3 reflects the thinking and exploring Jenna Benko did as she evaluated the elements and relationships she had previously analyzed.

RESEARCH

The above exercise involved analysis and evaluation according to your own knowledge, insight, and imagination. Often, however, the process of analytical inquiry draws from effective research. Consult Chapters 18 and 19 on methods of inquiry and

Figure 14.3:
Jenna Benko's
Evaluation of the
Irish Pub Photo:
Effects

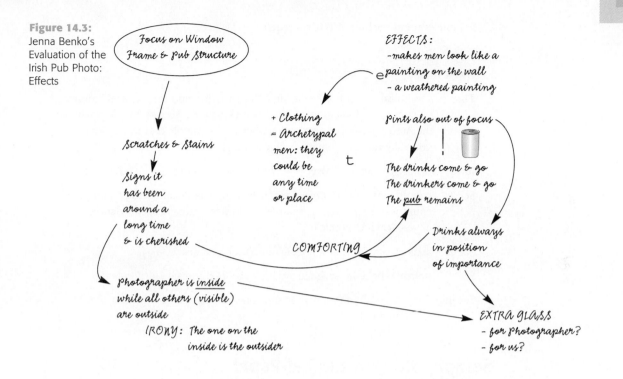

documentation. (Also see "Interviews" at the Text Enrichment Site, Chapter 18.) The following sample essay demonstrates student Gwen Kelley's analysis and evaluation of whether Canada should support the Kyoto Accord. This is the sort of complex topic that necessitates research.

From Preliminary Analysis and Evaluation Toward a Critical Paper

Once your evaluation begins to crystallize, you are ready to outline your paper.

Discover Your Thesis and Organize Your Support

As discussed in Chapter 5, you will emerge from your pre-writing (in this case, analysis and evaluation along with other techniques that help you to find your essay) with a thesis and outline of supporting points. In October 2002, at a time when then–prime minister Jean Chrétien was nearing a decision on whether to ratify the Kyoto Accord, Gwen Kelley was asked to analyze the issue and recommend a decision. She practised pre-writing techniques (Chapter 5), conducted research (Chapters 18 and 19), did some more pre-writing activities, and at last outlined her essay. Here is her preliminary thesis and supporting essay sections.

Sample student outline of critical paper

Let's Sign

Gwen Kelley

Th: On ethical grounds of protecting Mother Earth, and on practical grounds of sustaining the force that sustains us, let's sign the Accord; the detriments of the Accord do not appear major whereas the gamble that our emissions are not really causing climate change is too great.

Intro: history, background, overview of contentions, concessions to other side, thesis

Sec 1: concessions to main objections, which are a. political-ethical (exempted countries); b. practical (exempted countries, inconclusive evidence); c. practical (economic)

Sec 2: analogy of your mother being ill (ethical, practical)

Sec 3: potential benefits weighed against purported threats (all standards)

Sec 4: Recognize Alberta's concerns and concomitant need for Triple E Senate (all standards).

Sample Student Critical Paper

Kyoto Discord—Let's Be Wise, If Not Right or Rich

Following these introductory comments is the final draft essay that Kelley completed from her outline. You will find at least three important things to think about as you review this essay. We have just been discussing organizing and outlining, so we suggest that you pay attention to how Kelley structures and phrases her analysis. Marginal notes in black comment on the writing strategies she has applied. Another area of importance is how the writer has used and cited her sources. Marginal notes in green comment on documentation techniques according to MLA style (see Chapter 19). A third important thing to consider, as reader, is the impact of time.

In the next chapter, "Rhetorical Analysis," as well as in Chapters 18, "Research Methods," and 19, "Documentation," we discuss how important it is to consider when a particular essay or other form of information was authored. If the material was written some time ago, and especially if, like Kelley's essay, it deals with an issue that experiences rapid change, be sure to compare the context then and now. In the five years since Gwen Kelley wrote her paper, Paul Martin took over as Canadian prime minister, followed by Prime Minister Stephen Harper. George Bush is nearing the end of his second term as president of the United States and will soon step down. Ralph Klein resigned as premier of Alberta, replaced by the new Alberta Conservative Party leader Ed Stelmach. More importantly, the Kyoto Accord and climate change issues in general have undergone continual redefinition, resulting from ongoing research, debate, and public interest. The United Nations Integrated Panel on Climate

Change (IPCC) continues its major commitment to compiling, evaluating, and reporting on the evolving state of human knowledge of the environment (see http://www.ipcc.ch/). Intense media attention to climate change, reinforcing the appeals of high-profile speakers such as Al Gore (*An Inconvenient Truth*), has contributed to a general acceptance that human activity does affect the climate. Even George Bush has moderated his former rejection of that idea. The 60th General Assembly of the United Nations declared 2008 "International Year of Planet Earth," an observance aiming to raise $20 million from industry for environmental outreach efforts. Australia has changed its resistant attitude, while Canada, on the other hand, received the 2007 "Fossil" award for recalcitrance. These developments represent a new background quite different from the one that informed Kelley's analysis and ensuing argument. Her discussion may indeed remain valuable to how we think about this topic, but time has redefined the values to be found.

Sample Essay

Kyoto *Discord*—Let's Be Wise, If Not Right or Rich
Gwen Kelly

1   When American President Bill Clinton signed the 1997 Kyoto Accord, joining 37 other industrialized countries in commitment to a protocol that now calls for a carbon-emissions reduction of 3.5 percent by 2012 (over 1990 levels), American business immediately objected (Duff). Even the American Energy Department questioned the President (Duff). Clinton's opponents cited three main reasons: the failure to include developing countries; unconvincing scientific evidence; and the serious threat to the American economy. Canada, one of the 38 signatories, initially accepted the opinion of United Nations scientists: continued carbon emissions could contribute to greenhouse climate change and severe planetary disruption (Duff). With strong opposition from the United States and now from Alberta, Canada's prime minister Jean Chrétien must decide if he should ratify the Accord (Duff). While it is admittedly hard for us to know which scientist, which economist, and which politician to believe, the wisest course for Canada is to seek national consensus in support of Kyoto.

2   The objections to Kyoto were embraced by President George W. Bush who, upon succeeding Clinton, withdrew support for the Accord. On the first point, he argued that by exempting developing nations the Accord defeats its goals: emissions from non-participants will offset the sacrifices made by participants. In response, let us consider that notwithstanding lack of scientific agreement on this entire topic, it only follows that emissions reductions by 38 heavily industrialized nations will do some good, and it is better to have controls begin in the highly industrialized countries (where the levels of emissions are highest) than in the less industrialized ones. Western parties can build emissions controls into future industry agreements with non-Kyoto nations. A system of rewards can be implemented for those who join the Accord. Mr. Bush, however, also pleads unfairness: why should the developed countries be the ones hampered by new standards? But

Opening defines Accord and conflict.

Duff cited, through paraphrase.

Three main points introduced.

Basic issue raised.

Thesis statement/controlling idea.

Focus on first of three topics previewed. Opposition side first.

the President overlooks the massive advantages and influence of the West. Our standard of living is so much greater than that of the excluded countries that surely we can better sustain the challenge of adapting to Kyoto standards. This will even help others to catch up, an important consideration for political health. Given the vast lead that Western nations have over those in developing areas, the exemption of poorer nations from Kyoto standards simply represents awareness on our part of a need to pursue a higher level of political and economic equity. In the meantime, having 37 highly industrialized nations set an example is surely a formidable starting point, one that would be all the more powerful, of course, with the United States, the world's leading emitter of greenhouse gases.

3   On the second objection, lack of scientific assurance that carbon emissions harm the environment, President Bush presented a petition of 15,000 scientists opposed to Kyoto (SEPP). Yet these scientists remain themselves opposed by colleagues whose opinions have been accepted by 37 other countries. Just 450 pro-Kyoto scientists in each of the other 37 signatory nations would outnumber Bush's list. Winston Gereluk, coordinator of industrial relations at Alberta's Athabasca University, contends that the Kyoto "protocol is based on one of the most extensive scientific exercises in history," one that began well before the 1988 global climate-change meeting (A.15). With scientific opinion divided, to say the least, we might ask does the viewpoint of one nation encourage greater conviction than that of 37 nations? Certainly arguments from the pro-Kyoto side need to be more deeply considered.

4   The David Suzuki Foundation has gathered together views and evidence from the vast scientific sector discounted by Mr. Bush. Noting today's widespread scientific acceptance that global warming is a reality (0.2 degrees Celsius rise in temperature per decade) and that carbon emissions do contribute to this trend, the Foundation lists numerous scientific studies exploring the harmful consequences of global warming in three broad categories: extreme weather, imperilled ecosystems, and human health (*Climate Change: Impacts*).

5   Such far-reaching consequences have begun to emerge in Canada. On the subject of weather, let us consider the recent cases of drought, intense summer heat, and violent storms. Victoria, British Columbia, recorded half of its usual winter rainfall in 2000–01, its driest winter since 1900. As a result, the reservoirs of available water dropped by 30 percent (Deborah Walker, qtd in Davey). In 2002, Edmonton experienced its driest and hottest summer on record; unprecedented forest fires north of the city soon exhausted the normal firefighting budget.

6   Turning to imperilled ecosystems, it is estimated that by the end of this century, 45 percent of Canada's habitat could be lost, along with 20 percent of its wildlife species (Markham and Malcolm). The human health factor has also been widely considered by scientists, many of whom predict increased asthma and heart disease. In some cases, scientists offer these predictions despite political pressure to remain silent. In October 2002, Dr. David Swann, medical health officer for the southern Alberta Palliser Health Authority, was fired from his job after expressing support for the Kyoto Accord as a health benefit (Chambers A6). Political

denial cannot erase the real threat to health, however. As temperatures rise, there is also the threat of tropical diseases. Cases of mosquito-borne illnesses have recently occurred in North America. There may not be incontestable proof that carbon emissions cause these problems, but over the past 15 or 20 years, increasing numbers of reputable scientists have been making public statements to the effect that combustion of our standard fuels and global warming could be agents of dire change. Canadians seem to be reading and accepting these opinions. Seventy-eight percent of Canadians, including 65.6 percent of Albertans, supported ratification of Kyoto in a March 2002 poll by Decima Research (Chase A7). We know that all the people are not right all of the time—but is the majority right in this case?

author and page.

*Sources identified
by author and
page.*

7   Let us imagine that our mother became ill and one doctor said we must sacrifice personal income and suffer hardship to secure the right herbs to save her. Another doctor said there was no reason to be so worried, that we should go on making our usual income and not bothering to seek herbs. What would we do? Certainly the earth is our mother: we depend entirely upon the planet for our well-being. The air we breathe, if polluted, can harm and even kill us. This has been demonstrated in numerous scientific investigations. The earth nourishes us and all living things, so it is only right that we care for her. If there is a 50 percent chance, or even a lower chance, that the United Nations scientists are right and the Bush scientists are wrong, then it only makes sense to take the prudent course. Ignoring the possible consequences of global warming could mean no turning back. So let us say that while we may never be able to claim that by supporting Kyoto we are right, we can, like a loving child, strive to be wise.

*Appeal to ethics
and emotion,
using analogy.
Motherhood
appeal?*

*Writer ends anal-
ogy with "reason-
able" suggestion.
No certainty but
urges caution.*

8   Although Mr. Bush disagrees, the potential benefits to planetary well-being more than outweigh any possible costs of implementing Kyoto. This is so even if the worst-case economic fears of Kyoto opponents are realized. In 1997, the National Energy Department predicted that Kyoto would lower the American GDP by 4.1 percent; there would be 2.4 million fewer jobs by 2010 (Duff). Bad as that picture may be, it still looks better than the possible harm of greenhouse emissions. Opponents within Canada argue that unless the United States ratifies the Accord as well, Canada will be at an extreme economic disadvantage in competition with our already prodigious neighbour. On the other hand, pro-Kyoto advocates, such as the David Suzuki Foundation, argue that the consequences of global warming bring their own major economic problems. The costs of dealing with drought, floods, fires, water shortages, illnesses, and the like should be considered (*Climate Change: Impacts*). The Suzuki Foundation contends that ratifying Kyoto will stimulate the high-tech sector, bringing more jobs and net benefits to Canada (*Kyoto Protocol*). Stepping back from both sides of this economic debate, one may decide that predictions that the American and Canadian economies will significantly suffer or benefit from the Kyoto Accord may be as overstated as predictions that were made about the economic repercussions of the Free Trade Agreement. In reality, after all the extreme predictions of economic gains or losses arising from that agreement, some people benefited by it while others

*Opposition's view
of third point
summarized.*

*Source given by
author only.*

*In citations,
sources identified
by titles only. No
page numbers for
Web.*

had to find new work or adapt in their existing employment. Some sectors went up, others went down. There is still no consensus on whether the Free Trade Agreement overall helped or hurt our economies.

Detailed rebuttal of opposition's third point.

9   What does seem possible—and what the Suzuki Foundation does not seem to address specifically—is that the Alberta economy could pay a significant short-term cost in adapting to Kyoto. We should consider that since the 1960s, Alberta's major industry has been the exploitation of petroleum and other mineral resources. The tar sands of the Athabasca River are considered among the richest oil deposits in the world. Half of Canada's coal is mined in Alberta. Natural gas is another major resource. Despite diversification of its economy in Calgary and Edmonton, Alberta relies on these resources and feels deep psychological dependence on the energy sector. Resentment over the imposed National Energy Policy (NEP) of the 1980s remains strong. Vince Mullan, an Albertan writing online to CBC's program *Your Space* on May 16, 2002, suggests that there was a "huge loss of jobs in Alberta" due to the NEP, and that the same ramifications could follow with Kyoto. We might respond that Alberta, NEP notwithstanding, still has the highest standard of living on the planet, and that non-renewable resources cannot continue fuelling Alberta's economy forever—but regardless of the above-mentioned Albertan's facts or reasoning, his response signals how seriously that province feels both exploited and excluded from national decision-making. Alberta's premier, Ralph Klein, has threatened to boycott discussions of Kyoto unless his modified proposal on controlling carbon fuel emissions is accepted. So while supporting Kyoto is paramount, Ottawa, in response to Alberta's concerns about national alienation, should also show renewed interest in a Triple-E Senate, a long overdue measure that would extend more say to the regions.

No parenthetical citation—author cited in sentence, no page for online source.

Consideration for opposition restored (Alberta part of opposition). Prepares for concluding idea that political process in Canada unfair.

10   In conclusion, with the United States dominating world affairs, Canada is certainly wise to ratify Kyoto. If our nation supports, however modestly and diplomatically, a global balance of power and tenders an important vote for protection of the life source on which we all depend, our actions will resonate globally, perhaps influencing other nations to make a greater environmental commitment. Yet Canada's continued contribution to global well-being will be measured first in large part by its ability to settle political imbalances, perceived and real, within its own nation.

Works Cited

Chambers, Allan. "Doctor's Firing Tarnishes Alberta Stand." *Edmonton Journal* 8 Oct. 2002: A6.

Chase, Steven. "Kyoto Plan Backed by 78 Percent, Poll Says." *Globe and Mail* 1 Apr. 2002: A7.

Climate Change: Impacts. The David Suzuki Foundation. Oct. 2002 <http://www.davidsuzuki.org/Climate_Change/Impacts>.

Davey, Tom. "Edmonton Hosted Three Provinces at WCW and WA [Western Canada Water and Wastewater Association] Conference." *Environmental Science and Engineering.* Jan. 2002 <http://www.esemag.com/0102/wcw.html>.

Duff, Anna Bray. "Kyoto Accord Divides Business." *Investor's Business Daily* 13 Nov. 1998.

Gereluk, Winston. "Climate Science Faces Alberta-style Inquisition." *Edmonton Journal* 14 Oct. 2002: A.15.

Kyoto Protocol. The David Suzuki Foundation. Oct. 2002 <http://www.davidsuzuki.org/Climate_Change/Kyoto/>.

Markham, Adam, and Jay Malcolm. *Speed Kills: Rates of Climate Change Are Threatening Biodiversity.* 1 Sept. 2000. Oct. 2002 <http://www.panda.org/climate/spotlight/speedkills.cfm>.

Mullan, Vince. Comment. 16 May 2002. Oct. 2002 <http://cbc.ca/news/viewpoint/yourspace/kyoto_protocol.html>.

SEPP News Release: More Than 15,000 Scientists Protest Kyoto Accord. The Science and Environment Policy Project (SEPP). 21 Apr. 1998 <http://www.sepp.org/pressrel/petition.html>.

Reading other analytical essays is an excellent way to form a critical question to pursue your own essay on the same general topic. Here are some questions about Kelley's essay to help you pursue your own critical response to Canada's ratification of the Kyoto Accord.

Focus Questions

1. Imagine how you or others might have responded to this essay at the time it was written. In what specific respects has the passage of time modified your responses to this essay as you read it today?
2. Does this essay overlook possible counter-arguments? For example, Australia decided not to ratify the accord unless the United States also ratified it. By not mentioning this fact, does the essayist oversimplify the situation as one rogue country against all the others? Also, since Victoria experienced temperatures in 1900 equal to those in 2001, what makes the writer so certain that greenhouse gases caused the heat wave of 2001? Should this question have been recognized and addressed? Finally, China and India, both heavy polluters, were left out of the accord. Does the essayist oversimplify by implying that these countries are "non-industrial"?
3. Can you cite phrases that violate the recommendation not to use emotionally laden language in argumentation? (See Chapter 16.) How would you characterize most of the language in this essay?

4. On the issue of economics, how valid is the comparison to the Free Trade Agreement?

5. Do the listed Works Cited reflect a fair balance of views, pro and con, as well as more neutral, purely informational sources?

6. Did the essay to any extent change or challenge your own thinking on this topic? If so, how?

7. Look back to the discussion of logic and logical fallacies (Chapter 3). Is the thrust of this essay suitably logical? Can you detect any of the 10 listed logical fallacies? If so, explain why you believe your example is a fallacy.

8. Find an analogy in the essay. How crucial is it to the essayist's purpose? Explain. How successful do you consider this analogy? Explain.

9. Comment on any strategies you find particularly effective in this essay.

10. Consider the objectivity of public opinion polls. The writer overlooks mentioning that the Decima Research poll was commissioned by Greenpeace, a group that strongly supports the Kyoto Accord. In the autumn of 2002, the Alberta government flooded the province with brochures attacking the Kyoto Accord. The Alberta government then commissioned another poll within the province, and found that attitudes had shifted to around 72 percent now opposed to ratification of Kyoto. Concerning poll results, comment on the importance of recognizing who commissioned particular polls and what sorts of public propaganda campaigns preceded them. As a more recent example, in the spring of 2006 the right-leaning Fraser Institute released a study suggesting that Canada's commitment to the Kyoto protocols is far too expensive for any possible benefit attained. Not surprisingly, their findings contradicted the recommendations of most environmentalist groups.

11. As narrator of "The Rockies," an episode in the CBC series *Geologic Journey* (2007), David Suzuki observes that climates and geographies have always changed, according to natural cycles, and always will. The complex question, he says, is to what extent human activities are hastening the natural rate of change and thereby compromising adaptation. British author George Monbiot, for one, believes that human impact on the environment must be swiftly curtailed. Read his 2006 book *Heat: How to Stop the Planet from Burning* and also review our introduction to "The Doomsday Machines" (Reader, p. 505). Then try to decide how seriously we should heed Monbiot's warnings, and why.

As you can see, Kelley's essay employs point-by-point comparative method for purposes of analytical contrast (see Chapter 12). This is a dominant pattern in scholarly argumentation (see Chapter 16), whereby strongly opposing reasons on highly controversial questions are measured against yours throughout a piece of writing. A consensus-refutation pattern occurs as Kelley brings forward points on the opposition side, summarizes their arguments and concedes some value to them, but then refutes those points with her own views. You can also see in Kelley's analytical essay, as we previously observed, that emphasis on *reasons* is very important. You are called upon to demonstrate *causes and effects* in order to show the shortcomings of other positions and the merits of your own. It is therefore a very good idea to review cause-effect methods and comparison-contrast methods (see Chapters 10 and 12) as well as Chapter 16 dealing with the more formal application of these methods in the service of a fair, comprehensive, balanced debate.

Responding to Critical Ideas in an Essay

As you have seen in this chapter, forming a critical response entails considerable thinking on one's question, and almost always a fair degree of research (see Chapter 18). Sometimes, however, it can be helpful to write a tentative response without research, using just your current knowledge and experience. You will later explore and test your preliminary ideas by further inquiry, thereby ensuring that you have practised creative and original thinking before seeing what others think. Furthermore, there are critical-writing occasions when you cannot do research, such as examinations. In the following fictionalized scenario, student Lee Jennings is required to write a critical response to David Suzuki's argument(s) in "The Right Stuff" (Reader, p. 464). Unlike Gwen Kelley, whose assignment asked her to evaluate the Kyoto Protocol in Canada without necessarily focusing on the arguments of any one writer, Jennings must focus on the ideas put forward in just one essay. Jennings must therefore treat that one essay—or, in this case, at least, its arguments—as his subject for analysis and evaluation. Jennings must write approximately 400 words in no more than two hours, so he must work efficiently according to a system. He uses the following guidelines.

Guidelines for Responding to the Ideas in an Article, Essay, or Chapter

- Summarize the author's controlling ideas, reasons, and appeals (see Chapter 13).
- Note your initial responses and formulate questions about the author's ideas.
- Since you are focusing on ideas, pay especial attention to logic (see Chapter 3).
- Consider the standard(s) of evaluation you think are best applied to these ideas.
- According to your chosen standards, decide which parts of the arguments you consider sound and which you consider lacking.
- Give reasons for your viewpoints for and against.
- Develop your thesis to express the controlling idea of your response and its reasons (see Chapter 6).
- Structure your response by summarizing the text you are evaluating (in no more than two or three sentences), then stating your thesis and elaborating on your responses. If you agree with some of the essay but mainly take issue with it, recognize the parts you support first, then concentrate on what you consider the shortcomings. If you disagree with some of the thinking but mainly support it, recognize the points that concern you first, then concentrate on explaining what you believe is valid.
- Be careful to avoid the circular trap of simply re-stating the author's ideas as your explanation of why they are or are not worthy.

PRACTICE

Before reading the following critical response by Lee Jennings, follow the above steps yourself and write a 400-word evaluation of Suzuki's argument(s) in "The Right Stuff." When you have completed your response, read Lee Jennings's short essay and our marginal notes and commentary.

Note that this form of critical response (to analysis and arguments within a reading) may also be referred to as a "critique," "position paper," or similar term of that nature.

Critique of an Essay

"The Right Stuff"—If Only It Were That Simple
Lee Jennings

Student states controlling idea; previews reasons, direct-box style.

1   David Suzuki's "The Right Stuff" features the gracious, entertaining and informative style we have come to associate with this well-known host of *The Nature of Things.* But the essay fails to support its thesis that high school science courses should begin with sex education, because Suzuki spends too long on one personal anecdote and ignores or, at best, sweeps aside counterarguments.

Student touches on rhetorical analysis (writing techniques, appeals to reader).

2   Almost half of this seven-paragraph essay describes a trip Suzuki made to a certain high school in a "tough" northern town where he was to address 400 students in the school auditorium. Having dropped into the motel bar the night before his address, Suzuki was approached by the school science teacher, a prophet of doom, who predicted the so-called sex-crazed students would "tear [Suzuki] apart." The next day Suzuki greeted his young audience with the comment, "I'm a geneticist. I know you're basically walking gonads, so I'm going to talk about sex." The audience was hooked, and a lengthy, productive discussion of science emerged from this departure point. But Suzuki commits the fallacy of *post hoc, ergo propter hoc* by assuming that his remark caused this reaction. The reaction could have been caused by his charisma and celebrity. Furthermore, certain students might have been privately disturbed by his directness: one observer cannot determine how 400 students are responding on deeper levels.

See Chapter 3, fallacy of shared space and time.

Methods of respected figure with ethos must still be scrutinized.

3   This flaw of oversimplification mars Suzuki's essay in general. To give another example of this shortcoming, the writer argues that the hormonal changes of puberty inevitably disrupt high school students, causing their preoccupation with sex. But one might as well argue that social conditioning, fed by TV, video games, internet and the like—all heavily infused with appeals to sexual desire—influence teenage restlessness. The nature-nurture debate is surely far from settled. Suzuki concludes too hastily that teenage attitudes and interests are biologically determined.

Student reinforces topic sentence of this paragraph.

4   In a further hasty conclusion, Suzuki states that opponents of sex education in the schools have no intention of tutoring their children at home. This over-generalization could surely be refuted if we surveyed opponents of sex education in the schools. I know of two people who educate their children about sex at home, and who prefer that method of instruction. Another consideration that Suzuki overlooks is logistical: how can the schools, understaffed and overstressed, add the difficult subject of sex education to their curriculum? The high school staff I know say that they are already overworked and pressured to take on roles outside their expertise. The highly sensitive subject of sex education requires great care and knowledge of the young people involved. Unless governments suddenly increase grants to education or other sources of revenue appear, educators have their hands full with present curriculum responsibilities. So while Suzuki makes an excellent point that educators should respect their students and appeal to their interests, his argument for sex education is oversimplified.

> Evidence to refute conclusion given—here from personal experience.

> Student shifts focus to practical concern not acknowledged by proposal. Placing concern last gives added weight.

Word count: The computer word count for this response is 476 words, but short words like "the" and "by" are generally not meant to be included in assignment lengths. This essay, then, gives a good example of the length expected by a request for 400 words.

Commentary on Critical Response to "The Right Stuff"

> The student's critique might just as well have supported Suzuki's basic proposal and gone on to explain why, with reference to ethics, logic, and practical considerations.

The views in this critique may certainly be debated. We do not present it as the *right* response. In an opposing critical response, another student, Brian Mitchell, criticizes Jennings's response as misguided. Mitchell argues that Suzuki never intended his essay as a formal proposal report but rather as a catalyst to get parents thinking. He reminds Jennings that there are different levels of persuasion, which can be used for different purposes. Suzuki's, Mitchell suggests, was simply to influence thinking, not to implement immediate action. Mitchell believes that "The Right Stuff" succeeds in all that it set out to do, that it is up to the parents and others to whom Suzuki appeals to deal with the practical issues. You can read Mitchell's essay at the Text Enrichment Site under "Virtual Discussion Groups," sample paragraph posting for Discussion 2. Mitchell's response is titled "'The Right Stuff'—Let's Read It for What It Is."

Jennings's 400-word critique is simply an illustration of *how* you might prepare and present a first-draft critical response. Regardless of other opinions about Suzuki's proposal, however, here are some features of Lee Jennings's essay that we advocate for *all* critical responses to readings:

- a respectful view toward the source material, despite objections to its perceived weaknesses (see Chapter 16, "Argumentation," for more on respecting ideas you go on to oppose)
- an introduction recognizing the value of the author and the importance of the topic
- a brief introductory summary of Suzuki's thesis and main supporting points
- a clear indication of the central concern of the critique (does the essay acknowledge the complexities involved?)
- awareness of the author's work outside this reading as well as of related knowledge in the issues touched on here (the nature-versus-nurture debate, the relevance of current education policy and spending)
- attention to rhetorical features as a test of arguments, with an expectation that competing sides be given fair consideration (see Chapter 16 for more on fairness of inquiry)
- insistence on sustained logical thinking (see Chapter 3, "More About Logic")

Now let us look further at specific features of Jennings's critique.

The opening pays respect to strengths of the essay and provides further information of relevance (see the section on essay openings in Chapter 7). Since the assignment requires a short response (just 400 words), the writer moves quickly to the topic and thesis of Suzuki's essay (see Chapter 13, "The Summary," for a detailed breakdown of how to find an author's thesis). Jennings then clearly states his own thesis and suggests the nature of his supporting reasons (see Chapter 6 on thesis statements).

The body of the critical response uses fully developed, focused paragraphs matched to the reasons suggested in the thesis and organized to build effectively to a final climactic objection (see Chapter 6). The second paragraph elaborates on the anecdote and explains its shortcomings. From this paragraph flows the problem of oversimplification: the following (third and fourth) paragraphs offer further cases of this central problem. Since the response must be so short (around 400 words), the writer concludes with one reinforcing sentence at the end of the fourth paragraph rather than with an exhaustive conclusion (see Chapter 7 for more on types of conclusions).

Another feature of this sample response is that it pays close attention to the essay under study. It notes the precise length (seven paragraphs), since overdependence on a long anecdote is one of the main criticisms. This particular aspect of the critique draws upon the methods of rhetorical analysis (described in more detail in Chapter 15). For learning purposes, we often speak of responding to the ideas of an essay as opposed to responding to the rhetorical methods of that essay, but in fact, this separation is somewhat artificial. Meaning and form are intertwined; they cannot be entirely separated from each other. Some attention to form is usually helpful in all critiques of essays, even those critiques that concentrate, like Jennings's, on the arguments. By looking closely at Suzuki's form, Jennings picks out main points, such as Suzuki's apparent assumption that biology is the cause of behaviour. The student also shows an awareness of various logical fallacies, such as *post hoc, ergo propter hoc* (see Chapter 3), and various other forms of oversimplification. These types of fallacies may be imbedded in the structure and style of the essay (its rhetorical aspects) as well as in separate statements within it. Jennings uses as much rhetorical analysis as he needs to support his primary focus on assessing Suzuki's proposal.

A studious, moderate tone arises from this close, careful observation combined with use of third person (see Chapter 2 for features of tone). Judicious use of first person occurs in the fourth paragraph to add examples from personal experience. Since this assignment was presented as a simulated examination, with no access to research sources, the writer has used first-hand knowledge to identify an angle of criticism that could be solidified with further research. With more time and access to research sources, the writer might well drop the use of first person in these places by fortifying his response with other supports gained by wider inquiry.

PRACTICE
Expanding a Critical Response with Research

Read Chapter 18, "Research Methods" and "Interviews" at the Text Enrichment Site. Imagine how you would complete the following assignment. Expand Lee Jennings's essay by approximately 500 words, integrating research and adapting point of view to critical third person throughout. Consider whether an interview might be suitable, based on content in Jennings's original essay.

See the Text Enrichment Site for "The Right Stuff"— If Only It Were That Simple" (Lee Jennings's essay expanded by research). What do you think of the extra work Jennings has done? What is your response to our commentary on that additional work? Discuss your thoughts with your instructor and classmates.

PRACTICE
Ghostwriting for David Suzuki

Let's imagine the following scenario. David Suzuki has been invited to speak to the National Teachers Association. Although he has read the concerns raised by Lee Jennings and has heard that most of the teachers are opposed to his recommendation on grounds of workload, he wants you (his new speechwriter) to write his speech following Monroe's Motivated Sequence (see Chapter 16, p. 265). Since he trusts you as an advisor, he has asked you to determine precisely how to define the call to action. Outline his speech. Discuss your proposal with your coursemates and your instructor.

This exercise should be an illustration that the act of writing can never be separated from the act of preliminary decision-making, with key attention to audience, practical realities, and imaginative possibilities.

PRACTICE

Let's imagine that the head of a major school board has been invited to speak to a group of "concerned parents." This large group is deeply concerned about the school board's recent adoption of sex education classes patterned on the design presented by David Suzuki to lead from sex education to matters of science. Already there have been complaints of disturbed and offended students; school counsellors have advised that several students who experienced abuse in the past are anxious about having to attend. Parents and students with religious organizations have described the new classes as immoral and threatening to increase premarital sexual relations. Although teaching workloads have been addressed, some teachers have formed a lobby to express their concern about not feeling quali-

fied for the classes. Another lobby of teachers has questioned the underlying assumption that science education should become more generalist, as David Suzuki advocates in his proposal. The head of the school board has appointed you to write her speech. Feeling hopeless, if not outright despairing, you read Chapter 16 of this text on Rogerian argument and other forms of persuasion that seek to conciliate. You watch a video clip of Prime Minister Lester Pearson speaking to a hostile audience of Legionnaires who opposed his new Canadian flag. The head of the school board has given you permission to work some new ideas and strategies into her address. You may make up realistic possible details to enrich this scenario. Outline the speech. Discuss it with your coursemates and your instructor.

See the Text Enrichment Site for this chapter for further practice activities and material on critical discussion groups. You will find further student responses to Suzuki's essay and to Lee Jennings's critique.

CONCLUSION

In its ideal expression, the university encourages plurality of thought. While promoting rigorous forms of analysis and evaluation, our academies also recognize that critical interpretations—however well argued—are opinions, not facts (see more on fact versus opinion in Chapter 3). However, as we all know, things are not always ideal. If others do not seem to greet your ideas with open-minded acceptance, all the more reason to benefit from the methods explained in this chapter and in Chapter 16. With proper skill in critical thinking and persuasion, it is possible to overcome obstacles and objections by "acting on words."

Works Cited

Paul, Richard, and Linda Elder. *Critical and Creative Thinking.* Dillon Beach, CA: The Foundation for Critical Thinking, 2004.

Stewart, Kay, Chris Bullock, and Marian Allen. *Essay Writing for Canadian Students.* 4th ed. Toronto: Pearson, 2004.

Chapter 15
Rhetorical Analysis

Rhetorical analysis represents a special form of critical analysis (see Chapter 14). Rhetoric, as defined elsewhere in this text, means the art of using language. Rhetorical analysis therefore involves exploring how certain components in a piece of writing interact together, affect the reading process, and contribute to a deeper understanding of a related issue. We suggest that you imagine a piece of writing as an operational system with the ultimate purpose of creating a final meaning. You may picture a car engine, a bridge, a biological system . . . something based on principles of engineering, parts and processes, and dedicated to a certain function. In search of exactly how the process works in a particular text under study, you apply minute care to examine the parts and principles of the text and their process relationships. Your ultimate goal is to evaluate the writer's intended purpose—but to succeed you must first identify the components and interactions that suggest what that purpose is.

Since many students find it difficult to get started on a close study of how language functions in a piece of writing, this chapter provides recommended steps and examples. As you will discover, ability with rhetorical analysis serves students in all subjects that require advanced reading skills. Rhetorical analysis intensifies consciousness of words and meanings, a crucial step forward in your post-secondary experience.

TWO STAGES OF RHETORICAL ANALYSIS

Rhetorical analysis, as critical analysis in general, comprises two basic stages: analysis and evaluation.

Analysis: Breaking a Text Down into Parts and Relationships (Stage 1 of Critical Thinking)

As defined in Chapter 14, analysis involves breaking a subject down into its parts and relationships. Identifying and describing the important attributes of an essay is an application of Stage 1 critical thinking.

Here is a checklist of basic textual elements, principles, and process relationships to help you perform a preliminary identification of rhetorical components:

Who is the author and what biographical information is available on him or her?

Where was the work published?

What type of writing is this (investigative journalism, academic analysis, corporate persuasion, and so forth)?

Who is the intended audience?

What various public beliefs exist on the topic?

What various public beliefs existed on the topic at the time the piece was written?

What is the author's purpose?

What is the author's controlling idea?

What are the author's reasons? (controlling idea + reasons = thesis)

What specific methods of inquiry (research) have been used?

Where do you think you could find more information about the subject matter discussed?

What connections to the subject beyond the essay are included or implied?

How has the reading been organized and what rhetorical strategies and patterns are featured throughout and in separate parts?

What style and therefore tone does the reading use (kinds of words, lengths of sentences)?

PRACTICE

Select an essay from this text. Analyze it according to the above checklist. Fill in all parts of the checklist. Discuss your findings with your instructor and classmates.

A Process Description Consolidates Information from Your Checklist

Once you have considered the reliability of information in your checklist, you may find it helpful to summarize the important parts of that information into one or two paragraphs. These may use full sentences or simply use coherent note-making style. Your description in one or two paragraphs of what you have found in analyzing a selected essay is a form of *process description*. Chapter 11, "How-to Instructions, Process Description, and Definition," provides more information on this form (pp. 163–68), closely related to the summary (described in Chapter 13). A close detailed study of rhetorical elements should come before any intensified attempt to evaluate the *significance* of the writing. Therefore, you should fill in the above checklist and convert its findings into a short process description before you proceed to the second stage of evaluation.

> ## ♪ PRACTICE
>
> Read the essay "College Girl to Call Girl" in the Reader (p. 457). Fill in the checklist of essay attributes and relationships given on page 224. Convert your checklist into a rough-draft process description. Then turn to page 242 of this chapter to see Valerie Desjardins's note-form process description of "College Girl." Compare your description to hers. Discuss this comparison with your instructor and classmates.

Evaluating the Significance of Rhetorical Parts and Principles (Stage 2 Critical Thinking)

After you have studied a text closely and filled in the above checklist, you come to a preliminary idea of what that essay is attempting to say and how it pursues that goal. Depending on the complexity of the text, you may need to do more intense examination to test your preliminary ideas and only then to consider the *significance* of what you believe the author is attempting to do. This careful consideration of basic components can prove useful in alerting you to your own possible biased thinking, as the following example may demonstrate.

In 1995, John MacLachlan Gray published a book called *I Love Mom: An Irreverent History of the Tattoo*. While poking fun at the tattooed set of his day, he nevertheless expressed the controlling idea that those in the mainstream who deplored tattoos were snobs and less alive than the tattooed. Reading that book today, younger readers sometimes overlook that not so long ago tattoos were marginal. Gray wrote his book with the mistaken assumption that this marginalization would continue, but not with the belief that it should continue. Readers today who overlook the mainstream attitudes of 1995 come to a hasty conclusion that Gray's purpose was to disapprove of tattoos rather than to confront that disapproval. By ignoring that different attitudes existed in the past (often because we feel superior to those attitudes), we lose an important clue to help us gather a writer's purpose.

Upon thinking further about the elements in the above checklist, you may feel that the essay expresses a worthy thesis, but does so partly for the wrong reasons, or that it could do a better job of supporting its thesis. On the other hand, the opposite judgement might be more compelling. You might feel that the essay expresses a questionable thesis but actually does a superficially effective job of using rhetoric to convince others to accept its central idea. You might consider the thesis to be relatively uninteresting, yet supported by one or two points of interest that deserve further examination. You might consider the essay to be so subtle, deft, and complex that simply tracing its techniques and effects alone will provide you and your reader with an enriching journey. You may be most interested in pursuing a relationship between the style of the essay and its author, intended audience, critics, or historical or cultural context. In whatever case, a rhetorical analysis will assert some interesting relationships between the methods of a particular text and a related point of significance.

The emphasis in first-year rhetorical analysis often remains upon the writing itself. Through careful examination of the writing, the student seeks to understand, as fully as possible, what the author intends to convey, as well, perhaps, as what causes or effects the writing may have, and whether these seem intentional or not. First-year rhetorical evaluation generally decides on how well the writer's apparent goals have been met.

As with critical response in general, the standards you use to pursue your evaluation of aspects of style and their significance may be those of practicality (e.g., appeals of pathos, logos, and ethos and their effects upon readers); logic (e.g., consistency within the essay, see Chapter 3); aesthetics (pleasurable designs, patterns, and artistic methods); or ethics (e.g., whether the essay uses language to enrich an idea of value to others or to obscure possible harmful consequences, whether the author uses language in a way that respects relationships to other people and accountabilities involved in the occasion). In many cases, two or more of these standards may be called into discussion.

To help you apply standards suitable to your selected essay, we offer the following five specialized approaches. Based on what you have discovered in the first stage of your analysis, you may consider that one or more of the following specialized methods will assist you to move into the more intense stage of evaluation.

FIVE SPECIALIZED APPROACHES

The following five specialized approaches may assist you to add further detail to your Stage 1 analytical information; these specialized methods will most certainly guide you into Stage 2 evaluation.

- examining for appeals to logos, pathos, and ethos
- examining for use of the four classical canons of memory, invention, disposition, and style
- applying the criteria of a certain critic
- applying the Fog Index
- applying the methods of literary analysis

EXAMINING FOR APPEALS TO LOGOS, PATHOS, AND ETHOS

Examining an essay for appeals to logos, pathos, and ethos (also known as classical rhetorical analysis) is a specific type of rhetorical analysis, but it shares the same motivation as other forms: an interest in how authors use language to advance their thesis and convince their audiences of its merit. As we learned in Chapter 1, classical rhetoric refers to persuasive attributes as appeals: logos (logical or rational appeal), pathos (emotional appeal), and ethos (ethical appeal or writer credibility). In classical rhetorical analysis, then, the focus is on how effectively the author of the work being analyzed uses these appeals. Although there are many ways of analyzing various works, a classical approach is useful because the categories of appeal, while often overlapping, will help determine the development and organization of the analysis. A classical approach, like any of the other approaches to rhetorical analysis, works for analyzing not only writing like articles and essays, but any kind of persuasive work (from an advertisement to a film), anything in which the person producing the piece of work is trying to persuade his or her audience.

Chapter 1 outlines the various ways the appeals are used. Writers should use logical reasoning, providing evidence as support for the points they make. They will use induction and/or deduction in presenting the argument, and will follow various methods of logical development (comparison-contrast, cause-effect, definition, classification, process analysis, and examples). The evidence that writers use must be accessible to testing and verification. Evidence may take the form of facts, statistics, primary sources, and secondary sources. Ideally, writers use pathos to add to logos so that the audience is "touched" by the argument. The main rhetorical methods used to create emotional appeal are description (particularly figurative language) and narration. If pathos is overdone, however, the appeal can seem insincere and manipulative; writers also need to avoid using "trigger" or "loaded" words that may prove inflammatory. Finally, writers' ethos depends largely on how well writers have employed logos and pathos, as well as their demonstrated right to speak on the topic. They must be seen to share with their audience at least a fundamental understanding about what is right and what is wrong on the subject. Writers coming from unexpected angles on "sensitive" subjects must be particularly careful to establish their common ground of ethos with the audience. They should appear to have carefully weighed the pros and cons of a variety of perspectives before deciding on the one presented. The opposing perspectives must be treated fairly: their good points acknowledged, but any logical fallacies also pointed out.

In a classical analysis, you will choose the main ways the author has used these appeals and determine how and how *well* the appeals have been made. For the purposes of our discussion, we will assume that you will be analyzing a piece of writing. In order to assess the effectiveness of the author's use of appeals, you need to first determine the writing situation and purpose, as well as identify, as far as possible, the target audience(s). That's why you should try to find out what you can about where the piece of work first appeared and whether there is any evidence of responses to it. You should also have some knowledge of the author and of why he or she produced the work. Finally, it's important to remain aware of your own readers and their needs in understanding your analysis and being persuaded of its value. (See the checklist of questions to answer concerning an essay's parts and relationships, page 224).

For example, let's say that, as a class assignment, you are asked to write a rhetorical analysis of "The Ways of Meeting Oppression," which can be found in Chapter 10 (p. 144) and is an excerpt from Martin Luther King, Jr.'s book *Stride Toward Freedom*. You not only need to read the essay carefully for rhetorical strategies, but you also need to provide a context for your reading. You do some preliminary research and discover that the book documents the famous Montgomery Bus Boycott. After researching a bit more on the book and evidence of responses to the book, you decide King had two target audiences: African-Americans, particularly those who are interested in pursuing civil rights, and white audiences who need to be educated on "nonviolent resistance" and be made aware of the intentions of the activism King represents—perhaps even persuaded to join the movement based on their Christian beliefs. Now, you look for ways that King appeals to these audiences under the categories of logos, pathos, and ethos. Although you may already know quite a bit about King, his life and his beliefs, you may want to ensure that what you know is correct by researching biographical material for the time period.

Because the material easily available on King is abundant, you must decide to limit your search and sift through what you find so that only the most relevant to your time and space will be used. For example, even though you learn that King was stabbed by a black woman at a book signing of *Stride Toward Freedom* and that he and his family received numerous threats because of his activism, this material is not relevant to an analysis of this excerpt.

Here is a possible working outline of an approximately 1450-word analysis, consisting of six paragraphs:

Intro.	Background on King's book and responses, identification of target audiences, brief summary of the excerpt, identification of King's thesis, and a brief summary of the appeals used and an indication of their effectiveness
Body para. 1	Logos—first method
Para. 2	Logos—second and third method
Para. 3	Pathos
Para. 4	Ethos
Conclusion	
Works Cited	

Sample Essay

A Rhetorical Analysis of "The Ways of Meeting Oppression"
Eugenia Gilbert

The excerpt "The Ways of Meeting Oppression" is taken from Martin Luther King, Jr.'s book *Stride Toward Freedom,* published in 1958 by Harper & Row. The book introduced to America the man who took the stage as a civil rights leader when he became head of the Montgomery in Action committee, responsible for orchestrating the famous Montgomery Bus Boycott that lasted over a year and ended with new rights for African-American citizens. This book appealed to black audiences, particularly students and others who were looking for a blueprint to take action against oppressive and unjust laws, and to white audiences, who were curious about this new leader and wanting to know more about the tactics used in nonviolent demonstration, something King would be expanding and expounding on in the years to come. Thus, King's ethos is established as a civil rights leader with some success, and his audiences would be ready to listen to what he had to say, even if they did not completely agree with the aims or methods he describes. In "The Ways of Meeting Oppression," King outlines three methods used to deal with the unjust laws against black American citizens, beginning with the attitude of acceptance he has witnessed (the acceptance of oppression), then the response of defiant force, and finally, something that combines the peacefulness of acceptance with the resistance of violence: nonviolent resistance. Through the rhetorical modes of classification, definition, cause and effect, illustration, as well as precise and emotive language, King uses logos, pathos, and ethos effectively to persuade his audiences that nonviolent resistance is the path African-Americans must follow to gain equal rights.

Although this excerpt does not include research or statistics, there are plenty of examples of logos in the method of development and the use of evidence. From the first sentence, King sets up a logical structure, indicating his argument will be measured and based on reason. First, King organizes his essay by classification, defining and explaining the causes and effects of using the three methods of "meeting oppression." For each method, he provides illustrations that help readers understand how these methods work. For the first method, "acquiescence," he uses the example from the Bible of the Israelite slaves who grumbled at their freedom and preferred whatever security they had in Egypt. King's audiences of the 1950s, both black and white, would be very familiar with the story of Exodus and would certainly not be surprised to see a Baptist minister use it as an example. They might be more surprised to see him go on to refer to a passage from Shakespeare to explain the slaves' reluctance, and this allusion to a literary figure would help establish him as an educated man. To show that he is also in touch with the ordinary black Americans' suffering, he then quotes the guitarist to show "the type of negative freedom and resignation" that characterizes acquiescence. He follows with a logical argument ending with "[a]cquiescence is interpreted as proof of the Negro's inferiority"—a strong call to prove otherwise. For each method that he explains, he shows the effects of choosing this way to deal with the lack of civil rights.

King uses the same rhetorical strategies in discussing the second and third methods. In claiming that the second method, a response with violence, "is both impractical and immoral," he once again refers to a passage from the Bible, the one in which Peter draws a weapon to resist Jesus' capture at Gethsemane and is told to put the weapon aside. This, too, is a strong call to those of Christian faith not to use violence, even against injustice. King also quotes Gandhi, though perhaps his readers would not have recognized it, when he says "an eye for an eye leaves everybody blind." Although he cites no specific examples of the failure of violence as a method, he ends with the easily proven claim that "[h]istory is cluttered with the wreckage of nations" who choose this method of resistance. Finally, he continues to use logos effectively in describing the third method of meeting oppression: "nonviolent resistance." Here he introduces Hegel's dialectic, something that only his educated readers would be familiar with, but explained so that any reader could understand. The third way is explained as the synthesis of the first two, the peace without the violence, the results without the submission. By drawing on Hegel, King emphasizes his educational background and understanding, something that would help establish his ethos as well as show his ethical character, aiming for the best possible outcome, logically and morally. While his logical thesis can be seen as "[o]ppressed people deal with oppression in three characteristic ways," his persuasive thesis is that nonviolent resistance "[m]ust guide the actions of the Negro in the present crisis in race relations."

Since the outcome of his method of resistance is speculative and cannot be proven, King must go beyond logical reasoning and appeal to his readers' sense of justice and hope by using emotional appeals (pathos). While he uses figurative language more sparingly here than in some later famous publications, such as "Letter from Birmingham Jail" and his "I have a dream" speech, there are still plenty of examples of emotionally appealing language throughout the excerpt. He goes beyond proving the first two methods to be merely ineffective by emphasizing that the methods are immoral. Readers may be encouraged to feel guilty if they agree or to feel angry at the "coward[ice]" implied by acquiescence and the aftereffects of violence: "corroding hatred" and "bitterness." In the first way, non-resisters are aligned with "the way of the coward," as "evil as the oppressor," and "willing to sell the future of [their] children." In the second way, those children will "be the recipients of a desolate night of bitterness . . . [and] an endless reign of meaningless chaos." However, in the third way, resisters are aligned with "ris[ing] to the noble height of opposing the unjust system while loving the perpetrators of the system." War metaphors are used further to evoke a rallying cry to "arms": "the Negro can also enlist all men of good will in his struggle for equality," reinforcing his claim that "[t]he problem is not a purely racial one . . . but a tension between justice and injustice." Here the language should especially appeal to his white audience as well. Further, King claims that those involved in this method of resistance "can make a lasting contribution to the moral strength of the nation and set a sublime example of courage for generations yet unborn." The emotive language sends out a strong call to black readers, which was met by those who took up the call, such as black students involved in SNCC (Student Nonviolent Coordinating Committee) (Newfield). While King may be using bandwagon appeal to some extent, his use of logos balances the use of pathos, and his readers will not be tempted to be swayed by words alone.

King's ethos is established by the reason Harper & Row would publish his ideas: he was a rising civil rights leader who gained nationwide attention during the Montgomery Bus Boycott. In this excerpt, his ethos is increased by his balanced view, apparently careful weighing of options, and support for his observations throughout. He appears to have actually considered the other possibilities, which indicates lack of bias. He is seen to be of an ethical character himself, desiring justice and eschewing hatred, and throughout he emphasizes his connection to Christian belief. It is not surprising that a quotation from Bishop James A. Pike was noted on the book's cover—"May well become a Christian classic" (Cover)—and certainly this element would not only support King's ethos, but have wide appeal for his audiences as well.

The response to the book indicates that his appeals were successful in reaching his target audiences. He gained more credibility with white leaders (though not necessarily popularity—he probably showed himself as more dangerous to many) and with blacks who agreed with the methods, especially those who wanted to encourage his leadership and followers who were eager to continue and to try the methods. According to Kerry Taylor, one of the people involved in editing a volume of King's papers for publication by Stanford University, "*Stride Toward Freedom* essentially became the Bible for many activists following King's footsteps" (Dang). A contemporary reviewer claimed that, in this book, "King throws down a rigorous challenge to American white society and to Negroes. He calls on his fellow Christians to be Christians, his fellow democrats to be democrats, and he asks right-thinking whites and his fellow-Negroes to join him in refusing to cooperate with evil" (Isaacs). While the book may have evoked a variety of responses, it is clear that the excerpt would be persuasive because of King's expert use of logos, pathos, and ethos.

Works Cited

Cover of *Stride Toward Freedom* [photograph of original book cover]. n.d. The Martin Luther King, Jr. Research and Education Institute. 4 Jul. 2006 <http://www.stanford.edu/group/King/about_king/details/580917.htm>.

Dang, Jess. "Volume of King papers published—Ongoing Stanford project to anthologize King's letters, talks and sermons." *Stanford Daily* 9 May 2000. 4 Jul. 2006 <http://www.stanforddaily.com/article/2000/5/9/volumeOfKingPapersPublished-OngoingStanfordProjectToAnthologizeKingsLettersTalksAndSermons>.

Isaacs, Harold R. "Civil Disobedience in Montgomery." Rev. of *Stride Toward Freedom*, by Martin Luther King, Jr. *New Republic* 6 Oct. 1958: 19–20. Academic Search Premier. EPSCO. Mount Royal College Lib., Calgary, AB.

King, Jr., Martin Luther. "The Ways of Meeting Oppression." *Acting on Words*: *An Integrated Reader, Rhetoric, and Handbook*. Eds. David Brundage and Michael Lahey. 2nd ed. Toronto: Pearson, 2007. 144–45

Newfield, Jack. "The Student Left." *Nation* 10 May 1965: 491–95. Academic Search Premier. EPSCO. Mount Royal College Lib., Calgary, AB. 20 Jul. 2006.

Much of King's work has been studied in terms of rhetorical analysis. Some analysts use simple terms, such as those on a webpage for beginning students of rhetoric that shows the various appeals through colour-coding, an easy-to-follow visual way to see how King balances his appeals (available at <http://faculty.millikin.edu/~moconner/writing/king1a.html>); others use more detailed, sophisticated terms in journals of rhetoric, such as *Rhetoric & Public Affairs*. In your own assessment of the analysis above, did the student use every possible example, or only the main ones to make her point? For some students, the Biblical references may seem more aligned with pathos than logos because they would be emotionally evocative of religious belief, but for many of King's followers and audience, the references would be seen as historical, factual, and entirely logical.

✒ PRACTICE

Examine the following four essays from the Reader for logos, pathos, and ethos: "The Right Stuff" (p. 464), "The Other Canadians and Canada's Future" (p. 416), "A Liberal Education Is Key to a Civil Society" (p. 462), and "Canadians: What Do They Want?" (p. 467). Then see the Text Enrichment Site, Chapter 15, for classical rhetorical analyses (according to logos, pathos, and ethos) for each of these.

EXAMINING FOR USE OF THE FOUR CLASSICAL CANONS OF MEMORY, INVENTION, DISPOSITION, AND STYLE

Another helpful approach to textual analysis, one with a classical pedigree matching that of the logos, pathos, ethos approach, is to examine how a text observes the four canons of memory, invention, disposition, and style. Indeed, this approach involves some of the same reader-appeal awareness that we have laid out under the previous method. These two classically based methods are, in fact, reciprocally supporting. For example, when you investigate the matter of style, you will ask, among other things, if it appeals more to logos or pathos. To get you started using the four canons approach, all we really need to do is define what the ancients meant by "canon" and by the four types of canon. Then it is your job to read a text closely in search of how each of those four attributes is addressed (analysis) and how well it is addressed (evaluation).

Classical canon: "Canon" is one of those English words with various denotative meanings. In this case, the word refers to a basis for judgement, a principle, a standard or criterion.

Memory: Summing up a theme throughout much literature, American writer Henry Miller once called upon his readers to "remember to remember." He was thinking in particular of the human proclivity to "sweep things under the rug," to oversimplify and even sanitize history and the present. He was calling for general mindfulness. Memory refers to a firm knowledge of the subject matter, the context surrounding the writing. Clearly the canon of memory connects to the idea of ethos. Not all of the context around the essay can be directly included in the writing, of course, but when you research the topic yourself, do you sense that the writer has grasped the subject beyond the focus presented in the writing? Deciding if a piece of writing demonstrates memory usually draws significantly upon the evaluation stage of critical analysis: you must infer from certain statements and general tone whether the writer is expert in the world of the subject beyond his or her text. An important part of "memory," from the writer's perspective, is the question of knowing public beliefs on the topic (what Stephen Toulmin calls "warrants"). What assumptions seem to run through society and how do they connect to the particular discussion?

For example, in her essay "Non-Fiction Isn't Fact—Read with Care" (Reader, p. 485), Nina Varsava appears to "remember" (consider) that many us seem to believe that anything in print must be accurate, even as we also seem to believe that we are a society of independent-minded thinkers. In his essay "The Right Stuff," David Suzuki "remembers" (considers) that middle-class parents worry about their children's coming-of-age as a time when problems increase and communication decreases. These values or assumed beliefs may not be directly stated, but they are "remembered" by the writer, usually as a way to shape persuasions suited to the psychology of the audience. Memory is, in no small part, *audience* awareness as well as subject awareness.

Invention: By invention, the ancients meant the discovery of ideas and proofs. In other words, what type of *research* has the writer conducted and how specifically has the writer linked us to his or her sources of information and other methods of devising content? See Chapter 18, "Research Methods"; "Interviews" (at Chapter 18 on the Text Enrichment Site); and Chapter 19, "Documentation," for various methods of *invention*. In your study of a piece of writing, recognizing the kind of research that the writer conducted occurs in your analysis stage of critical analysis and evaluation. Deciding upon the apparent effectiveness or results of that kind of research represents the evaluation stage.

For example, in her process description of "College Girl to Call Girl" (see page 242), Valerie Desjardins notes that the writer, Sarah Schmidt, has conducted interviews but that she does not cite her sources of background studies and statistics; in contrast, more academic essays, such as "Beyond the Answers" (by Melanie Klingbeil, in Chapter 19, "Documentation") rigorously cite their sources. Desjardins does not go on to evaluate this possible shortcoming in "College Girl," but as a result of recognizing it, she did her own research to confirm that Schmidt's statistics concerning tuition hikes and off-street prostitution seemed to be accurate. If they had not been accurate, she would have dealt with that concern.

Disposition refers to order, arrangement, organization, forms, structure. This principle operates on the level of sentences, paragraphs, subsections, and the text as a whole. In our discussion of sentences in Chapter 2, we refer to the "Bermuda Triangle" of sentences, to the idea that information in the middle of sentences has less impact than words at the beginning and ending. Psychological studies have come to the same conclusion—people remember items at the beginning or the ending of a list. Performers at open stages or other variety shows often hope to be first or last in the line-up, in order to achieve more impact. In Chapter 2, we also ask you to compare the contrasting meanings expressed when a phrase like "kings and beggars" is reversed to "beggars and kings." The first form expresses the idea of literal kings who are spiritual beggars; the second expresses the idea of literal beggars who are spiritual kings. This is because terms that come last tend to modify or qualify those that come before them. Similar principles of impact and modification occur in terms of larger parts of a composition as well, of paragraphs, pages, and complete chapters or units.

While the meaning of disposition varies by culture, in Western approaches to writing, as we have seen, main ideas tend to be expressed in openings, especially in prominent places such as at the end of the opening. Breaking structure into discrete parts according to the development of new thoughts, proofs, and patterns of development through an essay (such as cause and effect, or comparison-contrast) can provide you with ways to move from analysis of parts to an evaluation of the intended purpose and meaning of those parts, as they function independently but also in unison with each other.

Style: Just as the concept of invention overlaps with that of memory, so the concept of style overlaps with that of disposition. By "style," the ancients referred primarily to the words chosen, whether formal or informal, general or technical, ironic or sincere, gentle or forceful. They referred to the tone that emerges from these choices, combined with choices made under disposition. Chapters 1 and 2 discuss words and their effects from various perspectives, including that of the history of English.

Effects of the Canons

Your reference to the four canons of memory, invention, disposition, and style will help you to isolate and thereby ponder the effects of each; this approach also allows you to consider writing as something of a musical composition, with different instruments at play, each contributing in its own way. After you have broken down the canons and considered each, you may often ask how the canons relate to each other in a way that serves, or perhaps fails to serve, the author's apparent intentions? Is there an inherent logic to the operation of the various canons throughout the whole? Thus you move from the analysis stage of identifying and defining the attributes of the canons to the evaluation stage of determining their efficacy and other effects.

Examples of Analysis and Evaluation Using the Four Canons

For a Stage 1 analysis of "College Girl to Call Girl," see Valerie Desjardins's process description on page 242. For her evaluation of Sarah Schmidt's intentions and degree of success, see " 'College Girl to Call Girl': Innocent Victims or Entrants in a Rat Race?" (Chapter 16, p. 258).

APPLYING THE CRITERIA OF A CERTAIN CRITIC

As we mentioned in Chapter 1 in discussing ethos, as a first-year student you understandably may view yourself as a junior researcher, not an expert; you may feel yourself limited in your ability to deliver an interesting, original interpretation, or to apply valid tools. While this self-doubt is likely exaggerated, applying ideas and criteria of another critic or group of critics can help get you started on your own analyses and assessments. This can also prove an excellent way to familiarize yourself with new theories or tools and to put them to the test.

Although we do not recommend excessive echoing of other critics, applying another's ideas *can* benefit even the most self-confident scholar. Needless to say, if the critic you select has presented particularly illuminating and important ideas, your exercise in applying and testing those (and the works they are meant to evaluate) can be highly rewarding. Well-known writers on writing include Linda Flowers, Peter Elbow, Natalie Goldberg, Annie Dillard, William Zinsser, and Wayne Booth. As you might imagine, a complete list of critics and rhetoricians worth your exploring (some in intriguing opposition to each other) would be far too long to include here. You will, however, find an essay by one representative of this field, Wayne Booth, in the Reader (p. 487).

PRACTICE

1. Read Wayne Booth's essay "The Rhetorical Stance" in the Reader (p. 487). Write a summary of its main points. Refer to the Text Enrichment Site for Chapter 13, "The Summary," for two sample summaries of this challenging essay. Once you are confident that you understand Booth's idea of three "corrupt stances," try to find one sample of each from various sources. Explain how each sample represents one of the three different corrupt stances. Discuss your evaluation with your instructor and classmates.

2. Read George Orwell's "Politics and the English Language" in the Reader (p. 471). Refer to the Text Enrichment Site for Chapter 13 , "The Summary," for two sample

summaries of this challenging essay. Once you are confident that you understand Orwell's central idea of what constitutes "bad" writing, try to find illustrations of it. Discuss your illustrations with your instructor and classmates.

3. Read Howard Richler's "The Seven Deadly Sins Are 'In' and Proud of It" in the Reader (p. 482). Identify his controlling idea and reason(s)—that is, his thesis. Then look for an example or two of writing that appears to illustrate the problem he identifies. Discuss your findings with your instructor and classmates.

APPLYING THE FOG INDEX

PhD in mathematics and professor emeritus at UCLA Robert Gunning authored the 1968 text *The Technique of Clear Writing* to promote readability. Gunning is best known, however, for the Fog Index, originally publicized through business publications such as the *Wall Street Journal*. As you will see, his system doesn't presume primarily to help us grasp meaning; its goal is to test and encourage clarity and ease of reading.

How to Use the Fog Index

1. From the writing you wish to analyze, take a passage of 100 words (or close to 100 words).

2. Count the number of sentences in the passage. You may count independent clauses that follow one another directly (i.e., after semicolons or colons or coordinating conjunctions followed by a comma).

3. Find the average number of words per sentence by dividing the number of words in your sample by the number of sentences.
4. Count the number of words (excluding proper nouns) of three syllables or more. Don't count verbs that reach three syllables by grammatical endings such as -es, -ed, or -ing. Exclude simple compounds like "shopkeeper."
5. Calculate the percentage of three-syllable words.
6. Add the average number of words per sentence to the percentage of three-syllable words.
7. Multiple the total by 0.4.
8. The resulting number is the years of formal schooling needed to easily read and understand the text from which your sample of writing has been taken.

✍ PRACTICE

Apply the Fog Index formula to the following two passages:

Passage 1—From "Brownie," Reader (p. 375)

One day I saw Brownie do something that shaped my view of animals forever. She saved my brother's life. It happened during cucumber-picking season when I was four years old. The whole family—my parents, six brothers, and one sister—had been out in the field all day working. Brownie had been watching over me and my nine-year-old brother, Ed, whenever he got tired of picking. By the time the sun was going down our Chevy flatbed was piled high with boxes of cucumbers. It was time to head home for dinner. Ed wanted to ride back on our older brother's bicycle, a big thing that he could barely control.

Passage 2—From "On Synchronicity," Reader (p. 426)

The result of the spatial experiment proves with tolerable certainty that the psyche can, to some extent, eliminate the space factor. The time experiment proves that the time factor (at any rate, in the dimension of the future) can become psychically relative. The experiment with dice proves that

moving bodies, too, can be influenced psychically—a result that could have been predicted from the psychic relativity of space and time.

The energy postulate shows itself to be inapplicable to the Rhine experiments, and thus rule out all ideas about the transmission of force. Equally, the law of causality does not hold—a fact that I pointed out thirty years ago. (Paragraphs 10–11)

Once you have the result, decide to what extent this formula seems to provide a reliable assessment of the readability of the two longer texts from which the passages have been taken. Is complexity a part of readability, and can a text be complex without scoring a high readability number according to the Fog Index?

When you have answered these questions, visit the Text Enrichment Site for Chapter 15, read our commentary on Passages 1 and 2, and read Kerry Li's essay "Quality or Quantity?" She applies the Fog Index to "On Synchronicity" and a short story by Bharati Mukherjee and discovers that the Jung essay has a much higher Fog Index than does the short story. Does this fact mean that the story is less complex than the academic essay?

Popular Uses of the Fog Index

For years, magazine editors have applied the Fog Index or similar readability measures to establish stylistic parameters for their publications. Writers hoping to place articles with various magazines would do well to study the Fog Index measure of the intended magazine. Without even reading your submission, an editor who adheres strictly to the Fog Index (and many do) will determine at a glance whether your manuscript deserves further consideration.

PRACTICE

Determine a Fog Index quotient for the following two essays: "A Liberal Education Is Key to a Civil Society" (Reader, p. 461) and "The Right Stuff" (Reader, p. 464). Also read George Orwell's essay "Politics and the English Language" (Reader, p. 471). You may then go to the Text Enrichment Site for Chapter 13, "The Summary," for two sample summaries of Orwell's challenging essay. Having followed these steps, answer the following questions:

1. To what extent does the Fog Index quotient for "A Liberal Education" and "The Right Stuff" add to your thinking about those essays? Explain.

2. In what ways does Orwell's essay support and/or oppose the apparent goals of the Fog Index? Explain.

3. Based on your use of the Fog Index to analyze "A Liberal Education" and "The Right Stuff," to what extent do you think it is a useful tool for rhetorical evaluation? Explain.

4. Discuss your answers with your instructor and classmates. Then read Colleen Leonard's essay "In Search of Clear Writing: A Use and Assessment of 'The Fog Index'" at the Text Enrichment Site for Chapter 15.

APPLYING THE METHODS OF LITERARY ANALYSIS

Rhetorical analysis commonly occurs in literary studies, as readers seek understanding through analysis and evaluation of words, sentences, patterns, and various literary devices. For an overview of specific tools used for literary analysis, see "Literary and Film Analysis" at the Text Enrichment Site for this chapter. Following are two sample essays of literary analysis—the first of a poem, the second of a song.

Analysis of a Poem

Percy Bysshe Shelley (1792–1822)—the husband of Mary Shelley, author of *Frankenstein*—remains a major voice of the British poetic tradition. Classified by literary critics as a Romantic, this poet is sometimes criticized for overly ornate language and fanciful ideas; but he is also recognized as a master craftsman, whose skills drew upon his remarkable dexterity in other languages. In keeping with the Romantic revolutionary consciousness, Shelley defied authority that he considered oppressive and was not afraid to question conventional beliefs and practices, even when the consequence was expulsion from Oxford University. The following much-anthologized poem tells of a certain tyrant and the ruins of a statue he had commanded be built to his greatness. Consider your own responses to this poem, then compare those to the literary analysis that follows.

Ozymandias
Percy Bysshe Shelley

I met a traveller from an antique land
Who said: Two vast and trunkless legs of stone
Stand in the desert. Near them, on the sand,
Half-sunk, a shattered visage lies, whose frown,
And wrinkled lip, and sneer of cold command,
Tell that its sculptor well those passions read
Which yet survive, stamped on these lifeless things,
The hand that mocked them and the heart that fed:
And on the pedestal these words appear:
"My name is Ozymandias, king of kings:
Look on my works, ye Mighty, and despair!"
Nothing beside remains. Round the decay
Of that colossal wreck, boundless and bare
The lone and level sands stretch far away.

(1818)

PRACTICE

Before reading the following analysis, consider how you would answer the following questions: what point of view does Shelley use in his poem, and what is the significance of that point of view? For a definition of point of view, see "Literary and Film Analysis" at the Text Enrichment Site for this chapter.

Sample Essay

Stone, Sand, and Syllables
A Legacy of Language in "Ozymandias"
Michael Lahey

Percy Bysshe Shelley's "Ozymandias" (1818) tells of a tyrant who has built a magnificent city and has then ordered a gigantic, domineering statue of himself to represent his achievement long after his death. This mighty statue, surviving for many years, possibly centuries, is now disintegrating in its last pieces in the indifferent desert. Although this poem seems to warn against the corrosiveness and emptiness of all vanity, even the vanity of conquerors who built ancient cities, the poem's underlying meaning is really much more ambiguous than such easy sermonizing. Rather than a straight-forward caution against arrogance, the poem—its title even—ironically shows how the legacy of Ozymandias still lives on, but not on his own imperious terms.

"Ozymandias" contains several illusions and reversals of presumption. The poem significantly opens with an important structural surprise—a speaker ("I") who immediately tells the reader that the entire poem is someone else's experience and observation: "I met a traveller from an antique land who said . . . " Usually, speakers (in poetry) and first-person narrators (in fiction) represent at least part of their own concerns, involvements and memories. Here, however, the speaker reports an experience second-hand: a poem about a random conversation about a stranger's experience. Despite the distancing effect of this frame narration (a speaker representing another speaker), the specific language of the poem that follows still makes readers feel as though they are present in this represented desert moment, the sand blowing back and forth. The fact is, however, the reader does not even know where this specific setting, this "antique land," is. Just as Ozymandias' boastful stone plaque commands people to "[l]ook on my works, ye Mighty, and despair," but points to nothing— to emptiness—the speaker's poem is only questionably there on its own terms. Instead, the poem is someone else's talk—either quoted or paraphrased or a dubious combination of the two—with only an uncertain degree or influence of the speaker's voice, the most important aspect, to comment on or conclude after the traveller's words.

Another quiet illusion of "Ozymandias" is that it supposedly reveals the folly of this despotic conqueror. Even though Ozymandias' great empire is gone, levelled by sand and wind, these last desert remnants of his presumed defeat to time and eternity still manage to stimulate the traveller to tell—and vividly—what he saw. Despite the nearly complete erosion of Ozymandias' architectural vision of himself, his legacy nonetheless lives on through the traveller's talk, then through this terse writing: this poem. The literary work entitled "Ozymandias," which has been published again and again internationally, thus contradicts its own apparent "lesson" or implication about the inevitable obliteration and insignificance of all people, whether powerful or powerless. The poem instead ensures that some people's words and deeds persist through history, as the tourist's sighting becomes the conversation that becomes literature. Since the poem replaces the statue, as language hardens into the permanence of writing, Ozymandias' memory survives, but not on the tyrant's original or forecasted terms.

Another significant complication about the nature of presumptions in "Ozymandias" occurs at the level of represented "voice," the source of any poem's literary language. Since Shelley's anonymous speaker is so quick to attribute the poem's language to the anonymous traveller, the reader must ask, exactly whose poem, whose language, is this? By the second line, the poem seems to become exclusively the traveller's expression rather than the speaker's. The punctuation of the colon conspicuously signals this shift—"[w]ho said: . . . " However, we can never be sure exactly how much of the poem emerges from the speaker's own language (when he either improvises from or perhaps loosely paraphrases the traveller) or the traveller's original language and specific imagery of the desert scene. In this tangled manner, the poem unfolds through a strange, slightly uneasy and uncertain co-authorship. In fact, "Ozymandias," despite its direct, clear, even deceptively simple language, exists as an indeterminate fusion of the words of not only *two* people (one person stating, but possibly embellishing and improving in eloquence what another has said), but *four* people, when the reader considers Ozymandias' own words quoted in the poem and originally "written" in stone by the obedient sculptor. While Ozymandias, the tyrant, was deeply invested in his sole ownership of territory, property, and achievement ("my works"), the poem that chronicles him has such an at once interlocked and diffuse authorship that it cannot be considered any one person's work or utterance, any one person's property.

Yet the most subtle reversal of presumption involves the undeniable reversal of power the poem performs. Power and authority move *from* the tyrant with his city, people, soldiers and resources *to* the sculptor with only his chisel and skill *to* the anonymous tourist *to* the speaker controlling through poetic writing the memory and meaning of Ozymandias' works and words. Notably, the speaker also shapes the several meanings involved in the act of writing about this Ozymandias: for instance, the meaning of collaborative writing, or of transforming history in its "messiness" into literature in its relative "neatness," or of offering a supposed lesson on colossal vanity even as that very lesson secures some cultural power and capital for the poet, Percy Bysshe Shelley. Shelley's famous poem, then, not only surprisingly affirms this dead tyrant's fantasy of historical immortality by representing him, but also—and arguably more powerfully—asserts its own immortality as a work of art, as authority shifts from tyrant to poet. Art, more than the immediacy of tyranny or even the longer crushing stretch of imperialism, shapes Ozymandias' persistence over time and precisely on an artist's terms. The poem's strongest irony (which can be defined as the distance between intentions and effects) is this reversal of power positions, where the formerly most dominate figure is now powerless to others' lasting representations.

For study questions on this essay, see the Text Enrichment Site.

Analysis of a Song

Songs, like poems, may provide fine subjects for rhetorical analysis, but choose carefully. You may wish to consider the interplay of the music with the words, or concentrate simply on the lyrics. If you choose to analyze a song lyric as an assignment in rhetorical analysis, check with your instructor first to be sure the subject seems sufficiently rich for the exercise. Song lyrics do not necessarily function successfully apart from their arrangements (or in some cases even with their arrangements).

PRACTICE

Imagine that you have been assigned to write a 1000-word essay on the following topic: "Does the Clash song 'The Card Cheat' serve or betray the spirit of punk? Explain."

To answer this question, you need to answer the following preliminary ones:

How is punk generally or commonly defined?
How does craft express theme in "The Card Cheat"?

Does theme in "The Card Cheat" accord with or further the spirit of punk?
Could or should this definition be somehow expanded or deepened?

Now see page 92 of Chapter 6 for Mark Simpson's song analysis in response to the above question.

EXPLAINING HOW AN EXCERPT RELATES TO A WORK AS A WHOLE

A common examination question in composition and literature classes, as well as in other courses in the humanities and liberal sciences, is to explain how a brief excerpt from an essay or other text relates to the work as a whole. Instructors often ask this question by presenting a list of excerpts from different course readings. They ask you to pick one of the excerpts, identify the reading from which it is taken, and then explain the significance of the excerpt to the reading as a whole. In this way they test whether you have familiarized yourself with the reading and also whether you understand how an essay works.

Definition of the Word "Excerpt"

An excerpt is a piece, a portion. It is a small part of a text lifted out of the text and reproduced. An excerpt may be presented with quotation marks around it to indicate that it is an exact reproduction of wording from another text, in other words, a quotation. This excerpt itself may or may not contain a quotation within it. Don't become confused if there is a quotation within the excerpt. Here is an example of an excerpt from "College Girl to Call Girl" (p. 457) as it might appear on an examination:

Sample excerpt from "College Girl to Call Girl"

"'You're looking at a very different kind of situation in the year 2000. Most people don't know what prostitution looks like. People have no clue,' says sex-trade researcher John Lowman, a professor of criminology at Simon Fraser University in Vancouver."

Reading the Excerpt Carefully—Understanding Quotation Marks

The first thing to realize is that in making up the examination, the instructor placed the usual double quotation marks around the excerpt to indicate that it is a direct word-for-word transcription from a text. Because the excerpt chosen also begins with an opening quotation mark indicating the exact words of Professor Lowman, quoted by Sarah Schmidt in her article, the instructor converts this double quotation mark into a single quotation mark. The reader sees the double quotation mark opening the excerpt followed by a single quotation mark and realizes that something has been quoted from somewhere else, and that the material being excerpted begins with a quotation. This is an example of how tiny punctuation marks provide crucial indications. Note that when Lowman's first quotation ends with the words "have no clue," the instructor making up the examination has reproduced the double quotation mark as a single quotation mark. This single quotation mark matches the single mark that indicated the start of Lowman's quoted statement. The words that follow are those of Sarah Schmidt, not John Lowman. These words end with "Vancouver."

Make sure you clearly understand what this assignment is asking you to do, and how the quotation marks provide clarity concerning whose words you are reading. Check with your instructor to ensure you understand the question as presented above. Then read on to follow our recommended steps in how to handle this assignment.

Steps in Preparing to Explain How an Excerpt Relates to the Work from Which It Has Been Taken

1. In the interests of care and thoroughness, fill in the checklist recommended for Stage 1 rhetorical analysis. This checklist covers the basic textual elements, principles, and relationships, and thereby helps you perform a preliminary identification of rhetorical parts.

    Who is the author and what biographical information is available?
    Where was the work published?
    What type of writing is this (investigative journalism, academic analysis, corporate persuasion, etc.)?
    Who is the intended audience?
    What various public beliefs exist on the topic?
    What various public beliefs existed on the topic at the time the piece was written?
    What is the author's purpose? (See the discussion on types of persuasive appeal in Chapter 16, p. 252.)
    What is the author's controlling idea?
    What are the author's reasons? (controlling idea + reasons = thesis)
    What specific methods of inquiry (research) have been used?
    Where do you think you could find more information about the subject matter discussed?
    What connections to the subject beyond the essay are included or implied?
    How has the reading been organized and what rhetorical strategies and patterns are featured throughout and in separate parts?
    What style and therefore tone does the reading use (kinds of words, lengths of sentences)?

    Step 2 is to write a process description of the essay. Step 3 is to write a summary of the essay. The process description draws upon the checklist, and the summary draws upon the process description.

2. Write or outline a short process description of the text that the excerpt comes from. Here is an illustration written by Valerie Desjardins.

    Outline—Process description of "College Girl"

    Investigative journalism; intended for general public audience; omits specific citations; unreferenced statistics—80 percent of prostitution is now off street and college tuition fees have risen 126 percent on average over nine years, both stats juxtaposed toward beginning; uses mostly examples—interviewees, four student prostitutes (one ex), escort service manager, police detective, novelist-researcher; main subject at beginning, middle and end is Stacy; Stacy shown by language, actions and comments by others to be self-deluding; outreach worker Bennett says toward end (impact location) that Stacy uses "rationalization"; John toward end (impact location) suggests the middle-class world is essentially one of imposed prostitution and denials; Lowman, sociology prof, suggests middle class is heavily into prostitution and denial (impact location at beginning where thesis of essay might be, after opening extended anecdote).

The details in your carefully observed process description (analysis of rhetoric) will assist you to finalize your summary of the main claim and supporting ideas of the reading as well as to be able to identify the excerpt as a specific form of rhetoric with a specific purpose related to the main purpose and to the thesis of the reading.

3.   Write or outline a short summary of the text that the excerpt comes from. (See Chapter 13 for more on writing a summary.)

> **Outline summary of "College Girl"**
>
> Thesis (main claim): (Controlling idea) Discreet off-street prostitution is significantly on the rise, (reasons) because middle-class students, confronted by rising costs and other pressures on the middle class, have entered the business.
>
> Supporting forms of evidence: Student prostitutes, sociologists, police officers, outreach workers, and other investigators into the issue all confirm the thesis. Statistics show off-street prostitution dominates the trade and college fees have risen by 126 percent.
>
> Assumed public attitude: The middle-class public in general denies or ignores this activity.
>
> Backing for assumed public attitude: Student prostitutes maintain appearances of not being prostitutes and apply rationalizations suggesting they are not doing anything wrong and that middle-class life is fine, as always.

> The summary sketches the main claims and supporting ideas. Your goal in explaining how an excerpt relates to the reading as a whole is essentially to show how the excerpt serves or furthers the purpose and thesis of the reading.

Preparing for an Examination

Many examination questions asking you to explain how an excerpt relates to a reading are not "open book." In other words, you have to come to the examination having already worked through the recommended three steps of checklist, process description, and summary at home. The summary and process description are short in order to focus you on precise answers as well as to help you remember the outstanding issues. Unless you have a photographic memory (and most of us don't), you need to boil the reading down to the key ideas and rhetorical details—the ones that will most likely be presented by or required through the excerpt.

Recognizing the Excerpt and Its Role

The first thing to ask yourself when you see the excerpt that comes from the reading is whether the excerpt is the thesis of the reading. Think of the thesis as the tallest tree in the forest. You feel a little lost, so to get your bearings you look for the tallest tree. In preparing for this exercise, you have written out the thesis (in your own words) and memorized it. If the excerpt from the reading does not appear to be the thesis, ask yourself what relationship it has to the thesis by placing it into one of the following three general categories:

1. A supporting idea (a major or minor premise in a syllogism, or a Toulmin warrant or backing for a warrant, or some idea similarly needed to give support to the controlling idea)
2. A tool of reasoning, explanation, intensification, or illustration (for example, an analogy, a figure of speech used to convey a certain conclusion that somehow supports the thesis, and so forth)
3. Evidence (the words of an authority, an example such as a character description or anecdote, data from some source, other detailed forms of proof)

Once you have chosen one of these three categories for the excerpt, be as specific as you can about the nature of the excerpt within that category and then ask yourself *where* the excerpt occurs. Place it in one of the following areas:

Introduction
Body (be as specific about where in the body as you can)
Conclusion

Chapter 7 of this text provides information on characteristics and functions of openings and conclusions. Chapter 4 covers basic features of paragraphs, and Chapter 10 reviews basic organizational forms used within body sections of readings. Information in those chapters will help you to see how an excerpt may be reflective of the words immediately surrounding it as well as of the reading as a whole. Note that the main point made by the student in the following sample excerpt relationship is how the excerpt relates to the thesis of the reading.

✒ PRACTICE

Here is a question you might find on an examination:

> "Identify which of the following excerpts comes from the reading 'College to Call Girl' and explain how the excerpt relates to the essay as a whole."

You might then be given a list of excerpts from different readings, each excerpt identified by a letter. Let's assume that the "College Girl" excerpt provided on page 241 is identified by the letter "d":

d) "'You're looking at a very different kind of situation in the year 2000. Most people don't know what prostitution looks like. People have no clue,' says sex-trade researcher John Lowman, a professor of criminology at Simon Fraser University in Vancouver."

If you haven't already done so, read the essay "College Girl to Call Girl" (Reader, p. 457) and write out your answer in one solid paragraph.

Some instructors might give you the choice to come prepared knowing one of several readings and allow you to choose the excerpt from the reading you wish to deal with. Other instructors might want you to be prepared to explain excerpts from several course readings. This question may be presented in various ways, but the underlying skills needed are the same.

Here is how you might answer the question in the Practice activity box, drawing upon the information you prepared for yourself in your checklist, process description, and summary preparations. Instructors usually request a short answer to this question, one solid paragraph. So you need to identify the relationship as *precisely* as you can.

Sample explanation of an excerpt relationship

Excerpt "d" comes from Sarah Schmidt's article of investigative journalism "College Girl to Call Girl," originally published in the Toronto *Globe and Mail*. This excerpt sets up the main claim of the article: that discreet off-street prostitution is significantly on the rise because middle-class students, confronted by rising costs and other pressures on the middle class, have entered the business. Professor Lowman's quoted words appear in a location of high impact near the opening, right after a lengthy character description of Stacy. Stacy is depicted as going about her typical moonlighting "business" as an off-street prostitute. Further descriptions of Stacy use words like "scores," suggesting that she is in essence a prostitute like any other, even though she is a middle-class student dressed like a middle-class student. Relying on interviews with student prostitutes, professors of criminology, and others connected to the field, Schmidt states that tuition fees have risen on average by 126 percent over nine years and that 80 percent of Canada's sex trade comprises off-street activity. Right after telling Schmidt that "[m]ost people don't know what prostitution looks like," Lowman goes on to say, "What we have is a <u>class-based</u> system of prostitution" (my underlining). This article implicitly argues the thesis stated above, supported by the investigative evidence of numerous interview subjects and an understood attitude that the middle-class public in general denies or ignores this activity. Quotation "d" drives home the actual situation—what is happening and what is denied—and thus prepares us to discover or infer reasons why this is happening and why it is denied. Because Schmidt uses detached third person, typical of investigative reporting, she does not state her own opinion. That of Professor Lowman, an authority quoted in a place of high impact, therefore carries especial weight.

(295 words)

✒ PRACTICE

Reread the preceding sample explanation of an excerpt relationship by Valerie Desjardins. Answer the following question:

Is there a topic sentence in this paragraph, one sentence that essentially answers the question?

We suggest that the essential answer does appear in one topic sentence. In this case, the topic sentence is the *second* sentence of the paragraph because the writer chose to use the opening sentence to identify where the excerpt appears. Some writers might subordinate the information in the first sentence within a longer opening topic sentence:

> Excerpt "d," which comes from Sarah Schmidt's article of investigative journalism "College Girl to Call Girl," originally published in the Toronto *Globe and Mail*, sets up the main claim of the article: that discreet off-street prostitution is significantly on the rise because middle-class students, confronted by rising costs and other pressures on the middle class, have entered the business.

If Desjardins had written either of these topic sentences and nothing else, she would deserve several marks for this section, as this explanation is so concise and specific. The other parts of the first paragraph are dedicated to expanding on this basic insight. Note that Desjardins has carefully shaped the paragraph according to the advice in Chapter 4 and has ended by reinforcing why the excerpt is important. The paragraph is about the excerpt, not about the essay in some general or vague sense. To answer this sort of question well, you have to have analyzed the reading with the thorough understanding that an essay is a process involving the operation and cooperation of various parts.

For further practice in this admittedly difficult and demanding skill, here are two more practice activities.

PRACTICE

Read the essay "Life in the Stopwatch Lane" (Reader, p. 451). See if you can explain in 150 to 200 words how the following excerpt from this reading relates to the essay as a whole.

c) "Time was, before the advent of car phones and digital clocks, we scheduled two kinds of time: time off and work hours. Not any more."

Student Explanation of the Above Excerpt

Nancy Corscadden wrote the following answer to the above excerpt on an Athabasca University composition examination in 2002. Corscadden did not have access to the reading during her invigilated exam, and time was limited.

Examination answer by Nancy Corscadden

In her wry classification essay, Amy Willard Cross identifies a new social group: the Busy Class. Members of the Busy Class are characterized by their complaint "I'm *soooo* busy," by their desire for expensive stuff, and by their penchant to divide time into smaller and smaller units. Excerpt "c" above ties these three features of the Busy Class into one bundle. Informal words and short, snappy phrasing relate to the short bursts of activity common to the Busy Class. Car phones and digital clocks represent the "expensive stuff" this class wishes to acquire.

Willard Cross anticipates further divisions of time by identifying the crude, by-gone classification of "time off and work hours." Her essay then goes on to list six categories the Busy Class has invented to demonstrate its concern for the importance of time off. The excerpt, thus, is an excellent introduction to Willard-Cross's thesis about ourselves in consumerist society: ironically, the more we invent intricate terms to describe our relationships apart from work, the less attention we pay to anything but making and spending money.

Commentary

Corscadden's answer draws from the elements of a concise process description and summary. She begins by observing that the tone of the essay is "wry" (ironic, tongue-in-cheek, playful). Willard-Cross combines a playful approach with the academic's interest in categories. Behind the classification approach, she is really concerned with a cause-effect relationship: what motivates busy people to subdivide time, especially time off work? As Corscadden observes, the excerpt anticipates the answer to this question (the thesis) by implying that addiction to consumerism has divided and isolated the human psyche. The apt quotation "I'm *soooo* busy" speaks to the unease and posturing underlying our actual attitude to time off. We know that personal time is an endangered species; we aren't about to do anything truly significant to stop that trend.

✒ PRACTICE

Read the essay "The Ways of Meeting Oppression," Chapter 10 (p. 144). See if you can explain in 250 to 300 words how the following excerpt from this reading relates to the essay as a whole.

a) "A second way that oppressed people sometimes deal with oppression is to resort to violence and corroding hatred."

Student Explanation of the Above Excerpt

The following answer to excerpt "a" above was written by Bernadette Cymbaluk on her mid-term examination at Blue Quills First Nations College in February 2006. Students could not look at the essay; they had to know it well going into the exam, and they had limited time in which to complete the response.

Examination answer by Bernadette Cymbaluk

Quotation "a" comes from Martin Luther King's essay "The Ways of Meeting Oppression." King argues that resorting to hatred and brutality is only a temporary, ineffective means of responding to mistreatment. He further argues that violence is impractical because it results in destruction for parties on both sides. It is also im-moral because it demeans the human race; violence seeks to "annihilate" rather than correct. In using violence as a tool against injustice, African-Americans consign their future generations to a legacy of chaos, loneliness, and bitterness. King argues that this is not the way.

In addition to hatred and violence, King explains, there are two other means of meeting oppression: consent and peaceful resistance. Living under the veil of injustice serves to wear on the spirit of the oppressed; eventually their lives are engulfed in "negative freedom and resignation." King argues that to cooperate with an unjust system is as evil as the act of oppression itself. Moreover, the African-American does not gain the respect of people everywhere by acquiescing to the way of the coward. King argues that the third and preferred way of dealing with oppression is peaceful resistance. African-Americans must embrace this method if they are to transcend racial injustice. In taking this path, they will find honour and their rightful place in society. They must meet their oppressor with unbending strength and courage.

King's essay uses classification-division as its structure. Its thesis is there are three ways of meeting oppression: acquiescence, violence and hatred, and peaceful resistance. Excerpt "a" gives strong support to King's main point; it elaborates on the second way, the method of hatred and brutality. The excerpt points to historical evidence, in that section of the essay, that countries engaging in violence have gained nothing but destruction itself.

(300 words)

Commentary on Bernadette Cymbaluk's Answer

Notice that Cymbaluk repeats the verb "argues" in describing the process of this essay. Chapter 13, "The Summary," recommends that you find precise verbs to convey, often in a single word, the rhetorical purpose and strategy of the essay being summarized.

Note that Cymbaluk has memorized and quoted from the essay words not repeated in the excerpt itself.

Cymbaluk does not give quite as much attention to rhetorical methods in her answer as we find in the previous excerpt relationship dealing with "College Girl." Given that King's essay is more direct and explicit than Schmidt's, Cymbaluk's greater attention to summarizing ideas and lessened attention to rhetorical methods make sense.

FINAL WORD

As we have seen, this ability to identify the role of an excerpt in relation to the overall meaning of the reading to which it belongs draws on summarization and rhetorical process description. Understanding what is said, especially in more ironic and sarcastic forms, requires drawing inferences from the figurative meanings of words and images, recognizing how tone contributes to meaning. This requires you to use your judgement about what the author is really saying—not the same thing as using your judgement to evaluate the reliability or merit of what the author is saying (which is the evaluative stage of critical thinking). Explaining how an excerpt relates to the whole is *not* an exercise in the evaluation stage of critical thinking. It *is* an exercise in summarizing skills and the analyzing skills involved in the first stage of critical thinking—breaking down subjects into their constituent parts and recognizing relationships between those parts.

Chapter 16
Argumentation

Like the words "critical evaluation" (see Chapter 14), the word "argument" as used in rhetoric does not designate what we think when we hear the word in typical daily conversation. When we hear someone say, "They are having an argument," we picture an emotional battle, a desire to get one's way, perhaps at the expense of fairness and consideration. "What's wrong with them?" we ask, noticing that a couple are no longer speaking to each other. "They had an argument," someone says. The word in daily usage suggests something that ends in bitterness and isolation. In rhetoric, however, the word refers to presenting one's carefully considered view—a view intended in most cases to be beneficial to all—in a way that considers others; one's goal is the opposite of bitterness and isolation—rather it is deepened awareness and possibly new thinking or even desired action taken on the part of your audience or reader.

A SUBCATEGORY OF PERSUASION

Argumentation is a subcategory in the large domain of communication known as persuasion. All forms of **persuasion** attempt to sway an audience to think or act a certain way. In the broadest and most basic sense, *all* writing is persuasive in seeking to convince us of its integrity. All successful authors persuade us of their ethos (see Chapter 1). A good personal essay, for example, persuades us that the writer really knows and in some way understands the place or experience being described. A fictionalized memoir such as "The Hockey Sweater" (p. 387) may not explicitly appeal to logos, but there is a compelling soundness in the effects—in certain conclusions—that the memoir stirs in the reader. The story appeals to emotions and ethics, but there is a world of logos under its surface. It implies various arguments, counterarguments, proofs, and the like. If we "believe" the story, even though we know it is partly made up, if we accept its implied thesis or theme, it is persuasive. In the study of communication and writing, however, the term "persuasion" most often refers specifically to appeals made by promoters or exponents seeking, for whatever reasons, in whatever contexts, to change thinking or behaviour related to a particular topic, often one of considerable controversy or choice.

Deciding *How Far* to Try to Influence Your Reader

Most persuasions focus, in general, on one of three possible goals:

- an increase of awareness (which may lead, naturally, to a change of attitude)
- a change of attitude (new way of thinking about a topic)
- a change of behaviour (new action[s] adopted)

These goals are sometimes said to entail differing levels of persuasion, with the first goal aiming for the lowest level of change and the third goal aiming for the highest. Clearly, all three goals will incorporate considerable awareness of the others. These three levels offer choices in answer to the important question, "How far should I try to influence my reader in this particular communication?"

Deciding *How* to Pursue Your Goal

Advertisers often pursue their goal of selling products or services through card-stacking (lying, omitting or evading facts, underplaying or overemphasizing issues, and so on). Propagandists seek to influence political decisions by similar marginalizing of logic and fairness. Argumentation, on the other hand, strives to persuade its reader through appeals that respect the full range of reasoning on the debate or controversy. One of the earliest known classical rhetoricians (Gorgias, BCE 483–375) maintained that while a seemingly weak argument could be shown to be stronger than a seemingly strong one, the orator (unlike today's advertisers or propagandists) had a duty to refute the other arguments, explicitly. While confident in its own view, argumentation features a moderate, respectful tone that recognizes opposing views. Recognizing those opposing views, argumentation aims to change thinking and often to promote a certain action. Its goal is persuasive, but it "plays fair." When you decide on argumentation over more biased forms, you consider the attributes and benefits that we discuss next.

MAIN ATTRIBUTES OF ARGUMENTATION

We sometimes use the term "formal" to define argumentation for reasons primarily related to the *occasion*. As Wayne Booth reminds us in his essay "The Rhetorical Stance" (p. 487), writing to persuade demands careful consideration of how the reader will react to how the ideas are expressed as well as to what they are. When you write an argument, you must imagine a reader opposed to your ideas. How can you change that person's awareness, thinking, or even behaviour? How you shape your discussion to introduce your view through well-timed appeals to the reader, how you choose words to avoid "loaded" language—these matters of "form" are critical.

In addition, argumentation developed from a tradition of oral speeches, often delivered under formal, even ceremonial, circumstances. Protocols (matters of social form) needed to be observed. Issues of social and political importance to many people often figured in these addresses. A formal argument is normally intended for many eyes and levels of officialdom. The style of your formal argument should consider multiple readers in various formalized circumstances. Tone and structure will therefore reflect a sense of characteristics suiting the public culture of ceremony, protocol, tact, and so on. Consult the tones chart on the inside back cover of this text and you will find that a formal level "assumes a higher level of education," uses explicit structure, and reflects "complex content organized by clear patterns." Such tones, as the chart further indicates, rely on data and logical formulations.

Benefits of Mastering Argumentation

Your command of argumentative methods will help you as a researcher to analyze your sources by identifying and evaluating basic elements of persuasions being made. Command of argumentative methods will also help you as a writer to test and critique your own arguments. Furthermore, many people regard the will and ability to handle even-handed argument to be the lifeblood of political freedom as defined by Western-style democracy. We might further suggest that this will and ability are especially important for Canada, a country of vast geography, pronounced regional differences, and necessary compromise.

How to Be Sure You Meet the Expectations of Argumentation

How do you go about developing an essay that meets the requirements of argumentation? Observe the following guidelines:

- Be sure your topic involves a strong controversy on which opinion is divided or on which the majority support a view opposed to yours.
- Identify a public occasion for which your essay will be used (instigating circumstances, audience, forum).
- Address readers whose views offer significant opposition to yours.
- Decide how far you can go in pushing readers to a call for action. Is it wisest simply to promote a new awareness or to take the extra step of specifying action to be taken? Try to push for as strong and specific a reader response as you think you can command.
- Consult compelling sources on the opposed side of the debate as well as sources that support your view (balance sources for and against in your list of references).
- Construct a tone that is fair-minded, respectful, moderate, and yet firmly persuasive.
- Appeal to ethos, pathos, and logos; however, be sure that logos operates effectively throughout.
- Adapt your voice to the features of formal style noted in the formal column of the tones chart on the inside back cover of this text.

- Follow the steps for analysis and evaluation (Chapter 14) and also apply one of the following four models for formal argumentation or a hybrid model that you and your instructor agree will suit the subject and occasion proposed for your essay.
- Be specific about the circumstances and purpose. Fill in the following form:

> Location of presentation or name of publication:
>
> Nature of audience—size, demographics, attitudes on the topic:
>
> Purpose of presentation or category of publication (e.g., letter to editor, editorial, feature article, etc.):
>
> Objective (for instance, "influence at least 25 percent of audience to . . . "):

An important part of defining your objective is deciding whether you should aim for a change of knowledge, a change of thinking, or a change of action. What results do you hope will follow from the change? Be as specific as possible. You may wish to shape your argumentation as an oral address (see Chapter 20). Thinking and writing in terms of oral presentations can be a useful way to remember that you are communicating; this helps you to recognize that the psychology of your readers or listeners is every bit as important to success as the more literary attributes of your work.

MODELS OF ARGUMENTATION

We offer the following four models:

- concession-refutation
- Toulmin's claim, support, and warrant
- Monroe's motivated sequence
- Rogerian conciliation

Concession-Refutation

A major emphasis in what the ancients called rhetoric and dialectic was placed upon recognizing (or conceding) arguments on the opposite side. In her essay "Should Cats Be Allowed to Roam?" (Chapter 6), Joyce Miller begins, "Many people believe that . . . " She concedes that there are compelling reasons to allow cats to roam; however, she goes on to name three undesirable effects of this roaming for the animals themselves. (The critical inquiry demanded of argumentation relies considerably on logical scrutiny of causes and effects, so it would be useful to review Chapter 10 [p. 140] in conjunction with your study of argumentative models.) Opening with what "some people think" or "most people think" occurs as well in Gwen Kelley's response to the Kyoto Accord (Chapter 14) and George Orwell's "Politics and the English Language" (Reader, p. 471). In all three of these named examples, the writers concede to the opposition in their introduction but then, as controlling idea, state a refutation. In different ways, the rest of their essay implies a continued dialogue with the view conceded, of course, arguing reasons for the view stated in the thesis. Deductive thesis placement can alienate opposed readers, but you, your classmates, and your instructor might think of occasions in which a concession followed by a deductive thesis and then by arguments supporting the refutation might work well as a persuasive tactic.

In any case, opening with a concession-refutation paragraph fulfills an important persuasive principle: the need to assure your reader that you are aware of other views and respect those views. Such an opening illustrates that you have put effort into your inquiry and given fair consideration to opposed views. Your intentions are serious and thoughtful. This alone may not win over readers opposed to your view, but it will help things off to a better start than would an immediate statement of your position. Now, to sharpen your skills in shaping concession-refutation, study the following examples and commentary.

Concession

In reports, research papers, and analytical as well as persuasive essays, you must sometimes concede a valid point or two against your own argument to establish credibility with your reader. Your argument or perspective may well be mostly valid or convincing, but sometimes a strong indisputable counterpoint still exists and therefore must be recognized—conceded. Gorgias (483–375 BCE) boasted that a counterpoint always exists and can be made the strongest argument, if you are clever enough to make it so.

Here are two short examples of concession followed by refutation:

Higher education is certainly helpful in any business career. Textbook learning, however, can never replace common sense, self-confidence, and good judgement, especially in the often rapid world of business developments.

Although The Rolling Stones were originally seen as great innovators in the spread of popular rock 'n' roll, their music over the last three decades has contributed only to their bank accounts, not to new ideas or new musicianship. They are essentially a nostalgia act.

Sometimes a longer concession is necessary. You may need to deal with opposing evidence in more detail. Whether your concession is brief or requires its own paragraph, be fair with these opposing points (never superficially dismissive), but also strategic to manage your argument effectively. You can fully concede an opposing point or fact, but then minimize its significance so your argument or analysis can develop unobstructed.

Here is a further example of concession followed by refutation:

Although much rap music glorifies violence, mindless materialism, and subjugation of women, rap's linguistic resourcefulness and representations of the dangers and despair of the urban underclasses still offer great social and artistic value. In fact, rap's negative aspects are part of the dangers and despair this music depicts.

By making a concession or two to some valid points that oppose your argument or view, you also avoid falling into some possible logical fallacies: hasty generalizations, false either-or divisions, or bandwagon appeals. (See the section on logical fallacies in Chapter 3.)

Let's say, for example, you want to argue that sports indisputably build strong character. You are ready to discuss numerous examples drawing on high school scenarios, inner-city transcendence, college scholarships, strict coaches as wise mentors, and physical training as a socially admirable form of self-knowledge and self-control. You must nonetheless address, even if only briefly, the far less inspiring fact that many amateur, college, and professional athletes often make headlines for their complete *lack* of character: whether for criminal convictions against professional football, hockey, and basketball players, for proven doping by Olympians and their coaches, or even for sexual assault. Furthermore, if you were to try to argue—by overgeneralizing—that sports "indisputably" build strong character, how can you credibly ignore or blithely dismiss certain actions by boxing's Mike Tyson, figure-skating's Tonya Harding, or hockey's Todd Bertuzzi?

It would be better to manage your necessary concession here as follows:

Even though, as Brigid O'Shaunessey points out, sports success "sometimes misleads a few athletes (at all levels) into dangerous delusions of vanity, invincibility or unaccountability" (29), the overwhelmingly positive effect of sports on the character of a majority of youths is not in dispute. Sports activity generally generates physical, emotional, and social health.

Several mediocre, semi-famous, and famous athletes have sometimes made the news for ridiculous, even criminal, activity over the years. Nonetheless, sports still offer proven ways for the average young person to build strong character through effort, responsibility, cooperation, improvisation, and self-reliance.

Once acknowledged, concessions allow you to conduct your argument effectively, fairly, and unobstructed.

Refutation

To "refute" means to disprove someone's analysis, opinion, or findings. An argument, analysis, or report may be refuted with a better, more thorough, or more accurate counter-argument or, just as often, with a valid observation not considered in the original writer's claims.

Here are some examples of refutation:

Although Mick Shrimpton asserts that technology has "far outpaced our legal system's ability to control it" (82), he has failed to consider that legions of legislators, ethicists, and activists constantly devise new laws and regulations to govern technology's developments and effects. Though Shrimpton is correct that the law lags behind technology's advancements, the legal system is neither helpless nor static.

Helen Collins, representing the South Bay Environmental Foundation, wrongly claims that the giant sea squid is "one of the rarest sea creatures" (67). International oceanographers and fishermen, in fact, often find the strange beaks and remains of these giant creatures, and sometimes more than one, in the bellies of whales. Collins is likely confusing the rarity of a human actually seeing these extremely deep ocean creatures with a presumption of their scarcity.

If a particular writer has manipulated statistics or offered only partial facts or neglected proper context, such misleading or incomplete aspects can and should be successfully challenged—refuted.

Here is another example along these lines:

Claim	The death penalty lowers the risk of violent crime; every nation should therefore allow such executions.
Refutation 1	According to Jolene Durden, no statistics "have ever reliably established that the death penalty acts as a deterrent for other prospective criminals" (34). Considering the nature of death penalty crimes, which are either psychotically violent, deeply asocial, or catastrophically evident of complete loss of self-control, one quickly sees that the perpetrator may never even consider the concept of such a deterrent. The death penalty, then, may more accurately be defined as society's revenge against a single violent criminal rather than any widespread deterrent.
Refutation 2	In some U.S. cases, according to Eloise Mennier, once a violent perpetrator realizes himself guilty of a death penalty crime, "his crimes continue and even escalate because he knows he can be executed only once" (82).

In these two preceding refutations, critics (secondary sources) help to bolster the counter-argument and prove the original claim wrong, short-sighted, or skewed.

Both concession and refutation will make your essays, research papers, and reports more thorough, mature, and fair. You should also think of concession and refutation as part of your writer's duty to address the necessity and challenges of accuracy.

As we have shown in these examples, a concession can be handled so that it does not weaken or undermine your own argument and view. A refutation can be constructed either through your own opinion and experience or with the help of external information (an expert's view or factual information).

Remember that a refutation is a solid *disproving*, not only another view or another interpretation. The following three examples illustrate the differences among statements of opinion, analysis, and refutation:

Opinion	Sue likes the Beatles, but I like the Bangles more.
Analysis	Many critics and fans overlook the serious tension in some of Springsteen's music between vigorous expression and sombre, even despairing, content.

Refutation   When Riley Murphy claims that no important films ever emerge from Canada, he reveals absolutely no awareness of the work of Atom Egoyan, Denys Arcand, and David Cronenberg.

Comparison-Contrast Model Blending Concession-Refutation and Critical Analysis

As our look at concession-refutation suggests, classical rhetoric essentially advocates a comparison-contrast approach (see Chapter 12), balancing examination and refutation of the opposing side with examination and endorsement of one's own side. Based on his study of classical argumentative texts, composition professor John Thompson provides the following model for formal argumentation:

1. My opponent says A is true (briefly allude to the reasons—concession).
2. A is not true; B is true for these reasons (summarize them—refutation).
3. Elaborate on the reasons for believing A is not true (refutation).
4. Elaborate on the reasons for believing B is true (refutation).
5. State final implications and reflections, perhaps even a call to action.

Depending on the length of your essay, steps 1 and 2 above can be placed in the introductory paragraph. Step 2 is the thesis statement (see Chapter 6), and may be phrased, eventually, as one complete sentence. Step 3 could be covered in one paragraph. Step 4—representing the essence of your argument—might take two paragraphs, leaving a fifth and final paragraph for Step 5. Note that steps 3 and 4 as outlined above represent **block style** in comparison-contrast essays. Alternatively, you could handle steps 3 and 4 in **point-by-point style**, interweaving them into paragraphs focused on *reasons* rather than on which side of the argument is in question. If the reasons given by A and B are essentially opposite views of the same topic (French immersion places a person between two languages, which is a good thing, as opposed to French immersion places a person between two languages, which is a bad thing), then you might decide that point-by-point structure is the better choice. This choice would help you avoid repetition more effectively than the block approach would. Here is how the same argument model would look in point-by-point arrangement:

Reason 1	A's position
	B's position
Reason 2	A's position
	B's position
Reason 3	A's position
	B's position

Find the comparative pattern that most avoids repetition, yet maintains equal consideration of the two sides. Remember to acknowledge the good points and reasoning on the side you are opposing; express a tone of fairness and respect even as you stress the reasons for your final position.

With its deductive thesis coming as the second point (in the first or second paragraph), Professor Thompson's model might suit a number of "hybrid" situations—that is, academic or literary occasions requiring considerable attention to critical analysis combined with persuasion. This model might suit occasions that do not involve an effort to incite action or confront highly emotional resistance, but deal with matters of logos, such as critical responses to books or essays. The following essay illustrates content, tone, and structure in the formal argumentative model proposed by Professor Thompson according to classical example. See Valerie Desjardins's process analysis of the essay "College Girl to Call Girl" in the Text Enrichment Site, Chapter 15. Desjardins was asked to develop her process analysis into the following critical response according to Professor Thompson's classical model for argument.

Sample Essay

"College Girl to Call Girl": Innocent Victims or Entrants in a Rat Race?
Valerie Desjardins

My opponent says A is true.

1   According to at least three people in our discussion group, Sarah Schmidt's article "College Girl to Call Girl" adopts a posture of journalistic detachment but really expresses the ideological view that prostitution is acceptable because its practitioners are forced into it, through no fault of their own. Certainly the article entices us to conclude that financial need has driven students to the world's so-called oldest profession because fees are said to have risen by 126 percent while "[o]ff-street prostitution has experienced a similar explosion" (para. 8). However, I think that Schmidt simply wishes to report that many student prostitutes themselves claim they have been driven to prostitution by the high cost of education. Far from condoning these students behind a mask of detachment, Schmidt is rather obvious at times in her almost snide suggestions that these students exemplify middle-class people in crisis, desperately redefining morality in order to keep up with the traditional yet unquestioned requirements of middle-class status.

A parenthetical citation with paragraph number helps the reader to place the reference.

A is not true; B is true for these reasons.

A is not true, for these reasons.

2   Why are my discussion group members misguided to conclude that Schmidt sees the student prostitutes as entirely innocent? To begin with, Schmidt herself never says that she thinks university fees have forced students into prostitution. When I pointed this out, my group-mates counter-argued that a 126 percent increase in fees is so immoral that it must be intended as sufficient evidence of the student prostitutes as innocent victims. Yet these same critics themselves believe that the student prostitutes should work hard at legal jobs and adopt other morally acceptable steps toward their goals, such as registering for distance programs part time and adopting patience. I agree with this myself. I asked my discussion group members, again, why they believe Schmidt does not appear to share our ethics. My group-mates admitted that Schmidt does not state explicit acceptance of the innocence argument by the student prostitutes but challenged me to show where she states explicit refutation. My answer was and is that although the author (like Shakespeare in his plays) does not directly state her personal opinion anywhere in the article, her rhetorical methods overwhelmingly suggest that she dismisses the student prostitute argument as social hypocrisy.

B is true for these reasons.

3   Examining Schmidt's methods according to the first classical canon of inquiry, we find that she has consulted a wide range of interviewees: four student prostitutes (one an ex-prostitute) as well as two professors, an escort service manager, a police detective, an outreach worker, and a novelist-researcher. Her interviewees are represented as endorsing the claim that within the increase of middle-class prostitution, more and more students see it as a way to cope with the "lean" years while working toward a "respectable" future. But only the students themselves claim that they are innocent victims. Presumably Schmidt consulted this range of people in order to uncover a range of ideas and thus encourage us to weigh various arguments. Is her presentation of the different views impartial?

Reason for believing B: classical canon of inquiry

4   If we examine the classical canon of disposition, we find that Schmidt has shaped her presentation to the disadvantage of the student prostitutes' argument. Disposition refers to organization of ideas, to structure. Openings and closings are powerful positions. The essay opens and closes with Stacy, placing considerable weight on her as the student prostitute representative. She is not a reliable figure for such an important position, as we will see further with reference to the canon of style. Continuing for now with an examination of structure, paragraph 6 also represents a powerful location. It is here that Schmidt moves from her opening descriptions of Stacy to another source, John Lowman, professor of criminology. His main point on the topic is that contrary to popular belief, we have a "class-based system of prostitution." Far from saying that student prostitutes are innocent, he suggests that they are (perhaps undeservedly) party to privileges denied to others. While Lowman's statement cannot be taken as Schmidt's, the author has chosen to place it right where her own thesis might appear in traditional essay structure. Furthermore, in organizing her interviewees, she has left John to the last, adding power to his statements. John's statements, in turn, link us to the classical canon of memory in a way that furthers a concern with social hypocrisy.

Reasons for believing B: classical canon of disposition

5   The classical canon of memory refers to awareness of the subject, to connections beyond the examples under our immediate gaze. John's references raise awareness that morality is not black-and-white, that life in general is a rat race. He implies that his father made choices that could be likened to those of a prostitute, placing business success over people and ethics. Through this strong positioning of John in the line-up of sources, Schmidt invites us to link the matter of student prostitutes to the bigger picture, outside the article, to the general rat race. A question is embedded in this positioning, further emphasized by John's bitterness and disillusion: if we seek to win by the rat race, can we wash our hands of it?

Reason for believing B: classical canon of memory

6   Returning to Stacy, we find someone who does wish to benefit by one thing and then wash her hands of it. Paragraph 25 summarizes Stacy's opinion that there is "a difference" between her and street prostitutes. She admits to not liking the work or her "customers," but feels she is superior to street prostitutes because, as she says, "I portray myself with a level of respect." In other words, not what one does but what one "portrays" is what matters. This sounds suspiciously like snobbery and hypocrisy as

Reason for believing B: classical canon of style

defined by John. Outreach worker Carolynn Bennet appears to agree as she describes Stacy's attitude as "rationalizations" (para. 26). Stacy's arguments *are* blatantly self-contradictory: on one hand, she agrees that prostitution is all the same (para. 25), but on the other she insists that this work is different and okay for her, presumably because she's more privileged than low-class prostitutes and perhaps because she feels more pressured than they to keep up appearances and "get ahead." As this paragraph has been pointing out, style, the classical canon dealing with language choices, strongly affects the depiction of Stacy. She "stumbled" (10) and she "scores" (11), words that imply considerable criticism. The word "score," drawn from street vocabulary, implies that Stacy is essentially like any other hooker, except that she's a self-deluding snob.

Final reflection and implication

Commentary on "Innocent Victims or Entrants in a Rat Race?"

7   Whether this means that she is more to blame for her dilemma than the culture that partly created her is another bigger and more difficult question. But accepting her as an intended embodiment of the endangered, conflicted middle-class today does follow from a careful examination of the classical canons underlying Schmidt's methods. The result is a picture bordering on satire, and as we know, satirists are not known for their moral equivocation.

Desjardins's essay, following Thompson's adapted classical model, states its thesis at the end of the introduction, according to deductive placement. This placement typifies exposition and analysis rather than those forms of persuasion that seek to win over the opponent before finally stating the contrary position. Desjardins writes to her professor and a community of students, not to various levels of officialdom for various formal reasons. Consequently, she emphasizes inquiry over persuasion. Concession-refutation forms the basis of this model, one intended to adapt classical practice to the needs of scholarship. In his essay "How to Write an Argumentative Paper," quoted at the website *Elements of Rhetoric,* Professor Jack Meiland writes that "college work, aimed at knowledge and understanding, consists in inquiry." Like Professor Thompson, he therefore believes in adapting argumentation as a tool of analytical thinking, evaluation, and reporting. The weight of one's inquiry and reasoning constitutes the argument, as in the example above.

Toulmin's Model of Argumentation

Modern rhetorician Stephen Toulmin introduced his model of argumentation with his 1958 book *The Uses of Argument.* The webpage "Toulmin's Analysis," expounding ideas from this book, asks the following most interesting question, followed by an astute observation:

Have you ever noticed that when you research both sides of a question, you find yourself being convinced first by one side, and then by the other? Each argument sounds good—at least while you are reading it. . . . [A]nd soon you may feel completely confused.

Toulmin's model helps you to identify the key parts of an argument so that each can be tested. This model therefore offers great value when it comes to appraising arguments. Of course, it offers a good choice for your own persuasive essays as well.

Three Parts of Any Argument

Toulmin maintains that every argument contains three essentials: the claim, the grounds, and the warrant. **Claims** present an assertion (e.g., "You should take the *Acting on Words* writing course"); **grounds**—data or evidence—offer proof (30 percent of people taking this course were able to spell their names consistently afterwards); **warrants** link the claims and the proof (people want to write well). Warrants may be implicit or explicit (unstated or stated). Toulmin believes that the weakest part of an argument is its weakest warrant (stated or implicit). If people don't want to write well, why take the course?

Toulmin identifies three other elements: qualifiers, rebuttals, and backing. A **qualifier** may be necessary to limit the claim, if the claim is to be valid. For example, the claim may need to be stated as "Those who wish to pursue university studies in the liberal arts and sciences should take the *Acting on Words* writing course." Why should *everyone* need to take it? Qualifiers tend to be words such as "most," "usually," "some," and "sometimes."

Rebuttals recognize that despite careful construction of the argument, there may still be counter-arguments that could be raised against it. This matches the awareness of concession-refutation, in which the concession is seen as a potential rebuttal in need of dismissing. A rebuttal against the claim that "Those who wish to pursue university studies in the liberal arts and sciences should take the *Acting on Words* writing course" might be the objection that the course textbook has several chapters printed upside-down and a large element of plagiarism. This anticipated counter-argument may be pre-empted by the assurance that "those who attend the course will receive new, improved, correct, and corrected editions of the text."

Backing represents the most important of all ingredients in the Toulmin model by offering support to the warrant. In the above example, the writing course promoters would think of as many solid reasons as possible to support the warrant that people want to write well. This support could be in the form of what Chapter 4 describes as "warm" and "cool" proofs—personal examples, anecdotes, even figurative language on the "warm" side, and various types of rigorously gathered and tested data on the "cool" side.

Example of Toulmin in Action

In the following somewhat fictionalized illustration, student Lorne Redshirt was challenged to identify and refute the central argument presented by Kim Pittaway in her essay "Crystal Balls" (Reader, p. 423). As a result of his "harrowing" experience, he wrote a personal reflective essay so that other students could benefit from the wisdom of his experiences.

Sample Essay

Toulmin and Me
or
How to Get an A- for that Essay You Couldn't Finish on Time
Lorne Redshirt

1 Professor Sikes (not his real name for reasons you will discover) told us we had to use Stephen Toulmin's model of argumentation to analyze an essay by Kim Pittaway, "Crystal Balls." People sure get away with off-colour puns in magazines like *Chatelaine,* where this essay was first published. Nothing against the pun, but I wasn't happy with the topic. I like to have my own say in how to evaluate an essay. However, Professor Sikes told us that we *had* to refute Pittaway's argument, using the criteria in Toulmin's book *The Uses of Argument.* It didn't sound too exciting.

2 One good thing, though—the professor put Toulmin's basic model on the board. The model states a claim or major proposition, such as "City Council should enact a bylaw to prevent cats from roaming." Then there are the grounds, consisting of data or other forms of evidence: "Over 500 citizens have signed a petition objecting to roaming cats using neighbourhood gardens as litter boxes." Then there is the warrant expressing common support for the claim and the evidence. In this example, the warrant would be that "Citizens in this society don't like their private property to be violated." You notice that I said in "this" society, because in my society we don't really believe in picket fences and private property. This leads me back to my problem with Professor Sikes's assignment.

3 I thought university was about sharpening your own points of view, not being told what to think. I'm not so sure I'm going to accept the concept of private property, just because that's how the professor's culture sees things. I wasn't so sure I wanted to disagree with Kim Pittaway, just because the teacher said I should. I had already looked over her essay "Crystal Balls," and I was pretty sure the author was saying that men and women should respect each other as equals. My own culture believes that, and I had the impression that today's mainstream culture was heading toward more or less the same understanding. But I really believe in respecting the teacher, too, differences aside, and I also needed to pass the course.

4 So I looked through my notes again. Professor Sikes said that it's really important to test backing for the warrant. For example, if the warrant is that "people want whiter teeth," then you really have to inquire around and see if that's true. I decided to read that essay by Kim Pittaway again to see if I could outline the three main parts of the model. Once I found the warrant, I could test that out.

5 The opening three paragraphs of the article give an anecdote—a supporting detail, not a main idea. The anecdote, however, implies a message that women in 1979 were overlooked by the patriarch. The anecdote sets up a concern about a lack of equality and respect between the sexes. Paragraph 4 gives a concession: Pittaway

concedes that it is human nature to want your own political group to "come first"; she says that "part of me" wants this. By this point, it's getting pretty obvious that she is heading us in the other direction: she's making the point that *fair-minded women realize that two wrongs don't make a right* [my italics]. If you read the article as closely as I did the second time, you'll see what I mean.

6   The second time through, I realized that Pittaway's main purpose in this essay is to give her opinion of a book by the anthropologist Helen Fisher. I realized that the claim was her opinion about the book. I worked out Toulmin's model for the essay as follows:

7   Claim: Don't bother with Helen Fisher's book because she wants the future to belong to women.

8   Grounds: Her book says so.

9   Warrant: Fair-minded women know that two wrongs don't make a right.

10   I was between girlfriends at the time, so all the girls in our class looked fair to me. So I asked them if they agreed or disagreed with this warrant. They said things like, "Feminists are warriors out for revenge, even if the revenge means further injustice." They said "we're past that" and "I agree with her friend who doesn't see the world in gender terms; I don't believe in stereotyping." I had all the evidence I needed to support the warrant and thereby show that Pittaway's argument was sound. I decided to "suck it up" and oppose the professor, as respectfully as I could. Maybe that's what he wanted, coming from that ancient Greek dialectic tradition. Maybe he was just testing us to see who was the bravest and would oppose him.

11   You can tell that nothing bad happened to me, because I'm telling this story—but it didn't turn out quite the way I expected. My Auntie knew about this essay I had to write, and the evening before it was due, she dropped by my place for tea. I decided to show her my courage. I asked her to read my draft. She read the "Crystal Balls" essay, too. After she was done with my essay, she pushed it back and said, "I hope you don't expect a pass for this."

12   "It's due tomorrow," I said. "I can't let Professor Sikes think I'm someone who never submits work on time."

13   Then Auntie took a book out of her bag and slid it across the table to me, with the back cover upwards, so I could see what the other critics had said. I noticed the following comment by the *Philadelphia Inquirer:* "Fisher's prediction of a more open and egalitarian order provides a compelling—and hopeful—vision for the future."

14   This kind of troubled me, because I thought "egalitarian" meant "equal."

15   "It does," my Auntie said. "Those reporters are 'inquirers,' so let's hope they actually read the book—not like this girl who says she 'couldn't get past the first chapter.' Or does that really mean she *wouldn't?*"

16   I cancelled plans to meet Mike at the video arcade and went to my bedroom with Fisher's book. I felt pretty rotten. Fortunately, Auntie was fresh in my mind.

I remembered her complaining that newspapers often use sensationalistic headlines. These headlines, she said, were what Wayne Booth calls "The Advertiser's Stance," aimed at an assumption or an emotion intended to hook readers, even if the idea of the headline is not at all what the writer is trying to say. What if the same were true about books for the general public? What if Pittaway had simply "jumped" on an over-simplified headline? Maybe Fisher wasn't trying to say that women were "first" in the sense that men were the losers.

17   I remembered a girl beside me in class who can go through a whole book in thirty minutes, picking out the main ideas according to headings and topic sentences and concluding sentences. I decided to give it a try. Not much more than an hour later (allowing one break to check Sportsnet for the Flames update), I made it through Fisher's 288 pages with enough evidence to show that she believed—with major qualifications for many exceptions—that women and men have different but complementary inherent strengths. I remembered an elder on our reserve who always says that there is no harm in women having their natural roles and men having their natural roles, but because European society isn't natural, that circle of balance has been broken.

18   I guess I started to realize that whether Fisher is right or wrong with some of her conclusions based on physiological research, she is not saying that women should take over the world.

19   By then it was almost midnight. Writing a full essay just wouldn't cut it, so I prepared the following paragraph:

20   Stephen Toulmin is probably correct that arguments won't hold much water without strong warrants. But I have learned a lesson: testing warrants doesn't mean you should overlook testing the grounds. Kim Pittaway claims that Helen Fisher claims that the future belongs to women. Well, my Auntie found Fisher's book for me (she says I can't find anything that isn't on internet or in the video arcade). I scanned all 288 pages of this book, and Pittaway came to a hasty conclusion by misrepresenting the grounds. The book simply says that the future belongs to a more balanced relationship, with women respected for their special strengths. I'm okay with that, but I'm too sleepy to give all the page citations. If I get a pass, even though I didn't finish my essay, it's thanks to my Auntie.

21   Next morning I just about crawled into 8 a.m. class. After all that work, I sure wasn't going to be late handing in my assignment. Professor Sikes really likes to play what he calls "hard ball." But there was a note saying class was cancelled. Again. Rumour had it that Professor Sikes believed a PhD in English shouldn't have to teach composition, especially not at 8 a.m. Nothing was open yet anyway, so I used the time to write out my essay in full, with citations. I got an A-. Professor Sikes wrote: "Good analysis, but work on the 15 Common Errors." With English class, you never have to worry about delusions of grandeur.

Monroe's Motivated Sequence

When you wish to stress the element of persuasion over that of inquiry, Monroe's motivated sequence, or some adaptation of it, might serve you well. Professor Alan Monroe introduced his motivated sequence in 1935 as a practical step-by-step approach for speakers wishing to move, in a single speech, from the level of raising awareness to that of inciting action. This model strongly influenced formulas for advertising letters and other types of persuasive written communications. Here are Monroe's five steps:

1. Arouse attention. Offer vivid stories or examples, startling facts, or eloquent statements by admired people with suitable ethos.
2. Demonstrate a need. Show that the situation you want to change is urgent. Arrange evidence to build intensity; tap into the motivation of your audience, so that they look forward to your solution to the problem.
3. Satisfy the need. Provide a way, or ways, to solve the problem you have demonstrated. Provide a clear plan of action. Show how this plan agrees with audience principles and desires.
4. Visualize the results. Create vivid images to represent the positive results that will follow. Perhaps create a vivid picture of what may happen if your action plan is not followed.
5. Call for action. Provide a challenge, an appeal, or a statement of personal commitment. "Give listeners something specific that they can do right away" (Osborn 458). Taking action to solve a problem is much like putting a canoe in motion—the first paddle strokes are the hardest. This part needs the most encouragement and support on your part as motivational speaker. When Martin Luther King, Jr. called upon African-Americans to register to vote, he had already arranged to have a sign-up table near the door of the assembly.

For a sample speech using Monroe's motivated sequence ("Language Arts or Language Departs?"), see the Text Enrichment Site, Chapter 16.

In Praise of Conciliation: Models that Privilege Ethos and Pathos

The "Golden Rule"—that grand ethical guideline apparent in so many traditions—counsels us to do to others as we would have them do to us. It follows that we *not* do to others what we would *not* want done to us. Most of us do not want our ideas or plans swept aside to be replaced by someone else's. So aggressive forms of persuasion, strong in logos, often fail to respect and sympathize with their audience. Given Canada's history of reaching numerous concessions and compromises, perhaps it's appropriate that we conclude this section on persuasion by considering approaches that place special importance on sympathizing with audiences and recognizing the ethical line in how and how much to entice them toward our own position.

Perhaps the best known persuasive model of this sort today is Rogerian argument. Less concerned with "winning" and "losing" than classical and Toulmin models, Rogerian argument emphasizes exploring common ground, building bridges, resolving differences, negotiating and achieving reconciliation. This form places special stress on respecting the audience. As described by the webpage "Rogerian Argumentation" "[t]his psychological approach encourages people to listen to each other rather than to try to shout each other down."

Psychologist Carl Rogers believed in "empathic listening." He encouraged potential speakers to attend actively to their audience, to enter into reasoning opposed to theirs, and to recognize the validity of those views. One hundred years before Carl Rogers, Rudolf Steiner placed similar value on the need to accept opposing arguments without responding with defensive or loaded language. This discipline he viewed as critical to growth as a person as well as a communicator. Many people from other places, times, and cultures would agree with the strategy of listening rather than confronting, with the effort to build bridges rather than win wars, with a willingness to accept gradual and partial change.

With its stress on the rights and feelings of the audience, the Rogerian model grants equality to ethos and pathos along with logos. Many people see this as a valuable corrective to the dominance of logos in academic and other institutions. We referred to this concern in Chapter 1, suggesting that immoderate emphasis on logos has resulted in unhealthy suppression of feelings and ethics. With its stress on reconciliation, Rogers's method seeks to avoid the spectacle of elected members of office shouting insults and gesturing obscenely before TV cameras while another tries to speak. Current disenchantment with oppositional-style party politics, particularly among the young, suggests a growing desire to transcend roadblocks created by stubborn, partisan allegiances. Rogers's approach offers a genuine will to expand the meaning of concession from simply defining a position to be refuted to recognizing the parameters of possible negotiation. Like other empathic approaches, Rogerian argument works with what the audience appears to allow and takes its shape from there.

Speechwriters commonly begin their texts with an anecdote connected to family, since we all come from families; they may use gentle humour touching on some other universal human situation. Rogerian speech builds from this general sort of starting point by valuing the audience's specific views on the main topic of discussion. Chapter 14 outlines four common standards of judgement: logical, practical, ethical, and aesthetic. If a speaker knows that his audience places utmost importance upon practical criteria related to the topic, then shifting to ethical or logical criteria could be interpreted as appearing morally superior or out of touch. A Rogerian speaker avoids such appearances by collaborating with the main concerns of the audience, by finding common ground within those.

An example of meeting the evaluative standards of your audience might be if you were on a police service promotion committee that included hardliners who still distrusted that female officers could do the job. Your appeal for promotion of a female candidate would not address work equity but demonstrated past performance.

According to the Rogerian approach, while you may not care for certain values of your audience, you must see beyond those to the ones you do share—in this case, a common belief in proven performance and the need for the right skills. You must keep those values in mind throughout, demonstrating how they will be respected and perhaps even furthered in certain ways. For instance, you might note that the female candidate led her recruit class in marksmanship and three other disciplines, took no sick days, and has attracted the attention of a larger police service interested in sharing her negotiation skills.

Speakers using a Rogerian model delay expounding their theses until they have recognized common ground, explained matters in a way that offers benefits to the audience, and shown continued respect for the audience's way of seeing things. You would not state your recommendation concerning the promotion until you had reviewed and explained all of the work history and current contexts in terms of performance only. You would concede to your audience's known dislike for equity hiring and promotion. In exchange, you would trust your audience to be prepared to reciprocate with a degree of concession as well.

Here is another simple illustration of Rogerian approach adapted from an example by Professor Patricia E. Connors:

- Your company has declared a freeze on office spending until the end of the year, but that is another six months away.
- You state your understanding and agreement with the spirit of this goal of increased savings.
- However, your current printer is slow, needs frequent repairs, and produces poor quality in comparison to that of its competitors.
- You do a cost analysis and find that sharing a superior printer with the other two offices on your floor will result in less expense to the company than if each of you continues with your current equipment. You anticipate increased profits through improved quality, and improved teamwork through cooperative contact. You show that in the new budget year, acquiring two new printers for the other two offices will result in no greater cost to the company than remaining with the status quo. You would not add the cooperative benefit if you knew your supervisor opposed that attitude toward the two other offices.

A persuasive written request to your supervisor would follow the above outline.

Some might object that Rogerian argument pursues "mere compromise," but sometimes inciting others to accept compromise while offering concessions in exchange is an important step forward. After all, Canada achieved and has retained its national standing in large part according to the oft-repeated "serenity prayer," asking for the courage to change the things we can, the serenity to accept those we can't, and the wisdom to tell the difference.

Former prime minister Lester B. Pearson (1897–1972), a Canadian famous for his empathic listening and negotiating expertise, faced a truly "tough" audience in 1964 when the Royal Canadian Legion invited him to talk to them, at its national convention in Winnipeg, about plans to replace the Red Ensign with a new Canadian flag. Keeping to his election commitments, Pearson was advocating the new flag (an earlier proposed model of the one we now fly); a majority of the Legionnaires felt passionately loyal to the Red Ensign, part of their British heritage and the symbol that they had fought for in the Second World War. Pearson's address demonstrated three main points of Rogerian argument, summarized by Professor Connors as follows:

- Show the audience that you understand their position.
- Specify the conditions under which you believe the audience's position is correct.
- Convince the audience that you and they share the same moral qualities (honesty, quality, good will, and the desire to solve the problem).

If you watch the recorded segment of Pearson's address to the sometimes rowdy Legionnaires (available at CBC Archives online as well as through the CBC video library), you will see that these three goals are easier to achieve when appealing for a new printer than when trying to change the central symbol of a country. Nevertheless, Pearson demonstrated utmost attention to all three of the above essentials of audience awareness and response. He recognized a strong British history in the flags flown by Canada in the two world wars, the Union Jack in the first and the Red Ensign in the second. When he acknowledged the Red Ensign, the audience rose in a standing ovation. While this expressed complete opposition to adopting a new flag, it allowed Pearson to comment on shared ground: a love of country including a common recognition of the primacy of national symbols. When interrupted by hecklers, Pearson demonstrated good nature and said, "It's all right, Mr. Chairman, this is a *veterans'* meeting." In response, he received a strong round of applause. Wearing his military badges, indications of his own loyal service in the First World War, Pearson demonstrated that he was a veteran, too—that he had fought for the same basic values. He demonstrated that he understood the audience's passion for the Red Ensign and that he shared their emotions of patriotism.

When he stated his thesis—that the time for a new flag had come—he was greeted by hostile booing. In dealing with this, he did several things to specify the conditions under which the audience's attachment to the Red Ensign was correct. He clearly expressed that this attachment was correct during the Second World War, when the flag was flown by Canada. By mentioning that the Union Jack (not the Red Ensign) had been flown in the First World War, when he had fought, he introduced the idea of time and change. He explained that in 1964, the country had five million or more French descendants and five million or more immigrants from countries other than France or Britain. When interrupted by a heckler who shouted "I don't agree," he replied, "That's good—you have that right." In this way, Pearson reminded his audience of a fundamental common value, fought for in the wars—democracy, the right of free speech followed by majority decisions through the parliamentary process. He built on this important condition.

Further invoking a fundamental value of soldiers—courage in the just cause—he read from a letter by a member of Parliament stating that it was the member's duty to vote according to the will of a majority of the people he represented. Pearson implicitly reminded his hostile audience that a condition of the Red Ensign was its representation of courage and freedom. He received grudging applause upon declaring that he was committed to facing the hard, controversial issues upon which the future depended. While defending the rights of his hecklers to free speech, Pearson then pointed out his equal right to explain *his* position. In pursing this explanation, he offered further respect and conciliation. He offered that the new model flag consisted of three maple leaves patterned on the Legion badge, to be framed by blue representing not only the two oceans but also the blue of the Legion scroll. He appealed, in his explanation, for his audience to recognize that the future must blend their sense of past heritage with a coming new nationhood embracing multiple cultures and histories as part of one.

Pearson surely realized that his hostile audience would not go away supporting the new flag or planning to vote for him again, if they had done so before. His goal was to go as far as he could—to plant the seeds of new awareness that over time might take root with some. According to his vision of a democracy of contending positions, he accepted that some would not agree. It was the duty of a statesman to use words to appeal to common understanding and purpose as best he could. As we know, his powers of negotiation and persuasion, which earned him Canada's first-ever Nobel Peace Prize, were not quite equal to achieving the flag of his vision, three joined maples leaves in red framed on either side by two bars of blue. But he did see the adoption of a truly Canadian flag, a colossal achievement in the face of fierce emotional resistance. During his peace negotiations surrounding the Suez Canal proceedings, Pearson had recognized that other countries did not separate Canada's positions from those of Britain. To achieve respect and achieve effective international persuasions, therefore, Pearson recognized a need to succeed with internal persuasions.

CULTURAL CONSIDERATIONS

Canada pre-1960 was a very different place from the country we know today. A great many ideas and patterns assumed to be the only way of doing things have made room—or been made to make room—for other varieties of thought and expression. The same is true, in general, of ideas today concerning rhetoric and persuasion.

Before leaving this topic of argumentation, we should consider, again, the importance of cultural factors in how we relate to rhetorical traditions. Certain cultures neither engage in nor admire the oppositional, sometimes intensive adversarial approach we discuss in this chapter, an approach vigorously taught in North American colleges and universities. See "Cultural Considerations" in Chapter 3 (p. 43) for more on this topic.

Focus Question

Does argumentation, as discussed in this chapter, indeed offer an approach preferable to or even different from those of "biased persuasion"?

Works Consulted

Connors, Patricia E. "How to Be Persuasive in Writing." 20 Aug. 2006 <http://www.stc.org/confproceed/PDFs/>.

Corbett, Edward P.J. "Review: *The Contemporary Reception of Classical Rhetoric: Appropriations of Ancient Discourse* by Kathleen E. Welch." JAC 11.1 (1991). 20 Aug. 2006 <http://jac.gsu.edu/jac/11.1/Reviews/1.htm>.

Monbiot, George. *Heat: How to Stop the Planet from Burning*. Toronto: Doubleday, 2006.

Osborn, Suzanne, and Michael Osborn. *Public Speaking*. 7th ed. Boston: Houghton, 2006.

"Rogerian Argumentation." 20 Aug. 2006 <http://www.winthrop.edu/wcenter/handoutsandlinks/rogerian.htm>.

Smith, David. "Burying the Hatchet in Language." *Reader's Choice*. Kim Flachmann, Michael Flachmann, and Alexandra MacLennan. 3rd Can. ed. Scarborough: Prentice Hall, 2000. 540–44.

"Toulmin's Analysis." 20 Aug. 2006 <http://owlet.letu/contenthtml/research/toulmin.html>.

"Toulmin's Argument Model." 20 Aug. 2006 <http://changingminds.org/disciplines/argument/making_argument/toul>.

Zarefsky, David, and Jennifer MacLennan. *Public Speaking Strategies for Success*. Canadian ed. CBC/Prentice Video Library, 1997.

Chapter 17

Essays in Exams

Courses in English, history, biology, philosophy, and psychology have exams that require essay writing. The exams are usually significantly weighted into your final grade. The challenge with writing these exam essays, unlike papers written at home, is that you must express a strong thesis, clear topic sentences, and a satisfactory conclusion, and employ correct syntax all within a set time limit. Many essay exams are two hours long and require you to write two essays. This type of exam therefore requires strong organizational skills. The following test-taking tips ought to help you plan to write your essays in the allotted time.

PRE-EXAM PLANNING

1. All written exams require pre-reading. The reading may include short fiction, agricultural reports, case studies, historical information, novels, or textbook chapters. However, your exam essay will probably focus on only a few of the selections you have read all term. Therefore, instead of rereading all of the items on your syllabus—you won't remember them all anyway—focus on reviewing those texts that apply best to the course objectives and main themes. By preparing fewer texts in more depth, you can write on them in more analytical detail. If your exam will emphasize wide course coverage, however, read more, perhaps all, texts on the syllabus. Broad coverage and concentrated knowledge are a difficult balance, so ask your instructors about *their* exam expectations to help you structure your pre-exam planning.
2. Identify possible topics. When studying at home, review the main topics covered on the syllabus. Focus on any prevailing themes or periods covered in detail during the course. Choose the main themes and issues around which you can focus most of your preparation.
3. Read your three or four selected texts with your chosen topics in mind. Set aside sheets of paper with the names of each of these texts as headings. As you read your selections, keep in mind the possible topics you identified in Step 2 and jot down any passages from the work that may apply to your topics.

4. By the end of your studying, you will have a sheet of paper for each text outlining the passages you may use to address a variety of possible essay topics. Some texts will appear better than others for certain topics. Take some time now to identify some "if . . . then" strategies—that is, decide "*if* the question is on 'this' subject, *then* I will use 'this' text."

5. Generate possible theses for your different study essays. Using the notes you have made and the quotations or passages you pulled from each text, write out an essay plan, including topic sentences. Once you've done this preparation, you're usually more prepared than you were to write the test.

Mnemonic Devices: Memory Tricks

When you have large amounts of information to organize and remember, you may wish to "bundle" that information temporarily through mnemonic devices, or "memory tricks." These strategies are highly individual; some include anagrams (say, "FANBOYS" for the seven coordinate conjunctions: *f*or, *a*nd, *n*or, *b*ut, *o*r, *y*et, and *s*o) or deliberately unusual expressions to encode larger, more serious blocks of information ("Portable Cross" to remember that Pierre La*Porte*, a Canadian politician, and James *Cross*, the British trade commissioner, were kidnapped [illegally trans*porte*d] by the FLQ terrorists during the October Crisis in 1970 in Quebec).

Some mnemonic devices may rely on personal memory, silly expressions, puns and wordplay, or even irreverent constructions that are best kept private. In economics, for another example, a "bear market" is a strong market with rising stock values, while a "bull market" is a weakened market with declining stock values. People commonly think of a *bear* as *rising* on its hind feet to show dominance, while a *bull lowers* its head when threatened.

WRITING THE EXAM

Once you are in the exam, plan your time effectively so you can finish the entire test.

1. When you receive the exam, read all the possible topics and questions. Look for topics that are similar to those you considered when you were preparing your study notes. Don't panic if nothing matches exactly. Much of your prepared information may be flexible enough to work in part or in other combinations to satisfy the exam's essay questions.

2. Decide within the first five minutes of the test which one or two topics you will write on. If the examination has other components (multiple-choice, short-answer, definition, fill-in-the-blank), choose your essay topics *first* and your mind will "work on them" as you write the other sections.

3. When you begin the essay portion of the test, first note how much time you have to write each essay. If you have an hour, divide your time carefully, roughly according to this model:

- up to 10 minutes for planning by integrating ideas from the notes, topic sentences, and theses you generated at home
- up to 45 minutes for writing
- 5 remaining minutes for looking the paper over for correct syntax, grammar, and clarity

If you use your *planning* time correctly at the beginning of the exam, you should have no problems sticking to this schedule in the test.

Key Words in Essay Questions

Analyze: Discuss, interpret, and closely examine the many components of a single text, concept, or situation. To analyze is to declare significance and implications, not merely to summarize.

Compare: Look at the similarities and, more important, the differences between two or more concepts, situations, or texts. Recognize both similarities and differences, but work toward a thesis emphasizing one or the other.

Contrast: Emphasize the differences between two concepts or texts. Set them in opposition in your discussion. One teacher of analytical writing once said, "A lot of things are like a lot of other things in this world, and that's why distinctions and contrasts are important."

Criticize: Analyze a given number of texts for comparative worth. Make judgements evaluating one against the other.

Define: Provide the meaning of crucial, often complex terms from the course. Be sure to state the exact limits of what is to be defined. Be brief, but articulate a precise meaning. Consider providing an example for pointed clarity.

Describe: Detail a given theme, genre, case, or set of circumstances. List the qualities and characteristics of the account you are rendering.

Discuss: This very broad term invites analysis, or cause-effect, or comparison-contrast to argue or debate an interpretation or set of circumstances. You can **define** central terms; list pros and cons, complexities, contrasting qualities, unexpected conditions or effects; or examine meaning and effectiveness.

Explain: Clarify by describing logical development, use, and effect. Give examples.

Illustrate: Use examples to explain a concept. Comparisons between works are effective here.

Interpret: Comment on a given text or situation by describing it and its issues. Then analyze it—what does it all mean? Describe comparisons and give examples.

Outline: Describe main themes, interpretations, characteristics, or events.

Relate: Show some broad and many specific connections between themes, ideas, or events. Establish a larger context in which to place your discussion.

Summarize: Briefly discuss or recount an event or discussion, including crucial ideas and facts and avoiding unnecessary details.

HOW TO HANDLE A DEMANDING EXAM IN ENGLISH COMPOSITION

English exams can be notorious for the amount of reading, summarizing, analyzing, and writing that they demand in what seems like too little time. In this section we describe a typical composition exam with four parts. We then use this specific exam as an example of how you need to bring a special approach to bear if you are to complete all sections effectively, within the allotted time.

Sample Exam Questions

Part A Essay—50 percent of exam mark
Choose one of the following topic questions below and write an essay of approximately 500 to 600 words, 4 to 5 paragraphs, 3 to 4 pages double spaced.

Part B Summary and Critical Response Paragraph—20 percent of exam mark
Read the essay below entitled. . . . In one short paragraph of 4 to 5 sentences, summarize the essay. In a second paragraph of 9 to 12 sentences, write a critical response to the essay. Your response will amplify, modify, or refute an idea in the essay, or examine some aspect of rhetoric and demonstrate its effect.

Part C Identifying and Explaining an Excerpt—10 percent of exam mark
Listed below are 12 excerpts from 12 readings on the syllabus of this course. Choose one of the excerpts and (1) identify the title and author of the reading from which the excerpt has been taken and (2) state the relevance of the excerpt to the essay as a whole. Your answer should comprise one effective paragraph of 10 to 12 sentences.

Part D Correct Common Errors—20 percent of exam mark

1. Most or all of the following 10 lines contain a typical error—no more than one per line. Making as few changes as absolutely necessary, correct the errors.
2. The following paragraph contains 10 of the 15 common errors. Correct these errors, making as few changes as absolutely necessary. Be sure your editing intentions are clear. Be sure to correct documentation style as well.

Time allowed for an exam like this might range from two to three hours. The following suggestions, tips, and advice assume that you have three hours to complete this exam. If that were two and a half hours or even two hours, you would apply the same steps and points of awareness that follow, but you would need to reduce the time taken by reducing time devoted to each section in proportion to the mark weight for that section.

Strategy for Answering the Above Sample Exam Questions

Be as Rested and Relaxed as You Can

We recommend, above all, that you have a good night's rest and try to relax (if exams make you nervous). The exam illustrated above does not throw any curve balls. The examiner simply wants to see your essay-writing, summarizing, critical thinking, and grammar skills in action. The marker likely won't expect your writing to be as fully polished or achieved as it might be if you had more time. The key is to create thoughtful point-form outlines/rough notes to help you organize and ensure that essentials are included.

Do Not Write Multiple Drafts

Go into the examination planning to write only one draft of the essay (one based on a thesis and topic sentence outline) and paragraphs. Double-space your writing; that way, you can go over it afterwards, making corrections between the lines. Your handwriting should be legible (assuming you are not working on a computer), but it is not necessary to aim for a calligraphy award.

Look Over the Whole Examination, Then Begin Planning Part A

Once you have received your examination and filled in any required administrative portions, look the whole exam over once; then decide on the essay topic you'd like to do for Part A, and think about it for a few minutes. In preparing to answer Part A, try to answer the following questions for yourself—and based on those answers, do a rough outline:

> Who is my audience?
> What is my purpose?
> Therefore, what should be my style and type of writing (e.g., personal, expository, analytical, persuasive)?
> What is my thesis?
> What is the topic/topic sentence in each of my three or four body paragraphs?
> What sort of supporting detail will I need to mention for each point made in each paragraph?

Your essay should demonstrate a clear, sufficiently detailed thesis (usually placed at the end of your opening paragraph) and at least three solid body paragraphs of 6 to 12 sentences each. Use good paragraph craft, so that each paragraph has focus, support, and a clear, effective relationship to your thesis. (Review the material in Chapter 4 on the 4 Fs.)

Double-Space Your Answers for A, B, and C

By double-spacing all of your writing on the exam, you provide space to insert revisions and make changes both as you go along and afterwards when you proofread the finished essay. You may certainly cross out certain phrases or lines. By double-spacing, you make the writing easier for your reader to take in. Do not worry about doing a second complete draft of any section. Use rough notes and an outline so that you can make do with just one draft. Do write as legibly as you can.

After Planning Part A, Get Parts B, C, and D Out of the Way

Once you have your outline for Part A, consider doing Parts B, C, and D to get them out of the way. As you work on those, ideas may come to you for the essay. Simply add to your rough notes for the essay as you do the other parts (if that method suits you).

Match the Time You Spend on Each Part to the Mark Value for That Part

Keep an eye on the time and be sure to start on the draft of your essay with at least 80 minutes to go for a three-hour exam. Don't worry about rewriting a second draft. For revision, go through and make corrections between the lines.

Use Your Dictionary Thoughtfully

If your course allows you to use a dictionary during the exam, be careful not to spend too much time with it. First, use your dictionary to check the precise meanings of any key words in assignment instructions. Then, once you reach the essay revision, use your dictionary to check spellings, if the time allows.

How to Prepare for Part B

Review Chapter 13, "The Summary," especially the 10 steps (p. 198). Also review Chapters 14, 15, and 16 on critical response in general and rhetorical response (a specific application of critical response). As preparation, also read the process description essay "Reading an Essay under Pressure" on the Text Enrichment Site, Chapter 11. You should use the scanning and skimming techniques described and illustrated in that essay to shorten the time it takes you to read the Part B essay as well as to intensify your comprehension of its main assertions and methods. In writing your summary of four or five sentences, concentrate on expressing the ideas in your own words—don't worry about perfecting the style of your answer as you would with more time at home. Show that you have recognized the controlling idea of the essay and its supporting reason(s). That is the essence of what the summary requires.

For the paragraph of critical response to the essay, again as briskly as you can, demonstrate knowledge of the steps of critical thinking described in Chapter 14, "Critical Analysis and Evaluation." In your "scrap" pages, brainstorm quickly about the elements you believe should figure in an analysis of the issue raised by the essay. Then brainstorm about a way to narrow your thinking as you evaluate some significant aspect of those elements. Choosing one or two (and no more) of the evaluative criteria suggested in Chapter 14 (p. 205) should help you to move expeditiously while deciding on a focus. Then work on the topic sentence of your critical response paragraph. Once you have that, the paragraph should flow naturally.

How to Prepare for Part C

See Chapter 15 (p. 241) for assistance with explaining how an excerpt relates to the essay from which it has been taken. Be sure you determine in advance how many of the course readings you are expected to know well for this part of the exam. The sample exam question for Part C above suggests that you need to know well just one of the 12 represented essays. Instructors who assign this question are often more interested in your understanding of the basic nature and process of an essay than in how many course essays you remember in detail. But some exams do require an extensive knowledge and memory of course readings—so be sure to know well in advance how many of the assigned course readings you need to review for the exam.

For the Part C question above, you would not try to remember all 12 essays! You would simply need to familiarize yourself in advance with one, breaking it down into its main parts. On Part C of the exam you would see a list of excerpts, one for each of the 12 essays given to you to choose from. You would choose the one excerpt you wished to explain. Chapter 15 gives detailed steps in how to prepare to write the sort of paragraph required by this exam question. Knowing that part of Chapter 15 should give you considerable confidence for handling this answer.

How to Prepare for Part D

To prepare for Part D, you can do the exercises in the 15 common errors (with answer keys) at the Text Enrichment Site under the Handbook, Section 3. If you have trouble understanding some of the explanations for the 15 common errors in the Handbook of this text, then you may need to brush up on how to identify basic parts of speech and sentence patterns. That basic review information is provided at the Site for the Handbook, Section 1; it is also readily available elsewhere online, in libraries, and in bookstores. If you have been working with your instructor's notations on your coursework, then you have likely made good progress in correcting the 15 common errors by this stage. Do not spend too long on this section. Answer the questions that you know and leave those that you do not know. Return to the incomplete ones later, if you have time.

Be Sure to Return Your "Scrap" or "Rough" Notes

Most, if not all, examination procedures require that you include all of your rough notes with the rest of the exam. This requirement has an important benefit for you in that a marker can quickly see evidence of your thinking and knowledge from your brainstorming and outlines. Even if you run out of time and fail to complete the essay, if you have provided an outline similar to those modelled throughout Chapters 9 to 16, an outline with a clear thesis and topic sentences, the chances are that you will receive sufficient marks for the incomplete writing to allow you a pass for the exam. If you find yourself with only 12 or so minutes remaining and not enough time to complete what you are writing, write a note to the marker that you are running out of time and demonstrate the rest in note form. This method often earns more marks than students realize. Resist any feeling of despair—make the most of the limited time available, and remember that it is limited for everyone. Providing clear, effective, knowledgeable outlines is one strategy to help you follow plans and provide evidence of plans.

Keep a Sense of Proportion

Remember that final exams rarely count toward a majority of your final mark for the course. The important thing is to pass. Of course do your best, but try not to allow worry about the exam to become overly disruptive to you. You must accept that almost no one leaves an exam feeling satisfied that all parts went perfectly, because it is not the nature of exam conditions to promote perfection. The intention is to test general knowledge of the course teachings, and by following the tips recommended here, you should certainly be able to demonstrate that you have achieved the level of knowledge and ability required for an exam such as the one illustrated above.

Success Does Not Mean Perfection in All Points of the Marking Rubric

Marking schemes or rubrics for English essays generally cover five categories: content, organization and flow, style and tone (adapting to purpose), grammar and spelling, and mechanics (punctuation, spacing, documentation technique, and so forth). Polishing and perfecting all of these aspects under exam pressures may not be realistic. A wise strategy is to provide a strong base of content and structure and simply do the best that you can with the other aspects.

Section 3   Research and
Documentation

INTRODUCTION

In the following two chapters you will learn what sources are, how they are classified, how they must be evaluated and integrated for scholarly purposes, and how they must be cited. What are the pitfalls of online sources? When and how do you summarize, paraphrase, and quote sources? What is the basic citational principle used by most documentation systems, such as that of the American Psychological Association (APA) or Modern Language Association (MLA)? The following two chapters answer these crucial questions and more.

 We strongly recommend that in conjunction with referring closely to Chapters 18 and 19 you also read "Evaluating Sources" at the Text Enrichment Site, Chapter 18.

There is much detail to absorb in what lies ahead. To regain perspective as you increase your sense of how to research and cite sources, you will find it valuable to consult the following checklist on a regular basis. Also read and carefully reread the following caution to avoid the appearance of plagiarism.

Common Research Errors in First-Year Papers

1. A final list of sources appears but the paper lacks in-text attributions of any sort. The reader has no idea how the listed material has been integrated. Although such papers may not reflect deliberate cheating, they can be classified as plagiarism.
2. The paper makes references to Wikipedia and other online sources that lack reliable ethos (no cited author, unreliable author[s], or have no identified host organization or contact person, an unreliable host organization, or uncritical uses of sources that "have something to sell").
3. The paper presents an idea from another source as its own (plagiarism).
4. Facts have been stated as common knowledge, when they are not, and therefore require citation.
5. When integrating material, the paper fails to make the most appropriate choice among summarizing, paraphrasing, or quoting.
6. Names of the authors or works referred to are misspelled (which reflects lack of focus, intention, or interest).
7. Quotation marks are omitted around short quotations or they are incorrectly inserted around longer quotes (four lines or 40 words) that are set off from the text as block quotes.
8. The paper uses the now outdated footnote system to cite references.
9. The paper fails to acknowledge that words quoted from one source were in fact quoted by that source from yet another source.
10. The paper fails to represent sources offering a balance of different points of view on the topic.
11. Too many sources have been used (perhaps including some of dubious value).
12. The paper does not reflect the latest current information on the topic.
13. The writer has misunderstood the ideas in the sources.
14. The writer has handed control to the research sources while the actual writer remains on autopilot.
15. In-text attributions appear, but there is no final list of sources.

Avoid the Appearance of Plagiarism

Any loose or hasty attitude toward full and accurate citation of your sources may lead to charges of plagiarism. (Chapter 19 goes into more specific detail on ways to ensure that your summaries, paraphrases, and quotations are properly attributed.) When you plagiarize someone else's work, you are presenting his or her ideas or words in your own writing as though they were your own. Academic institutions consider plagiarism a serious offence, one that can result in academic failure or even expulsion. Many students plagiarize without intending to because they haven't learned when and how to document their sources, or because they have developed bad note-taking and composition habits that lead to plagiarism. In fact, some students claim to have gone through high school blissfully unaware that they were plagiarizing virtually in every essay and research assignment they ever wrote.

It is very important to learn the rules and expectations for documenting sources before you find yourself in the unpleasant situation of dealing with an accusation of plagiarism. Make yourself aware of your institution's definition of plagiarism. Treat that definition like a law.

Although this serious caution may raise anxiety, as long as you credit your sources where credit is due and learn how to do that according to accepted convention, you should not encounter problems in your research. The principles and methods are simpler than they may seem. To ensure that you acknowledge ideas other than your own in the text of your essay, simply be sure that you give the source author's last name with the idea and be sure to list the source at the end of your paper in alphabetical order according to surname of authors. That one practice is all you need as a foundation. Use the following chapters with diligence, and you will soon have many fine research essays standing on a solid base.

Chapter 18
Research Methods

Students commonly think of research papers as specialized forms of writing. As this section recognizes, research writing *does* involve specialized elements; however, all that really separates a "research paper" from other academic essays is the *extent* of the preliminary investigation. Your dominant purpose may be to share first-hand observation, to organize secondary-source information, to analyze an issue, to argue a certain viewpoint, or to combine two or more of these purposes. First-year research papers typically aim to present up-to-date information as reliably and clearly as possible (basic expository style), to weigh and decide upon varying opinions and conclusions (analysis), and to argue a perspective, often on a controversial topic (persuasive). Any combination of the types of writing previously described in this Rhetoric could be used. So as you proceed to learn and practise the techniques specific to this form of writing, continue to shape your work according to the general guidelines for all good writing.

See "Evaluating Sources" at the Text Enrichment Site, Chapter 18, for an essay on the special problems of evaluating sources.

TYPICAL SOURCES

Sources may include academic writing, historical accounts, government reports, statistics, microfilm, interviews, and legal and medical opinions. Exploring all of this information without becoming lost or overwhelmed can be a challenge. This section of the text recommends you follow clear stages and provides details for the various formal techniques of integrating information. (Chapter 19, "Documentation," explains how to acknowledge your sources.)

If you proceed in a systematic way, you should attain a feeling of solid achievement as you complete your work. Be prepared to spend time on a research paper, remembering that this type of writing, based on a vigorous inquiry, is central to many professional activities. Research skills will take time to master, but they will serve you well.

PRACTICE

Consider the possible merits and limitations of the following sources. Compare and contrast the natures of these different sources.

- a report by Statistics Canada
- a government report by a specially appointed commission into an area of concern, such as problem gambling
- government facts sheets that describe a particular program and present basic data on its operation
- a corporate report
- a pamphlet by Greenpeace
- a newsletter by REAL Women
- a call for academic papers on an alleged "turn to ethics" in American literary criticism with an invitation

to answer whether such a turn would be "good" for anyone in Canada
- George Monbiot's book *Heat: How to Stop the Planet from Burning*
- Noah Richler's book *This Is My Country, What Is Yours: A Literary Atlas of Canada*
- a personal interview with a chemical engineer
- a personal interview with a gambling addict
- a Greek text of historical and cultural information written in 600 BCE
- a European text of historical and cultural information written in 1450 CE
- a story of tribal origin handed down through oral tradition

STEPS IN YOUR RESEARCH PROCESS

As we said, a research paper requires several major steps from beginning to completion:

- You have to locate, select, organize, and synthesize your background sources.
- You have to arrange your paper as a cohesive body of research from these various sources and perspectives.
- As well, you probably have to present your own particular analysis or argument—and emerge with a viewpoint that is your own.

Since a research paper requires your investigation and representation of other people's analyses, you need to consider some crucial factors that would not affect your non-research essays, such as *long-term scheduling* and careful *note-keeping* from your secondary sources.

GETTING STARTED

Break down the writing of a research paper into several steps. This is true for experienced research scholars or for first-year students. Each step requires some planning, from getting organized to narrowing your topic to proofreading the final draft. Some instructors may request a **proposal** and/or a **working thesis statement** and/or an **outline** and/or a proposed **Works Cited page** to ensure that you observe the necessary stages and to start you moving in the right direction. More than anything, be aware as you begin that a good research paper can take you as long as a month or six weeks to prepare.

Scheduling

You cannot pull a research paper together in one night, though many students have tried. Since you have to locate and evaluate several credible sources, you will probably need at least three weeks of hard work for a serious effort. Students who do not thrive on stress may need more time. A weak research effort will be immediately obvious, so plan ahead. As instructors usually view a polished research paper as a measure of academic commitment, you might think of this project as the consolidation of your previous efforts in a course or an opportunity to expand or reconsider an earlier essay or idea that arose in the course. Check with your instructor if you wish to expand on an earlier paper. Your research paper should differ significantly and be substantially deeper than the course paper you wish to build on. Writing is never a linear process, so the valuable experience of revisiting previous work to improve on it can develop your appreciation of the writing process and even your sense of yourself as a writer.

A Five-Step Provisional Model

What follows is a provisional model for a long-term research and writing schedule. We will explain specifics later, after this snapshot of the approach.

Step 1: *Settle on your topic,* even if only generally at first. What further angle or subcategory of your topic would you like to invest your time and effort in? Can you find sufficient background sources? Have you looked around? Are you genuinely interested in your topic? Why?

Step 2: Once you have found your specific area (say, masculinity in two recent African-American novels, the return of social vision to Canadian politics, the influence of women in Canadian business, Kennedy's rationale for committing troops to Vietnam, or representations of authority in three rap songs), you need to *gather specific research material* on your topic. As you conduct your research, you will likely continue to adjust or redefine your selected topic, based on those research findings. Keep notes that thoroughly document all useful information and details from your source material (authors, titles, publishers, places of publication, and dates). Carefully record all exact quotations with their page numbers. Also write yourself little reminders for further possible areas of discussion in your paper. Try to outline a draft version, either in point form, in a topic-sentence tree, or in some provisional paragraphs.

Step 3: Now that you have read through both general sources and more specialized discussions on your topic, you will make some longer draft notes that contain quite a few quotations that can help your discussion. You can always delete or shorten some of these quotations later. Some quotations should be solid evidence, while some could be argumentative views that you may either support or challenge with other views on the subject. Some other references you may not use directly—verbatim, or word for word—but indirectly. With these, you want to offer a responsible, accurate paraphrase that you still attribute in the paper by citing the author's name and the page of his or her work where you found it. You probably have narrowed your topic sufficiently now to have a **working thesis**, a specific position on your topic that you can establish (expository) or argue (persuasive) confidently. Based on your reading and notes, you can now *develop your outline* into a fuller draft version of your paper: you will have provisional topic sentences in place by now to guide your paragraphs. You are probably ready to rewrite soon and refine this draft version into your research paper.

Step 4: *Rewrite your first draft.* Present your established thesis clearly and confidently in your introduction. In the paper's body paragraphs, present your supporting evidence and assert what you see as the implications of that thesis. You may wish to add footnotes or endnotes to include brief supporting or explanatory information.

Step 5: *Edit that draft for submission.* Check and recheck all quoted material for accuracy. Look at your topic sentences to check their relevance to and support of your thesis statement. Are your own voice and perspectives strong in the paper? What do you conclude at the discussion's end?

SELECTING YOUR TOPIC

For your research paper, your instructor may give you only one topic to research or provide you with choices or ask you to select your own topic. Whether you have been assigned choices (and therefore must provide an answer to a specific question) or an open topic (and must propose your own question and decide *when* you have answered it), select a subject that interests you. Select one for which you can find sufficient research material as well.

Settle on a topic you can research in no more than four weeks. Look for a topic that does not place you in a corner for available sources. You must always be prepared to find a compromise between your interests and the sources available to you. In part, this compromise may be further defined by your school's library and computer capabilities. If you are pressed for time, you are probably best advised to select a topic that you know has been widely written about, such as the influence of computing on education, or globalization and its consequences, or the representation of childhood and youth in J.D. Salinger's fiction.

If you stay flexible at this stage, you should be able to pursue at least some aspects of your interests, while making a practical choice based on the available sources. Be true to your own curiosities; a research paper that bores you will also bore your reader. As well, a research paper that you half-heartedly write only to complete the course may end up reading like a barely connected string of quotations without any centre.

Here are some sample research essay topics that include a range of social, historical, literary, and business interests:

- diet and nourishment issues: meat, vegetables, junk food, vitamins, meal replacements
- male and female body images: size, health, media, fears, bodies and/as machines

- increased musical instruction and discussion in schools: from Mozart and Mahler to Muddy Waters, Bob Marley, and Metallica
- marketing to youth: strategies, ethics, social convergence
- Vimy Ridge in WWI: are Canadians expendable in a global conflict?
- prenuptial agreements and support payments
- sexual knowledge and social circumstance in Alice Munro's "Thanks for the Ride" (Reader, p. 376)
- men's and women's "lifestyle" magazines: content, presumptions, market, private and social fantasies
- Middle East conflict: history as ongoing negotiation
- the 1960s and 1970s: still going strong, but why?
- influenza, infection, antibiotics, and super-bugs: the cure as the ailment?
- police brutality, pepper spray, freedom of speech, police helicopters, social control: the rise of the authoritarian state?
- "are we ourselves?": Canadian community values and private lives or regional and national self-perceptions
- natural resource management: fish, forest soil, ozone, water, crops
- consumer protections, advertising frauds
- Canadian self-employment: benefits and perils

Many examples on this list are very broad topics. You would need to narrow those topics to a more specific issue within the general topic area. Remember that you will need to assert a **thesis statement** in your final draft, so develop a strong view on a particular angle of the topic.

Narrowing Your Topic

After you have picked a subject for which you can locate some sources, you are on your way. Having a subject, however, does not mean you have a specific research topic. You need to narrow your interest to a particular angle. The First World War itself is far too large to serve as a first-year research topic. However, a smaller category within that topic would lead to an interesting research project. How about the strategic effect of propaganda or counter-intelligence in one battle or stage of the conflict?

By narrowing your topic and investigating a specific area of inquiry within your general topic, you can move closer to several goals at once. You will eliminate extra reading that may be either too general or too specific in a direction that differs from yours. You will move toward a working thesis, a position on your topic. While narrowing your research topic from a large area of interest to a specific line of inquiry may seem difficult, this step requires only that you first ask yourself, "What is my main concern?" "What am I most interested in?" and "How would I prefer to spend my research time?" As you read some initial secondary sources, you will begin to develop a sense of what specific topic you would like to pursue.

Here are some further brief examples of how you might move quickly from general topic areas to working research topics, from a large category of interest to a research subcategory:

Violence in Sports

- NHL violence in the last two years
- soccer-crowd violence in last two World Cups
- women's hockey and football leagues
- boxing's future/changing gender roles
- criminal records of NBA and NFL athletes

Business Concerns in an International Economy

- controls of inventory in a multinational company
- the internet's impact on specific areas of retail, manufacturing, and/or wholesale
- changes in specific business laws and recent effects
- Employment Insurance and proposals for revised cost-sharing between employees and employers
- cyber-commerce

EXPLORING SOURCES

The Information Age is an unrelenting blizzard of uneven and uncertain information. Finding the way to genuinely useful and accurate information is every researcher's challenge and goal. This brief guide will help you get started.

Your College or University Library

Your college or university library is usually the best place to start your search for good, reliable sources. Take advantage of the resources available in your own library. Almost all libraries offer free assistance in the form of information sessions, classes, or individual consultation with reference librarians; these sessions can be extremely helpful to students new to college or university research. Most librarians are happy to help you as long as you are polite and patient. Saying "please" and "thank you" is often a productive strategy to ensure assistance with research questions and problems.

Library Catalogues

While library catalogues vary, you will find certain strategies applicable in most situations. You will want to try more than one way of accessing your topic, by various keywords, subject headings, words in titles, etc. If your searches are pulling up hundreds of sources, narrow your search. Use two keywords instead of one ("vampire and literature" or "vampire and film" instead of just "vampire") or identify a more specific topic ("Dracula" or "Bela Lugosi"). Conversely, if your searches on a topic are pulling up only one or two sources, try synonyms or related words ("pregnancy," "birthing," "midwife," "childbirth," "motherhood," "nursing") or broaden your topic term ("horror film" instead of only "John Carpenter's *Halloween*" or "scientific entrepreneur" instead of only "marketing of lab mice").

Specialized Databases

To find a journal article, you will probably have to use one of your library's specialized electronic databases. Some specialized databases provide abstracts (summaries of articles) or even full articles, while others simply give you a list of articles and their sources. Find out from your library or your instructor which databases are used in your subject area. Some examples are ERIC (for education), MLA (for literature), Medline (for medicine and biosciences), and PsychINFO/PsychLIT (for psychology).

Encyclopedias and Dictionaries

Encyclopedias and dictionaries can help introduce you to your subject by defining terms, summarizing facts, and sometimes providing an overview of the main issues associated with your topic. Although these reference works are a good place to start a writing assignment, never stop there; reference books never provide enough depth for a college or university writing assignment. You must be more active in your research efforts.

Encyclopedias can be general or specialized. General encyclopedias cover numerous topics from a wide range of fields. Because of their broad scope, they do not cover subjects in the detail of specialized encyclopedias and dictionaries. Many of the most up-to-date general encyclopedias are now available in electronic form. *Encyclopedia Britannica* (available online at <http://www.britannica.com>) and the electronic encyclopedia *Encarta* (<http://encarta.msn>) are just two examples.

You will find specialized encyclopedias and dictionaries useful when beginning your research on a topic. Some of these contain articles of several pages in length, written by experts in the field, while others contain shorter entries with highly specific information on specialized topics. Examples include the *Dictionary of Literary Biography*, *The Encyclopedia of Social Work*, *The International Dictionary of Films and Filmmakers*, and *The Gale Encyclopedia of Native American Tribes*.

Be sure to check the year of publication of any encyclopedia you are using. Some older college and university libraries have reference works dating back several decades. These sources may be extremely well researched and fascinating in their own right, but they can also be catastrophically out of date for your purposes. Research and representation of many subjects (such as mental illness, narrative techniques in fiction, Aboriginal cultures) have changed significantly over the decades, so make sure you examine the most recent sources available in your school library or online.

Do not use Wikipedia or similar reader-generated encyclopedias. They simply cannot be relied upon to ensure the ethos demanded of an encyclopedia. They may have remained current, and they may be accurate, but no assurances of those required qualities exist in the anonymous reader-generated model.

Books

Scholarly books form a solid basis for most college and university research papers. Often, you will need to read only two or three chapters of the books to gather valuable information. These chapters can provide serious, consistent, current, in-depth information on major ideas and research on your topic. They can help you to find and narrow your issue. Most college and university libraries specialize in scholarly or academic books appropriate for research papers, but not all books on your topic might be good sources for your particular paper. (Our discussion of evaluating sources later in this chapter will help you choose the right books.)

Journals

Articles in journals are usually your best source of information for a brief and highly specialized discussion of a topic. However, journal articles are sometimes written for experts in a particular academic field, so you may find some of the terms difficult to understand. You may have to decide whether you need to understand some of this terminology in order to write about your subject. Often, you can consult a special dictionary on theoretical terms or perhaps another article on the troubling term itself ("first-person confessional narrative," "diegesis," "setting," "autoeroticism," "isothermic," "historiography," "hip hop," "Tom Jones"). The authors of journal articles engage in specific arguments based on issues particular to their field.

Newspapers and Magazines

Articles in newspapers and magazines are often both more superficial and more accessible than articles in academic journals because the former generally address a wider audience. Sometimes you can use these general-interest articles as appropriate sources along with other more specialized sources for a research paper, especially if your topic is very recent and people have not had time to publish on it in longer books and scholarly journals. Reviews and interviews from newspapers and magazines, for instance, can be useful sources of beginning information. On the other hand, if your assignment requires that you draw on scholarly articles from academic journals in a proposed field, do not rely on newspapers or magazines. The journalists who write articles in newspapers and general-interest magazines such as *Maclean's* or *Cosmopolitan* are usually on assignment and have with no particular expertise in the areas they cover for those days; so they are not the most reliable sources when you are investigating serious developments in research or scholarly debates on a given subject. Some specialized magazines, however, such as *The Economist*, *New Scientist*, and *Scientific American*, are well researched and well respected by experts in the field and may be good places to begin your research.

Interviews and Personal Experiences

Interviews and personal experiences can add an interesting, surprising, and original dimension to your research paper. For example, one student may gain substantial insights for an essay on contemporary Jewish literature (Mordecai Richler, Philip Roth, Cynthia Ozick, Saul Bellow) by interviewing her grandparents, who may have survived Nazi internment camps, oppression, and/or migration. Another student may success-fully incorporate his own Japanese-Canadian experiences in a study of some of the strengths and problems of Canadian multiculturalism. Interviewing has much to offer (when properly balanced with other sources) yet tends to be underutilized. For more on interviewing, see "Interviews" at the Text Enrichment Site, Chapter 18.

Be aware, however, that personal experiences are not always easy or appropriate to include in research papers, especially if you are very emotional about the experi-ence. Before you include a personal experience in a research paper, ask yourself whether that experience contributes to the paper, provides an illuminating example, or will distract your reader from your point. Also, some instructors may object to your including personal experiences, while others strongly encourage it. If you are not sure where your instructor stands on the politics of personal comments in a research paper, discuss your ideas with him or her.

The Internet

The World Wide Web can provide vast quantities of information on many subjects, particularly those that are current. Students who are comfortable with the internet (or who start their essays after conventional libraries are closed) may be tempted to use it as their only source of information. Usually, however, this is not advisable. Certainly many websites provide stimulating discussions and well-researched, reliable information, but just as many are poorly researched, inaccurate, and otherwise misleading. Some websites, even those posted by people with "PhD" after their name, contain unattributed words from other sources—that is, plagiarism. There are very few occasions when it is appropriate for you to use the World Wide Web as your only source of information. ***Use the web for its strength (currency)—don't use it as a crutch.***

Research on the web works best for introducing you to recent topics, since the internet is the international up-to-date medium. The information it provides on history, complex topics, or less popular subjects tends to be sketchier. When in doubt, consult recommended library sources before you turn to the internet, so you will have a better understanding of the credibility of the materials you find there.

Internet Search Engines

If you are looking for information on the World Wide Web, you will probably use an internet search engine. Most browsers have default search engine settings with several other search options available as well. Each search engine works somewhat differently, so the same word or phrase may give you different results. Try out several search engines to see which one you like best. Your choice may also depend on your starting point. For example, if you have only a general idea of a subject for a research paper but not a precise topic, a search engine like Yahoo, which classifies information by subject heading, may be helpful. Conversely, if you have a very specific topic in mind, a search engine such as AltaVista, which scans websites for precise phrases or word combinations, will probably work best.

Note that some search engines, such as AltaVista and Hotbot, use a robot and an indexer to seek information and perform keyword searches. Others, such as Yahoo and Webcrawler, are directories with professional editors who index sites. These search engines allow you to search by subject as well. Experience and experimentation will show you which engines give you the best results for various assignments. Here are some URLs for search engines:

- <http://www.yahoo.com>
- <http://www.altavista.com>
- <http://www.google.com>
- <http://www.excite.com>
- <http://www.webcrawler.com>
- <http://www.questia.com>
- <http://www.infoseek.com>
- <http://www.hotbot.com>

Narrow your search by using options such as "all the words" or "the exact phrase." Although search engines vary in what they find and in the exact instructions for finding information, all of them have Help files to help you narrow your search to a manageable size. Note that some search engines can carry out Boolean searches as well, so that they can be more easily narrowed down using the following terms:

- By typing "music AND copyright," you search with both terms in that order.
- By typing "music OR copyright," you broaden your search by searching either term separately.
- By typing "music AND copyright NOT Napster," you now eliminate documents with the word "Napster" in them.
- By typing "music copyright," you confine your search to these two words grouped together.

- By typing "music NEAR copyright," you retrieve documents in which these terms are within 10 words of each other (on some engines, such as AltaVista).

Keep track of reference sites for writers. For no cost, you can find many guides and resource materials here (and in associated links). A good, academically credible source you might like to search further for general information is the Voice of the Shuttle, at <http://vos.ucsb.edu>.

Saving Material You Find on the Internet

It is often a good idea to download material from a website onto your computer or a disk. You can do this with a simple right-click of your mouse. This step is important because websites may change from day to day, and the material you find today may not be accessible to you tomorrow. Keep a log to document when you referenced specific websites.

To avoid plagiarizing, take "notes" by cutting from a website you visit but pasting in another font, so that you can tell where your words stop and another's words begin. Record important websites among your "Bookmarks" or "Favourites" for easy reference. Always record the date on which you retrieved certain information from the web. Download and keep a copy of the online material you are considering citing.

✒ PRACTICE

1. Look up the same topic in three different encyclopedias or dictionaries, including at least one general and one specialized source. What are the strengths and weaknesses of each? Which source would be the best for getting you started on a research paper?
2. Choose a specific topic that interests you, such as performance-enhancing drugs in sports, medical marijuana, vampire films, or the Nuremberg trials. Try to find four articles on the subject: two from newspapers or magazines and two from academic journals. How helpful would these different sources be for writing a research paper on that topic?

Primary and Secondary Sources

Most areas of study make an important distinction between primary and secondary sources. **Primary sources** are the initial materials you are working with—a work of literature, a philosophical treatise, a historical document, or data you gather directly from an experience. Working directly with these sources allows you to come up with your own interpretation or analysis of them. The primary source or sources are *what* you are writing about, the topic of the paper.

Secondary sources are other writers' interpretations, analyses, or discussions of an event, an issue, or a primary source. Interpretations of literary or musical works, discussions of film, and political analyses of an international speech are all examples of secondary sources.

If you are writing a term paper on Alice Munro's story "Thanks for the Ride," for example, that text is your primary source. A scholarly discussion of that story, such as an article entitled "Summer Desires in Munro's 'Thanks for the Ride,'" would be a secondary source. If you were to analyze Canada's tax structure, the body of facts of our taxation system would be the primary source, whereas a piece of writing discussing an aspect of those facts, such as an essay called "GST and Other Irritating Taxation Techniques," would be your secondary source. If you were to conduct an interview with a retired taxation official from the Canada Customs and Revenue Agency on his or her view of certain flaws and possible improvements in the taxation system, then that interview would also be a secondary source.

Sometimes it can be a little tricky to identify the primary source. In fact, in some research situations what might usually be a secondary source can become your primary source if you decide to write your paper on that secondary source! If you wish to write a paper or a review on attitudes in literary criticism toward female characters in recent Canadian short stories, for example, the pieces of literary criticism you examine would be your primary sources, since these articles are the texts that your research paper addresses. Similarly, a paper on the 1991 Gulf War would have to rely on a factual account of this event as the primary source, but a paper on *one* writer's interpretation of this war would use that writer's work as the primary source.

Primary Source	Secondary Source
Mavis Gallant's "My Heart Is Broken" (story)	"Romance and Self-Esteem in Mavis Gallant's 'My Heart Is Broken'" (scholarly article)
Travis Horncastle's "Gulf War Syndrome" (research article)	Other articles, other research on Gulf War syndrome

EVALUATING SOURCES

You should always be careful about your sources. There is no need to take home every single book or other publication on your subject, or, on the other hand, to select randomly from the shelf. Good researchers look through a range of sources related to their topics, and use only some of these to write their papers. Evaluating your sources carefully before you use them will save you time on research and make your paper better. See "Evaluating Sources" at the Text Enrichment Site, Chapter 18.

When you assess a secondary source, you measure its relevance and usefulness to your project. Take into account the secondary source's **date of publication** (are its points and conclusions current or outdated?), its **scope** (is it too general or too specialized?), and its **Works Cited page** (MLA), **References page** (APA), or **Bibliography** (is it a well-researched discussion or a one-sided "opinion" piece?). You might also be able to find other potential sources listed in one good secondary source's Works Cited or References page. Using such "cross-referencing" is an effective and common research technique.

When you first evaluate a source, "read" quickly—not as an involved reader, but as a research scanner—moving rapidly through the source's main argument to see if you can use it productively. (See "Reading an Essay Under Pressure" at the Text Enrichment Site, Chapter 11.) Will it support your paper? Does it provide evidence and facts you can build on? Can you perhaps contend against the source's opinions and findings? Do you suspect errors, gaps, or bias in it?

Here are five questions to help you evaluate a source:

1. What is the source's main point, claim, or argument?
2. What is the author's perspective and/or tone (for/against/objective)?
3. Can you summarize the author's evidence?
4. Do you agree or disagree (or a little of both) with the author's point?
5. What questions does the source leave fully or partially unanswered or, equally important, completely unasked—in *your* opinion?

You should also look carefully at each source's table of contents and index (if a book), abstract (if an article and if available), introductory chapter or introductory paragraph, and Works Cited or References page. Sometimes these brief sections can help eliminate a useless source or generate new directions and new secondary sources in your research.

One advantage in using a college or university library is that some of the work in evaluating sources has already been done for you. Librarians, professors, and instructors who have a good idea of the sources their students need will have selected these books. If you use only a public library to do your research, you will have to be more careful; many sources there are intended primarily for high school students, hobbyists, or general-interest readers, and they may not be extensive enough for a college or university research paper.

Ask yourself these three questions to help you choose your sources well:

1. *Is the source written for researchers?* Does the book seem to be written for college or university students or for more advanced researchers in the field? Generally, your sources should be pitched just above your own current level of understanding, not a step or two below. You should be learning as you conduct your research. Many students are too easily put off by secondary sources that seem somewhat difficult. If you use a source that simplifies issues too much, you may not gain an understanding of the twists and turns of your subject, or the various debates within it. On the other hand, you need not struggle with a ferociously specialized source way beyond a first- or second-year student's level of comprehension, that is, a source that assumes a large body of knowledge you simply do not have yet. If you are writing a paper on the medical uses of marijuana, for instance, but you do not have a background in biology or medicine, expect to have to deal with some unfamiliar terminology, but don't waste valuable time

agonizing over highly specialized scientific articles obviously intended for an audience of MDs and PhDs. Use such articles if you can, but if you feel lost, put them aside for more immediately useful material.

2. *Is the source relevant to my topic?* Always check the introduction, table of contents, and the index to make sure that the source really contains the information you need. If the source has only a couple of pages relevant to your topic, you can photocopy these for a mention in your paper or perhaps a footnote or an endnote, and keep looking.

3. *What is the secondary source's position?* Remember that many published articles are only interpretations of facts and developments rather than completely objective evaluations. The authors of secondary sources offer their expert opinions as persuasively as possible, but remember that the entire secondary source may be only that one person's view, not the whole truth. Be careful as a researcher to distinguish the facts from the perspectives. While using the facts of the primary source or the view of another secondary source, you may be able to argue against or to qualify the perspective presented in any one particular secondary source.

Reading as a Researcher

A great deal of published research (secondary sources) contains aspects of both explicit and implicit interpretation. By definition, all interpretations contain significant aspects of **subjective knowledge:** personal experience, embedded perspectives, and professional attitudes toward what counts as evidence and toward what counts as a reasonable conclusion. You will come across many disputes between these different authors of secondary sources—all perhaps examining the same primary source—on the basis of the different interpretative strategies they employ. This tension is part of any research territory.

As a junior researcher reading the work of more experienced researchers, you need to be aware of the significant (and even sometimes trivial) ways your sources disagree with each other. Always be prepared to challenge these expert views. Sometimes the "experts" make mistakes in basic facts. Sometimes they draw arguably, or even blatantly, wrong conclusions from ambiguous premises. Sometimes they offer a wildly belligerent opinion or whimsical conclusion with which you have every right to disagree.

If you can "debunk"—that is, successfully challenge, expose, and overturn—a published or established view, you have performed one of the most important and respected functions of a researcher. The larger social function of all research is to locate a true account—a fair, just view.

Evaluating Sources on the Internet

Many of the strategies for evaluating printed sources apply equally to the World Wide Web. What is the source's authority? What is the source's background research? Does the source have a bias?

The web raises additional concerns:

- *Can you find out who is responsible for the site?* Do the individual organizations responsible for the site tell you anything about themselves? Are they established academics, teachers, or researchers? What if they are only grade 11 students who harbour deep resentment over the cultural underestimation of Duran Duran? How can you compare the merits of one source and another on the internet?
- *Is the site connected to a university or college?* Some of the best research sites are based in academic institutions and are entirely sound sources for academic research. However, be cautious about using information posted by other students, who may be designing superficial websites or posting weak drafts of eventually mediocre papers for their own courses. If the document seems to be composed by someone who does not know anything about writing, evidence, essay structure, analysis, or documentation, then steer clear of the site.
- *Is the site trying to sell you something?* If it presents research on something that it also tries to sell, chances are the research is biased in its favour. For example, if a pharmaceutical company posts information about a drug they sell, they will predictably select information that presents the drug in a positive light. Although some of the research may be reliable, look at other sources as well to give you a sense of balance.
- *When was the site last updated?* If the site has not been updated for one or two years, its owner might have abandoned it. In any event, a site that has not been updated for some time is usually not a particularly good source of information.
- *Is the site just a cheap collection of flashy graphics?* Remember that you are looking for information in your research, not splashy nonsense. Evaluate the text or substance of the site. In some cases, the graphics may be exactly what you need for your research, yet often they have little or no bearing on the content or substance of the site.

✒ PRACTICE

1. Find four websites on a specific topic you would like to research. Evaluate the strengths and weaknesses of each. How are some sources appropriate and some not for a research paper?

2. In groups, compare notes on various websites. Talk about the best and worst sites. Can you tell which sites were written by knowledgeable people and which sites were written by charlatans? What do the best websites have in common?

3. In groups, discuss how some websites have bamboozled many people with needless or misleading information. Evaluate the internet's usefulness in your experience.

4. How do you define "information"? In groups, debate this definition and the ways it may differ from "fact," "knowledge," and "common sense."

NOTE-TAKING FOR RESEARCH PURPOSES

As you read into your topic area, you need to take exact notes of your findings. Many researchers first make their notes on regular paper and then later condense the most vital information to a small card: perhaps a useful quotation, a brief two- or three-sentence summary of an article or chapter, or a particular author's central argument. You can easily rearrange and add to these cards later to reflect changes in your outline—and your outline will certainly change as you add and delete the information you collect and tighten your points and topic sentences to represent your revised thesis.

In this preliminary research stage, remember to record all source information precisely. The author's name, the source title, publisher, year, city of publication, and page numbers are crucial information. If there are errors in your research paper at this level, you will undermine your credibility as a researcher. All your quotations also need to be exact, so be careful when transcribing your initial notes, when condensing your longer notes to points on cards, when incorporating that information into various drafts, and when summarizing or paraphrasing source material. Remember you will have to attribute all summaries and paraphrases to your source by the author's name and the page number, though you will not necessarily quote that author's very words.

Following is a hypothetical example of a handy research card that you might produce from some of your initial reading and note-taking as you work toward shaping your thesis statement and an outline for your paper:

Sample Research Note Card

Tucker, Susan A. *The History of Boxing*. Toronto: McEwan Publishing, 1998.
- Chapter Five, "Mike Tyson's Presence," most relevant to my paper, especially the points about "social justification for bad behaviour," p. 134.
- Tucker asserts "only in professional boxing or crime could someone like Tyson flourish financially" (142).
- "Tyson himself seems genuinely confused about why his aggression is tremendously rewarded in the ring, but socially and legally denounced outside the ropes" (149).
- boxing a "circus or art" (151)?

The card contains all the necessary source information (author, title, city of publication, publisher, and date), as well as four exact quotations with their correct page numbers. You may later decide not to use all the quotations in your final draft, but these quotations may help you develop your thinking and initial draft for a research paper tentatively entitled, for example, "Sports Justifications for Bad Behaviour" or "Social Tolerance and Mike Tyson." This brief set of notes with page numbers on the research note card will save you from substantial rereading, since you will be able to relocate useful areas of discussion in the source quickly.

Photocopies from Secondary Sources

Some students photocopy significant articles and book chapters, in whole or part, when collecting their research materials. This may be useful later, when your outline and drafts are under way and expanding. You can later condense the photocopied information in the form of either direct quotations or attributed paraphrases on your note cards for integration into your drafts. Or you may draw in more detail from the photocopy if you need to expand a certain part of your discussion at a later stage of revision.

Reflecting Critical Reading in Your Notes

We have already looked at the importance of evaluating your sources. We stressed that when you read your sources and take notes for a research paper, you should approach those sources actively and critically. Look for facts that back your argument, but do not disregard facts that challenge your view. Also try to develop your own ideas. Your notes should reflect (1) helpful information (facts, strong views on your selected subject, some useful quotations), (2) perhaps a couple of more provocative quotations (and whether you agree or disagree), and (3) your opinions and analysis. It is important to keep the facts, perspectives, and specific language of your sources separate from your own language and views. Note-keeping should be meticulous.

When reading and taking notes as a researcher, be conscious of your own responses to the sources you find and your impression or interpretations of the texts and facts at hand. These are important in pulling together your own thesis and overall research paper.

Here is a summary of the strategies we have discussed to assist you when reading and taking notes from research sources:

- Use the introduction, conclusion, and table of contents to provide an overview of the secondary source's argument and to point you to the chapters and sections most relevant to your topic. The introduction or first chapter often states the author's thesis and goals, a preview of the argument, and sometimes even a summary of each chapter.
- Distinguish carefully between the author's interpretation and your own interpretation. You are gathering facts and evidence to support your own arguments, while you also assert your interpretation clearly and confidently. Remember that your view may or may not agree with your various sources' interpretations. (See "Fact or Opinion?" in Chapter 3, "More About Logic.")
- Keep track of disagreements among your sources. Whether your sources disagree with one another outright or differ only slightly in interpretation of the same events or texts, such discrepancies could lead you toward an

interesting topic or thesis. You should also think about which argument you find more convincing and why.

- Keep track of your own impressions and reactions to what you read. Do you agree or disagree with the ideas? Do any facts or assertions seem strange, surprising, or completely wrong? Do you notice a bias in the writer's perspective? Do you object to any particular point or interpretation? Does the author seem to take certain points for granted or overlook certain possibilities?

- Note the source's critical or theoretical perspective. Some authors will acknowledge their critical perspective directly within the first few pages; others will leave you to work it out. An awareness of your source's theoretical assumptions or framework—textual, contextual, poststructuralist, environmental, feminist, and conservative are some examples—will help you understand the source's argument and possible limits. You do not have to agree with a source's theoretical perspective in order to use it as part of your paper. In fact, if you strongly disagree with its perspective, reading the source may give you important insight into the other side of the issue and help you sharpen your own argument. (See Chapter 14, "Critical Analysis and Evaluation," and Chapter 16, "Argumentation.")

SUMMARIZING, PARAPHRASING, AND QUOTING

As you begin to expand your outline into full paragraphs, the three main techniques you will use to refer to your sources (thereby providing the supporting detail required in your paragraphs) are summarizing, paraphrasing, and quoting. Knowing when and how to apply these three basic techniques represents a major part of your work as a mediator of research sources. With experience, you will be able to decide in the researching and note-taking stage whether the best way to convey a certain point is to summarize, paraphrase, or quote.

Summarizing

A summary is an extremely compressed representation of a longer text. Compared to a paraphrase, a summary is a far more sweeping re-statement. A paraphrase usually teases out the fuller meanings and implications, while a summary encapsulates one or two crucial points from the original texts as briefly as possible. We have discussed summarizing in Chapter 13, so here we will review only crucial points and offer examples for your consideration.

When summarizing, be prepared to capture the single point or points of a text that, in your view, summarize that text most fully. By necessity, summaries do not include many details. Thus, you need to be bold in your willingness to compress and still be accurate. For example:

Shakespeare's *Macbeth* examines the political and psychological costs of sacrificing integrity for unrestrained ambition.

Anne Murray's song "Snowbird" seems to express regret for the coming of winter, but really expresses the disillusionment of lost love.

Even in slightly longer summaries, most details, people, events, and characters involved have been omitted. The point of the summary is to make one quick point that you will draw on or expand later in your essay.

Historical Summary

The late prime minister Trudeau, responding officially to the urgent requests of the premier of Quebec and the mayor of Montreal, invoked the War Measures Act in peacetime to contain the perceived threat of the FLQ against the elected government.

Literary Summary

Margaret Atwood's novel The Handmaid's Tale depicts a future post-nuclear world where radiation and environmental damage have resulted in mass infertility. Militarized Christian fundamentalists have formed the government (now a "theocracy" rather than a democracy). Handmaids are the few young fertile women and must live in servitude for the purpose of attempted procreation with government and military officials.

PRACTICE

Summarize a well-known movie in three or four sentences. Show your summary to a friend or classmate and see whether that person would agree or disagree that your summary accurately represents the main point or theme.

Paraphrasing

A paraphrase represents a specific point or expression drawn from another source. It differs from a summary by representing a more concentrated section of a selected text. A paraphrase attempts to capture accurately a particular idea in a particular moment of the text, whether, for example, a poem, scholarly article, history book, or song. A paraphrase is a close, faithful representation of the original.

As we discuss later in this chapter, there are good reasons not to overuse direct quotations from your sources. For one thing, reflecting too many other voices can create confusion and lose your own voice. For another, you may become lazy and let the other writers do the talking while your mind drifts out of the discussion. Putting another writer's words into your own words helps you to maintain consistent tone and control of the discussion. A summary achieves this, but so does a paraphrase. When the details of the material you wish to report are important, then a paraphrase serves you better than a summary, which must reduce the material to its essence only. Our examples below provide invented statements from hypothetical sources followed by paraphrases of the original statements.

Source

J. Tosako, 1999: "Some argue that tuition hikes are not offset by a slightly increasing number of scholarships and bursaries that offer limited sums" (113).

Paraphrase

Despite the availability of limited funds for post-secondary entrance students, some experts argue that these limited scholarships and bursaries are still insufficient to make up for tuition increases (Tosako 113).

Source

P. Murphy, 1998: "Statistics Canada surveyed three thousand individuals between the ages of 17 and 25, and determined that 42 percent of the population eligible for post-secondary entrance was forced to work nearly full-time to support full-time school costs or else not attend because of low funds" (7).

Paraphrase

Murphy's findings that nearly half of eligible post-secondary students must work full-time to cover costs (7) are supported by Tosako's recent findings on underfunding (113).

Once you have listed all your authors' central positions from your sources, you may find both similarities and differences in their perspectives. These will help you construct your argument. Group some sources together and support your claims about their similarities or differences by summarizing or paraphrasing this research.

Now you can probably develop a series of provisional topic sentences. Use them to organize paragraphs of your essay draft, making sure to support the topic sentence with your chosen evidence. Be alert to any changes in your own perspective. You may revise not only the topic sentences, but also the way you position your argument and your supporting evidence. Through this work, you will produce your first complete draft.

Original (excerpt from poem)

I should have been a pair of ragged claws / Scuttling across the floors of silent seas

—T. S. Eliot, "The Love Song of J. Alfred Prufrock," 1917

Inaccurate paraphrase

Prufrock wishes he had big claws so that he could run fast on the bottom of the ocean, feeling happy and alive.

This inaccurate paraphrase imposes invented facts and notions on these two quoted lines. First, the original lines state "ragged claws," not "big claws." This paraphrase error misconstrues the poem's language, representing the speaker as somehow feeling powerful ("big claws"), yet the original words, "ragged claws," strongly imply bare survival, turbulent existence, and perhaps even a sense of future doom. The hasty paraphrase entirely erases the bleak aspects of a failing struggle conveyed within the poet's choice of words.

As well, the paraphrase's "run fast" completely misrepresents the action of "[s]cuttling" in the original line. "Scuttling" implies an intentional but highly inefficient movement: strenuous, makeshift, even frantic. "Run fast," as an inaccurate paraphrase, carelessly deletes such invoked "scuttling" connotations, arbitrarily replacing them with the student's projected image of athleticism, speed, efficiency, and joy.

Last, the paraphrase's closing description, stating that the poem's speaker would feel "happy and alive" in this ocean scene, is an entirely superimposed observation rather than a factually or contextually accurate re-statement of anything in the original lines. Be careful not to adjust paraphrases to "speak" your own view; instead the paraphrase must accurately reflect its original quoted text.

More accurate paraphrase (the two lines literally)

Prufrock here wishes to be nothing more than some kind of crustacean, scraping its way for its entire existence across the sea bottom. Prufrock also wishes for escape to the endless silence of the ocean floor.

More accurate paraphrase (within context of entire poem)

Rather than live in his pretentious, upper-class, paralyzing, and gossipy social world, Prufrock wishes he could become a simple creature of purely instinctive existence in a silent world of Nature, possibly even an undiscovered part of that world. Prufrock's wish indicates that he is prepared (or so he says) to trade a gracious but empty life of privilege and culture for an unthinking but uncomplicated anonymity. He would also trade all his human consciousness for the peace of having no consciousness.

✒ PRACTICE

Paraphrase the following two excerpts from a poem and a secondary source. These paraphrases can be presented to your instructor for comment, discussed with classmates during group work, or exchanged within the class as a whole, using multiple photocopies.

Poem Excerpt

> She fears him, and will always ask
>   What fated her to choose him;
> She meets in his engaging mask
>   All reasons to refuse him;

—E. A. Robinson, "Eros Turannos," 1916

Secondary Source Excerpt

In particular, compositional balance [in film noir] within the frame is often disruptive and unnerving. Those traditionally harmonious triangular three-shots and balanced two-shots, which are borrowed from the compositional principles of Renaissance paintings, are seldom seen in the better film noir. More common are bizarre, off-angle compositions of figures placed irregularly in the frame, which create a world that is never stable or safe, that is always threatening to change drastically and unexpectedly. . . . And objects seem to push their way into the foreground of the frame to assume more power than the people. (65)

—Janey Place and Lowell Peterson, "Some Visual Motifs of *Film Noir*," in *Film Noir Reader*, eds. A. Silver and J. Ursini, 1996

> **Tip:** A good paraphrase always carefully represents the telling details of the original quotation. Often, especially with compressed and literary language, the paraphrase may be longer than the original quoted lines.

There are two further areas of difficulty that complicate paraphrasing efforts:

Ambiguous Words and Phrasings

Ambiguous words and phrasings are everywhere and there are few places to hide from them. For example, if you were to paraphrase the line "an abundance of trout is suddenly biting off the coast of Vancouver," would you represent this occurrence as a happy opportunity for good fishing or as an unprecedented marine disaster? The slightly alarming phrase "biting off the coast" creates the ambiguity here.

Let us say this following sentence appeared in a year-end business report for a large corporation: "In the last year's busy and changing international economy, our company only faced two new lawsuits." Does this sentence mean that the only business this particular company engaged in was defending itself against lawsuits? Or does the sentence mean, despite all its other activities in the busy and changing international economy, only two lawsuits arose? Presumably the incorrect placement of the word "only" in the sentence creates this ambiguity.

Idiom

Imagine that the following sentence is to be paraphrased by someone who does not speak English as a first language and has just started English lessons:

> I <u>ran into Lisa</u> the other day and she asked me <u>to give her a hand</u>, but I said I was <u>wiped out</u> and wanted <u>to call it a day</u>.

The four idiomatic phrases here that most North American English speakers take for granted can pose serious comprehension, let alone paraphrasing, difficulties. Taken literally, the sentence makes little sense. Literature, music, political statements, and film dialogue from other cultures (even other cultures in the English language, such as Irish, Australian, and U.K. English) can pose paraphrasing problems.

Quoting

In his writing workshops, writer Clark Blaise used to point out that quotations in a short piece of writing contain enormous force. A quotation, of course, is a word-by-word accurate transcription of someone else's exact words. It is signalled by surrounding quotation marks—"like this." Notice how the quotation marks draw extra attention to the words quoted. Quotations represent high impact locations; they carry weight. As Blaise used to tell his writing students concerning quotations, in short pieces of writing, less is more— even essays of 20 pages may be considered relatively short pieces of writing. You will gain considerable effect by using quotations, especially if you select them with extreme care. If someone has worded something in a clumsy way, why not summarize or paraphrase? If someone has said something in 30 words when 15 would have done, why quote the entire 30 words? Remember Clark Blaise's advice and intersperse quotations in your work with care, using only the choicest, most crucial words.

Later in this chapter we say more about how to integrate quotations smoothly into your paper. During the researching and note-taking stage, the key consideration is to look for quotable words that seem to represent the essence of what someone is saying. Copy or retain those words with extreme care for accuracy.

SHAPING YOUR WORK

Two important steps, as your note-taking proceeds, are **finding a working thesis** and **outlining a possible structure**.

Developing a Working Thesis

As you find new information or decide to emphasize a different angle or point in your analysis of a selected topic, your outline and your thesis will likely change, often only slightly but sometimes extensively. In either event, a working thesis will help you shape your early drafts.

If you have decided to work on the topic of a recent Canadian tuition increase, for example, you may have researched the public's changing attitudes toward education over the last three or four decades. You may decide to research the possibility that the idealistic approach of encouraging individual promise and identifying it through constant classroom dialogue, argument, student experience, and frequent teacher-student interactions has shifted to a new corporate model of processing students as customers at arm's length. There are recent studies—both in the form of books and articles in education journals—that even attempt to define what a college or university may be or should be. There are certainly plenty of newspaper and magazine articles on the social effects of tuition increases: on how financial obstacles to post-secondary education change the fabric of democracy, on how high tuition may be seen as gatekeeping on the dubious basis of socio-economic class, and how the increasing emphasis on money in exchange for knowledge can only perpetuate the generational cycles of "haves" and "have-nots." You might take the opposite view, however, based on your experience, and locate research sources to support your view.

Because the subject of post-secondary education has become one of Canada's most pressing concerns, your essay will have both academic and social implications. Here are some examples of how you might move from this general topic to a working thesis on it:

Tuition increases and their effects

1. Tuition increases change the social composition of the student body. Do tuition increases create unnecessary exclusion? And how might increases affect the future of Canadian society?

2. Is education vital to democracy and freedom? Could tuition increases threaten those ideals?
3. Tuition increases reflect the increasing financial responsibility young people and their families must accept in the pursuit of education. Is there a limit?
4. Do tuition increases threaten to turn education into just another luxury consumer product? Is education a right or a privilege?

You will develop your working thesis, whatever your perspective is, as you work through your reading and form reactions to it. Keep asking yourself where you stand in relation to what you read. Question and challenge the perspectives of the authors you encounter in your research.

You can develop your outline—topic sentences, paragraph subjects, paragraph sequence, use of evidence, and quoted material from sources—after you have settled on your working thesis. Your outline, with this working thesis, will lead you into a draft, which will allow you to develop that working thesis further. Remember that as you develop your essay's content and form, you will adjust your thesis, topic sentences, and emphasis accordingly. (See Chapter 6 for more guidance on this formative stage of essay development.)

Outlining

Once you've chosen a working thesis for your paper, you can begin the outlining process to prepare for writing your first draft. First, take a look at the research you have already done and try to find further readings that focus on your own emerging perspective, whether they support or dispute your thesis. As you read, keep your working thesis in mind and how it compares or contrasts with other authors' perspectives and how those authors compare and contrast with each other.

You may now be able to construct the brief outline to represent the shape of your essay. Write down the main points from your different sources and state how they either support or refute the basis of your chief assertion. For each point, try to represent a different source. You may wish to propose a topic sentence that asserts some point to be expanded into a paragraph later—your perspective in relation to the other researchers' conclusions and claims.

Sample Student Outline for Research Paper Defining and Understanding "Introversion"

For the completed essay and further commentary on how it has handled citations, see Chapter 19 (p. 322).

Working title: Introversion: The Dreaded Other
Colleen Leonard

Introductory paragraph: Present example of five-year-old Adam whose loner behaviour after school worries his parents. Describe his behaviour. Is there something "wrong with him"? Parents read a couple of books recommended by the guidance counsellor [Leonard introduces the idea of more information to follow from research sources]. State controlling idea: After reading these books, the parents understand there is nothing "wrong" with Adam: he is simply introverted.

Second paragraph topic sentence: "[T]he terms introversion and extroversion became known in psychology through Carl Jung's theory of Psychological Types (1921), and were defined as two "complementary orientations to life" (Myers & Briggs Foundation, n.d., p. 7). Define Jung's original ideas and show how scientific studies and findings since then seem to support that he was accurate—people do seem to be born with biological preferences. Examples: M. O. Laney's *The Introvert Advantage* case study; Garcia, brain scan research; and Myers-Briggs–type indicator adapted from Jung and widely considered accurate and useful. Point: Jung's introvert-extrovert dichotomy has merit and both impulses are valuable. So why does society seem to consider introversion an affliction?

Third paragraph topic sentence: Part of this attitude may be due to the influence of Sigmund Freud. Laney's critique of Freud's emphasis on "narcissism" and his idea that the point of psychological development is to "find gratification in the world of external reality" (p. 26)." Laney's critique of the *Dictionary of Psychology*, showing biased language favouring extroversion over introversion. End with the most dramatic example—Webster's *New World Thesaurus* defining introvert as "a brooder, self-observer, egoist, narcissist, solitary lone wolf, and loner" (qtd. in Laney, 2002, pp. 50–51).

Fourth paragraph topic sentence: It is not hard to understand why introversion might be considered the less desirable of the two if using the definitions above within North American culture. Survey North American cultural values that predominantly elevate extroversion and devalue introversion: using Crozier (1990), examine confusion of extroversion with 1. shyness and 2. schizoid disorders.

Fifth paragraph topic sentence: If, however, introversion is inborn, why do studies find only 25 percent of the North American population to be introverts? Consider Jung's idea of the collective consciousness of a people. He seemed to allow for an interaction between innate and culturally conditioned responses. Laney's point about "rugged individualism"—drive—introverts are a threat to North American myths.

Sixth paragraph topic sentence: A final factor contributing to the negative perception of introversion is that certain studies seem to find extroverts to be "happier" than introverts (Laney, 2002). Discuss Laney's perceptions of flaws in these studies.

Final paragraph topic sentence: In conclusion, it seems there are a number of misconceptions that contribute to the "bad press" that introverts get in North America. Reflect on the combination of misconceptions and extroversion dominance as potentially harmful to the esteem of introverts. One result is the need for introverts "to develop extra coping skills" (Laney, 2002, p. 6). Misconceptions need to be challenged by everyone, however—with harmful, inaccurate ideas, everyone loses. Note that introverts comprise the majority of the gifted population (Gallagher, 1990; Hoehn & Birely, 1988).

In rough form, Colleen's outline integrates the parts of her research that she has reviewed, reconsidered, and decided to use. She has given herself directions about what to cite, when and where. She has included direct quotations where she thinks she might want to use them. How precisely she cites her sources will be guided by her purpose, as it has now emerged.

As you can see, that purpose is to define introversion in order to uncover harmful misconceptions about it and replace those with accurate ideas about what introverts have to offer. Refining her strategy further, she has determined a need to begin the body of her essay with a brief history of the term, something that will require a paragraph. Her following paragraphs not only look at misunderstandings but do so from the point of view of causes: what has caused the misunderstandings and how did they spread? Later in the outline she acknowledges a complicating question—if introversion is innate and meant to be a complement to extroversion, why are 75 percent of the North American population extroverted? She offers possible answers—again referring to her sources—and concludes by reviewing the harm caused by inaccurate ideas. This clear sense of strategy and purpose throughout her outline has allowed her to "plant" her citations where they make sense. Now that she knows when and where she wishes to cite her sources, *how* will she handle those citations? The answer is that she will recognize the benefits of summarizing, paraphrasing, and quoting, and will decide, at the drafting stage, when one offers more benefits than the others.

THE DRAFTING STAGE—INTEGRATING QUOTATIONS

As you move from note-taking and outlining to drafting, one of the challenges you face is how to integrate the quotations you have gathered. Any quotations you use must fit smoothly into the flow of your own sentences. You need to punctuate carefully when including quotations, as if the quoted words were a natural part of your own sentence. If you use a long quotation (four typed lines or more, MLA style, or 40 words or more, APA style), try to precede the quotation with an independent introductory clause followed by a colon. This allows your reader some preparation—a breath—before plunging into the long quotation. Such longer quotations are always set off from the rest of the text by block indentation and do not require quotation marks.

Integrating a long quotation

Despite popular opinion, lemmings are a sturdy, independent species, as Cornelia Zahl observes:

> Investigators are interested in lemmings' seasonal movements, but of even more pressing interest to scientists are the little creatures' population explosions. These significant population increases occur every three or four years, sometimes astounding even the most experienced lemming experts. Lemmings, in fact, are among the most prolific of mammals. Sometimes the

weasel population on the tundra starts to soar, since the lemmings, as small rodents, are staples of some carnivore diets. (41)

Note that the period appears before the page citation in parentheses at the end.

If, on the other hand, you want to use only a short part of a quotation, you might begin the sentence with a few words of your own and finish the sentence by incorporating the significant element from your source. Students tend to rely far too much on long quotations—in some cases, because these fill in the word count and get the paper "over with." That is a poor reason for choosing a block quotation. If you do use a long quotation, it had better be for a really important reason. A general rule of thumb is to quote only the choicest words and to handle the remaining idea through summary or paraphrase.

Integrating short quotations

Franklin is only one of several biochemists who claim that "working with Dr. Kostner was like being in daily contact with an unpredictable force of nature" (274).

Although Lisa-Marie Grierson maintains that society will eventually turn away from the computer, "coming to this point of anti-technological enlightenment will take decades and perhaps a century" (79).

In the second example above, the comma appears before the quotation simply because that is how the sentence would normally be punctuated. This comma separates the introductory dependent clause from the main or independent clause, which is the quotation here. Remember that you should not use any extra punctuation with a quotation when normal grammatical usage would not require that punctuation. In our first example above, no punctuation was required to work the quotation into the sentence's own language and syntax.

Watch for the extremely common mistake of creating a comma splice when introducing the quotation.

Comma splice

Some critics of Wong Kar-Wai's film *Chungking Express* find the camera technique purposefully distracting in order to complicate the representation of the characters, "the shifting and jarring camera work, which sometimes imitates a public area surveillance camera, tries to capture the rushing momentum in daily big city life, as well as the two main characters' emotional isolation" (Bugden 18).

The way to fix this punctuation error is to replace the comma directly before the quotation with a colon (:). This colon will set off the quotation, which is an independent clause, from the writer's own preceding independent clause that introduces it.

Square Brackets

Square brackets appearing within a quotation indicate that a capital letter has been either added or removed or that a word or phrase has been added or changed.

Although Paul Hewson argues that "Big Rock [beer] tastes fresh and crisp . . ." [s]atisfying Canadian beer-drinkers is always a challenge" (30).

Here, the essayist has added the word "beer" in square brackets to clarify exactly what the brand name "Big Rock" indicates and has also used square brackets to indicate that a capital "S" has been changed to a lower-case "s," allowing the essayist to shape the quotation within the syntax of his or her own sentence.

Ellipses

The three periods after "crisp" in the above example are called **ellipses** and indicate that some words have been omitted. Three periods form ellipses within a quotation; however, an ellipsis that appears at the end of a sentence still requires the period.

> Pamela J. Salzwedel argues that "Heathcliff in Emily Brontë's *Wuthering Heights* experiences a crisis as a boy because of sudden socioeconomic realization, but returns to the scene of his trauma as a wealthy and vengeful man . . . " (69).

Punctuation and Quotation

As prescribed by MLA or APA style (Chapter 19), the period follows the parentheses of the page reference. If there are no page references in parentheses, place commas and periods inside your quotation marks. Colons and semicolons should be placed outside your quotation marks, but only if they are not part of the quotation.

> E. L. Doctorow's 1971 novel *The Book of Daniel* is "a law-literature classic"; it explores the Rosenberg case during U.S. Cold War frenzy.

If your quotation runs into another sentence and the quotation does not need to be indented into a block note, the quotation marks straddle the two sentences.

> Fraser's book *Violence in the Arts* boldly contends that "our attitudes towards violence are deeply confused. The organized violence in the film *The Godfather* seems to have audience support" (19).

Fair Use

In general, small changes using square brackets and ellipses can be made within quotations from your sources, provided these changes do not alter or manipulate the quotation's original meaning. In a quotation, you must represent the author's view fairly.

Original quotation

"The U.S. trade embargo against Cuba stands as a colossal contradiction to the new principles of international free trade. A continuing embargo shows that rather than functioning as a fair and globally open economic plan, free trade is only what the U.S. government says it is at any given moment" (Kostyrenko, *Free Trade and Its Political Contradictions*, 232).

Unfair, misleading use

"The U.S. trade embargo against Cuba . . . function[s] as a fair and globally open economic plan . . . " (232).

Fair use

"The U.S. trade embargo against Cuba [reveals that] . . . free trade is only what the U.S. government says it is at any given moment" (232).

Use Only Significant Quotations

Remember to include only significant quotations in the final draft. A research paper is not supposed to be merely a smorgasbord of various quotations, quickly strung together until you have reached the required word limit. Be selective. Your voice and your perspective on the topic are supposed to be the most important dimensions in your college and university research paper. Your research source should be *integrated* into your own considered view of a text or topic rather than allowed to dominate the paper. Let your reader see clearly, in detail and with articulated implications, where you stand on the topic or text you are examining.

Weak integration of sources (sample paragraph)

Jim Simpson contends that the musical *The Sound of Music* "raises important questions about the fragile triumph of private happiness in the face of turbulent international events" (53). Mary Ciccione seems to disagree: "*The Sound of Music*, as pleasant as the singing is, addresses nothing of any substance, even more blatantly than *Willy Wonka and the Chocolate Factory*, a film musical about chocolate" (178). However, Julie Andrews's optimism, according to Burton Bachman, "allows viewers to believe in the healing-power of music, especially the singing voice as a sign of hope" (22). I guess I agree with some of these points, but not with all of them.

Better integration of sources with essayist's perspective

Critics continue to be divided on the thematic importance of the film musical *The Sound of Music*. Although Mary Ciccione argues that the film "addresses nothing of any substance" (178), Bachman's view is that Julie Andrews's optimism "allows viewers to believe in the healing-power of music, especially the singing voice as a sign of hope" (22). Simpson also agrees that the film has substance, since it raises "important questions of the fragile triumph of private happiness in . . . turbulent international events" (53).

See "How to Avoid Quotation Overcrowding" at the Text Enrichment Site, Chapter 18, for more advice on dealing with quotations.

Distinguishing Between Source Material and Your Own Views

Here are hypothetical examples of two pieces of writing drawing from the same research note card. The first essayist falls into inadvertent plagiarism because he borrows language and points from the source without full acknowledgment. The second essayist shows care in separating the secondary source's argument and language from his own views and language.

Incorrect use of quotation

Ondaatje's poem "Letters and Other Worlds" explores how the turbulent, solitary father cannot communicate, at any level, with his diverse family, though, as Peters points out, he "could write so beautifully" (147).

Sample Note Card

Source: "The central question of Michael Ondaatje's poem 'Letters and Other Worlds' is why the turbulent, solitary father could not communicate, at any level, with his family, though he could write so beautifully." (Meghan T. Peters, "Ondaatje's Frightening Family View," *York Experiments*, Vol. 8, No. 2, p. 147)

As you can see, most of the language of the secondary source ends up in the student's own sentence and most of it is not acknowledged. This is plagiarism and can lead to serious consequences.

Correct use of quotation

Although Meghan Peters correctly points out that Ondaatje's poem "Letters and Other Worlds" examines an unpredictable father who cannot communicate with his family, "though he could write so beautifully" (147), Peters overlooks the often complex, painful, and withdrawn relationship many creative people have with the world.

In the preceding example, Peters's language and point are attributed fully to her, and the student takes the opportunity to express his opinions of what Peters's perspective may overlook in an interpretation of Ondaatje's poem.

Such proper handling of your secondary sources—through accurate quotations, attributed paraphrases, sharp distinction between your ideas and those of others, fair use of context, square brackets, and ellipses, and smooth integration of quotations within your own writing—will contribute to an effective research paper.

FINAL WORDS

This chapter has, indeed, presented a wide array of detail. Much of it can be called upon as needed according to your stage in the process. The main thing to remember from start to finish with a research assignment is that success depends upon finding and evaluating suitable sources, then citing those in line with your purpose and according to the particular effects of summarizing, paraphrasing, and quoting. Each use of a source must provide a specific acknowledgment, one that links your reader via the author's surname to more information on that source in your final list of sources. Chapter 19 provides more information on how that process of "documenting" is handled, whether by the Modern Language Association system (MLA) or the American Psychological Association system (APA). The following checklist summarizes and reinforces the main points made in this chapter.

✔ CHECKLIST of Steps to a Successful Research Paper

1. Make a realistic schedule that considers not only reading and rereading your sources, but also drafting and rewriting your paper.

2. Select, then narrow, your topic; define your point of interest, your specific research context.

3. Define crucial terms in your instructor's assignment, your selected research topic, and your subsequent research. You may have to research your terms to pursue your project.

4. Gather preliminary research and resume narrowing your topic and angle of inquiry.

5. Gather and evaluate secondary sources.

6. Take notes: ideas, issues, authors, titles, dates, summaries of arguments, paraphrases, quotations (with page numbers).

7. Create your outline on paper: main points, your position, topic sentences, and paragraphs.

8. Refine your working thesis, then adjust topic sentences and parts of your paragraphs accordingly.

9. Combine your analysis and opinion with your material, solidifying your own position on the research. Keep your position distinct from those of your sources.

10. Draft, document, revise, proofread—be sure you have avoided the 15 common errors listed in section 3 of the Handbook.

Chapter 19
Documentation

Why document sources? Documentation is taken very seriously in academic writing. When you document your sources, you credit other researchers' work that appears in some way in your own essays. Your readers need to distinguish between others' work and your own. Proper documentation informs your readers exactly what sources you decided to work with, what their positions are, and how these sources differ from your own ideas and language. Providing a list of your sources at the end of your essay without giving specific citations in the body of your essay, where aspects of those sources have been used, creates an appearance of plagiarism.

ASSISTING YOUR READER AND AVOIDING THE APPEARANCE OF PLAGIARISM

By clearly acknowledging everything you take from sources and providing complete information on those sources, you give valuable background to your reader and avoid any appearance of plagiarism. See the introduction to this section (p. 280) for an important caution concerning possible perceptions of plagiarism.

FORMS OF DOCUMENTATION

The preferred form for citations and bibliographic entries varies considerably among disciplines. Publications in the humanities and arts generally use the Modern Language Association (MLA) style of documentation. Editors in the social sciences prefer the American Psychological Association (APA) style. These two styles are regarded as the most widely used forms of documentation, but there are many others, including the University of Chicago style. Later in this section we present examples of MLA and APA style, as we have done throughout various other parts of this Rhetoric. We do not, however, represent the many other styles, nor provide complete information for all documentation scenarios concerning the two most widely used styles that we have presented as illustrations. It is your responsibility to find out what form of documentation is used by the publication in which you intend to place your work (or which style your instructor prefers). You should then supplement the information provided here by referring to a complete manual for the style required.

These manuals are available in most college or university bookstores, as well as the reference section of your college or university library. The most recent versions of APA and MLA documentation guidelines appear in the following publications (listed in MLA style, by the way):

- Gibaldi, Joseph. *MLA Handbook for Writers of Research Papers.* 6th ed. New York: Modern Language Association of America, 2003.
- *Publication Manual of the American Psychological Association.* 5th ed. Washington, D.C.: American Psychological Association, 2001.

MLA and APA forms are both based on the use of short parenthetical citations within the text. This basic technique is explained in more detail below.

WHEN TO DOCUMENT

Many students have the wrong impression. They believe they need to acknowledge their sources only when quoting directly from a text. This presumption is very misguided. Any time you use another person's idea or phrasing in an essay of yours, you have to acknowledge your source. This idea or phrasing is someone else's work and someone else's property. (When a work is published, copyright sometimes reverts from the author to someone else.) You must acknowledge sources when you quote directly, summarize, paraphrase, or otherwise use someone else's ideas. Sometimes you even have to acknowledge sources for factual information, not only opinions and interpretations.

You do not need to document sources for factual information that is considered common knowledge either to the public or in your field. Some examples of common public knowledge include Columbus's arrival in North America in 1492, Pierre Trudeau's service as a Canadian prime minister, Alice Walker's writing the novel *The Color Purple,* Newfoundland's joining Canada last among the provinces, and Leonard Cohen's writing sad songs. Sometimes it is difficult to know what would be considered common knowledge, but one indication would be that all the sources you have consulted agree on the facts. If you are doubtful about what counts as common knowledge, be safe and cite your source.

PARENTHETICAL CITATIONS WITHIN THE PAPER

MLA and APA styles of documentation work on the same principle: inserting short citations in the body of the essay within parentheses. These brief citations point to full ones listed at the end of your paper, usually by linking the last name of the author in the body of your essay to the first word of the related biblio-graphic entry in the alphabetical list. Some of the most common types of citations are provided below.

MLA Parenthetical Citations Within the Paper

The MLA system requires that you provide your citation's page number in paren-theses after the quotation. You must also provide the author's name if it is not already included in your sentence. If you refer to more than one work by the same author, you should also include in the parentheses a short version of the title, such as one key word.

> Winters argues unconvincingly that Hamlet "was written by Queen Elizabeth" (17). [Here there is no need to repeat the author's name in parentheses, so just include the number of the page on which this quotation can be found.]

> One critic even suggests that Hamlet was written by Queen Elizabeth (Winters 17). [Here the author's name is also supplied in parentheses because it does not appear in the sentence.]

> In her most recent article, however, Winters backs away from her earlier claims that Hamlet was written by Queen Elizabeth (<u>Reconsideration</u> 175–76). [Here a short version of the article's title is given because now more works than one by Winters are listed in the Works Cited list for the essay.]

More Parenthetical Citation Tips for MLA Style

- Use "qtd. in" (for quoted in) for quotations taken from an indirect source:

  > James Bone wrote that London resides in "the appearance of great shadows where there can be no shadows, throwing blackness up and down" (qtd. in Ackroyd 110).

- Shorten publishers' names. Use "Pearson" rather than "Pearson Education."
- Use regular numerals to indicate act and scene in plays (Lear 2.2). Use Roman numerals (lower case) only for pages from a preface, introduction, or table of contents.
- Use only the name of the first person listed when citing a source by more than three people:

  > Gold et al. suggest that Canada is more than the sum of its parts (27).

Contrary to popular belief, the first underground railroad between the U.S. and Canada existed to free slaves held on Canadian territory (Walker 19). [Here the citation is to little-known information.]

> **Tip:** Note that in APA style, a *comma* separates author, publication date, and page number in the parentheses, while in MLA style, *no comma* separates author and page number in the parentheses. Note also that APA uses the abbreviation "p." before the page number, while MLA does not.

APA Parenthetical Citations Within the Paper—Emphasis upon the Date

The APA system requires that you provide not only the author's name and a page number or numbers, but also the date of the work in the body of your paper. Supply information in parentheses when it is not already part of your sentence. In the APA system these parentheses are placed within the sentence, right after the reference to the article or study:

In 1996, Hintz studied the intellect of mice. [There is no need for a page number here because there is no direct quotation, and the summary is very general.]

A recent study of the "previously underestimated intellect of mice" (Hintz, 1996, p. 56) proved that mice are smarter than seagulls. [Both author and date must be included in parentheses with the page number if the author and date do not appear in the sentence.]

Hintz (1996) argued that mice are not as large as they seem close up. [The author is part of the sentence, so only the date must be provided in parentheses. Note that this date appears right after the author's name.]

Three recent studies of the intellect of mice (Hintz, 1996; Lamb, 1994, 1997) have shown that mice have not yet discovered electricity or television. [Here is an example of how you would cite more than one study in parentheses. In this case, you are referring to one study by Hintz and to two studies by Lamb, conducted in different years.]

MLA FULL CITATION IN THE FINAL REFERENCES PAGE

Entries in a bibliography in MLA style are listed on a separate page under the heading "Works Cited" (see the sample research paper in MLA style that follows). All authors are listed alphabetically by surname. The author's last name appears first, followed by a comma, followed by his or her full first name, and then a period. Then the title of the work appears: a book title is italicized or underlined; an essay title in a scholarly journal appears in quotations, and the name of the journal, italicized or underlined, follows the essay title. With scholarly articles, volume and issue numbers follow the title of the journal, followed by the date in parentheses, a full colon, and the page spread (the article's first and last page). Here are some examples of common MLA citations:

Book

Axelrod, Alan. <u>Elizabeth I, CEO: Strategic Lessons from the Leader Who Built an Empire.</u> Englewood Cliffs, NJ: Prentice Hall, 2000.

Article in a journal or magazine

Kelly, Philip F. "The Geographies and Politics of Globalization." <u>Progress in Human Geography</u> 23 (1999): 379–400. [The 23 in this case refers to the issue number. If the periodical also has a volume number—for example, 135—the entry would appear as follows.]

Kelly, Philip F. "The Geographies and Politics of Globalization." <u>Progress in Human Geography</u> 135.23 (1999): 379–400.

Article in an essay collection (including names of editors)

Partington, Angela. "The Designer Housewife in the 1950s." <u>A View from the Interior: Feminism, Women and Design</u>. Ed. Judy Attfield and Pat Kirkham. London: Women's Press, 1989. 206–14. [When citing a reading in a multi-purpose text such as *Acting on Words,* treat the author of the reading as the author and Brundage and Lahey—for example—as the editors. If you are citing parts of the Rhetoric written by Brundage and Lahey, then treat them as the authors.]

Booth, Wayne C. "The Rhetorical Stance." *Acting on Words: An Integrated Rhetoric, Reader and Handbook.* 2nd ed. Ed. David Brundage and Michael Lahey. Toronto: Pearson, 2009. 488–93. [The page span of the reading is included at the end.]

Article in a newspaper

Tibbetts, Janice, and Kate Jaimet. "Trudeau Dead at 80." <u>Edmonton Journal</u> 29 Sept. 2000: A1.

Book by a group or corporate author

American Psychological Association. <u>Publication Manual of the American Psychological Association</u>. 5th ed. Washington: APA, 2001.

Book or film review

Ebert, Roger. Rev. of <u>Jesus of Montreal</u>, dir. Denys Arcand. <u>Chicago Sun-Times</u> 18 July 1990: E4.

Website

Walker, Alice. "Letter from Alice Walker to President Clinton." 26 Oct. 2000 <http://www.igc.apc.org/cubasoli/awalker.html>.

Note that all lines subsequent to the first line of each entry are indented five spaces, a format known as a "hanging indent." Also double-space both within and between your entries on the Works Cited page.

If your source is written or edited by two or three people, format the full citation as follows:

Gold, Eleanor, Eli Sky, and James Cedar. <u>Views of Canada.</u> Toronto: Maple Leaf, 2000.

If your source is written or edited by more than three people, give the name of the first-listed person followed by "et al." (meaning "and others"):

Gold, Eleanor, et al. <u>Views of Canada.</u> Toronto: Maple Leaf, 2000.

For more information on how to document online sources in MLA style, see the MLA website at www.mla.org/style.

APA FULL CITATION IN THE FINAL REFERENCES LIST

Entries on the References page in APA style are listed on a separate page at the end of the essay under the heading "References." (See the sample research paper in APA style later in this section.) Like MLA style, APA uses the hanging indent format, with the first line of an entry flush left, but all subsequent lines of that entry indented five spaces. Again like MLA, double-spacing is used between and within entries in APA. The author's last name appears first, followed by his or her initials, rather than the full first name. Then the date of publication follows in parentheses. The entries on this References page should appear in alphabetical order according to author surname. The APA style for the References page is a highly detailed format and requires the additional rules:

- Underline or italicize titles and subtitles of books and journals.
- Do not place titles of articles in quotation marks.
- Capitalize only the first word of a book or article title [this does *not* apply for book or article titles within the body of the essay].
- List all authors' names rather than use "et al."
- Separate two or more authors' names with an ampersand (&), not the word "and."
- Underline or italicize volume numbers of journals.
- Use the abbreviation "p." (or "pp." for plural) before page numbers of newspaper articles and works in anthologies, but not before page numbers of either scholarly journal articles or magazine articles.

Here are some common examples of APA style:

Book

Axelrod, A. (2000). *Elizabeth I, CEO: Strategic lessons from the leader who built an empire.* Eaglewood Cliffs, NJ: Prentice Hall.

You need to underline or italicize the title of the book, but capitalize only the title's first letter, the first letter after a colon, and any proper names. Next, list the place of your publication, followed by a colon. The publisher's name should appear after the colon. Close the citation with a period.

Article in a journal

Kelly, P. F. (1999). The geographies and politics of globalization. *Progress in Human Geography, 23,* 379–400.

Article titles appear in much the same form as a book title in APA style. Only the first letters, the first letter after a colon, and the proper nouns are capitalized. The title of the journal, however, shows each important word capitalized. Note that the page numbers of the article are listed from first to last page. No abbreviation for "page" or "pages" is included with journal articles. The volume number, as well as the title of the journal, is underlined or italicized in this style.

Article in an essay collection

Partington, A. (1989). The designer housewife in the 1950s. In J. Attfield & P. Kirkham (Eds.), *A view from the interior: Feminism, women and design* (pp. 206–214). London: Women's Press.

Lahey, M., & Sarantis, A. (2008). Words and bullets: A rhetorical analysis of E.A. Robinson's "Richard Corey." In D. Brundage and M. Lahey (Eds.), *Acting on words: An integrated rhetoric, reader, and handbook* (pp. 437–439). Toronto: Pearson.

If the article or essay was published a significant time before its republication in the collection you are referring to, indicate that fact as follows:

Orwell, G. (2008). Politics and the English language. In D. Brundage and M. Lahey (Eds.), *Acting on words: An integrated rhetoric, reader, and handbook* (pp. 471–481). Toronto: Pearson. (Original work published 1946.)

An alternative solution used by some is the following:

Orwell, G. (1946). Politics and the English language. In D. Brundage and M. Lahey (Eds.), *Acting on words: An integrated rhetoric, reader, and handbook* (2009, pp. 471–481). Toronto: Pearson.

In the References list, APA style does not require quotation marks to enclose the titles of articles. Capitalize only the first words and proper nouns. To identify the book, supply the editors, the book title, and the publication information after the title of the article. Note that it is important to identify any editors as well as authors by including "(Ed.)" for "editor" and "(Eds.)" for "editors" after those editors' names. APA style requires the symbol "&" rather than "and" when the work has more than one author or editor. If the articles are contained in a book rather than in a journal, use the abbreviation "pp." for "pages" and place the listing of inclusive pages in parentheses after the book title, as in our title. Remember that the appropriate abbreviation for a single "page" is simply "p." For plural "pages" it is "pp."

Article in a newspaper

Tibbetts, J., & Jaimet, K. (2000, September 29). Trudeau dead at 80. *Edmonton Journal*, p. A1.

A newspaper article requires the year and the day of publication after the author's or authors' names. List the information in parentheses, with the year first. If you can find no author for the article, begin with its title, and then give the date and other information. Note that the name of the newspaper is underlined or italicized to indicate that it is a publication. The page number follows after a comma with the abbreviation "p." for "page."

Website

Walker, A. (1996). Letter from Alice Walker to President Clinton. Retrieved October 26, 2000, from http://www.igc.apc.org/cubasoli/awalker.html

A website is cited in a manner similar to that of a book. Begin with the author's name, if available. Follow this by the date in parentheses, then the title. As with most items on the References page, separate each item with a period. After the title, provide the information to enable the reader to find the article online, including your date of retrieval (since the information might well have changed or even disappeared since that date).

Name the host if the document is in a large and complicated website, such as a university site:

Writing a research paper. Retrieved December 18, 2001, from University of Alberta Libraries website: http://www.library.ualberta.ca/library_html/help/ pathfinders/ respaper.html

For more information on how to document online sources in APA style, go to www.apastyle.org/elecref.html. You will find updated information there on how to deal with electronic media in your essays.

FOOTNOTES AND ENDNOTES

A handy device for providing extra information briefly in your essays, especially research papers, is the footnote or endnote. *Footnotes* appear at the foot (or bottom) of the relevant essay page, three line spaces below your last line of text. *Endnotes* appear at the end of the essay, on a separate page entitled "Notes" or "Endnotes." This page appears just before your last page, where you list your sources.

In an MLA-style essay, you can use either footnotes or endnotes, but not both. In APA-style research papers, you rarely use footnotes; you list the endnotes on a separate page following the last page of the essay, before the References page. APA strongly discourages content footnotes, preferring additional information to be handled in an appendix or the text itself. Copyright permission notations are sometimes given in footnotes.

In MLA style, the first line of each footnote is indented five spaces, and any remaining lines in the footnote are flush against the left-hand margin. The footnote is single-spaced, but double-space between each footnote if you are including more than one on a single page. In both MLA and APA styles, the notes or endnotes (in contrast to the footnotes) are double-spaced.

Designate a footnote or endnote using a superscript number:

> Elephant herds in Kenya are fluctuating because of uneven government protections and surges of poaching.[3]

The footnote related to this point then appears with its corresponding number at the bottom of the page or, if you are using endnotes, at the end of the essay—but before your Works Cited page, if you quoted sources.

Footnotes and endnotes usually function in three ways:

1. providing other references
2. supplying further factual content
3. advancing related observations to bolster argument

Footnotes and endnotes can supplement your discussion effectively and economically.

Footnote and Endnote Usage (Hypothetical Examples)

Britain's Royal Family continues to face damaging public exposure. The Duchess of York, Sarah Ferguson, seems prepared to become a spokesperson for almost anything to fend off her financial troubles,[1] while the young Royal Princes, William and Harry, continue to be ejected from London nightclubs for unruly behaviour. Furthermore, a former assistant to one of the chauffeurs for the late Diana, Princess of Wales, has recently given a controversial interview about Diana's alleged belief in intergalactic abductions.[2] Meanwhile, many senior members of British Parliament are raising legal questions about abolishing the Queen's traditional immunity to prosecution because of decades of unpaid parking tickets accrued by her carriage and horses during various royal processions.[3]

Footnote or endnote #1 (other references, in MLA style)

[1] For a detailed discussion of the Duchess of York's previous financial troubles, see Theodore E. Bear's "Sarah's Creditors in a New Royal Age," *Monarchy Quarterly* 3.2 (1998): 114–27, and Ja-Yoon Kim's *Duchess for Hire* (Toronto: Pentium Press, 2001).

Footnote or endnote #2 (further content)

[2] This account has been vigorously denied by spokespeople for Buckingham Palace. As well, the chauffeur's former assistant has recently told BBC News that he was misquoted, claiming that he said "ablutions," not "abductions."

Footnote or endnote #3 (further observations or argument)

[3] I believe, along with several constitutional law experts, that the Queen's complete legal immunity, as well as the Royal Family's blanket immunity, from ever being called to testify in court, has no place in a modern England. Legal immunity actually damages their credibility rather than protecting it in the eyes of the public.

THE FINAL EDIT

Having produced a more polished draft, and carefully integrated quotations, proper citations, and bibliographic references, you should proof your work and perform any necessary final editing. Here are two sample research papers that have passed through all steps to their final form.

Sample Student Research Paper Using APA Documentation

APA requires paginated title page. Abbreviated title appears as header five spaces to left of page number.

Full title of essay appears in upper and lower case with no underlining or other marks, double-spaced and centred in upper third of page.

Author name centred in approximate middle of page.

In lower third of title page, centre course information, instructor name, and submission date.

Introversion:

The Dreaded Other

Colleen Leonard

English 1112

Professor Jill Deschamps

March 12, 2006

Introversion: The Dreaded Other

1   When five-year-old Adam gets into the car after school dismissal, his parents know to wait until later to ask him about his day. They have discovered that he prefers simply to listen to music during the drive home. Once home, he usually unpacks his latest library book, and then escapes to the privacy of the family room to play with some toys and unwind. After some time playing alone, he then becomes vocal and social with his family for the rest of the evening. Since this is Adam's first year at school, his parents were worried at first when he was uncommunicative, and would resist their efforts to get him to "open up" and talk about his day.

2   "Could there be something wrong at school?" they wondered. They decided to observe him at school, and noticed that he tends to prefer to be invited to join a group, rather than just jump in. He also seemed to prefer interacting with small groups of children. Adam's teacher reported that the boy was doing well in all respects, and appeared to enjoy school. After reading a couple of books recommended by the school guidance counsellor, the parents came to understand that there was nothing "wrong" with Adam; he was simply *introverted.*

3   The terms *introversion* and *extroversion* became known in psychology largely due to Carl Jung's theory of Psychological Types (1921), and define two "complementary orientations to life" (Myers & Briggs Foundation, n.d., p. 7). Jung believed that people had innate tendencies towards either the "inner world of concepts and ideas": introverts, or the "outer world of people and things": extroverts (Briggs Myers, 1980, p. 7). Scientific studies and findings now show that Jung's theory may have been accurate; people do seem to be born with innate preferences. For example, in *The Introvert Advantage* (2002), psychotherapist M. O. Laney highlights the findings of a twin study by N. Segal, a researcher, which reveal remarkable similarities in the personality traits of adult twins raised in completely different environments and without contact with each other. Other studies reported in the American *Journal of Psychiatry* have shown, through brain scanning (as cited in Garcia, 1999), that introverts and extroverts have blood flow differences in the brain. In addition to the biological findings supporting the idea of different inborn temperaments, the Myers-Briggs Type Indicator (MBTI), a personality inventory tool based on Jung's 'type' theory, has been in widespread use for many years and is widely acclaimed by educators and human resources officers to have merit. If, however, the concepts of

Quotation marks around "open up" signal colloquialism..

Quotation marks enclose parents' thought—a direct question.

Note date right after source.

Note page or paragraph number with author(s) and date right after quotation from source..

Author first identified by initials and surname.

Mentioning place of publication increases ethos of studies..

introversion and extroversion are generally recognized as innate and natural orientations, then why is it that introversion seems to be considered the less desirable orientation—and more like an *affliction*—in North America?

4   It is likely that some of the feeling that extroversion is a "more healthy" orientation is due to the significant influence of Sigmund Freud. In spite of a period of collaboration between Jung and Freud, they parted ways over a disagreement, after which Freud referred to introversion only in relation to mental disorders. For example, Laney refers to Freud's writings on narcissism, where he emphasized the narcissist "turning inward away from the world" (2002, p. 26), and also Freud's belief that the success of psychological development was to "find gratification in the world of external reality" (p. 26). Conversely, Jung felt that both extroversion and introversion were normal and natural points on a continuum, and not pathological unless these orientations were all-pervasive. It would appear that Freud's outlook on introversion is still more prevalent than Jung's, as evidenced in our language. In *The Introvert Advantage,* Laney provides some of the following examples: the *Dictionary of Psychology* defines introversion as " . . . orientation inward toward the self. The introvert is preoccupied with his own thoughts, avoids social contact and tends to turn away from reality" (p. 49). The same dictionary defines extroversion as " . . . a tendency to direct the personality outward, the extrovert is social, a man of action, and one whose motives are conditioned by external events" (as cited in Laney, p. 50). Many other dictionaries use similarly negative definitions for introversion. One particularly striking example is by Webster's *New World Thesaurus,* which defines an introvert as " . . . a brooder, self-observer, egoist, narcissist, solitary lone wolf and loner" (as cited in Laney, pp. 50–51).

5   It is not hard to imagine why introversion might be considered the less desirable of the two orientations, if using the definitions above, and especially in North American culture where the ideal qualities are those associated with extroverts (loves to chitchat, likes to be the centre of attention, a "people person," feels energized and eager from social interactions, talks a lot, enjoys knowing a lot of people). The need for reflection, solitude, a reserved attitude, enjoys ideas more than people, small circle of deep friends, are not traits we hear praised or valued much, and in some cases can be mistaken for pathological tendencies. For instance, there is confusion around normal introverted traits and somewhat similar traits that are exhibited by people with anxiety and personality disorders. Shyness is often thought to be the same thing as introversion, but it is not, though certainly introverts can be shy. Studies have differentiated shyness from

Disagreement is common knowledge. See Jung (p. 426).

Date of Laney's book before page, since date not cited earlier in paragraph. Note Laney quotes from Freud.

Leonard clarifies that she quotes from Laney, who quotes from dictionary.

Quotation marks around "people person" signal professional and popular jargon.

introversion (Crozier, 1990.) Shy people have social anxiety, which is a fear of social activities, but introverts prefer solitary activities for reasons other than fear. It is possible to be a shy extrovert. People with schizoid disorders also avoid contact with people and tend to isolate themselves; however, as with shyness, this is due to fear. When introverts prefer solitude, it is generally to reflect and restore their energy, which becomes drained from too much social interaction.

6   In North America, it is estimated that around 75 percent of the people are extroverts and 25 percent are introverts (Rauch, 2003, p. 2), and so it is possible that part of the bias against introversion may simply be due to percentages. In other words, the qualities of extroversion are considered more "normal" because that is the way most people are in our culture, and therefore extroverts set many of the benchmarks of "normal" traits. Laney points out, "America was built on rugged individualism and the importance of citizens speaking their minds. We value action, speed, competition, and drive" (2002, p. 5). Does this, then, call the basic definition of introversion as an innate and complementary orientation into question? The Myers & Briggs Foundation webpage (n.d.) reports that "distribution" of the standard personality types, which feature introversion and extroversion, shows different yet similar patterns across cultures. The foundation reports research suggesting that the expression of introversion in different cultures may vary. Perhaps there is room to consider an interaction between innate and culturally conditioned traits, a pull toward the norm that could, over time, repress if not erase certain innate traits that do not affirm the culture's norms. Perhaps some introverts, rather than deal with a self-image of being deviant, reply to personality typology with the answers they have grown to feel are most acceptable?

7   This possibility seems arguable when considering a final factor contributing to the negative perception of introversion: certain studies have reported that extroverts are "happier" than introverts. Surely this idea could have an influence on attitudes in society in general and on the self-image of introverts. Whether this idea is actually true, however, is another question. Laney (2002) argues that these studies are flawed because the types of questions used to measure happiness are not suitable to use with both introverts and extroverts. For example, in response to a question asking a participant to rate the importance of a statement such as "I like to be with others," an introvert may choose "not important" to happiness. Extroverts might interpret this response to mean that an introvert must be unhappy, because to an extrovert "not wanting to be with others" would be a sign of depression. But to introverts, not being with others does not imply that they are depressed, but simply that they enjoy

No page numbers cited because refers to entire study.

Cites article in *Atlantic Monthly* but also online. Online pages cited in References.

Webpage does not give date, so "n.d."

Since Laney is paraphrase, page number optional.

solitude. It seems that different things make introverts and extroverts happy, so questionnaires would have to be devised accordingly in order to gauge accurately which group is "happiest."

8   In March 2003, J. Rauch published "Caring for Your Introvert" in the *Atlantic Monthly*. As a result of that article, media went on to dub Rauch the figurehead of the so-called new introverts' rights movement. On February 14, 2006, S. Stossel of the *Atlantic* reported that "Rauch has received more mail in response to [his 2003 *Atlantic*] article than for anything else he has written" (p. 1). In addition, Rauch's 2003 article on introversion, now on the *Atlantic* website, continues to draw "more traffic than any other piece [the magazine] has posted" (Stossel, p. 1). In conclusion, as Stossel notes in his follow-up interview with Rauch, there continue to be a number of misconceptions that contribute to the reputation that introverts have in North America. In Rauch's words, as reported by Stossel, introverts are "one of the most misunderstood and aggrieved groups in America, possibly the world" (p. 1). These misconceptions, together with a society where the majority are extroverts, have led to a bias that can be damaging to the self-esteem of introverts. This prejudice also requires introverts to "develop extra coping skills in life because there will be an inordinate amount of pressure on them to 'shape up,' and act like the rest of the world" (Laney, 2002, p. 6). If these misconceptions are not challenged, then extroverts lose as well, because it seems that introverts also have a great deal of value to offer to society. For example, it is interesting to note that though extroverts tend to dominate in many spheres, according to several studies and observers, introverts comprise the majority of the gifted population (Hoehn & Birely, 1988; Gallagher, 1990; Stossel, p. 2). While this reverse claim may no doubt do much for the self-esteem of beleaguered introverts, it seems most reasonable to conclude that both introverts and extroverts have their own sets of innate gifts, and contributions to offer. Whether introverts should truly be considered as more gifted than others, in the words of Stossel citing Rauch, they *should* be seen simply as "a different kind of normal" (p. 1).

Common knowledge from media.

Square brackets signal minor change to quote.

List multiple sources if fact or claim supported by more than one.

References

Briggs Myers, I., and Myers, P. B. (1980). *Gifts differing.* Palo Alto, CA: Consulting
Psychologists Press.

> No quotation marks for titles of essays and articles. Italicize or underline book titles.
> Capitalize only first word of title and subtitle, plus proper nouns.

Crozier, W.R. (Ed.). (1990). *Shyness and embarrassment: Perspectives from social psy-*
chology. New York: Cambridge University Press

> No specific essay in collection identified because in-text citation is to introductory
> remarks by Crozier. When citing a specific essay, use author's name and include
> pages.

Myers & Briggs Foundation. (n.d.). Multicultural use of the MBTI® instrument. Retrieved
March 1, 2006, from http://www.myersbriggs.org/more-about-personality-type/
international-use/multicultural-use-of-the-mbti.asp

> Use essay-title style for webpage title. Give date information was retrieved; download
> and archive material cited.

Gallagher, S. A. (1990). Personality patterns of the gifted. *Understanding Our Gifted,* 3(1),
11–13.

> Article title first, then journal title. Volume number is "3," followed by issue number
> "(1)." Symbols "pp." do not precede academic journal pages.

Garcia, T. (1999). Brain activity indicates introverts or extroverts. News in Science. ABC.
Retrieved March 1, 2006, from http://www.abc.net.au/science/news/stories
/s21104.htm

> Treat name of web feature as journal title. List hosting corporation, ABC, as publisher.

Hoehn, L., & Birely, M. K. (1988). Mental process preferences of gifted children. *Illinois*
Council for the Gifted Journal, 7, 28–31.

> No issue number here—journal is continuously paginated ("7" is volume number); "28–31"
> refers to pages in volume of journal.

Laney, M. O. (2002). *The introvert advantage.* New York: Workman.

Rauch, J. (2003, March). Caring for your introvert: The habits and needs of a little-under-
stood group. The *Atlantic Monthly* online, 291(2), 1–4. Retrieved March 1, 2006, from
http://www.theatlantic.com/doc/200202/rauch

> Pages here refer to online article. Better to obtain print version and supply those page
> numbers.

Stossel, S. (2006, February 14). Introverts of the world, unite! A conversation with
Jonathan Rauch. The *Atlantic Unbound* online. Retrieved March 1, 2006, from
http://www.theatlantic.com/doc/200602u/introverts

> Material entirely online. Day and month given. If print magazine, no day given.

Connections: Strong Points in Leonard's Use of Sources

1. Awareness of **time**: Leonard has found that her central term traces back to Carl Jung's work in 1921 and remains, in 2006, a "hot" media topic as well as a subject of ongoing scientific study. Seeking the most up-to-date scholarly and media interest, Leonard gives prominence to the 2002 book of researcher Dr. Marti Olsen Laney as well as to the even more current *Atlantic Monthly* and *Atlantic Unbound* pieces by Rauch and Stossel.

2. Awareness of the need for **credibility**: Four of Leonard's sources are by recognized professional researchers whose findings have been published by credible presses or recognized academic journals.

3. Awareness of the need for **recoverability**: Only one of Leonard's sources (the item in *News in Science*) seems likely to disappear from its website, and that source does refer to an academic journal where the cited studies were published. A reader could track down the studies. The *Atlantic Unbound* interview, not published in printed form, is likely to remain available for some time through the *Atlantic* online archive. The *Atlantic Monthly* citation is to a text that was also published in the print magazine, and the month, year, volume, and number of the print publication have been provided, though the page numbers refer to the online version.

4. Awareness of **balance and variety**: Leonard refers to the Myers & Briggs print publication as well as to the Foundation's website. While this source certainly has "something to sell" (to cite George Monbiot), it also represents a long-standing commercial and professional instrument based on Jung's original formulation. While this source alone would be entirely insufficient, including it together with other disinterested sources adds an important awareness.

5. Awareness of **documentation norms**: Leonard has closely followed all the guidelines in the *Publication Manual of the American Pyschological Association*, fifth edition.

Connections: Areas for Improvement

This is clearly an excellent essay, well written and documented, but are there specific ways in which you think Leonard's use of sources might be strengthened? Explain.

PRACTICE

An outline of Leonard's essay is provided in Chapter 18, page 304. Before consulting that outline, make your own outline of her essay with attention to the main purpose, methods, and content of each paragraph. Provide the controlling idea and reasons and the topic sentences for each paragraph. Does Leonard state her reasons together with her controlling idea, or does the reader gather in the reasons paragraph by paragraph? Once you have completed your outline, read Leonard's outline and decide how it compares to yours. Would you make improvements to either outline? Explain.

Sample Student Research Paper Using MLA Documentation

Melanie Klingbeil's University of Alberta English 101 research essay on two poems by William Butler Yeats and two poems by Emily Dickinson offers an example of textual analysis drawing upon helpful secondary-source quotations. Also, note that a strong writer's voice marshals the research.

The numbers 1 to 7 at various places in the margins signal areas where we offer follow-up comments. These follow-up comments are provided under the subsequent heading "Connections: Areas for Improvement" following the essay.

Melanie Klingbeil
Professor Lahey
English 101
24 March 2002

No separate title page for MLA. Student name, instructor, course, and date are at top of page, flush left.

Selected Poems of Emily Dickinson and W. B. Yeats: Beyond the Answers

First letters of major words capitalized. No underline or italics.

1   Only without the universal questions of this world, without the mysteries that baffle great minds, and without the existence of contradictions, would the world be able to exist without philosophy. Mesmerized by their shared belief that there is more to understand than they already do, the poets Emily Dickinson (American) and W. B. Yeats (Irish) tried to walk through a door of understanding that could lead them into the realm of philosophy. Their contemplation and their philosophies emerged as poetry. Examples of their poetry prove that they were both capable philosophers, that they both vigorously contemplated realities beyond the fundamental world of material reality. Consider some titles of their works: Dickinson's "I know that He exists" (160) and "This world is not conclusion" (501); Yeats's "Byzantium" (1323) and "The Second Coming" (1320). Interpretations of these works can establish the differences between their two philosophies: where Dickinson questions religion, Yeats creates his own; where Dickinson considers the effects of the belief on the believer, Yeats puzzles over what shapes all human consciousness. What significance does this difference between the two poets truly bear? How does the distinction work? Interpreting these poems can lead to answers to these questions. I will consider what is at stake for both poets, and what, in their lives, accounts for their philosophical inclinations in order to explain what truly matters about the differences between Dickinson and Yeats.

Usual MLA style is "I Know that He Exists," with major words capitalized. Instead, Klingbeil respects Dickinson's way of writing her titles. Numbers in parentheses refer to pages in primary sources, listed under authors' names in Works Cited. Quotation marks close sentence, then parenthetical citation appears, followed by period.

Biographical information common knowledge—no citation.

2   The church was a part of Dickinson's early life. She understood the doctrines of Christianity and the practices of traditional religion. This understanding brought her to question, then reject the church. When the church claimed to have all the answers, Dickinson came up with new questions. How was Christianity an issue for Emily Dickinson? What would Christianity have taken from her were it not for her philosophy? Dickinson could not live as though she had the answers to the transcendental questions that troubled her, nor could she live as though she would ever attain them. Her poetry nourished her: with sanity, her contentment, her peace. As a critic has noted, "Dickinson lived with doubt without ever despairing" (Ferlazzo 31).

Note author name cited, then page of quotation. Period follows final parenthesis.

3   Dickinson's poem "I know that He exists" affirms not only her spiritual beliefs, but also the persistent disbeliefs that consume her. Her affirmation of her disbeliefs held her to an unconventional integrity—that all strong faith requires an ingredient of uncertainty in order for it to exist. Faith, by definition, must struggle with doubt.

1

Klingbeil 2

This uncertainty the church often ignores. The poem's first line, however, obviously makes a statement of faith. Dickinson acknowledges the separation God has from man by describing how He hides his "rare life / From our gross eyes." She thus affirms her belief in a supernatural being; she endorses a deity that seems no different than conventional Christianity's. Kimpel points out that other distinctions, however, between Dickinson's spiritual view and that of organized religion's eventually resulted in her social rejection:

> What she rejected, on the other hand, was their version of religion. . . . Her disparagement of their self-satisfied attitude about their own understanding of the nature of God was, consequently, their provocation for ostracizing her from the "converted" and the "saved." (209)

Dickinson's faith emerges in her poetry not from what she knows about God, but from what she does not know about Him. Once her faith is affirmed in her poetry, Dickinson then suddenly expresses a profound perplexity over the possibility that this God plays a cruel game with his believers by offering salvation as nothing more than a joke: "Would not the fun / Look too expensive? / Would not the jest / Have crawled too far?" To deny this cosmic possibility would be to deny the spiritual uncertainties that engulf the human condition. For Dickinson, denying the uncertainties and anxieties of the human condition would be blasphemous, more so than questioning God's existence or God's intentions.

While Dickinson examines the personal uncertainties of spiritual beliefs, Yeats seeks broader answers to the metaphysical questions of the universe. Yeats pursues a life of fascination with metaphysics and the occult. Studying his philosophical poetry is much like taking a journey through a luminous spirit world. This is Yeats's non-institutional religion—a deep philosophy influenced by the realm of metaphysics. As one critic puts it, "Everywhere, he felt, was incontrovertible evidence of an invisible but eminently active spirit world" (Unterecker 19). But what was the value of this fascination to Yeats? Beckson, quoting Symons, one of Yeats's colleagues, points out that Yeats pursued the mysterious instinct to become an artist: "'he discovers immortal moods in mortal desires'" (128). These "mortal desires" underlie the purposes of Yeats's poetry. These desires reveal what was at stake for Yeats in his passion for metaphysics.

"Byzantium," for example, says more about the poet than most readers may realize. Yeats connects the flesh-and-blood reality of the twentieth century to the reality (that he believed) of the supernatural. The first stanza concludes with the clashing of two contradictions, but only through their clash do they truly become distinct: "A starlit or a moonlit dome disdains / All that

2

3

4

5

6

Quotation from primary source, and poem already identified. Sentence identifies words as first line.

Quotation four lines or more set off. No quotation marks. Period before parentheses.

See "Literary and Film Analysis," website, Chapter 15, on quoting from poetry.

Following academic style, writer introduces quotation.

Smooth handling of Symons reference.

man is, / All mere complexities, / The fury and the mire of human veins." Yeats
describes one of his major symbols, the full moon, which represents   5
full and complete consciousness: all that the mind can become. For the human
mind to attain such a supernatural feat, it must escape the constraints of this material
world—reality as we know it. This elevation was Yeats's aim, his ambition, his necessity
to become a great metaphysician and poet. This ambition is what the poem tells us
about the poet. The contradiction between this world and the one beyond, Yeats
points out, clashes as the "moonlit dome disdains." Only when the potential transcendental consciousness looks down upon its current, lesser state does either become
truly defined. This potential consciousness Yeats longed for. His belief that he could
in fact attain it was what was at stake for Yeats. According to Unterecker, "[o]nly, Yeats
believed, if he could discover the design of the world of spirit would the pattern of the
world of matter in which he felt himself to be trapped make sense" (23). Yeats's only
way to preserve the spirituality he felt at stake was to manifest his intellectual escape
from the confines of material reality into his philosophy and his poetry.

> Square brackets used
> to change capital
> letter to lower case.
>
> Author's name not
> cited because in
> sentence.

7   Dickinson's unusually solitary life accounts for her deep introspection and her
heightened state of self-awareness. Dickinson might have been considered a
recluse, yet as Richard Sewall observes, "she kept in vital touch throughout her life
with all the people she loved and with many who just interested her" (521). This
private, yet expressive life allowed Dickinson to think philosophically about the
internalized world of faith. By ceaselessly pondering and challenging herself over
the nature and existence of the supernatural, Dickinson explored the concept of
the sublime. She considered such transcendental concepts with amazement, only
because she realized her own minute existence relative to it. Her poem "This world
is not conclusion" describes the struggle of a believer trying to reconcile daily experience with the conception of a higher, divine, more perfect reality. This is the
human struggle of knowing of the existence of a spiritual world, but perhaps lacking
the ability to absorb it: "A sequel stands beyond, / Invisible, as music" (lines 2–3).
Dickinson by no means claims that the sublime is simple:

> Again, in block quo-
> tation, period *before*
> citation.

> The poet admirably characterizes the inaccessibility of this reality
> which is transcendent of the physical world and transcendent alike to
> the sensory experiences of which the human being is capable. It is, in
> other words, "invisible." (Kimpel 229)

8   Dickinson's words pose another dimension to this struggle. By comparing
the "invisible" to music, she speculates that perhaps internalizing the sublime is
no more difficult than engaging with the presence of invisible, yet real music.
The poem continues with a firm statement that logic and faith are not to be
confused. When it comes to believing in something that is invisible, "Sagacity
must go" (line 8). This ambiguous statement could have two meanings.

"Sagacity" is defined as shrewdness, or keen perception. One could interpret the poet's statement as one of disdain for those who believe in something that is invisible. In this view, to have faith means to throw aside all rational thought. The opposing, but equally valid interpretation of this line would commend those who do not require logic in order to have faith—those people who can successfully internalize the sublime. Dickinson's poem strongly suggests that the human spirit does indeed possess the capacity to embrace more than a material world. The capacity to spiritually embrace the unknown, however, does not require keen perceptive skills. In fact, "sagacity" is irrelevant; it fails to offer human beings any guarantees about spirituality. The last two lines of the poem describe the irony of the nature of human existence: we have an immense ability to sense a connection between ourselves and a "divine" force but, at the same time, we have no sure means of defining that force: "Narcotics cannot still the Tooth / That nibbles at the soul" (lines 19–20). Neither timeless doctrines and intellectual theologies, nor structured religions (the "Narcotics") are capable of soothing or distracting us from the continual uncertainties (the "Tooth") that press upon the human soul. Narcotics are numbing; they induce sleep. Dickinson suggests that a rigid system of belief actually destroys and undermines, rather than nourishes, our spirituality and our philosophical sensibilities. Dickinson's introspective, yet socially aware life accounts for her philosophy that focuses on the hope for the human condition in reality. Her poetry offers a brief meditation on the effects of the possibilities of an unknown world, the sublime, on a soul that exists in a material world.

9   As Dickinson contemplates the Cosmos from her human standpoint, Yeats attempts to imagine the opposite. Yeats contemplates the fate of the human condition from the position of the Cosmos. Yeats's intricate poetry never directly acknowledges the human soul—the soul of the individual. Instead, his poem "The Second Coming" vividly and intensely describes the onset of the new millennium—the chaotic onset of the second antithetical period. The entire poem penetrates into the horror that Yeats prophesies. Where does this horror come from? The Spiritus Mundi, a predominant concept of Yeats's philosophy, accounts for his fear. It releases the antithetical beast: "The Second Coming! Hardly are those words out / When a vast image out of *Spiritus Mundi* / Troubles my sight" (lines 11–13). The Spiritus Mundi represents the soul of the world, the spirit of all human consciousness. Yeats no longer separates the supernatural world from this one. The two realities become one. The soul of the world is, in fact, the source of the release of the beast. Yeats's apocalyptic images in the beginning of the poem do not centre on any physical details that appeal to our senses. Rather, the events he describes are conceptual and abstract, suggesting that what the speaker "sees" is the product of a mental

6

Since lines from primary-source poem, reader can find collection under Primary Sources, Works Cited.

world: "The ceremony of innocence is drowned; / The best lack all conviction, while the worst / Are full of passionate intensity" (lines 6–8). Although the title of the poem alludes to the biblical prophesy of the return of the Saviour, Yeats's vision emerges not from an all-powerful deity, but from a source that is embedded in the human mind. Yeats designates humans as the source of their own chaos. Perhaps our minds and imagination have far more power than we are apt to realize. Yeats obviously believed just that.

10   At this point, considering the meaning of Yeats's philosophy is meaningless without considering Yeats's life and work. What could possibly account for his complicated and horrific vision? Yeats's world was full of political chaos and upheaval. An Irish nationalistic movement was taking place, but Yeats's class and personal beliefs prevented him from ever completely participating in it. Perhaps he never felt as though he belonged to his own social reality because of this personal exclusion. MacGloin criticizes Yeats for not being more accountable to the social conditions around him:

> William Butler Yeats's world was devastated, doomed, and unredeemable. His work is, in part, the marvel of a long personal anguish in its loss—a threnody—that by its obsessive and particularized nature allowed little compassion for the living. (484)

11   MacGloin's argument falls apart, however, once one considers the reason for Yeats's philosophy rather than only the philosophy itself. The existence of Yeats's poetry says something different than the poetry itself. It reflects a deep emotional awareness of his human condition, the conditions of his turbulent world. Yeats's poetry allowed the little compassion he had to remain. Yeats's poetry is a demonstration of his own conception of clashing contradictions. The clash of his reality with his philosophy signified the distinction he tried to make between them.

12   The beauty of philosophy lies in the combination of discipline and creativity it conceives. Logic, science, and even religion, in contrast, attempt to bear evidence for the separate proofs these areas of thought require to progress. Unfortunately, this sort of evidence might also terminate the seeking of spiritual development. Dickinson and Yeats, although very different, travelled this philosophical road through their poetry. While Dickinson expresses what spiritual change happens with her as a human being, Yeats theorizes about the effects that human consciousness has on the universe as a whole. Their philosophical searches exemplified how aspects of their lives accounted for their specific thoughts about their existence. Dickinson acknowledged in her poetry her belief that evidence for faith does not exist. In life, her refusal to join the church represented her refusal to diminish the concept of faith. For Yeats, his philosophy was his only means of coping with the politically unstable world around him.

Klingbeil 6

He was mesmerized by the possibilities of a spiritual world, simply because he was horrified by the material world around him. He does not look at the world of beyond from an individualistic point of view. It is almost as though Yeats tries to write to us from beyond that spirit world; his poetry gives him a place in that world—a claim to a part of it. Another beauty of philosophy.   7

Works Cited

Beckson, Karl. "'The Tumbler of Water and the Cup of Wine': Symons, Yeats and the Symbolist Movement." <u>Victorian Poetry</u> 28.1 (1990): 125–33.

For articles in academic journals, first author's name, then article title in quotation marks; next title of journal, underlined or in italics. Volume number is "28"; issue number is "1." Year of publication follows in parentheses, then colon introduces pages.

Ferlazzo, Paul J. <u>Emily Dickinson.</u> Boston: Twayne Publishers, 1976.

Kimpel, Ben. <u>Emily Dickinson as Philosopher</u>. Lewston: Edwin Mellen, 1994.

MacGloin, T. P. "Yeats's Faltering World." <u>Sewanee Review</u> 95.1 (1996): 470–84.

Sewall, Richard B. "In Search of Emily Dickinson." <u>Michigan Quarterly Review</u> 23.1 (1984): 514–27.

Unterecker, John. <u>A Reader's Guide to William Butler Yeats</u>. London: Billing & Sons, 1959.

Primary Sources

Dickinson, Emily. "I know that he exists." *The Complete Poems of Emily Dickinson.* Ed. Thomas H. Johnson. Boston: Back Bay, 1976. 160.

Copies of these poems available in many books and accessible online, yet best to provide source used. Textual and pagination differences occur from edition to edition, so listing primary-source edition ensures accuracy. Above, "160" refers to page of poem.

---. "This world is not conclusion." *The Complete Poems of Emily Dickinson.* Ed. Thomas H. Johnson. Boston: Back Bay, 1976. 501.

When author listed for two or more entries, MLA uses three hyphens.

Yeats, W. B. "Byzantium." *The Norton Introduction to Literature.* 7th ed. Ed. Jerome Beatty and J. Paul Hunter. New York: Norton, 1998. 1323.

---. "The Second Coming." *The Norton Introduction to Literature.* 7th ed. Ed. Jerome Beatty and J. Paul Hunter. New York: Norton, 1998. 1319.

If two or more entries by same author, arrange according to alphabetical order of titles.

Connections: Strong Points in Klingbeil's Use of Sources

1. Awareness of **time:** Different subjects experience different rates of academic activity and change. How psychologists define and interpret introversion, for example, undergoes continual modification, through widespread use of instruments such as the Myers-Briggs Typology Indicator®. Controversial political issues, such as maintaining English as the one official language of the United States, result in frequent new pronouncements and commentaries from the various advocacy groups involved and from related scholarly books (much in demand due to popularity of the topic). Computer programming and fields related to science and technology tend to change on a weekly, even daily basis; research and development drives these disciplines. Contemplation of spiritual and philosophical ideas in poets of the past, however, tends to move at a much slower rate, with fewer new titles "hitting the presses." Thus when you note that Klingbeil's most recent source is 1994 (she wrote her paper in 2003), this does not indicate a lack of research, as it might if the subject had been introversion or English as the official language of the United States. In fact, Klingbeil researched for any current information on her topic in journals and academic presses. What she found and used is up to date by the standards of her particular topic. Furthermore, she did not neglect earlier work that she found worthwhile. Ignoring the past in the name of the myth of progress is particularly inappropriate in humanities areas that should realize the importance of history.
2. Awareness of the need for **credibility:** All of Klingbeil's sources are by recognized professional scholars whose findings have been published by credible presses or recognized academic journals.
3. Awareness of the need for **recoverability:** All of Klingbeil's sources are in books and journals, and therefore recoverable.
4. Awareness of **balance and variety:** Within the parameters of her topic, Klingbeil reflects balance and variety by considering a number of different views and interpretations.
5. Awareness of **documentation norms:** Klingbeil has closely followed all the guidelines in the *MLA Handbook for Writers of Research Papers,* sixth edition.

Connections: Areas for Improvement

As thoughtful and well documented as this sample essay is, we know that most of our writing can still use some improvements. Review Klingbeil's essay with attention to its methods and especially to its connections to its research sources and surrounding ideas. Offer any suggestions you can for small improvements. Then read our following comments, numbered in relation to the numeric marginal notations on the essay.

1. It might be a good idea to identify the significance of the title "Byzantium" in a footnote here or to work a definition into the essay's introduction. The student does provide the Biblical significance of the title later in the essay, but perhaps moving it closer to the beginning would help readers grasp Yeats's reference.

2. Would a little further explanation here help the reader understand the context of Dickinson's "social rejection" based on religious grounds? Alternatively, a brief footnote comment might provide some historical details to describe Dickinson's situation in her community.

3. Here, Klingbeil has decided to provide a longer quotation in block format. Using three block quotations through a paper of this length places her on the border of too many block quotations. She has balanced the longer quotations with shorter, incorporated ones, however. Be careful not to resort to an abundance of block quotations simply to eat up essay space.

4. The student might briefly mention here the source for this information on Yeats's "fascination with metaphysics and the occult." As well, a working definition of "metaphysics" would help the reader see how the essayist (and Yeats) understand this specific term. Remember to recognize opportunities for careful definitions of specific and crucial terms as important moments of communication and persuasion in your writing.

5. This analysis of the full moon in Yeats's poetry is insightful and persuasive. In an additional sentence in the paragraph, Klingbeil might show either how the moon appears in another instance of Yeats's poetry (a brief reference to one other poem would be sufficient) or how she first became aware of this symbol's implication.

6. A footnote further explaining these theological terms and notions would certainly help clarify these very specific references.

7. Melanie concludes her last paragraph with a deliberate sentence fragment. This stylistic choice, at the end of such a formal essay, has the effect of surprising the reader by making expression visceral as well as cerebral. Some editors and instructors, however, might consider this as pushing the limits of acceptable academic style too far.

🖋 PRACTICE

Design an outline for this essay along the lines of the outline provided for "Introversion: The Dreaded Other" in Chapter 18 (p. 304). Be sure to incorporate the controlling idea and its reasons. Try to identify each topic sentence and the method and main purpose of each paragraph. Has Klingbeil organized and connected her discussion in an effective, purposeful manner?

FINAL WORDS

Diligence, discipline, and patience are indeed required for you to master academic research and documentation. More special situations occur in practice than we can possibly cover in this relatively short space. What we have covered here should serve most if not all of your needs at the first-year level, but if you are serious about future scholarly work, you will obtain the *MLA Handbook for Writers of Research Papers,* sixth edition, the *Publication Manual of the American Psychological Association,* fifth edition, or the style guide required by your field of study. You will then refer to it on a regular basis.

Oral
Presentations

INTRODUCTION

Many of us face the task of writing and delivering oral presentations. These may take the form of student seminars, business meetings, or addresses at community, political, or family gatherings. Speechwriting has much in common with essay writing, but there are some notable differences, as it must account for oral dynamics. Developing and delivering your presentation includes more than just writing your text or notes. You need to account for audience needs by preparing for oral delivery and practising the skills that ensure a successful presen-

tation. The following chapter helps you with both writing and delivering your oral presentation so that it achieves its purpose and builds your enthusiasm for further oral communication.

Guidelines and examples in the following chapter are supplemented by student sample speeches and related information at the Text Enrichment Site, Chapter 20. Another sample speech, "Language Arts or Language Departs," may be found at the site under Chapter 16.

Chapter 20
The Oral Presentation

Presentation audiences have particular needs, and these needs place special demands on the speaker. The following chapter outlines five ways in which you, as a speechwriter, can assist your audience. It also provides special tips to deal with the four different modes of presentation. Finally, it provides detailed assistance with how to develop and deliver a presentation using any of the modes.

FIVE WAYS TO ASSIST YOUR AUDIENCE AS SPEECHWRITER

In many ways, writing for public speaking is similar to writing an essay. You still need to know your audience and to structure your speech around a direct-list thesis statement containing a manageable number of points. You need an introduction, a conclusion, and smooth transitions. There are, however, important differences between writing for the page and writing for oral presentation.

When you write a speech, always keep in mind that the audience will be listening to the **rhythms** and **enunciations of a voice**, not reading text. Your audience cannot go back and check words or ideas that they have trouble grasping. Although an oral presentation makes special demands on you as an author, you can help your listeners in a number of ways.

1. First, *use informal conversational language* that is appropriate to your purpose and to your audience. Use terminology that is familiar to that group. For instance, if you are addressing a group of horse owners, it would be appropriate to use the technical phrase "centre the pommel of the saddle over the withers." A group of novice riders would be confused and eventually alienated by these terms if you continued your speech without explaining them. Use short sentences. Sentence fragments are acceptable in oral speech and can be used to great effect.
2. *Emphasize colourful, concrete language.* Your audience will remember word pictures more easily than extended abstract ideas. Use your word pictures to give vitality to your concepts.

3. *Use previews, repetition, and internal summaries* to present your points clearly and remind the reader of their importance. Make sure that you have included concise internal summaries sufficient for a *listening* audience to make the connections between your main points and between these main points and the overall thesis.
4. In most cases, you will want to **state your thesis clearly** in the introduction and again in the conclusion.
5. A speech has no footnotes, so, for ethical reasons, *cite sources of information and quotations* as you speak. Vary the ways you introduce your quoted material: "One expert, Susan Smith, contends that . . . ," "As Peter Brown points out . . . , " and "According to Melanie Jones . . . ." Such variety will keep your listeners alert to the sometimes multiple voices in your presentation.

Simple, concrete language, internal summaries, and short, uncluttered sentences will help to give your points impact for the listening audience.

MODES OF ORAL PRESENTATION

The four modes of oral presentation are

- extemporaneous
- manuscript
- memorized
- impromptu

Each of these modes is useful in certain situations, although the extemporaneous approach is generally the most effective.

Extemporaneous Presentations

In the extemporaneous mode, you speak with only key words and phrases written on file cards to remind you of your main points. This approach allows you to maintain eye contact with your audience and move freely as you speak, yet you have cues to keep you from losing your place. Extemporaneous speaking usually sounds the most natural. The section below, entitled "Developing the Oral Presentation," will look at ways you can prepare a speech to be presented extemporaneously. See the Text Enrichment Site, Chapter 20, "Sample Speeches," for the full text speeches, working outlines, and key-word outlines for two student presentations.

Reading from Manuscript

In some circumstances, you may wish to read from a full-text manuscript. This mode of delivery is most often used when speeches are televised (usually read off a teleprompter) or in situations where exact wording is crucial. For example, Pierre Elliott Trudeau was known for his smoothly delivered, colourful extemporaneous speeches. But his address to the nation on October 16, 1970, when he announced his decision to invoke martial law in Montreal, was very different. He delivered this televised speech seated at a desk, reading from a carefully worded manuscript that he held in his hand. He used this delivery to signal to viewers that he was in control of the situation and that his plan, like his speech, had been carefully thought through. You can view the speech at <http://archives.cbc.ca/IDCC-1-71-101-618/conflict_war/october_crisis/>.

This sense of careful planning is one of the strengths of using a manuscript when speaking. If you speak with authority, an oral presentation from a prepared manuscript can enhance both your perceived control of the situation and your material. This style does have weaknesses, however. One of these is the loss of eye contact. We have all seen local commercials featuring merchants who are not used to reading from teleprompters. Their eyes look glazed and move from side to side as they read. It takes practice to make yourself appear to be speaking to the viewer. Reading from a paper interferes with eye contact between speaker and audience even more. A class of public-speaking students who viewed the Trudeau speech said his quick glances away from the text and up to the camera made him look "shifty" and as if he were "hiding something." This effect can occur whether the speech is televised or delivered live. A second weakness, one regularly demonstrated by the local commercials mentioned above, is that most people sound stilted or monotonous when they read. Modulate your voice as naturally as possible during manuscript delivery and mark your text ahead of time for words you would like to pronounce more emphatically or more softly. You may also wish to mark the text where natural pauses occur. Finally, if you lose your place, it can be difficult to find it again. If you choose to deliver a speech with a manuscript, highlight or underline important points and rehearse the speech thoroughly so that you can maintain as much eye contact as possible.

Memorized Presentations

Some professional speakers present speeches from memory. This allows the speaker to maintain eye contact while retaining precise wording. For most people, however, this is a dangerous method. People who are not professional speakers or actors usually use a sing-song voice when they speak material they have memorized. If you forget part of a memorized speech, you risk a long and embarrassing pause while you try to remember your chain of words. Either of these problems may cause your audience to remember the speech in a way you'd rather they didn't. (If you do go blank, improvise—rephrase your last idea and keep talking until your text comes back to you.)

You may wish to memorize parts of an extemporaneous speech. Speakers often like to memorize the introduction, the thesis statement, and the conclusion. This gives you the strengths of precise wording and eye contact, but is not so sustained a memory task as to allow problems to present themselves.

Impromptu Presentations

In business meetings or informal gatherings, you may be called upon to "say a few words" unexpectedly or to respond to a point that has been made. In such cases, you need to make an impromptu presentation. Even in these situations, you can and should structure your thoughts. Jot down a few notes if you have time. Decide what your objective is and state it as clearly as possible. That will serve as your thesis statement. Think of one or two points and evidence to support your thesis. Summarize your thesis and your main points as you conclude. Listeners will appreciate your ability to present your thoughts in a simple, concise, structured way.

If you are a member of a community business association, for example, and you are suddenly invited to respond to a concern about liquor laws during a brief meeting, you may be best advised to organize your thoughts around the implications of any changes to or violations of current liquor restrictions. Examples from the community's experience would help illustrate your points. In such an impromptu address, the audience would understand you are speaking provisionally, not offering shaped conclusions, but ideas to be discussed.

Each of these means of presenting an oral speech is useful in certain situations. One speech may use several modes: the body of the speech may be delivered extemporaneously while the introduction and conclusion are memorized, quotations and statistics read, and questions answered impromptu. As the extemporaneous mode is the most effective in most situations, the following section will focus on developing that form of speech.

DEVELOPING THE ORAL PRESENTATION

For many people, anxiety is the first obstacle to overcome for a good oral presentation. In fact, a survey conducted by *Psychology Today* (quoted by Lyle W. Mayer in *Fundamentals of Voice and Diction,* 10th ed., 1994) found that many people are more afraid of public speaking than they are of death. So if you are nervous, recognize that most people share your feelings. Also realize that "nerves" can help you focus and energize your presentation as you control and channel them rather than allow them to control you. Remember that your **preparation,** your **practice,** and your **focus** are the essential elements in developing a good oral presentation. Whether you are a nervous speaker or not, these three elements are essential for a successful delivery of your carefully written speech, and your attention to them will see you through a case of nervous hesitation.

Preparation

Be absolutely sure you have done your homework, including all the research you would do for any good piece of writing. You may find the following steps helpful:

- Write out a full outline of your speech.
- Highlight the key words and phrases that the audience must hear in order to understand your message.

- Make up cue cards for yourself. Write just the key words and phrases. You may wish to write out the full text of your thesis statement and any quoted material and statistics, but keep these as brief as possible.

Practice

Perhaps the most valuable advice that can be given to a speaker is to practise, practise, practise! Most oral presentations are not rehearsed enough. Speakers who go over their speeches too little in advance undermine their messages as well as themselves. Practise your speech until you can run through it smoothly, using only your cue cards for reference. Practise in front of a mirror to find the best hand gestures to emphasize your points while appearing natural and to eliminate excessive, distracting body language. If you will present while standing, practise standing, making sure your posture is straight but relaxed and that you don't fall into bad habits of fidgeting or shifting from side to side. If you will be seated when you speak, practise a good seated posture that helps you appear confident. Again, try to avoid excessive hand gestures or fidgeting that will advertise any discomfort.

You may wish to make a videotape of one of your practice runs. Or you may wish to round up a sympathetic audience of friends or family members. Even a child or a pet (other than a goldfish) can help you work at making eye contact and varying your voice to gain and hold attention.

As well as rehearsing the text of the speech and your presentation of it, prepare for questions the audience may ask you and practise your answers. Give special consideration to tough questions that may come up so that you will answer them confidently. Even if exact or even similar versions of the questions you have anticipated do *not* arise, you will usually be able to use parts of your prepared answers for other, unanticipated questions.

Focus

There are several techniques you can use to focus on the task at hand rather than on your butterflies as presentation day draws near. The most commonly used techniques are controlled breathing, simple kinetic exercises, and visualization. Whether you are nervous or not, these techniques can help you achieve peak performance.

Breathing

The beauty of breathing exercises is that you can do them lying on your back in a darkened room or seated at a boardroom table surrounded by others. The following is a simple progression that will help you to concentrate.

First, just notice your breath—is it fast and high in your chest? Begin to slow it down. Breathe deeply into your diaphragm (or belly). Feel your bottom ribs swing out and up slightly as you inhale. Once your breath is low and slow, count silently as you inhale and exhale. Start inhaling, for a count of two, hold for a count of two, and exhale for a count of three. Work up to inhale for a count of eight, hold for a count of eight, and exhale for a count of ten. The count should be slow enough to be relaxing, yet not so slow that you run out of air. If you feel light-headed, return to normal breathing.

Kinetic Exercises

You can also use this technique while lying on the floor or discreetly while in a room full of people. Find a relaxed position, seated or lying down. If you are alone, close your eyes. Use the breathing exercises until your breath is relaxed. Starting with your toes and working up to your face, clench and release each muscle group in your body. Hold each set of muscles for a slow count of 10 before relaxing them. Let yourself feel the release for a moment before you move on to the next group of muscles, working your way slowly up your legs, trunk, arms and hands, to neck and head. Pay special attention to places where you hold tension; the shoulders and the jaw are the greatest tension points for many of us.

Visualization

Many professional and top-ranking athletes include visualization in their training. Visualization allows you to rehearse your "event" (in this case, your speech) in a relaxed, positive way that reinforces the correct techniques, making errors in your presentation less likely. It is good to try a visualization in the final day or two before you present. You can also do a mini-visualization on the spot if you find yourself losing confidence just before you are to speak. To practise visualization privately, find a relaxed position, seated or lying down. Close your eyes. Run through the breathing exercises and the kinetic sequence. When you feel relaxed, picture yourself in a favourite place where you feel safe and content, perhaps a sandy beach by the ocean. Enjoy the image for a moment. Relax into the sand. Feel the sun's warmth on your face and body. Hold on to the relaxed feeling as you picture yourself preparing to leave. See yourself packing everything you need for the presentation. You remember everything. You arrive at the space where you will present in plenty of time. You check it out and set everything up. It all goes smoothly. Watch your audience arriving. You are relaxed, they are friendly. It is your time to speak. You feel confident and prepared. Visualize yourself delivering your entire speech smoothly. (Do not check your notes or speak out loud—just watch the "movie" of your own polished presentation.) Watch the audience. They are clearly interested. As you finish, they applaud. You smoothly and constructively answer their questions. After you close, they compliment you on the effectiveness of your speech. Open your eyes and hold on to that happy, confident feeling.

If, in the moments before you speak, you start to feel anxious, guide yourself back to your positive visualization. Remember that few problems are beyond your ability to cope with in the context of your presentation. If you forget your speech, you have your cue cards. If you cannot answer a question, replying with an honest

"I don't know" can be very effective in sustaining your audience's respect when you follow it with an assurance that you will find the information. Most important of all, see yourself succeeding.

Committed preparation, practice, and focus will help make your presentation an experience that is more pleasant for you and more effective for your listeners. In the longer term, there are many other ways to build your presentation skills.

PRESENTATION SKILLS: VOICE AND BODY

Your voice and body are tremendously important in communicating your presentation. You cannot escape them. They will affect the audience's perception of your message, so use them to fullest advantage. Develop vocal flexibility and physical expressiveness. You can incorporate the following exercises into your rehearsals of one important presentation; you will find they become more effective if you do them over time. If your chosen career involves a lot of public speaking, you may want to consider joining an organization or speaking group where you can hone your skills continually with experienced speakers. If you have speech problems (nasal voice, soft consonants, etc.) or are very inhibited physically, classes in voice, yoga, tai chi, or even kick-boxing can make a big difference in the way your presentations are received.

Voice

Using volume, rate, pitch, and articulation appropriately is as important in public speaking as it is in singing. Speakers who know how to make these vocal qualities work for them deliver many otherwise questionable presentations convincingly. On the other hand, audiences overlook many thoughtful arguments in presentations when the speakers mumble in a monotone or hurriedly spit out their points. In oral presentations the speaker's voice will either contribute to or detract from the spoken content. There is no third alternative.

Volume

As for the volume of your voice, first of all you must be *audible*. Ask the audience if everyone can hear you, especially if you will be speaking without a microphone. Most people speak too softly when addressing a group. Unless you have been told you have a loud voice, always speak at a level that feels too loud without yelling. If you are soft-spoken, speak loudly every time you practise your speech.

A speaker who tries to be loud by straining the throat sounds shrill rather than confident. Learn to support your voice from the diaphragm. Start by breathing deeply. Use your diaphragm (just above your stomach) to push the air out slowly. After you have done this a few times silently, do the same on a hiss, then on an "ahhhh." As you build strength in the muscles between your ribs and your abdomen, start reading your text at a comfortable, fairly loud level. Each time you do the exercise, read further on one breath, always stopping before you start to strain. If you are unsure where your diaphragm is or how to get started, consult a singing teacher or a voice coach.

Rate

The rate or pace of your speech is also very important. Second to insufficient volume, *racing*—speaking at a rushed rate—is the most common way speakers lose their audiences. If you race because you are nervous, use pauses to force yourself to slow down, even writing "pause here" on your cue cards. If your speech is running long, skip parts. **Do not race.** It is far better for the listeners to get some of your points than none. When you practise, speak more slowly than you normally do. Ask a friend to listen to you run through your speech and signal to you if you are going too fast.

Pitch

Another essential characteristic of speech is your pitch. Most people speak within a very narrow range, seldom using the upper and lower parts of their registers. So think of your presentation as a kind of performance, which it is. Think of pitch as a dramatic instrument that can help establish your presence and your content. Listen to a speaker you find interesting. You will likely notice that he uses a wider range of pitch than most of us do in day-to-day conversation. You too can develop this ability through practice.

Articulation

Clear articulation is extremely important when an audience is relying on your oral delivery of information. You can confuse your listeners by phonetically substituting a "D" for a "T" when you are explaining unfamiliar terms. Over the long term, you will find tongue-twisters that feature consonants both enjoyable and useful for sharpening up overly casual articulation. Say each tongue-twister several times; the first time, say it slowly to exaggerate each sound, then increasingly speed it up, but don't lose the clear consonants. Follow up by running through your speech, exaggerating the consonants.

Variation of Volume, Rate, and Pitch

Vary your volume, rate, and pitch when you practise your presentation at home. See what effect you create when you slow down and when you speak loudly or softly in making important points. Use the higher and lower parts of your range. Exaggerate. Move from deep down to high and squeaky. Race through some parts, slow to a crawl for others. Whisper a significant point or yell it like an old-time preacher.

Have fun with your whole presentation. After you have done this a few times, run through the speech in a normal speaking voice, holding on to the vocal variations that you found effective.

After you have practised bringing these examples of vocal variety into your speech, tape your presentation and check for crisp articulation and interesting, natural-sounding modulation. You will begin to recognize your speaking voice as a responsive instrument, a device valuable in expressing your prepared content and furthering your career.

Body Language

People take in far more information through their eyes than their ears. Body language is therefore an important tool for any presenter. Eye contact and facial expression, posture and gesture all send important signals to your audience.

Eye Contact

Novice speakers find making eye contact with audience members difficult, but such communication is essential to establishing rapport. Speakers who make eye contact appear friendly, confident, and candid about their messages (even if they are not). If you are nervous about eye contact, practise at home with someone you know. If you present to a small group, make eye contact at some point with each person. If you present to a group of more than 20 people, divide the audience mentally into four parts. If you make eye contact with at least one person in each quadrant, the entire audience will feel included. Choose a sympathetic-looking person to look at if you are nervous, although don't stare at one person too much or you may make him or her more nervous than you are. If there is a bright light on you and the audience area is dim, make "eye contact" where you know someone will be.

Facial Expression

Facial expression also counts for a great deal in public speaking. Smile as soon as you begin your presentation. This will warm the audience to you and make you feel more confident. Smile where appropriate throughout the presentation. It will make a big difference in the listeners' perception of you and your message. In one study customers in a bank were asked to estimate the time they had spent waiting in line for a teller. Those whom the teller had greeted with a smile after their wait in line underestimated their total wait time; the other customers, who received no greeting smile, overestimated their time in line! If you tend not to smile when you are nervous, you may want to add "smile" on your cue cards at strategic spots.

Posture

A good, relaxed posture will also help you appear competent and confident. As you stand, picture your feet sinking into the floor and the crown of your head being gently pulled up by a string hanging from the ceiling above you. You want to avoid a stiff, military posture and at the same time avoid rounded shoulders, slouching, or hunching. You also want to keep track of what your feet are doing—imaginatively sinking them into the floor—comfortably—to anchor you and help you avoid aimless pacing. Note whether you are speaking at a podium that is open at its bottom and allows the audience a full view of your legs and feet. Speakers can often appear purposeful and strong above the podium, while their feet are fidgeting, twisting around each other, and even slipping their shoes on and off! On a raised platform, your busy feet and not your words will become the focal point of your presentation. Change your posture occasionally, of course, but exercise some physical self-discipline to create a minimum of distractions from your presentation.

Feel free to move away from the podium, however. A podium forms a barrier between you and the audience. Leaving it and crossing the stage or floor toward the audience can be a powerful way to emphasize a point, as well as to enact your sense of comfort with your material and the audience itself. By demonstrating this degree of comfort, you will put the audience at its ease, and its members will be more likely to remember your particular presentation as both enjoyable and convincing.

Gestures

Gestures can greatly enhance a speech by making ideas visible. Keep them simple and natural, to amplify, not compete with, the points you are making in your presentation. For instance, an inclusive gesture on "all of us" visually underlines the meaning. Holding up fingers to count off your main points dramatizes the organization of your presentation. If you are not accustomed to "talking with your hands," decide on a few effective gestures and practise them as you run through your speech. Remember not to overdo gestures, however, since excessively "talking with your hands" can belie a lack of faith in the power of your words and your ability to inform and convince through language, logic, analysis, and argument.

Your hands are very influential as you speak. Trembling hands are one of the most common giveaways of nervousness, and one of the most upsetting to speakers. As you speak, your hands shake and the paper rattles. This makes you self-conscious, so the paper rattles more. You cannot stop the trembling, but you can make it irrelevant if you use large file cards rather than paper for your notes. Without the rattling paper, neither the audience nor you will be distracted from your message. Ideally, you will speak from a key-word outline, so all the notes you need should fit on several cards. If you are speaking from a manuscript, place either the whole text or the bottom half flat on your desk or podium to anchor it and keep your hands from shaking. Contact with a steady surface will steady you.

Stretching, breathing, and relaxation exercises will all help you transform the stiffness of your nerves into the fluidity of effective movement, just as vocal exercises will make your voice more flexible and interesting to listen to. You can do these exercises as part of your preparation for a single speech; you will find them more effective if you make them part of your long-term routine.

PRESENTATION AIDS

As you move into final preparations, consider how you have incorporated presentation aids into your speech. These include all visual and audio aids, including PowerPoint, transparencies, objects, videotapes or audio tapes, and even your own appearance. Visual aids can be especially helpful in keeping your audience with you.

Computer-Generated Aids

Computer-generated aids are effective—*if* you know how to use them. However, many presentations begin late or are delivered with distracting technical difficulties, because the speaker is unfamiliar with the program or the room (the outlet, the best place to project, or the best place to stand without blocking the audience's view). Nervous speakers sometimes fidget with a computer mouse, projecting a cursor that wanders distractingly over the image at the front of the room. If you are unfamiliar with the PowerPoint program but must use it, seek a knowledgeable assistant to run the program while you present—and be sure to practise with this person ahead of time. Above all, be prepared to present the speech without the presentation aid if you run into insurmountable technical difficulties. For instance, make a handout of the PowerPoint slides. Your audience will admire your courage and appreciate your consideration of their time.

Ten Tips for Using Visual Presentation Aids

1. Limit the number of aids you use so that they enhance your presentation without overwhelming it.
2. Keep your visual aids simple and uncluttered.

   - Use bulleted lists rather than sentences, with no more than six bullets to a list.
   - Simplify maps so they show only the features relevant to your presentation.
   - Make graphs as simple as possible and use clearly contrasting colours.
   - Use charts that contain the minimum of information you need to get your point across.

3. Ensure all lettering is legible and can be seen from the back of the room.
4. Talk to the audience, not to the aid.

5. Avoid blocking your own aid.
6. Reveal points only as you make them in your speech, or the audience will stop listening to you as they read ahead.
7. Decide on your strategy for distributing a handout; unless you have set up this written material so that the audience uses it to follow you point by point, distribute it when you are finished talking (for the same reason given in point 6). Reproduce photographs large enough that people at the back of the room can see them. Do not pass them around, as this will divide the audience into pockets of people concentrating on them rather than on what you are saying.
8. Do not plan to speak over recorded sound unless it is extremely soft.
9. Keep aids out of sight until you need them.
10. Make sure you have practised with and are in control of the aid. For example, always check that an overhead projector has a spare bulb. Avoid using live animals unless you know you can focus audience attention back on you; a litter of kittens will make a much bigger impact than you do and can quickly get out of control, but a well-trained adult dog may be helpful in a speech about seeing-eye dogs.

Your Appearance

Consider your appearance a powerful presentation aid, too. Dress with your audience in mind. Your T-shirt and jeans would likely alienate a corporate board of directors, while a business suit could have the same effect on an audience of inner-city teens. If you are uncertain of the social atmosphere or your audience's expectations of dress code, seek middle ground: wear dress pants or a simple skirt, dress shoes, and plain shirt with a blazer you can easily remove or keep on for adding or reducing formality on the spot.

Nine Things to Do on the Day You Present

1. Arrive in plenty of time. Check out the room if it is unfamiliar to you, to make sure it has all the resources you need. Arrange and set up your presentation aids, so you won't keep your audience waiting while you fiddle with them later.
2. Keep your visualizations positive. Breathe.
3. When you begin, smile at the audience, and establish eye contact with them individually. Stay in touch with them. If they look puzzled or bored, interact with them if possible: ask if there are any questions, or whether you need to explain anything again. Your honest interaction will keep the audience with you.

4. Speak conversationally. Very few audiences actually want you to fail. In your position, they would be nervous, too. Speaking to them as if they were ordinary people (which they are) will relax both you and them.

5. Find ways to make your presentation interesting as well as informative. Make jokes that illuminate the topic (generic jokes such as "ladies and germs" are rarely effective). Use natural gestures. Vary your voice. Use presentation aids.

6. Rephrase questions aloud as the audience asks them, since people at the back usually cannot hear the people at the front. Answer questions thoroughly, and do not be afraid of admitting you do not have the answer or that you may not have made up your mind on an issue. You may even use the question as an opportunity to strengthen your connection with your listeners by asking if there is anyone else in the audience who could answer.

7. Respect your time limit out of consideration to the audience and any other speakers, and signal clearly when you are drawing to a close. The only thing worse than a speaker who goes on and on is one who repeatedly says "And in conclusion," and then goes on and on.

8. Thank the audience and exit graciously. Save the introspective post-mortem for later.

9. When you do your self-examining post-mortem, look for the strengths, especially if you are usually hard on yourself. Allow yourself to enjoy your strong points and build on them for next time. Audiences enjoy listening to speakers who enjoy speaking!

THE PRESENTATION

In summary, there are many naturally gifted speakers in the world. You may wish to improve your speaking style by emulating one of them, but you need not *be* one of them to be an effective speaker. Respect your audience as you prepare your oral presentations. Carefully word and structure your work to make it effective as spoken text, both in its information and its argumentation. Develop your ability to use your voice and body to enhance your message. Plan your presentations thoroughly, including your presentation aids. Your listeners will appreciate your respect for them and will receive your message as warmly as it deserves.

FINAL WORD

The principles in this chapter will enrich your writing as well as your speaking; future success may depend at least as much upon the one as upon the other.

Section 5   Revising

INTRODUCTION

Revising contributes far more to a successful essay than many student writers initially realize. Depending on the amount of research required for your paper, pre-writing and drafting stages will certainly absorb a substantial portion of your time. Nevertheless, you should spend at least 15 percent of your overall writing time on the final phase—revising.

To assist your work as self-editor, the following chapter offers three main steps: sharpening impact at key locations, correcting grammar, and perfecting style.

For each step, we connect you to the other parts of this text that directly support the specific editing principles involved. You should find this an efficient, simple way to gather what you have learned from this text into a final review and polish of your essays. Given all the work involved in pre-writing and drafting, why settle for lowered marks—even failure, or rejection by a publisher—simply because you did not take the final steps to perfect your work? Put in that 15 percent (or more) of revising time that all professional writers dedicate to their work.

Chapter 21
Revising

Revising contributes as much to a successful essay as pre-writing and drafting. Think of revising as analogous to delivering an email. You may write the message, but if it sits in your drafts folder, it fails to cross the line from private record to wider communication. "Sending" the message, in this analogy, means executing three main editing steps that, taken together, may require several hours of work, depending on the assignment and your readiness as editor. We recommend revising your essays according to the following three steps.

THREE STEPS OF REVISION

- Sharpen key locations.
- Correct grammar.
- Perfect style.

This text and its Text Enrichment Site provide the tools you need for each of these three steps. The following discussions of each step begin with a listing of the main parts of this text that most directly serve your work for the step concerned.

SHARPEN KEY LOCATIONS

Key locations are introductions and thesis statements, topic sentences, and conclusions. The following sections assist with these topics:

Thesis statements	Chapter 6
Topic sentences	Chapter 4 and Chapter 6
Introductions and conclusions	Chapter 7

PRACTICE
Sharpening Key Locations—Thesis Statement

Decide if the following essay contains an effective thesis statement. If not, what would you do as editor to provide or sharpen a thesis statement? Refer to the Text Enrichment Site for this chapter to find our suggested editing improvements as well as to access more detailed instruction on revising.

Sample Essay

Beginning Riders: The Untold Story

Joyce Miller

When a beginning rider mounts a horse for the first time, the rider feels awkward, unbalanced, and unsure of what to do. The horse feels exactly the same way.

The horse may adopt the attitude of a middle-aged family pet who belongs to the new rider's neighbour, best friend, or relative. This horse spends its days dreaming in the field, the carefree succession broken only for the odd pleasure ride. The horse doesn't much care what gets on its back, so long as the mounted thing doesn't expect much expenditure of energy. While the new rider tries several times to swing a leg high enough to get on without dislocating a hip, the horse catches a few winks. At an uncertain tap from the rider's heels, the horse ambles five feet, then lowers its head to graze. This process is repeated several times. Thirty minutes later, the ride ends twenty feet from where it began. The rider is a little frustrated, but no mishaps have occurred and the horse's state of zen remains undisturbed.

A higher level of energy and more experience with beginning riders creates a horse with a foreman mentality. This is usually a lesson or trail horse. The horse knows what needs to be done, quickly senses that the rider doesn't know what needs to be done, and sets out to do it as efficiently as possible. Intelligent new riders realize this and, with great relief, hand over control to the most competent member of the team. This works great until the horse decides it is time to a) return to its stall, b) visit with friends, or c) clear the three-foot jump in the centre of the ring. The rider may come out of this ride embarrassed, but the worst injury is usually to the ego.

A third attitude belongs to the horse no beginner should ride, and few do for long. This horse may be the "really calm cutting horse" on Uncle Fred's ranch; the "excellent young prospect" being sold cheap by a dealer; or the high-octane, under-used acreage horse whose owner is sure he's safe to ride, although she's never been on him, because the previous owner was a thirteen-year-old (never mind that she was a thirteen-year-old provincial barrel racing champ). Such a horse has lots of energy, a lively imagination, and complete inexperience with beginning riders. The sensation of 100 to 200 pounds of yanking, wobbling weight on his back brings to life a race memory of killer cougars. He makes an instant, life-saving decision which would win him a berth in the Kentucky Derby if only anyone were there with a stopwatch, and if only he still had a rider on his back. This is definitely the most painful introduction to riding, but strangely enough, there are some riders who don't give up.

Despite frustration, terror, and/or pain (or perhaps because of them), the stubborn novice rider persists until he or she no longer flops on the horse like a sack of ill-sorted potatoes. The magic day arrives when balance and technique come together. Riding becomes almost effortless; the horse seems to respond to the thought of the rider. Best of all, it is clear that the horse enjoys the experience.

Sharpening Key Locations—Topic Sentences and Conclusion

Now that you have thought about revising to sharpen the thesis statement for the above essay, decide if you would make any revisions to the topic sentence of paragraphs, and why.

Then decide if there is anything you might do in the conclusion to sharpen the main idea of the essay.

See the Text Enrichment Site, Chapter 21, for our suggestions in response to this exercise.

More on Revision of Topic Sentences

We have said elsewhere, in Chapter 4, "Paragraph Skills," that effective topic sentences need to hit their pages running. A good topic sentence announces the subject of its paragraph, but a very good topic sentence also asserts a rationale for its position that the paragraph then explores.

Good topic sentence

The Tragically Hip are an exceptional band.

Better

The Tragically Hip are an exceptional band because of poetic, often surprising lyrics, rich vocal power, and energetic musicianship.

Good topic sentence

Canada's most famous medical discovery is insulin.

Better

Insulin, Canada's most famous medical discovery, allowed Dr. Frederick Banting to bring diabetes patients back from the edge of death in 1922.

Good topic sentence

Prague isn't the only historically interesting part of the Czech Republic.

Better

Prague is only one of several dozen towns with carefully preserved medieval architecture in the Czech Republic.

These stronger topic sentences have "analytical spin": they articulate the significance of their own observations. This quality is a bit tricky and may take time to incorporate into your writing habits. You can successfully produce effective topic sentences through committed revision.

PRACTICE
Sharpening Key Locations—Topic Sentences

First-year composition student Caren I. Jameson has written a draft essay arguing a highly unusual, controversial view: "Euthanasia should be made legal and be decided by a hospital administrator's holding of a raffle after all those patients wishing for euthanasia put their names, to be drawn at random, into a hat." Your task is to go through Caren's draft essay revising the first few sentences of each paragraph in order to refine *one* effective topic sentence for each paragraph.

Before this work, you wisely decide to revise her thesis statement for diction and conciseness. You express her thesis effectively as follows: "Euthanasia should be legalized and administered through a raffle for all declared candidates." Now you work with the opening of her draft paragraphs, which appear below. For our suggested topic sentence revisions, see the Text Enrichment Site for this chapter.

Caren's Paragraph Openings

Paragraph #1

Euthanasia is serious. No one person should ever bear such bureaucratic responsibility for decisions such as these that affect such a large number of others. The wishes of the suffering patients need to be heard and respected, however.

Paragraph #2

Who can say what's morally right? So, what authority can decide a view, one way or the other? If the patient is dying painfully, beyond the help of medicine and the comfort of family, his or her view might be the most informed view.

Paragraph #3

Life is very random. We didn't choose our parents, our genetics, our talents, and often our disposition. Let me tell you about that someday. Philosophically speaking, randomness is fair because it's a neutral quality. A raffle best represents this random quality of life.

Paragraph #4

A euthanasia raffle will thus satisfy the winners. It will alleviate guilt, indecision, and responsibility in the authorities. This will also be true for administrators. A raffle will imitate the quality of life itself, which is random.

More on Revision of the Introduction

A clear, terse introduction will go a long way to helping you organize your subsequent discussion and to gaining your reader's interest and confidence. Strive to achieve both compression in your language and pointed direction in your analysis for an effective introduction. Always revise and hone your thesis statement with care as the introduction's most important sentence.

> ## PRACTICE
> ### Sharpening Key Locations—Introductions
>
> Revise the following sample introduction for conciseness, clarity, and a more chiselled thesis statement. Then see the Text Enrichment Site, Chapter 21, for our suggestions.

Sample introduction

Video lottery terminals, available to the public, pose a danger for many of the vulnerable people who are playing them. They are often located in bars, where people tend to drink and lose some of their best judgement about how to spend their money and their time. They sometimes pay out money, but over a year, what would someone who likes to play them, spend annually? Probably a lot more than you would think. The government, bars, and casinos may make money from VLT machines, but not the players, especially those who start to become addicted. Does society have a duty to intervene with new laws and regulations when people's choices harm themselves only and not really anyone else? Should society ban video lottery terminals?

More on Revising Conclusions

We discuss conclusions on pages 102–05 of the Rhetoric. Whether you or your instructor wishes your paper to end with a *suggestive* or *exhaustive* conclusion is an important point to discuss before you hand in the paper for grading. In either case, your conclusion needs to signal that the essay has come to an effective and satisfactory end. Presumably, you have built a case for your view and are ready to close the discussion.

Three tips can help you revise a draft conclusion:

1. Try to avoid repeating your thesis in exactly the same words. Be more resourceful. Your reader will already know your thesis if you have stated it clearly in your introduction and have developed focused topic sentences to guide your body paragraphs.

    If you have written an essay arguing that Don Cherry unfortunately functions in Canadian culture more as an entertaining buffoon than as a seasoned ex-player, experienced coach, sports historian, and respected strategist, then your thesis statement might appear as something like this: "Cherry's clownish presence and loudmouth ranting degrade a sport that, to some people, is a form of culture."

    Your conclusion should either pursue a final implication of this view of Don Cherry *or* completely rephrase this assertion, probably taking some of the essay's overall discussion into account. Here are sentences from possible conclusions.

    Weak (repetitive)

    Therefore, Cherry's clownish antics and loud rants do nothing but degrade a winter sport that some Canadians see as a form of culture.

    Revised (exhaustive)

    Cherry's self-presentation, though mildly entertaining, finally hurts the image of a world sport that has successfully outgrown a shouting bully.

    Revised (suggestive)

    A final implication of Cherry's regularly scheduled rants is that young players, especially children, may think that hockey continues to be a sport that embraces its lowest common denominator—dim-witted aggression—instead of its highest levels of controlled speed, masterful timing, passing and defensive skills, and shooting accuracy.

2. Avoid adding such startling new information that you, in effect, set up a new body paragraph. New information, new implications, or new dimensions in your argument can be introduced, but only with care. The result will be a *suggestive* conclusion: it must still remember and clearly relate to the thesis of the essay.

Let us say you are completing an essay on the representation of romance in the music of Johnny Cash. Let us say you have argued that Cash, unlike many singers (except, for example, for Sinead O'Connor, The Eagles, and Barry White), contends that romance and love require great personal responsibility. Some possible conclusions might unfold as follows:

Weak conclusion (because of startling new information)

Johnny Cash also recorded a cover of Bob Dylan's "It Ain't Me, Babe." Cash's version, slower, vocally deeper, reveals more ethical and emotional dimensions within a failing relationship than even Dylan's original recording, which seems to skim along on lighter romantic and courtship differences.

Revised conclusion

Cash's work always presents romantic love as the serious endeavour of life, not escapism from it. He treats love as an ethical expression throughout his music. Cash's work, including [here you would mention a song or songs you have mentioned in your essay], quietly reflects the multiple, demanding dimensions of deep love that most popular music often superficially misrepresents.

This revised conclusion economically addresses your essay's earlier discussion, even though it may resourcefully restate it. The weaker conclusion does not attempt to resolve the issues of its discussion but instead acts as a brand new body paragraph. Though interesting, it does not signal and summarize any ending or implication. Remember that your conclusion must perform its primary function: to resolve the preceding discussion.

3. Avoid overstating the scope and significance of your earlier discussion. Many students panic as they conclude, and they offer sweeping claims when they could finish their essays nicely with controlled, understated summaries. If your conclusion claims more than the arguments have, your writing—your evaluation and your sense of things—will appear unreliable or, worse, reveal that you think your reader is gullible.

PRACTICE
Sharpening Key Locations—Revision of the Conclusion

Revise the following draft conclusion, keeping in mind some of the revision strategies we have discussed.

Then see the Text Enrichment Site, Chapter 21, for our suggestions.

Sample conclusion

To conclude, self-employment is thus far more difficult and riskier than one would think sometimes. The problem of small resources makes competition with corporations tough. A new study claims governments do not take individual small business seriously until after five years. Making and maintaining business networks is also difficult, since most of your time is usually spent completing what work or contracts you have already. Even the problems of insurance and benefits are worrisome. Therefore, despite a self-employed person's being his or her own boss and taking lunch breaks whenever, there are reasons why 70 percent of first-year businesses fail and many people falsify tax claims and don't give much time or money to charities anymore.

CORRECT GRAMMAR

Given that many students lack a conscious command of grammar, part of the revising phase should include efforts to learn more about common errors and to find and correct those in the essay. The Handbook in this textbook assists you with grammar.

An efficient method of revising your essays for grammar is to test for the 15 common errors. Finding and correcting these should eliminate 90 percent or more of your grammar concerns. You can sharpen your awareness of these common points of grammar by trying some of the quizzes at the Text Enrichment Site. Refer to the answer key for each quiz to see which of the errors you need help with. The quiz answer keys provide references to appropriate parts of Section 3 of the Handbook. Sections 1 and 2 of the Handbook define and illustrate the terms used in the explanations of the common errors. If you aren't sure what a certain explanatory term means, check its definition in either Section 1 or Section 2. If the principle remains unclear, consult your instructor or someone with sound grammar knowledge. Revision requires that you have sufficient knowledge of grammar to be able to find and correct your deviations from standard usage.

♪ PRACTICE
Correcting the 15 Common Errors

Edit the following two paragraphs making as few changes as necessary to remove the common errors.   Then see our revised version at the Text Enrichment Site, Chapter 21.

Sample Writing

Paragraph One: Correct for the 15 Common Errors

The Soprano's have all the features of a Shakespearian history play, as defined by Norrie Epstein; battlefield heroics, familial relationships, feisty characters, power politics and covert scheming (151). Like Prince Harry overcoming Hotspur in Henry IV, Part 2 Tony prevailed over an attempted assassination (episode 12), so did Chris (episode 21). This is where Chris almost died, so bravery was much on display. Shakespeares use of domestic scenes are paralleled in *The Sopranos* by similar scenes of family relationships involving Tony, Carmela, Meadow, Anthony Junior, and various other members of the extended crime "family." Feisty Shakespearean characters such as Hotspur, Falstaff, and Mistress Quickly find their modern counterparts in *Sopranos* regulars like Chris, Uncle Junior, and Janice. Each has their own feisty manner. In particular, Tony resembled Henry IV in their concealing of private anguish beneath a mask of political action. On the matter of power politics, Shakespeare's histories began with the question of whom will succeed to power, and would there be an answer to the bitter feud which occurred between the houses of Lancaster and York. Similarly, *The Sopranos* begins with the death of the local crime boss, Jackie Aprile, Sr., a consequential power vacuum, and problems of how to gain control according to the old code of honour which only has kept its meaning for Tony. Comparing Shakespeares' language to language in *The Soprano's,* a parallel exists in many visual and linguistic puns and double entendres such as the name of the informant character Pussy (executed at the end of season two). This is little observed, it seems. An essay on the topic, however, is upcoming. Uniting all of these similarities is the strong appeal that both the histories and *The Sopranos* has for their audiences, we envy the rich and the powerful, the vicarious thrill of sin and danger is experienced, in the ruthless main characters the same moral compromise which governs our own lives are recognized. A shared worldview despite the different time periods.

Work Cited

Epstein, *Norrie. Friendly Shakespeare: A Thoroughly Painless Guide to the Best of the Bard.* Penguin: New York, 1993.

Sample Writing

Paragraph Two: Correct for the 15 Common Errors, Misspellings, Etc.

Eighties music is not as bad or culturally frightening as many people say. Although its hard to defend Duran Duran. One band, Cameo had a great funk song entitled "Word Up" in the early Eighties. Two other band's styles from this decade have defined alot of modern music here and now; U2 and REM. Besides these two examples of writerly talent and innovative musicianship we need to really remember that some of Tom Petty's, AC/DC's, Bananarama's, and, of course Guns n' Roses' best work appeared in the Eighties. However the mysterious problem of all those one-hit or two-hit wonders are a concern to any true connoisseur of this decade's music, for instance: 'Til Tuesday's "Voices Carry," A-Ha's "Take On Me," Adam Ant's "Goodie Two Shoes," The Bangles' "Walk Like an Egyptian," Fine Young Cannibals' "Good Thing," and Glass Tiger's "Don't Forget Me [When I'm Gone]." Did these artists' managers suddenly run out of ideas, were they abducted by extra-terrestrials or by Lou Reed and Iggy Pop? Considering Elton John's recent work, is it better too burn out then fade away?

PERFECT STYLE

To make sure that your style is appropriate and consistent, refer to the following parts of the text:

Tone (word choice, sentence structure)	Chapter 1, Chapter 2, Chapter 16 (persuasive appeals shaped to purpose) Tones chart (inside back cover)
Paragraph craft	Chapter 4
Sentence craft	Handbook, Section 3, Common Errors 1, 5, 11, 12, and 14
Citations	Chapter 19

More on Revising for Style

As Chapters 1 and 2 explain, through careful word choice, you need to establish and maintain your level of language in service to the purpose and audience for your essay. You also need to review your sentences to ensure that they are not too informal and that they are contributing through effective rhythm, patterns, and impact points. A particularly important part of revising for style is to improve conciseness.

Conciseness is a form of beauty, yet few people are spontaneously concise writers. Conciseness is sometimes difficult to achieve even in subsequent drafts of a paper. You can accomplish this conciseness after you return to your writing with a stronger sense of what you are trying to express; economy of expression will match clarity of concept. Conciseness also requires a little editorial perspiration, some sweat in the compression of your expression! Once you have your draft—have worked towards some observations, assertions, implications, paragraph form—you will be surprised to reread and see how much more economical you can be with words.

Conciseness requires your elimination of unnecessary words and phrases. Delete clunky phrases such as "in terms of," "about the question of," "are indicative of," and "to consider in the context of," which clutter up your sentences and your potentially terse and crisp expression.

Remember that much redundancy also results from a hasty disregard for logic. Delete unnecessary restatements of what you have already said or clearly implied.

PRACTICE
Perfecting Style—Revising for Conciseness

Revise the following passage for conciseness, spontaneously co-composed in a brief inkshedding session by two first-year students, Helen Allingham and Otto Graph. Then see the Text Enrichment Site, Chapter 21, for our suggestions.

Sample Writing

Paragraph A: Revise for Conciseness

In terms of the very many persistent concerns about the question of our ongoing water safety after the frightening scare over health in the Canadian town of Walkerton, Ontario, many people, including all Canadians, need to start to consider the many facts about all this. The expectations that we have formed that our water will always be safe and hazard-free for us to drink are indicative of how we tend to rely far too much on the bureaucratic assurances that are given to us by people who work in the government agency. Like our other natural resources, water is a valuable resource that we cannot take for granted or fail to consider in the context of supply.

PRACTICE
Perfecting Style—Revising for Conciseness

Revise the following interesting (but wordy) assertions appearing as part of a first draft by British exchange student Patsy Kensit-Murphy for a community affairs paper entitled "There's No McDonald's in Camden Town." Once you are done, see the Text Enrichment Site, Chapter 21, for our suggestions.

Paragraph B: Revise for Conciseness

McDonald's is continuing to enjoy its great degree of success in fast-food products on a scale that could be accurately described as global. But why, given that more and more people are continuing to become vegetarians or at least are concerned to some extent about their nutrition, veggie intake, and cholesterol, why does such a company prosper? Firstly, to begin, a lot of their business success seems to be relying on the use of their slick, but merely image-driven advertisements: it's strange that there is little talk in these beautiful ads of factual nutritional wholesomeness, considering how McDonald's sells food for families and young people. Secondly, the price the company charges is always right. If a customer is worried about today's prices (like I am), McDonald's prices are appealing to customers. But what if the final outcome is that the deliberate lies of many promises in media join together with the appealing incentive of low price to make people forget their best interests?

PUTTING IT ALL TOGETHER—USING ALL THREE STEPS TO EDIT AN ESSAY

The final part of this chapter provides an example of a student's first draft as it has evolved from a preliminary topic sentence tree. We have added notes on how the thesis statement and topic sentences have been organized into a fully written draft. As a final exercise, go through this draft carefully according to the three editing steps recommended in this chapter. What further sharpening, correcting, and perfecting would you do?

        When you have completed your revisions, see the Text Enrichment Site, Chapter 21, for our suggestions and further commentary.

Introduction to Sample Student Essay

What if you are interested in writing a brief analysis arguing, say, that World Wrestling Entertainment is a form of soap opera? Your paper will likely rely partly on **classification** (arguing that WWE is, surprisingly enough, part of a television genre widely known as the soap opera), partly on **definition** (defining what a soap opera is and how WWE displays some of these characteristics), and partly on **comparison and contrast** techniques to organize your paragraphs.

After you have worked through a point-form list, inkshedding, diagramming, or a topic-sentence tree in the pre-writing stages, you are ready to begin a draft of your discussion. Your topic-sentence tree for this analysis may look something like our diagram. The optional numbers attached to each topic sentence in the tree here would be added only later, as your draft takes shape and you make decisions about which topic sentences to use, which ones—possibly—you might want to combine, and the order in which they should appear in your draft.

After constructing your topic-sentence tree, you can write a first draft of your paper. The topic sentences in your tree diagram need not appear in the order you have thought of them; move them around as necessary and modify them in your draft. As you work on this draft, you may find that your essay structure changes slightly with any new insights and developments. In fact, some of your tentative topic sentences from the topic-sentence tree may not even appear later as topic sentences, but may become points in a paragraph organized by other topic sentences. Such flexibility and shape-shifting are skills you learn in the process of drafting and revising.

Your main aim in sketching a topic-sentence tree and in composing a first draft is to start developing your argument: (1) working thesis (the main claim or point), (2) the paragraph structure with provisional topic sentences, and (3) the significance of your observations. Your first draft of an analysis of the WWE as soap opera might unfold something like our example. The working thesis statement and topic sentences are underlined in the sample essay to emphasize their presence as the frame—the backbone—of the essay.

Figure 21.1

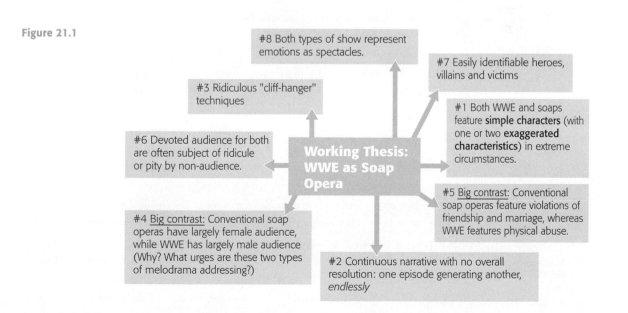

The First Draft

Working thesis.

Topic sentence #1
from tree diagram.

Topic sentence #2
from tree diagram.

Topic sentence #3
from tree diagram
now incorporated
into the paragraph.

Topic sentences
#4 and #5 from
tree diagram now
combined.

World Wrestling Entertainment is really only a kind of soap opera. It is a big soap opera for a mostly male audience. WWE, like all soap operas, is about melodrama because of the exaggerated situations and extreme feelings. Although WWE is different in some ways from regular soap operas, there are lots of similarities.

Both WWE and daytime soap operas present lots of characters in painful, often exaggerated circumstances. The characters in both are always in some trouble, distress, or crisis. In both the wrestling world and the usual soap operas, there seems to be a whole lot of betrayal. The situations are the same over and over: someone lies or cheats on somebody in the daytime soaps and someone sneaks up on someone in the WWE and hits him with a chair. The situations are all pretty extreme, but also almost the same from week to week. It's all about simple characters with one or two exaggerated characteristics getting in trouble or causing trouble.

Another thing these two types of shows have in common is there's no overall conclusion or else the show would end as a series. Different problems get concluded, sure, but one thing spins into another and one big problem creates other ones for next week, next month, next year. When someone's marriage ends in the soaps, it often comes out that years of adultery are the reason. However, the cheating might be between a sultry corporate businesswoman and her shifty accountant, who would falsify all their expense accounts because he was obsessed with going to fancy spas in a bikini with her, and now the company's stockholders are suddenly demanding an investigation that might also reveal that none of the company's new products meets safety standards. In WWE, a tag-team match turns bad when one of the partners is sucker-punched by a masked wrestler who is not even supposed to be in the ring. He climbs in because one of the other wrestler's brothers—also a wrestler—jumped on him last week from the top turnbuckle minutes before their match was supposed to start. There's lots of indiscriminate pushing in the ring until somebody gets hit with a garbage can while the ref was advising someone else about time restrictions for the bout. This cheap shot wins the match, but the revenge will probably come next week. In both soaps and wrestling, the episodes are cliff-hangers to deliberately set up lots of other related episodes, so the stories are continuous, unlike other television shows that usually resolve each episode before a new one next week.

Despite similarities, there are some important contrasts between the wrestling and daytime soap opera worlds. Soap operas have largely female audiences, while WWE has mostly male audiences. Soap operas usually dramatize family problems and betrayals in friendships and relationships. But wrestling makes fun of physical aggression and bodily pain. The soaps look at emotions in the context of social and private life, while the WWE presents the pain of comic book make-believe physical abuse in male competition. These differences make the melodrama of soap operas seem more realistic, at least as far as their characters' problems relating in some way to the viewers' fears and perhaps hopes. So, while the women's soaps exaggerate and exploit a lot of genuine adult fears, the wrestling really only represents the immature boy's perspective of a schoolyard bullying tournament.

With all these easily identifiable heroes, villains, and victims, the daytime soaps and WWE have a big devoted audience. Unfortunately, the people of these audiences are often ridiculed by people who are not fans. The fans are not necessarily silly, but perhaps are enjoying the simplistic characters in one crisis after another. The formulas please the viewers. This is because there are occasionally surprising variations in the same plots and themes. This requires real innovation. There are links between differences in the sex of the separate audiences and the differences in the types of fears and fantasies of the two types of melodrama. These differences in content reveal that the men and women who like melodrama seek different types in order to entertain themselves. However, both sexes seem to enjoy seeing emotions represented as spectacles.

Topic sentences #6 and #7 combined.

Topic sentence #8 repositioned as concluding sentence.

FINAL WORDS

Exercises such as those in this chapter can certainly help you to kick-start your thinking and skills as an editor. Ultimately, however, the best way to improve is to edit your own work carefully. Use past and present revising suggestions from your instructor and peer editors. See "Peer Editing" at the Text Enrichment Site, Chapter 21, for illustrations of how to give and accept editing suggestions. Improving as a self-editor takes time, patience, and disciplined time management. For every essay, it is important to schedule in enough time for several hours of careful revising. As you schedule your pre-writing, drafting, and revising time, allow at least a couple of days between drafting and revising. Time away from the essay provides a fresh eye and increased objectivity. You will be able to do a much better job as self-editor if you have allowed yourself a break from the essay as well as some rest and recreation. Budget your editing time so that you spend at least an hour on each of the three recommended steps of revision. This professional discipline will begin to pay you back with the pride of fully achieved writing and improved marks.

THE
READER

INTRODUCTION

In the following four Reader sections, you will find personal and critical writing that deals with connections between self-identity and place, times, family, and many other aspects of life and thought. Literary work, popular books and magazine pieces, student essays, and other forms of writing are represented. None of the following pieces perfectly demonstrate the five-paragraph short academic essay form that we have modelled in the Rhetoric, but part of your work as a student is learning to negotiate your way through a wide range of forms and ideas. Regardless of the specific form of writing, all of the pieces in this Reader illustrate to greater or lesser degrees the basics of good writing. These basics have much in common with those of good driving: a sense of purpose, careful respect of distance and relationships, and a concern to signal to others where one is going. See if that isn't true throughout the selections that follow. Take note of places where you believe this isn't always true, and try to define why.

You will find topics and themes of relevance to university students as well as to anyone interested in what it means to be Canadian and human. We believe you should find much to admire and emulate in the following works. For each reading we have provided a short introduction of background information as well as follow-up questions and further sources, all intended to help you make useful connections among these pieces, rhetorical information elsewhere in the text, and your own growth as a reader and writer. We have organized the four Reader sections according to a general curve: from primarily evocative works to pieces more intent on changing what readers know, to still others intent on changing how readers think (and perhaps what they will do as a consequence). None of these purposes is necessarily separate from the others: what we consider the fundamental purpose of a piece of writing is a matter of its relative and immediate emphasis. However, we offer this basic lay-out—from personal to overtly critical—as a reminder, once again, that writing is about choices related to communication, about shaping information and ideas in the interests of some new state of being in one's self, one's reader, and one's world.

Review Summarizing and Rhetorical Analysis

To help you benefit from these selections to the fullest, read Chapter 13, "The Summary," and Chapter 15, "Rhetorical Analysis," in the Rhetoric. These chapters describe the importance of active reading, with detailed guidance on how to write a summary and a rhetorical process description. You will probably be asked to write at least one summary as part of your writing assignments, but it is also a good idea to write a brief summary of any selection that particularly interests you or that has been selected for class or group discussion. Check with your instructor and classmates to see how successfully you are capturing the main intents, strategies, and ideas of the different selections. The first step to becoming a stronger reader and thinker is learning how to write a successful summary. For help with analyzing the short stories, see "Literary and Film Analysis" on the Text Enrichment Site for Chapter 15.

If writing may be likened to breathing out, then reading is breathing in. All good writers realize it is not possible to do one without the other. We hope our selections help to make your reading as valuable as it can be, by gaining your interest as well as furthering your personal, academic, and community growth.

Section 1 Storytelling:
Narration and
Description

In college or university, you will likely be expected to produce analytical and persuasive writing closer in style to that demonstrated in Sections 2, 3, and 4 of the Reader than to the type featured in Section 1. Nevertheless, the following examples should inform your academic writing. First, these samples illustrate a command of narration and description, techniques examined in Chapter 8 and Chapter 9 of the Rhetoric and in "Literary and Film Analysis" on the Text Enrichment Site, Chapter 15, as valuable for all forms of writing. Notice how precisely a story such as "Thanks for the Ride" describes its setting, how economically a story such as "The Hockey Sweater," using just the right balance of slower and swifter sections, propels us forward in anticipation of what happens next. Whether or not you have room for personal writing in your current English or communications course, you will gain by considering the techniques demonstrated in these samples, by recognizing the unity of voice, tone, mood, and purpose that informs them. You will no doubt recognize the writer's underlying commitment to the topic and theme: no one else but the particular writer in question could have handled the material in quite the same way. Like good researchers adding to communal knowledge, personal writers add their original voices to the communal story.

In his essay "The Rhetorical Stance" (p. 487), Wayne C. Booth raises the problem of the "entertainer's stance," an attitude of self-indulgence that may seem engaging but that detracts from attention to the deeper, broader topic. According to Johnny Moses, a Nootka storyteller raised on the west coast of Vancouver Island, when people ask why there is no word for *I* or *me* in his language, he tells them that the grandmothers say it's "because the ego is so big it doesn't need a name." The word *ego*, for *self*, was made famous through the writings of Austrian psychologist Sigmund Freud (1856–1939). Freud characterized the ego as that part of the self which moderates between the sometimes unruly, disruptive forces of self-interest—the id—and those of broader social awareness and even repressive self-censure—the superego. Traditional academic wisdom says that using third person and "detached" tone overcomes or at least mitigates the risk of undue emphasis on the writer. But is this academic solution to the danger of "entertainer's stance" as simple as it sounds?

We have mentioned elsewhere that third-person style may achieve a surface appearance of dispassionate integrity that does not hold up when one digs into it. Furthermore, first person does not inevitably result in a compromised commitment to truth or what we imagine as truth, far from it. There is a Sufi saying that until one tells the story of one's life, simply and briefly, one cannot purposefully proceed to less personal communication. The following selections, though using first person, express a primary concern not with self (the inevitable lens) but with relationships to others: to nature, to family, friends, adversaries, and lovers, and to communities local and large. We will find, in the various depictions of these relationships, concerns with topics such as education, gender, generation, race, faith, work, dislocation, politics, global upheaval, and perception. The first-person approach, while it requires care to avoid the "entertainer's stance" defined by Booth, by no means belittles the topic. Some would argue that this stance, in fact, deepens the discussion, whether implied or explicit.

In this spirit, some writing instructors encourage personal writing, often in the form of personal essays, sometimes in more casual forms, such as the journal (described in Chapter 5 of the Rhetoric). While first person does not suit many analytical occasions, it has the advantage of reminding writer and reader that authors are always present in their writing, and that ultimately they are accountable. (See George Orwell's essay on the evasive nature of third-person bureaucratese, of passive voice, on page 471). First person reminds us as writers to deal with primary matters of meaning to self, which must be acknowledged. In scholarship, first-person journal responses to readings and research encourage students to find relevance, to take personal ownership of issues, to explore meaningful connections, to increase awareness of personal responsibility. The essential skill of putting ideas into one's own words is valuably practised in personal writing. We think you will find that the essays in this section provide excellent and enjoyable models of that essential skill and of personal reflection and response.

Roger Fouts This brief memoir describes how Fouts's pet dog sacrificed her life to save his brother. Fouts went on to earn a PhD and to perform groundbreaking research into communication with chimpanzees. Continuing Jane Goodall's resistance to the traditional approach, which views animals as completely detached from humans, Fouts developed a 30-year friendship with Washoe, the chimp at the heart of his book *Next of Kin*. In that book, Fouts chooses first-person voice, in keeping with his belief that animal research must embrace a personal aspect. His approach invites debate concerning the decision to communicate scientific research and analysis in a popular, personal style. "Brownie" has been excerpted from *Next of Kin*.

Brownie

1   My closest animal companion was our dog, Brownie. Feisty and fiercely loyal, Brownie was a fixture of our household. She needed us and we needed her. In addition to guarding the house, she baby-sat the youngest kids in the fields during the harvest season.

2   One day I saw Brownie do something that shaped my view of animals forever. She saved my brother's life. It happened during cucumber-picking season when I was four years old. The whole family—my parents, six brothers, and one sister—had been out in the field all day working. Brownie had been watching over me and my nine-year-old brother, Ed, whenever he got tired of picking. By the time the sun was going down our Chevy flatbed was piled high with boxes of cucumbers. It was time to head home for dinner. Ed wanted to ride back on our older brother's bicycle, a big thing that he could barely control. My parents said OK and Ed headed out on the bike, chaperoned by Brownie. Twenty minutes later, the rest of us clambered onto the truck and left the field with my twenty-year-old brother, Bob, driving.

3   It was the dry season, six months or so since the last rain, and the dirt road was blanketed with four or five inches of chalky dust. As the truck drove along the well-worn tire ruts in the road, it kicked up a huge cloud of dust that covered us on all sides, making it impossible to see more than two feet ahead or behind. After going along for a while, we suddenly heard Brownie barking very loudly and very persistently. We looked down and we could just make her out next to the front fender. She was snipping at the right front tire. This was very strange behavior. Brownie had come to the fields hundreds of times and had never once barked at the truck. But now she was practically attacking it. My brother Bob thought this was odd but didn't give Brownie much thought as he plowed ahead even as her barking became more frenzied. Then, without further warning, Brownie dove in front of the truck's front tire. I heard her shriek, and I felt a thump as we drove over her body. Bob hit the brakes, and we all got out. Brownie was dead. And right there in front of the truck, not ten feet away, was Ed, stuck on his bike in the deep tire rut, unable to escape. Another two seconds and we would have run him down.

4   Brownie's death was devastating to all of us. I had seen animals die before, but this one was my nearest and dearest friend. My parents tried to explain that Brownie had only done what either of them would have done for us. No one doubted for a second that Brownie had sacrificed her own life to save my brother's. She saw a dangerous situation unfolding, and she did what she had to do to protect the boy she had been baby-sitting for so many years. Had she not acted, the course of our family's life would have been very different.

For Further Thinking

1. "No one doubted for a second that Brownie had sacrificed her own life to save my brother's." Is this view of a dog's behaviour consistent with your own experiences and observations?

2. By telling this personal story in a book on chimpanzee behaviour, Fouts signals his personal relationship to his work. Do you feel this personal writing style in an academic work compromises the author's objectivity? Why or why not?

3. Is this memoir fundamentally narrative, descriptive, or reflective?

4. Review our discussion of thesis statements in Chapter 6 of the Rhetoric. Do you feel this personal essay has an explicit or implicit thesis statement? Explain.

Looking Back and Ahead

1. As a memoir, Fouts's essay has strong connections to other selections in this section, including "The Hockey Sweater" and "The King and I." If you have not already done so, describe what you consider the central qualities of this form of writing.

2. Read John Markoff's "The Doomsday Machines" (p. 505). Do you think Roger Fouts would take some of the concerns in this article seriously?

3. Much scientific writing uses a detached style that Fouts has chosen not to use in his book on Washoe the chimpanzee. Is it an oversimplification to suggest that more use of the personal style in scientific writing might help guard against the dangers described in "The Doomsday Machines"?

Alice Munro On the prowl for two young women and a good time, two out-of-town young men cruise into Mission Creek, Ontario, population 1700, described by a fly-speckled sign in Pop's Cafe as follows: "Gateway to the Bruce. We love our children." George, the aggressive older cousin, matches Dick with Lois, a girl of few but choice words. A much older Dick—later in time—narrates the account of his own voyage to sexual experience with the more knowing Lois and his observations of her.

Alice Munro was born in Wingham, Ontario, in 1931 and has remained emotionally close to her place of birth. Much of her fiction concerns the social restrictions experienced by characters in a rural world reflecting her own. "Thanks for the Ride" first appeared in *The Tamarack Review* and was later collected in *Dance of the Happy Shades* in 1968. Munro has been twice awarded the Governor General's Award for fiction; she is the first Canadian to have received the Canada-Australia Literary Prize, and has also received the U.S. National Book Critics Circle fiction prize for the short-story collection *The Love of a Good Woman*. She is widely regarded as one of Canada's finest writers and among the world's best short-story writers.

Thanks for the Ride

1   My cousin George and I were sitting in a restaurant called Pop's Cafe in a little town close to the Lake. It was getting dark in there, and they had not turned the lights on, but you could still read the signs plastered against the mirror between the fly-speckled and slightly yellowed cutouts of strawberry sundaes and tomato sandwiches.

2   " 'Don't ask for information,' " George read. " 'If we knew anything we wouldn't be here' " and " 'If you've got nothing to do, you picked a hell of a good place to do it in.' " George always read everything out loud—posters, billboards, Burma-Shave signs, " 'Mission Creek. Population 1700. Gateway to the Bruce. We love our children.' "

3   I was wondering whose sense of humour provided us with the signs. I thought it would be the man behind the cash register. Pop? Chewing on a match, looking out at the street, not watching for anything except for somebody to trip over a crack in the sidewalk or have a blowout or make a fool of himself in some way that Pop, rooted behind the cash register, huge and cynical and incurious, was never likely to do. Maybe not even that; maybe just by walking up and down, driving up and down, going places, the rest of the world proved its absurdity. You see that judgment on the faces of people looking out of windows, sitting on front steps in some little towns; so deeply, deeply uncaring they are, as if they had sources of disillusionment which they would keep, with some satisfaction, in the dark.

4   There was only the one waitress, a pudgy girl who leaned over the counter and scraped at the polish on her fingernails. When she had flaked most of the polish off her thumbnail she put the thumb against her teeth and rubbed the nail back and forth absorbedly. We asked her what her name was and she didn't answer. Two or three minutes later the thumb came out of her mouth and she said, inspecting it: "That's for me to know and you to find out."

5   "All right," George said. "Okay if I call you Mickey?"

6   "I don't care."

7   "Because you remind me of Mickey Rooney," George said. "Hey, where's everybody go in this town? Where's everybody go?" Mickey had turned her back and begun to drain out the coffee. It looked as if she didn't mean to talk any more, so George got a little jumpy, as he did when he was threatened with having to be quiet or be by himself. "Hey, aren't there any girls in this town?" he said almost plaintively. "Aren't there any girls or dances or anything? We're strangers in town," he said. "Don't you want to help us out?"

8   "Dance hall down on the beach closed up Labour Day," Mickey said coldly.

9   "There any other dance halls?"

10   "There's a dance tonight out at Wilson's *school*," Mickey said.

11   "That old-time? No, no, I don't go for that old-time. *All-a-man left* and that, used to have that down in the basement of the church. Yeah, *ever'body swing*—I don't go for that. Inna basement of the *church*," George said, obscurely angered. "You don't remember that," he said to me. "Too young."

12   I was just out of high-school at this time, and George had been working for three years in the Men's Shoes in a downtown department store, so there was that difference. But we had never bothered with each other back in the city. We were together now because we had met unexpectedly in a strange place and because I had a little money, while George was broke. Also I had my father's car, and George was in one of his periods between cars, which made him always a little touchy and dissatisfied. But he would have to rearrange these facts a bit, they made him uneasy. I could feel him manufacturing a sufficiency of good feeling, old-pal feeling, and dressing me up as Old Dick, good kid, real character—which did not matter one way or the other, though I did not think, looking at his tender blond piggish handsomeness, the nudity of his pink mouth, and the surprised, angry creases that frequent puzzlement was beginning to put into his forehead, that I would be able to work up an Old George.

13   I had driven up to the Lake to bring my mother home from a beach resort for women, a place where they had fruit juice and cottage cheese for reducing, and early-morning swims in the Lake, and some religion, apparently, for there was a little chapel attached. My aunt, George's mother, was staying there at the same time, and George arrived about an hour or so after I did, not to take his mother home, but to get some money out of her. He did not get along well with his father, and he did not make much money working in the shoe department, so he was very often broke. His mother said he could have a loan if he would stay over and go to church with her the next day. George said he would. Then George and I got away and drove half a mile along the lake to this little town neither of us had seen before, which George said would be full of bootleggers and girls.

14   It was a town of unpaved, wide, sandy streets and bare yards. Only the hardy things like red and yellow nasturtiums, or a lilac bush with brown curled leaves, grew out of that cracked earth. The houses were set wide apart, with their own pumps and sheds and privies out behind; most of them were built of wood and painted green or grey or yellow. The trees that grew there were big willows or poplars, their fine leaves greyed with the dust. There were no trees along the main street, but spaces of tall grass and dandelions and blowing thistles—open country between the store buildings. The town hall was surprisingly large, with a great bell in a tower, the red brick rather glaring in the midst of the town's walls of faded, pale-painted wood. The sign beside the door said that it was a memorial to the soldiers who had died in the First World War. We had a drink out of the fountain in front.

15   We drove up and down the main street for a while, with George saying: "What a dump! Jesus, what a dump!" and "Hey, look at that! Aw, not so good either." The people on the street went home to supper, the shadows of the store buildings lay solid across the street, and we went into Pop's.

16   "Hey," George said, "is there any other restaurant in this town? Did you see any other restaurant?"

17   "No," I said.

18   "Any other town I ever been," George said, "pigs hangin' out the windows, practically hangin' off the trees. Not here. Jesus! I guess it's late in the season," he said.

19   "You want to go to a show?"

20   The door opened. A girl came in, walked up and sat on a stool, with most of her skirt bunched up underneath her. She had a long somnolent face, no bust, frizzy hair; she was pale, almost ugly, but she had that inexplicable aura of sexuality. George brightened, though not a great deal. "Never mind," he said. "This'll do. This'll do in a pinch, eh? In a pinch."

21   He went to the end of the counter and sat down beside her and started to talk. In about five minutes they came back to me, the girl drinking a bottle of orange pop.

22   "This is Adelaide," George said. "Adelaide, Adeline—Sweet Adeline. I'm going to call her Sweet A, Sweet A."

23   Adelaide sucked at her straw, paying not much attention.

24   "She hasn't got a date," George said. "You haven't got a date have you, honey?"

25   Adelaide shook her head very slightly.

26   "Doesn't hear half what you say to her," George said. "Adelaide, Sweet A, have you got any friends? Have you got any nice, young little girl friend to go out with Dickie? You and me and her and Dickie?"

27   "Depends," said Adelaide. "Where do you want to go?"

28   "Anywhere you say. Go for a drive. Drive up to Owen Sound, maybe."

29   "You got a car?"

30   "Yeah, yeah, we got a car. C'mon, you must have some nice little friend for Dickie." He put his arm around this girl, spreading his fingers over her blouse. "C'mon out and I'll show you the car."

31   Adelaide said: "I know one girl might come. The guy she goes around with, he's engaged, and his girl came up and she's staying at his place up the beach, his mother and dad's place, and—"

32   "Well that is certainly int-er-esting," George said. "What's her name? Come on, let's go round and get her. You want to sit around drinking pop all night?"

33   "I'm finished," Adelaide said. "She might not come. I don't know."

34   "Why not? Her mother not let her out nights?"

35   "Oh, she can do what she likes," said Adelaide. "Only there's times she don't want to. I don't know."

36   We went out and got into the car, George and Adelaide in the back. On the main street about a block from the cafe we passed a thin, fair-haired girl in slacks and Adelaide cried: "Hey stop! That's her! That's Lois!"

37   I pulled in and George stuck his head out of the window, whistling. Adelaide yelled and the girl came unhesitatingly, unhurriedly to the car. She smiled, rather coldly and politely, when Adelaide explained to her. All the time George kept saying: "Hurry up, come on, get in! We can talk in the car." The girl smiled, did not really look at any of us, and in a few moments, to my surprise, she opened the door and slid into the car.

38   "I don't have anything to do," she said. "My boy friend's away."

39   "That so?" said George, and I saw Adelaide, in the rear-vision mirror, make a cross warning face. Lois did not seem to have heard him.

40   "We better drive around to my house," she said. "I was just going down to get some Cokes, that's why I only have my slacks on. We better drive around to my house and I'll put on something else."

41   "Where are we going to go," she said, "so I know what to put on?"

42   I said: "Where do you want to go?"

43   "Okay, okay," George said. "First things first. We gotta get a bottle, then we'll decide. You know where to get one?" Adelaide and Lois both said yes, and then Lois said to me: "You can come in the house and wait while I change, if you want to." I glanced in the rear mirror and thought that there was probably some agreement she had with Adelaide.

44   Lois's house had an old couch on the porch and some rugs hanging down over the railing. She walked ahead of me across the yard. She had her long pale hair tied at the back of her neck; her skin was dustily freckled, but not tanned; even her eyes were light-coloured. She was cold and narrow and pale. There was derision, and also great gravity, about her mouth. I thought she was about my age or a little older.

45   She opened the front door and said in a clear, stilted voice: "I would like you to meet my family."

46   The little front room had linoleum on the floor and flowered paper curtains at the windows. There was a glossy chesterfield with a Niagara Falls and a To Mother cushion on it, and there was a little black stove with a screen around it for summer, and a big vase of paper apple blossoms. A tall, frail woman came into the room drying her hands on a dishtowel, which she flung into a chair. Her mouth was full of blue-white china teeth, the long cords trembled in her neck. I said how-do-you-do to her, embarrassed by Lois's announcement, so suddenly and purposefully conventional. I wondered if she had any misconceptions about this date, engineered by George for such specific purposes. I did not think so. Her face had no innocence in it that I could see; it was knowledgeable, calm, and hostile. She might have done it, then, to mock me, to make me into this carica-ture of The Date, the boy who grins and shuffles in the front hall and waits to be presented to the nice girl's family. But that was a little far-fetched. Why should she

want to embarrass me when she had agreed to go out with me without even looking into my face? Why should she care enough?

47   Lois's mother and I sat down on the chesterfield. She began to make conversation, giving this the Date interpretation. I noticed the smell in the house, the smell of stale small rooms, bedclothes, frying, washing, and medicated ointments. And dirt, though it did not look dirty. Lois's mother said: "That's a nice car you got out front. Is that your car?"

48   "My father's."

49   "Isn't that lovely! Your father has such a nice car. I always think it's lovely for people to have things. I've got no time for these people that's just eaten up with malice 'n envy. I say it's lovely. I bet your mother, every time she wants anything, she just goes down to the store and buys it—new coat, bedspread, pots and pans. What does your father do? Is he a lawyer or doctor or something like that?"

50   "He's a chartered accountant."

51   "Oh. That's in an office, is it?"

52   "Yes."

53   "My brother, Lois's uncle, he's in the office of the CPR in London. He's quite high up there, I understand."

54   She began to tell me about how Lois's father had been killed in an accident at the mill. I noticed an old woman, the grandmother probably, standing in the doorway of the room. She was not thin like the others, but as soft and shapeless as a collapsed pudding, pale brown spots melting together on her face and arms, bristles of hairs in the moisture around her mouth. Some of the smell of the house seemed to come from her. It was a smell of hidden decay, such as there is when some obscure little animal has died under the verandah. The smell, the slovenly, confiding voice—something about this life I had not known, something about these people. I thought: my mother, George's mother, they are innocent. Even George, George is innocent. But these others are born sly and sad and knowing.

55   I did not hear much about Lois's father except that his head was cut off.

56   "Clean off, imagine, and rolled on the floor! Couldn't open the coffin. It was June, the hot weather. And everybody in town just stripped their gardens, stripped them for the funeral. Stripped their spirea bushes and peenies and climbin' clemantis. I guess it was the worst accident ever took place in this town.

57   "Lois had a nice boy friend this summer," she said. "Used to take her out and sometimes stay here overnight when his folks weren't up at the cottage and he didn't feel like passin' his time there all alone. He'd bring the kids candy and even me he'd bring presents. That china elephant up there, you can plant flowers in it, he brought me that. He fixed the radio for me and I never had to take it into the shop. Do your folks have a summer cottage up here?"

58   I said no, and Lois came in, wearing a dress of yellow-green stuff—stiff and shiny like Christmas wrappings—high-heeled shoes, rhinestones, and a lot of dark powder over her freckles. Her mother was excited.

59   "You like that dress?" she said. "She went all the way to London and bought that dress, didn't get it anywhere round here!"

60   We had to pass by the old woman as we went out. She looked at us with sudden recognition, a steadying of her pale, jellied eyes. Her mouth trembled open, she stuck her face out at me.

61   "You can do what you like with my gran'daughter," she said in her old, strong voice, the rough voice of a country woman. "But you be careful. And you know what I mean!"

62   Lois's mother pushed the old woman behind her, smiling tightly, eyebrows lifted, skin straining over her temples. "Never mind," she mouthed at me, grimacing distractedly. "Never mind. Second childhood." The smile stayed on her face, the skin pulled back from it. She seemed to be listening all the time to a perpetual din and racket in her head. She grabbed my hand as I followed Lois out. "Lois is a nice girl," she whispered. "You have a nice time, don't let her mope!" There was a quick, grotesque, and, I suppose, originally flirtatious, flickering of brows and lids. "Night!"

63   Lois walked stiffly ahead of me, rustling her papery skirt. I said: "Did you want to go to a dance or something?"

64   "No," she said. "I don't care."

65   "Well you got all dressed up—"

66   "I always get dressed up on Saturday night," Lois said, her voice floating back to me, low and scornful. Then she began to laugh, and I had a glimpse of her mother in her, that jaggedness and hysteria. "Oh, my God!" she whispered. I knew she meant what had happened in the house, and I laughed too, not knowing what else to do. So we went back to the car laughing as if we were friends, but we were not.

67   We drove out of town to a farmhouse where a woman sold us a whisky bottle full of muddy-looking home-made liquor, something George and I had never had before. Adelaide had said that this woman would probably let us use her front room, but it turned out that she would not, and that was because of Lois. When the woman peered up at me from under the man's cap she had on her head and said to Lois, "Change's as good as a rest, eh?" Lois did not answer, kept a cold face. Then later the woman said that if we were so stuck-up tonight her front room wouldn't be good enough for us and we better go back to the bush. All the way back down the lane Adelaide kept saying: "Some people can't take a joke, can they? Yeah, stuck-up is right—" until I passed her the bottle to keep her quiet. I saw George did not mind, thinking this had taken her mind off driving to Owen Sound.

68   We parked at the end of the lane and sat in the car drinking. George and Adelaide drank more than we did. They did not talk, just reached for the bottle and passed it back. This stuff was different from anything I had tasted before; it was heavy and sickening in my stomach. There was no other effect, and I began to have the depressing feeling that I was not going to get drunk. Each time Lois

handed the bottle back to me she said "Thank you" in a mannerly and subtly contemptuous way. I put my arm around her, not much wanting to. I was wondering what was the matter. This girl lay against my arm, scornful, acquiescent, angry, inarticulate and out-of-reach. I wanted to talk to her then more than to touch her, and that was out of the question; talk was not so little a thing to her as touching. Meanwhile I was aware that I should be beyond this, beyond the first stage and well into the second (for I had a knowledge, though it was not very comprehensive, of the orderly progression of stages, the ritual of back- and front-seat seduction). Almost I wished I was with Adelaide.

69   "Do you want to go for a walk?" I said.

70   "That's the first bright idea you've had all night," George told me from the back seat. "Don't hurry," he said as we got out. He and Adelaide were muffled and laughing together. "Don't hurry back!"

71   Lois and I walked along a wagon track close to the bush. The fields were moonlit, chilly and blowing. Now I felt vengeful, and I said softly, "I had quite a talk with your mother."

72   "I can imagine," said Lois.

73   "She told me about that guy you went out with last summer."

74   "This summer."

75   "It's last summer now. He was engaged or something, wasn't he?"

76   "Yes."

77   I was not going to let her go. "Did he like you better?" I said. "Was that it? Did he like you better?"

78   "No, I wouldn't say he liked me," Lois said. I thought, by some thickening of the sarcasm in her voice, that she was beginning to be drunk. "He liked Momma and the kids okay but he didn't like me. *Like me,*" she said, "What's that?"

79   "Well, he went out with you—"

80   "He just went around with me for the summer. That's what those guys from up the beach always do. They come down here to the dances and get a girl to go around with. For the summer. They always do.

81   "How I know he didn't *like* me," she said, "he said I was always bitching. You have to act grateful to those guys, you know, or they say you're bitching."

82   I was a little startled at having loosed all this. I said: "Did you like him?"

83   "Oh, sure! I should, shouldn't I? I should just get down on my knees and thank him. That's what my mother does. He brings her a cheap old spotted elephant—"

84   "Was this guy the first?" I said.

85   "The first steady. Is that what you mean?"

86   It wasn't. "How old are you?"

87   She considered. "I'm almost seventeen. I can pass for eighteen or nineteen. I can pass in a beer parlour. I did once."

88   "What grade are you in at school?"

89   She looked at me, rather amazed. "Did you think I still went to school? I quit that two years ago. I've got a job at the glove-works in town."

90   "That must have been against the law. When you quit."

91   "Oh, you can get a permit if your father's dead or something."

92   "What do you do at the glove-works?" I said.

93   "Oh, I run a machine. It's like a sewing machine. I'll be getting on piece-work soon. You make more money."

94   "Do you like it?"

95   "Oh, I wouldn't say I loved it. It's a job—you ask a lot of questions," she said.

96   "Do you mind?"

97   "I don't have to answer you," she said, her voice flat and small again. "Only if I like." She picked up her skirt and spread it out in her hands. "I've got burrs on my skirt," she said. She bent over, pulling them one by one. "I've got burrs on my dress," she said. "It's my good dress. Will they leave a mark? If I pull them all—slowly—I won't pull any threads."

98   "You shouldn't have worn that dress," I said. "What'd you wear that dress for?"

99   She shook the skirt, tossing a burr loose. "I don't know," she said. She held it out, the stiff, shining stuff, with faintly drunken satisfaction. "I wanted to show you guys!" she said, with a sudden small explosion of viciousness. The drunken, nose-thumbing, toe-twirling satisfaction could not now be mistaken as she stood there foolishly, tauntingly, with her skirt spread out. "I've got an imitation cash-mere sweater at home. It cost me twelve dollars," she said. "I've got a fur coat I'm paying on, paying on for next winter. I've got a fur coat—"

100   "That's nice," I said. "I think it's lovely for people to have things."

101   She dropped the skirt and struck the flat of her hand on my face. This was a relief to me, to both of us. We felt a fight had been building in us all along. We faced each other as warily as we could, considering we were both a little drunk, she tensing to slap me again and I to grab her or slap her back. We would have it out, what we had against each other. But the moment of this keenness passed. We let out our breath; we had not moved in time. And the next moment, not bothering to shake off our enmity, nor thinking how the one thing could give way to the other, we kissed. It was the first time, for me, that a kiss was accomplished without premeditation, or hesitancy, or over-haste, or the usual vague ensuing disappointment. And laughing shakily against me, she began to talk again, going back to the earlier part of our conversation as if nothing had come between.

102   "Isn't it funny?" she said. "You know, all winter all the girls do is talk about last summer, talk and talk about those guys, and I bet you those guys have forgotten even what their names were—"

103   But I did not want to talk any more, having discovered another force in her that lay side by side with her hostility, that was, in fact, just as enveloping and impersonal. After a while I whispered: "Isn't there some place we can go?"

104   And she answered: "There's a barn in the next field."

105   She knew the countryside; she had been there before.

106   We drove back into town after midnight. George and Adelaide were asleep in the back seat. I did not think Lois was asleep, though she kept her eyes closed and did not say anything. I had read somewhere about *Omne animal,* and I was going to tell her, but then I thought she would not know Latin words and would think I was being—oh, pretentious and superior. Afterwards I wished that I had told her. She would have known what it meant.

107   Afterwards the lassitude of the body, and the cold; the separation. To brush away the bits of hay and tidy ourselves with heavy unconnected movements, to come out of the barn and find the moon gone down, but the flat stubble fields still there, and the poplar trees, and the stars. To find our same selves, chilled and shaken, who had gone that headlong journey and were here still. To go back to the car and find the others sprawled asleep. That is what it is: *triste. Triste est.*

108   *That headlong journey.* Was it like that because it was the first time, because I was a little, strangely drunk? No. It was because of Lois. There are some people who can go only a little way with the act of love, and some others who can go very far, who can make a greater surrender, like the mystics. And Lois, this mystic of love, sat now on the far side of the car-seat, looking cold and rumpled, and utterly closed up in herself. All the things I wanted to say to her went clattering emptily through my head. *Come and see you again—Remember—Love—*I could not say any of these things. They would not seem even half-true across the space that had come between us. I thought: I will say something to her before the next tree, the next telephone pole. But I did not. I only drove faster, too fast, making the town come nearer.

109   The street lights bloomed out of the dark trees ahead; there were stirrings in the back seat.

110   "What time is it?" George said.

111   "Twenty past twelve."

112   "We musta finished that bottle. I don't feel so good. Oh, Christ, I don't feel so good. How do you feel?"

113   "Fine."

114   "Fine, eh? Feel like you finished your education tonight, eh? That how you feel? Is yours asleep? Mine is."

115   "I am not," said Adelaide drowsily. "Where's my belt? George—oh. Now where's my other shoe? It's early for Saturday night, isn't it? We could go and get something to eat."

116   "I don't feel like food," George said. "I gotta get some sleep. Gotta get up early tomorrow and go to church with my mother."

117   "Yeah, I know," said Adelaide, disbelieving, though not too ill-humoured. "You could've anyways bought me a hamburger!"

118   I had driven around to Lois's house. Lois did not open her eyes until the car stopped.

119   She sat still a moment, and then pressed her hands down over the skirt of her dress, flattening it out. She did not look at me. I moved to kiss her, but she seemed to draw slightly away, and I felt that there had after all been something fraudulent and theatrical about this final gesture. She was not like that.

120   George said to Adelaide: "Where do you live? You live near here?"

121   "Yeah. Half a block down."

122   "Okay. How be you get out here too? We gotta get home sometime tonight."

123   He kissed her and both the girls got out.

124   I started the car. We began to pull away, George settling down on the back seat to sleep. And then we heard the female voice calling after us, the loud, crude, female voice, abusive and forlorn:

125   "Thanks for the ride!"

126   It was not Adelaide calling; it was Lois.

For Further Thinking

1. Define the story's point of view as precisely as you can. How does this point of view contribute to the mood and theme of the story?

2. Find a section of the story in which Munro uses comparison-contrast to reveal the characters of Dick and George. What characteristics emerge from this passage of comparison?

3. The French writer Émile Zola (1840–1902) propounded a theory of "naturalism." Subjects are to be observed by the writer as if by a scientist observing specimens in a laboratory. Human will is not free but rather governed by external forces. To what extent does Munro's story fit into the realm of naturalism?

Looking Back and Ahead

1. In tone, how does "Thanks for the Ride" compare with Douglas Coupland's excerpt "The Sun Is Your Enemy" (p. 390)? What other similarities and/or differences do you find in these two stories?

2. Read Robertson Davies's essay "The Pleasures of Love" (p. 431). Discuss his view of love in that essay in reference to the view Munro's characters appear to have. How does the attitude Davies expresses compare to the attitude implied by Munro in "Thanks for the Ride"?

3. Read David Suzuki's essay "The Right Stuff" (p. 464). One argument against teaching sex education in junior high or high school is that it promotes sexual promiscuity among youth. What contribution to this debate does "Thanks for the Ride" suggest?

4. How are class and sexuality tangled up as sources of identity and power in the story?

Roch Carrier One of Quebec's foremost writers, Roch Carrier (b. 1937) has achieved success in a remarkable range of forms: novels, short stories, children's fiction, plays, screenplays, and poetry. He sets much of his fiction in rural Quebec and characteristically deals with fears of the English, with hypocrisy, and with ironic reversal. Like Michel Tremblay, Carrier is widely read in North America as well as abroad. He has served as executive director of the Canada Council for the Arts and as National Librarian of Canada.

The following story accurately reflects 1950s Quebec. One man, Maurice "Rocket" Richard (1921–2000), number 9 of the Montreal Canadiens, symbolized the pride and aspirations of French-speaking Quebecers. In March 1955, Clarence Campbell, president of the National Hockey League, suspended Richard for striking a referee; his decision provoked the "Richard Riot," identified by some historians as the beginning of Quebec's nationalist movement.

The Hockey Sweater

1   The winters of my childhood were long, long seasons. We lived in three places— the school, the church and the skating-rink—but our real life was on the skating- rink. Real battles were won on the skating-rink. Real strength appeared on the skating-rink. The real leaders showed themselves on the skating-rink. School was a sort of punishment. Parents always want to punish children and school is their most natural way of punishing us. However, school was also a quiet place where we could prepare for the next hockey game, lay out our next strategies. As for church, we found there the tranquility of God: there we forgot school and dreamed about the next hockey game. Through our daydreams it might happen that we would recite a prayer: we would ask God to help us play as well as Maurice Richard.

2   We all wore the same uniform as he, the red, white and blue uniform of the Montreal Canadiens, the best hockey team in the world; we all combed our hair in the same style as Maurice Richard, and to keep it in place we used a sort of glue—a great deal of glue. We laced our skates like Maurice Richard, we taped our sticks like Maurice Richard. We cut all his pictures out of the papers. Truly, we knew everything about him.

3   On the ice, when the referee blew his whistle the two teams would rush at the puck; we were five Maurice Richards taking it away from five other Maurice Richards; we were ten players, all of us wearing with the same blazing enthusiasm the uniform of the Montreal Canadiens. On our backs, we all wore the famous number 9.

4   One day, my Montreal Canadiens sweater had become too small; then it got torn and had holes in it. My mother said: "If you wear that old sweater people are going to think we're poor!" Then she did what she did whenever we needed new clothes. She started to leaf through the catalogue the Eaton company sent us in the mail every year. My mother was proud. She didn't want to buy our clothes at the general store; the only things that were good enough for us were the latest styles from Eaton's catalogue. My mother didn't like the order forms

included with the catalogue; they were written in English and she didn't understand a word of it. To order my hockey sweater, she did as she usually did; she took out her writing paper and wrote in her gentle schoolteacher's hand: "Cher Monsieur Eaton, Would you be kind enough to send me a Canadiens' sweater for my son who is ten years old and a little too tall for his age and Docteur Robitaille thinks he's a little too thin? I'm sending you three dollars and please send me what's left if there's anything left. I hope your wrapping will be better than last time."

5   Monsieur Eaton was quick to answer my mother's letter. Two weeks later we received the sweater. That day I had one of the greatest disappointments of my life! I would even say that on that day I experienced a very great sorrow. Instead of the red, white and blue Montreal Canadiens sweater, Monsieur Eaton had sent us a blue and white sweater with a maple leaf on the front—the sweater of the Toronto Maple Leafs. I'd always worn the red, white and blue Montreal Canadiens sweater; all my friends wore the red, white and blue sweater; never had anyone in my village ever worn the Toronto sweater, never had we even seen a Toronto Maple Leafs sweater. Besides, the Toronto team was regularly trounced by the triumphant Canadiens. With tears in my eyes, I found the strength to say:

6   "I'll never wear that uniform."

7   "My boy, first you're going to try it on! If you make up your mind about things before you try, my boy, you won't go very far in this life."

8   My mother had pulled the blue and white Toronto Maple Leafs sweater over my shoulders and already my arms were inside the sleeves. She pulled the sweater down and carefully smoothed all the creases in the abominable maple leaf on which, right in the middle of my chest, were written the words "Toronto Maple Leafs." I wept.

9   "I'll never wear it."

10   "Why not? This sweater fits you . . . like a glove."

11   "Maurice Richard would never put it on his back."

12   "You aren't Maurice Richard. Anyway, it isn't what's on your back that counts, it's what you've got inside your head."

13   "You'll never put it in my head to wear a Toronto Maple Leafs sweater."

14   My mother sighed in despair and explained to me:

15   "If you don't keep this sweater which fits you perfectly I'll have to write to Monsieur Eaton and explain that you don't want to wear the Toronto sweater. Monsieur Eaton's an *Anglais*; he'll be insulted because he likes the Maple Leafs. And if he's insulted do you think he'll be in a hurry to answer us? Spring will be here and you won't have played a single game, just because you didn't want to wear that perfectly nice blue sweater."

16   So I was obliged to wear the Maple Leafs sweater. When I arrived on the rink, all the Maurice Richards in red, white and blue came up, one by one, to take a look. When the referee blew his whistle I went to take my usual position.

The captain came and warned me I'd be better to stay on the forward line. A few minutes later the second line was called; I jumped onto the ice. The Maple Leafs sweater weighed on my shoulders like a mountain. The captain came and told me to wait; he'd need me later, on defense. By the third period I still hadn't played; one of the defensemen was hit in the nose with a stick and it was bleeding. I jumped on the ice: my moment had come! The referee blew his whistle; he gave me a penalty. He claimed I'd jumped on the ice when there were already five players. That was too much! It was unfair! It was persecution! It was because of my blue sweater! I struck my stick against the ice so hard it broke. Relieved, I bent down to pick up the debris. As I straightened up I saw the young vicar, on skates, before me.

17   "My child," he said, "just because you're wearing a new Toronto Maple Leafs sweater unlike the others, it doesn't mean you're going to make the laws around here. A proper young man doesn't lose his temper. Now take off your skates and go to the church and ask God to forgive you."

18   Wearing my Maple Leafs sweater I went to the church, where I prayed to God; I asked him to send, as quickly as possible, moths that would eat up my Toronto Maple Leafs sweater.

For Further Thinking

1. Make an outline of the narrative structure of this story. Does it have specific parts and connections between the parts? How do these work?
2. What would you state as the theme of this story? See "Literary and Film Analysis" on the Text Enrichment Site, Chapter 15, for a definition of *theme*.
3. Although the story deals with barriers between French and English, hockey is often said to be "in the blood of all Canadians," a force of unification beyond the power of politicians and business leaders. What do you think of this perception?
4. What are your own connections with the narrator of the story? Is his childhood significantly different from yours? Explain.
5. Discuss the commingling of hockey and religion in this story.

Looking Back and Ahead

1. Compare the narrative voice of this memoir-like story to that of Douglas Coupland's excerpt "The Sun Is Your Enemy" (p. 390). What are the similarities and differences?
2. Compare the young narrator of this fictional memoir to the young Michel Tremblay of "The King and I" (p. 399). What are the important similarities and differences?
3. Do you think Roch Carrier, like Michel Tremblay in his younger years, would vote "yes" to Quebec independence? Explain your answer.
4. Although "The Hockey Sweater" is fiction, it has strong connections to non-fiction memoirs in this text, including "Brownie" and "The King and I." If you have not already done so, describe what you consider the central qualities of the memoir.

Douglas Coupland Douglas Coupland, born in Baden-Baden, Germany, on a Canadian Forces Base in 1961, is a visual artist who is also well known as the author of *Generation X*, *Shampoo Planet*, *Life After God,* and *jPod,* amongst many others. His other artistic successes include writing and performance credits for the Royal Shakespeare Company, Stratford-upon-Avon, England, and his film *Everything's Gone Green* (2006), as well as art exhibitions in North America, Europe, and Asia. Coupland is known for providing an unusual perspective on social phenomena, often a postmodern perspective that Coupland himself attributes to his education as a visual artist. After being repeatedly falsely accused of being a meteorite collector, he has recently taken up the hobby of collecting meteorites. "The Sun Is Your Enemy" is the opening chapter of *Generation X*.

The Sun Is Your Enemy

1   Back in the late 1970s, when I was fifteen years old, I spent every penny I then had in the bank to fly across the continent in a 747 jet to Brandon, Manitoba, deep in the Canadian prairies, to witness a total eclipse of the sun. I must have made a strange sight at my young age, being pencil thin and practically albino, quietly checking into a TraveLodge motel to spend the night alone, happily watching snowy network television offerings and drinking glasses of water from glass tumblers that had been washed and rewrapped in paper sheaths so many times they looked like they had been sandpapered.

2   But the night soon ended, and come the morning of the eclipse, I eschewed tour buses and took civic bus transportation to the edge of town. There, I walked far down a dirt side road and into a farmer's field—some sort of cereal that was chest high and corn green and rustled as its blades inflicted small paper burns on my skin as I walked through them. And in that field, when the appointed hour, minute, and second of the darkness came, I lay myself down on the ground, surrounded by the tall pithy grain stalks and the faint sound of insects, and held my breath, there experiencing a mood that I have never really been able to shake completely—a mood of darkness and inevitability and fascination—a mood that surely must have been held by most young people since the dawn of time as they have crooked their necks, stared at the heavens, and watched their sky go out.

* * * * *

USE JETS
WHILE YOU
S T I L L
C A N

3   One and a half decades later my feelings are just as ambivalent and I sit on the front lanai of my rented bungalow in Palm Springs, California, grooming my two dogs, smelling the cinnamon nighttime pong of snapdragons and efficient whiffs of swimming pool chlorine that drift in from the courtyard while I wait for dawn.

4   I look east over the San Andreas fault that lies down the middle of the valley like a piece of overcooked meat. Soon enough the sun will explode over that fault and into my day like a line of Vegas showgirls bursting on stage. My dogs are watching, too. They know that an event of import will happen. These dogs,

I tell you, they are so smart, but they worry me sometimes. For instance, I'm plucking this pale yellow cottage cheesy guck from their snouts, rather like cheese atop a microwaved pizza, and I have this horrible feeling, for I suspect these dogs (even though their winsome black mongrel eyes would have me believe otherwise) have been rummaging through the dumpsters out behind the cosmetic surgery center again, and their snouts are accessorized with, dare I say, yuppie liposuction fat. *How* they manage to break into the California state regulation coyote-proof red plastic flesh disposal bags is beyond me. I guess the doctors are being naughty or lazy. Or both.

5   This world.

6   I tell you.

7   From inside my little bungalow I hear a cupboard door slam. My friend Dag, probably fetching my other friend Claire a starchy snack or a sugary treat. Or even more likely, if I know them, a wee gin and tonic. They have habits.

8   Dag is from Toronto, Canada (dual citizenship). Claire is from Los Angeles, California. I, for that matter, am from Portland, Oregon, but where you're from feels sort of irrelevant these days ("Since everyone has the same stores in their mini-malls," according to my younger brother, Tyler). We're the three of us, members of the poverty jet set, an enormous global group, and a group I joined, as mentioned earlier, at the age of fifteen when I flew to Manitoba.

9   Anyhow, as this evening was good for neither Dag nor Claire, they had to come invade my space to absorb cocktails and chill. They needed it. Both had their reasons.

10   For example, just after 2:00 a.m., Dag got off of shift at Larry's Bar where, along with me, he is a bartender. While the two of us were walking home, he ditched me right in the middle of a conversation we were having and darted across the road, where he then scraped a boulder across the front hood and windshield of a Cutlass Supreme. This is not the first time he has impulsively vandalized like this. The car was the color of butter and bore a bumper sticker saying WE'RE SPENDING OUR CHILDREN'S INHERITANCE, a message that I suppose irked Dag, who was bored and cranky after eight hours of working his McJob ("Low pay, low prestige, low benefits, low future").

11   I wish I understood this destructive tendency in Dag; otherwise he is such a considerate guy—to the point where once he wouldn't bathe for a week when a spider spun a web in his bathtub.

12   "I don't know, Andy," he said as he slammed my screen door, doggies in tow, resembling the lapsed half of a Mormon pamphleting duo with a white shirt, askew tie, armpits hinged with sweat, 48-hour stubble, gray slacks ("not pants, *slacks*") and butting his head like a rutting elk almost immediately into the vegetable crisper of my Frigidaire, from which he pulled wilted romaine leaves off the dewy surface of a bottle of cheap vodka, "whether I feel more that I want to punish some aging crock for frittering away my world, or whether I'm just upset that

the world has gotten too big—way beyond our capacity to tell stories about it, and so all we're stuck with are these blips and chunks and snippets on bumpers." He chugs from the bottle. "I feel insulted either way."

McJOB: A low-pay, low-prestige, low-dignity, low-benefit, no-future job in the service sector. Frequently considered a satisfying career choice by people who have never held one.

13   So it must have been three in the morning. Dag was on a vandal's high, and the two of us were sitting on couches in my living room looking at the fire burning in the fireplace, when shortly Claire stormed in (no knock), her mink-black-bob-cut aflutter, and looking imposing in spite of her shortness, the effect carried off by chic garnered from working the Chanel counter at the local I. Magnin store.

14   "Date from hell," she announced, causing Dag and I to exchange meaningful glances. She grabbed a glass of mystery drink in the kitchen and then plonked herself down on the small sofa, unconcerned by the impending fashion disaster of multiple dog hairs on her black wool dress.

15   "Look, Claire. If your date was too hard to talk about, maybe you can use some little puppets and reenact it for us with a little show."

16   "Fun*nee*, Dag. Fun*nee*. God. *Another* bond peddler and *a*nother nouvelle dinner of seed bells and Evian water. And, of *course*, he was a survivalist, too. Spent the whole night talking about moving to Montana and the chemicals he's going to put in his *gasoline* tank to keep it all from decomposing. I can't keep doing this. I'll be thirty soon. I feel like a character in a color cartoon."

POVERTY JET SET: A group of people given to chronic traveling at the expense of long-term job stability or a permanent residence. Tend to have doomed and extremely expensive phone-call relationships with people named Serge or Ilyana. Tend to discuss frequent-flyer programs at parties.

17   She inspected my serviceable (and by no means stunning) furnished room, a space cheered up mainly by inexpensive low-grade Navajo Indian blankets. Then her face loosened. "My date had a low point, too. Out on Highway 111 in Cathedral City there's this store that sells chickens that have been taxidermied. We were driving by and I just about fainted from wanting to have one, they were so cute, but Dan (that was his name) says, 'Now Claire, you don't *need* a chicken,' to which I said, 'That's not the point, Dan. The point is that I *want* a chicken.' He thereupon commenced giving me this fantastically boring lecture about how the only reason I want a stuffed chicken is because they look so good in a shop window, and that the moment I received one I'd start dreaming up ways to ditch it. True enough. But then I tried to tell him that stuffed chickens are what life and new relationships was all about, but my explanation collapsed somewhere—the analogy became too mangled – and there was that awful woe-to-the-human-race silence you get from pedants who think they're talking to half-wits. I wanted to throttle him."

18   "Chickens?" asked Dag.

19   "Yes, Chickens."

20   "Well."

21   "Yes."

22   "Cluck cluck."

23   Things became both silly and morose and after a few hours I retired to the lanai where I am now, plucking possible yuppie fat from the snouts of my dogs and watching sunlight's first pinking of the Coachella Valley, the valley in which Palm Springs lies. Up on a hill in the distance I can see the saddle-shaped form of the home that belongs to Mr. Bob Hope, the entertainer, melting like a Dali clock into the rocks. I feel calm because my friends are nearby.

24   "Polyp weather," announces Dag as he comes and sits next to me, brushing sage dust off the rickety wood stoop.

25   "That is just too sick, Dag," says Claire sitting on my other side and putting a blanket over my shoulders (I am only in my underwear).

26   "Not sick at all. In fact, you should check out the sidewalks near the patio restaurants of Rancho Mirage around noon some day. Folks shedding polyps like dandruff flakes, and when you walk on them it's like walking on a bed of Rice Krispies cereal."

27   I say, "Shhhh . . ." and the five of us (don't forget the dogs) look eastward. I shiver and pull the blanket tight around myself, for I am colder than I had realized, and I wonder that all things seem to be from hell these days: dates, jobs, parties, weather. . . . Could the situation be that we no longer believe in that particular place? Or maybe we were all promised heaven in our lifetimes, and what we ended up with can't help but suffer in comparison.

28   Maybe someone got cheated along the way. I wonder.

29   You know, Dag and Claire smile a lot, as do many people I know. But I have always wondered if there is something either mechanical or malignant to their smiles, for the way they keep their outer lips propped up seems a bit, not false, but *protective*. A minor realization hits me as I sit with the two of them. It is the realization that the smiles that they wear in their daily lives are the same as the smiles worn by people who have been good-naturedly fleeced, but fleeced nonetheless, in public and on a New York sidewalk by card sharks, and who are unable because of social convention to show their anger, who don't want to look like poor sports. The thought is fleeting.

30   The first chink of sun rises over the lavender mountain of Joshua, but three of us are just a bit too cool for our own good; we can't just let the moment happen. Dag must greet this flare with a question for us, a gloomy aubade: "What do you think of when you see the sun? Quick. Before you think about it too much and kill your response. Be honest. Be gruesome. Claire, you go first."

31   Claire understands the drift: "Well, Dag. I see a farmer in Russia, and he's driving a tractor in a wheat field, but the sunlight's gone bad on him—like the fadedness of a black-and-white picture in an old *Life* magazine. And another strange phenomenon has happened, too: rather than sunbeams, the sun has begun to project the odor of old *Life* magazines instead, and the odor is killing his crops. The wheat is thinning as we speak. He's slumped over the wheel of his tractor and he's crying. His wheat is dying of history poisoning."

32   "Good, Claire. Very weird. And Andy? How about you?"

33   "Let me think a second."

34   "Okay, I'll go instead. When I think of the sun, I think of an Australian surf bunny, eighteen years old, maybe, somewhere on Bondi Beach, and discovering her first keratosis lesion on her shin. She's screaming inside her brain and already plotting how she's going to steal valiums from her mother. Now *you* tell *me*, Andy, what do you think of when you see the sun?"

HISTORICAL UNDERDOSING: To live in a period of time when nothing seems to happen. Major symptoms include addiction to newspapers, magazines, and TV news broadcasts.

HISTORICAL OVERDOSING: To live in a period of time when too much seems to happen. Major symptoms include addiction to newspapers, magazines, and TV news broadcasts.

35   I refuse to participate in this awfulness. I refuse to put people in my vision. "I think of this place in Antarctica called Lake Vanda, where the rain hasn't fallen in more than two million years."

36   "Fair enough. That's all?"

37   "Yes, that's all."

38   There is a pause. And what I *don't* say is this: that this is also the same sun that makes me think of regal tangerines and dimwitted butterflies and lazy carp. And the ecstatic drops of pomegranate blood seeping from skin fissures of fruits rotting on the tree branch next door—drops that hang like rubies from their old brown leather source, alluding to the intense ovarian fertility inside.

39   The carapace of coolness is too much for Claire, also. She breaks the silence by saying that it's not healthy to live life as a succession of isolated little cool moments. "Either our lives become stories, or there's just no way to get through them."

40   I agree. Dag agrees. We know that this is why the three of us left our lives behind us and came to the desert—to tell stories and to make our own lives worthwhile tales in the process.

For Further Thinking

1. Based on this opening chapter of *Generation X*, define "Generation X" as a social category. Rely only on the characterizations, activities, attitudes, writing style, and choices revealed in this chapter.

2. What is the significance of the title of this chapter?

3. Examine some of the jargon or terms used. Can you create definitions of these terms based on their context in the story chapter?

4. There is a lot of focus on material items and consumer culture—décor, clothing, etc.— what do you think the purpose of this focus is? What is the purpose of the chicken anecdote that Claire tells Andy?

5. How is this chapter organized? In other words, how does Coupland develop a type of thesis in the organization and presentation of various information, characterization, and conversation?

Looking Back and Ahead

1. Like many of the authors in this section, Coupland uses narrative in order to further a larger purpose. How do Coupland's narrative strategies compare to Munro's "Thanks for the Ride"?

2. Read Kim Pittaway's essay "Crystal Balls" (p. 423). Compare the attitude in Pittaway's essay that people should be valued for their individual talents, gender aside, to Coupland's chapter, in which individuality plays a particular role. Do you think that Pittaway and Coupland are revealing similar views?

Evelyn Lau Evelyn Lau appeared on the Canadian literary scene in 1989 at the age of 18 with the publication of *Runaway: Diary of a Street Kid*, an emotionally intense and brutally honest chronicle of her own life as a runaway, drug addict, and prostitute in Vancouver. While many thought Lau to be a one-hit wonder, she has since proven her literary worth with a number of publications of poems, short stories, and novels, many of which return to the theme of her own dysfunctional and dangerous youth as a street kid. Lau is particularly good at sketching characters. Note how she manages different characterizations in this essay of her own quest to buy a condominium unit. Also note the way in which Lau includes a number of emotional scenarios, while still chronicling the process of buying property.

I Sing the Song of My Condo

1   Late in the spring of last year, my fancy turned to thoughts of real estate and I joined the growing ranks of Canadians in their 20s who were looking for their first homes.

2   I had been a renter since I was 16 and I never wanted to deal with a landlord again. Instead, I wanted to know what it was like to worry if I spilled wine on my carpet, to agonize over the exact placement of a picture before pounding a nail in my wall, to open a closet door or rest my forehead against a kitchen cabinet and think, "I own this."

3   I went to the bank with a bundle of tax returns under my arm to prequalify for a first mortgage. After a long meeting during which the bank manager and I peered morosely at a computer screen and juggled numbers for savings, RRSPs and a writer's erratic income into a yearly figure, I walked out with a brochure titled Information for First Homebuyers in my hand.

4   The people depicted in the brochures were not like anyone I knew. The women were blond, with sunny smiles, and their husbands looked both chiseled and paternal. They were engaged in chummy family activities, like washing the dog or puttering in the garden, with the help of their model children. A white picket fence stood in soft focus in the background.

5   I knew then I wanted to live in the world of the mortgage brochures, which never showed these middle-class people lying awake among twisted sheets in their new master bedrooms or throwing up into their ceramic sinks from panic at hefty mortgages and rising interest rates. I wanted to sing the love song of the middle class. I wanted this to be the song of myself—a litany of mortgage payments and car payments, the weeping and gnashing at tax time, maximum RRSP payments and mutual funds, credit cards and credit's twin, debt.

6   Laura Cavanagh, the real-estate agent I acquired through a friend's connections, was an outgoing woman with tanned skin, long hair and hips so slim it seemed impossible she had two teenaged children. The male realtors we met in front of apartment buildings always held her hand for a beat too long and fastened their eyes upon hers with much intent and private meaning.

7   Together we toured a depressing number of 500-square-foot one-bedrooms listed by young married couples who had just had their first baby. Their apartments smelled of sour milk and spoiled food, and in the bedrooms a crib took up whatever space the double bed did not already occupy. The vendor's agent would gamely point out that new carpets weren't that expensive, really, and if I enlisted the help of friends I could easily strip away the velvet-textured and dung-coloured wallpaper. He would flick on all the light switches and then exclaim, "And look at how bright this unit is!" I became increasingly dejected at what my savings could afford in Vancouver, when I knew the same amount could buy a house, with acreage attached, in Saskatoon. Laura, however, remained true to her business card's slogan—"The realtor with a positive attitude"—and came to my apartment several times a week to show me yet another suite.

8   Over the months I grew fond of her. She was different from some of the other agents we encountered, who drove gold Mercedes and who staggered about in high heels and silk scarves, arrived late for appointments and then whipped us through the apartment while their pagers and cell phones incessantly beeped and rang. Laura held my hand when I made my first offer—and my second, third and fourth, all unsuccessfully—and comforted me after I had spent another sleepless night over interest-rate calculations.

9   As summer passed into fall, I discovered that acquiring a real-estate agent was like acquiring a stray kitten or a runaway child—it was a lifetime commitment. She reminded me of little Gertrude in John Cheever's *The Country Husband*, with her uncanny knack of showing up in places I did not expect. I would open my front door on a Saturday morning to pick up the paper and there she would be, showered and perfumed, standing in the hallway and proffering the latest figures on a suite in which I had expressed a moment's interest. See, here's its sales history, its current assessment. Would I like to see it in 15 minutes? She would be wearing such a brave smile that I could only admire her and never find it in my heart to turn her away.

10   Meanwhile, my friends, who were older and therefore wealthier, were actually buying places. I went to a friend's house-warming party with a smile of congratulations on my face and envy in my heart. My former foster parent bought a penthouse with 12-foot ceilings in a new building; another friend purchased an actual house with the help of his well-off parents. I went to a cocktail party at his parents' home, where a hundred guests fit neatly into the kitchen. I was surrounded by half a dozen empty bedrooms, Jacuzzis and soaker tubs and murderous chandeliers in the marble foyer. Resentment blazed in me.

11   Now when I walked the streets of Vancouver, I glared up at the high windows of the condominiums and felt the owners were not as special as me, nor as deserving. When I gave poetry readings, I looked out at the audience and wondered how many of them owned their own homes. It came to me that I had rarely wanted anything this much before.

12   One afternoon Laura took me to the opening of a converted building where she said the suites were priced below market value. Balloons were tied to the gates and hedges, and dozens of would-be buyers stood about the grounds, gazing up at the suites with their brochures shielding their eyes.

13   The display suite was bustling with activity—realtors wearing suits and flustered smiles, the women with green eye-shadow and trailing a scent of White Shoulders. They paced back and forth with their clients, pulling out calculators to demonstrate price per square foot and the amount of monthly payments. Even as I sat there, someone called out that suite 312 had just been sold and 105 down the hall, and they were expecting an offer on 210.

14   The cell phones rang and rang and the anxiety of the buyers became a frenzy of panic. It was a fever that sparked smiles on the faces of the realtors. Offers were recklessly written, and a slim-waisted woman in a floral dress who represented the financing company stepped forward to give or withhold her approval.

15   I was tempted by the display suite, which was small but fully renovated, boasting a marble fireplace and slate tiles. Loden wallpaper in the bathroom was printed with female Greek statues clutching scraps of fabric to their breasts. I realized that the suite was a good bargain, but as I sat on the rented leather couch I found I could not pull out my chequebook and write an offer, not without at least a night's reflection.

16   "In all good conscience, I can say you aren't going to lose money on this one," Laura said, but I was immobilized with terror. An hour later she drove me home. I spent the evening drinking heavily and calculating my finances.

17   The suite was priced within my range, and by the light of morning I had decided I would make my move. I went back to the suite where I had sat on the couch and looked around my new home—this was where I would put my desk, my bed. I approached the sales agent—a beefy, blond man with a distracted air and an incessantly warbling pager—and said I would buy the display suite.

18   "Oh. That was sold yesterday," the man said, already turning away.

19   I surprised myself with my own reaction—it was grief. I very nearly heard the crack of my heart breaking. This was not the relief I felt when one of my previous offers had fallen through; this was my *home* being taken away.

20   I stumbled out in a daze and walked the three kilometres home, wiping away tears with the back of my hand the whole way. It seemed my song would be a different one after all, it would be the song of Rainer Maria Rilke's *Autumn Day*: "Whoever has no house now will never have one." It was all very well for Rilke—he had owned houses. He had written his famous elegies while staying in Princess Marie von Thurn and Taxis-Hohenloe's castle. I wished bankruptcy, illness and death upon whoever had bought my suite.

21   What surprised me for weeks afterward was how entirely alike this feeling of bereftness was to losing the person you love. Somehow the real, intelligent, sensible desire to buy a first home and stop paying rent had mutated over the

months into an obsession that was like a woman's obsession for a man who had deserted her, whom she could love only at a distance.

22   When I slept I was tortured by dreams in which I walked through beautiful apartments that were within my price range, then just as I pulled out my cheque-book I would wake up. Several times I dreamed I bought an apartment with three balcony doors but no balconies, and I knew that one day I would open the doors, step out and fall to my death. In another, I had just moved into a new condominium and discovered that with the removal of the previous owner's furniture and pictures, I could see that the walls were pocked with holes the size of my fist.

23   Over the course of a year, my realtor and I saw 50 suites. I sat on 50 strangers' sofas, looked into their cupboards, sniffed inside their refrigerators, inspected their drapes and light switches. I checked the drains in their balconies and flushed their toilets. I looked for my own books on their bookshelves and was dismayed by the rows of American bestsellers or educational texts I found there. I peered into their closets and discovered if the owners were people who shopped in vintage stores or Sears or Holt Renfrew.

24   Once I saw the apartment of a little old lady whose obsession was turtles—troops of ceramic, glass and jade turtles filed across every available counter and desktop. She owned an aquarium of turtles, posters of turtles, a bedspread with a turtle stitched on it.

25   After 12 months of searching, I no longer believed I would purchase anything soon. I had visions of my realtor and me setting out at the turn of the millennium to look at our 300th suite.

26   When at last I found the right place, it happened so suddenly that the frustrations of the year vanished overnight. I went to an open house on Sunday and on the Monday Laura presented my offer. It was accepted that afternoon. She stopped by to give me the news and when she came down the hallway her eyes were shining.

27   "You have a home now," she said.

28   The rest of the week flashed by in a blur of telephone calls and meetings with the bank manager. I signed contracts, read by-laws and city council meeting minutes and certified deposit cheques. It was so stressful that I felt disconnected from reality. I vacillated between happiness, numb panic and a great, swelling pride. I had never been in debt for anything before, had never even owned a car or a computer, and now here I was committing myself to a $100,000 mortgage for 650 square feet. I had made a decision that was going to affect the rest of my life.

29   I take possession of the suite at the end of June, just days before my 24th birthday. I may never sleep again. But at last I'm a homeowner.

For Further Thinking

1. Explain Lau's title for this essay. How does the title's literary allusion potentially affect the way in which this essay is read?

2. Examine Lau's use of imagery. Pick out one or two examples in which Lau is able, through her imagery, to critically examine consumer culture and humanity's love/hate relationship with it.

3. Explain how Lau organizes this essay. Is there an organizational pattern or strategy at play here?

4. What aspect of Lau's identity is made evident throughout? What is the significance of her discovery of herself as one who, in her own words, "had rarely wanted anything this much before"?

5. Examine Lau's concluding paragraph. It is very short and concise. How does it still manage to connect to the essay's larger themes?

Looking Back and Ahead

1. Like many of the essays in this section, "I Sing the Song of My Condo" is written from a deeply personal, autobiographical point of view. Which essays does it have the most in common with in its content, diction, and effect on the reader?

2. Read Douglas Coupland's "The Sun Is Your Enemy." How does Lau's characterization of herself compare to characters of a similar age in Coupland's first chapter of his novel? What values do they have in common? Where do they differ? What might account for these differences?

3. Roch Carrier's "The Hockey Sweater" can be compared to Lau's essay in that both characters feel that some of their identity and being is at stake when their connections to material items are threatened. Explain.

Michel Tremblay In this wry memoir, one of Quebec's most renowned writers describes how, on his fourteenth birthday, he gained the courage to bluff his way into an R-rated film, *The King and I*.

Best known for his plays, Tremblay had to wait three years before anyone would produce his landmark drama *Les Belles-Soeurs* (*The Sisters-in-Law*, 1965). Its use of *joual* (informal, everyday French, sometimes regarded as debased) and accurate depictions of east-end working-class society were not deemed appropriate for literature. Many critics have also said that Tremblay is too preoccupied with Quebec concerns; however, his wide popularity outside the province suggests that focusing on what he knows and cares about has only enhanced his appeal. "The King and I" comes from *Bambi and Me*, a collection of 12 autobiographical narratives, each centred around a film. In recent years, Tremblay has dismayed ardent Quebec nationalists by reconsidering his earlier support for political separation.

The King and I

1 On the day I turned fourteen, June 26, 1956, I decided that from now on I was going to go to movies with the adults, even though I didn't meet the age requirement. I'd had enough of animated cartoons, lives of saints, edifying melodramas or Heidi coming down from her mountain to take care of a little cripple in town. I wanted to see Susan Hayward in her strapless gowns, Lana Turner in her fuzzy sweaters, Marilyn Monroe lying in her Niagara Falls. At the

time I wasn't very interested in French films, I saw too many on television, and I was getting sick of Fernandel's faces, Georges Guétary's quavery voice and the tralala of Suzy Delair.

2   At the Palace theatre they were advertising a musical comedy entitled *The King and I* which I'd never heard of but which immediately grabbed my attention: in the ad in *La Presse*, a beautiful woman wearing a wide satin gown was dancing in the arms of what appeared to be a half-naked Indo-Chinese man. That was all I needed to make up my mind and I set out with pounding heart to mount an assault on a movie theatre that had the reputation of being invincible if you were under sixteen.

3   I hadn't yet made the mistake of my brother Bernard who'd drawn on a moustache once to get into the Passe-Temps with our aunt Robertine, only to be met with the cashier's laughter. She'd regretted her action as a matter of fact when my father's sister decided to come to her nephew's defense with her stentorian voice and her flowery language. On Mont-Royal Street people were still talking about it. No, I was dressed simply: blue pants, short-sleeved white shirt, red V-neck, my Pat Boone shoes. I probably looked like a cartoon version of a real little gentleman.

4   From my window on the St. Catherine Street tramway I could see the ad for the film, the same one but in colour, and my courage failed me. If besides asking me my age, the cashier demanded some ID . . . if she called the police . . . if I landed in jail because I'd wanted to see a film that, in the end, was really too "adult" for me. . . . I stayed on for a few stops and got off at Ogilvy's. It was barely ten-thirty a.m. (the first showing was at eleven) and I was already sweating. I walked back as far as Eaton's, across the street from the Palace, and stood on tiptoe to try and see what the cashier looked like. . . . Impossible, needless to say. I crossed the street, avoiding the cars and streetcars that were coming in tight ranks in both directions.

5   She didn't look particularly easy-going. I pretended to be checking out the photos—which were very beautiful actually, glossy and sharp and made you want to see the damn film even more—while I kept glancing furtively towards the glass cage. The cashier was old, fat, serious, and she handed out the tickets like some rare and precious manna, gesturing broadly and staring hard at the customer. She wasn't there to enjoy herself and she let you know it.

6   Did that mean I was sentenced to another two years of Heidi and her goat and her fat neighbour?

7   Deciding I'd been standing there too long, the cashier took a coin and started rapping it against her glass cage, gesturing to me to move on. I must have looked like a depraved child who stands around in front of dirty pictures, so I took off, my shoulders hunched and my tail between my legs.

8   It was a quarter to eleven and my birthday was already ruined.

9   I needed consolation.

10   I darted into Eaton's and headed straight for the record department on the fifth floor.

11   At that time you could buy classical recordings on the Remington and Plymouth labels for the huge sum of ninety-nine cents. They all sounded equally bad and had probably been recorded in studios the size of match-boxes, but I made do with them because I didn't know anything else, my budget being, to say the least, limited. I already owned a fairly impressive collection, basics like the inevitable suites from *Carmen* or *Peer Gynt* and excerpts from *Swan Lake,* but also some works that were less obvious for a neophyte of fourteen— Bruch's violin concerto, for instance, or Stravinsky's *Pulcinella.* I also had Mozart's *Così* sung by second-rate German singers with flowery names like Elsie Plümaacher, whose Italian sounded hilarious. But I didn't mind, I was learning, I liked everything, I thought it was all sublime, I cried like a calf over Saint-Saëns' ballet music for *Samson and Delilah* as much as over the first chorus of Bach's *St. John Passion.*

12   I was going then to work off my frustration and for another twenty-four cents, buy a fine classical recording that would bring me dozens and dozens of hours of listening instead of the hypothetical pleasure of watching the lady in the long dress dance with the half-bare-naked Siamese man. Obviously I'd decided that *The King and I* wasn't worth risking jail for and that, in any event, it would probably bore me to death.

13   Eaton's record department had listening booths for customers where I'd already spent quite a lot of time choosing among three or four records, often unable to make up my mind; I was known there and the salesladies liked me because I was probably their only teenage customer who bought something besides the records of Patti Page or Gale Storm.

14   That morning though I was out of luck, there was a new girl at the cash register whom I seemed to be disturbing, so much did she look as if she wanted to be somewhere else.

15   And our conversation got off to a very bad start.

16   "Could you open this record for me please, I'd like to listen to it." She looked at me as if I were a dog turd on a velvet cushion.

17   "Sorry, I don't speak French."

18   I knew it was store policy for people to speak English but there was no way that girl was an Anglo, absolutely no way! The accent, the face, the hairdo, the clothes, the gum—it was all straight from the Plateau Mont-Royal or the Faubourg à mélasse. She was a carbon copy of my cousin Lise who worked next door at Kresge's, who used to tell us how people would order a cheese sandwich in English and she'd bring them a ham sandwich in French . . . and that most of all, nobody was going to make her speak English if she didn't feel like it! Except that the Eaton's salesgirl had decided to play the game.

19   She wasn't much older than I was, she was a long way from twenty in any event, and I decided to stand up to her.

20   "Don't make me laugh, you're as French as I am. . . . Anyway, I don't want a conversation, I just want you to open this record. . . ."

21   She raised her eyebrows in circumflex accents and shook her head. And in her best English accent came out with an "I beg your pardon," that emerged from her lips like the most elegant *joual*.

22   I couldn't help laughing.

23   "Look, make a little effort, okay, I know you aren't English so why keep trying?"

24   The salesgirl leaned across the counter towards me.

25   "What the hell do you want, you little creep, you want me to lose my job?"

26   She glanced furtively to her right and pretended she was busy at the cash register.

27   Near the escalators, some manager or other was watching us suspiciously, not even bothering to hide his dismal performance as an underpaid spy out to catch *in flagrante delicto* two francophones who were communicating in their language. I got the picture in an instant: the constant humiliations, the harassment, the small and pitiful capitulations. I felt sorry for her. And for me.

28   "Okay, pretend I talked English to you. He didn't hear us."

29   I felt like an asshole. So did she.

30   She ripped the cellophane off the record sleeve and held it out with an extremely stupid look on her face.

31   "Think you're smart, eh? Just wait till you're in my shoes!"

32   As I headed for the listening booth I came across the record of *The King and I* in the place of honour on the display racks. I picked it up, looked at it from every angle. It looked fantastic!

33   Of course I wanted to listen to it. On my way back to the cash register to have it opened, I noticed the spy who'd come to stand next to the salesgirl, smiling ferociously as he watched me come back. They weren't going to make me speak English with them! When I got to the counter I showed the salesgirl the record, totally ignoring the manager, I tore the cellophane myself with my thumb the way I'd seen her do with the other record, then I turned my back on them.

34   It was a very small victory, a victory by omission rather than a genuine active resistance, but I was still very proud of myself.

35   Unlikely as it may sound, what follows is absolutely true.

36   I don't remember anything about the classical record, all I know is that it didn't interest me and I didn't spend much time with it.

37   I put *The King and I* on the turntable, hoping the music would be worthy of the album cover. The opening was pleasant enough in the Oriental-American style of the fifties, but it didn't really grab me and I nearly put the record back in its envelope. Then came the first song, "I Whistle a Happy Tune." The words leaped out at me like a message that Anna, the English school-mistress who had just arrived in Siam to teach the king's children, was sending out to me personally across time, a record, a film, a song, and I was blown away:

38   "Whenever I feel afraid
I hold my head erect
And whistle a happy tune

So no one will suspect
I'm afraid."

39   The song was addressed to me personally! The secret was in its off-hand manner. If I wanted to get inside that theatre I had to be the opposite of the beaten dog who goes and hides in the corner so he'll be forgotten before he even gets scolded for doing something wrong! I had to be so off-hand the cashier would feel she had to let me in even though she could see I wasn't sixteen yet. Most of all, she mustn't know I was terrified of her. I shouldn't have run away, I should have faced up to her—holding my head erect.

40   I sped back to return the two records, telling the salesgirl in a superior tone: "They're boring!" and ran to the theatre without stopping.

41   The dragon was still at her post; there was no one going inside because the film had started ages ago. The cashier was listlessly leafing through a magazine while she waited for the next wave of customers who wouldn't turn up for an hour at least. I gathered up the small amount of courage I still had despite my wobbly legs, the sweat running down my back, my rapidly pounding heart and the lump in my throat and I managed to arrive at the ticket booth whistling, just like on the record. It wasn't very loud, but you could hear it. I don't know if you could really call it casual, but I hoped it would give the illusion. Bravely, I dropped my seventy-five cents in front of her, looking her straight in the eye. "Please God, don't let her recognize me! Don't let her create a scandal so I have to defend myself in English, I can't speak it well enough and I don't want to be laughed at on top of everything else!" Inwardly I was the Krakatoa about to erupt, but outwardly I wanted to give the impression I was someone for whom going to the movies was nothing out of the ordinary, a critic maybe, yes, why not, a rather blasé critic who's stuck with seeing this film he doesn't really want to see and he's going now, just before noon, so he won't ruin an entire day. Someone who couldn't care less if they let him in or not, because this film, really. . . . She probably didn't look at me or else she admired my nerve enough to disregard her rules and her convictions, but the fact remains that I ended up holding a ticket without having hell open up at my feet or lightning strike my slender little body. It was almost too easy, I hesitated for a fraction of a second before walking away from the cashier.

42   I had a ticket for *The King and I* two years early!

43   I'll always remember the state of euphoria I was in as I climbed the thickly-carpeted stairs. I looked at myself in the huge mirror that ran along the banister on both sides, multiplying my reflection infinitely. . . . Though I looked like a little bum! A little bum in his Sunday best who wants access to something he's unworthy of. . . . How could I deceive anybody? I was still whistling but my mouth was frozen, I felt as if never again would I be able to relax the muscles in my lips.

44   The ticket-taker didn't even look at me and I went down into the theatre deep in a Nirvana whose intensity measured 8.5 on the Richter scale.

45   It was a wall-to-wall screen, Cinemascope in all its splendor, and a Siamese ballet as revised by Rogers and Hammerstein was unfurling its extravagance while Rita Moreno intoned: "Run, little Eva, run!" I raced to the most anonymous seat, the one where nobody ever sits because it gives you a headache, and let myself be swallowed up for two and a half hours by the faintly sickening but oh so reassuring syrup of the colours, the music, the dances, the songs, the sets, the stunning dresses worn by Deborah Kerr (who would be the great idol of my teenage years, at least till the arrival of Shirley MacLaine in *Some Came Running*), and the seductive outfits worn by Yul Brynner.

46   I was thrilled, moved, and I swore that from now on I was going to movies "for adults" at least once a week. No more silly kids' stuff for me; starting now, the global production of movies, at least whatever made it to Montreal, was mine. I was an adult.

For Further Thinking

1. Do you, like Tremblay, have memories of an incident that publicly marked your passage into adulthood? How does your experience resemble his? How does it differ?

2. Comment on how the memoir combines psychological and political obstacles.

3. Describe the structure of this memoir. Is it simply rambling and episodic, or does each new event play into the underlying concern? Explain.

4. How would you describe the mood and tone of this essay? Give examples of elements that contribute to this effect.

5. Talking about *Bambi and Me* with David Homel of *Books in Canada* magazine, Tremblay said, "Each chapter was like a step forward for the character, a discovery of fear, of sexuality, of art. . . ." Is this true of "The King and I"? If so, explain how.

Looking Back and Ahead

1. Tremblay remembers when French was considered inferior to English, when even French employees in the "posh" English-owned stores had to pretend their preferred language was English. How much does this history influence the society suggested by Roch Carrier in "The Hockey Sweater" (p. 387)?

2. As a memoir, Tremblay's essay has strong connections to other selections in this text, including "Brownie" and "The Hockey Sweater." If you have not already done so, describe what you find to be the central qualities of this form.

Melisa-Maurice P. Janse van Rensburg Melisa-Maurice P. Janse van Rensburg's "Not like the Movie" is a personal essay that contrasts a student writer's girlish expectations with her real-life experiences as a young nurse. The violence of the St. James Church massacre in Cape Town on July 25, 1993 had a profound impact on the writer as well as on the national psyche of South Africa. From the point of view of a rescue worker, Janse van Rensburg describes the gruesome aftermath of the attack on a Sunday-evening Christian church service of approximately 1400 white South Africans by the Azanian People's Liberation Army (APLA) who burst through the church doors and opened fire on the congregation with automatic weapons. The APLA attributed the assault to an act of a war against apartheid. The perpetrators have since been granted amnesty by the Truth and Reconciliation Commission, a court-like body assembled after the fall of apartheid in South Africa.

This essay is an example of creative non-fiction, a genre that has gained considerable popularity in contemporary literary communities.

Not like the Movie

1   Her hair blew in the wind, surrounding her like a thick, black mane. The camera zoomed in, focusing on the single tear in her eye as she cried for her true love, lying beside her—dead. She had been a nurse in the Second World War; he was a pilot, shot down over enemy soil but rescued and brought back into her care to be nursed back from near death. That old black and white film is where my love first breathed. My love for men in uniform and my love for nursing flourished in such romantic and such dramatic scenes.

2   As a child I dreamt of being a nurse. I would serve man on the front lines of war, marry a dashing young pilot and, after the war, return as a heroine. I would save many lives while at war, without regard for my own safety. Then we would have two kids, a dog and a white picket fence. Did I mention my dad's bosom swollen with pride as he pinned the Purple Heart on my chest? I imagined a parade in my honour, perhaps even a holiday or a street named after me. I would be the best nurse ever; move over Florence.

3   Years later I remembered this fantasy. The smell of the ocean cut the air, the sun burned my back, and a gentle breeze cooled me as I walked home from nursing school. At the time, terrorism and violence were all around us. Our patients included 13-year-old boys shot after killing two policemen, and the man in Forensic Psychiatry who had murdered and eaten a small child. I stood at the top of the hill, overlooking the Atlantic ocean, and I wept. An old cliché boomed through my mind: "Be careful what you wish for." Dramatic? Yes. Romantic? Not at all.

4   I started nursing school in January 1993. I had returned to Cape Town after living in the Transvaal for a number of years. I started nursing school because my mother told me to. I had no idea where I wanted to be or which career path to follow. Going to school full time while doing practicums in the hospitals gave me a great balance of academic and hands-on experience. It also gave me a home away

from home. All the nursing students lived in "res." The independence and liberty were great. We partied all night, and we slept through lectures all day. It was pretty unremarkable as far as student life goes.

5   One particular Sunday evening, life changed. My reality shifted. A couple of the girls and I had made our way along the Pipe Trail. This trail ran along the sunny side of Chapman's Peak, an extension of Cape Town's world-renowned Table Mountain, where two oceans collide with one another. It's about a four-hour hike, not too strenuous, and surrounded by magnificent trees that date back centuries. We flirted with the boys along the trail and giggled like sixth-graders when they flirted back. We were about a half hour from the end of the trail when dense towers of cumulonimbus clouds thundered and roared in off of the ocean with an ominous fury. I remember looking out of the window on the drive home. I gazed at the black sea feeling small, insignificant and yet, calm and peaceful. Life was perfect. Then we neared the hospital where we lived.

6   Ambulances raced past us, and crowds of people stopped in the streets. There was panic in the air. I was frantic as I tried to find a radio station that might tell us what was happening. Then we heard. There had been a massacre at St. James Church, just two blocks from where we were. They were asking all staff from Victoria Hospital to report for duty immediately. "Mass casualty . . . AK-47s . . . Hand grenades . . ." These were the only words I heard. Conny and I looked at each other in horror, and she turned her beat-up, little Golf in the direction of St. James Church.

7   We were among the first to respond to the call. People staggered around crying, sobbing, and screaming. Dads searched frantically for their kids; sisters searched frantically for their brothers, and everywhere there was chaos. Fear enveloped me. Fear forced me to breathe through the layers of silence that had grabbed hold of my mind. It demanded that I extract courage from the depth of my now-wounded soul. The air was heavy with the smell of gunpowder and burning flesh. As if God himself was responding to this tragedy, lightning strobed across the sky; it illuminated church-goers as they made their way out of the building. A deluge of rain poured from the sky, adding to the assault. We were cold, wet and terrified. The Fire Department had arrived but the firemen just stood around whispering to one another. I hadn't noticed myself run toward the church entrance until a police officer tried holding me back.

8   "I'm a nurse," I screamed at him. "I work at Victoria Hospital: let me through." He waved us on, instructing us to help where we could. "Oh, dear God," I heard myself whisper as we ran inside.

9   I knelt beside a young man who had been killed instantly—a single bullet hole through his head. I moved on to the next victim, then the next, and the next. I was in a daze. I was on autopilot. A mother, Marita, who had twice survived cancer, now lay dead. She had been shot in the chest at close range. She would be buried on her birthday. Gerard had thrown himself on a hand grenade immediately before it exploded and ripped apart his husky, 21-year-old body.

That is how July 25th, 1993, ended for me; for others, it simply ended. There were 11 dead and 50 more wounded.

10   The following day brought about a new reality that felt contrived. It was a reality where people were safe to worship and meet with friends. Children were free to ride their bicycles around the neighbourhood, and voiceless screams were absent from my dreams. The all-night parties resumed and the nightmares returned while I slept through lectures. The Pipe Trail saw more of us and we continued to flirt with the boys along the way. I went on to complete my nursing diploma. I never spoke of that night.

11   Hoping to escape those memories, I packed a small bag, boarded an aeroplane, and crossed the African continent arriving at London's Heathrow Airport. The air was palatable and smelled different. It smelled of sweet peas and fresh, crisp watercress, and it smelled like liberty. I remember disembarking after my overnight flight, and feeling determined to find an escape from the hatred and the imprisoning politics in South Africa. I spent two years in London, England. A year of that was spent taking care of the elderly in their homes, which allowed them to maintain some independence. The second year I spent caring for two young boys as a live-in nanny. All this time I studied different fields related to psychiatry. In retrospect, I think that I was trying to understand the workings of the evil that has destroyed, and continues to destroy, so many lives. I had decided that Canada was the perfect country to live in and focused on finding a way to immigrate. When I left London for Canada, it was with a few letters of the alphabet behind my name and a fluffy little white feather in my hat.

12   Nearly eight years have passed since I arrived in Canada. I have been institutionalized by Tim Horton's, and although I don't skate very well, I proudly support the Calgary Flames. Two years ago, I stood before God and more than 100 witnesses and humbly pledged allegiance to the Queen. I spent a year studying to become a Licensed Practical Nurse and now I work at Foothills Hospital in Calgary. It's a hard job physically, emotionally and mentally. Our Health Region suffers from poor staffing and an ever-growing geriatric population. Still, peace and sleep continue to elude me at times, and I lie awake, listening to my husband's peaceful breathing. Geography cannot replace that part of me that died back in 1993.

13   Being a nurse has defined me in many ways. The experience has taken me to many places where I have seen many things. I hope it will remain a large part of my life. I never did marry a pilot, and my husband and I are struggling to maintain our second pregnancy. We don't yet have a dog, nor do we have a white picket fence around our home. There has been no parade in my honour, and no street named after me. My hair tangles in the wind and the only thing purple on my chest is blueberry jam stains left by my little boy. My dad is proud of me, and sometimes I feel proud of myself, too. I am proud that I have found the strength to forge forward over all the hurdles in life and that I continue reaching for my dream—to serve our fellow man.

For Further Thinking

1. How many different tones can you pick out in this essay? Where does the tone of the essay change and why?

2. The writer contrasts her expectations of what a nursing career would be like with her real-life experience. Can you think of a similar encounter in your life whereby your experience of something did not match your expectations of it? Would a similar essay format be an appropriate form in which to write about it?

3. The writer tells us that she came to Canada "determined to find an escape from the hatred and the imprisoning politics in South Africa," from the outcomes of apartheid. As we know, many political refugees arrive here annually, and for many Canada is a land of peace and equality. But those with a different angle on Canada and its history, to cite Daniel David Moses, speak of its "white-washed identity" (96). Within Native circles in this country, it is a well-accepted fact that the Canadian Department of Indian Affairs with its reserve system gave South Africa its "inspiration for apartheid" (Moses 140). Should Canadians be doing more to resolve their own legacy of racial apartheid, and if so, what should those things be?

Looking Back and Ahead

1. Roch Carrier writes nostalgically about "the winters of [his] childhood" spent on the hockey rink. How does Jance van Renburg use nostalgia in "Not like the Movie"? What effect does it have on the reader?

2. Is Jance van Renburg's relationship to Canada in "Not like the Movie" similar to Pamela Swanigan's relationship to Canada as described in her essay "I Am Half-Canadian" (p. 411)? How and how not?

3. How do we define violence? Read "Canada's 'Genocide'" (p. 443) and "Saskatchewan's Indian People—Five Generations" (p. 166). Is there a possibility that Jance van Renburg's essay leaves an impression of Canada as too much like the official movie most of us have been raised to believe in (tolerant, non-racist, peaceful)? Must we see blood flowing in our own communities in order to judge whether violence is occurring?

4. Read Martin Luther King Jr.'s essay "The Ways of Meeting Oppression," in Chapter 10 (p. 144). His recommendations suggest the philosophy of Mahatma (Great Soul) Gandhi (1869–1948) and the ideal of "passive civic resistance." In your experience, what percent of humanity do you think is liable to understand and act upon this philosophy? Does your answer have implications for social policy here and elsewhere? Explain.

5. Read Nina Varsava's "Non-fiction Isn't Fact—Read with Care" (p. 485) and consider Jance van Renburg's essay as creative non-fiction: are the fictional techniques an impediment to reliability? Explain your answer.

Work Cited

Moses, Daniel David. *Pursued by a Bear: Talks, Monologues, and Tales.* Toronto: Exile Editions, 2005.

Section 2   Did You Know?

As in Section 1, some of the readings in Section 2 use the first person, but generally the purpose of work in the following pieces has shifted from the expressive and evocative purpose of Section 1 to a primary concern with exposition. The following pieces, unlike personal essays or short stories, identify their topics explicitly and use more formal means than those used in Section 1 to pursue the discussion. Chapters 9 to 13 in the Rhetoric are particularly relevant to the following readings. Also relevant is Wayne Booth's concern with what he calls the "pedant's stance" and the "advertiser's stance" (see pages 489–91). When you write on a topic with a primary purpose to relay and explain information and perhaps also with a purpose to evaluate and argue a position on the topic, you could be in danger of adopting either one of those faulty stances.

The "pedant's stance" occurs when the writer places such technical attention on the subject that "deadly dull" writing results. You need to consider how you might keep the discussion lively without overusing more personal and entertaining techniques, such as first person. The "advertiser's stance" could occur when you wish to argue an evaluation but do so without giving fair consideration to other views, to the full picture. Instead of being fair to the topic, you could appeal to the reader for agreement based on reasons apart from logic and fairness. As you study the readings in Section 2, consider how the writers deal with the challenge of treading between these two undesirable stances that can afflict writers of exposition, analysis, and evaluation.

Another concern as we approach the matter of writing that wishes to inform us of truths on a certain topic is the old philosophical question: what is truth? Whether this problem is really any greater than it ever was or not, it feels greater today, for reasons that we should consider, at least to some further extent.

In his study of William Shakespeare (1564–1616), biographer Park Honan argues that the greatly celebrated Renaissance poet was deeply concerned with "a fracturing of the medieval unity and a loss of a faith that once bound together Western Europe" (344). This concern is echoed and intensified in a famous British poem of the late Victorian period, "Dover Beach." In that work, Matthew Arnold (1822–88) laments the loss of universal faith; science has undermined the literal truth of religion without substituting clear, absolute answers. The poet's only touchstone of meaning becomes that of personal relations. Echoing this sentiment yet again some 100 years later, American songwriter Paul Simon wrote, "I stand alone without beliefs; / The only truth I know is you." At times, Canada showcases this problem as a result of official multiculturalism, maintaining what the writer Bharati Mukherjee pejoratively refers to as hyphenated identity. Novelist Mordecai Richler (1931–2001) represents just one of many Canadian writers who have expressed a concern with the process of having to define one's own moral standards, one's own authority, in a world where values, beliefs, and faiths now vary drastically from person to person. Given this situation and the cult of rugged individualism that helped forge North American popular mythologies, are we in danger of entering a free-fall free-for-all, devoid of collective values? What implications does this situation have for the problem of audience awareness? To compound the confusion is the fact that humanity has never had such wide and easy access to so much information—but we don't always know how much of it is grounded, and how we are to tell whether it is or not.

This section of the Reader will not restore absolute objective truth or one universal audience. However, it will demonstrate common ways that people of different beliefs working in different fields go about organizing information for specific readers. As we have said, this section concentrates particularly on samples of writing produced by writers whose goal (regardless of whether they use the third or first person) is to focus on a body of information and an issue.

Readings in Section 2, like those in Section 1, deal with issues of identity, generational, social, and cultural experience, as well as people's relations to nationhood and learning. As in Section 1, questions for further thinking and for comparisons to other essays in the Reader are listed after the readings.

Work Cited

Honan Park, *Shakespeare: A Life.* Oxford: Oxford University Press, 1999.

Pamela Swanigan How do you define a Canadian? What does it mean to be a citizen of this country? Answers often consider cultural pluralism, social security, and "niceness," as well as naïveté, provincial mediocrity, and hypocrisy—depending on whom you ask. In any case, it could probably be said with some fairness that few people on this planet have a harder time putting their sense of national identity into words. Born and raised in the United States, half Black, half White, Pamela Swanigan, an expatriate American and former professional sports writer, offers her views on what makes Canadians distinct. Her article appeared in *Saturday Night* magazine, January 27, 2001.

I Am Half-Canadian

1 In times of deep national self-reflection, and even on the other two days of the year, I tend to think there's nothing wrong with being Canadian that being an ex-American wouldn't fix. We expat Americans are probably the happiest Canadians around, taking Air Canada convolutions and hospital waiting lists as minor burbles of an admirable system. Some of this is probably indoctrination—our upbringing inclines us to be patriotic—but more of it, I think, is inoculation, particularly against that great pox of the Canadian psyche, the so-called identity crisis.

2 Not that we don't experience Canadian society as amorphous and callow, like everyone else; just that we can see these qualities are only a "crisis" in the same way that Vancouver is part of the Pacific Northwest—which is to say, strictly by American reference points. Conventional wisdom holds that the U.S. attained its cohesive culture by leaping into the nation-forging crucible of war at every opportunity, whereas Canada, having chosen a more peaceable route, remains (to use Robert Fulford's words) "an art object, an abstraction—a piece of fiction, perhaps."

3 Philosophical footsy-playing aside, what ex-Americans know that other Canadians do not is that America has historically used a less, shall we say, traditional method to maintain its self-definition. America treats identity as a zero-sum proposition: you can be this, but only if you're not that. Canadians may worry that we sketchily define ourselves by what we are not, but Americans suffer the opposite problem: everyone's forced to pick one definition and stick to it. As such, Americans have become the most highly summarized people on the planet; if this makes their national fabric a tightly woven one, it also makes it one of a largely synthetic fibre.

4 Take, for instance, a typical American employment form, such as the one I recently received from a college in California. "Federal and state mandates require that we compile summary data on the gender and ethnicity of the applicants," it declares, before assuring you that although it is about to elicit personal information from you, nobody will ever use any of it for any purpose that could remotely affect your life. It then offers six choices of what it calls "ethnic background" (a category that wanders happily between skin colour, continental origin, language, and state residency) and exhorts, "Please check only one." You may be

black, white, Hispanic, Asian, Hawaiian, or American/Alaskan Indian. Or again, you may not, in which case you're out of luck. (By contrast, the Canadian census form allows you to check as many boxes as you like.)

5   Americans are required to pigeonhole themselves in this manner at every turn: on college applications, insurance forms, medical forms, military forms, and in many states used to have to do so on their driver's licences. As cultural conception goes, it's about as organic as a Kraft Singles slice.

6   Nor is this fixation a recent contrivance: America has taken a (literally) black-and-white view of identity from the day it was born. Marriage or propagation between blacks and whites was outlawed in nearly every state during the antebellum years, and in almost half of them it remained a crime until 1967. (Fortunately for my black father, my white mother, and my sister and I, California was not one of them, though my mother was disowned and our house in Oakland was torched.) The "one-drop" rule, which states that any person of traceable African ancestry is legally black, had become law nationwide by the 1850s, and variations of it still exist throughout the country. To this day, as sociologist F. James Davis writes, "'racially mixed' is not an accepted racial category in the United States for a child who has any black ancestry at all. One is either white or black." (I tried saying I was "both" once, in an NBA locker room at the beginning of my sports-writing career, and set off a debate that ended with Michael Jordan saying gravely, "You want to know what you are, Pam? You are 'other.'")

7   Though racial identity is the big bugaboo in the U.S., nationality has been fashioned into a similar kind of straitjacket. Canadian brain-drainees may be surprised to find that their new government used to forbid, and still does not recognize, dual citizenship, and that indeed, their new American compatriots regard anything beyond a passing fondness for one's origins as vaguely seditious. My American-born stepfather got some insight into U.S. attitudes about national identity last summer, on a family trip to San Francisco, when U.S. customs officials hauled him into an interrogation room at the Vancouver Airport and searched his luggage. "Is it because I'm a known socialist?" he asked hopefully. (At the time, he held a minor post in the provincial NDP cabinet and was eager for any sop to his ego.) The customs officials growled back, "How did you lose your American status?" When he told them that he had voluntarily relinquished it in order to become a Canadian citizen, they searched him thoroughly. And then they sent his luggage to San Luis Obispo.

8   Granted, the crenellations of the boxed-in American national psyche can be fascinating; I myself used to find them the most mysterious and seductive questions of identity in the world. (This was before we had both the Tories *and* the Alliance.) But envy-prone Canadians might also want to note that to many ex-Americans, living in Canada is like getting out of jail, and that perhaps if there is a crisis, it is only the natural crisis of freedom. I can't speak for central Canada, with its 350-year-old Euro-colonial foundation, but here in Vancouver almost everybody has some major ambiguity or conflict or multiplicity of heritage;

we swim around in our fluid identities like Alice in her pool of tears, battling and occasionally appreciating our aggregate citizenships and the expansive versions of our selves. It's unsettling and often distressing, yes; West Coast Canadian culture is uncongenial and unsophisticated, true; and no one who has lived here for very long could fail to notice the indecisiveness about identity that, especially among young white males, amounts to an epidemic. But to American-Canadians, who know something about the most proximate alternative, this is exactly the way it should be.

For Further Thinking

1. What do you think of Swanigan's conclusion that "to many ex-Americans, living in Canada is like getting out of jail, and that perhaps if there is a crisis, it is only the natural crisis of freedom"? Ill at ease with this free-fall state of identity, Clark Blaise believes that "unstable identities are 'preying' at the moment on Canada."[1]

2. Make a list of the various points that Swanigan treats through comparison-contrast (Chapter 12, "Comparison-Contrast," can help).

3. Swanigan refers to a comment made to her by American basketball superstar Michael Jordan. Is she simply name-dropping or does Jordan's presence have a significant bearing on her thesis? Explain.

4. Swanigan admits that she cannot speak for the central eastern regions of Canada and that her assessment of Canadian identity applies mainly to Vancouver. Do you think her conclusion, if valid, can be stretched to apply across the country?

5. Does Canadian immigration policy and practice treat members of all races equally? You may need to do some research to shape and defend your opinion. You may also wish to interview people.

6. Swanigan's family home in Oakland was "torched" because her White mother married a Black man. For Canadian readers, this may reinforce our officially accepted idea that the United States mistreats African-Americans and that Canada does not. However, in an essay called "The Quebec Experience: Slavery 1628–1834," Dorothy Williams examines Canada's history of racial attitudes with attention to our era of legalized slavery (which many Canadians seem to know little or nothing about). For a version of Williams's essay, see *Boundaries of Identity*, Les Éditions Yvon Blais, 1989. What other examples of Canadian racial injustice can you think of? Are we, in reality, any better than other countries in providing rights and freedoms? Explain.

Looking Back and Ahead

1. Read Pat Deiter-McArthur's "Saskatchewan's Indian People—Five Generations," in Chapter 11 (p. 166). Do you feel this article raises valid challenges to the conclusions Swanigan suggests?

---

[1] Clark Blaise, qtd. in "U.S./Canadian Writers' Perspectives on the Multiculturalism Debate," *Canadian Literature* 164 (Spring 2000): 88.

2. Swanigan suggests that the group of Canadians most insecure in their identity is young White males. What do you think of this opinion? If you feel there is some truth to it, how does this observation tie in to the thesis of Susan McClelland's "The Lure of the Body Image" (p. 447)?

3. Writer Bharati Mukherjee left Canada disgusted with the racism she felt here. In contrast, she prefers the United States. She doesn't want to be a hyphenated anybody, just an American. On the Text Enrichment Site, Reader Section 2, "I Am Half-Canadian," in the section For Further Reading, we list other sources where you can pursue Mukherjee's views on this topic. Compare her opinion to Swanigan's. How do you explain and perhaps reconcile these two opposite claims?

Diane Mooney   As Canada's youngest province (it entered Confederation in 1949), Newfoundland is this country's oldest point of European contact. The population resides mainly on the island of Newfoundland, principally on the Avalon Peninsula. By contrast, Labrador, on the mainland, is sparsely populated. Rated well below Canada's other regions on the United Nations "quality of life" scale, Newfoundland risks sliding even further behind as politicians in the richer provinces pressure Ottawa to reduce or discontinue federal equalization payments from rich to poor.

In the following essay, marine biology student Diane Mooney takes us on a tour of major linguistic regions, combining classification-division, spatial process, and descriptive process to celebrate the range of cultures and languages in her home province. A trained environmental technician, Mooney grew up along the rugged shores of Newfoundland. She calls herself "an avid tourist of the island . . . where there is always a new culture and dialect to discover." If you have never visited Newfoundland, talk to some of your classmates who have been there, to prepare you for reading this essay.

Newfoundlandese, If You Please

1   I learned recently that people who visit Newfoundland become fascinated with our unique dialect. If they travel to different areas of the island, they quickly realize that every little nook and cranny, of which there are many, has its own specific sound. Not too long ago I travelled to the Port au Port peninsula on the province's West Coast. Here, the inhabitants are French descendants and speak with an odd accent, Newfoundland French, I guess. Being from an Irish settlement on the East Coast, I had difficulty understanding their speech as they did mine. All the different descendants in Newfoundland play a major role in our dialect. It seems as though our ancestors, who came from many different areas, never quite lost their own speech: they all just adapted to the lives they settled into. There were many settlements all along the coast and inland across the island, all with a different adaptation of English. As Baldwin says in his essay "If Black English Isn't a Language, Then Tell Me, What Is?" "people evolve a language." He was referring to the African Americans of the United States. The same can be said for the Irish, English, British, and French of Newfoundland. The difference is that they didn't just evolve into one, they evolved into one with many different variations.

2   Starting with the Avalon Peninsula of the East Coast of Newfoundland, with which I am most familiar, it is easy to tell who first settled in what area simply by their speech. The Southern Shore of the island is Irish, and to this day you can hear an Irish accent in their voices. People on the Southern Shore refer to their fathers as "daa." Whether this is an Irish thing or just a Southern Shore thing, you won't hear it anywhere else in the province. You may look even deeper into each individual community. Some are all Catholics and came from one area of Ireland with their own dialect; others are all Anglican coming from a different area of Ireland with another dialect. However, there are very few Anglicans on the Southern Shore; the Catholics drove out most.

3   Not too far away in the Trinity-Conception area, again they are mainly Irish—Anglican Irish. The dialect here can be quite difficult to understand. A number of areas drop their "h's" and this is one of them. For example, "I'm goin' 'ome to clean me 'ouse de once." Translation: "I am going home to clean my house now." "De once" means it is going to be done immediately—at once. To a visitor from outside the province or even to someone from within the province this can also be very difficult to understand, especially with the speed of Newfoundland speech. All Newfoundlanders talk fast; this is just a given.

4   Moving off the Avalon into Central Newfoundland we have moved out of the fishing communities into logging and mining towns; mainly fishermen who moved inland in winter to hunt and log when they couldn't fish settled in these areas. The settlements there today are pretty mixed with dialects coming from all over. One area in particular always uses "we" and "I" when making references to themselves instead of "us" and "we." For example, "Be careful or they'll come after we or I." Translation: "Be careful or they will come after us." Again something that can be very confusing and interesting to the non-native.

5   Most of Newfoundland believes that the West Coast of the island is trying to sound like mainlanders. They say "eh" a lot and have a slight twang in their speech. In reality though, it probably goes back to when the French settled, which is still so strong on the Port au Port peninsula.

6   The Northern Peninsula, which is very large and stretched out but not heavily populated, seems to be in a world of its own. Some communities drop their "h's" while others add extra "h's." For example, "First you put your happles in the hoven and you bake 'em on 'igh." Translation: "First you put your apples in the oven and you bake them on high." Some others on the tip of the Northern Peninsula, which is so close to Quebec, have a tendency to slip into some French dialect as well.

7   Taking in only major sections of the province, any tourist can see clearly that Newfoundland has many different descendants and therefore many different dialects. As Baldwin suggests, when so many different languages are put together, they have to come up with a way to communicate that everyone can understand. Because Newfoundland is so spread out, a language evolved and each little cove and inlet adapted its own version.

For Further Thinking

1. What other island could be said to offer a different dialect for every new "nook and cranny"? How is this of relevance to Mooney's focus on variety?

2. Would you say that you speak English fast or slowly? Is your accent difficult for others? How have your ancestry and region shaped your style of English?

3. Is there a common Canadian English—truly distinct from the language of the United Kingdom, Commonwealth countries, and United States—or does our country simply have pockets of regional speech?

4. In your own words, express Mooney's thesis as completely and precisely as you can.

5. From what you know of Newfoundland—and you could always add to that knowledge with a little further research—how important do you think its forms of English have been to its cultural life?

Looking Back and Ahead

1. Think of someone you know who emigrated to your community from a country that speaks little or no English or that speaks a different form of English from yours. Would this person's language difficulties be heightened or lessened in Newfoundland? Why or why not?

2. Read George Orwell's "Politics and the English Language" (p. 471). Would he approve of the French dialect that Mooney finds included on the Northern Peninsula? What do you think of his opinion on this matter?

3. On the whole, do you think the types of English that Mooney describes lend themselves to the political abuses described by Orwell? Why or why not?

4. Read the chapter from Douglas Coupland's novel *Generation X* (p. 390). The generation he portrays in that novel is located circa 1990 in California. Do you imagine that the generational features of Newfoundland's young adults in 1990 were like those of the young Californians Coupland describes? Are differences between Californian young adults and those of Newfoundland less pronounced today than may have been the case 20 years ago? Do you think the world is headed toward a global culture where the distinctions of a Newfoundland will have all but disappeared?

Habeeb Salloum   Observing that non-French and non-British Canadians constitute 37.5 percent of the country's population, Habeeb Salloum believes these "others" are to many observers "an unknown force in Canadian society." The author summarizes the history of immigration to Canada, pointing out that before Trudeau chose the road to multiculturalism, immigrants were expected to assimilate. The more different they were from the predominant society that they found here, the more they were taunted. Those who were visibly different could not escape this fate. In this March 1997 essay, Salloum acknowledges the usual criticisms of multiculturalism, but concludes that on the whole it has had a "beneficial and civilizing effect."

The non-Anglo population of Vancouver is now 30 percent of the whole and that of Toronto is 60 percent. Ironically, some of those most opposed to multiculturalism are themselves the descendants of immigrants, while most university-educated people of British background support the policy. Salloum concludes that multiculturalism protects self-esteem over an assimilation period of three generations, but that assimilation most definitely occurs, and that descendants of non-British immigrants become more "Anglo" than those whose ancestors came from the British Isles. Salloum is a Canadian author and freelance writer specializing in Canadian, Arab, Far Eastern, and Latin American topics.

The Other Canadians and Canada's Future

1   In Canada's province of Quebec, a majority, perhaps, of the inhabitants are convinced that they must act to protect their language and culture. A good section of these go much further, and seek an independent nation. On the other hand, in the English-speaking part of the country, especially in western Canada, the vast majority of people feel that the French, defeated in 1759 on the Plains of Abraham, have no claim to nationhood. This much publicized conflict was discussed by J.A.S. Evans in his article, "The Present State of Canada," in the September 1996 issue of *Contemporary Review*. These views are tempered by those of the remaining non-French and non-British Canadians—about 37.5 per cent of the population. These communities from many ethnic groups, who, with the French Canadians, form the majority of Canada's population, are to many observers an unknown force in Canadian society.

2   For nearly a half century, Canada has been living under the threat of Quebec separation. During this long period of tension between English—about 34.5 per cent—and French Canadians—about 28 per cent of the population—the immigrant minorities have been in a dilemma. Traditionally the overwhelming majority, even in Quebec, became integrated into "Anglo" society. (In Canada the "English" include a large number of Scots who have played a crucial role in the country's history.) However, in that province during the last few decades, this tendency to assimilate into dominant English culture has caused much friction, has raised concerns among French Canadians and has given rise to debates throughout Canada.

3   Amid these pressures, how do the Canadian minorities whose origins can be traced to countries from the four corners of the world see the Canada of the future? For an answer, one must travel back in history to the beginning of this [twentieth] century, when non-French and non-British Europeans in large numbers along with a few Asiatics begin to immigrate to Canada. In that period, assimilation of the minority ethnic groups, without regard to their desires, was the order of the day. In one or, at the most, two generations, the dominant Anglo-Saxon culture and language melted into its folds—not always happily—the vast majority of the sons and daughters of these immigrants.

4   No one in those days, when ethnic epithets and other derogatory terms were used to taunt immigrant groups, would ever visualize the multicultural

Canada of our times where all Canadians are treated equally. Peoples of all racial origins, in today's Canada, are encouraged to romanticize their ethnic history and, hence, to feel "at home." Canadian society has become, at least on the surface, a truly cultural mosaic.

5   However, in the past, it was very different. For the early immigrants and their offspring, the coercion to assimilate into the dominant society was overwhelming. This took many forms. Prejudice, discrimination, racial slurs and subordination into the dominant English culture, all had their effects on the newcomers. In the early years of this [twentieth] century, the acceptance of diversity—people who held unfamiliar customs and values—was not even in the cards.

6   Some of the ethnic groups, like the Dutch, Germans, Scandinavians and many of the Lebanese, assimilated quickly; others, like the Chinese, Greeks, those from the Baltic nations of Estonia, Latvia and Lithuania, and Ukrainians preserved their identity for several generations. However, all the racial minorities through interaction, but mainly through education, in no more than three generations, had totally melted into the governing English society or, to a much lesser extent, French culture in Quebec. In the process of assimilation, many members of the ethnic groups lost confidence in their identity, self-esteem and pride in their racial origin as they were absorbed into the dominant society. Even after receiving their citizenship and becoming new Canadians, usually because of their accents, many were labelled with the derogatory term DPs (displaced persons).

7   Others, if they remained visible like the blacks and Asiatics, were never accepted as true Canadians. One need only bring to mind the sad fate of Japanese Canadians during the Second World War: they had their property confiscated while their total population was interned. "Black Syrian! Black Syrian!" These epithets during my own school years were daily taunts. In those years, the school was a painful place for a child of non-British origin. To escape the daily verbal persecution, I, like the sons of many other immigrants of foreign origin, tried to hide my identity, making believe that my forefathers came from the British Isles.

8   All this changed when Canada's controversial Prime Minister, Pierre Trudeau, set the country on the road to "Multiculturalism within a Bilingual Framework" policy. His vision and that of the Liberal government at that time was this rule: "Canada's many ethnic and racial groups living in harmony while retaining their cultures—a prop to the English-French nucleus of the country." The government believed that "multiculturalism" would bolster the equality of all Canadians, encourage participation of minorities in social institutions and strengthen the allegiance of ethnic groups to the communities in which they lived. "Multiculturalism" would co-exist with bilingualism as a "defining characteristic" of Canadian society.

9   Trudeau theorized that in a bilingual, multicultural Canadian nation the Anglo-Canadians would have to retire to their proper place, instead of

interpreting Canadian identity in their own British terms. As a result, he assumed genuine power sharing would follow. Rather than the American melting pot idea of assimilation into the dominant ethnic group, Canada would become a land of ethnic pluralism—a cultural mosaic of many peoples, forging unity from diversity.

10   In 1971, a policy of multiculturalism was officially adopted, legitimizing the self-conception of Canada as resting on pluralist foundations. Government policy thereafter encouraged one country, two languages, many cultures. Legislation became an instrument to legitimize and manage a diverse population within a state apparatus. It officially formalized a multicultural nation and Canada became the world's only official multicultural society. "Ethnic diversity," "ethnic pluralism," "multi-ethnic" and "poly-ethnic" were now acceptable phrases. In 1988, Canada's multiracial and multi-lingual mélange was strengthened further by the passage of the Multicultural Act which emphasized "positive race relations." With its enactment, the country moved to the forefront of nations in dealing with ethno-racial diversity in a politically acceptable manner.

11   Among some of the ethnic groups, multiculturalism was accepted with great enthusiasm. In the 23 October 1978 issue of the Saskatoon *Star-Phoenix*, it was reported that at a Ukrainian fund-raising dinner in the city, one of the speakers stated: "Canada's unique characteristic and strength is multiculturalism." He went on to say: "Canadians have abandoned the futile evangelism of patriotic nationalism. Instead, every Canadian can enjoy the joy and pride of his cultural roots, recognized, respected and accepted as a worthwhile contributor to Canadian society."

12   On the other hand, "multiculturalism" has proved to be a controversial social policy. From the very beginning, some groups wanted to emphasize language; others religion; while a number zeroed in on folklore. Opinion varied among the ethnic societies as to how much ethnicity and interaction among other cultural groups were to be stressed. At the inception of multiculturalism, critics said that it was a ploy by Trudeau and the Liberal Party to control and manipulate ethnic groups and was only a vote-getting gimmick. Subsidizing the ethnic groups to teach their own languages, which multiculturalism supported, would, according to many at that time, retard the immigrants' assimilation into the English or French societies.

13   In the ensuing years, many denounced multiculturalism as counterproductive, irrelevant, unworkable and an expensive frill which would impede assimilation—a guise to destroy British traditions and the English language. Some asserted that it would increase the risk of racial conflict; others described it as a cultural zoo: the zoo keeper—the government—would manipulate the inhabitants.

14   Yet, on the whole, multiculturalism, despite its critics, has had a beneficial and civilizing effect on Canada. It has shaped the country's collective identity as a generous and tolerant nation, enhancing the quality of life for all its inhabitants. It has become a system of achieving national consensus without the loss of integrity—a setup which all Canadians can buy into as equals. No country in the world has ventured as far as Canada into the field of ethnic interaction.

15   Contributing an inclusive sense of common citizenship, official multiculturalism, harnessing the power of the over ten million Canadians who are neither English nor French, has defused mounting Quebec pressure on federalism; blunted American influences on Canadian cultural space; enhanced the country's cultural richness; and, with the demise of Anglo-conformity, filled the void in the Canadian cultural identity. Without doubt, it has elevated Canada to the ranks of progressive countries in the judicious management of ethnic relations.

16   By the encouragement of self-confidence, self-worth and a feeling of pride in their ethnic origin, multiculturalism has helped the immigrants succeed in their social and economic life and has made them feel at home. There is no better indication of how self-image determines the future of the country than when I visited the northern Alberta Arab community of Lac La Biche in the late summer of 1996. "I love it here! In this town we prospered and here we have established our roots." Khalil Abughoush, owner of the IGA supermarket in Lac La Biche, was full of enthusiasm when talking about his small northern city. Like his fellow countrymen—20 per cent of the town's 3,000 inhabitants are of Arab-Lebanese origin—he had come to seek his fortune in this northern Alberta resort. In Canada's multicultural society, Abughoush, like the majority of immigrants and their descendants, felt at home. As he prospered he felt no coercion to fit in, no pressure to leave his culture behind. There is no question that "multiculturalism" has succeeded, to a great extent, in making Canada's newcomers feel at home, with the exception of many of the visible minorities. For the latter, multiculturalism has been only of marginal benefit. It has failed to combat racism and discriminatory practices. Even though today one of the major priorities of multiculturalism is the elimination of racism, unofficially, the dominant Anglo and French societies continue to see visible minorities as different, not equal, and an unstable factor in Canadian society. These visible minorities at present constitute 6.3 per cent of the population—expected to rise to 10 percent by the year 2000. In the large urban centres, they have become an important segment of the population. The non-Anglo population of Vancouver is 30 per cent and that of Toronto 60 per cent—20 per cent of which are visible minorities.

17   Even more forgotten by multiculturalism are Canada's "First Nations Peoples." Even though there is a widespread consensus that the country's Indigenous Peoples have been treated unfairly, they remain as the bottom stratum in Canadian society. To them, multiculturalism has brought very little benefit. In the Canada of today, for Asiatics, Africans and Aboriginals, skin colour acts as a substantial barrier to integration. The question, asked in the 2 September 1979 issue of the *Toronto Daily Star* by its columnist Richard Gwyn, persists: "How many non-whites will prove too many for the stability of Canadian society?" Even more pointedly, Stella Hryniuk, in *Twenty Years of Multiculturalism*, quotes a Canadian of French and Haitian descent as asking, "Am I a Canadian when I feel Canadian, or when others say I am a Canadian?"

18   Nevertheless, for the majority of immigrants, multiculturalism, costing the government annually a mere dollar per Canadian, has benefited the country. A good number of newcomers believe that government funding of multicultural events like dance-fests and ethnic centres will preserve their culture forever. Ethnic gatherings such as Caravan and Caribana in Toronto, Dragon Boat Races in Vancouver, Folklorama in Winnipeg and Heritage Day in Edmonton romanticize the newcomers' history and identity and offer them a feeling of belonging. Cultural community life is more visible in Canada today than in any other country.

19   However, ethnic ceremonies and dances do not change the reality that the Canadian power structure remains English and French, around which circumnavigate lesser satellite cultures. Assimilation still goes on apace, but in a more humane manner. The difference between the Canadian "mosaic" and American "melting pot" is not overwhelming—both have the same aim: assimilation. The preservation of ethnic cultures in both countries is still very dependent on new replenishment by way of immigration. Through education and intermarriage, the overwhelming majority have assimilated into mainly the English culture—by the third generation over 85 per cent. Unlike earlier in this century, they willingly melt into the host society as they ethnically dance themselves out of existence. Our family, whose members, in the main, live in western Canada, are an excellent example of this assimilation. Out of its eight members, only two married Arabs. Today, my nieces and nephews are Carletons, McWhirters and McCallums who know very little about their partially Arab origin. Their views about Canada and its future are those of the dominant Anglo society.

20   In western Canada, where non-French, non-British and non-Native origins constitute nearly half of the population, "English only" is supported by the majority of the inhabitants. The descendants of the "black Syrians" are now the most vocal opponents of multiculturalism. To them, all the new immigrants are taking away the Canadians' jobs and bringing a foreign element into Canadian society. The same view is held by many descendants of immigrants. They are multiculturalism's most vocal critics. The backlash against cultural retention comes, in the main, from assimilated members of ethnic communities. Strangely, support for cultural maintenance is strongest among university graduates of British origin.

21   The views about the future of Canada among the vast majority of these descendants of immigrant groups is more "Anglo" than those whose forefathers came from the British Isles. With the passing of the third generation, the countries of their origin are, I would say, to the majority, unknown. The legacy of their fathers to Canada are a few foods like falafel, hummus, pizzas and wonton soup. However, as they disappear, because of multiculturalism, they retain their self-esteem. Overwhelmingly, their view of Canada and its future is that of the Anglo Canadians.

For Further Thinking

1. David Suzuki, a third-generation Japanese-Canadian, makes statements in his autobiographical book *Metamorphosis* (1987) that certainly seem to support Salloum: "we children didn't understand the old culture, and didn't have the slightest interest—we were Canadians." From people you know, or perhaps your own experiences, do you think Salloum's theory is correct?

2. It is often observed that those who come to Canada see its strengths and value its beauty more highly than native-born Canadians. Is there some truth to this? Is complacency a Canadian problem?

3. What is your opinion of Canada's attitude toward immigration? What is your view on the value of new immigrants to the Canadian future?

Looking Back and Ahead

1. How does Pamela Swanigan's discussion fit with the ideas developed in this essay (see "I Am Half-Canadian," page 411)?

2. Read "Canada's 'Genocide'" (p. 443), an article intended in part to remind Canadians of our general neglect and mistreatment of Native communities. In a speech in Vancouver, April 2007, former governor-general Adrienne Clarkson pursued the theme that "we are all treaty people." By that, she meant that Europeans made legal and ethical commitments to First Nations in exchange for the lands now possessed and used by non-Aboriginals. These obligations were inherited by the independent government of Canada. Discuss the obligations as well as the rights of citizenship, and consider the difficulties people from other countries (as well as those born here) sometimes have in understanding Canada's unresolved history with its original inhabitants.

3. Read "Not like the Movie" (p. 405) and imagine what difficulties the author might have experienced in settling in her new community. Then imagine a new arrival to Canada who speaks English as a second language and who would be considered a "visible minority." If you can, think of someone you know. Do you think the author of "Not like the Movie" and this other person would have the same basic chance of smooth acceptance? What sorts of variables might come into play in addressing this highly hypothetical question?

4. In a personal essay comparing Canada and the USSR under communism, published in the first edition of *Acting on Words,* a Russian immigrant offered several criticisms of Canadians, including that we seem too materialistic and too obsessed with being "nice." Some Canadian readers responded that if this writer thinks we are too "nice" (i.e., guarded) and not as passionate about life and philosophy as Russians (even when under the constraints of communism), then she should go back to Russia. What do you think about this rather typical reaction to immigrants who "dare" to criticize "us"?

Kim Pittaway Responding to anthropologist Helen Fisher's book *The First Sex: The Natural Talents of Women and How They Are Changing the World*, Pittaway expresses dissatisfaction with the author's thesis. She feels that Fisher is really saying, "The future belongs to women! Let's honour our foremothers and kick some testosterone butt." Fisher emphasizes that men's and women's brains have developed differently, with women superior at synthesis or "web thinking," skills demanded by the future. Pittaway argues that the next generation of women has moved beyond a confrontational battle-of-the-sexes approach, which she says "takes us backward instead of forward, to a place where we can only conceive of winning if someone else loses. Our foremothers didn't work to get a place at the table so that they could make the boys eat in the kitchen." Pittaway's essay represents a form of persuasive analysis. In preparing to read this selection, you might wish to review our discussion of critical analysis in Chapter 14 of the Rhetoric.

Crystal Balls

1   It was close to midnight on a New Brunswick New Year's Eve. The eve of a new decade, 1979. An Oscar Peterson LP spun on the turntable, but no one could hear it: the room was filled with laughter, cigarette smoke and the clink of glasses and plates piled high with Mom's lasagna. Then Dad posed the question: not the usual "What are your resolutions?"—too boring—but "What will your life be like in 2000?" I don't remember a single word uttered by any of my parents' guests because I was too busy trying to figure out what I was going to say. Finally, my turn came—and Dad skipped right over me. It was my mom who noticed me giving him the evil teenage eye. "Tom, Tom, wait a minute—you missed Kim," she said. And so I made my predictions: in the year 2000, I'd be 35 (more than twice my age at the time and inconceivably distant to my 15-year-old brain). I wouldn't be living in Moncton—I'd be someplace big, maybe Halifax. I'd be a journalist or a movie director. And I'd be married with kids.

2   Halifax lost out to Toronto. The only movie directing I do is when I pause the VCR to replenish the chip bowl, and the husband and kids. . . . [L]et's just say news reports on efforts to extend ovarian viability catch my eye and my no-blind-dates rule has been rescinded. I got "journalist" and "35" right though.

3   Twenty years later, we're heading into the most-hyped New Year's Eve ever. And the question "Where will we be?" is echoing in my head.

4   What does the future hold for Canadian women? Peering into the new millennium, I'm tempted to be a "woman first" cheerleader. Part of me wants to shout "The future belongs to women! Let's honour our foremothers and kick some testosterone butt."

5   I wouldn't be alone, either. In her new book *The First Sex: The Natural Talents of Women and How They Are Changing the World*, anthropologist Helen Fisher argues that the future does indeed belong to women: that men's and women's brains have developed differently; that we are better at "synthesis" or "web thinking"—gathering facts and insights from a wide range of sources and experiences—while men are stuck with one-step-at-a-time linear thinking and a more

limited view. Basically, this means women can listen to the radio traffic report, feed the cat and make breakfast all at the same time, while the guys tend to do one thing at a time. Try asking a man a question while he's reading the newspaper, says Fisher, and you'll get a firsthand demonstration of one-track brains. Women also have better language and people skills and more acute senses, and all of that means tomorrow is ours for the asking.

6   I couldn't get past the first chapter of Fisher's book. The fact is, I don't want the future to belong to women. That sort of ownership bothers me. For one thing, it sounds too much like the flip side of the lines used to keep women in their place in the past. "Women make excellent workers when they have their jobs cut out for them, but . . . they lack initiative in finding work themselves," said a bulletin issued in 1943 to male supervisors in the transportation industry. "Be tactful when issuing instructions or in making criticisms. Women can't shrug off harsh words the way men do," it continued. I have the reprint pinned to my bulletin board as a reminder of how far we've come. (I harbour a special affection for management tip No. 3: "General experience indicates that 'husky' girls—those who are just a little on the heavy side—are more even-tempered and efficient than their underweight sisters.") I'm sure the women in my family—and probably yours too—heard a variation on those lines.

7   I think of my mother and grandmothers as trailblazers, though I'm sure they'd never have described themselves that way. Catherine Gillis, my mother's mother, studied at Halifax's Mount Saint Vincent University and worked with my grandfather in every business he ever ran. Edna Pittaway, my father's mother, was a working mom long before the phrase was coined: she worked in a factory soldering knick-knacks. My mother, Marie, just retired after 40 years as a nurse and a teacher, two stereotypical pursuits—but not so stereotypically, she brought home a paycheque that always equalled my dad's.

8   My grandmothers saw the working world change from a time when women were hired only because the men were off fighting a war to an age when their granddaughters (my sister and me and our cousins) could pick and choose from a world of options. In my mother's lifetime, the advances can be seen in the slogans used to fight for change: "Equal pay for work of equal value." "Freedom of choice," "No means no"—phrases that defined then-revolutionary ways of thinking about what it means to be female.

9   But I'm not ready to add "The future belongs to women" to the list. It offers a limited view of what the possibilities really are and takes us backward instead of forward, to a place where we can only conceive of winning if someone else loses. Our foremothers didn't work to get a place at the table so that they could make the boys eat in the kitchen.

10   The possibilities of the future are so much broader than a women-first focus allows. As I look into the future, I'm taking my cue from a friend who calls me on it every time I start a sentence with a gender-based generalization, such as "Men always . . ." or "Women tend to. . .".

11   She's in her 20s, and while the gap in our ages is small, it's big enough that her view of the world is different from the one I grew up with. She, like many women her age, doesn't define her world in gender terms.

12   Sure, she sees the differences, but she's more likely to chalk them up to individual rather than gender attributes. She doesn't seem to feel the need to fight to be heard—perhaps because she's grown up entitled to speak.

13   She's aware that rich white guys still make up the lion's share of the world's business and political leaders. She knows that paycheques aren't genderless. But she's figured out that the next stage of the battle of the sexes, to use that quaintest of terms, isn't about winning and losing, top and bottom; it's about being who you were meant to be in a world that celebrates each individual's unique gifts. After all, who wants to be on top all of the time?

14   This New Year's Eve, after I've checked my supply of spring water, batteries, canned food and cash, I'll pose a question to my co-celebrants: "What will your life be like in 2020?" Sure, 2020 is only a baby step into the new millennium, but predictions are tricky and I'm reluctant to push past the 20-year frontier. There will be laughter, the clinking of glasses and even the stray whiff of cigarette smoke coming from the porch, as we take our turns peering into the future. And I promise not to skip over my dad when it's his turn to speak.

15   What will my life be like in 2020? I think I might be in Halifax. Directing a movie. And getting ready for the birth of my first child. Where will you be?

For Further Thinking

1. Can you point to an era or a culture where equality existed or exists between the sexes? Will the patriarchy, if it gives way entirely, be replaced by a matriarchy?

2. Is Pittaway devising her own form of political correctness; that is, if women *are* demonstrably better than men at certain key functions, should we deny this evidence only because it offends our notions of equality or hopes for the status quo future?

3. What is your attitude to the so-called battle of the sexes? Do you feel your attitude on this topic differs significantly from that of your parents, friends, and/or your children?

4. Are differences in behaviour and abilities between the sexes a matter of nature or nurture? Explain your view.

5. Has feminism accomplished its goals, as Pittaway suggests? Are we ready for a society that is "gender blind"? Should we be ready for a society that is "gender blind"?

Looking Back and Ahead

1. Is Lois's experience in Alice Munro's "Thanks for the Ride" (p. 376) specific to young women of her time and place only? If sexism explains part of Lois's problem, has the matter been resolved?

2. How does Pittaway's conception of time compare or contrast to that of other authors in our Reader? Is the future better, worse, or static?

3. Chapter 13 offers advice on finding the controlling idea and supporting reason(s) of an essay (p. 191). Review that advice and see if you can identify Pittaway's central claim (controlling idea), grounds (evidence, support), and warrant (supporting the claim and evidence, a general value or attitude that we suppose to be true). Pages 260–61 of Chapter 16 provide more explanation of assertions, grounds, and warrants. Write just one sentence for each of these parts of the argument model. When you are done, compare your answers with the student essay in Chapter 16, page 261, "Toulmin and Me or How to Get A- for That Essay You Couldn't Finish on Time." If your answers are quite different from those in the student essay, discuss these differences with your classmates and/or instructor.

Carl Jung Psychology—the study of the human mind—was not regarded as its own discipline until the early twentieth century. Austrian therapist Sigmund Freud (1856–1939) is generally recognized as the "father of modern psychology" and psychoanalysis. In 1906 Freud met a Swiss explorer in the new field, Carl Jung (1875–1961), and served as this young man's mentor for about seven years. Major differences between the two emerged, however, when Jung defended his belief in psychic realities and metaphysical subjects, which Freud rejected.

Jung's idea of the collective unconscious—a reservoir of cultural memories, dreams, and myths— led him to explore comparative religions, alchemy, the *I Ching*, and astrology.[2] He cast horoscopes of his patients, hoping to use the insights of astrology in combination with his own psychotherapeutic ideas; he also made a statistical study of the relations between the horoscopes of marriage partners, described in his work *Synchronicity: An Acausal Connecting Principle* (1955). Jung's ideas on personality are the basis of today's widely used Myers-Briggs Type Indicator, and his form of psychotherapy has influenced a wide range of artists and writers, including Canadian writer Robertson Davies (1913–1995). Have a look at "The Pleasures of Love," p. 431.

On Synchronicity

1 It might seem appropriate to begin my exposition by defining the concept with which it deals. But I would rather approach the subject the other way and first give you a brief description of the facts which the concept of synchronicity is intended to cover. As its etymology shows, this term has something to do with time or, to be more accurate, with a kind of simultaneity. Instead of simultaneity we could also use the concept of a *meaningful coincidence* of two or more events, where something other than the probability of chance is involved. A statistical—that is, a probable—concurrence of events, such as the "duplication of cases" found in hospitals, falls within the category of chance. Groupings of this kind can consist of any number of terms and still remain within the framework of the probable and rationally possible. Thus, for instance, someone chances to notice the number on his street-car ticket. On arriving home he receives

---

[2] Colin Wilson, *The Occult* (London: Hodder & Stoughton, 1971) 324.

a telephone call during which the same number is mentioned. In the evening he buys a theatre ticket that again has the same number. The three events form a chance grouping that, although not likely to occur often, nevertheless lies well within the framework of probability owing to the frequency of each of its terms. I would like to recount from my own experience the following chance grouping, made up of no fewer than six terms:

2   On April 1, 1949, I made a note in the morning of an inscription containing a figure that was half man and half fish. There was fish for lunch. Somebody mentioned the custom of making an "April fish" of someone. In the afternoon, a former patient of mine, whom I had not seen for months, showed me some impressive pictures of fish. In the evening, I was shown a piece of embroidery with sea monsters and fishes in it. The next morning, I saw a former patient, who was visiting me for the first time in ten years. She had dreamed of a large fish the night before. A few months later, when I was using this series for a larger work and had just finished writing it down, I walked over to a spot by the lake in front of the house, where I had already been several times that morning. This time a fish a foot long lay on the sea-wall. Since no one else was present, I have no idea how the fish could have got there.

3   When coincidences pile up in this way one cannot help being impressed by them—for the greater the number of terms in such a series, or the more unusual its character, the more improbable it becomes. For reasons that I have mentioned elsewhere and will not discuss now, I assume that this was a chance grouping. It must be admitted, though, that it is more improbable than a mere duplication.

4   In the above-mentioned case of the street-car ticket, I said that the observer "chanced" to notice the number and retain it in his memory, which ordinarily he would never have done. This formed the basis for the series of chance events, but I do not know what caused him to notice the number. It seems to me that in judging such a series a factor of uncertainty enters in at this point and requires attention. I have observed something similar in other cases, without, however, being able to draw any reliable conclusions. But it is sometimes difficult to avoid the impression that there is a sort of foreknowledge of the coming series of events. This feeling becomes irresistible when, as so frequently happens, one thinks one is about to meet an old friend in the street, only to find to one's disappointment that it is a stranger. On turning the next corner one then runs into him in person. Cases of this kind occur in every conceivable form and by no means infrequently, but after the first momentary astonishment they are as a rule quickly forgotten.

5   Now, the more the foreseen details of an event pile up, the more definite is the impression of an existing foreknowledge, and the more improbable does chance become. I remember the story of a student friend whose father had promised him a trip to Spain if he passed his final examinations satisfactorily. My friend thereupon dreamed that he was walking through a Spanish city. The street led to

a square, where there was a Gothic cathedral. He then turned right, around a corner, into another street. There he was met by an elegant carriage drawn by two cream-coloured horses. Then he woke up. He told us about the dream as we were sitting around a table drinking beer. Shortly afterward, having successfully passed his examinations, he went to Spain, and there, in one of the streets, he recognized the city of his dream. He found the square and the cathedral, which exactly corresponded to the dream-image. He wanted to go straight to the cathedral, but then remembered that in the dream he had turned right, at the corner, into another street. He was curious to find out whether his dream would be corroborated further. Hardly had he turned the corner when he saw in reality the carriage with the two cream-coloured horses.

6   The *sentiment du déja-vu* is based, as I have found in a number of cases, on a foreknowledge in dreams, but we saw that this foreknowledge can also occur in the waking state. In such cases mere chance becomes highly improbable because the coincidence is known in advance. It thus loses its chance character not only psychologically and subjectively, but objectively too, since the accumulation of details that coincide immeasurably increases the improbability of chance as a determining factor. (For correct precognitions of death, Dariex and Flammarion have computed probabilities ranging from 1 in 4,000,000 to 1 in 8,000,000). So in these cases it would be incongruous to speak of "chance" happenings. It is rather a question of meaningful coincidences. Usually they are explained by precognition—in other words, foreknowledge. People also talk of clairvoyance, telepathy, etc., without, however, being able to explain what these faculties consist of or what means of transmission they use in order to render events distant in space and time accessible to our perception. All these ideas are mere names; they are not scientific concepts which could be taken as statements of principle, for no one has yet succeeded in constructing a causal bridge between the elements making up a meaningful coincidence.

7   Great credit is due to J.B. Rhine for having established a reliable basis for work in the vast field of these phenomena by his experiments in extrasensory perception, or ESP. He used a pack of 25 cards divided into 5 groups of 5, each with its special sign (star, square, circle, cross, two wavy lines). The experiment was carried out as follows. In each series of experiments the pack is laid out 800 times, in such a way that the subject cannot see the cards. He is then asked to guess the cards as they are turned up. The probability of a correct answer is 1 in 5. The result, computed from very high figures, showed an average of 6.5 hits. The probability of chance deviation of 1.5 amounts to only 1 in 250,000. Some individuals scored more than twice the probable number of hits. On one occasion all 25 cards were guessed correctly, which gives a probability of 1 in 298,023,223,876,953,125. The spatial distance between experimenter and subject was increased from a few yards to about 4,000 miles, with no effect on the result.

8   A second type of experiment consisted in asking the subject to guess a series of cards that was still to be laid out in the near or more distant future. The time factor was increased from a few minutes to two weeks. The result of these experiments showed a probability of 1 in 400,000.

9   In a third type of experiment, the subject had to try to influence the fall of mechanically thrown dice by wishing for a certain number. The results of this so-called psychokinetic (PK) experiment were the more positive the more dice were used at a time.

10   The result of the spatial experiment proves with tolerable certainty that the psyche can, to some extent, eliminate the space factor. The time experiment proves that the time factor (at any rate, in the dimension of the future) can become psychically relative. The experiment with dice proves that moving bodies, too, can be influenced psychically—a result that could have been predicted from the psychic relativity of space and time.

11   The energy postulate shows itself to be inapplicable to the Rhine experiments, and thus rules out all ideas about the transmission of force. Equally, the law of causality does not hold—a fact that I pointed out thirty years ago. For we cannot conceive how a future event could bring about an event in the present. Since for the time being there is no possibility whatever of a causal explanation, we must assume provisionally that improbable accidents of an acausal nature—that is, meaningful coincidences—have entered the picture.

12   In considering these remarkable results we must take into account a fact discovered by Rhine, namely that in each series of experiments the first attempts yielded a better result than the later ones. The falling off in the number of hits scored was connected with the mood of the subject. An initial mood of faith and optimism makes for good results. Scepticism and resistance have the opposite effect: that is, they create an unfavourable disposition. As the energic, and hence also the causal, approach to these experiments has shown itself to be inapplicable, it follows that the affective factor has the significance simply of a *condition* which makes it possible for the phenomenon to occur, though it need not. According to Rhine's results, we may nevertheless expect 6.5 hits instead of only 5. But it cannot be predicted in advance when the hit will come. Could we do so, we would be dealing with a law, and this would contradict the entire nature of the phenomenon. It has, as said, the improbable character of a "lucky" hit or accident that occurs with a more than merely probable frequency and is as a rule dependent on a certain state of affectivity.

13   This observation has been thoroughly confirmed, and it suggests that the psychic factor which modifies or even eliminates the principles underlying the physicist's picture of the world is connected with the affective state of the subject. Although the phenomenology of the ESP and PK experiments could be considerably enriched by further experiments of the kind described above, deeper investigation of its bases will have to concern itself with the nature of the affectivity involved. I have therefore directed my attention to certain observations

and experiences which, I can fairly say, have forced themselves upon me during the course of my long medical practice. They have to do with spontaneous, meaningful coincidences of so high a degree of improbability as to appear flatly unbelievable. I shall therefore describe to you only one case of this kind, simply to give an example characteristic of a whole category of phenomena. It makes no difference whether you refuse to believe this particular case or whether you dispose of it with an *ad hoc* explanation. I could tell you a great many such stories, which are in principle no more surprising or incredible than the irrefutable results arrived at by Rhine, and you would soon see that almost every case calls for its own explanation. But the causal explanation, the only possible one from the standpoint of natural science, breaks down owing to the psychic relativization of space and time, which together form the indispensable premises for the cause-and-effect relationship.

14   My example concerns a young woman patient who, in spite of efforts made on both sides, proved to be psychologically inaccessible. The difficulty lay in the fact that she always knew better about everything. Her excellent education had provided her with a weapon ideally suited to this purpose, namely a highly polished Cartesian[3] rationalism with an impeccably "geometrical" idea of reality. After several fruitless attempts to sweeten her rationalism with a somewhat more human understanding, I had to confine myself to the hope that something unexpected and irrational would turn up, something that would burst the intellectual retort into which she had sealed herself. Well, I was sitting opposite her one day, with my back to the window, listening to her flow of rhetoric. She had had an impressive dream the night before, in which someone had given her a golden scarab—a costly piece of jewellery. While she was still telling me this dream, I heard something behind me gently tapping on the window. I turned round and saw that it was a fairly large flying insect that was knocking against the window-pane from outside in the obvious effort to get into the dark room. This seemed to me very strange. I opened the window immediately and caught the insect in the air as it flew in. It was a scarabaeid beetle, or common rose-chafer (*Cetonia aurata*), whose golden-green colour most nearly resembles that of a golden scarab. I handed the beetle to my patient with the words, "Here is your scarab." This experience punctured the desired hole in her rationalism and broke the ice of her intellectual resistance. The treatment could now be continued with satisfactory results.

15   This story is meant only as a paradigm of the innumerable cases of meaningful coincidence that have been observed not only by me but by many others and recorded in large collections.

---

[3] This adjective derives from the name René Descartes (1596–1650). Sometimes considered the "father" of modern philosophy, the French mathematician attempted to make philosophy "scientific," in keeping with the empirical values of his time. His system emphasized doubt, skepticism, and a denial of feelings. For an interesting critical interpretation of Descartes's influence on today's world, see Albert Borgman, *Crossing the Postmodern Divide* (Chicago: University of Chicago Press, 1992).

For Further Thinking

1. In Chapter 11 of the Rhetoric, "definition" is the last of the purposes and organizational patterns discussed. This is because the act of defining a complex concept may call upon any of the other patterns of writing we discuss. Skim the essentials of Chapters 9 to 12. How many other expository patterns can you find in Jung's passage?

2. Have you ever been thinking of a friend you haven't spoken to in a long time, only to find out that he or she has just left or will soon leave you a message? Have you had dreams or insights about the future that were proven true? What is your opinion of psychic experiences in general? What is your opinion of the "scarab" experience reported by Jung?

3. Jung suggests that the "psychic factor . . . modifies or even eliminates the physicist's picture of the world." Have the recent discoveries of quantum mechanics altered this picture sufficiently to reconcile the "psychic factor" and the "physicist's picture"?

4. Do you think Jung's misgiving about universities' excluding certain subjects is a valid concern today?

5. Do you think an acceptance of psychic reality is culturally determined to some extent? Explain.

Looking Back and Ahead

1. Many cultures believe that spirits are real and active. While we tend to consider such beliefs as exclusive to Aboriginal societies, in fact, many Europeans and non-Aboriginal North Americans have asserted a belief in spirits. What do you think Sigmund Freud might have thought of this belief? How do you think Jung might have responded? Perhaps conduct some brief research on both thinkers before offering your response.

2. Read John Markoff's "The Doomsday Machines" (p. 505). It is sometimes said that whereas the East concentrates on inner reality and being, the West most values exterior action and time (rapid change). Has the West listened too little to the Jungs of the world, and paid too little attention to inner reality while pursuing external systems without the necessary inner resources to handle them?

3. Read Robertson Davies's, essay "The Pleasures of Love," following. In what ways and for what reasons can you imagine Davies embracing the values and beliefs of Jung?

Robertson Davies Novelist, playwright, raconteur, and essayist, Robertson Davies (1913–95) grew up in Thamesville, Ontario, the son of a journalist. He was educated at Upper Canada College, Queen's University, and Oxford. After a spell as a professional actor, he edited *Saturday Night* magazine in Toronto and then the Peterborough *Examiner*. In 1961 he was appointed Master at Massey College, University of Toronto, where he remained until retirement. He died at the age of 82 on December 12, 1995.

In 1971, the *Penguin Companion to English Literature*, edited in England, pronounced that Davies's "urbanity and elegance are unique in [English] Canadian fiction." But the qualities Canadian readers appreciate in his work are also those of his journalistic background—a sharp eye for the detail and spirit of small-town Ontario. His best-known work remains *Fifth Business*, a finely crafted and graceful novel. Raised a Protestant, Davies nevertheless had an abiding interest in the more mysterious side of religious experience and in explorers of the psyche like the Swiss psychotherapist Carl Jung (1875–1961).

The Pleasures of Love

1   Let us understand one another at once: I have been asked to discuss the pleasures of love, not its epiphanies, its ecstasies, its disillusionments, its duties, its burdens or its martyrdom—and therefore the sexual aspect of it will get scant attention here. So if you have begun this piece in hope of fanning the flames of your lubricity, be warned in time.

2   Nor is it my intention to be psychological. I am heartily sick of most of the psychologizing about love that has been going on for the past six hundred years. Everybody wants to say something clever, or profound, about it, and almost everybody has done so. Only look under "Love" in any book of quotations to see how various the opinions are.

3   Alas, most of this comment is wide of the mark; love, like music and painting, resists analysis in words. It may be described, and some poets and novelists have described it movingly and well; but it does not yield to the theorist. Love is the personal experience of lovers. It must be felt directly.

4   My own opinion is that it is felt most completely in marriage, or some comparable attachment of long duration. Love takes time. What are called "love affairs" may afford a wide, and in retrospect, illuminating variety of emotions; not only fierce satisfactions and swooning delights, but the horrors of jealousy and the desperation of parting attend them; the hangover from one of these emotional riots may be long and dreadful.

5   But rarely have the pleasures of love an opportunity to manifest themselves in such riots of passion. Love affairs are for emotional sprinters; the pleasures of love are for the emotional marathoners.

6   Clearly, then, the pleasures of love are not for the very young. Romeo and Juliet are the accepted pattern of youthful passion. Our hearts go out to their furious abandonment; we are moved to pity by their early death. We do not, unless we are of a saturnine disposition, give a thought to what might have happened if they had been spared for fifty or sixty years together.

7   Would Juliet have become a worldly nonentity, like her mother? Or would she, egged on by that intolerable old bawd, her Nurse, have planted a thicket of horns on the brow of her Romeo?

8   And he—well, so much would have depended on whether Mercutio had lived; quarrelsome, dashing and detrimental, Mercutio was a man destined to outlive his wit and spend his old age as the Club Bore. No, no; all that Verona crowd were much better off to die young and beautiful.

9   Passion, so splendid in the young, wants watching as the years wear on. Othello had it, and in middle life he married a young and beautiful girl. What happened? He believed the first scoundrel who hinted that she was unfaithful, and never once took the elementary step of asking her a direct question about the matter.

10   Passion is a noble thing; I have no use for a man or woman who lacks it; but if we seek the pleasures of love, passion should be occasional, and common sense continual.

11   Let us get away from Shakespeare. He is the wrong guide in the exploration we have begun. If we talk of the pleasures of love, the best marriage he affords is that of Macbeth and his Lady. Theirs is not the prettiest, nor the highest-hearted, nor the wittiest match in Shakespeare, but unquestionably they knew the pleasures of love.

12   "My dearest partner of greatness," writes the Thane of Cawdor to his spouse. That is the clue to their relationship. That explains why Macbeth's noblest and most desolate speech follows the news that his Queen is dead.

13   But who wants to live a modern equivalent of the life of the Macbeths—continuous scheming to reach the Executive Suite enlivened, one presumes, by an occasional Burns Nicht dinner-party, with the ghosts of discredited vice-presidents as uninvited guests.

14   The pleasures of love are certainly not for the very young, who find a bittersweet pleasure in trying to reconcile two flowering egotisms, nor yet for those who find satisfaction in "affairs." Not that I say a word against young love, or the questings of uncommitted middle-age; but these notions of love correspond to brandy, and we are concerned with something much more like wine.

15   The pleasures of love are for those who are hopelessly addicted to another living creature. The reasons for such addiction are so many that I suspect they are never the same in any two cases.

16   It includes passion but does not survive by passion; it has its whiffs of the agreeable vertigo of young love, but it is stable more often than dizzy; it is a growing, changing thing, and it is tactful enough to give the addicted parties occasional rests from strong and exhausting feeling of any kind.

17   "Perfect love sometimes does not come until the first grandchild," says a Welsh proverb. Better [by] far if perfect love does not come at all, but hovers just out of reach. Happy are those who never experience the all-dressed-up-and-no-place-to-go sensation of perfection in love.

18   What do we seek in love? From my own observation among a group of friends and acquaintances that includes a high proportion of happy marriages, most people are seeking a completion of themselves. Each party to the match has several qualities the other cherishes; the marriage as a whole is decidedly more than the sum of its parts.

19   Nor are these cherished qualities simply the obvious ones; the reclusive man who marries the gregarious woman, the timid woman who marries the

courageous man, the idealist who marries the realist—we can all see these unions: the marriages in which tenderness meets loyalty, where generosity sweetens moroseness, where a sense of beauty eases some aridity of the spirit, are not so easy for outsiders to recognize; the parties themselves may not be fully aware of such elements in a good match.

20   Often, in choosing a mate, people are unconsciously wise and apprehend what they need to make them greater than they are.

21   Of course the original disposition of the partners to the marriage points the direction it will take. When Robert Browning married Elizabeth Barrett, the odds were strongly on the side of optimism, in spite of superficial difficulties; when Macbeth and his Lady stepped to the altar, surely some second-sighted Highlander must have shuddered.

22   If the parties to a marriage have chosen one another unconsciously, knowing only that they will be happier united than apart, they had better set to work as soon as possible to discover why they have married, and to nourish the feeling which has drawn them together.

23   I am constantly astonished by the people, otherwise intelligent, who think that anything so complex and delicate as a marriage can be left to take care of itself. One sees them fussing about all sorts of lesser concerns, apparently unaware that side by side with them—often in the same bed—a human creature is perishing from lack of affection, of emotional malnutrition.

24   Such people are living in sin far more truly than the loving but unwedded couples whose unions they sometimes scorn. What pleasures are there in these neglected marriages? What pleasure can there be in ramshackle, jerrybuilt, uncultivated love?

25   A great part of all the pleasure of love begins, continues and sometimes ends with conversation. A real, enduring love-affair, in marriage and out of it, is an extremely exclusive club of which the entire membership is two co-equal Perpetual Presidents.

26   In French drama there used to be a character, usually a man, who was the intimate friend of husband and wife, capable of resolving quarrels and keeping the union in repair. I do not believe in such a creature anywhere except behind the footlights. Lovers who need a third party to discuss matters with are in a bad way.

27   Of course there are marriages that are kept in some sort of rickety shape by a psychiatrist—occasionally by two psychiatrists. But I question if pleasure of the sort I am writing about can exist in such circumstances. The club has become too big.

28   I do not insist on a union of chatter-boxes, but as you can see I do not believe that still waters run deep; too often I have found that still waters are foul and have mud bottoms. People who love each other should talk to each other; they should confide their real thoughts, their honest emotions, their deepest wishes. How else are they to keep their union in repair?

29   How else, indeed, are they to discover that they are growing older and enjoying it, which is a very great discovery indeed? How else are they to discover that their union is stronger and richer, not simply because they have shared experience (couples who are professionally at odds, like a Prime Minister and a Leader of the Opposition, also share experience, but they are not lovers) but because they are waxing in spirit?

30   During the last war a cruel epigram was current that Ottawa was full of brilliant men, and the women they had married when they were very young. If the brilliant men had talked more to those women, and the women had replied, the joint impression they made in middle-age might not have been so dismal. It is often asserted that sexual compatibility is the foundation of a good marriage, but this pleasure is doomed to wane, whereas a daily affectionate awareness and a ready tongue last as long as life itself.

31   It always surprises me, when Prayer Book revision is discussed, that something is not put into the marriage service along these lines—"for the mutual society, help, comfort and unrestricted conversation that one ought to have of the other, both in prosperity and adversity."

32   Am I then advocating marriages founded on talk? I can hear the puritans, who mistrust conversation as they mistrust all subtle pleasures, tutting their disapproving tuts.

33   Do I assert that the pleasures of love are no more than the pleasures of conversation? Not at all: I am saying that where the talk is good and copious, love is less likely to wither, or to get out of repair, or to be outgrown, than among the uncommunicative.

34   For, after all, even lovers live alone much more than we are ready to admit. To keep in constant, sensitive rapport with those we love most, we must open our hearts and our minds. Do this, and the rarest, most delicate pleasures of love will reveal themselves.

35   Finally, it promotes longevity. Nobody quits a club where the conversation is fascinating, revealing, amusing, various and unexpected until the last possible minute. Love may be snubbed to death: talked to death, never!

For Further Thinking

1. What do you think of the statement that love cannot be analyzed, that it "is the personal experience of lovers. It must be felt directly"?

2. "Love takes time"—is this true? With age, are people prepared to settle for less in love or, conversely, do they expect more?

3. Davies introduces a striking metaphoric comparison to emphasize his thesis. What is that comparison?

4. What is Davies's major recommendation for achieving the pleasure of love?

5. How would you define the style of this essay? What are its features?

Looking Back and Ahead

1. Contrast the style of this essay to that of Pamela Swanigan's "I Am Half-Canadian" (p. 411). Consider that both essays were published in the same magazine, but 40 years apart.
2. Compare the style of this essay to that of Kim Pittaway's "Crystal Balls" (p. 423), published in a popular magazine 39 years after Davies's essay appeared.
3. How might Douglas Coupland's chapter "The Sun Is Your Enemy" (p. 390) be interpreted in light of Davies's thesis in this essay?

Michael Lahey and Ari Sarantis In the following essay of critical analysis and evaluation, Michael Lahey and Ari Sarantis respond to the famous poem "Richard Cory" by E. A. Robinson. Robinson published his poem in 1897. Paul Simon and Art Garfunkel brought it back to public awareness with their song adaptation in the 1960s. Chapter 14, "Critical Analysis and Evaluation," Chapter 15, "Rhetorical Analysis," and especially "Literary and Film Analysis" at the Text Enrichment Site for Chapter 15 all provide useful background reading to help you to appreciate or write a literary analysis. We now provide a sketch of Edwin Arlington Robinson followed by his poem "Richard Cory."

Edwin Arlington Robinson was born in 1869 in Head Tide, Maine; he is a distant descendant of the famous British writer Anne Bradstreet. He established himself as one of America's most important poets, winning the Pulitzer Prize for poetry three times: in 1921, 1924, and 1927. In 1929, he was awarded a gold medal by the American Institute of Arts and Letters for his poetic accomplishments. *Children of the Night* is generally considered Robinson's best-known book of poems. Also well known are the poems in his Arthurian trilogy, *Merlin*, *Lancelot*, and *Tristram*. Despite his accomplishments, Robinson's success was not easily made. He and his family suffered a series of emotional, physical, and financial misfortunes; it is Robinson's own brushes with tragedy that give him his keen insight and sympathy for many of his poetic characters. He is able to portray these individuals in all of their raw humanity without judgement, and in the process invites the reader also to sympathize with the often tragic plight of humanity: personal failure, frustrated desire, and pure bad luck. Robinson died in 1935.

While reading Robinson's poem, take note of the form, its use of conventional poetic structure, and the way in which its content challenges conventionality (for its time) by addressing subject matter not generally considered worthy of poetry. Then think about what the poem means to you before you read the essay.

Richard Cory

Whenever Richard Cory went down town,
We people on the pavement looked at him:
He was a gentleman from sole to crown,
Clean favored, and imperially slim.

And he was always quietly arrayed,
And he was always human when he talked;
But still he fluttered pulses when he said,
"Good-morning," and he glittered when he walked.

And he was rich—yes, richer than a king—
And admirably schooled in every grace;
In fine, we thought that he was everything
To make us wish that we were in his place.

So on we worked, and waited for the light,
And went without the meat, and cursed the bread;
And Richard Cory, one calm summer night,
Went home and put a bullet through his head.

Words and Bullets: A Rhetorical Analysis
of E. A. Robinson's "Richard Cory"

1   Edwin Arlington Robinson's poem "Richard Cory" could be mistaken for an easy
text. It seems structurally unremarkable, almost like a small-town conversation,
and thematically commonplace: the painful truth of despair underlying the
superficial appearance of fulfillment, a presumed completeness. Yet the poem, on
closer scrutiny, offers structural and linguistic opportunities for considerable
analysis and interpretation. This poem is at once highly accessible and deceptively
complex. It uses specific language choices and language patterns to reveal the sad,
fantasy relationship between Richard Cory and the townspeople.

2   Although a student usually focuses most of his or her analysis on a poem's
(or a song's) content, a rhetorical analysis more closely examines the strategies of
the language. A rhetorical analysis explores how meaning can be created so subtly, even slyly, by word choices that it seems to spring wholesale, "naturally,"
from the page. A rhetorical analysis examines how such meaning derives from or
is construed by virtue of the words themselves, either through specific word
choice (**diction**), through relationships to other words (**rhythm, alliteration,
conceptual sameness, contradiction, rhyme**) or through types of meaning
(whether **denotative**—direct—or **connotative**—implied, emotional, political).
A poem's rhetorical structure relies partly on the literary devices the poet uses to
generate, even complicate, the poem's content. An insightful rhetorical analysis
would thereby reveal how the structure and the reader's sense of content are by
no means mutually exclusive, but that the structure generates and deepens content. Often, however, it is difficult to isolate one from the other. A poet's calcu-
lated repetition of a word, synonym, or even rhythm at certain points in the
poem likely has structural and substantive significance. Rhetorical analysis,
therefore, can reveal, sometimes unsettlingly, exactly how much of what a reader
might consider as the transparent, indisputable content is really the effect of the
rhetoric, of language strategies.

3   Robinson's "Richard Cory," composed uniformly of four stanzas of four lines,
changes its pacing from stanza to stanza to reflect the speaker's awe of, then

investment in, then baffled disappointment with Richard Cory. The first four lines establish a public scene and mood with Richard Cory as a revered communal figure, almost valuable public property. He is "down town," where "we people," apparently the entire community, "looked at him." The poet's language here starkly sets Richard Cory apart from, rather than as part of, the group—on a stage, whether he wants to be or not. As with a stage, the curtain rises on the poem, so to speak, and the rapt audience (both townspeople and reader) watches a person who is treated like a spectacle.

4   With the second stanza, however, the poem starts to flow faster. This sense of slightly urgent movement occurs in part through Robinson's skilful uses of **anaphora** (repetition of a word or words at the beginning of successive clauses or sentences) and of **epistrophe** (repetition of a word or words at the end of successive clauses or sentences). These language devices, whether noticed by the reader or not, nonetheless create a rhythmic effect that paces the language, quickening it in this second stanza to reflect the town's excitement that someone like Richard Cory would ever be in their midst.

5   This beginning (anaphoric) repetition initiates the second stanza, creating chanting, hymnal effect. Consider the first two lines: "*And he was always* quietly arrayed, / *And he was always* human when he talked." Then note how seamlessly Robinson follows this chanting effect with three instances of epistrophe, an ending repetition, which appears here as a recurrent phrasing: " . . . was always human *when he talked*; / But still he fluttered pulses *when he said*, / 'Goodmorning,' and he glittered *when he walked*." This chanting pattern—repetitive language—suggests the townspeople's accelerated, nearly breathless worship of Richard Cory. Then the poet returns to his established beginning repetition (anaphora) with "*And he was* rich . . . / *And* admirably schooled." This return to the anaphora deliberately coincides with the reader's visual return to the left side of the page upon finishing the second stanza and beginning the third, essentially locking the reader into a language pattern that mirrors the way the town is locked into a pattern of static perception regarding Mr. Cory. These many repeated "ands," appearing in succession in stanza two, three and four, also contribute to the poem's casual, conversational, familiar tone. The "ands" represent the informality of spontaneous conversation, a democratic notion through language of "the people," but here also represent inferiority, not equality, increasing their sense of unbridgeable social distance from this rich, aristocratic citizen, who, unlike the townsfolk, is "admirably schooled in every grace." In fact, this democratic phrasing of "we people" ironically excludes Richard Cory from community. So E.A. Robinson's subtle language choices—from "we people" and the informal, folky repetition of "and" to Richard Cory's initial presentation as spectacle—quietly perform the deep tensions of inclusion and exclusion that the poem explores.

6   The anaphoric (beginning) repetitions, which give the poem its subtle, chanting hymnal quality, in turn define and articulate that collective, communal "voice" in the poem. This is an instance where a rhetorical analysis—how the

poem is specifically built by selected words—now shades into a substantive analysis of what the meaning may be. While only one direct speaker articulates the poem, that person is speaking on behalf of a collective, further developing the point of Cory's exclusion from that collective, the impoverished townspeople: "*We people* on the pavement looked at him"; "[i]n fine *we thought* that he was everything"; [s]o on *we worked*." This repetitive phrasing further establishes the two oppositional social identities in the poem: the anonymous collective and the glorious Richard Cory. Interestingly, these phrasings seem to empty democracy of its potential for strong personal identity.

7   So, the question arises, why do the people invest so much intense speculation about happiness and personal completeness in this one person? The poem's speaker even uses distinct emblems of royalty—"crown," "imperial," "glittering"—and then takes this regality one explicit step further: "[a]nd he was rich—yes, richer than a king." In this particular line, Robinson's word choice and especially word patterning actually seem to dramatize a quick verbal exchange *outside* the written poem, a *paratextual* conversational moment. The speaker's slightly but suddenly interrupted utterance, signalled by the poem's only use of dashes and then followed by the insistent word "yes" suggest the speaker suddenly takes a cue from someone else in a group of listeners to be more accurate about the degree of Cory's wealth.

8   Robinson begins the final stanza by bringing the reader out of the collective speaker's communal reverie to harsher facts. The pleasant current of praise for Cory carrying the reader through the almost breezy second and third stanza suddenly fades. As hard times resume their full, immediate emphasis, the statement "[s]o on we worked"—in its succinct phrasing yet ceremonial rhythm—summarizes both the burden of physical toil and its accepted continuity over the course of their lives. This "light" they passively wait for may be a metaphor for hope or change, but, significantly, one only helplessly invoked externally, from beyond them and their own resources. More grimly, the light may be the peaceful compensation of death, a cessation at last of life's struggles. The "light" may even indicate Richard Cory, who comes down town and flutters pulses when he says "Good-morning." As the townspeople go without the "meat," a traditional metaphor for feasting, and curse the "bread," a traditional metaphor for the crude necessities, they articulate unsatisfied lives, wanting what they believe they cannot have, having only what they do not appreciate, but need. Robinson's rhetorical strategy here hinges on a beautiful series of compressions, where three instances of single words—"light," "meat," "bread"—manage to represent poignantly much larger, even universal ideas of social, economic, and emotional longing.

9   As the thought of Richard Cory enters the final stanza in the third line, the serenity of "one calm summer night" seems to represent if not life's potential fullness, then perhaps a fulfilling balance quietly achieved in quiet lives. The reference to the summer night's calmness, a soothing moment of potential hope, also disarms the reader as Richard Cory's suicide suddenly occurs, an outcome all the more unexpected for the poem's previous word choices.

For Further Thinking

1. How does the town presume it knows certain facts about Richard Cory? How does E. A. Robinson's poem examine not just Richard Cory, but also the gap between our knowledge and our presumptions about most people with whom we interact (or think we interact)?

2. What tensions between aristocracy and democracy emerge through word choices? Does the speaker's disproportionate language suggest a resentment of democracy's forced equality, theoretical anonymity, and membership among the masses?

3. Compare and contrast Simon and Garfunkel's song version of this poem with the far more gritty version by a young Van Morrison, recorded when he sang for a band called Them.

4. How does Robinson use Richard Cory as an unknowable presence? How is the poem an irresolvable mystery?

Looking Back and Ahead

1. At the Text Enrichment Site, go to "Literary and Film Analysis" under Chapter 15. There you will find information on analyzing poems and songs. Then write your own short analysis and evaluation of a song. You might want to consider one of the existing musical adaptations of "Richard Cory."

Section 3 Problems and Solutions

As a post-secondary student, you are vitally engaged in preparing for your future—most obviously, for your career, but surely no less for your role as a person and citizen. Many of us, young and old, would agree that today's younger generation, on the whole, has encountered different challenges and complexities than those who graduated in the 1960s and 1970s. A Southam News feature of February 2001 consulted a panel of philosophers, ethicists, and religious studies professors for their views of the most pressing issues facing humanity in the next 10 years (Todd). The panel identified major concerns related to the environment, computers, genetic engineering, nuclear arms, and nationalism, along with rising social dilemmas—an increasing gap between rich and poor, immoderate work patterns, and a perceived increase in callousness. They all pointed, as well, to an issue we discussed in our introduction to Section 2 of this Reader, colliding values and beliefs: "With globalism and immigration bringing cultures closer together, whose ethical system will we follow?" (Todd).

A number of such concerns were raised by writers in the previous section of the Reader, but in this section, which deals again with the main themes we have visited in Reader Sections 1 and 2, you will find writers using language specifically to outline problems, to weigh choices, to assert their own values, and in some cases to propose solutions. Rhetorically, the following selections relate to the aims and methods discussed under "Critical Analysis and Evaluation" (Chapter 14) and, to some extent, under "Argumentation" (Chapter 16), so it would be a good idea to review those parts of the Rhetoric. Again, you will not find simple or incontestable answers—but you will, most likely, come to appreciate the importance of analytical and argumentative skills in preparing for a future of complexity and challenge.

In this section of the Reader, the expository purpose of Section 2 has intensified to a greater insistence on arguing an analytical position. In other words, the argumentative edge of Section 3 is somewhat more pronounced. This raises a concern with what Wayne Booth calls "the advertiser's stance" (p. 491) which occurs, says Booth, when the writer uses various unfair and unreasonable appeals to convince the reader. As you work with the following essays, consider in what ways they have or have not avoided this unsound stance.

Work Cited

Todd, Douglas. "Our Top 10 Moral Issues." *Edmonton Journal* 11 Feb. 2001: E5.

Michael Downey "Canada's 'Genocide'" chronicles the Sixties Scoop adoptions in which thousands of Native children were removed from their biological homes and relocated into White families by the Canadian government. Downey discusses the impact of one such child seizure on the life of Carla Williams, who suffered not only the trauma of being separated from her parents, home, community, and cultural identity, but also severe abuse under the custody of her adoptive family. Downey suggests that the collective impact of separating thousands of Native children from their homes and cultures was an effectively genocidal practice. While the Canadian government has offered an official apology for the infamous abuses suffered in residential schools and dedicated funds toward healing strategies for individuals and communities, no such apology or action plan has been proffered to the children, families, and communities of the Sixties Scoop. Canada's First Nations people still experience disproportionately high rates of adoption.

The article originally appeared April 26, 1999, in *Maclean's* magazine, a long-running periodical that has been offering news, opinion, and analysis on topical Canadian issues—from survival during the Depression to the current obesity epidemic—for over 100 years.

Canada's "Genocide": Thousands Taken from Their Homes Need Help

1   Carla Williams was 4 when the authorities knocked on the door and took the terrified Manitoba native youngster away from her parents forever. It was 1968, and Williams was thrust into a white society where nobody spoke her native tongue. Three years of cultural confusion later, she was adopted by a family that then moved to Holland. There the young girl was permitted no contact with her grieving parents back in Canada. Subjected to emotional and sexual abuse, she had three babies by the age of 16—two of them, she says, by her adoptive father, and one was given up for adoption. Finally, after her descent into alcohol, drugs and prostitution, the Dutch government received an official request from Canada to have her returned. Williams left Amsterdam in 1989 at the age of 25, shouting, "I'm going home!" She arrived back in Canada too late to meet the parents she had barely known: after the removal of three of their children, her native mother and father committed suicide.

2   Williams, now a saleswoman in Winnipeg, has had considerable success in turning her life around. But a new study being prepared for release next week sheds light on a tragically disruptive program that saw thousands of young natives removed from their families for three decades starting in the 1950s. Children from native communities in British Columbia, Alberta and Ontario as well as Manitoba were routinely shipped to non-native foster homes or adoptive families far from their homes. Most of the 3,000 from Manitoba alone and many from the other provinces went to the United States, where placement agencies often received fees in the $15,000 to $20,000 range from the adoptive parents. One Manitoba judge has branded the child seizures "cultural genocide," and they do seem to fall well within

the United Nations post–Second World War definition of genocide, which includes "forcibly transferring children of [one] group to another group."

3   Now, after almost a year of hearings, a report will be delivered this week to the funding body, a joint committee of aboriginal groups and a unique partnership of four Ontario government ministries. Prepared by an aboriginal social agency, Native Child and Family Services of Toronto, and Toronto-based consultants Stevenato and Associates and Janet Budgell, the report is expected to examine the history of what authorities called the "apprehensions" of native children, which continued into the early 1980s. The practice is sometimes referred to as the Sixties Scoop because the numbers peaked during that decade.

4   The seizures were carried out by child welfare agencies that insisted they were acting in the children's best interest—simply moving them into a better environment than they were getting in their native parents' home. Forced apprehensions of native children in fact began up to five generations earlier with the creation of residential schools, which functioned more as alternative parenting institutions than educational facilities. Those strict boarding schools effectively incarcerated native children for 10 months of the year.

5   Unfortunately, many of the students returned from residential schools as distant, angry aliens, lacking emotional bonds with their own families. Having missed out on nurturing family environments, they were ill prepared to show affection or relate to their own children when they became parents—as most did at an early age. Then, in the 1950s and 1960s, the federal government delegated responsibility for First Nations health, welfare and educational services to the provinces, while retaining financial responsibility for natives. With guaranteed payments from Ottawa for each child apprehended, the number of First Nations children made wards of the state skyrocketed. In 1959, only one per cent of Canadian children in custody were native; a decade later the number had risen to 40 per cent, while aboriginals made up less than four per cent of the population.

6   Ultimately, it became clear that the seizures were doing terrible damage to uncounted numbers of young natives. "It was perhaps—perhaps—done with the best of intentions," says David Langtry, current assistant deputy minister of Manitoba's child and family services. "But once it became recognized that it was the wrong thing to do, changes were made to legislation." A process introduced in 1988, he says, assures that an aboriginal child removed from a family will be placed in a new home according to strict priorities, turning to a non-native placement only as a last resort.

7   As previous investigations in other provinces have shown, the Sixties Scoop adoptions were rarely successful and many ended with children committing suicide. The new Ontario report will undoubtedly refer to formal repatriation programs already in place in Manitoba and British Columbia—as well as Australia, where there was a similar seizure of aboriginals—with a view to helping others return to Canada, find their roots and locate their families. The study will also set the stage for new programs aimed at healing the collective native pain and perhaps, in time, the deep-rooted anger.

8   Individual stories of the Sixties Scoop paint a heart-wrenching picture. Sometimes, whole families of status and nonstatus Indian or Metis children were separated from each other, never to meet again. Names were changed, often several times. They were shipped thousands of kilometres from their people and denied contact with their parents, siblings or communities or information about their heritage or culture. Some were enslaved, abused and raped. And no Canadian body has ever officially taken responsibility, or apologized, for the policies.

9   *Maclean's* has learned that the new report will be soft on blame but frank about the extent of the tragedy still gripping native parents and plaguing the thousands of survivors who lost their names, language, families, childhood and, above all, their identities. It will seek faster access to adoption records to speed repatriation. However, Sylvia Maracle, a member of the committee of the umbrella group that funded the study, says repatriations are only a partial remedy. "We need to bring them back into the native circle," she says, "in a way that is comfortable for them." The decision to commission the study recognized the bitterness felt by all native people, says Maracle, who is Mohawk. "We are grieving," she says, "we are angry and we must do something to at least start the healing and in a holistic way."

10   Joan Muir would agree. "I was taken away from my family because my grandparents were alcoholics," says the Vancouver resident, now 33, "and placed with adoptive parents who were—as social workers had noted on my records prior to adoption—known alcoholics and racists." Muir says she was raised to be ashamed of her native status. "It just hit me a couple of years ago, that it's OK not to hide it anymore," she says. "Now that I'm away from my adoptive parents, I'm allowed to be native."

11   The report will also refer to the tragic story of Richard Cardinal, a northern Alberta Metis forcibly removed from his family at age 4. Over the next 13 years, he was placed in 28 homes and institutions. In one, he was beaten with a stick for wetting the bed. Another provided a bed just two feet wide in a flooded basement. One entire Christmas Day, while his adoptive family celebrated the holiday, Cardinal was kept outside in the cold, staring in. His suicide attempts began when he was 9. At his 16th foster home, aged 17, he nailed a board between two trees and hanged himself.

12   Toronto social worker Kenn Richard, a coauthor of the report, says it outlines the history of the seizures through the words of people who experienced them firsthand. But he feels strongly that the practice was only one part of a long history of wrongheaded and disastrous policies towards Canada's native population. "It's the legacy of child welfare in this country," says Richard, "that we have dysfunctional families and a deep anger among aboriginals."

13   In the late '70s, Manitoba's native leaders rebelled against the permanent loss of their children. "This was cultural genocide," concluded Manitoba family court Judge Edwin Kimelman, called on to investigate the seizures in 1982. "You took a child from his or her specific culture and you placed him into a foreign culture without any [counselling] assistance to the family which had the child. There's something drastically and basically wrong with that." That year, Manitoba

banned out-of-province adoptions of native children and overhauled its child welfare system. Native child welfare authorities were established across Canada.

14   The task of repairing the damage is still under way. Lizabeth Hall, who grew up in a native family and now heads the B.C. repatriation program, was shocked at the loss of identity among those removed from their native community. "People have called and asked, 'Can you just tell me what kind of Indian I am?'" says Hall. "It made me cry. I'd like Canadians to know what happened and why. Non-natives always 'justify' their protection of natives; they don't realize the racism in that."

15   At a 1992 B.C. government hearing into the Sixties Scoop seizures, a First Nations elder addressed Canada's history of "protecting" aboriginals. "For 30 years," said the elder, "generations of our children, the very future of our communities, have been taken away from us. Will they come home as our leaders, knowing the power and tradition of their people? Or will they come home broken and in pain, not knowing who they are, looking for the family that died of a broken heart?" Those are questions that new repatriation and education programs could help answer.

For Further Thinking

1. Is the title of this article apt? How does the use of the word "genocide" inform your expectations of the article? What effect do the quotation marks around the word "genocide" produce? Does "Canada's 'Genocide'" (the title and the article) suggest that the removal of Native children from Native homes during the second half of the twentieth century is a rare blight in Canada's history?

2. A few years ago in a Canadian newspaper, a young Native man wrote that he had been adopted by a White family who were kind and loving. He wanted to protest the popular idea—repugnant to him—that every adoption of a Native by non-Natives is genocide. In her one-woman play *Moonlodge*, Blackfoot writer-actor Margot Kane portrays with deep affection the Ukrainian woman who adopted her. Some adoptions occur with full consent of the biological parents who remain welcome to visit their child. Is there a danger of all adoption of Native children being painted with the same brush? From your own experience or from research, decide what you think about coming to generalized judgements on this question.

3. In 1998, one year prior to the publication of "Canada's 'Genocide,'" the Canadian government offered a Statement of Reconciliation, which admitted culpability for the creation and administration of residential schools and apologized to those who suffered abuses within them. No such apology has been offered regarding the Sixties Scoop adoptions. Would such an apology be empowering to victims of the adoptions?

4. In "Canada's 'Genocide'" Downey looks toward future "programs aimed at healing the collective native pain." Have gains been made since the publication of his article in this respect? What sources would you use to do a follow-up on Downey's article?

5. In an April 2007 speech in Vancouver, former Canadian governor general Adrienne Clarkson pursued the theme that "we are all treaty people." By this she meant to remind non-Natives that legal and ethical agreements recognized an exchange of lands for rights and payments. Do you think such a reminder was necessary? Explain.

6. Will Ferguson, like his brother Ian (*Village of the Small Houses*), grew up next to a Native reserve, experiencing far more interaction with Native people than the typical Canadian. In his book

Why I Hate Canadians, Will Ferguson describes Native peoples as "our *burakumin*, our Third Solitude" (117), a "caste created by fiat" (118). Ferguson's view supports the claim of genocide or at least attempted genocide: "In Canada, one of the wealthiest most prosperous countries in the world, we have created an entire, racially segregated subclass, our very own Third World" (118). Do some research into the history of Native peoples from contact onward. Having done that, consider that when Canadians are polled on issues of uppermost importance to them, the condition of Native communities and relationships to those communities never seem to emerge as significant to those polled. What conclusions should we draw from this?

Looking Back and Ahead

1. Both Downey's "Canada's 'Genocide'" and Malissa Phung's "Building Blocks" (Chapter 9, p. 136) discuss historically racist policies administered by the Canadian government. However, Downey's article about the Sixties Scoop adoptions is a factual report whereas Phung's article about the Chinese Head Tax policies is a factual account framed by a personal response. What reasons might each of these authors cite for making these rhetorical choices?

2. Read "Saskatchewan's Indian People—Five Generations" in Chapter 11 (p. 166). How does the timing of the "scoop" described in Downey's article tie in with the historical stages of Native experience reported by Pat Deiter-McArthur?

3. Read "Not like the Movie" (p. 405), a memoir of the St. James Church massacre in Cape Town, South Africa, an attack that the Azanian People's Liberation Army (APLA) attributed to an act of war against apartheid. Although Downey's article refers to a program of adoption of Native children into White homes, this program operated with the tacit idea that a White home is better than a reserve home, reserves being thought of as part of Canada's Third World. Within Native circles in this country, it is a well-accepted belief that the Canadian Department of Indian Affairs with its reserve system gave South Africa its "inspiration for apartheid" (Moses 140). How do you explain a policy of marginalizing people into what writer Harold Cardinal called "prisons of grass" on one hand and, with the Sixties Scoop, taking their children away for adoption into "mainstream" homes on the other?

Susan McClelland   This article, from *Maclean's*, February 22, 1999, examines extreme measures some men are taking to achieve the "beefcake look." Example and interview, statistical reports on steroid use, and cause-effect analysis are combined to assemble various explanations for why men feel compelled to look muscular. McClelland also considers consequences and suggests alternatives.

The Lure of the Body Image

1 The year Ralph Heighton of Pictou, N.S., turned 30, he decided to lose some weight. At five-foot-nine, pushing 210 lbs., Heighton says when he stood in front of the mirror, he knew something wasn't working. He joined the YMCA in the nearby town of New Glasgow, started taking nightly walks and altered his diet, cutting out the late-night pizzas and pitas with spiced beef, onions and sauce. Now, at 34, Heighton fluctuates around the 185-lb. mark and has converted one of the three

bedrooms in his new two-storey home into a gym, complete with weights and a tattered heavy bag bound by duct tape. Heighton, a wildlife technician with Nova Scotia's Department of Fisheries, says he has achieved his goal of feeling better. Though still single, he says bashfully that he thinks he has never looked as good—which was one of his key reasons for getting in shape. "The magazines sort of force this body image on you of what it means to be a physically fit person," says Heighton. "Whether we want to admit it or not, this image is what we want to look like."

2   The idealized male body image nowadays is beefy and muscled, as epitomized in the Calvin Klein underwear advertisements showcasing the bulging pecs and rippling abdomen of Antonio Sabato Jr. And like Heighton, hundreds of thousands of men in Canada are flocking to gyms and health clubs in the quest to look buffed and toned. There are signs, however, that some men are taking the image to extremes. Statistics on steroid use show an alarming number of male teenagers across the country are using the substance illegally simply to put on muscle. Men are increasingly being diagnosed with eating disorders. And plastic surgeons report a general increase in men seeking their services to improve their appearance. "This is an early warning," said New York City author Michelangelo Signorile, whose book *Life Outside* chronicles the history of body image among homosexual men. "This 'cult of masculinity' isn't just in gay culture as so many like to believe. It envelops the entire culture. It is an obsessive devotion to an ideal."

3   Although worshipping the body is hardly new, the emphasis on the beefcake look has evolved gradually in North America over the past 100 years. Both Signorile and Brian Pronger, a philosopher in the Faculty of Physical Education at the University of Toronto, say that many men, straight and gay, adopted a more masculine appearance after the Oscar Wilde trials in the 1890s associated effeminate behaviour with homosexuality in the popular mind. Pronger and Signorile also say that women's suffrage and, later, the modern feminist movement caused men to covet a larger appearance as a means of defending men's status. "As women take up more space in traditionally masculine places," says Pronger, "some men feel compelled to take up more in order to maintain their position."

4   It takes a lot of sweating and spending to achieve a hard-body look. According to a 1995 report published by the Canadian Fitness and Lifestyle Research Institute, men spend more than twice as much as women in all categories related to fitness, including clothing, exercise equipment, membership fees and instruction. Brad Whitehead, who works for one of the largest distributors of creatine, a controversial supplement that increases the energy capacity in muscles, says sales have increased 130 per cent since 1997.

5   Calvin Klein and other underwear merchants are not alone in using men with buffed bodies to sell products. Other advertisers include Coca-Cola, Nike and Marlboro, which has introduced a bulkier version of its original "Marlboro Man." As well, magazine stands now offer dozens of titles devoted to health, fitness and muscle, tantalizing readers with snappy headlines like "Great abs in eight weeks." Their pages are adorned with ads featuring big, bulky men selling muscle-building supplements.

6   One of the sad consequences of the push towards a hyper-masculine image is that it can rarely be obtained without the use of potentially harmful drugs. A 1993 study conducted for the Canadian Centre for Ethics in Sport concluded that four per cent of males aged 11 to 18—as many as 83,000 young Canadians—used anabolic steroids in 1992 and 1993. In the study, which involved 16,169 high-school and elementary students, one in five reported that they knew someone who was taking anabolic steroids. Among the reasons given for their use, nearly half said it was to change their physical appearance. That contrasted starkly with previously held notions that steroids were used mostly to increase athletic performance, says Paul Melia, the Centre's director of education. "The reality for most of these young men, even if they do get on a regimen of weight train-ing, is that they are not going to look like these picture boys," said Melia. "And sustaining that look is a full-time job."

7   In a downtown Toronto gym, Mike, a 32-year-old former bodybuilder and weight lifter and a longtime user of anabolic steroids, says as many as four out of five of the 18- to 25-year-old men using the facility are on the illegal drugs. When he started using steroids 16 years ago, Mike says, he was part of an elite group of men who took them for competitive reasons. "Today it is for the body image," he says. "And these kids stack—they add steroid upon steroid, thinking they are going to get a certain look. They take this stuff, go out to night clubs, get drunk and mix everything together. It's all for image."

8   Mike says one result of working out seriously can be that, no matter how big their muscles get, men start thinking they are still not big enough. It is a phenomenon dis-turbingly similar to cases of eating disorders among women who believe they are too big, no matter how thin they get. Maintaining a hard body takes not only a regimen of heavy workouts, but also a dedication to eating right and at times dieting to avoid gaining fat, says Mike. And psychologists across the country say one result of those self-imposed pressures is an increased incidence of eating disorders among men. According to Dr. Howard Steiger, a clinical psychologist and director of the eating disorder program at Douglas Hospital in Montreal, surveys have shown that five to 10 per cent of eating disorder sufferers are men. He says most people with eating disorders have unstable self-esteem. He also says there are increasing sociocultural pressures on men to connect their self-esteem to body image. While there are no new national figures, specialists in many centres say that bulimia nervosa, characterized by binge eating and vomiting, is on the rise in men. "What you find," says Steiger, "are people who diet too much, who condition too much, and what you are doing is setting up this pressure of hunger—a constant state of undernutrition that even-tually leads to bulimic-type eating patterns."

9   In addition to steroid use and erratic eating behaviour, John Semple, secre-tary treasurer of the Canadian Society of Plastic Surgeons, says he believes men are increasingly having plastic surgery to alter their body image. Dr. Bill Papanastasiou, a plastic surgeon in Montreal, estimates that only 10 per cent of his patients were male when he opened his practice 13 years ago. Today, it is as high as 15 to 20 per cent. In Halifax, plastic surgeon Dr. Kenneth Wilson says one

of the most common surgeries he does for men is liposuction. For Nathan Estep, a 27-year-old from Detroit who spent $1,800 in Pontiac, Mich., in 1997 to have liposuction done on his waistline, the surgery has transformed his life. Since he was 10, Estep was a constant dieter, at times bulimic, and for many years tried to control his weight using diet drugs including Dexedrine, ephedrine and laxatives. Today, Estep says he can walk proudly, with his shirt off and with no hint of any fat from his childhood returning. "I was a fat kid—I had fat in the wrong places," he says. "The first thing I did after the liposuction was go to the beach, take my shirt off and eat a pint of Häagen-Dazs. I feel like a new man."

10   According to Pronger, who has been studying the philosophy of physical fitness for five years, a person with a hard, fit body considers it a signal of discipline and a capacity for hard work. "When you see somebody who is overweight," he says, "often the response is how did they let themselves get like that." The mistaken presumption, he adds, is that the person doesn't have the discipline to be a productive citizen. One of the solutions, says Pronger, is to teach children to look at body images in the same critical way they are told to consider art and literature—to be able to recognize what has merit. "If we were doing the same with physical education, people could learn to have a different reaction to these extreme body images," he says. "They would say, 'Hey, I don't want to be part of this pressure to fall in love with a highly commercialized image.'"

For Further Thinking

1. Do you think McClelland's article overstates the problem of steroid abuse among boys and men? Explain.

2. Critics such as Jean Kilbourne, author of *Deadly Persuasion* (1999) and her film series *Killing Us Softly* (1979–2000), have pointed out how advertising presents distorted images of women, stressing two myths: the sex goddess or the perfect homemaker. The *Maclean's* article states, "One of the sad consequences of the push towards a hyper-masculine image is that it can rarely be obtained." Is the unrealistic portrayal of men in advertising as damaging as the portrayal of women?

3. How effectively do you feel the article has used studies and statistics?

4. What do you think of McClelland's suggested alternatives and solutions?

Looking Back and Ahead

1. McClelland quotes Dr. Howard Steiger as saying that 5 to 10 percent of those suffering eating disorders are men, and there is widespread professional opinion that bulimia nervosa is on the rise in men. See Leanna Rutherford's "An Anorexic's Recovery," Chapter 8 (p. 120), for more information on eating disorders.

2. McClelland's article ends with reference to the dangers of falling in love "with a highly commercialized image." What possible connection can you find between this article and George Orwell's "Politics and the English Language" (p. 471)?

Amy Willard Cross   The post-war version of the American dream is that anybody willing to work hard—or with the good sense to marry a hard-working man—can achieve material success: a nice home in the suburbs, an automobile, an annual vacation, and a gleaming, well-provisioned refrigerator. Today, many are disillusioned with this dream. "Isn't there more to life?" is a common query of those contemplating the daily grind. Many feel trapped inside the rat race—as though they are working toward goals that were never their own. Is it time to re-evaluate our priorities? How can we measure what we've gained against what we've lost? Do we need a new dream? Perhaps North American angst is simply one trapping of an over-indulged society, one that always pines for more while multitudes struggle to obtain the barest necessities of life.

In 1899 American economist Thorstein Veblen published *The Theory of the Leisure Class.* The book provides a critique of modern (Victorian) consumerism and of what Veblen defined as the new Leisure Class. In "Life in the Stopwatch Lane," Amy Willard Cross also critiques modern life and defines a new demographic that she dubs "the Busy Class," or for short, "the Busies." She asks, "How has replacing free time with more billable hours affected society?"

Cross is the author of two books: *The Summer House: A Tradition of Leisure* and *Summer in America*. Both books are about retreating to the slower rhythms of cottage country.

Life in the Stopwatch Lane

1   If time is money, the rates have skyrocketed and you probably can't afford it. North Americans are suffering a dramatic time shortage since demand greatly exceeds supply. In fact, a recent survey revealed that people lost about 10 hours of leisure per week between 1973 and 1987. Maybe you were too busy to notice.

2   Losing that leisure leaves a piddling 16.6 hours to do whatever you want, free of work, dishwashing or car-pooling. In television time, that equals a season of 13 *thirtysomething* episodes, plus $3\frac{1}{2}$ reruns. Hardly enough time to write an autobiography or carry on an affair.

3   How has replacing free time with more billable hours affected society? It has created a new demographic group: the Busy Class—who usurped the Leisure Class. Easy to recognize, members of the Busy Class constantly cry to anyone listening, "I'm *soooooo* busy." So busy they can't call their mother or find change for a panhandler. Masters of doing two things at once, they eke the most out of time. They dictate while driving, talk while calculating, entertain guests while nursing, watch the news while pumping iron. Even business melts into socializing—people earn their daily bread while they break it.

4   In fact, the Busies must make lots of bread to maintain themselves in the standard of busy-ness to which they've become accustomed. To do that, they need special, expensive stuff. Stuff like call waiting, which lets them talk to two people at once. Stuff like two-faced watches, so they can do business in two time zones at once. Neither frenzied executives nor hurried housewives dare leave the house without their "book"—leather-bound appointment calendars thick as bestsellers. Forget hi-fis or racing cars, the new talismans of overachievers also work:

coffee-makers that brew by alarm; remote-controlled ignitions; or car faxes. Yet, despite all these time-efficient devices, few people have time to spare.

5   That scarcity has changed how we measure time. Now it's being scientifically dissected into smaller and smaller pieces. Thanks to digital clocks, we know when it's 5:30 (and calculate we'll be home in three hours, eight minutes). These days lawyers can reason in 1/10th of an hour increments; they bill every six minutes. This to-the-minute precision proves time's escalating value.

6   Time was, before the advent of car phones and digital clocks, we scheduled two kinds of time: time off and work hours. Not any more. Just as the Inuit label the infinite varieties of snow, the Busy Class has identified myriad subtleties of free time and named them. Here are some textbook examples of the new faces of time:

7   *Quality time*. For those working against the clock, the quality of time spent with loved ones supposedly compensates for quantity. This handy concept absolves guilt as quickly as rosary counting. So careerist couples dine à deux once a fortnight. Parents bond by reading kids a story after nanny fed and bathed them. When pressed for time, nobody wastes it by fighting about bad breath or unmade beds. People who spend quality time with each other view their relationships through rose-coloured glasses. And knowing they've created perfect personal lives lets the Busy Class work even harder—guilt-free.

8   *Travel time*. With an allowance of 16.6 hours of fun, the Busy Class watches time expenditures carefully. Just like businesses do while making bids, normal people calculate travel time for leisure activities. If two tram rides away, a friendly squash game loses out. One time-efficient woman even formulated a mathematical theorem: fun per mile quotient. Before accepting any social invitation, she adds up travel costs, figures out the time spent laughing, drinking and eating. If the latter exceeds the former, she accepts. It doesn't matter who asks.

9   *Downtime*. Borrowed from the world of heavy equipment and sleek computers, downtime is a professional-sounding word meaning the damn thing broke, wait around until it's fixed. Translated into real life, downtime counts as neither work nor play, but a maddening no-man's land where *nothing* happens! Like lining up for the ski-lift, or commuting without a car phone, or waiting a while for the mechanic's diagnosis. Beware: people who keep track of their downtime probably indulge in less than 16 hours of leisure.

10   *Family time*. In addition to 60-hour weeks, aerobics and dinner parties, some people make time for their children. When asked to brunch, a young couple will reply, "We're sorry but that's our family time." A variant of quality time, it's Sunday afternoon between lunch and the Disney Hour when nannies frequent Filipino restaurants. In an effort to entertain their children without exposure to sex and violence, the family attends craft fairs, animated matinees or tree-tapping demonstrations. There, they converge with masses of family units spending time alone with the kids. After a noisy, sticky afternoon, parents gladly punch the clock come Monday.

11   *Quiet time.* Overwhelmed by their schedules, some people try to recapture the magic of childhood when they watched clouds for hours on end. Sophisticated grown-ups have rediscovered the quiet time of kindergarten days. They unplug the phone (not the answering machine), clutch a book and try not to think about work. But without teachers to enforce it, quiet doesn't last. The clock ticks too loudly. As a computer fanatic said, after being entertained at 16 megahertz, sitting still to watch a sunset pales by comparison.

12   As it continues to increase in value, time will surely divide into even smaller units. And people will share only the tiniest amounts with each other. Hey, brother, can you spare a minute? Got a second? A nanosecond?

For Further Thinking

1. What, if any, sources does Cross cite in "Life in the Stopwatch Lane?" How does her decision to reference, or not to reference sources, affect her argument?

2. The definitions of "work" and "leisure" have changed significantly in the last 50 years, especially in regards to child-rearing, and for no-one as much as women. Elaborate.

3. Who is Cross's audience? Does her article speak to Canadians across different ethnic and class boundaries?

4. How does the North American workweek compare to that of other countries?

5. The Amish define two kinds of time, "slow" and "fast." Slow time refers to the phases of the day or the cycles of the season. Fast time refers to clock time. What do you think is the purpose and possible effect of this distinction? Can you think of other people who differentiate between time in a similar manner?

6. Cross presents a problem but no defined solution. What do you believe is needed to free us from life in the stopwatch lane?

Looking Back and Ahead

1. Both "Life in the Stopwatch Lane" and "Subtraction by Addition: When More Adds Up to Less" (below) criticize growing social trends toward accumulating wealth at the expense of other values. Does one piece provide a more exacting critique than the other? How?

2. Compare "Life in the Stopwatch Lane" with "The Doomsday Machines" by John Markoff (p. 505). How are they thematically different and/or similar? How does each writer's tone affect the seriousness of his or her message?

Carey Goldberg Since the Second World War, North Americans have grown up in an era of unprecedented wealth and material affluence. The Baby Boomers dropped their spending money on Beatles records and Coca-Cola. Generation Xers must have bottled water, Ikea furniture, and jogging strollers. Generation Y flaunts iPods, Xboxes, flip-phones, and flip-flops. Is it any small sign of our times that these generations are defined and identified largely as target markets?

Not everybody is able to make ends meet, and the gap between the rich and the poor is steadily widening. But by international standards we are awash in belongings. SUVs, DVDs, lip gloss, camera-phones, plush toys, patio sets, hair dryers, designer jeans, snowboards, drum kits, treadmills, Christmas lights, throw pillows: it's no wonder that one of today's fastest-growing industries is storage. Even your average suburban house pet is likely to have more possessions than one could count on both hands.

So why aren't we, and our pets, wildly happy? Anxiety, depression, obesity, and heavy debt-loads are as ubiquitous as hand-held massagers, Prozac, processed food, and limited-time-only credit card offers. In this article from the *Boston Globe,* writer Carey Goldberg reports on the findings of researchers in the field of emotional wellness and the effects materialism has on general well-being.

Subtraction by Addition: When More Adds Up to Less

1   As a Lexington, Mass., psychologist and couples therapist, Aline Zoldbrod is all too familiar with this picture: a husband and wife no longer connect.

2   They are so exhausted from the pursuit of "nice things"—a big house, private school for the kids, fancy cars—that they are time-starved and depleted. Life is luxurious but unsatisfying and simply no fun.

3   Zoldbrod said it is not only her clinical experience that tells her such clients are on the wrong track, it's a growing body of research.

4   Using statistics and psychological tests, researchers are nailing down what clerics and philosophers have preached for millenniums: materialism is bad for the soul. Only, in the new formulation, materialism is bad for your emotional well-being.

5   In recent years, researchers have reported an ever-growing list of downsides to getting and spending—damage to relationships and self-esteem; a heightened risk of depression and anxiety; less time for what the research indicates truly makes people happy, like family, friendship and engaging work. And maybe even headaches.

6   "Consumer culture is continually bombarding us with the message that materialism will make us happy," said Tim Kasser, a psychology professor at Knox College in Illinois who has led some of the recent work. "What this research shows is that that's not true."

7   The research is more nuanced than that, of course. For people who are living paycheque to paycheque, more money unquestionably brings greater well-being. And for the comfortable, a raise or a new purchase can certainly feel good—for a little while, anyway. Also, economic research indicates that a hunger for money can motivate people to perform better and even more creatively.

8   There is also a question of cause and effect. Feelings of insecurity incline people toward materialistic values, the research suggests, and that insecurity can also lead to relationship troubles and other problems associated with a materialistic lifestyle.

9   But Kasser argues that when people turn to material things to feel better, they compound the problem, because they seek experiences that "don't do a very good job of meeting their psychological needs."

10   Researchers generally measure materialism through surveys (How much do you agree or disagree with statements like "The things I own say a lot about how I'm doing in life"?) or by statistically analyzing test subjects' ratings of different values in terms of their importance.

11   Ed Diener, a University of Illinois psychology professor and happiness expert, said in an e-mail that he has found that "those who value material success more than they value happiness are likely to experience almost as many negative moods as positive moods, whereas those who value happiness over material success are likely to experience considerably more pleasant moods and emotions than unpleasant moods and emotions."

12   Studies show that poor people who emphasize materialistic goals are especially likely to be unhappy, while in some studies, materialistic rich people show fewer ill effects, presumably because they are meeting more of their goals. But even for the better-off, materialism can create a nagging appetite that can never be satisfied, since no matter how much a person gets, there will always be someone with more.

13   Materialism becomes "a more difficult goal than many," Diener said, "because it is open-ended and goes on forever—we can always want more, which is usually not true of other goals such as friendship. With friends, we have them and enjoy them but usually are not taught that we keep needing more."

14   There's also an opportunity cost to chasing the wrong goals, said Daniel Gilbert, a Harvard psychology professor who focuses on people's flawed ability to predict their emotional reactions. When people spend their effort pursuing material goods in the belief that they will bring happiness, he said, they're ignoring other, more effective routes to happiness.

15   So why is materialism so common? The trouble is that the error is subtle. "If it were the case that money made us totally miserable, we'd figure out we were wrong" to pursue it, Gilbert said. But "it's wrong in a more nuanced way. We think money will bring lots of happiness for a long time, and actually it brings a little happiness for a short time."

16   Some research has also found that when people focus on money, status and things, they are more likely to treat other people as objects, to have shorter, shallower friendships, and to feel competitive rather than cooperative with others, Kasser said.

17   Boston College professor Juliet Schor warns that the danger of materialism extends to children as well. Her study of metropolitan Boston school children, published in 2004 in her book *Born to Buy*, found that the more consumerist children became, the likelier they were to suffer from low self-esteem, depression and anxiety. They also became more prone to headaches and stomachaches.

18   Schor said her research shows that parents can "immunize" their children against materialistic values by reducing young people's exposure to media, eating dinner together—particularly home-cooked food—limiting junk food, and teaching money management through allowances.

19   Whether warnings from social scientists will make a dent in popular consuming values remains to be seen. Kasser compared the expanding pool of data on the potential harm of materialism to the data on lung cancer caused by smoking. Preachers had long called smoking "the devil's work," he said, but it was only when the cancer connection was proved scientifically that smoking really began to wane.

20   Gilbert of Harvard, however, is skeptical. "Let's try. Let's give them the data. Let's shout it from the mountaintops," he said. "But let's not be too surprised when all the people in the valley nod their heads knowingly and then go on to covet a Porsche and a new home and tickets to the Super Bowl."

For Further Thinking

1. Interview an older person about what kinds of changes he or she notices in the number of possessions a person "needs" now in comparison to "back in their day."

2. "Consumer culture is continually bombarding us with the message that materialism will make us happy," says Tim Kasser of Knox College. What examples of this message can you think of? Through what types of media are you personally most likely to be bombarded with consumerist messages?

3. What is the opposite of consumer culture? How could an anti-materialistic lifestyle be cultivated in today's society? Is it possible? Is it desirable?

4. Among the researchers and scientists Goldberg cites is Ed Deiner, a "psychology professor and happiness expert." Is researching "happiness" and "well-being" a viable scientific pursuit?

5. After the September 11, 2001, attack on the World Trade Center (dubbed "9–11" by the media), American President George W. Bush and New York Mayor Rudolph Giuliani both adjured New Yorkers and Americans to show their resistance to "terrorism" by continuing to shop. What do you think of this?

6. Are capitalism and democracy the same things? Why or why not?

Looking Back and Ahead

1. Compare Goldberg's "Subtraction by Addition" with Cross's "Life in the Stopwatch Lane" (p. 451) and Richler's "The Seven Deadly Sins Are 'In' and Proud of It" (p. 482). Which authors rely heavily on sources without furnishing their own opinions on the subject of consumption? Who strikes a strong ethical stance against excessive consumption? Which authorial position is most effective to you as a reader?

Sarah Schmidt   Observing that tuition fees over nine years have risen on average by 126 percent—far more rapidly than inflation or the minimum wage—Schmidt finds "a growing number of middle-class women" who are turning to that oldest of professions to make it through their school years. Drawing upon interviews, Schmidt describes students working in all forms of Canada's off-street prostitution trade, which now accounts for 80 percent of the country's sex trade. Consulting a number of sources, including police detectives, escort service managers, sociologists, and other researchers, she ends by asking whether this practice is unavoidable, as some of her subjects claim.

This article originally appeared in 2000 in the *Globe and Mail*. Since Schmidt presented this problem, educational fees have continued to escalate.

College Girl to Call Girl

1   Stacy is dealing with all the typical end-of-term pressures of university: term-paper angst, exam anxiety, career stress. And by day, she is indeed a typical, perhaps model student, working at her co-op job placement and visiting the library at York University in Toronto to prepare for a career in advertising.

2   But at around eight, most evenings, Stacy heads out to pay the bills.

3   And this 25-year-old, from an upper-middle-class Oakville, Ont., home, doesn't serve up coffee at Starbucks. Though she grew up much like any suburban child of a chartered accountant and a homemaker—bedtime stories, piano lessons, cottage weekends, trips to Disneyland—Stacy now goes out on "calls," as many as six times a night, condoms in hand, to pleasure clients as a prostitute.

4   Most men expect intercourse. A few are satisfied with oral sex. The odd one—either "really drunk or really lonely," she says—just wants to talk. But she doesn't call herself a hooker, and she doesn't wear high heels, fishnet stockings or short skirts. As a student "escort," Stacy dresses like any college girl going out to the movies or a bar. That's the way the men like it.

5   For a growing number of middle-class youths graduating this spring, prostitution isn't seen as a shameful trap, but as a means of making it through the lean student years on the way to a respectable career. Escorts like Stacy are dispatched by agencies to upscale hotel rooms, private homes and even offices. She may turn tricks, but in her own mind she is far away from the streets and alleys and whores desperate for $20 for a fix. She serves mostly professionals, who can afford the house call.

6   "You're looking at a very different kind of situation in the year 2000. Most people don't know what prostitution looks like. People have no clue," says sex-trade researcher John Lowman, a professor of criminology at Simon Fraser University in Vancouver. "What we have is a class-based system of prostitution. Just like you have a hierarchy of food services, you have a hierarchy of sex services."

7   Over the last nine years, tuition fees in Canada have risen on average by 126 per cent, far more rapidly than inflation and the minimum wage. About

half of the student population graduates with an average debt load of $25,000, up from $8,000 in 1990.

8   Off-street prostitution has experienced a similar explosion, and many Canadian cities have cashed in by charging annual licensing fees to "massage parlours," "escort agencies" and "encounter counsellors." Researchers estimate that off-street prostitution now comprises approximately 80 percent of Canada's sex trade. And students work in every part of it, from phone sex and stripping up to turning tricks. Ads in weekly newspapers promote "College Cuties," "Adorable Students," "University Girls," and "Hot College Hard Bodies."

9   Fifteen years ago, such ads were unheard of. This year alone, escort ads in the *Montreal Mirror*, for example, have increased by 50 per cent. Since 1995, they've increased five-fold in Victoria's *Monday Magazine*. Even NBC's new megahit, *The West Wing,* has featured a subplot about a Washington, D.C., law student who doubles as a high-priced call girl.

10   For her part, Stacy stumbled into the business three years ago. She knew someone else who was doing it. She was ineligible for student loans because she had defaulted on a previous one, and her stepfather did not want to pitch in. "There's no way a $7-an-hour job is going to pay my rent and tuition. It's not possible."

11   Escort work is far more lucrative: Stacy scores $170 for a one-hour call, $130 for a half-hour (the agency keeps $80 and $70 in each case). On the other hand, it's also a lot more demanding than steaming up a latte while wearing a funny hat.

12   "I remember the first time, I felt sick," recalls Stacy. And it has not gotten much easier with time. "It's not something I want to be doing. I hate it."

13   "People think, 'Students? Not students!'" says sociologist Cecilia Benoit. "They think of sex workers as marginal women, women who are down and out. It ain't like that."

14   The University of Victoria professor, in partnership with the Prostitution Empowerment and Education Society of Victoria, is undertaking a study on the health conditions of the city's off-street sex-trade workers. Findings so far show that some come from troubled backgrounds, but many don't, and their control over working conditions also varies. The danger of assault or murder is certainly lower than it is for street prostitutes.

15   Stacy's boyfriend knows how she pays her bills. "He doesn't like it, but he doesn't make me feel bad about it." Otherwise, she doesn't discuss it with family or friends.

16   Still, Detective Bert O'Hara of the Sexual Exploitation Squad of the Toronto Police Services observes that off-street sex work has "become more socially acceptable." In the past, it occurred in cheap motels; now, it's in private homes and commercial establishments. When Det. O'Hara and his colleagues take a peek inside, they find a range of participants: housewives earning extra cash, students covering their bills, single moms making grocery money.

17   Police continue to focus on the more visible, and cheaper, blue-collar street prostitution, Lowman says, while "men with money can buy sex with impunity." And at this end of the sex trade, both sides get to pretend they're just having a normal social interaction, at least to a degree.

18   Louis, manager of a Montreal escort service, knows students sell well to a particular class of men. His Baby Boomers' Playground serves up "young female students for your utmost fantasy," according to the ad. It's a perfect match: The clients, middle-aged professionals, prefer to mix sex with intelligent talk, not just idle chatter, Louis says.

19   Harvard grad Bennett Singer came to the same conclusion when he investigated the sex industry to research a novel he co-authored about his alma mater. *The Student Body,* to be released in paperback next month, is based on a real-life prostitution scandal that rocked the prestigious Brown College in 1986. "They enjoy an intelligent conversation with a young, refined person with an active mind," says Singer, executive editor of *Time Magazine's* education program.

20   Anna, the daughter of a businesswoman and an academic, was recruited a few years ago to pursue graduate work at one of Canada's leading research institutions, but a financial and personal crisis led her to work as a "high-end call girl." Her clients' educations matched her own.

21   And you can see why they would fall for Anna's quick wit, wholesome face, welcoming eyes and a warm smile. As an escort, she dressed business-casual, "so we could get past the front desk." Her first client, "a virgin who didn't want to be a virgin anymore," made it easier for her to break into the business.

22   "I still felt cold, though," she says, and she never got over that feeling. She just "put on a happy face," even on the night she had seven calls. "I was in total shock. That night was a bit stunning."

23   Still, she says she actually met one man, a broker, whom under different circumstances she would have dated. "My God, you're like a girlfriend," Anna remembers him saying. Unlike most, he "needed a full connection. He was so nice."

24   University of Toronto student and former escort Alicia Maund has heard similar coping strategies from Toronto's sex-trade workers. "They say, 'He's a banker. It's at the King Eddie [a high-class hotel], so it's okay.'"

25   Stacy is a case in point. "To me, there's a difference," she says. "It's not prostitution. I realize in essence everybody's doing the same thing, but I portray myself with a level of respect." That doesn't mean she's all that fond of her regulars, though. "They like to think we have something. I just fake it. I don't want these people to know me. I don't want to be friends with them."

26   Carolyn Bennett shakes her head at Stacy's rationalizations. "Whatever way you look at it, it's prostitution. You still get paid for sex," says the outreach worker for the Halifax-based Stepping Stone Association, a drop-in centre for street prostitutes.

27   John, a general-studies college student and former sex worker in Vancouver, agrees completely. "It's a cop-out," he says. "I don't mind being called a hustler." Before he started hustling, minimum-wage work was "killing my spirit," he says,

and his parents, a nurse and labourer, couldn't really help out. He was saddled with a growing student loan when his girlfriend, also a student, introduced him to the idea of escort work.

28   "It really freaked me out initially. It was unimaginable for me. It seemed horrible, but I was totally desperate for money."

29   John has floated in and out of the massage business since 1996. There, the rules were clear: the rub-down always includes a hand job, but nothing else. But he had more flexibility as an independent. On outcalls, "I charged what I could get away with," he says, which sometimes exceeded $150 an hour.

30   Though he was raised with "traditional values" in the suburbs, John, like many young, educated sex workers, is also a bit of an adventurist. "To have someone project a fantasy onto you, for the purposes of the hour, to see you as the fantasy, that's powerful. I think there's something that draws me in."

31   Nonetheless, at first he didn't tell anyone. "I didn't want to deal with them trying to comfort me, or seeing me differently." Today, most of his friends know, but not his parents. "It would kill my mom. It would kill them both." They're still wrestling with his bisexuality, he says, though he feels like his father should understand. "He's done the worst jobs."

32   John is facing a more immediate decision, though. He's been out of the business for a while, but a friend at the University of British Columbia has a regular client that would like to add John to the equation. "I have to figure that out for myself and my partner. But I could sure use the money."

33   His caution makes sense. For many students, it seems, the real stigma in sex work is tied to how long you do it. Anna only lasted six weeks—her parents intervened when they found out, and gave her "total freedom, total choice and support." She still sounds a bit stunned by the experience. "It was a very healthy choice in a bizarre situation. Had I stayed longer, it would have hurt me," says Anna, now a high-tech professional.

34   Another reason to get out quickly is to minimize the risk of running into former clients in later life. Anna says she would pretend not to recognize them. "People don't deal with the issue well." But she also wishes people would "get over their hang-ups," she says. "It's just a job."

35   Maybe so, but Stacy would rather land that advertising job after graduation and put this kind of work behind her for good. "I don't want to be doing this," she says. "I want to do something for myself. I know I'm an intelligent person."

For Further Thinking

1. Is Schmidt shaping a story simply to fulfill a perceived reader demand for sex and drama, or has there truly been a significant increase in the number of university students turning to off-street prostitution to pay the bills?

2. Review our section on examples in Chapter 10 of the Rhetoric. Does "College Girl to Call Girl" use this kind of organizational approach effectively? Explain.

3. What is your opinion of Schmidt's implication that the students she spoke with reveal self-delusion, as well as a form of snobbery?

4. What is your opinion of Schmidt's research on this article? Is there any point she could or should have pursued more thoroughly?

5. In response to those who look down on prostitutes, certain writers and social critics maintain that the most common form of prostitution is marriage. Morley Callaghan developed this theme in the novel *Such Is My Beloved*, for instance. What does this claim mean, and is there any truth to it?

Looking Back and Ahead

1. Read Douglas Coupland's "The Sun Is Your Enemy," the opening chapter of *Generation X* (p. 390). Do you think any of the attitudes expressed by Stacy and the other student prostitutes in Schmidt's article can legitimately be connected to attitudes of the Baby Boom, Generation X, or Generation Y? Explain.

2. Read "I Sing the Song of My Condo" by Evelyn Lau (p. 395). Lau burst onto Canada's literary scene with *Runaway: Diary of a Street Kid* in which she describes her experiences as a prostitute. Compare Lau's attitudes in her essay to those of Stacy in Schmidt's article. How are they apparently similar? How are they apparently different? What significance do you find in this comparison?

3. Describe Lois's attitude toward sex in Alice Munro's "Thanks for the Ride" (p. 376). Compare her attitude to that of Stacy. Are their attitudes more similar than different? Consider possible reasons for their attitudes.

4. Read George Orwell's essay "Politics and the English Language" (p. 471). When discussing and conducting business, university sex-trade workers apparently use a different sort of language from those "on the street." Could this educated language promote self-delusion? Give examples.

5. For an analysis of Schmidt's essay, see student Valerie Desjardins's essay in Chapter 16 (p. 258). Before reviewing this response by Desjardins, however, try to summarize Schmidt's essay and shape your own critical thesis in response to it. Your thesis should contain your controlling idea and your reason(s) for that idea. You may compare your summary to that of Valerie Desjardins in Chapter 15 (p. 243). Desjardins wrote her critical response (in Chapter 16) after working out her process description and summary (Chapter 15, pp. 242–43).

James Downey Past president of the University of Waterloo, Downey refers to studies reported by Robert Putnam and his co-authors in *Making Democracy Work* (1993). The studies strongly link economic development to the quality of social organizations: "The communities which succeeded socially and economically did not become civil because they were rich, but rather became rich because they were civil." Downey goes on to note "the growing sense in Canada, and Ontario particularly, that this kind of social capital has been depleted." He observes that many people now feel a sense of disenfranchisement, but that it is too easy simply to blame government and business leaders. He argues that it would be "better and truer" if we all accepted responsibility, starting with our universities. He appeals to us to remember that "ideals should lie at the heart of the university." He calls upon university members—particularly those in the humanities and social sciences—to "lead by example" through practising engaged citizenship.

A Liberal Education Is Key to a Civil Society

1   Perhaps the most compelling argument for the value of a liberal education is that, without the application of the knowledge and values it embodies, civil society would be impossible. And without civility the quest for prosperity becomes both aimless and fruitless. If this argument is not being well advanced these days, it may be in part because the usual defenders of liberal education, humanists and social scientists, are not matching rhetoric with example in the community closest to them: the university.

2   Civility, as I am using it, is not a series of grace notes or decorative features added to social interaction. Nor is it a matter of feeling good or being nice towards each other. It is something more fundamental to the workings of successful communities and nations. In *Making Democracy Work,* Robert Putnam has described studies which strongly link economic development to the quality of social organizations in the community. Putnam made an historical analysis of a number of Italian communities and concluded that the ones which succeeded socially and economically did not become civil because they were rich, but rather became rich because they were civil. The best predictors of success, he concluded, were strong traditions of civic engagement as reflected by voter turnout, newspaper readership, and active membership in community organizations and networks that are organized horizontally not hierarchically. Putnam described these aspects of civic engagement as social capital, a type of capital that is augmented, not depleted, by use.

3   There is a growing sense in Canada, and Ontario particularly, that this kind of social capital has been depleted, the result in part of severe and often crude economic measures governments and corporations have taken to balance budgets, contain costs, and increase productivity. Economic disparities have grown, and so too has the sense of disfranchisement many feel. It is easy to be critical of government and business leaders in all this, but it would be better and truer if we all accepted greater responsibility, starting with ourselves, in universities.

4   What is true for communities in general is no less true for universities. The social capital represented by associations and networks of civic engagement is a precondition for academic development and effective governance. An institution that relies on mutual respect and assistance is simply more effective at achieving its ends than an oppositional, distrustful community. Social capital in the collegium, no less than in the community at large, is built from an investment of time and commitment by individuals—people who first make the effort to understand the issues and then take an active, citizen role in their resolution.

5   Many in the academy feel that this capital has been eroded on our campuses in recent years, although they are not agreed on the cause. Some blame it on size, some on the divided loyalties of professors, some on the increased emphasis on individual rights at the expense of collective obligations, and some on chilly climates of one sort or another. Whatever the root cause, it seems clear that mutually reinforcing corporatism and unionism have waxed while the spirit of community and civic engagement has waned. Waned too has any strong sense that universities have a role in society that transcends the simple formula of teaching, research, and service, or any sense at all that our ideals oblige us to become exemplary societies ourselves. Humanists and social scientists have been much better at social deconstruction than at reminding colleagues of the ideals that should lie at the heart of the university.

6   As it bears on the education universities provide, it should be acknowledged that no set of academic disciplines has a monopoly on the knowledge and values of which I speak. A liberal education only makes sense in a modern university and contemporary society if its concepts, principles, and ideals are built into the curricula of all undergraduate programs. Ironically, I believe that engineering and some other professional programs may be doing a better job of this than many programs in arts and social science, which assume they are liberal but in fact are quite narrowly specialized and leave students without a sufficiently broad base of skills, knowledge and outlook for a meaningful engagement as citizens. Which is to say that if we who profess ourselves to be humanists and social scientists wish to defend and promote the ideals of a liberal education in a hard-edged materialist culture, we must be prepared to lead by example, starting with our own universities—the programs we offer, the academic citizenship we practise.

For Further Thinking

1. Would you agree that when today's college students choose courses, the pressure to make prudent career choices takes precedence over personal interest in particular subjects? Must economics always take priority over personal growth and exploration for students?

2. Would you agree that on today's campuses "mutually reinforcing corporatism and unionism have waxed while the spirit of community and civic engagement has waned?" Do your instructors seem engaged or to be merely fulfilling the contractual obligations of "corporatism and unionism"?

3. Downey is concerned that many students today receive too narrow an education, and that without breadth of knowledge, one's capacity as a citizen is limited. What is your response to this idea?

4. What forces do you believe are working against the sort of broad, "liberal" education experience Downey would like to see for tomorrow's learners?

5. Would Downey's essay be stronger if he were more specific? Is he naïve to believe individuals ought to value (or even historically have placed) community ahead of self-interest?

Looking Back and Ahead

1. Read John Markoff's "The Doomsday Machines" (p. 505). Is there a similarity between the situation of eroding liberal education and that of problems that could be lying in wait if certain economic and technological changes are not made? Further, is there a possible causal relationship between eroding liberal education and attitudes toward environmental disorders?

2. If Robert Putnam is correct that communities become rich because they are civil, why don't today's political and business leaders take a much stronger interest in renewing liberal education? How are long-term and short-term goals at possible odds?

3. Read "The Pleasures of Love" (p. 431). If Davies is right on how to sustain a pleasing marriage, what sort of education would most enable the effort he feels is needed?

4. Discuss a possible relationship between Downey's thesis and Roger Fouts's in "Brownie" (p. 375).

David Suzuki The popular TV host of the *Nature of Things* and *A Planet for the Taking*, David Suzuki probably needs little introduction. Born in 1936 in Vancouver, a third-generation Japanese-Canadian (Sansei), he trained as a geneticist, joining the staff of the University of British Columbia in 1963. In 1969 he was appointed full professor of zoology. Three times consecutively (1969–72), he was awarded the Steacie Memorial Fellowship as Canada's most outstanding research scientist.

Suzuki believes it is crucial for ordinary people to understand science, and that it is quite possible for them to do so, at least enough to participate in ethical debate. He understands the power of talking to people as equals and makes exhaustive use of television, radio, and newspaper columns to pursue this vital dialogue. Suzuki's ongoing commitment to the ethics of science and to holistic approaches may be his greatest legacy in a field often characterized by self-reference.

The following article on sex education is taken from a collection called *Inventing the Future* (1990). To give the issue some historical context, consider that in 1967 Canada still had a law forbidding the dissemination of birth control information. Today, sex education is available in some secondary schools, but not all. Consider what was the case in your own experience and what is the case for schools in your community today.

The Right Stuff

1   Years ago I read a marvellous book entitled *Is There Life After High School?* In spite of the title, it was a serious comparison of human relationships at different stages in life. The study revealed that impressions formed in high school are more vivid and indelible than those formed at any other time in life. The author described how people in their seventies and eighties who had difficulty remembering most of their associates in university and at work would instantly recall most of their classmates by name while leafing through their high school yearbooks. In the analysis [by] the author, high school society is divided into

two broad categories, the innies and the outies. The innies were football and basketball players and cheerleaders who set the whole social climate of the school. The outies were all the rest, the majority of the student body, most of whom lusted to be innies. I sure hope it's different today because that description fits my recollection of high school and it was awful. But I'm getting off the point.

2   Those high school memories are so intense because that is the time when puberty occurs. The enormous physiological changes that take place in response to the surge of new hormones through the body completely transform both anatomy and mind. I always feel kids lose about half their intelligence for a few years in response to that blast of hormones. Relationships change radically. Suddenly parents change from protective, loving gods to dictatorial wardens incessantly imposing restrictions and criticizing everything. A pubescent teenager perceives adults and members of their own age group with totally new eyes. It's not surprising then that attitudes to school, courses and studying also change dramatically.

3   In the early 1970s, I visited a small northern town to judge a science fair. Back then, it was a tough town with a transient population of men working in the oil fields and a high proportion of Native people. The night I arrived, I dropped in to the bar of the motel and a man came over and said, "I hear you're going to talk to the students at the high school tomorrow." When I affirmed it, he shocked me by adding, "They'll kill you. I'm the science teacher there and I can tell you that all they think about is sex, drugs and cars. They'll tear you apart."

4   Well, he really scared me. I immediately formed images of a blackboard jungle, filled with switchblades and drug-crazed hoods. The next day when I walked into that auditorium, it was with great trepidation. There were 400 teenagers in the gym, about a third of them Indians. They looked pretty normal, but I had been warned and knew they were just biding their time before turning into raving animals.

5   So I began by saying, "I'm a geneticist. I know that you're basically walking gonads, so I'm going to talk about sex." That opener caught their attention. I started with the beginning of human life by describing eggs and sperm, talked about chromosomes and the X and Y basis for sex determination and went on from there. The kids were dead silent and attentive. I talked for about an hour and then opened it up for questions. I was astounded at the range of topics we covered. We discussed drugs and chromosomes, test-tube babies, amniocentesis and cloning. The principal finally had to step in to dismiss the group an hour and a half after that.

6   Science education in high school should be designed around sex and human biology. It's a shock every time I hear that a school board has caved in to pressure and kept sex education out of schools. I am sure opponents of sex ed have no intention of providing that information to their own children. In a time of easy access to the most explicit films, videos, magazines and books, who can believe it's better to keep youngsters ignorant by denying them some accurate facts? They're going to get all kinds of anecdotal, apocryphal stuff about sex from their peer group, anyway.

7   By starting their instruction with human sexuality and reproduction, teachers will be able to go on to practically every other subject in science. It just takes a hard look from a different perspective. After all, we are not trying to train future scientists (only a small percentage of high school graduates will go on in science), yet all of them will be able to use information that science can provide for the rest of their lives. And you can bet they will remember those lessons vividly in their life after high school.

For Further Thinking

1. In your own words, what is the thesis of this essay? Do you agree with it? Why or why not? (See Chapter 13 of the Rhetoric for our suggestions on how to find the thesis of this essay and how to summarize the other main ideas.)

2. Review the discussion of "Logic and Logical Fallacies" in Chapter 3 of the Rhetoric. Are there any such fallacies in "The Right Stuff"? Explain.

3. In his book *Metamorphosis*, Suzuki writes, "We make a great mistake by associating the inheritance of physical characteristics with far more complex traits of human personality and behaviour" (13). But in "The Right Stuff," doesn't he associate adolescent behaviour entirely with the physical characteristic of puberty and its hormones? Is he contradicting his own more complex understanding of cause-and-effect?

4. Suzuki gives his opponents little voice in "The Right Stuff." Are there strong reasons that you can think of for *not* teaching sex education in high school?

5. In paragraph 4, Suzuki notes that a third of the teenagers were Indians. How do you think he intends this comment to be taken? Is it an unnecessary, potentially offensive reference, such as "the female police officer found a blood-stained glove at the scene"?

6. Al Gore (*An Inconvenient Truth*) won the 2007 Nobel Peace Prize for his advocacy of environmental healing. Should David Suzuki have more rightly received the honour of such a nomination? On the other hand, are prizes simply tools of the Edward Bernayses of the world? (Bernays was Sigmund Freud's nephew, the little-known figure who concocted various strategies to hook people on consumer goods and similar diversions, such as awards shows.)

Looking Back and Ahead

1. Read John Markoff's "The Doomsday Machines" (p. 505). Would Suzuki be more likely to side with or against the "informed sources" who foresee dangers in a number of scientific fields, including Suzuki's own field of genetics?

2. Would Suzuki support or contradict Habeeb Salloum's conclusions in "The Other Canadians and Canada's Future" (p. 416)?

3. Chapter 14 of the Rhetoric contains a sample critique of "The Right Stuff." Should the student writer of that critique have acknowledged that Suzuki's "essay" was in fact a newspaper opinion piece for the *Globe and Mail*? Is it fair to criticize Suzuki for failing to respond to potential counter-arguments?

Margaret Atwood In this article, commissioned in 1982 by *Mother Jones* magazine to explain why so many Canadians appear to be anti-American, Atwood suggests that Canada is to the United States as Gaul was to Rome. She appeals to her American readers to imagine what it would be like to be dominated by Mexico: 75 percent of the books they bought and 90 percent of the films they watched would be Mexican, and the profits would flow across the border to Mexico. Revolution against economic control, Atwood surmises, is one of the few home-grown American products that is definitely not for sale and export. She allows that Canadians helped this situation come into being, but the main concern, she feels, is that Americans "seem not to know that the United States is an imperial power and is behaving like one."

Canadians: What Do They Want?

1   Last month, during a poetry reading, I tried out a short prose poem called "How to Like Men." It began by suggesting that one start with the feet. Unfortunately, the question of jackboots soon arose, and things went on from there. After the reading I had a conversation with a young man who thought I had been unfair to men. He wanted men to be liked totally, not just from the heels to the knees, and not just as individuals but as a group; and he thought it negative and inegalitarian of me to have alluded to war and rape. I pointed out that as far as any of us knew these were two activities not widely engaged in by women, but he was still upset. "We're both in this together," he protested. I admitted that this was so; but could he, maybe, see that our relative positions might be a little different.

2   This is the conversation one has with Americans, even, uh, *good* Americans, when the dinner-table conversation veers round to Canadian-American relations. "We're in this together," they like to say, especially when it comes to continental energy reserves. How do you *explain* to them, as delicately as possible, why they are not categorically beloved? It gets like the old Lifebuoy ads: even their best friends won't tell them. And Canadians are supposed to be their best friends, right? Members of the family?

3   Well, sort of. Across the river from Michigan, so near and yet so far, there I was at the age of eight, reading *their* Donald Duck comic books (originated, however, by one of *ours*; yes, Walt Disney's parents were Canadian) and coming at the end to Popsicle Pete, who promised me the earth if only I would save wrappers, but took it all away from me again with a single asterisk: Offer Good Only in the United States. Some cynical members of the world community may be forgiven for thinking that the same asterisk is there, in invisible ink, on the Constitution and the Bill of Rights.

4   But quibbles like that aside, and good will assumed, how does one go about liking Americans? Where does one begin? Or, to put it another way, why did the Canadian women lock themselves in the john during a '70s "international" feminist conference being held in Toronto? Because the American sisters were being "imperialist," that's why.

5   But then, it's always a little naive of Canadians to expect that Americans, of whatever political stamp, should stop being imperious. How can they? The fact is that the United States is an empire and Canada is to it as Gaul was to Rome.

6   It's hard to explain to Americans what it feels like to be a Canadian. Pessimists among us would say that one has to translate the experience into their own terms and that this is necessary because Americans are incapable of thinking in any other terms—and this in itself is part of the problem. (Witness all those draft dodgers who went into culture shock when they discovered to their horror that Toronto was not Syracuse.)

7   Here is a translation: Picture a Mexico with a population ten times larger than that of the United States. That would put it at about two billion. Now suppose that the official American language is Spanish, that 75 percent of the books Americans buy and 90 percent of the movies they see are Mexican, and that the profits flow across the border to Mexico. If an American does scrape it together to make a movie, the Mexicans won't let him show it in the States, because they own the distribution outlets. If anyone tries to change this ratio, not only the Mexicans but many fellow Americans cry "National chauvinism," or, even more effectively, "National socialism." After all, the American public prefers the Mexican product. It's what they're used to.

8   Retranslate and you have the current American-Canadian picture. It's changed a little recently, not only on the cultural front. For instance, Canada, some think a trifle late, is attempting to regain control of its own petroleum industry. Americans are predictably angry. They think of Canadian oil as *theirs*.

9   "What's mine is yours," they have said for years, meaning exports; "What's yours is mine" meaning ownership and profits. Canadians are supposed to do retail buying, no controlling, or what's an empire for? One could always refer Americans to history, particularly that of their own revolution. They objected to the colonial situation when they themselves were a colony; but then, revolution is considered one of a very few home-grown American products that definitely are not for export.

10   Objectively, one cannot become too self-righteous about this state of affairs. Canadians owned lots of things, including their souls, before World War II. After that they sold out, some say because they had put too much into financing the war, which created a capital vacuum (a position they would not have been forced into if the Americans hadn't kept out of the fighting for so long, say the sore losers). But for whatever reason, capital flowed across the border in the '50s, and Canadians, traditionally sock-under-the-mattress hoarders, were reluctant to invest in their own country. Americans did it for them and ended up with a large part of it, which they retain to this day. In every sellout there's a seller as well as a buyer, and the Canadians did a thorough job of trading their birthright for a mess.

11   That's on the capitalist end, but when you turn to the trade union side of things you find much the same story, except that the sellout happened in the

'30s under the banner of the United Front. Now Canadian workers are finding that in any empire the colonial branch plants are the first to close, and what could be a truly progressive labor movement has been weakened by compromised bargains made in international union headquarters south of the border.

12   Canadians are sometimes snippy to Americans at cocktail parties. They don't like to feel owned and they don't like having been sold. But what really bothers them—and it's at this point that the United States and Rome part company—is the wide-eyed innocence with which their snippiness is greeted.

13   Innocence becomes ignorance when seen in the light of international affairs, and though ignorance is one of the spoils of conquest—the Gauls always knew more about the Romans than the Romans knew about them—the world can no longer afford America's ignorance. Its ignorance of Canada, though it makes Canadians bristle, is a minor and relatively harmless example. More dangerous is the fact that individual Americans seem not to know that the United States is an imperial power and is behaving like one. They don't want to admit that empires dominate, invade and subjugate—and live on the proceeds—or, if they do admit it, they believe in their divine right to do so. The export of divine right is much more harmful than the export of Coca-Cola, though they may turn out to be much the same thing in the end.

14   Other empires have behaved similarly (the British somewhat better, Genghis Khan decidedly worse); but they have not expected to be *liked* for it. It's the final Americanism, this passion for being liked. Alas, many Americans are indeed likable; they are often more generous, more welcoming, more enthusiastic, less picky and sardonic than Canadians, and it's not enough to say it's only because they can afford it. Some of that revolutionary spirit still remains: the optimism, the 18th-century belief in the fixability of almost anything, the conviction of the possibility of change. However, at cocktail parties and elsewhere one must be able to tell the difference between an individual and a foreign policy. Canadians can no longer afford to think of Americans as only a spectator sport. If Reagan blows up the world, we will unfortunately be doing more than watching it on television. "No annihilation without representation" sounds good as a slogan, but if we run it up the flagpole, who's going to salute?

15   We *are* all in this together. For Canadians, the question is how to survive it. For Americans there is no question, because there does not have to be. Canada is just that vague, cold place where their uncle used to go fishing, before the lakes went dead from acid rain.

16   How do you like Americans? Individually, it's easier. Your average American is no more responsible for the state of affairs than your average man is for war and rape. Any Canadian who is so narrow-minded as to dislike Americans merely on principle is missing out on one of the good things in life. The same might be said, to women, of men. As a group, as a foreign policy, it's harder. But if you like men, you can like Americans. Cautiously. Selectively. Beginning with the feet. One at a time.

For Further Thinking

1. In her discussion, Atwood refers to the possibility that then-president Ronald Reagan might blow up the world. From today's perspective, does that suggestion, and therefore her whole article, appear exaggerated or, at best, biased? Are nuclear fears less or more real today?

2. Canada added its voice to those from Europe issuing stern objections to President George W. Bush for backing out of the 1997 Kyoto Accord as well as the non-proliferation arms agreement of the early 1970s. The United States then attacked Iraq against the will of the United Nations, likely violating international law. Could Atwood use the Bush administration as further proof of her main point: that "the world can no longer afford America's ignorance" in its activities as an imperial power? Do you agree with Atwood (writing in 1982) that America's national self-imaging and active international presence are mere "ignorance"?

3. Do you accept Atwood's analogy of the United States to men and Canada to women in the power politics of relationships? (See our discussion of analogy under "Comparison-Contrast," Chapter 12; also see faulty analogies under the section on logical fallacies in Chapter 3.) The Canadian band The Guess Who reversed this metaphor in their song "American Woman." What are the meanings and implications of these two opposed national metaphors?

4. Do you, like Atwood, know individual Americans who seem great, yet do you also object to the attitudes of the United States as a whole? Explain your view.

5. Make two columns on a sheet of paper. On one side, list the qualities you consider Canadian. On the other, list those you consider American. Now, from either side, select those traits you consider an ideal combination. Is there any way Canadians and Americans could take this list and draw the best from each other?

6. In April 2007, Al Gore, then a nominee for the Nobel Peace Prize (which he went on to win), chided Canada publicly for its dreadful record on the environment, a criticism fully supported by environmental author George Monbiot and by the United Nations. Would Margaret Atwood consider Gore's comments as American imperialism? What do you think she should say to him?

Looking Back and Ahead

1. How do the arguments, evidence, and politics (values) of Pamela Swanigan, author of "I Am Half-Canadian" (p. 411), compare/contrast to Atwood's opinions in this essay?

2. Based on the social and sexual politics of "Thanks for the Ride" (p. 376), what might Alice Munro think of the young man's comment to Atwood that "[w]e're both in this together"?

4. In what possible ways do "College Girl to Call Girl" by Sarah Schmidt (p. 457) and "Saskatchewan's Indian People—Five Generations" by Pat Deiter-McArthur (p. 166) provide counterpoints to Atwood's essay? See Chapter 14 of the Rhetoric, "Critical Analysis and Evaluation," Chapter 15, "Rhetorical Analysis," and Chapter 16, "Argumentation," for a discussion of various methods of analysis and for evaluations of arguments.

5. Compare Atwood's essay to "The Lure of the Body Image" (p. 447). If you were to write a five-paragraph essay comparing these two, what outline would you use? See Chapter 12, "Comparison-Contrast," for some ideas in answer to this question.

George Orwell Born Eric Arthur Blair in Motihari, India, in 1903, George Orwell went on to a life many describe as sadly short; certainly it was a life of hardships, ill health, and grim sights. Orwell began his writing career as a voluntary tramp, experiencing first-hand the life of the homeless. It was only by the end of his life, after *Animal Farm* and *1984*, that he found financial success. By that time he had served in the Indian Imperial Police force in Burma (now Myanmar) for six years and fought for the Republican forces in the Spanish Civil War to liberate Spain from the Fascists. Orwell, however, had grown disillusioned with the infighting of the Communists. *The Road to Wigan Pier* (1937) and *Homage to Catalonia* (1938) expressed some of that disillusion. But his two most visionary works condemning human folly were the allegorical beast fable *Animal Farm* (1945) and the speculative nightmare or dystopia *1984* (1949). In 1950, the year of his death, Orwell published *Shooting an Elephant and Other Essays*. This collection of non-fiction uses personal experience combined with rigorous analysis.

In one of these essays, "Politics and the English Language," Orwell argues that the English of his day is becoming vague, stale, and thoughtless, and that this condition contributes to gradual political degeneracy. His image for writing was the window, a clear pane. It doesn't attract any attention to itself; consequently, we see sharply what it focuses us to see. According to Orwell, this form of writing is the key to social and political regeneration.

Politics and the English Language

1   Most people who bother with the matter at all would admit that the English language is in a bad way, but it is generally assumed that we cannot by conscious action do anything about it. Our civilization is decadent and our language—so the argument runs—must inevitably share in the general collapse. It follows that any struggle against the abuse of language is a sentimental archaism, like preferring candles to electric light or hansom cabs to aeroplanes. Underneath this lies the half-conscious belief that language is a natural growth and not an instrument which we shape for our own purposes.

2   Now, it is clear that the decline of a language must ultimately have political and economic causes: it is not due simply to the bad influence of this or that individual writer. But an effect can become a cause, reinforcing the original cause and producing the same effect in an intensified form, and so on indefinitely. A man may take to drink because he feels himself to be a failure, and then fail all the more completely because he drinks. It is rather the same thing that is happening to the English language. It becomes ugly and inaccurate because our thoughts are foolish, but the slovenliness of our language makes it easier for us to have foolish thoughts. The point is that the process is reversible. Modern English, especially written English, is full of bad habits which spread by imitation and which can be avoided if one is willing to take the necessary trouble. If one gets rid of these habits one can think more clearly, and to think clearly is a necessary first step towards political regeneration: so that the fight against bad English is not frivolous and is not the exclusive concern of professional writers. I will come back to

this presently, and I hope that by that time the meaning of what I have said here will have become clearer. Meanwhile, here are five specimens of the English language as it is now habitually written.

3   These five passages have not been picked out because they are especially bad—I could have quoted far worse if I had chosen—but because they illustrate various of the mental vices from which we now suffer. They are a little below the average, but are fairly representative samples. I number them so that I can refer back to them when necessary:

(1)   I am not, indeed, sure whether it is not true to say that the Milton who once seemed not unlike a seventeenth-century Shelley had not become, out of an experience ever more bitter in each year, more alien [sic] to the founder of that Jesuit sect which nothing could induce him to tolerate.

—Professor Harold Laski (Essay in *Freedom of Expression*)

(2)   Above all, we cannot play ducks and drakes with a native battery of idioms which prescribes such egregious collocations of vocables as the Basic *put up with* for *tolerate* or *put at a loss* for *bewilder.*

—Professor Lancelot Hogben (*Interglossa*)

(3)   On the one side we have the free personality: by definition it is not neurotic, for it has neither conflict nor dream. Its desires, such as they are, are transparent, for they are just what institutional approval keeps in the forefront of consciousness; another institutional pattern would alter their number and intensity; there is little in them that is natural, irreducible, or culturally dangerous. But *on the other side,* the social bond itself is nothing but the mutual reflection of these self-secure integrities. Recall the definition of love. Is not this the very picture of a small academic? Where is there a place in this hall of mirrors for either personality or fraternity?

—Essay on psychology in *Politics* (New York)

(4)   All the "best people" from the gentlemen's clubs, and all the frantic fascist captains, united in common hatred of Socialism and bestial horror of the rising tide of the mass revolutionary movement, have turned to acts of provocation, to foul incendiarism, to medieval legends of poisoned wells, to legalize their own destruction of proletarian organizations, and rouse the agitated petty-bourgeoisie to chauvinistic fervour on behalf of the fight against the revolutionary way out of the crisis.

—Communist pamphlet

(5)   If a new spirit is to be infused into this old country, there is one thorny and contentious reform which must be tackled, and that is the humanization and galvanization of the B.B.C. Timidity here will bespeak canker and atrophy of the soul. The heart of Britain may be sound and of strong beat, for instance, but the British lion's roar at present is like that of Bottom in Shakespeare's *Midsummer*

Night's Dream—as gentle as any sucking dove. A virile new Britain cannot continue indefinitely to be traduced in the eyes, or rather ears, of the world by the effete languors of Langham Place, brazenly masquerading as "standard English." When the Voice of Britain is heard at nine o'clock, better far and infinitely less ludicrous to hear aitches honestly dropped than the present priggish, inflated, inhibited, school-ma'mish arch braying of blameless bashful mewing maidens!

—Letter in *Tribune*

4   Each of these passages has faults of its own, but, quite apart from avoidable ugliness, two qualities are common to all of them. The first is staleness of imagery; the other is lack of precision. The writer either has a meaning and cannot express it, or he inadvertently says something else, or he is almost indifferent as to whether his words mean anything or not. This mixture of vagueness and sheer incompetence is the most marked characteristic of modern English prose, and especially of any kind of political writing. As soon as certain topics are raised, the concrete melts into the abstract and no one seems able to think of turns of speech that are not hackneyed: prose consists less and less of *words* chosen for the sake of their meaning, and more and more of *phrases* tacked together like the sections of a prefabricated hen-house. I list below, with notes and examples, various of the tricks by means of which the work of prose-construction is habitually dodged:

5   **Dying Metaphors.** A newly invented metaphor assists thought by evoking a visual image, while on the other hand a metaphor which is technically "dead" (e.g., *iron resolution*) has in effect reverted to being an ordinary word and can generally be used without loss of vividness. But in between these two classes there is a huge dump of worn-out metaphors which have lost all evocative power and are merely used because they save people the trouble of inventing phrases for themselves. Examples are: *Ring the changes on, take up the cudgels for, toe the line, ride roughshod over, stand shoulder to shoulder with, play into the hands of, no axe to grind, grist to the mill, fishing in troubled waters, on the order of the day, Achilles' heel, swan song, hotbed.* Many of these are used without knowledge of their meaning (what is a "rift," for instance?), and incompatible metaphors are frequently mixed, a sure sign that the writer is not interested in what he is saying. Some metaphors now current have been twisted out of their original meaning without those who use them even being aware of the fact. For example, *toe the line* is sometimes written *tow the line.* Another example is the *hammer and the anvil*, now always used with the implication that the anvil gets the worst of it. In real life it is always the anvil that breaks the hammer, never the other way about: a writer who stopped to think what he was saying would be aware of this, and would avoid perverting the original phrase.

6   **Operators *or* Verbal False Limbs.** These save the trouble of picking out appropriate verbs and nouns, and at the same time pad each sentence with extra

syllables which give it an appearance of symmetry. Characteristic phrases are: *render inoperative, militate against, make contact with, be subjected to, give rise to, give grounds for, have the effect of, play a leading part (role) in, make itself felt, take effect, exhibit a tendency to, serve the purpose of, etc., etc.* The keynote is the elimination of simple verbs. Instead of being a single word, such as *break, stop, spoil, mend, kill,* a verb becomes a *phrase,* made up of a noun or adjective tacked on to some general-purpose verb such as *prove, serve, form, play, render.* In addition, the passive voice is wherever possible used in preference to the active, and noun constructions are used instead of gerunds (*by examination of* instead of *by examining*). The range of verbs is further cut down by means of the *-ize* and *de-* formations, and the banal statements are given an appearance of profundity by means of the *not un-* formation. Simple conjunctions and prepositions are replaced by such phrases as *with respect to, having regard to, the fact that, by dint of, in view of, in the interests of, on the hypothesis that*; and the ends of sentences are saved from anticlimax by such resounding common-places as *greatly to be desired, cannot be left out of account, a development to be expected in the near future, deserving of serious consideration, brought to a satisfactory conclusion,* and so on and so forth.

7   **Pretentious Diction.** Words like *phenomenon, element, individual* (as noun), *objective, categorical, effective, virtual, basic, primary, promote, constitute, exhibit, exploit, utilize, eliminate, liquidate,* are used to dress up simple statement and give an air of scientific impartiality to biased judgments. Adjectives like *epoch-making, epic, historic, unforgettable, triumphant, age-old, inevitable, inexorable, veritable,* are used to dignify the sordid processes of international politics, while writing that aims at glorifying war usually takes on an archaic colour, its characteristic words being: *realm, throne, chariot, mailed fist, trident, sword, shield, buckler, banner, jackboot, clarion.* Foreign words and expressions such as *cul de sac, ancien régime, deus ex machina, mutatis mutandis, status quo, gleichschaltung, weltanschauung,* are used to give an air of culture and elegance. Except for the useful abbreviations *i.e., e.g.,* and *etc.,* there is no real need for any of the hundreds of foreign phrases now current in English. Bad writers, and especially scientific, political and sociological writers, are nearly always haunted by the notion that Latin or Greek words are grander than Saxon ones, and unnecessary words like *expedite, ameliorate, predict, extraneous, deracinated, clandestine, subaqueous* and hundreds of others constantly gain ground from their Anglo-Saxon opposite numbers.[1] The jargon peculiar to Marxist writing (*hyena, hangman, cannibal, petty bourgeois, these gentry, lacquey, flunkey, mad dog, White Guard,* etc.) consists largely of words and phrases translated from Russian, German or French; but the normal way of coining a new word is to use a Latin or Greek root with the appropriate affix and, where necessary, the *-ize* formation. It is often easier to make up words of this kind (*deregionalize, impermissible, extramarital,*

non-fragmentatory and so forth) than to think up the English words that will cover one's meaning. The result, in general, is an increase in slovenliness and vagueness.

8   **Meaningless Words.** In certain kinds of writing, particularly in art criticism and literary criticism, it is normal to come across long passages which are almost completely lacking in meaning.[2] Words like *romantic*, *plastic*, *values*, *human*, *dead*, *sentimental*, *natural*, *vitality*, as used in art criticism, are strictly meaningless, in the sense that they not only do not point to any discoverable object, but are hardly ever expected to do so by the reader. When one critic writes, "The outstanding feature of Mr. X's work is its living quality," while another writes, "The immediately striking thing about Mr. X's work is its peculiar deadness," the reader accepts this as a simple difference of opinion. If words like *black* and *white* were involved, instead of the jargon words *dead* and *living*, he would see at once that language was being used in an improper way. Many political words are similarly abused. The word *Fascism* has now no meaning except in so far as it signifies "something not desirable." The words *democracy*, *socialism*, *freedom*, *patriotic*, *realistic*, *justice*, have each of them several different meanings which cannot be reconciled with one another. In the case of a word like *democracy*, not only is there no agreed definition but the attempt to make one is resisted from all sides. It is almost universally felt that when we call a country democratic we are praising it: consequently the defenders of every kind of régime claim that it is a democracy, and fear that they might have to stop using the word if it were tied down to any one meaning. Words of this kind are often used in a consciously dishonest way. That is, the person who uses them has his own private definition, but allows his hearer to think he means something quite different. Statements like *Marshal Pétain was a true patriot*, *The Soviet Press is the freest in the world*, *The Catholic Church is opposed to persecution*, are almost always made with intent to deceive. Other words used in variable meanings, in most cases more or less dishonestly, are: *class*, *totalitarian*, *science*, *progressive*, *reactionary*, *bourgeois*, *equality*.

9   Now that I have made this catalogue of swindles and perversions, let me give another example of the kind of writing that they lead to. This time it must of its nature be an imaginary one. I am going to translate a passage of good English into modern English of the worst sort. Here is a well-known verse from *Ecclesiastes*:

> I returned and saw under the sun, that the race is not to the swift, nor the battle to the strong, neither yet bread to the wise, nor yet riches to men of understanding, nor yet favour to men of skill; but time and chance happeneth to them all.

10   Here it is in modern English:

> Objective consideration of contemporary phenomena compels the conclusion that success or failure in competitive activities exhibits no tendency to be commensurate with innate capacity, but that a considerable element of the unpredictable must invariably be taken into account.

11   This is a parody, but not a very gross one. Exhibit (3), above, for instance, contains several patches of the same kind of English. It will be seen that I have not made a full translation. The beginning and ending of the sentence follow the original meaning fairly closely, but in the middle the concrete illustrations—race, battle, bread—dissolve into the vague phrase "success or failure in competitive activities." This had to be so, because no modern writer of the kind I am discussing—no one capable of using phrases like "objective consideration of contemporary phenomena"—would ever tabulate his thoughts in that precise and detailed way. The whole tendency of modern prose is away from concreteness. Now analyse these [previous] two sentences a little more closely. The first contains forty-nine words but only sixty syllables, and all its words are those of everyday life. The second contains thirty-eight words of ninety syllables: eighteen of its words are from Latin roots, and one from Greek. The first sentence contains six vivid images, and only one phrase ("time and chance") that could be called vague. The second contains not a single fresh, arresting phrase, and in spite of its ninety syllables it gives only a shortened version of the meaning contained in the first. Yet without a doubt it is the second kind of sentence that is gaining ground in modern English. I do not want to exaggerate. This kind of writing is not yet universal, and outcrops of simplicity will occur here and there in the worst-written page. Still, if you or I were told to write a few lines on the uncertainty of human fortunes, we should probably come much nearer to my imaginary sentence than to the one from *Ecclesiastes*.

12   As I have tried to show, modern writing at its worst does not consist in picking out words for the sake of their meaning and inventing images in order to make the meaning clearer. It consists in gumming together long strips of words which have already been set in order by someone else, and making the results presentable by sheer humbug. The attraction of this way of writing is that it is easy. It is easier—even quicker, once you have the habit—to say *In my opinion it is a not unjustifiable assumption that* than to say *I think*. If you use ready-made phrases, you not only don't have to hunt about for words; you also don't have to bother with the rhythms of your sentences, since these phrases are generally so arranged as to be more or less euphonious. When you are composing in a hurry—when you are dictating to a stenographer, for instance, or making a public speech—it is natural to fall into a pretentious, Latinized style. Tags like *a consideration which we should do well to bear in mind* or *a conclusion to which all of us would readily assent* will save many a sentence from coming down with a bump. By using stale metaphors, similes and idioms, you save much mental effort, at the cost of

leaving your meaning vague, not only for your reader but for yourself. This is the significance of mixed metaphors. The sole aim of a metaphor is to call up a visual image. When these images clash—as in *The Fascist octopus has sung its swan song, the jackboot is thrown into the melting pot*—it can be taken as certain that the writer is not seeing a mental image of the objects he is naming; in other words he is not really thinking. Look again at the examples I gave at the beginning of this essay. Professor Laski (1) uses five negatives in fifty-three words. One of these is superfluous, making nonsense of the whole passage, and in addition there is the slip *alien* for *akin*, making further nonsense, and several avoidable pieces of clumsiness which increase the general vagueness. Professor Hogben (2) plays ducks and drakes with a battery which is able to write prescriptions, and, while disapproving of the everyday phrase *put up with*, is unwilling to look *egregious* up in the dictionary and see what it means; (3), if one takes an uncharitable attitude towards it, is simply meaningless: probably one could work out its intended meaning by reading the whole of the article in which it occurs. In (4), the writer knows more or less what he wants to say, but an accumulation of stale phrases chokes him like tea leaves blocking a sink. In (5), words and meaning have almost parted company. People who write in this manner usually have a general emotional meaning—they dislike one thing and want to express solidarity with another—but they are not interested in the detail of what they are saying. A scrupulous writer, in every sentence that he writes, will ask himself at least four questions, thus: What am I trying to say? What words will express it? What image or idiom will make it clearer? Is this image fresh enough to have an effect? And he will probably ask himself two more. Could I put it more shortly? Have I said anything that is avoidably ugly? But you are not obliged to go to all this trouble. You can shirk it by simply throwing your mind open and letting the ready-made phrases come crowding in. They will construct your sentences for you—even think your thoughts for you, to a certain extent—and at need they will perform the important service of partially concealing your meaning even from yourself. It is at this point that the special connexion between politics and the debasement of language becomes clear.

13   In our time it is broadly true that political writing is bad writing. Where it is not true, it will generally be found that the writer is some kind of rebel, expressing his private opinions and not a "party line." Orthodoxy, of whatever colour, seems to demand a lifeless, imitative style. The political dialects to be found in pamphlets, leading articles, manifestos, White Papers and the speeches of under-secretaries do, of course, vary from party to party, but they are all alike in that one almost never finds in them a fresh, vivid, home-made turn of speech. When one watches some tired hack on the platform mechanically repeating the familiar phrases— *bestial atrocities, iron heel, bloodstained tyranny, free peoples of the world, stand shoulder to shoulder*—one often has a curious feeling that one is not watching a live human being but some kind of dummy: a feeling which suddenly becomes stronger at moments when the light catches the speaker's spectacles and turns them into blank

discs which seem to have no eyes behind them. And this is not altogether fanciful. A speaker who uses that kind of phraseology has gone some distance towards turning himself into a machine. The appropriate noises are coming out of his larynx, but his brain is not involved as it would be if he were choosing his words for himself. If the speech he is making is one that he is accustomed to make over and over again, he may be almost unconscious of what he is saying, as one is when one utters the responses in church. And this reduced state of consciousness, if not indispensable, is at any rate favourable to political conformity.

14   In our time, political speech and writing are largely the defence of the indefensible. Things like the continuance of British rule in India, the Russian purges and deportations, the dropping of the atom bombs on Japan, can indeed be defended, but only by arguments which are too brutal for most people to face, and which do not square with the professed aims of political parties. Thus political language has to consist largely of euphemism, question-begging and sheer cloudy vagueness. Defenceless villages are bombarded from the air, the inhabitants driven out into the countryside, the cattle machine-gunned, the huts set on fire with incendiary bullets: this is called *pacification*. Millions of peasants are robbed of their farms and sent trudging along the roads with no more than they can carry: this is called *transfer of population* or *rectification of frontiers*. People are imprisoned for years without trial, or shot in the back of the neck or sent to die of scurvy in Arctic lumber camps: this is called *elimination of unreliable elements*. Such phraseology is needed if one wants to name things without calling up mental pictures of them. Consider for instance some comfortable English professor defending Russian totalitarianism. He cannot say outright, "I believe in killing off your opponents when you can get good results by doing so." Probably, therefore, he will say something like this:

> While freely conceding that the Soviet regime exhibits certain features which the humanitarian may be inclined to deplore, we must, I think, agree that a certain curtailment of the right to political opposition is an unavoidable concomitant of transitional periods, and that the rigours which the Russian people have been called upon to undergo have been amply justified in the sphere of concrete achievement.

15   The inflated style is itself a kind of euphemism. A mass of Latin words falls upon the facts like soft snow, blurring the outlines and covering up all the details. The great enemy of clear language is insincerity. When there is a gap between one's real and one's declared aims, one turns as it were instinctively to long words and exhausted idioms, like a cuttlefish squirting out ink. In our age there is no such thing as "keeping out of politics." All issues are political issues, and politics itself is a mass of lies, evasions, folly, hatred and schizophrenia. When the general atmosphere is bad, language must suffer. I should expect to find—this is a guess which I have not sufficient knowledge to verify—that

the German, Russian and Italian languages have all deteriorated in the last ten or fifteen years, as a result of dictatorship.

16   But if thought corrupts language, language can also corrupt thought. A bad usage can spread by tradition and imitation, even among people who should and do know better. The debased language that I have been discussing is in some ways very convenient. Phrases like *a not unjustifiable assumption*, *leaves much to be desired*, *would serve no good purpose*, *a consideration which we should do well to bear in mind*, are a continuous temptation, a packet of aspirins always at one's elbow. Look back through this essay, and for certain you will find that I have again and again committed the very faults I am protesting against. By this morning's post I have received a pamphlet dealing with conditions in Germany. The author tells me that he "felt impelled" to write it. I open it at random, and here is almost the first sentence that I see: "(The Allies) have an opportunity not only of achieving a radical transformation of Germany's social and political structure in such a way as to avoid a nationalistic reaction in Germany itself, but at the same time of laying the foundations of a co-operative and unified Europe." You see, he "feels impelled" to write—feels, presumably, that he has something new to say—and yet his words, like cavalry horses answering the bugle, group themselves automatically into the familiar dreary pattern. This invasion of one's mind by ready-made phrases (*lay the foundations, achieve a radical transformation*) can only be prevented if one is constantly on guard against them, and every such phrase anaesthetizes a portion of one's brain.

17   I said earlier that the decadence of our language is probably curable. Those who deny this would argue, if they produced an argument at all, that language merely reflects existing social conditions, and that we cannot influence its development by any direct tinkering with words and constructions. So far as the general tone or spirit of a language goes, this may be true, but it is not true in detail. Silly words and expressions have often disappeared, not through any evolutionary process but owing to the conscious action of a minority. Two recent examples were *explore every avenue* and *leave no stone unturned*, which were killed by the jeers of a few journalists. There is a long list of flyblown metaphors which could similarly be got rid of if enough people would interest themselves in the job; and it should also be possible to laugh the *not un-* formation out of existence,[3] to reduce the amount of Latin and Greek in the average sentence, to drive out foreign phrases and strayed scientific words, and, in general, to make pretentiousness unfashionable. But all these are minor points. The defence of the English language implies more than this, and perhaps it is best to start by saying what it does *not* imply.

18   To begin with it has nothing to do with archaism, with the salvaging of obsolete words and turns of speech, or with the setting up of a "standard English" which must never be departed from. On the contrary, it is especially concerned with the scrapping of every word or idiom which has outworn its usefulness. It has nothing to do with correct grammar and syntax, which are of no importance

so long as one makes one's meaning clear, or with the avoidance of Americanisms, or with having what is called a "good prose style." On the other hand it is not concerned with fake simplicity and the attempt to make written English colloquial. Nor does it even imply in every case preferring the Saxon word to the Latin one, though it does imply using the fewest and shortest words that will cover one's meaning. What is above all needed is to let the meaning choose the word, and not the other way about. In prose, the worst thing one can do with words is to surrender to them. When you think of a concrete object, you think wordlessly, and then, if you want to describe the thing you have been visualizing you probably hunt about till you find the exact words that seem to fit it. When you think of something abstract you are more inclined to use words from the start, and unless you make a conscious effort to prevent it, the existing dialect will come rushing in and do the job for you, at the expense of blurring or even changing your meaning. Probably it is better to put off using words as long as possible and get one's meaning as clear as one can through pictures or sensations. Afterwards one can choose—not simply *accept*—the phrases that will best cover the meaning, and then switch round and decide what impression one's words are likely to make on another person. This last effort of the mind cuts out all stale or mixed images, all prefabricated phrases, needless repetitions, and humbug and vagueness generally. But one can often be in doubt about the effect of a word or a phrase, and one needs rules that one can rely on when instinct fails. I think the following rules will cover most cases:

(i)   Never use a metaphor, simile or other figure of speech which you are used to seeing in print.
(ii) Never use a long word where a short one will do.
(iii) If it is possible to cut out a word, always cut it out.
(iv) Never use the passive where you can use the active.
(v)   Never use a foreign phrase, a scientific word or a jargon word if you can think of an everyday English equivalent.
(vi) Break any of these rules sooner than say anything outright barbarous.

19   These rules sound elementary, and so they are, but they demand a deep change of attitude in anyone who has grown used to writing in the style now fashionable. One could keep all of them and still write bad English, but one could not write the kind of stuff that I quoted in those five specimens at the beginning of this article.

20   I have not here been considering the literary use of language, but merely language as an instrument for expressing and not for concealing or preventing thought. Stuart Chase and others have come near to claiming that all abstract words are meaningless, and have used this as a pretext for advocating a kind of political quietism. Since you don't know what Fascism is, how can you struggle against Fascism? One need not swallow such absurdities as this, but one ought to recognize that the present political chaos is connected with the decay of language, and that one can probably bring about some improvement by starting

at the verbal end. If you simplify your English, you are freed from the worst follies of orthodoxy. You cannot speak any of the necessary dialects, and when you make a stupid remark its stupidity will be obvious, even to yourself. Political language—and with variations this is true of all political parties, from Conservatives to Anarchists—is designed to make lies sound truthful and murder respectable, and to give an appearance of solidity to pure wind. One cannot change this all in a moment, but one can at least change one's own habits, and from time to time one can even, if one jeers loudly enough, send some worn-out and useless phrase—some *jackboot, Achilles' heel, hotbed, melting pot, acid test, veritable inferno* or other lump of verbal refuse—into the dustbin where it belongs.

Notes

1. An interesting illustration is the way in which the English flower names which were in use till very recently are being ousted by Greek ones, *snapdragon* becoming *antirrhinum*, *forget-me-not* becoming *myosotis*, etc. It is hard to see any practical reason for this change of fashion: it is probably due to an instinctive turning-away from the more homely word and a vague feeling that the Greek word is scientific.

2. Example: "Comfort's catholicity of perception and image, strangely Whitmanesque in range, almost the exact opposite in aesthetic compulsion, continues to evoke that trembling atmospheric accumulative hinting at a cruel, an inexorably serene timelessness. . . . Wrey Gardiner scores by aiming at simple bull's-eyes with precision. Only they are not so simple, and through this contented sadness runs more than the surface bitter-sweet of resignation." (*Poetry Quarterly*)

3. One can cure oneself of the *not un-* formation by memorizing this sentence: *A not unblack dog was chasing a not unsmall rabbit across a not ungreen field.*

For Further Thinking

1. Orwell's purpose seems quite clearly persuasive—to convince us that although our language is troubled, if we consider the full nature and outcome of bad language we can start to do something about it. See the description of argumentative structure and techniques in Chapter 16 of the Rhetoric. In what specific ways does Orwell apply principles of argumentation?

2. What other structures does he apply from the expository array? (See Chapter 9 of the Rhetoric for more on expository patterns.)

3. To appreciate fully the mood of the world when Orwell worked on this essay, do a little research on the Second World War. Talk to some people who remember that time, perhaps some who served overseas. See also Professor John Simkin's website "The Second World War" at <http://www.spartacus.schoolnet.co.uk/author.htm>.

4. If you were to divide this essay into sections, how many would there be in the body? Is it possible to find a thesis statement toward the beginning of the essay that in fact lays out the sections to follow?

Looking Back and Ahead

1. The main character of Orwell's novel *1984* works for a government department that routinely falsifies records and uses the language of "doublespeak." This particular department is called the Ministry of Truth. Can you give examples in today's world of words that express a reality opposite to their denotative meaning?

2. "Parody" refers to imitation (typically an exaggeration or distortion) of something with an intent to ridicule. Orwell uses parody when he imagines what would happen if a bureaucrat tried to express a passage from the Bible. A much more gentle parody occurs in the final scene of Roch Carrier's "The Hockey Sweater" (p. 389). Can you identify how parody functions in that instance?

3. Read "Newfoundlandese, If You Please" (p. 414). What do you think of Orwell's admonition that we exclude all "foreign" words from our English? How would that affect us in most parts of Canada, taking Montreal as just one example?

4. See the Text Enrichment Site, Chapter 13, for two sample summaries of Orwell's essay. Before looking at those, see if you can rough out your own summary of "Politics and the English Language." Then compare your work with the two samples at the website.

Howard Richler   In eighteenth-century London, the unfashionable artist and poet William Blake noted bitterly that "commerce grows on every tree." What would he say today! Studies indicate that overworked members of our society typically do not demand reduced work hours—they demand higher wages. Star athletes who 30 years ago would have earned no more than civil servants now pull in millions of dollars a year. Certain individuals in the United States and other "developed" nations have personal fortunes greater than the wealth of entire countries. The music and film industries seem to be flogging youth more than ever. Advertisers target younger and younger people, thinking of them not as developing human beings but simply as mindless consumers. Multinational corporations, exploiting cheap labour in poor countries, exert increasing influence over all institutions. Universities feel increasing pressure to treat students purely as consumers and education as a product on the shelf. As consumerism marches on—pandering to escalating levels of selfishness—many critics believe our society has become spiritually bankrupt.

Howard Richler writes a language column for the Montreal *Gazette*. In the following essay from his collection *A Bawdy Language*, he argues that with the dominance of corporatism, few words have escaped strong overtones of commerce, yet the language situation does not really disturb us since we have recently placed positive, or at least neutral, meanings on words related to all seven deadly sins. Process writing plays an important role in this essay, as Richler traces the evolution of various words from feudal times forward.

The Seven Deadly Sins Are "In" and Proud of It

1   "We *profited* from their misfortune—no, let me rephrase that, it sounds too mercantile. We *benefited*—no, that's not right—we have *gained an advantage*—no!—well, you know what I'm trying to say." A friend was relating to me a

discussion she heard recently during a religious service. She said the speaker was trying to convey a sense of spiritual accomplishment but was stymied by the seemingly capitalistic nature of the verbs he employed.

2   Moneyed words are so central to our lives that any verb our hapless discussant used to communicate a sense of acquisition would have had the capitalist taint he was trying to eschew. The words *obtain*, *earn*, and *procure* carry the same connotation. In the long history of the English language, this mercantile sense wasn't always prevalent. But with the demise of feudalism and the ability of the common man to sell his labor freely, the need for new terms to reflect the new economic realities arose.

3   Usually, when a new field of endeavor arises, a jargon comes along with it. This specialized vocabulary serves as a shibboleth to a certain group and thus helps demarcate those who should be included in the select group and those who should be excluded. This did not happen, however, with words in the economic sphere. The vocabulary of capitalism is laced with words from other domains. Words like *account*, *budget*, *business*, *company*, *consumption*, *demand*, *duty*, *income*, *interest*, *market*, *pay*, and *purchase* all existed previously and were adapted to describe the new economic system. Probably the reason a selective vocabulary didn't develop was because of the centrality of these words to everyone's existence.

4   Many of these words once had radically different meanings. For example, when you *paid* a creditor, you weren't paying him, rather you were "pacifying" him. *Purchase* originally meant "to take by force." In Old French, *un enfant de perchas* was a term for a bastard; the implication is that a bastard is the product of a rape.

5   The end of feudalism necessitated new interpretations of words. *Service* was no longer an obligation, and many of the words to describe service and servants became pejorative terms. For example, a *knave* was originally just a term for a lower-class male child, and a *lackey* was a term for a footsoldier. Conversely, words that denoted a high status, like *noble* and *gentle*, came to possess a higher moral value.

6   With the ability to sell one's labor freely, words began to take on new connotations. Originally *fortune* referred only to chance; it didn't develop its sense of "great wealth" until the end of the sixteenth century. The point is that *fortune* was no longer seen as being controlled by others but now could be controlled by an individual.

7   Some words originally had a communal rather than an individual sense. *Wealth* once had the sense of communal wellness still displayed in the word *commonwealth*. By the sixteenth century it was used to describe an abundance, but it was not until the eighteenth century that it obtained its primary association with money. *Profit* was also originally associated with a community as opposed to an individual, but the focus changed with the growing tide of capitalism. Just as the "common weal" gave way to private wealth, communal profit gave way to individual profit.

8   M.M. Poston, in *The Medieval Economy and Society*, points out that profit and economic expansion in feudal days [were] inhibited by the concept of a "just price." This price was more than an injunction against excessive profit. Since the Church was essentially a conservative institution dedicated to preserving the status quo, "[i]t linked the price system with the divinely ordained structure of society, by defining a 'just' price as that which would yield the makers of goods and their sellers sufficient income to maintain them in their respective social ranks."

9   With the movement to a more secular society, equality first became an assumption, and then an inherent right of all men. According to Raymond Williams, in *Keywords*, *equality* is first used in the fifteenth century in reference to physical quantities, and in the sixteenth century to refer to equivalence of rank. The suggestion of "freedom" is thus one that is limited to the aristocracy. It is only with the French and American Revolutions that the term acquires a universal sense.

10   The advent of capitalism led to the amelioration of many words. In feudal times, to be *free and frank* implied only that one was not bound to a master. *Generous* suggested a noble lineage and not nobility of spirit, and, according to the OED, " 'liberal' was originally the distinctive epithet of those arts and sciences that were considered worthy of a free man."

11   This is not to imply that our more secular society is a morally superior one. Geoffrey Hughes, in *Words in Time,* postulates that the seven deadly sins—pride, wrath, envy, lust, gluttony, avarice, and sloth—are generally all seen, if not as virtues, then as neutral concepts. Pride is seen in a positive light, vanity has been ameliorated by terms like *vanity case*, and anger is seen as often justified. Envy and avarice are concomitant with capitalism, and lust, gluttony, and sloth are seen as facets of the "good life." No word better sums up this dramatic shift than the word *luxury*. In the fourteenth century, it had the sense of "lasciviousness" or "lust." By the seventeenth century, it had acquired a sense of habitual use of what is choice or costly, and it wasn't until the nineteenth century that it obtained its modern sense of contributing to sumptuous living.

12   But who knows? Now that the conspicuous consumption of capitalism is endangering our resource-depleted planet, perhaps one day *luxury* will regain its rapacious sense.

13   For goodness' sake, let's put the sin back in the Seven Deadlies!

For Further Thinking

1. Find one or two paragraphs that demonstrate process writing. Explain the rhetorical nature of the passage you have selected. See the sections on process description in Chapter 11, if necessary, for discussion of this form.

2. Do you think it is true that we use a type of doublespeak whereby we denude words of their original ethical and moral history? How does this process compare to the

doublespeak Orwell plays with in his novel *1984* (1949)? If you haven't read that novel, we describe its concept of doublespeak under "Looking Back and Ahead," following the previous selection (p. 482).

3   What current advertisements and/or songs use formerly negative or at least ambiguous words in new, supposedly enticing ways and contexts?

Looking Back and Ahead

1. What are the connections—based on language as a subject—between Richler's essay and the previous one by George Orwell?
2. Are there connections between Richler's essay and Diane Mooney's "Newfoundlandese, If You Please" (p. 111)? How does "culture" exert force on language, but perhaps differently, according to both authors?
3. Is there common thematic ground between this essay and Douglas Coupland's chapter "The Sun Is Your Enemy" (p. 390)? Explain.
4. Discuss the connections between this essay and "Subtraction by Addition: When More Adds Up to Less" by Carey Goldberg (p. 453) and "Life in the Stopwatch Lane" by Amy Willard Cross (p. 451).

Nina Varsava   Nina Varsava is an English major at the University of Alberta; this article first appeared in the University of Alberta's student newspaper *The Gateway*. In this essay, Varsava discusses the nature of fiction, non-fiction, and truth, and James Frey's *A Million Little Pieces*. Varsava questions the media's reaction to the discovery that not all of the events depicted in Frey's memoir are "true" and cautions the reader to read responsibly.

Non-fiction Isn't Fact—Read with Care

1   Suppose I tried to write a memoir—to build a coherent and convincing narrative out of a fragmented memory—but I screwed up a detail and someone proved its falsity. Am I now a fraud, a con artist? Because one of my details is untrue does it mean that my whole story is a lie, and can *I* even know which details are fact and which are fiction if all I have to rely upon is my (imperfect) memory? How can any piece of writing ever legitimately fit into the categories of memoir, autobiography, biography, or even history for that matter? Narratives about the past are based on reconstructed memories and records, and many details are lost, obscured, or fabricated over time—intentionally or not.

2   The current controversy surrounding James Frey's *A Million Little Pieces* got me thinking more about the absurdity of the unwavering fiction/non-fiction divide. Since an investigative internet site, "The Smoking Gun," disclosed evidence in January showing that Frey's best-selling memoir is bloated with fiction, the

public and the media have been in a state of stunned outrage. Readers feel unlawfully duped by the book that was deceptively published as non-fiction, and are filing lawsuits against Frey and his publisher.

3   Oprah chose *A Million Little Pieces* for her book club in October, and publicly praised Frey's courageous and inspiring narrative. But after learning that Frey had wickedly manipulated the truth, Oprah was irate. She had him, as well as his Random House publisher, Nan Talese, on her talk show, where she confronted them with her indignation.

4   Reproaching Talese, Oprah stated that, "if you're publishing it as a memoir, I think the publisher has a responsibility because as a consumer, the reader, I am trusting you. I'm trusting you, the publisher, to categorize this book [appropriately]." However, Oprah also asserted that Frey's memoir "reads so sensationally that you can't believe all this happened to one person." Nevertheless, she took the narrative as gospel until she was presented with authoritative evidence to the contrary. Have some faith in yourself, Oprah; if something is stamped as fact but is entirely unbelievable, then maybe you should consider not believing it!

5   Oprah's reliance on authority exemplifies the public's blind and passive acceptance of what is said by those in power. When you're reading a memoir, a newspaper article, a history book, or whatever, you have the right—and I think responsibility—to say, "Wait a minute . . ." when something seems questionable, even if the writer or publisher has greater "authority" on the issue than you. At all times, we need to approach critically what's presented as fact; if we don't, then we ourselves are at least partly to blame when we are duped by the authorities.

6   I've been shocked by readers' and the media's reactions to the discovery of fictitious elements in Frey's book, and have been led to feel that maybe the category of non-fiction has to be deconstructed entirely. If people actually take all non-fiction to be nonnegotiable truth, then it's a dangerous category indeed.

7   On Oprah's show, Talese wonderfully simplified the problematic nature of autobiography when she said that she can't "get inside another person's mind." "Well, that's my point, Nan," retorted Oprah, "Otherwise then anybody can just walk in off the street with whatever story they have and say this is my story." Well that's the point of autobiography, Oprah. You're the only one who has the authority to write your own, and with respect to many details, no one can ever really know whether you're lying or not.

8   It's ridiculous to demand that publishers investigate the minutiae of to-be "non-fiction" for its truth value. Non-fiction would never be published because the necessary investigations would be endless and, in fact, impossible.

9   Non-fiction has never been synonymous with truth. Once a moment of temporality is over, it can never be directly accessed, and the mediations of our memories are never infallible. However, I don't think this means that all "non-fiction" writing is illegitimate or dismissible. While one apparent solution would

be to categorize all works with questionable details as fiction, this would quickly become absurd, as I can't actually think of any non-fiction that wouldn't include details that were questionable to *someone*.

10   We could dismantle the category of "non-fiction" entirely, but this would detrimentally clump together two categories that are, generally speaking, significantly distinct, even if this distinction is shaky. Instead, I think we should accept and be constantly aware that the fiction/non-fiction divide is blurry at best. If we see non-fiction for what it is—a reconstruction of imperfect memories and scattered records—then we can appreciate the light it sheds on the truth, while critically engaging with its often questionable content.

For Further Thinking

1. Varsava's essay seems to tackle of number of important points in a short space. What rhetorical strategies does she use to accomplish this? (Definitions of these strategies can be found in Chapters 9 to 16 of the Rhetoric.)

2. Varsava begins her essay with a hypothetical scenario. Her thesis does not appear until later in the essay. What is Varsava's main argument (controlling ideas and reasons)? Can you think of other incidents similar to the controversy over James Frey's book that this same argument might also apply to?

3. According to Varsava's discussion, how should we as readers understand the category of non-fiction so as to have realistic expectations of a text's "truth value"?

4. Do you agree with Varsava's chastisement of Oprah's view of this debacle? What onus does the reader have according to the example that Varsava is making of Oprah's own reaction?

Looking Back and Ahead

1. Compare Varsava's argumentative method with other essays in this section, such as "The Seven Deadly Sins Are 'In' " (p. 485) and "Logic Will Betray Mankind Long Before Robots Do" (p. 509). How do the various methods compare? Which methods are more effective than others?

Wayne C. Booth Born in 1921 in American Fork, Utah, Wayne C. Booth received his PhD in literature from the University of Chicago in 1950. He went on to become a distinguished professor of English, serving as president of the Modern Languages Association in 1982. His major published work, *The Company We Keep: An Ethics of Fiction* (1988), examines in depth and detail his long-standing concern with the relationship of writer and reader. Now retired, Booth is working on a rhetoric of religious discourse.

Booth's essay "The Rhetorical Stance" uses various structures, notably comparison-contrast and cause-effect, to define his idea of the ideal "stance" or relationship to take with one's reader.

The Rhetorical Stance

1   Last fall I had an advanced graduate student, bright, energetic, well-informed, whose papers were almost unreadable. He managed to be pretentious, dull, and disorganized in his paper on *Emma*, and pretentious, dull, and disorganized on *Madame Bovary*. On *The Golden Bowl* he was all these and obscure as well. Then one day, toward the end of the term, he cornered me after class and said, "You know, I think you were all wrong about Robbe-Grillet's *Jealousy* today." We didn't have time to discuss his objections, so I suggested that he write me a note about them. Five hours later I found in my faculty box a four-page polemic, unpretentious, stimulating, organized, convincing. Here was a man who had himself taught freshman composition for several years and who was incapable of committing any of the more obvious errors that we think of as characteristic of bad writing. Yet he could not write a decent sentence, paragraph, or paper until his rhetorical problem was solved—until, that is, he had found a definition of his audience, his argument, and his own proper tone of voice.

2   When I think back over the experiences which have had any effect on my own writing, I find the great good fortune of a splendid freshman course, taught by a man who believed in what he was doing, but I also find a collection of other experiences quite unconnected with a specific writing course. I remember the professor of psychology who pencilled one word after a peculiarly vacuous paper of mine: *Bull*. I remember the day when P.A. Christensen talked with me about my Chaucer paper and made me understand that my failure to use effective transitions was not simply a technical fault but a fundamental block between him and my meaning. His off-the-cuff pronouncement that I should *never* let myself write a sentence that was not in some way *explicitly* attached to preceding and following sentences meant far more to me at that moment, when I had something I wanted to say, than it could have meant as part of a pattern of such rules offered in a writing course. Similarly, I can remember the devastating lessons about my bad writing that Ronald Crane could teach with a simple question mark on a graduate seminar paper, or a pencilled "Evidence for this?" or "Why this section here?" or "Everybody says so. Is it true?"

3   Such experiences are not, I like to think, simply the result of my being a late bloomer. At least I find my colleagues saying such things as "I didn't learn to write until I became a newspaper reporter" or "The most important training in writing I had was doing a dissertation under old Blank." Sometimes they go on to say that the freshman course was useless: sometimes they say that it was an indispensable preparation for the later experience. The diversity of such replies is so great as to suggest that before we try to reorganize the freshman course, with or without explicit confrontations with rhetorical categories, we ought to look for whatever there is in common among our experiences, both of good writing and of good writing instruction. Whatever we discover in such an enterprise ought to be useful to us at any level of our teaching. It will not, presumably, decide once

and for all what should be the content of the freshman course, if there should be such a course. But it might serve as a guideline for the development of widely different programs suited to the widely differing institutions in which we work.

4   The common ingredient that I find in all of the writing I admire—excluding for now novels, plays, and poems—is something that I shall reluctantly call the rhetorical stance, a stance which depends on discovering and maintaining a proper balance among three elements: the available arguments about the subject itself; the interests and peculiarities of the audience; and the voice, the implied character, of the speaker. I should like to suggest that it is this balance, this rhetorical stance, difficult as it is to describe, that is our main goal as teachers of rhetoric. Our ideal graduate will strike this balance automatically in any writing that he considers finished. Though he may never come to the point of finding the balance easily, he will know that it is what makes the difference between effective communication and mere wasted effort.

5   What I mean by the true rhetorician's stance can perhaps best be seen by contrasting it with three corruptions, unbalanced stances often assumed by people who think they are practicing the arts of persuasion.

6   The first I'll call the **pedant's stance**: it consists of ignoring or underplaying the personal relationship of speaker and audience and depending entirely on statements about a subject—leaving out, that is, the notion of a job to be done for a particular audience. It is a virtue, of course, to respect the bare truth of one's subject, and there may even be some subjects which in their very nature define an audience and a rhetorical purpose so that adequacy to the subject can be the whole art of presentation. For example, an article on "The Relation of the Ontological and Teleological Proofs," in a recent *Journal of Religion,* requires a minimum of adaptation of argument to audience. But most subjects do not in themselves imply in any necessary way a purpose and an audience and hence a speaker's tone. The writer who assumes that it is enough merely to write an exposition of what he happens to know on the subject will produce the kind of essay that soils our scholarly journals, written not for readers but for bibliographies.

7   In my first year of teaching I taught a whole unit on "exposition" without ever suggesting, so far as I can remember, that the students ask themselves what their expositions were *for.* So they wrote expositions like this one—I've saved it, to teach me toleration of my colleagues: the title is: "Family Relations in More's *Utopia.*"

> In this theme I would like to discuss some of the relationships with the family which Thomas More elaborates and sets forth in his book, *Utopia.* The first thing that I would like to discuss about family relations is that overpopulation, according to More, is a just cause of war.

And so on. Can you hear that student sneering at me, in this opening? What he is saying is something like "you ask for a meaningless paper, I give you a meaningless paper." He knows that he has no audience except me. He knows that I don't want to read his summary of family relations in *Utopia,* and he knows that I know that he therefore has no rhetorical purpose. Because he has not been led to see a question which he considers worth answering, or an audience that could possibly care one way or the other, the paper is worse than no paper at all, even though it has no grammatical or spelling errors and is organized right down the line, one, two, three.

8   An extreme case, you may say. Most of us would never allow ourselves that kind of empty fencing. Perhaps. But if some carefree foundation is willing to finance a statistical study, I'm willing to wager a month's salary that we'd find at least half of the suggested topics in our freshman texts as pointless as mine was. And we'd find a good deal more than half of the discussions of grammar, punctuation, spelling, and style totally divorced from any notion that rhetorical purpose to some degree controls all such matters. We can offer objective descriptions of levels of usage from now until graduation, but unless the student discovers a desire to say something to somebody and learns to control his diction for a purpose, we've gained very little. I once gave an assignment asking students to describe the same classroom in three different statements, one for each level of usage. They were obedient, but the only ones who got anything from the assignment were those who intuitively imported the rhetorical instructions I had overlooked—such purposes as "Make fun of your scholarly surroundings by describing this classroom in extremely elevated style" or "Imagine a kid from the slums accidentally trapped in these surroundings and forced to write a description of this room." A little thought might have shown me how to give the whole assignment some human point, and therefore some educative value.

9   A complete and pedantic divorce of writing from human purposes is revealed in a recent publication of the Educational Testing Service, called "Factors in Judgments of Writing Ability." In order to isolate those factors which affect differences in grading standards, ETS set six groups of readers—businessmen, writers and editors, lawyers, and teachers of English, social science, and natural science—to reading the same batch of papers. Then ETS did a hundred-page "factor analysis" of the amount of agreement and disagreement, and of the elements which different kinds of graders emphasized. The authors of the report express a certain amount of shock at the discovery that the median correlation was only .31 and that 94% of the papers received either 7, 8 or 9 of the 9 possible grades.

10   But what *could* they have expected? In the first place, the students were given no purpose and no audience when the topics were assigned. And then all these editors and businessmen and academics were asked to judge the papers in a complete vacuum, using only whatever intuitive standards they cared to use. I'm surprised that there was any correlation at all. Lacking instructions, some of the students undoubtedly wrote polemical essays, suitable for the popular press; others no doubt imagined an audience, say, of *Reader's Digest* readers; and others wrote with the English teachers as implied audience. An occasional student with real philosophical bent would no doubt do a careful analysis of the pros and cons of the topic assigned. This would be graded low, of course, by the magazine

editors, even though they would have graded it high if asked to judge it as a speculative contribution to the analysis of the problem. Similarly, a creative student who has been getting As for his personal essays would write an amusing, colorful piece, graded "F" by all the social scientists present, though they would have graded it high if asked to judge it for what it was.

11   One might as well assemble a group of citizens to judge students' capacity to throw balls, say, without telling the students or the graders whether altitude, speed, accuracy, or form was to be judged. The judges would be drawn from football coaches, jai alai experts, lawyers, and English teachers, and asked to apply whatever standards they intuitively apply to ball throwing. Then we could express astonishment that the judgments did not correlate very well, and we could do a factor analysis to discover, lo and behold, that some graders concentrated on altitude, some on speed, some on accuracy, some on form—and the English teachers were simply confused.

12   One effective way to combat the pedantic stance is to arrange for weekly confrontations of groups of students over their own papers. We have done far too little experimenting with arrangements for providing a genuine audience in this way. Short of such developments, it remains true that a good teacher can convince his students that he is a true audience, if his comments on the papers show that some part of dialogue is taking place. As Jacques Barzun says in *Teacher in America*, students should be made to feel that unless they have said something to someone, they have failed; to bore the teacher is a worse form of failure than to anger him. From this point of view we can see that the charts of grading symbols that mar even the best freshman texts are not the innocent time savers that we pretend. Plausible as it may seem to arrange for more corrections with less time, they inevitably reduce the student's sense of purpose in writing. When he sees innumerable W13s and P19s in the margin, he cannot possibly feel that the art of persuasion is as important to his instructor as when he reads personal comments, however few.

13   The first perversion, then, springs from ignoring the audience or over-reliance on the "pure" subject, whatever that could be. The second, which might be called the **advertiser's stance**, comes from *under*valuing the subject and overvaluing pure effect: how to win friends and influence people.

14   Some of our best freshman texts—Sheridan Baker's *The Practical Stylist*, for example—allow themselves on occasion to suggest that to be controversial or argumentative, to stir up an audience, is an end in itself. Sharpen the controversial edge, one of them says, and the clear implication is that one should do so even if the truth of the subject is honed off in the process. This perversion is probably in the long run a more serious threat in our society than the danger of ignoring the audience. In the time of audience-reaction meters and pre-tested plays and novels, it is not easy to convince students of the old Platonic truth that good persuasion is honest persuasion, or even of the old Aristotelian truth that the good rhetorician must be master of his subject, no matter how dishonest he may decide ultimately to be. Having told them that good writers always to some

degree accommodate their arguments to the audience, [a teacher must] explain the difference between justified accommodation—say changing *point one* to the final position—and the kind of accommodation that fills our popular magazines, in which the very substance of what is said is accommodated to some preconception of what will sell.

15   At a dinner about a month ago I sat between the wife of a famous civil rights lawyer and an advertising consultant. "I saw the article on your book yesterday in the Daily News," she said to me, "but I didn't even finish it. The title of your book scared me off. Why did you ever choose such a terrible title? Nobody would buy a book with a title like that." The man on my right, whom I'll call Mr. Kinches, overhearing my feeble reply, plunged into a conversation with her, over my torn and bleeding body. "Now with my *last* book," he said, "I listed 20 possible titles and then tested them out on 400 businessmen. The one I chose was voted for by 90 percent of the businessmen." "That's what I was just saying to Mr. Booth," she said. "A book title ought to grab you, and *rhetoric* is not going to grab anybody." "Right," he said. "My *last* book sold 50,000 copies already; I don't know how this one will do, but I polled 200 businessmen on the table of contents, and . . ."

16   At one point I did manage to ask him whether the title he chose really fit the book. "Not quite as well as one or two of the others," he admitted, "but that doesn't matter, you know. If the book is designed right, so that the first chapter pulls them in, and you *keep* 'em in, who's going to gripe about a little inaccuracy in the title?"

17   Well, rhetoric is the art of persuading, not the art of seeming to persuade by giving everything away at the start. It presupposes that one has a purpose concerning a subject which itself cannot be fundamentally modified by the desire to persuade. If Edmund Burke had decided that he could win more votes in Parliament by choosing the other side—as he most certainly could have done—we would hardly hail this party-switch as a master stroke of rhetoric. If Churchill had offered the British "peace in our time," with some laughs thrown in, because opinion polls had shown that more Britishers were "grabbed" by these than by blood, sweat, and tears, we could hardly call his decision a sign of rhetorical skill.

18   One could easily discover other perversions of the rhetorician's balance—most obviously what might be called the **entertainer's stance**—the willingness to sacrifice substance to personality and charm. I admire Walker Gibson's efforts to startle us out of dry pedantry, but I know from experience that his exhortations to find and develop the speaker's voice can lead to empty colorfulness. A student once said to me, complaining about a high school teacher, "I soon learned that all I had to do to get an A was imitate Thurber."

19   But perhaps this is more than enough about the perversions. Balance itself is always harder to describe than the clumsy poses that result when it is destroyed. But we all experience the balance whenever we find an author who succeeds in changing our minds. He can do so only if he knows more about the subject than we do,

and if he then engages us in the process of thinking—and feeling—it through. What makes the rhetoric of Milton and Burke and Churchill great is that each presents us with the spectacle of a man passionately involved in thinking an important question through, in the company of an audience. Though each of them did everything in his power to make his point persuasive, including a pervasive use of emotional appeals that have been falsely scorned by many a freshman composition text, none would have allowed himself the advertiser's stance; none would have polled the audience in advance to discover which position would get the votes. Nor is the highly individual personality that springs out at us from their speeches and essays present for the sake of selling itself. The rhetorical balance among speaker, audience, and argument is with all three men habitual, as we see if we look at their nonpolitical writings. Burke's work on the Sublime and Beautiful is a relatively unimpassioned philosophical treatise, but one finds there again a delicate balance: though the implied author of this work is a far different person, far less obtrusive, far more objective, than the man who later cried *sursum corda* to the British Parliament, he permeates with his philosophical personality his philosophical work. And though the signs of his awareness of his audience are far more subdued, they are still here: every effort is made to involve the *proper* audience, the audience of philosophical minds, in a fundamentally interesting inquiry, and to lead them through to the end. In short, because he was a man engaged with men in the effort to solve a human problem, one could never call what he wrote dull, however difficult or abstruse.

20   Now obviously the habit of seeking this balance is not the only thing we have to teach under the heading of rhetoric. But I think that everything worth teaching under that heading finds its justification finally in that balance. Much of what is now considered irrelevant or dull can, in fact, be brought to life when teachers and students know what they are seeking. Churchill reports that the most valuable training he ever received in rhetoric was in the diagramming of sentences. Think of it! Yet the diagramming of a sentence, regardless of the grammatical system, can be a live subject as soon as one asks not simply "How is this sentence put together?" but rather "Why is it put together in this way?" or "Could the rhetorical balance and hence the desired persuasion be better achieved by writing it differently?"

21   As a nation we are reputed to write very badly. As a nation, I would say, we are more inclined to the perversions of rhetoric than to the rhetorical balance. Regardless of what we do about this or that course in the curriculum, our mandate would seem to be, then, to lead more of our students than we now do to care about and practice the true arts of persuasion.

For Further Thinking

1. What does Booth achieve with the opening anecdote?
2. Where do you feel Booth first states his thesis?
3. What rhetorical method of elaboration is anticipated in the paragraph following his thesis statement?

4. Prepare a diagram or outline of this essay in which you break it into main sections. How do we recognize transitions between sections?

5. From your own experience as a writer, do you think Booth's definition makes sense? Explain.

Looking Back and Ahead

1. Can you find essays or portions of essays in the Reader that illustrate degrees of the pedant's stance, the advertiser's stance, and the entertainer's stance? You might wish to range beyond the Reader as well to look for other examples.

2. Are there two or three selections in the Reader that you would hold up as fine examples of a rhetorical stance achieved as Booth defines it? Explain your choices.

3. Rough out a summary of Booth's essay. Then compare your work to the sample summaries of "The Rhetorical Stance" on the Text Enrichment Site, Chapter 13.

Section 4 For and Against

The following four essays complete our Reader with an emphasis on formal argument, that is, on arguments that explicitly oppose each other's positions on a matter of controversy. Chapter 16 of the Rhetoric pertains to this final Reader section, although Chapters 14 and 15, on analysis and evaluation, are certainly relevant as well. As we say in various places throughout this text, your work in college or university involves a combination of critical thinking and argument. The four essays represented here emphasize the prevalence of analytical writing that hones a distinctly argumentative edge.

While the essence of argument is refuting other views and promoting yours, scholarly style encourages tolerance and moderation toward views you may ultimately oppose. It encourages fair-mindedness: that is, you are urged to consider other ways of looking at issues, and to respect those ways, before settling on your own. In a society of varied beliefs, an attitude of tolerance is very important. The word "argumentation" may seem to connote conflict and opposition, but may be more usefully conceived as a technique toward reconciliation. Public debate helps identify various worthwhile ideas, from which, with effort, consensus may eventually be achieved. For all the divisions and tensions within Canada, our country was founded and has survived—in the face of numerous obstacles—as the result of key agreements attained through public debate. Your careful consideration of the divergent opinions expressed in the following section may well lead you to formulate new thoughts and insights based on a synthesis of various different positions. As you express those new ideas, keep in mind that a standard way to maintain fairness and balance while also shaping your insights is the technique of concession-refutation discussed in Chapter 16. In the following four essays, consider to what extent and how effectively the writers have exercised concession-refutation. Also consider whether they avoid what Wayne Booth calls "the advertiser's stance" (p. 491).

Janice Procée and Gail Deagle   The next two essays, both by part-time students who are also health care professionals, argue opposing sides of the debate on euthanasia: are there times when society should deem it acceptable to end a human life as an act of mercy?

The Canadian Criminal Code outlaws the counselling or abetting of suicide. In May 1988, the first-ever conviction was laid against a Canadian doctor, Maurice Genereux, for having assisted suicide. As an indication of the high level of emotion often triggered in this debate, the Crown lawyer called Dr. Genereux the "Darth Vader of doctors." In the early 1990s, Sue Rodriguez, a woman suffering from Lou Gehrig's disease, appealed for the right to a dignified death through a doctor's assistance. The Supreme Court denied her petition. In February 1994, she ended her life with a mixture of morphine and Seconal, administered by an unknown doctor. An MP in British Columbia, Svend Robinson, an advocate of legalized euthanasia, was at her side, but was later not charged. This case, re-told by the 1996 TV movie *The Sue Rodriguez Story*, generated considerable public attention regarding whether euthanasia is compassion or crime.

The issue intensified with the Robert Latimer case. A northern Saskatchewan farmer, Latimer confessed to having killed his severely disabled 12-year-old daughter Tracy by carbon monoxide poisoning. There is disagreement over the degree of extended pain his daughter was suffering. Restricted by a form of cerebral palsy, Tracy did not seem to have a mental capacity beyond six months of age. She was far from being able to express what she might have wished. Tracy had undergone numerous medical interventions. Latimer's defence was that she would have endured endless, painful, futile operations and procedures, and that she would have suffered constant pain. Those critical of his action maintain that the girl was not in constant suffering and that he rejected the full extent of medical assistance available. In January 2001, after two trials by jury, appeals, a retrial owing to faulty procedure, and a refused request by the jury for a softened term, Latimer was sentenced to life in prison with no parole for 10 years. To some, this penalty shows the government of Canada and the judicial system as cruel, inflexible, and far behind the Netherlands, which allows doctor-assisted euthanasia under specified conditions.

Janice Procée   At the time of writing this essay, Janice Procée worked in a busy Ontario emergency department. Her essay illustrates the use of research as well as argumentation. Note her use of APA documentation style. In submitting papers using APA, you need a separate title page (not shown here). You number the title page "1"; you number the following pages in order beginning with "2" for the first page of your essay proper. You also provide a running head on every page at the top right, to the left of the page number. See Chapter 19 for more on APA style.

The Case for Active Euthanasia

1   Active euthanasia is a complex and diverse issue. This particular form of euthanasia is the "purposeful shortening of human life through active or direct assistance" (Darbyshire, 1987, p. 26). Personal and ethical dilemmas have surrounded this subject for decades, even centuries. Pro-life activists, including various churches, strongly oppose any type of assistance for people wishing to end their lives. Modern medical technology has advanced to such a degree, however, that terminally ill patients are not just living longer—they are dying longer. Through personal and work experiences as a nurse, I have found myself swaying in favour, within strict safeguards, of the right to die with dignity.

Author's surname links reader to entry in References. Date comes right after surname. Page number needed for direct quotations.

2   The debate against euthanasia is heard from religious lobbyists and other pro-life organizations. The Catholic Church, for example, believes that only God has the right to determine our fate, and we are trying to "play God" (Ellis, 1992, p. 34). "God giveth life, and only God can take life away" (Humphry, 1986, p. 5). The opposition groups fear that if euthanasia were legalized it would lead to widespread chaos and wrongful deaths. One dilemma is that if patients cannot express their desires, others may contravene their true wishes. Should a family member, a medical professional, or the caregiver have the final say? There is also great concern about organ donation, about patients not always receiving appropriate treatment because their organs are so desperately needed: "Transplant doctors circled like vultures around young, head-injured accident victims" (Trevelyan, 1992, p. 36). While these concerns may indeed be seen as legitimate, interestingly, there is no debate from pro-life groups regarding the issue of extreme measures to keep someone alive.

3   Before modern technology was introduced, people died by natural means without aid of life support systems. By allowing artificial respirators, feeding tubes, and a multitude of medications, we too are interfering with the natural death process, altering a life. Those opposed to the perceived cruelty of euthanasia should consider that to sustain a life that cannot breathe, eat, or function on its own is even more cruel. It is also a form of "playing God."

4   I work at the Royal Victoria Hospital in Barrie, Ontario, my home town. RVH serves a population of approximately 200,000 people. During the past two years that I have worked there I have been privy to many heart-wrenching situations involving patients who have determined their own demises through alternative means. This choice is never easy or without pain to others. Absolute prohibition of that choice, however, may simply intensify the pain of the choice individuals feel driven to make.

5   On one of my 12-hour shifts we had a patch call from an ambulance transporting a 67-year-old man who had sustained a self-inflicted single gunshot wound to the head. The ER trauma team prepared for the incoming patient. The paramedics arrived and were performing CPR [cardio-pulmonary resuscitation] when the team of doctors and nurses took over. The trauma team worked diligently for 30 to 40 minutes trying to sustain this gentleman's life; however, the gunshot would prove to be fatal. It was a highly charged emotional atmosphere as the family stood by and witnessed the passing of their loved one. Further investigation revealed that this man had recently been diagnosed with terminal cancer. He had chosen to take an active role in his own death. This unexpected choice had a devastating effect on the people he left behind. If given an informed choice, he might very well not have chosen such a violent means of death. For example, he could have learned more about the disease process and the length of survival and could have chosen to medicate himself until such time as he was past the point of pain management, and then been assisted by a professional during his final passing.

6   This past year I lost an aunt to terminal cancer. The cancer ravaged her body for over a year; we watched this horrible and crippling disease take away

the strong vital person we knew her to be. She was routinely brought into the hospital where I work, and each time I saw less and less of the person I knew. The last few months of her life were nearly impossible for both her and the family to bear. She would lie in her bed, unable to move, gasping for air, begging God to take her. Yet she still showed other signs of clinging to life.

7   This is definitely not a black-and-white issue. Earlier I mentioned a need for safeguards. Although I agree with euthanasia as a choice for consenting adults, I do not agree with its being implemented for babies, disabled persons who are unable to express their concerns, coma victims, or other people who cannot express their wishes. A society more open to the complexities surrounding this issue, however, would allow us to have personal transition orders in place. Those of us who do not wish to see life extended by the aid of machines in cases where recovery is not possible, who do not wish to feel a burden to those around us, could make that preference known in writing. We should have a choice about our final days while we are still competent to make decisions.

References

Darbyshire, P. (1987). Whose life is it, anyway? *Nursing Times, 83*(45), 26–29.

Ellis, P. (1992). An act of love. *Nursing Times,* 88(37), 34–35.

Humphry, W. (1986). *The right to die: Understanding euthanasia.* London: Bodley Head.

Trevelyan, J. (1992). Or an admission of failure? *Nursing Times,* 88(37), 36–37.

Here, no quotation marks, italics, or underline for essay title. Capitalize only first words of essay title and subtitle, plus proper nouns. Periodical title is italicized or underlined and all major words capitalized. Volume number is italicized, issue number roman in parentheses. Page span not preceded by "pp."

Essay title set as in previous entry. If same title appears in *body* of essay, then title takes quotation marks, and major words are capitalized. As in previous entry, no "pp." included. If essay were part of a book, then "(pp. XX–XX)" would precede place of publication.

Title of book italicized or underlined, but only first words of title and subtitle capitalized. In *body* of essay, all major words of book title capitalized and, as in References, title is italicized or underlined. References-list style for book is same for reports, brochures, monographs, and audiovisual media.

For Further Thinking

1. What do you consider the strong points of Procée's essay?

2. Are her points organized as effectively as possible? Why or why not?

3. Are there any weak points here? Has she supported all her claims with sufficient, detailed evidence? Are there any opinions stated as facts and thus left unsupported? Has she omitted anything surrounding the debate that, by its absence, could appear as a deliberate evasion?

4. Comment on her tone. Is it firm yet inclusive and respectful of the other side? Are there any moments of excess emotion or any propaganda techniques? (See Chapter 3 for a discussion of various propaganda techniques.)

Looking Back and Ahead

1. Based purely on rhetorical effectiveness, do you consider this essay more or less effective than Gail Deagle's "Euthanasia Reconsidered," which follows?

2. Examine Procée's references and compare them to Deagle's. Do you feel either of these writers has better references? If so, why? Could you suggest additions to the references in either case?

Gail Deagle At the time she wrote this paper, Gail Deagle was a part-time nursing student living in Grande Prairie, Alberta. Her paper illustrates the use of research as well as argumentation. Like Janice Procée, Deagle uses the APA style of documentation. See Chapter 19 for more information on this style.

Euthanasia Reconsidered

1   Discussions on controversial topics such as euthanasia, physician-assisted suicide, and the withdrawal or withholding of medical treatment are commonly held within our homes, workplaces, and governments. The last several decades have seen an increase in right-to-die activist movement groups across the nation. This is in part a result of many people being afraid that the tremendous advances in medical therapy available may expose them to unnecessary and extraordinary treatment, which would serve only to prolong their suffering in the face of death. Society's beliefs about end-of-life care and the right to make personal choices are changing. At one time, it was considered immoral and unethical to assist or aid a person to escape from pain and suffering of a terminal illness by means of euthanasia or suicide. Many people now feel they have the right to choose voluntary death in the terminal stages of their illnesses when they are no longer able to cope. Our nation is under great pressure by citizens and activist groups to legalize euthanasia. I believe that the legalization of euthanasia would lead to abuse of that legislation.

2   Once legalized, euthanasia would become a commonplace method of dealing with serious and terminal illnesses. One of the reasons for this is that medical and technical advances in palliative care and pain control would be threatened with the sanctioning of euthanasia as a method for relieving pain and suffering. We would see an eventual decline in available funds and resources for palliative care. In the state of Oregon, where euthanasia has been legalized, there has been a reduction of funds allocated to those essential services required for the care of the terminally ill. The same has been found in the Netherlands, where euthanasia is also a legal option. Post-implementation studies have shown that terminally ill patients are presented with fewer options for community-based, end-of-life care. Because supportive services in the Netherlands have been reduced, people tend to seek out end-of-life options. An important point to consider is that when given options, most people will not exercise their option of euthanasia when they have adequate pain control and end-of-life care.

3   Another point to consider is that it is entirely feasible that our government may choose the least expensive route of care in dealing with the terminally ill. Members of the International Anti-Euthanasia Task Force have addressed their fears that legalized euthanasia might be abused: "The cost effectiveness of hastened death is undeniable. The earlier a patient dies, the less costly is his or her care" (Torr, 2000, p. 115). It has been shown that in the Netherlands, medical treatment

options are frequently withheld from those who require palliative treatment. They are left to seek out the services of physicians who will assist them in succumbing to an early death. In Oregon, health management organizations (HMOs) are planning to cover the cost of assisted suicide and, as stated earlier, have reduced funding available for palliative care.

4   Not only do our governments hold a significant amount of authority in determining how our health-care needs are met, but physicians possess incredible power as well. Barney Sneiderman, a professor in the Faculty of Law at the University of Manitoba, is concerned that physicians have the potential to abuse guidelines when they take on the role of judge and jury (1994, p. 102). Legalization would enhance the power of control for doctors, not the patients where the control is intended. Where there is legislation approving euthanasia, there are no guarantees to safeguard against possible abuse. The Netherlands model of euthanasia is one we should be watching closely when determining possibilities of abuse after legalization. Explicit guidelines were set up in that model, but those guidelines are not being followed in the fashion intended. There is nothing in place to protect citizens from abuse. That country has found that there has been a progression from the people for whom euthanasia was initially intended to those who are receiving it now. Initially, the terminally ill were the only recipients of physician-assisted suicide or euthanasia. There has been a rapid progression to include those who are chronically ill, those with psychological afflictions, and finally those who are unable to make or communicate decisions for themselves. There are on average 130,000 deaths per year in the Netherlands, 1,000 of which a doctor actively caused or hastened without the patients' request.

5   Rather than requests for euthanasia being initiated by the patient, as the guidelines require, requests in the Netherlands most commonly come from family members of patients. Families become exhausted with caregiving, as there are few resources available for assistance. Given the option, many people choose to have their loved ones put to death instead of continuing the burden of caregiving. If euthanasia is legalized in Canada, the requests for assistance in dying should come voluntarily from individuals when they feel they can no longer cope with the burdens of the dying process. As seen in the Netherlands model, however, many will request assistance when they see themselves as burdens or nuisances. The next step is that requests for euthanasia will come from family or friends, as the patient is increasingly perceived as a burden on them. The reduced value placed on a life in our society and reduced available resources would play a role in this progression. In 1997, the Hemlock Society issued a press release "which asked that family members and other agents be able to procure court orders to kill *a demented parent, a suffering severely disable* [sic] *spouse, or a child* if their lives are *too burdensome to continue*" (Torr, 2000, p. 137, italics in original).

6   Our society has a declining value for human life. Our abortion policy proves that we are a society that already accepts ridding ourselves of unwanted lives. Our

society is one of convenience. Mothers who are inconvenienced by the prospect of giving birth to a child have an abortion. Family members inconvenienced by the duty of caring for one of their own who is terminally ill could seek euthanasia with or without the patient's knowledge or consent.

Within paragraph, do not include year in subsequent references to study if source is clear.

7   The disabled are wary and fearful that our country will legalize euthanasia. The apparent devaluation of human life brings fear to disabled persons that they will be killed against their will. Adolf Hitler set a mandate to "grant those who are by all human standards incurably ill a merciful death" (Torr, 2000, p. 118). The need for hospital beds during the war spurred Hitler to secretly euthanize the incurably insane and those with advanced senility or other conditions that caused the individual to be a burden on society. Diane Coleman (as cited in Torr, p. 134), founder and president of Not Dead Yet, claims that our society demonstrates significant prejudice against disabled persons, that society views the disabled as better off dead. She feels Dr. Jack Kevorkian is seen as a hero, which is the reason he has not been convicted of his crimes (Torr, p. 134). The majority of people Kevorkian has performed euthanasia on are those with disabilities, not with terminal illnesses. As quoted by Torr, Coleman goes on to say the following:

"As cited in" indicates study discussed in secondary source.

> According to Stephen Drake, Not Dead Yet's leading expert on Kevorkian, *the press have ignored his primary agenda to push for a class of human beings on which doctors can do live experimentation and organ harvesting. In his book,* Prescription Medicide, *he writes that assisted suicide is just a first step to achieving public acceptance of this agenda.* In written testimony that Kevorkian submitted in his first trial, he said, "*The voluntary self-elimination of individual and mortally diseased or crippled lives taken collectively can only enhance the preservation of public health and welfare . . .* " (p. 134, italics in original)

8   Given the trends seen in the Netherlands and hearing testimony from those advocating legalization of euthanasia, the disabled population has just cause to feel threatened.

In essay body, title of audiovisual program is underlined or italicized; major words capitalized.

9   The value we place on human life, particularly that of the disabled, was evidenced when Mike Wallace of the television program *60 Minutes* interviewed a disabled woman on television. During the interview, he questioned her about whether she felt she was a burden to society and openly discussed the costs of her health care. Similar comments to any other minority groups would never have been tolerated.

Here, Law Reform Commission identified as author; links to alphabetical entry in References.

10   Depression is a common reason for requesting assisted suicide in the Netherlands. In 1982, the Law Reform Commission in Canada defined the word "euthanasia" as "the act of ending the life of a person, from compassionate motives, when he is already terminally ill or when his suffering has become unbearable" (p. 17). My concern is with the terminology "unbearable suffering." It is not specified that the person must be terminally ill *and* be suffering unbearably. Will someone challenge the legal system with charges of discrimination because euthanasia is reserved only for those people with terminal illnesses? Euthanasia

is provided in the Netherlands, ambiguously enough, for people suffering mental anguish. An example is a woman distraught over the loss of her 20-year-old son four months earlier. Dutch courts ruled that mental suffering is grounds for euthanasia. It is suggested that a more appropriate treatment for depression is counselling and/or medication (Robinson, 2001). Diagnosis of depression can be difficult, but the condition is very treatable.

11   The process of legalization of euthanasia most certainly raises moral and ethical questions and concerns for all citizens in Canada. It is important that we look at the models already in place to evaluate their effectiveness and drawbacks. There is strong evidence to suggest that the same abuse of euthanasia as occurs in the Netherlands model would inevitably occur in Canada. Intentions behind strict guidelines have not been sufficient in enforcing the Netherlands' program. Involuntary euthanasia and the killing of people with afflictions other than terminal illnesses are occurring despite guidelines to the contrary. It is irresponsible to think that Canada would not see the same issues arise. There is a natural progression from euthanasia for those who are terminally ill and make a request for assistance to the eradication of a life that does not fall within those parameters.

References

Law Reform Commission of Canada. (1983). *Report on euthanasia, aiding suicide and cessation of treatment*. Ottawa: Supply and Services Canada.

Robinson, B. A. (2001). Euthanasia and physician assisted suicide: The verbal battle over euthanasia. *Religious Tolerance Org*. Retrieved April 25, 2001, from http://www.religioustolerance.org/euthanas.htm

Sneiderman, B., & Kaufert, J. M. (Eds.). *Euthanasia in the Netherlands: A model for Canada?* Brandon, MB: University of Manitoba. Legal Research Institute.

Torr, J. D. (2000). *Euthanasia: Opposing viewpoints*. San Diego: Greenhaven.

Identify date when information retrieved. Also download and archive information.

For Further Thinking

1. What do you consider the strong points of Deagle's essay?

2. Are her points organized as effectively as possible? Why or why not?

3. Are there any weak points here? Has she supported all claims with sufficient detailed evidence or citations? Are there any opinions stated as facts and thus left unsupported? Has she omitted anything surrounding the debate, which by its absence could appear as a deliberate evasion?

4. Comment on her tone. Is it firm yet inclusive and respectful of the other side? Are there any moments of excess emotion, any propaganda techniques? (See Chapter 3 in the Rhetoric for discussion of various propaganda techniques.)

5. Comment on Deagle's use of sources. Might she have gone further in acquiring certain sources? Explain.

Looking Back and Ahead

1. Based purely on rhetorical effectiveness, do you consider this essay more or less effective than Janice Procée's "The Case for Active Euthanasia" (the preceding essay)?
2. Examine Deagle's references and compare them to Procée's. Do you feel either of these writers has better references? If so, why? Could you suggest additions to the references in either case? See Chapters 18 and 19 for help with this question.

John Markoff and Bryce Clayton   The history of science abounds with luminaries and kooks. Often the most effective element in sorting out the former from the latter is the unfurling of time. In 1600 the Catholic Church burned cosmologist Giordano Bruno at the stake for the heresy of advocating the heliocentric view of the universe previously suggested by Nicolaus Copernicus (1473–1543). In 1616, cardinals of the Inquisition formally condemned the heliocentric "heresy" and suppressed Galileo Galilei who was using a newly developed telescope to support that theory. Louis Pasteur (1822–95) struggled ardently to convince a hugely skeptical medical community that microscopic organisms called "germs" cause disease. His controversial ideas included the insistence that prior to performing surgery, doctors should wash their hands. Until just recently, scientists predicting global warming trends were dismissed as alarmists and quacks. Today, the scientific community unequivocally believes that the earth revolves around the sun, that germs indeed exist and cause disease, and that threats posed by climate change are absolutely real. Even George W. Bush and the prime minister of drought-ridden Australia now concede that global warming poses a "problem." Yesterday's kooks become today's luminaries. But just as easily, today's luminaries become tomorrow's kooks, sometimes dire ones at that. Technologies such as nuclear power and DDT were welcomed wholesale into a civilization gazing optimistically towards a utopian future. Harmful consequences of innovations may be discovered only after catastrophe strikes.

The twentieth century witnessed an unprecedented explosion of technological growth that continues into this new millennium. Robotics, nanotechnology, and genetic engineering are just a few new technologies whose impacts have yet to be fully absorbed. In "The Doomsday Machines," John Markoff briefs his readers on some of the potential doomsday scenarios that supposedly could arise in connection with these new branches of scientific application, scenarios imagined by what Markoff calls "serious scientists and researchers."

The very term "doomsday" reminds us that fearing the end of the world, or at least the end of humanity, has ancient roots. In England, for example, a comprehensive land and resources survey of 1086 became known as the *Doomsday Book*, a title intended to celebrate the survey's thoroughness by comparison to the Biblical Day of Judgement when God was supposedly to judge all deeds and, perhaps not incidentally, end the world. In his 1924 classic history of the Middle Ages, Johan Huizinga refers to the people of that time as perennially "aggravated by the obsession of the coming end of the world" (21). Colin Wilson suggests that the cryptic prophecies of Nostradamus (1503–66), which the media and popular press publications rather than academics take to foresee a coming apocalypse, assumed a medieval belief that the earth would last 7000 years. In 1654, Archbishop James Usher used Biblical references to presume the earth's creation as October 26, 4004 BCE. By that reckoning, the twenty-first century begins the culmination of the final thousand years, the Millennium, foreseen as a time of wars and other catastrophes. Fears once driven by religion, however, now seem just as likely to be driven by views of technology. In the months leading up to January 1, 2000, for instance, thousands and possibly even millions of people stockpiled provisions and took various other drastic actions, convinced that so-called Y2K computer seize-ups would shatter life as we know it. It seems that we worry about chimeras while overlooking genuine threats.

One of many far-sighted authors who urged readers to come to grips with genuine threats was Mary Shelley. In her 1818 novel, published when she was merely 21 years of age, young Victor Frankenstein loses his mother to death; consumed by grief, he vows to overcome this nemesis of mankind. Applying the new scientific force of his age—electricity—he succeeds in charging life into a Creature assembled from body parts stolen from graves and charnel houses. The story switches to the Creature's point of view, and we realize that this lonely, unnamed being longs for love and acceptance. He is the ultimate outcast of literature—and the tragic outcome of his story is, of course, inevitable. For those uneasy with the direction of scientific research and invention, the story is a powerful metaphor of reckless application.

In the following magazine article, John Markoff provides further fuel for those on the doom side of the debate over science. His sources, referred to as a "representation of serious scientists," illustrate a willingness, perhaps an increasing willingness, on the part of those in science to open their own field to serious critical, ethical scrutiny. After the scientific concerns of the twentieth century, it seems that many in today's world are heeding the warning of works such as *Frankenstein*.

John Markoff John Markoff is a senior journalist who has been nominated three times for a Pulitzer Prize by his employer, the *New York Times*. He has been reporting on computers and technology since the seventies. His book publications include *The High Cost of High Tech* (1985). Markoff also teaches at Stanford.

The Doomsday Machines

1   In the space of three short decades, the computer chip industry has come to resemble the Sorcerer's Apprentice.

2   The exponential growth in computing power has produced stunning advances in a range of sciences and engineering fields ranging from decoding the human genome to the design of machines that can outplay the best human chess player.

3   And that in turn has led to exuberant predictions of a dawning of vast new Information Age utopias.

4   Sentient intelligent machines are as close as three decades away, many industry leaders believe; smart materials that can repair themselves and genetically coded immortality may also be just around the corner.

5   Given the hype and relentless optimism, perhaps it's not surprising that serious scientists and researchers have begun to explore darker, less inviting visions of the future.

6   This month an unlikely new doomsday prophet has emerged.

7   In an essay in *Wired* magazine, a popular forum for high-technology boosterism, Bill Joy, the chief scientist at Sun Microsystems, warns that the human species may be on the verge of collective suicide.

8   "The 21st-century technologies—genetics, nanotechnology and robotics—are so powerful that they can spawn whole new classes of accidents and abuses," he writes.

9   Joy is hardly a Luddite, but his gloomy pronouncements fit squarely into a long tradition of apocalyptic warnings about technology run amok, dating back to ancient Greeks, and voiced more recently in a millennial laundry list of threats, including nuclear winters, global warming, ozone depletion, marauding comets, the dispersion of deadly biological toxins by the Japanese Aum Shinrikyo cult in Tokyo subways, as well as the spectre of Y2K calamities sending civilization back to smoky caves.

10   As harrowing as all those threats may have appeared, for Joy and others the worst is yet to come.

11   The new danger, they argue, is self-replication, the technique at the heart of both modern biotechnology and the relatively new field of "material sciences" (the creation of advanced materials such as new ceramics or liquid crystal displays), which has the capacity for both tremendous good as well as destruction. The fears fall in three broad areas.

Robotics

12   The science fiction writer Isaac Asimov once described a world in which advanced machines, even if their intelligence vastly exceeded that of humans, could be programmed so they would never intentionally take any action that would harm people.

13   Now a number of writers and scientists are suggesting a more ominous, Darwinian scenario in which super-intelligent machines might evolve along with, and ultimately compete with, human society.

14   Consider a future world in which robots operate with microprocessors a million times more powerful than today's.

15   Hans Moravec, a robotics scientist at Carnegie Mellon University, conjures images in his writings of totally automated factories and networks that will emerge as soon as 2020.

16   These robotic systems will be able to program themselves and compete vigorously with humans for resources, perhaps creating self-sufficient artificially intelligent economies that could squeeze humans out of existence. (Think about a factory that decides to create an army of Robocops.)

17   Another computer scientist, Vemor Vinge, says machine intelligence will awaken sometime between 2005 and 2030, a date he calls "the singularity."

18   Vinge argues that this evolutionary watershed might accelerate progress well beyond human control.

19   Others suggest that the Internet may someday reach a critical mass of interconnections that at the least might exhibit some kind of chaotic behaviour,

perhaps even some kind of sentience. The problem, of course, is that such a system might be intelligent but not rational, thrashing around like a newborn baby—turning off power systems or launching missiles at random.

Nanotechnology

20   Nanotechnology refers to mechanical engineering on a molecular scale. The holy grail for nanotechnologists [is] sub-microscopic chemical or mechanical machines called assemblers that can reproduce and repair themselves.

21   There are already many industrial examples of micro-assemblers. For example, Polymerase Chain Reaction, the exponential amplification of DNA fragments, has become a standard tool of biotechnologists.

22   And recently IBM researchers described a process that permits chemical assemblers to self-assemble tiny magnetic particles into a perfectly aligned array of dots, each composed of several thousand atoms, for future disk drives.

23   Joy believes that within several decades, similar advances will lead to incredibly low-cost solar power, vastly more powerful computers and cures for everything from cancer to the common cold.

24   But here's the catch: in the wrong hands, or perhaps accidentally, nanotechnology could open a Pandora's Box.

25   This nightmare has long been the stuff of science fiction. Readers of Kurt Vonnegut's 1963 novel *Cat's Cradle* may remember "ice-nine," the final creation of the story's scientist, Felix Hoenikker.

26   Ice-nine was solid at room temperature. In other words, the molecules of H_2O in ice-nine had "discovered" a way to stack up to form a crystalline solid at temperatures where other molecules of H_2O were still in a liquid phase.

27   This contagious modification ultimately freezes the world's oceans. For several decades now, however, nonfictional scientists have been toying with the different ways that H_2O molecules can stack together.

28   And in real life, it might be possible to create tough omnivorous bacteria that could out-compete real bacteria. Spread by the wind, like blowing pollen, they could be designed to replicate swiftly and reduce life on earth to dust in a matter of days, according to Eric Drexler, one of the nation's principal advocates for nanotechnology. (Drexler advocates the construction of a series of high technology "shields" to ward off these kinds of threats.)

Genetic Engineering

29   While both robots and nanotechnological weapons are at least a generation away, genetic weapons are not. Joy and other scientists have begun to warn of near-term terrorist threats based on genetically engineered biological weapons.

30   "Much of the talk about information-based weapons is baloney," said Edward Feigenbaum, the former chief scientist of the U.S. Air Force.

31   "But biological terrorism is real and the government is beginning to take steps to defend against it."

32   Some scientists are worried both about the spectre of genetic experiments accidentally escaping into the population and also what Joy calls a "white plague" (a reference to another science fiction novel, by Frank Herbert)—genetically engineered bioweapons that could be targeted on a specific region or race.

33   It doesn't end there—there are even more exotic technological threats.

34   Last year a brief media frenzy broke out over speculation that the Brookhaven National Laboratory's Relativistic Heavy Ion Collider could create an artificial black hole that would devour the earth in a matter of minutes.

35   Scientists insisted that such fears were unfounded, yet as Armageddon scenarios go, it was a doozy. Earlier this month several physicists filed suit in federal court to stop the experiment.

36   Of course, it could be that Joy is wrong. After all, it is possible to take comfort in the thought that despite several thousand years of predictions of impending doom, the human species is, by and large, thriving. Still, it is a bit unsettling.

37   Perhaps Mark Twain put it best: "I'm all for progress. It's change I can't stand."

For Further Thinking

1. Consider your own personal experiences with the effects of science, technology, and medicine. Have they been good, bad, or a mixture of both?

2. What rhetorical patterns predominate in Markoff's article? (See Chapters 9 to 16 of the Rhetoric for a discussion of structures.) Should we have catalogued this article, as we have, in this section of the Reader, as exposition?

3. What would the science students and teachers you know say about this article by Markoff?

4. How would you describe the tone of this article?

5. Do you think science will bring a good or bad future, or some variation? Explain and illustrate with an example for each point.

6. In paragraph 9, Markoff refers to the "spectre of Y2K calamities." How did you feel about Y2K in 1999? How do you feel about it now?

7. Does Markoff manipulate his reader? If so, what strategies does he use to that purpose? Why is it easy to miss the sorts of problems that Clayton, in his following critical response, attributes to Markoff's essay?

Looking Back and Ahead

1. Read George Orwell's essay "Politics and the English Language" (p. 471). Rhetorically, how similar is that essay to Markoff's? Consider both structure and purpose.

2. Many North American Natives envision a harsh future of environmental malaise if the current order continues. In the fall of 2007, Alberta media began reporting on contamination flowing downstream in the Athabasca River, carrying polycyclic aromatic hydrocarbons from oil sands mining releases. Napthenic acids are another concern, but serious health risks for people of the Fort Chipewyan area began as early as the 1950s with dioxins

and furans released by pulp mills. In the 1960s the BC government erected the Bennett Dam on the Peace River, without consulting communities that could be affected. Water levels at Fort Chip dropped roughly 1.5 metres, killing off thousands of muskrats. For years, communities there have suffered from other industrial releases, such as arsenic, copper, lead, nickel, zinc, radium, and uranium. In a November 2007 CBC radio report, a Native community member was quoted as saying, "Your way of making money is our way of dying." Technology, the offspring of science, clearly seems driven by "our way of making money." Read "Saskatchewan's Indian People—Five Generations" in Chapter 11 (p. 166). Is destruction of life on the land an inevitable consequence of science and technology? What things do you think could and perhaps should be done to address the concerns of communities such as those around Fort Chip?

3. Read Gwen Kelley's essay in support of the Kyoto Accord, in Chapter 14 (p. 211). What do you imagine the scientists who supported George W. Bush's rejection of the accord would think of Markoff's essay?

Bryce Clayton   In response to the fears that Markoff outlines, Bryce Clayton's English course essay "Logic Will Betray Mankind Long Before the Robots Do" raises criticisms of bias and illogic. Clayton insists that Markoff oversimplifies the technology he discusses and fails to create "an effective analysis that requires examination of both sides of the argument." Bryce Clayton is an engineering student.

Logic Will Betray Mankind Long Before the Robots Do

1   On March 19, 2000, the fate of society was predicted; the end of the human species was assured by its own ingenuity. At least this was the message delivered in the essay "The Doomsday Machines" published in *The New York Times* by John Markoff. Markoff is quick to point out many dark aspects of technology that are indeed dangerous; powerful new technologies and innovations do have the potential to extinguish life with incredible speed and efficiency. Yet something as intricate as modern technology cannot be summarized so easily; there are too many shades of grey. How can something so complex be so simple? Also, an effective analysis requires examination of both sides of the argument which Markoff doesn't consider. Markoff fails to analytically investigate and present the threats posed by advanced technology through his bias, logic, and examples.

2   Questions and concerns floating around "the singularity," the instant when machines become conscious, are transforming into matters of "when" instead of "if." Markoff presents this event as the moment when machines will begin competing and eventually either enslaving or destroying mankind. Markoff refers to a computer scientist and science fiction writer, Vernor Vinge, who first proposed this event, and many other computer scientists, such as Ray Kurzweil, agree

with Vinge. Ray Kurzweil is considered to be one of the foremost experts in artificial intelligence by many esteemed colleagues, such as Bill Gates, founder of Microsoft. While Vinge sees the singularity driving the evolution of technology at a rate beyond human comprehension to the point of helplessness, Kurzweil foresees a future in which the sudden, exponential growth in technology following artificial intelligence will in fact be mankind's salvation. After interviewing Kurzweil, journalist Drake Bennet of the *Boston Globe* reported " . . . [Kurzweil believes] advances in nanotechnology [from technological growth] will allow us to ward off disease and senescence and to manufacture all the goods we want for a pittance . . . aging and poverty may hardly exist" (E5). Such a contrasting view of the birth of sentient machines is not even hinted at in Markoff's "The Doomsday Machines."An event as unprecedented as the singularity cannot be predicted with any accuracy. To condemn it as the beginning of an end is a gross over-simplification.

3   A semi-conscious internet shutting down entire infrastructures and firing nuclear missiles is a frightening yet ridiculous image. Markoff alludes to what has become known as "ghosts in the machine," bizarre reactions from unfinished code and hidden viruses, which may arise when the internet becomes so vast that it crosses the borderline into sentience. This notion has become a popular theme for science fiction writers, but does exist, most commonly in the form of viruses resurfacing long after anti-virus software has learned to defeat them. Markoff rightly ignores the viruses; these are deliberate attempts made by programmers to cause harm, not technology run amok as he fears. However, to suggest that the internet will achieve intelligence by simply having a sufficient number of connections is illogical. Unless specific programs are utilized, two processors cannot affect each other: the idea that millions of mindless processors will suddenly communicate and produce intelligence is so statistically remote it is practically impossible. Even if such a connection is made, current security measures such as firewalls and network passwords provide more than adequate defence. While programs that can bypass these defences do exist, they are the man-made viruses with specific intentions. The random code aspect of the "ghosts" is mostly a fantasy devoid of the capacity to defeat network securities. Computer programming works on a very simple premise: "on or off" binary language. All computer circuits function on an "on or off" principle and combinations of these on/ off signals produce a desired result. An unclear, unfinished line of code lacks the combination to provide any result. Complex programs that require repetition in the lines of code, such as search programs, utilize functions known as loops. Each time a loop is completed, the data it has acquired is stored in the computer's memory. In D.S. Malik's C++ programming textbook, the author states that "a loop that continues to execute endlessly is called an infinite loop. To avoid an infinite loop, make sure that the loop's body contains statement(s) that assure that the exit condition . . . will eventually [occur]" (202). An unclear loop will completely consume the computer's memory at which point the computer crashes. This

is just one of countless examples of how poorly written code can crash a computer. The fears of inexplicable behaviour emerging from the internet are premised according to "ideal" computers and situations instead of real computers. Markoff also avoided applying a name to the experts who have this fear, simply referring to them as "other scientists." The threat of a chaotic, semi-conscious internet cannot be considered valid if no one is willing to attach his or her name to the notion.

4   Markoff's choices of examples are particularly suspicious; they quickly reinforce his message, but after examination prove to either be irrelevant or even contradictory. One of Markoff's first examples is of the Aum Shinrikyo cult that released biological toxins in the Tokyo subway. The most sinister aspect of this attack is the helplessness of those exposed to these toxins: there was no defence available for the victims. This example elicits a blind and deeply emotional response to the dangers of technology, but fails to prove technology's responsibility for the act. A sociopath will be a danger to others no matter what technology is available to him. Assaulting people in mobs or the successful derailment of a train would have produced the same result; advanced biomedical technology was a flashy alternative. The next example chosen by Markoff was potential Y2K conflicts. The use of this example is particularly strange as the issues around Y2K never occurred. The scientific community rallied and quickly removed all potential dangers. Markoff reminds the reader of mankind's resilience with this example, not of our vulnerabilities. Fully automated factories are very close to reality as suggested in "The Doomsday Machines." However, to assume these factories will begin producing armies goes against logic. A logical, artificial intelligence would see that the continual production of machines would only deplete resources and further drain finite power sources.

5   Another source of Markoff's fears is the new field of nanotechnology. Alarms over engineered super-bacteria are being raised in many science fiction movies and novels such as *Twelve Monkeys* and *Cat's Cradle*. Markoff refers to Eric Drexler, who has been dubbed as the father of nanotechnology, as an example of an expert who warns of nanobots that could destroy all life on earth in days. Yet Markoff himself states that Drexler is a leading figure advocating the development of nanotechnology in the United States and that Drexler recommends that protective measures be established, not that the entire field of nanotechnology should be abandoned.

6   The most damaging aspect of Markoff's article is that it is based on an essay written by Bill Joy, chief scientist of Sun Microsystems. By first leaving the reader in the dark concerning what Sun Microsystems is, Markoff immediately damages his argument. Without any background information, Markoff gives Joy, an accomplished computer scientist and cofounder of a respectable networking firm, the little credibility of a Catholic preaching Islam. While Joy may be knowledgeable in a related area, he isn't necessarily an expert. Joy himself states, "I am more a computer architect than a scientist" (2) in the essay Markoff refers to. Such examples present shock value and can be quite persuasive at first glance, but the foundations of Markoff's arguments are crippled by insubstantial analogies.

7   Markoff may have tried to style his *New York Times* article to snare the reader's attention rather than to give a hard, analytical look at the growth of technology. Constant over-simplifications and worst-case scenarios may be far fetched, but are excellent eye-grabbers. Due to this, the casual reader may finish with a sense of dread and fear concerning the not so distant future, but discerning readers will recognize the shock value that Markoff intends and achieves.

8   Any research conducted must pass ethics committees, and as new dangers are recognized, new defences and safety measures are established. Dangers will constantly arise from new innovations, but often society benefits from these discoveries in unexpected ways. Nuclear bombs are arguably the most terrifying examples of dangerous technologies, but from their creation scientists have developed nuclear power plants and better understand the workings of the smallest particles.

9   Logical fallacies and shaky arguments keep "The Doomsday Machines" from becoming an analytical essay; there are no clean, unbiased facts.

Works Cited

Bennett, Drake. "Seeing the Really Big Picture." *Edmonton Journal* 27 Nov. 2005: E5.

Joy, Bill. "Why the Future Doesn't Need Us." *Wired Magazine* 8.04 (2000). Apr. 2007. <http://www.wired.com/wired/archive/8.04/joy.html>.

Malik, D. S. *C++ Programming: From Problem Analysis to Program Design.* Boston: Course Technology, 2002.

Markoff, John. "The Doomsday Machines." *Acting on Words: An Integrated Rhetoric, Reader, and Handbook.* 2nd ed. Ed. David Brundage and Michael Lahey. Toronto: Pearson, 2009. 505–08.

For Further Thinking

1. Give your definition of science. Is it synonymous with technology? If not, what is the difference between science and technology? What is the relationship between them?

2. Identify Clayton's main criticisms of Markoff's essay. Are they valid? Which points do you agree with? Which do you disagree with?

3. Define Clayton's tone in response to Markoff's "The Doomsday Machines." Use examples from the text to support your definition. Is this tone appropriate? Why or why not?

4. What sort of language (diction) does Clayton use? Give examples. Is this language always appropriate and effective?

5. Are Markoff's own opinions on the likelihood of catastrophe ensuing from the technologies he discusses in "The Doomsday Machines" discernible? Clayton asserts that Markoff predicts "the end of the human species" in his *New York Times* article. Does Markoff actually make such predictions? Is Markoff reporting on the opinions of others, making his own claims, or both? And Clayton?

6. Clayton insists that "an effective analysis requires examination of both sides of the argument, including points that Markoff doesn't consider." Is Clayton justified in calling Markoff's

article one-sided and biased? Does Clayton's essay provide "an effect analysis" that fairly examines "both sides of the argument"?

7. Clayton paraphrases Markoff's article without directly quoting him. Is this strategy effective? Does Clayton accurately paraphrase Markoff? Why might Clayton have chosen to paraphrase rather than to quote?

8. What other branches of current technology would you name as representing areas of potential harm? For example, some people deplore the genetic engineering of food and attendant monopolistic takeover of our food supply.

9. If you are a science fiction buff, you probably know of fiction, TV shows, and films that portray the future in opposite lights: some optimistic, some pessimistic. Think of two science fiction texts that contain contrasting views of technology. Summarize the two views. Is one more believeable than the other, or are they both oversimplified? What might have led the two authors to their particular views? Explain. If you can't think of texts but are interested in this question, consider a comparison of *The Time Machine* by H. G. Wells and *Walden Two* by B. F. Skinner.

Looking Back and Ahead

1. Read David Suzuki's essay "The Right Stuff" (p. 464), and think back to your own high school classes in science. Did those classes leave you with favourable or unfavourable ideas of what science and technology may mean to the future? What does Suzuki's view of that question appear to be? Do you share it or not, and why?

2. How is technology currently connected to other forces—politics, commerce, law, and so forth?

3. How would you like to see the future come to terms with the current ongoing explosion of technology?

INTRODUCTION

THE HANDBOOK covers the most common mechanical problems that arise in student writing. To be sure, it is simply a brief primer, reminder, and reference. You and your instructor will want to supplement this section with further exercises and examples. Our immediate goal is to introduce you to the principles and terminology that will help you understand an instructor's advice and identify grammatical functions. For ease of understanding, we have used the same terminology in the Rhetoric. With these condensed basics, you should begin to edit your own work more thoroughly and confidently.

Since the goal of college and university work is not simply to learn and apply rules but to think critically, we strongly encourage you to read "Language Arts or Language Departs?" on the Text Enrichment Site, Chapter 16, and "The Five Myths About Grammar" on the site under Handbook. The five myths suggest that grammar is (1) impossible to understand and apply, (2) dry and boring, (3) superficial, (4) limited to right and wrong, and (5) irrelevant to freedom, democracy, and respect for community. But if you think that grammar is superficial, you should consider the fact that misusing a single comma could cost an organization over a million dollars. A huge loss of money tied to one wrong comma happened in 2006, and it was by no means a unique incident. Give the essay "Five Myths About Grammar" a chance—go to the Text Enrichment Site, look under the Handbook section, read the essay carefully, and then decide if these five myths are or are not harmful assumptions.

Finally, on the Text Enrichment Site under Handbook, see the short essay "Scruffy Shoes and Job Interviews." It provides a pointed reminder that failure to apply standard usage in your writing can be as harmful to your success as a careless appearance when you present yourself for work.

The following three sections define principles that every writer works with daily.

1. Forms (Including Nine Parts of Speech)
2. Punctuation Terms
3. Fifteen Common Errors

We explain the terms and provide examples for each grammar principle. With a little attention to the rationale of these principles and terms, you should find them fairly easy to grasp. Remember, however, that almost everyone seems to feel embarrassed about his or her lack of knowledge on this subject, and therefore hesitates to ask questions. The most useful thing you can do after exploring your instructor's references to various terms in this handbook is to ask questions and clarify the principles. Work with the preliminary and supplementary information and methods on the Text Enrichment Site to help put the following information into a more clear, purposeful, overall picture.

Section 1 Forms
(Including Nine Parts of Speech)

As suggested in "The Five Myths About Grammar" (on the Text Enrichment Site under Handbook), words are like actors: they have their own identities, but they also play roles, and some words may change their function, their relationship to other words, and the sentence as a whole. Sometimes words change "parts" or "roles" without taking on any altered form whatsoever. Sometimes words add or lose endings and thereby change their ability to play different functions. The following types of words and players will be briefly defined and illustrated in this section: nouns, verbs, adjectives, adverbs, pronouns, phrases, clauses, modifiers, conjunctions, articles, subjects, predicates, objects, participles, gerunds, infinitives, prepositions, subject and object complements, comparatives and superlatives, and interjections.

1. NOUNS

Nouns are naming words. They name persons, places, things, and concepts. Often nouns end in the suffixes *–ence, –ance, –ism,* or *–ity.* Nouns may be made possessive by adding an apostrophe and usually *–s.*

Plural or Singular

noun

Many nouns may be either *plural* (more than one thing indicated) or *singular* (one thing indicated).

> **Examples**   bands, band

In the case of *collective* nouns, a single unit (treated as a singular subject) contains more than one thing.

> **Example**   The <u>team</u> prepares for the big game.

Some other collective nouns are *union, group, tribe, family,* and *herd.*
  Count nouns name things that can be counted and therefore expressed in singular or plural form.

> **Examples**   one woman, three women, 20 cities, six trees

Non-count or *mass nouns* name things that cannot be counted and seldom have plural forms. These are often abstract nouns, grouped items, food and drink, or natural elements.

> **Examples**   hopelessness, traffic, flour, air

Articles (or Determiners) and Nouns

The article (also called a *determiner*) *a* is used before a singular count noun when your reader or you do not know its specific identity, and when no other noun marker, such as a possessive pronoun, precedes the noun. The article *the* (also a determiner) is used before a noun when your reader knows its specific identity, except for plural or non-count nouns meaning "in general" or "all" or proper nouns.

Examples   The shopkeeper spoke to <u>a</u> customer on the telephone.

Fires can result from <u>the</u> smallest of sparks.

Four Main Types of Nouns

Nouns can be classified as four types: *proper, common, concrete,* and *abstract.*

A) *Proper nouns*, unlike all other nouns, are indicated by an initial capital letter. These "capital letter" nouns are the names of people, places, and some things.

Examples   Katrina, Salmon Arm, Charter of Rights and Freedoms

B) *Common nouns* name general groups, places, people, or things.

Examples   vegetables, cities, witness, instrument

King Arthur was an early <u>king</u> of England.

C) *Concrete nouns* name things perceived by the five senses.

Examples   muffin, sandpaper, perfume, sky, thunder

D) *Abstract nouns* refer to intangible concepts or values (things not perceived by the five senses).

Examples   love, truth, indecisiveness, pity

There is some overlap between categories: persons and proper nouns (Lisa), places and proper nouns (Cape Breton), and concrete and abstract words (tomorrow).

2. VERBS

Verbs are action words (*jump, realize, write*). Verbs also express states of being (Peter Gabriel *is* here). A transitive verb is followed by an object that completes its meaning (They *found* the keys). Intransitive verbs do not require objects (We *listened*).

Verb Tense

Verbs have different tenses: present, past, future. Each of these categories has sub-categories. *Uninflected* verbs (the infinitive) are expressed this way: to think, to feel, to understand. In order to express the time of action (tense) as well as to connect with the subject, verbs take on various regular or irregular endings and, in some forms of tense, helping or auxiliary words. A helping or auxiliary word (*am, had, could, would*

verb

have, etc.) together with the verb is referred to as the **predicate** (e.g., *is talking, had been talking, will have been talking*). For more on predicates (*verb + auxiliary or auxiliaries*), see number 12 following.

Examples	I <u>think</u>.
	She <u>thinks</u>.
	I <u>thought</u>. [irregular verb form to express past tense]
	She <u>calls</u> the meeting to order. [regular verb ending]
	She <u>called</u> the meeting to order. [regular verb ending to express past tense]
Present tense	They <u>run</u>. [simple present—a conjugated verb expressing actions or conditions happening now]
	Helen <u>has decided to exercise</u> better judgement. [present perfect—actions or conditions that began in the past but continue in the present]
	Lisa <u>is rowing</u>. [present progressive—an auxiliary verb and participle expressing ongoing actions or conditions]
Past tense	Anthony <u>fell</u> on the sidewalk. [simple past—actions or conditions that occurred in the past]
	We <u>had left</u> the movie theatre before Melanie and Kirsten realized they had forgotten to call Mr. Salinger. [past perfect—actions or conditions that occurred in the past but were completed before some other past actions or conditions occurred.]
	The happy couple <u>were dancing</u> to swing music. [past progressive—ongoing actions or conditions that occurred in the past]
Future tense	Jim and Tammy <u>will sell</u> their Nashville house. [simple future—actions or conditions that have yet to occur]
	Cirque du Soleil <u>will have given</u> countless performances in Las Vegas over the next two years. [future perfect—current actions or conditions that will be completed by some definite time in the future]
	Batman and Robin <u>will be waiting</u> for the Riddler to send another clue by next week. [future progressive—actions or conditions that will occur in the future]

Verb Mood

The form a verb takes can also show (besides a time period) the **mood** of the verb: how the action is viewed by the speaker. The *indicative* mood states a fact or asks a question (e.g., *I am going to the lake. Are you coming to the reunion?*). Some grammar texts consider the asking of a question as a separate mood: the *interrogative*. The *imperative* mood expresses a command (e.g., *Submit your assignment by Wednesday.*). The *subjunctive* mood expresses doubt, wish, or conditionality (e.g., *I don't think you should* *go to the party. She wishes she were older. If she were sixteen, she could go. Her brother talks as if he were in charge of the house.*). For several decades, however, the convention of altering forms of the verb "to be" for subjunctive mood has been weakening (e.g., *I wish I was rich* is now often written instead of the more formal *I wish I were* rich).

Verb Voice

The form a verb takes can also indicate voice: whether the doer of the action is presented as the doer of the action (*active voice*) or simply implied (*passive voice*). *She filed the complaint* is written in the active voice, whereas *A complaint was filed* is in the passive voice. In the latter example, the noun "complaint" functions as the grammatical subject of the sentence, even though the real doer is *she* or someone else not named. Passive and active voice can operate in any time and tense (e.g., *She files the report. A report will be filed. A report will have been filed.*).

Transitive and Intransitive Verbs

Some verbs (*transitive*) require an object for a complete thought to be expressed (e.g., *She threw a strike.*). Other verbs (*intransitive*) do not require an object to express a complete thought (e.g., *She celebrated.*). Your dictionary uses the abbreviation "tr." to denote transitive verbs and "intr." to denote intransitive verbs. Some verbs may be transitive or intransitive, depending on how they are being used (e.g., *She celebrated her perfect game.*).

For more detailed information on verbs, see the appendixes at the end of this section, "Appendix A: Twelve Verb Tenses" and "Appendix B: Irregular Verbs."

3. ADJECTIVES

adj

Adjectives modify nouns or pronouns. Adjectives tell the reader *what kind* and *what quantity*. Adjectives may be identified by various suffixes, including *–able, –ible, –ile, –ive, –ous, –ar, –ic, –ent, –ant, –ful,* etc.

Example   The <u>busy</u> accountant checked her <u>various</u> forms to determine which of the <u>five</u> <u>corporate</u> files needed <u>careful</u> review in the <u>busy</u> days <u>ahead</u>.

In the *positive, comparative,* and *superlative,* adjectives change.

Examples	**Positive**	**Comparative**	**Superlative**
	hot stove	hotter stove	hottest stove
	reasonable idea	more reasonable idea	most reasonable idea
	good student	better student	best student

> **Tip:** Most academic and business writers use adjectives only sparingly to maintain a formal tone. Personal and creative writers of fiction and non-fiction may use adjectives more frequently to intensify expression and effects. Advertising overuses adjectives to the point of meaninglessness: "colossal blowout bonanza sale."

> **Tip:** Adjectives created by the past participle form of a verb take an –*ed* ending.

Incorrect	She was bias.
Correct	She was biased.
Explanation	If you rely on how statements sound in conversation, you may not hear certain syllables being pronounced, or sometimes speakers leave off syllables that are meant to be used. We would not say, "The car was stole." We would say, "The car was stolen." *Stolen*, like *biased*, is the past participle of the verb functioning as an adjective.

4. ADVERBS

Adverbs modify verbs, adjectives, other adverbs, and entire clauses. Adverbs tell the reader *how* and *in what way*. Adverbs may be identified by the suffix –*ly*, though not all adverbs end in –*ly*, and not all words ending in –*ly* are adverbs.

> **Example**   Unexpectedly, the musician resourcefully sampled some Sly and the Family Stone, subtly but insistently, in her new song in a very bold way.

Like adjectives, many adverbs change form from the *positive* degree to express the *comparative* and *superlative* degrees.

> **Example**   intelligently, more intelligently, most intelligently

> **Tip:** As with adjectives, adverbs should be used sparingly in formal writing (academic and business composition), and can appear more frequently in personal and creative writing.

5. PRONOUNS

Pronouns take the place of nouns. When the pronoun stands in for a noun, that noun is then called the *antecedent* or *referent*.

The eight categories of pronouns are personal, demonstrative, relative, reflexive, intensive, interrogative, indefinite, and reciprocal. We cover only personal and relative pronouns here.

Personal pronouns refer to specific persons or things. They agree in number and gender with the nouns they represent. Personal pronouns have three *cases*, including subjective and objective. *Case* refers to the inflectional form taken by pronouns (or the possessive form of nouns) to indicate their function in a group of words.

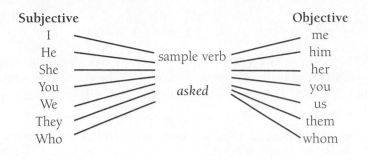

Pronoun case is determined by whether the pronoun functions as a subject or an object. Decide this according to the pronoun's relation to a verb or a preposition.

Examples   subj verb obj   infin   obj
(*verb*)   I *asked* <u>them</u> *to visit* <u>her</u> at her new job.

                   subj   verb obj
                   <u>They</u> *drove* <u>him</u> to Vancouver for ice cream.

                                      prep obj
Examples   The sale of the car will be left up *to* <u>her</u>.
(*preposition*)

                               prep   obj
                   The study group consisted *of* Dionna, Xiu, and <u>me</u>.

The possessive case of pronouns occurs when the pronoun is used as an adjective (e.g., *her* dog, The dog is *hers*.).

Relative pronouns (*who, which, whose, whom, that*) introduce adjective clauses. They refer to the noun or pronoun that the clause modifies.

Examples   The runner, <u>who</u> had an early burst, has dropped back in the last two kilometres.

                   The physics principle <u>that</u> we reviewed last week will be on the exam.

> **Tip:** *That* and *which* differ because *that* introduces restrictive clauses while *which* introduces non-restrictive clauses.

Example   The Clint Eastwood movie <u>that</u> needs more scholarly attention is 1971's *Dirty Harry*. This film, <u>which</u> is set in San Francisco, explores violence and urban alienation.

Some writers, however, occasionally use "which" with restrictive clauses.

(Please note that in the above example an apostrophe is used to indicate possession. The term "1971" is used as an adjective to describe the film; that is, *Dirty Harry* is a film *of* or *belonging to* 1971. Note, however, that the plural form to indicate an entire decade simply adds an "s," but no apostrophe: the 1970s. This is the same as adding an "s" to the singular word "book" in order to indicate additional "books.")

6. PHRASES

Phrases are groups of words that do not contain a conjugated verb and that function in some way as a unit to serve as a noun or modifier. There are various types of phrases, including gerund phrases, infinitive phrases, participial phrases, appositive phrases, and prepositional phrases.

As a noun   Becoming a lifeguard takes many hours in the pool. [This is a gerund phrase: the present participle here (verb ending in –*ing*) functions as a noun and, in this case, as the subject of the sentence.]

As a noun   To err is human. [This is an infinitive phrase, and the infinitive here functions as the sentence's subject.]

As a modifier   Linked by prison handcuffs, Sydney Poitier and Tony Curtis were fugitives in the film *The Defiant Ones*. [In this participial phrase, "linked" is the participle. Participial phrases always function as modifiers.]

As a modifier   Emily Brontë's novel, known as *Wuthering Heights*, was her only published novel. [This is an appositive phrase, which names the noun preceding it.]

As a modifier   The bowl of fresh kiwi and grapes looks refreshing. [This is a prepositional phrase, which modifies the noun "bowl" (a bowl of what?). A prepositional phrase begins with a preposition and ends with a noun or pronoun. The subject of the sentence is "bowl," not the prepositional phrase that modifies it.]

modifier

7. CLAUSES

A clause is a group of words containing a subject and a verb or predicate. There are two types of clauses: *independent* (which have subjects and predicates and can stand alone as sentences) and *dependent* (which have subjects and predicates but cannot stand alone as sentences). Dependent clauses function as adverbs, adjectives, or nouns.

Independent clause   A cigar smells. [subject + conjugated verb]

                          The blues singer, an experienced Chicago musician, looked above the crowd while she performed a famous Lightning Hopkins song. [subject + conjugated verb]

Dependent clause   The teachers, since they were undecided about the strike action, asked for more information.

8. MODIFIERS

A modifier qualifies other words, providing extra information. Modifiers may be adjectives (*tall, inexpensive, startled*), adverbs (*very, quickly, tightly*), articles (*the, a*), phrases (*of the valley*), or clauses (*which frightens Uncle Jim*).

Example   Soaked in rain, the young postal worker walked steadily toward the tall building, which was built in 1965.

Tip: Watch out for misplaced modifiers, which do not clearly refer to the words they seek to modify. You will produce meanings you do not intend!

Examples   Last year, Sigourney only smoked two packs of cigarettes. [Is that *all* she did all year? Or, more likely, did she smoke *only* two packs last year?]

Tasha presumed in Seattle that everyone liked playing Crazy Eights. [Did "Tasha presume *in Seattle*" or did she presume that "everyone *in Seattle*" liked this card game?]

9. CONJUNCTIONS

Conjunctions are joining words. They link words or word groups, expressing the relations between these elements. There are three types of conjunctions: coordinate, subordinate, and correlative.

conj

A) There are seven *coordinate conjunctions* (*for*, *and*, *nor*, *but*, *or*, *yet*, *so*). They can be remembered as the acronym "FANBOYS." These conjunctions may be used to combine two independent clauses into one sentence (known as a compound sentence). A comma falls before the coordinating conjunction, in order to clarify for the reader that a new clause is about to begin.

Examples   Moby is an interesting musician, <u>but</u> he is not as interesting as Miles Davis.

The gifted photographer Yousuf Karsh created portraits of many famous people, <u>yet</u> he did not photograph Pat Benatar or Barbara Carter.

B) *Subordinate conjunctions* introduce dependent clauses and express relations between dependent clauses and independent clauses. The type of sentence represented by the following example (*independent clause* + *subordinating conjunction* and *subordinate clause*) is called a *complex* sentence.

Example   We didn't realize Elvis Presley was a truck driver before he became a recording artist, <u>although</u> we thought we knew a lot about him.

Some subordinate conjunctions include *after*, *although*, *as*, *because*, *before*, *even though*, *if*, *once*, *rather*, *than*, *since*, *that*, *though*, *unless*, *when*, *whenever*, *where*, *whereas*, and *while*.

C) *Correlative conjunctions* appear as pairs of conjunctions that join word groups. Some correlative conjunctions include *both . . . and*, *either . . . or*, *neither . . . nor*, *not . . . but*, *not only . . . but also*, and *whether . . . or*.

Example   <u>Both</u> porpoises <u>and</u> chimpanzees are very intelligent creatures.

> **Tip:** The words or word groups joined by correlative conjunctions must be grammatically parallel.

D) *Adverbial conjunctions* (or *conjunctive adverbs*) are used to add information (*furthermore, moreover, likewise*), provide contrast (*however, nevertheless*), show results (*consequently, therefore*), or show an alternative (*otherwise*). These may occur as a non-restrictive modifier set off by commas in the midst of a statement (*She is the smallest student in the school. She is, however, the fastest runner.*). These may also follow a semicolon in compound sentences that combine two independent clauses using a semicolon (*She is the smallest student in the school; however, she is the fastest runner.*).

> **Tip:** When used following a semicolon to introduce a second independent clause, the adverbial conjunction is followed by a comma, indicating that it is an introductory element.

> **Tip:** Grammarians of yore used to forbid starting a sentence with a coordinating or adverbial conjunction. Even when that rule was imposed (and some people still abide by it), achieved writers "broke" it frequently. A better rule is to exercise stylistic discretion in when and why you start a sentence with either of these types of conjunctions.

subj

10. ARTICLES (DETERMINERS)

An article is a modifier appearing before a noun, adjective, or adverb. The three articles are *a*, *an*, and *the*. *A* and *an* are general, while *the* is specific.

Examples   <u>An</u> enzyme may be <u>the</u> source of this scientific mystery. [general (*an*) and specific (*the*)]

<u>The</u> old piano needs tuning. [specific]

> **Tip:** *An* should appear before words beginning with vowel sounds or a silent "h." *A* should appear before words beginning with consonant sounds or a sounded "h" (<u>a</u> history lesson, <u>an</u> hour).

11. SUBJECTS

A subject is one of two main parts of a sentence, the other being the predicate. There are simple subjects, complete subjects, and compound subjects.

A) A *simple subject* is a noun or pronoun that performs an action or is acted upon.

Examples   The <u>movie</u> *was filmed* in black and white. [subject acted upon]

The <u>car</u> *turns* right on the red light. [subject performing action]

> **Tip:** To find the simple subject of a sentence when it is part of a noun phrase, imagine a line scoring out the preposition and the words following it (e.g., *The Night ~~of the Long Knives~~ was a nuisance to Pierre Trudeau.*). The noun phrase in this example is *Night of the Long Knives,* but the simple subject is *Night.* The preposition is *of.* See section 17 below for more on prepositions. This point on how to recognize the simple subject as opposed to the complete subject is necessary, because the verb of the subject agrees with the simple subject only. One would not inflect the verb to agree in number with the nearest noun. It would be incorrect to write *The Night of the Long Knives were a nuisance to Pierre Trudeau.*

B)   A *complete subject* includes the simple subject and any words that modify it.

Example   The <u>tall mechanic with the beard</u> fixed the Volkswagen van.

C)   A *compound subject* is two (or more) simple subjects joined by a coordinate conjunction or correlative conjunction.

Example   <u>Alfred Hitchcock and Ridley Scott</u> have made interesting movies.

pred

> **Tip:** In some sentence constructions, the subject may not appear at the beginning of your sentence, nor appear in subject-verb sequence.

Examples   Where *does* <u>Lionel</u> find all those novels? [question]
                   <small>verb</small>

        <small>verb</small>
Don't *call* Patricia! [command—"you" is implied subject]

        <small>verb</small>
Here *are* some <u>Torontonians</u>. ["there" and "here" reverse subject-verb order to verb-object]

      <small>verb</small>
It *is* a rainy <u>day</u>.

Writers sometimes use the expletives—also called *dummy words*—*there* or *it* combined with forms of the verb *to be* in order to control pace and emphasis in certain sentences. In the last example above, the actual subject *day* comes at the end of the sentence. Avoid expletives unless they seem the natural choice.

12. PREDICATES

There are three types of predicates: *simple predicate* (which is the main verb), *complete predicate* (the main verb and its auxiliaries, including objects or complements and their modifiers), and *compound predicate* (two or more verbs that have the same subject and are linked by a coordinating conjunction or a correlative conjunction).

A) Simple predicate

Example   The runner <u>stumbles</u>.

B) Complete predicate

Example   Lydia <u>will have represented her client to the best of her limited ability</u>.

> **Tip:** In this example of a complete predicate, those words that indicate action, tense, and mood (*will have represented*) are followed by the direct object (*client*, the word that is the answer to the question *whom did she represent?*) and two adverbial modifying phrases (*to the best, of her limited ability*). Being able to subdivide complete predicates helps you to remain alert to specific functions within the combinations that a complete predicate may comprise.

C) Compound predicate

Example   The Halifax driver <u>signalled a left turn</u>, <u>slowed the school bus</u>, and <u>turned on the flashing green traffic light</u>.

> **Tip:** The inflected form taken by verbs and auxiliaries in a predicate may express tense, mood, and voice. These matters are explained under Verbs (pp. 519–21).

13. OBJECTS

There are two types of objects: *direct* and *indirect*.

A direct object (DO) is a word or word group that names the person or thing acted upon by the subject. A direct object can answer the questions *what?* or *whom?* about the verb.

Examples   Lisa laced <u>her figure skates</u>.

Russell Crowe pushed <u>another bar patron</u>.

An indirect object (IO) is a noun or pronoun that can answer the question *for whom? to whom? to what?* or *for what?* about the verb.

Examples   Stephanie helped her classmates <u>for her teacher's sake</u>.

Marc sold his drum set <u>to the highest bidder</u>.

14. PARTICIPLES

A participle is a verb form with either *–ing* or *–ed* on the end. Participles function as adjectives and appear as either *present* participles or *past* participles.

Examples   The <u>oncoming</u> ocean liner parted the cold waves. [present participle]

Now <u>stalled</u>, the car slowed the traffic on Sherbrooke Street. [past participle]

15. GERUNDS

A gerund is a verbal form that ends in *–ing* and functions as a noun. A gerund can be a subject or an object.

Subject   <u>Napping</u> is sometimes necessary.

Object   We know <u>swimming</u> does not require a swimsuit.

> **Tip:** Gerunds appear in the same form as present participles, but present participles function as *adjectives* while gerunds operate as *nouns*.

Examples   <u>Hoping for more peace</u>, the neighbour went on a <u>fishing</u> trip. [participle phrase and present participle (adjectives)]

<u>Fishing</u> takes more skill than bingo. [gerund (noun)]

16. INFINITIVES

An infinitive consists of the form of the verb preceded by "to" (*to* lift, *to* photograph, *to* kiss). We conjugate infinitives to derive specific verb forms (I lift, she photographs, they kiss).

Infinitives may function as subjects or objects of verbs.

Examples   <u>To dream</u> is courageous. [subject]

The cook wants <u>to relax</u>. [object]

The doctors hope <u>to find</u> the problem soon. [object]

> **Tip**: In efforts to treat English as Latin, grammarians of yore used to forbid the splitting of an infinitive (e.g., Don't say, *I am going to sweetly sing.* Say, *I am going to sing sweetly.*). The *Oxford English Dictionary* now recognizes that there are times when writers legitimately break this old rule.

17. PREPOSITIONS

Prepositions are connectors that express relationships between nouns or pronouns (or verbs or adjectives serving as nouns) and the other words in a sentence. They are primarily function words. Prepositions include the following words: *about, above, across, after, among, around, as, at, before, behind, below, beside, between, beyond, down, for, from, in, into, near, of, off, on, onto, over, toward, under,* and *within.*

A prepositional phrase begins with a preposition and ends with a noun or pronoun.

Examples   The agreement <u>between the accountants</u> has been signed.

          The bowl <u>of fruit</u> sits on the kitchen table.

> **Tip:** Remember to make your verb agree with your simple subject (bowl), not any noun in the prepositional phrase.

                      subj   prep phrase   verb

Example   This *collection* <u>of fishing rods, old comic books, and toys</u> *has* sentimental value.

> **Tip:** In efforts to treat English as Latin, grammarians of yore used to forbid ending a sentence with a preposition (e.g., Do not say, *Whom are you singing to?* Say, *To whom are you singing?*). This rule still makes basic sense in that it recognizes the end of a sentence as an impact location. Why place a small connective word in a point of importance? A more useful rule for today, however, is that you should avoid ending sentences with a preposition except when it seems natural to do so.

> **Tip:** One of the trickiest aspects of English is mastering the correct preposition to use with various words in order to express one of two or more meanings that could be conveyed by that word.

comp

Examples   Contending *with* rude customers is part of being a food server.

          Contending *for* improved quality is part of the new manager's agenda.

          This movie was adapted *from* the book.

          The script was adapted *by* a new writer.

          She has not yet adapted *to* life in Hollywood.

There are many prepositions and many different meanings conveyed by the same words if followed by different prepositions. Consult other, more comprehensive usage references if you have problems deciding which preposition expresses your intended meaning.

18. SUBJECT AND OBJECT COMPLEMENTS

A subject complement is a word or word group that follows a *linking verb* and identifies or describes the subject. Linking verbs are forms of being and include the verbs *be*, *seem*, *appear*, *stay*, *look*, *become*, *sound*, *taste*, *feel*, and *smell*.

                     linking verb   subj compl

Examples   This flower *smells* <u>like a mixture of talcum powder and fresh rain</u>.

                     linking verb

          This milk *seems* sour.

An object complement is a word or word group that follows a *direct object* and identifies or describes that object.

                                         DO   obj compl

Example   The CBC reporter called the author's *work* <u>self-centred</u>.

19. COMPARATIVES AND SUPERLATIVES

Comparatives are forms of adjectives and adverbs that describe a relation between *two* items or concepts.

Example   Irvine Welsh, who wrote *Trainspotting*, is a <u>better</u> writer than Jane Owen, who wrote *Camden Girls*, in describing the modern urban dance club in the United Kingdom.

A superlative is the form of an adjective or adverb that describes the relationship between *more* than two items or concepts.

Examples   Muhammad Ali is still the <u>most</u> spiritual and influential of all heavy-weight champion boxers.

                        Barbara Frum was the <u>best</u> of all CBC interviewers in the 1970s and 1980s.

> **Tip:** Usually, the comparative of one-syllable adjectives is formed by adding *–er* (small, small*er*), while the superlative of many one-syllable adjectives can be formed by adding *–est* (kind, kind*est*). Adjectives with two or more syllables can often be handled by adding *more* for the comparative and *most* for the superlative (*more* frightening, *most* frightening).

> **Tip:** Be alert that there are many irregular comparatives and superlatives (little, less, least).

> **Tip:** In formal writing, try to include *both* parts of your comparison in your sentence. [not *Canada is the best*, but *Canada is the best country <u>of those I have experienced</u>*]

inter

20. INTERJECTIONS

Isolated words or phrases expressing emotion are interjections, and although they are not independent clauses, usually they are permitted to stand alone as complete utterances.

Examples   *Alas*, poor Yorick! (*Hamlet* 5.1.171)

                        O, brave new world. . . . (*Tempest* 5.1.186)

                        Holy hole in a doughnut, Batman!

Appendix A
Twelve Verb Tenses

There are 12 verb tenses in English. The verb action can take place in the past, the present, or the future. There are usually word clues that indicate when the verb action occurs. Within each of these times there are four different situations.

1. *Simple tenses* occur at a particular point in time, or on a repeated or habitual basis.
2. A *progressive* or *continuous tense* indicates that the action takes place over time, and these tenses always use part of the verb "be" as the first part of the verb phrase and end with the main verb + *ing*.
3. A *perfect tense* indicates an action that ends before another action, always uses part of "have" as the first part of the verb phrase, and ends with the past participle of the main verb.
4. A *perfect progressive tense* indicates an action that happened over time and ends before another action. A perfect progressive tense starts with the relevant part of the verb "have" followed by "been" and ends with the main verb + *ing*.

If you remember these basic rules, you can always identify the verb tense being used, or use the verb tense you need without having to continually refer to a textbook or a table. Meanwhile, a chart like the one shown here can provide a quick and easy reference until you feel comfortable using the various verb tenses.

Also pay attention to the time clues in the following chart; while some of them can be used with more than one verb tense, they do restrict the number of possibilities and help you to understand which verb tense is being used, or which verb tense you should use.

Some examples:

simple past	yesterday
simple present	every day
simple future	tomorrow
past progressive	while
present progressive	now

Note: This appendix was prepared by Veronica Baig and is reprinted with the permission of Athabasca University.

Active Verb Tenses

	Past	Present	Future
Simple	*an action that ended at a point in the past*	*an action that exists, is usual, or is repeated*	*a plan for future action*
	cooked	**cook/cooks**	**will cook**
(time clue)*	He cooked yesterday.	He cooks dinner every Friday.	He will cook tomorrow.
Progressive be + main verb + ing	*an action was happening (past progressive) when another action happened (simple past)*	*an action that is happening now*	*an action that will be happening over time, in the future, when something else happens*
	was/were cooking	**am/is/are cooking**	**will be cooking**
(time clue)*	He was cooking when the phone rang.	He is cooking now.	He will be cooking when you come.
Perfect have + main verb	*an action that ended before another action or time in the past*	*an action that happened at an unspecified time in the past*	*an action that will end before another action or time in the future*
	had cooked	**has/have cooked**	**will have cooked**
(time clue)*	He had cooked the dinner when the phone rang.	He has cooked many meals.	He will have cooked dinner by the time you come.
Perfect progressive have + be + main verb + ing	*an action that happened over time, in the past, before another time or action in the past*	*an action occurring over time that started in the past and continues into the present*	*an action occurring over time, in the future, before another action or time in the future*
	had been cooking	**has/have been cooking**	**will have been cooking**
(time clue)*	He had been cooking for a long time before he took lessons.	He has been cooking for over an hour.	He will have been cooking all day by the time she gets home.

12 tenses

*Time clues: These are words that give some information about when an action occurs. Many words are time clues; some can be used to indicate a number of tenses.

If you learn to recognize these time clues, you will find them very helpful. Note that some time clues can be used with more than one verb tense and also that this table is not a complete list of all the time clues that can be used with all of the tenses.

Time Clues and Verb Tenses

Simple	Simple past	Simple present	Simple future
	yesterday	every morning/day/etc.	tomorrow
	last year/month/etc.	always	tonight
	before	usually	next week/month/etc.
	for five weeks/days/etc.	frequently	soon
	one year/month ago	sometimes	in the future
Progressive	**Past progressive**	**Present progressive**	**Future progressive**
	while	now	when
	when	right now	after
		this week/minute/etc.	as soon as
			before
Perfect	**Past perfect**	**Present perfect**	**Future perfect**
	before	until now	by the time you go
	already	since	(somewhere)
	by the time	ever	by the time you do
	until then/last week/etc.	never	(something)
	after	many times/weeks/years/etc.	already
		for three hours/minutes/etc.	
Perfect progressive	**Past perfect progressive**	**Present perfect progressive**	**Future perfect progressive**
	before	for the past year/month/etc.	by the time
	for one week/hour/etc.	for the last two months/	for 10 days/weeks/etc.
	since	weeks/etc.	by
		up to now	
		for six weeks/hours/etc.	
		since	

Appendix B
Irregular Verbs

There are a number of irregular verbs in English; they are irregular in the simple past form and/or the past participle. Rather than learning each verb separately, you can put many of the verbs into a group of verbs that change their forms in similar ways. If you are in any doubt about a verb—about whether it is irregular or not, or about the exact form that an irregular verb takes—refer to your dictionary. Many dictionaries contain a supplement listing a large number of irregular verbs alphabetically; they all indicate in the main listing whether a verb is irregular and, if so, the form(s) it takes.

Group I Verbs
- The verb name, the simple past, and the past participle forms are all different.
- The past participle forms ends in **n**.
- The vowel changes in the simple past and the past participle.

Note: V = vowel, C = consonant

	Change	Verb name		Simple past		Past participle
I A	i ➟ a ➟ u	begin	➟	began	➟	begun
I B	o/a ➟ e	blow	➟	blew	➟	blown
I C	double vowel ➟ o	break	➟	broke	➟	broken
I D	vowel ➟ o (past)	drive	➟	drove	➟	driven
I E	a ➟ oo (past)	take	➟	took	➟	taken

Group I Verbs

I A	I B	I C	I D	I E
i ➡ *a* ➡ *u*	*o/a* ➡ *e*	VV ➡ *o*	V ➡ *o* (past)	*a* ➡ *oo* (past)
begin	blow	bear	arise	forsake
drink	draw	break	drive	mistake
forbid	grow	choose	ride*	shake
ring	know	freeze	rise	take/undertake
shrink	throw	speak	stride*	
sing		steal	tread*	
sink		swear	write*	
spring		tear		
stink		wear		
swim		weave		

* The spelling of these past participle are, respectively, "ridden," "stridden," "trodden," and "written."

Other Group I Verbs

Verb name		Simple past		Past participle
be	➡	was/were	➡	been
bite	➡	bit	➡	bitten
do	➡	did	➡	done
eat	➡	ate	➡	eaten
fall	➡	fell	➡	fallen
fly	➡	flew	➡	flown
get/forget	➡	got/forgot	➡	gotten/forgotten
give/forgive	➡	gave/forgave	➡	given/forgiven

(continued)

Other Group I Verbs (continued)

Verb name		Simple past		Past participle
go	⟹	went	⟹	gone
hide	⟹	hid	⟹	hidden
lie	⟹	lay	⟹	lain
see	⟹	saw	⟹	seen
swell	⟹	swelled	⟹	swollen
wake	⟹	woke	⟹	woken

Group II Verbs

The simple past and past participle forms are the same.

irr verb

	Change	Verb name		Simple past/Past participle
II A	*ee/ea* ⟹ *e/ea** + *d*	feed	⟹	fed
II B	*e* ⟹ *o* + *ld*	sell	⟹	sold
	ay ⟹ *ai* + *d*	say	⟹	said
	i ⟹ *ou* + *nd*	find	⟹	found
II C	*ee/ea* ⟹ *e* + (C) + *t*	keep	⟹	kept
II D	*i/a* ⟹ *u* + (*n*) + *g/k*	sting	⟹	stung
II E	final *d* ⟹ *t*	sen**d**	⟹	sent

* Spelling may not change but vowel sound does change.

(continued)

Group II Verbs

II A		II B		II C	II D	II E
ee/ea ➟ *e/ea* + d*		*e* ➟ *o + ld* *ay* ➟ *ai + d*	*i* ➟ *ou + nd*	*ee/ea* ➟ *e + (C) + t*	*i/a* ➟ *u + (n) + g/k*	final *d* ➟ *t*
flee	sell	lay	bind	creep	cling	bend
bleed	tell	pay	find	feel	dig	build
breed		say	grind	keep	fling	lend
feed			wind	kneel	hang**	send
hear				leave***	stick	spend
lead				meet	sting	
read*				sleep	strike	
speed				sweep	string	
				weep	swing	
					wring	

irr verb

* Spelling may not change but vowel sound does change.

** "Hang" means "to fasten or attach from above." In the other meaning of "hang," "to hang a person," it is a regular verb.

*** Spelling changes, "leave" to "left."

Other Group II Verbs

Verb name	➟VV + *ght*	Past/Past participle*	Verb name	➟ *d*	Past/past participle	Verb name	➟*o/u*	Past/Past participle
bring	➟	brought	have	➟	had	shine	➟	shone
buy	➟	bought	hold	➟	held	spin	➟	spun
catch	➟	caught	make	➟	made	win	➟	won
fight	➟	fought	prove	➟	proved**			
seek	➟	sought	slide	➟	slid			
teach	➟	taught	stand	➟	stood			
think	➟	thought						

(continued)

Other Group II Verbs (continued)

Other Verbs		
deal	➡	dealt
light	➡	lit
lose	➡	lost
mean	➡	meant
shoot	➡	shot
sit	➡	sat

* Spelling is *au/ou*, but pronunciation remains the same.
** "Proven" is also acceptable for the past participle.

Group III Verbs
The simple past is different from the other verb forms; the past participle is the same as the infinitive.

Verb name		Simple past		Past participle
become	➡	became	➡	become
come	➡	came	➡	come
run	➡	ran	➡	run

irr verbs

Group IV Verbs
The verb form stays the same in the infinitive, the simple past, and the past participle.

Verb name	Simple past	Past participle
bet	bet	bet

Other Group IV Verbs

bid	cut	let	set	split
burst	fit	put	shed	spread
cast	hit	quit	shut	thrust
cost	hurt	rid	slit	upset

Group V Verbs

The simple past is the same as the verb name; the past participle is different.

Verb name	Simple past	Past participle
beat	beat	beat**en**

Section 2 Punctuation Terms

There are few punctuation marks available to writers. However, by varying your patterns of punctuation, you can keep your writing fresh and vital.

The forms of punctuation are the period, comma, semicolon, colon, apostrophe, quotation marks, parentheses, dash, slash, brackets, ellipses, question mark, and exclamation mark.

1. PERIOD [.]

The period provides the full stop at the end of sentences. A period brings order to writing, letting readers know when your sentence has ended. Pico Iyer, a travel writer, refers to the period as the dot that brought the world of writing to its senses. Correct use of the period shows that you recognize independent clauses.

Examples   Wayne Gretzky works on behalf of several charities. He is still an energetic, enthusiastic person.

Office flirting, a delicate matter, raises professional and ethical questions. Consequences and power relations must be considered.

2. COMMA [,]

The comma has many uses and may be considered the all-around utility player of punctuation. Commas can simply *separate* elements in your writing, or commas can also *set off* elements in your writing.

A)   Commas separate elements in a *list* (three or more items).

Examples   Pope John Paul II was the first pope to preach in a Lutheran church, visit England since before the time of King Henry VIII, address a Muslim audience of 80,000 people, re-establish diplomatic relations between Israel and the Vatican, and ask other religions and peoples to forgive the Catholic Church for its historical sins against them.

Pizza ingredients may include pepperoni, tomatoes, feta cheese, black olives, mushrooms, or onions.

Tip: Some people place a comma before the *and* or *or* as the list draws to a close, and some people don't. Whether you do or not, be consistent through your paper or report.

However, there is sometimes a reason of clarity to use the comma before *and* or *or* in a list of items. Consider these:

Examples   The theatre conference featured well-known artists including Linda Griffiths, Ann-Marie MacDonald, and Mump and Smoot.

The theatre conference drew well-known artists including Linda Griffiths, Ann-Marie MacDonald, Tomson Highway, and Drew Hayden Taylor.

Explanation: Mump and Smoot are a team, and therefore may be considered as a single entity, such as Laurel and Hardy or Gilbert and Sullivan. Highway and Taylor are individual artists, not a team. Placing the comma before the *and* allows the writer to clarify that the final item is not considered united with the one before it. Leaving out the comma clarifies that the last two items *are* considered part of one item in the list. This code will not work if you choose never to use the comma before the *and* or *or*.

B)   Commas separate *independent clauses* that are joined by *coordinate conjunctions* (for, and, nor, but, or, yet, so). The comma is placed before the coordinate conjunction.

Examples   Some doctors and nutritionists claim vitamin supplements are necessary for a healthy diet, but other experts claim bottled vitamins enrich only manufacturers and urine.

Parenting deeply changes most people, so it is not surprising that watching children grow compels parents to grow as well.

C)   Commas separate *parts of dates and addresses*.

Examples   On March 10, 1978, a beagle named Barney ran away.

All fan mail for Donny Osmond for his Halifax and Toronto performances in *Joseph and the Amazing Technicolor Dreamcoat* may be sent to his Canadian agent at 2602 Agnes Street, Toronto, Ontario M2A R9A.

Tip: No comma appears before the postal code.

D)   Commas set off a sentence's *introductory qualifier* (whether word, phrase, or clause). The comma separates this introductory element from the independent (or main) clause to help the reader recognize these two parts of the sentence.

Examples   When the government clerk Igor Gouzenko defected from Russia to Canada in 1945, he brought with him 109 secret documents that revealed a highly developed spy ring operating effectively out of Canada.

Named the Gouzenko Affair, this unexpected international revelation forced Canada to confront Cold War espionage as both a global and a domestic activity.

E)   Commas set off *non-restrictive qualifiers*. These are qualifiers that add extra, but not essential, information to the sentence.

Examples   Herb Alpert and the Tijuana Brass, a world-famous horn band, recorded the songs "A Taste of Honey" and "Tijuana Taxi" in the late 1960s.

Retro fashions, which have somehow managed to compress the forties, fifties, sixties, seventies, and eighties into one strangely layered moment of expression, present beautiful opportunities of expression and discovery through comparison and contrast.

F) Commas also set off *transitional expressions*, *parenthetical expressions*, *direct address*, and *interrogatives*.

Examples   Dr. Schaeffer is, thirdly, a fine poet. [transitional]

He was, of course, overlooked. [parenthetical]

Daphne, it's my round for beer, isn't it? [direct address *and* interrogative]

> **Tip:** Watch out for mistaking *restrictive qualifiers* for non-restrictive qualifiers. You cannot remove a restrictive qualifier from a sentence without changing the meaning of the subject or noun being qualified.

Example   The car insurance that we discussed provides full coverage for our van.

3. SEMICOLON [;]

Semicolons join related independent clauses.

Examples   In some parts of South Korea, spicy dog soup remains a popular delicacy; this is mostly among the older generations.

David Bowie issued his own investment bonds several years ago; they were financially backed by the future royalties on his music.

Sometimes, a semicolon can be used to separate complex items in a list where each item in that list already features a comma or commas for qualification. This use of the comma is called internal qualification.

Example   The judges include Chief Justice Beverley McLachlin, who is from Pincher Creek, Alberta; Justice Claire L' Heureux-Dubé, who often sides with the state rather than the accused; and Justice Andrew MacKay, who used to be president of Dalhousie University in Halifax, Nova Scotia.

4. COLON [:]

A colon is used after an independent clause to introduce a list, clause, phrase, or single word. An independent clause must precede the full colon, however.

Examples   We worried about one thing all year: money.

The following cartoon characters will appear at the charity event: Tweety Bird, Sylvester the Cat, Space Ghost, Kamandi, Betty and Veronica, and Lex Luther.

Full colons are also used in memo headings, titles, bibliographical entries, and time notations.

Examples   The Vulnerable Self: State Power in Kafka's *The Trial* [essay title]

To: Jon Bon Jovi [memo]

From: Melanie Moustafa [memo]

5. APOSTROPHE [']

Apostrophes signal the possessive case and also act as substitutes for letters in contractions. There are two types of possessive case: the singular ('s) and the plural (s').

Examples   The carjacker's attempt was thwarted by a passerby. [singular possessive]

The two biology teachers' attempts to coach the volleyball team were welcomed. [plural possessive]

They don't charge GST here. [contraction]

Tip: Individual possession by two or more owners requires an apostrophe for each noun.

Example   Both Susan's and Nancy's parties went late into the night.

Tip: Joint possession requires one apostrophe.

Example   Sid and Nancy's party went late into the night.

Tip: Most style guides now recommend against an apostrophe to form the plural of numbers.

Incorrect   Grammar went out in the 1960's.

Correct   Grammar went out in the 1960s.

6. QUOTATION MARKS [" "]

Quotation marks are used for direct speech, textual quotations, and some titles (stories, newspaper articles and scholarly articles, songs, poems, speeches, chapters of books, radio programs). Sometimes quotation marks also set off certain words as ironic or as special terms.

Examples   Michael Ondaatje's poem "Letters and Other Worlds" examines emotional distances. [title]

Kofi Annan, the former United Nations secretary-general, said, "The use of child soldiers in Sierra Leone continues to concern all nations." [direct speech]

Faulkner wrote that "between grief and nothing, I'll take grief." [textual quotation]

> **Tip:** Quotations of more than four lines require block quotation format, which is indented from the left margin and requires no quotation marks.

> **Tip:** Punctuation with quotation marks can be a little tricky. Put semicolons and colons *outside* closing quotation marks. Put commas and periods *inside* your closing quotation marks, unless you include a line or page reference in parentheses after the quotation. With such a reference, place the punctuation *after* the closing parenthesis.

Examples   "They paved over paradise," sang Joni Mitchell.

Some deep-water divers experience "shallow water blackout"; that is, sudden unconsciousness in the final moments of ascent.

The "belief in life elsewhere in the universe is widely held" (173), according to Davis Marble and Mavis Darby in their article "Life Elsewhere."

7. PARENTHESES [( )]

Parentheses are rounded enclosing marks, sometimes mistakenly referred to as brackets (which are actually square and look like this: [ ]). Parentheses are sometimes used to enclose non-essential (non-restrictive) information.

Example   Britney Spears (whose website was once visited more than any other) championed virginity while taking sexually suggestive appearance to a new extreme.

Parentheses are also used to provide abbreviated terms for items.

Example   We attended the fourteenth annual Canadian Information Technology Security Symposium (CITSS).

Terms to be replaced by abbreviations should be used in full the first time they occur in a piece of writing, followed as above by the abbreviation in parentheses. Thereafter the short form is used.

8. DASH [−]

The dash is the Evel Knievel of punctuation marks—a freewheeling, daredevil, expressive stretch. The dash can substitute for many other punctuation marks, but should be used sparingly in formal writing. The dash can set off non-restrictive and parenthetical elements (as commas can), can introduce a list, phrase, clause, or single word (as a colon can), can join two independent clauses (as a semicolon can), and can signal an interruption (usually in creative writing).

Examples   The white T-shirt worn by itself—popularized initially by Marlon Brando and James Dean—has become widespread rather than a rebellious or anti-establishment statement. [setting off a non-restrictive]

Etiquette lessons can become quite detailed—when to bring a gift, when to write a thank-you card, how formal to be on a first date, what shoes are suitable for a wedding. [introducing a list]

The African famine continues—the G8 must take steps to avoid human catastrophe. [joining two independent clauses]

9. SLASH [/]

The slash or solidus is seldom used in formal writing. It usually separates lines of poetry and song lyrics in quotations, numbers in abbreviated dates, overlapping calendar years, and sometimes paired terms.

Examples   Be shrewd my eyes / Lest you shall reveal / The sadness of my nature / And the truth of what I feel. [separating lines of poetry]

Every voter should be familiar with his/her candidate's political beliefs. [paired terms: note that use of *his/her* is usually awkward]

10. BRACKETS [ ]

Brackets are not used often, but they are very important in research papers when you have to insert a word or phrase to help the quoted syntax, to identify people, events, or action, to make connections within quotations after you have omitted some elements for the sake of brevity, or to clarify references.

Examples   "When he [Peter Parker] says that he knows now that a radioactive spider gave him unusual powers, he realizes his life has changed forever."

"It [consumer culture] manipulatively forces children and youth to make identity choices based on commodities before developing a full sense of identity" (47), according to a recent report conducted at the University of Western Ontario.

[]

You may occasionally see the Latin word *sic* enclosed in editorial brackets within a quotation.

Example   "She was always so tired that she would just lay [*sic*] on the couch all day."

The speaker has confused the verbs "to lie" and "to lay" (meaning to place an object). Correct usage would be "she would just lie on the couch all day." The inserted word *sic*, Latin for "thus," indicates that the quoted wording, though incorrect, remains faithful to the original source.

Brackets may occasionally also be used to enclose further parenthetical elements that occur within existing parentheses.

Example   She told him that her mother (a mysterious woman with complex motives [some of which were even now under investigation] and boundless energy) was returning from Europe that very evening.

Such awkward constructions are best avoided.

11. ELLIPSES [. . .]

When words are omitted from a quotation, three spaced ellipsis dots express this change—this gap—in the original material.

Original   "Doctors and nutritionists have cited the influence of the long Canadian winter, a geographical aspect, as a major contributing factor in the steady depletion that amounts to a shortage of vitamin D in Canadians."

Revised with ellipses   "Doctors and nutritionists . . cit[e] . . . the long Canadian winter . . . as a major contributing factor in the . . . shortage of vitamin D . . . ."

Tip: If an ellipsis occurs at the end of a sentence, the three spaced dots are followed by the period to end the sentence, amounting to four dots.

12. QUESTION MARK [?]

The question mark appears after a question.

Examples   Who disagrees that golf knickers are foolish?

Why wasn't Rachel the academic valedictorian?

Sometimes a declarative statement can seem like a question, but it isn't.

Example   The controversy focuses on whether or not Christina Aguilera is a responsible female role model.

13. EXCLAMATION MARK [!]

Exclamation marks or points supposedly emphasize strong expression. The problem, however, is that so many young writers are tempted to use exclamation points to emphasize almost anything (!!) that this punctuation mark has been rendered meaningless!

Example   Some doctors claim that drinking eight glasses of water a day may not be enough!

Tip: Keep exclamation points to a bare minimum and try to express strength or urgency through your language and your ideas.

Section 3 Fifteen Common
Errors

FIFTEEN COMMON ERRORS

Most usage errors in first-year essays fall into one of the following 15 common categories. Removing these 15 errors from your work will significantly improve your writing in all its forms.

We encourage your instructor to indicate occurrences of these errors in your writing by using the "CE" abbreviation and adding the pertinent number. CE 8 includes six sub-categories represented by the letters *a, b, c, d, e,* and *f*. When you find one of the common errors pointed out, first read the brief explanation of that error. Then, if necessary for clarification, refer to background terms and principles presented in Sections 1 and 2 of this Handbook. For example, the explanation of a comma splice refers to two independent clauses. Look in Section 1 for a definition of the terms *clause* and *independent clause*. The more familiar you become with Sections 1 and 2 of this Handbook, the more efficiently you will be able to find supporting explanations of terms used in the following discussions. We do not use terms simply for the sake of using them; in order to understand various basic principles, you need to know something about the following basic parts of speech: *noun, pronoun, subject, verb, clause, phrase,* and *modifier (adjective, adverb, or phrase behaving as an adjective or adverb)*. Finally, keep asking questions until the principle is clear and you can begin to apply it in editing your work.

To improve your understanding of the 15 discussions in this section, you may find it helpful to visit the Text Enrichment Site, read the information, and try the related practice exercises listed under the two following headings: "Preparing to Solve the 15 Common Errors" and "Solving the 15 Common Errors—Quizzes and Answer Keys." You will find the *Acting on Words* Text Enrichment Site at <http://www.pearsoned.ca/brundage/>.

A Word About Spell-Checks and Grammar-Checks

Neither computer spell-checks nor grammar-checks are reliable. They might be compared to an inflated inner tube for the young person who is learning to swim. Too much reliance on a tool that supposedly does the activity for you can prevent you from internalizing the skills you need to handle the activity on your own. That, in turn, reduces your thinking—and post-secondary education is all about thinking, isn't it?

1. SENTENCE FRAGMENT

sf

A *sentence fragment* is a group of words that is not a sentence. At its minimum, every sentence must form an independent clause; that is, it must have a subject and a predicate.

Example   Marissa misunderstands.

With a subject ("Marissa") and a conjugated verb ("misunderstands"), we have an independent clause, a complete sentence. Although most sentences will contain more than just a subject and verb, these two elements represent the simplest form of sentence. A sentence fragment is mistakenly missing one or both of these two elements.

Sentence fragment (missing subject and verb) Not for a while.

Corrected   The *bus* <u>will</u> not <u>stop</u> for a while.

Sentence fragment (missing subject) Agrees, however, that some changes are necessary and should be made soon.

Corrected   *Jennifer* agrees, however, that some changes are necessary and should be made soon.

Sentence fragment (missing conjugated verb) John, hoping for a better job in the accounting field in either Nova Scotia or Ontario.

Corrected   John *hopes* for a better job in the accounting field in either Nova Scotia or Ontario.

Sentence fragment (dependent clause) Although U2 has often altered their musical style by introducing more futuristic technotronic sounds into some songs.

Corrected   U2 has often altered their musical style by introducing more futuristic technotronic sounds into some songs.

2. COMMA SPLICE AND FUSED SENTENCE

A comma splice is a frequent writing error committed by using a comma to join two independent clauses, "splicing" them together. The comma by itself is not considered a strong enough piece of punctuation to join or coordinate two independent clauses.

Comma splice   Cathy likes to read *People* magazine, Helen likes to read stock reports.

Corrected #1   *While* Cathy likes to read *People* magazine, Helen likes to read stock reports.

Corrected #2   Cathy likes to read *People* magazine, *but* Helen likes to read stock reports.

Tip: Here are the four most common ways to correct a comma splice:

1. Add one of the seven coordinate conjunctions (mnemonic device FANBOYS) after the comma joining the two independent clauses.
2. Keep the comma but change one of the independent clauses into a dependent clause.
3. Delete the comma and separate the independent clauses with a semicolon instead.
4. Delete the comma and use a period instead to make the two independent clauses into two sentences.

CS

A fused (or run-on) sentence occurs when two or more grammatically complete thoughts follow one another with no punctuation. As the following example indicates, this problem may be thought of as the comma splice without the comma:

Fused sentence	Cathy likes to read *People* magazine Helen likes to read stock reports.
Corrected #1	*While* Cathy likes to read *People* magazine, Helen likes to read stock reports.
Corrected #2	Cathy likes to read *People* magazine, *but* Helen likes to read stock reports.
Corrected #3	Cathy likes to read *People* magazine; Helen likes to read stock reports.

3. SUBJECT-VERB AGREEMENT PROBLEM

In English, subjects and their verbs agree in number. If your subject is singular, then your verb form should be singular. If your subject is plural, then your verb form should be plural.

Subject-verb error	The lawyer for the nurses, doctors, technicians, and medical students involved in the series of medical errors are prepared to admit guilt on behalf of his clients.
Corrected	The *lawyer* for the nurses, doctors, technicians, and medical students involved in the series of medical errors <u>is</u> prepared to admit guilt on behalf of his clients.
Subject-verb error	The long Canadian winter, including snowstorms, ice storms, short days, nearly Arctic temperatures, and unpredictable windchills, require great endurance and patience.
Corrected	The long Canadian *winter* . . . <u>requires</u> great endurance and patience.

> **Tip:** Watch out for collective nouns that function grammatically as singular nouns, but represent more than one person or unit (e.g., *government*).

Subject-verb error	The group of electricians, welders, and carpenters vote tonight for a change in negotiations.
Corrected	The *group* of electricians, welders, and carpenters <u>votes</u> tonight for a change in negotiations.

Remember, since there is only *one* group here, "group" is a singular subject, although it may represent many people.

4. PRONOUN PROBLEM—AGREEMENT, REFERENCE, OR UNWARRANTED SHIFT WITHIN PARAGRAPH

Pronouns need to *agree* in number and gender with the nouns they represent, sometimes called their referents or antecedents.

Incorrect pronoun   Since the candles are not on sale, it is too expensive.

Corrected   Since the <u>candles</u> are not on sale, *they* are too expensive.

"They," a plural pronoun, refers correctly in number to the plural noun "candles."
    The most typical pronoun-agreement error is misuse of *their*.

Incorrect pronoun   Everyone in the class used *their* textbook.

Corrected #1   All the students in the class used their textbook.

Corrected #2   Everyone in the class used *his or her* textbook.

> **Tip:** Indefinite pronouns such as *person, one, any, each, either, neither*, and words ending in *–one, –body,* and *–thing* require singular pronouns such as *she* or *he*. When possible, replace the indefinite singular pronoun with a plural noun, as illustrated above: *All the students* in the class, instead of *everyone*. This avoids the exclusionist choice (of using *he* rather than *she* or *she* rather than *he*) as well as the clumsy choice of *he or she*. Use of *their* with indefinite pronouns is beginning to be sanctioned, but many readers still object to it. You are best to avoid this usage in your academic writing.

Pronouns should also *refer* clearly to their intended referents so that a reader has no confusion over what that particular pronoun represents. If you have more than one choice, consider that pronoun unclear or sometimes even incorrect.

Unclear pronoun reference   The difference between these corporate and government deductions in the three financial reports, prepared by rival accounting firms, raises a troubling question about the senator's travel expenses and a possibly illegal discount. <u>This</u> is very suspicious. ["This" = ?]

You have several options in clarifying the unclear pronoun reference, "This," depending on your intended meaning.

n/pn agr

Corrected #1   This <u>difference</u> is very suspicious.

Corrected #2   This <u>corporate and government discrepancy</u> is very suspicious.

Corrected #3   This <u>rivalry between accounting firms</u> is very suspicious.

Corrected #4   This <u>possible illegal discount</u> is very suspicious.

> **Tip:** "This" is a relative pronoun and may refer to a condition or state rather than specifically to a noun.

Example   It's raining today. This is good for the crops.

Unclear pronoun reference Helen told Viola that *her* purse had gone missing.

Clarify whose purse has gone missing. Is it Helen's or Viola's? It is better to repeat words, if necessary, than to allow serious ambiguity caused by unclear pronoun reference.

Corrected   Helen told Viola that Viola's purse had gone missing.

Use "who," "whom," and "whose" when the referent/antecedent is human.

Example   I spoke to the man that took the tickets.

Corrected   I spoke to the man who took the tickets.

Some grammar-checks mistakenly recommend *that* instead of *who* when the antecedent is human. Don't rely on grammar-checks!

Finally, pronouns should not shift in person or number within a paragraph, except for justified reasons. Such changes tend to disrupt tone (using *I* and *you* is more informal than using the third-person) and perspective (are we looking at the matter from a first-person viewpoint, a third-person viewpoint?). In conversation, speakers typically use "you" or "they" to mean *everyone, people*, etc. In writing, more care and consistency are needed. See "Focus Your Point of View: Avoid Unwarranted Shift in Person," Chapter 4, pages 51–52.

5. DANGLING PARTICIPLE

Dangling participles do not match the subjects or nouns they intend to qualify. A participle is a verb form ending in *–ing* or *–ed*. Participles and participle phrases modify nouns. When a participle or participle phrase appears at the beginning of a sentence, it functions as an introductory qualifier for the subject that should follow it directly.

Dangling participle   Skating hard, the open net loomed up ahead of the hockey player.

Corrected   Skating hard, *the hockey player* saw the open net loom up ahead.

Dangling participle   Flipping through the magazine, the recent articles on new bands seemed irrelevant to David Bowie.

Corrected   Flipping through the magazine, *David Bowie* thought the recent articles on new bands seemed irrelevant.

> **Tip:** Ask yourself who or what is performing or experiencing that participle and then check to see if an appropriate subject or noun directly follows the participle or participle phrase.

dp

6. MISPLACED MODIFIER

Be alert to what your modifiers are qualifying. Be sure they modify what you intend to qualify rather than modify any noun or concept haphazardly.

Misplaced modifier   The Diabetes Foundation, a quiet killer, needs donations for further research.

Corrected   The Diabetes Foundation needs donations to fight *the disease, a quiet killer*.

Misplaced modifier   If mowed regularly by highway crews, many more elk and deer might be visible from the Trans-Canada Highway through the field grass.

Corrected   Many more elk and deer might be visible from the Trans-Canada Highway if the field grass were mowed regularly.

7. PRONOUN CASE PROBLEMS

Case refers to the different forms that personal pronouns take to indicate their function in a group of words. Many people use the incorrect form of personal pronouns, especially when trying to sound formal. Personal pronouns have three cases: *subjective*, *objective*, and *possessive*. Problems usually arise, however, in deciding simply between the subjective and objective forms.

Determining whether the case of a personal pronoun should be subjective or objective depends on the pronoun's relation to either (a) the relevant verb or (b) the relevant preposition. The relevant verb determines whether the pronoun is a subject or an object, depending on how the pronoun functions with that verb. A subject pronoun takes the subjective form (*I, she, he, they*), while an object pronoun takes the objective form (*me, her, him, them*).

Pronoun Case with Verb

Examples   Ian <u>asked</u> Tim, Cliff, and *me* for some fitness advice.

Tracy Q. <u>kissed</u> Tina and *him* on their cheeks.

pro

"Me" is the objective form of the pronoun because it is the *object* of the verb "asked" in the first example. "Tina and him" are the *objects* of the verb "kissed" in the second example, so "him" appears as an objective pronoun. Pronoun case with a preposition follows a simple rule: the objective form of pronoun follows any preposition unless that pronoun is simultaneously the subject of a verb.

Pronoun Case with Preposition

Example   Stephen left a lot of the research up <u>to</u> Ravi, Tasha, and *me*.

"Me" takes the objective form because it follows the preposition "to." Often, you have to deal with pronoun case in relation to both verbs and prepositions.

Example   *She* <u>told</u> *him* <u>to ask</u> *them* to leave the choice of gifts up <u>to</u> Steve Miller, Peter Frampton, and *me*.

"She" is the subject, performing the verb "told," and so appears in the subjective form of the pronoun. "Him" and "them" are objects of the verb "told" and of the infinitive "to ask," respectively, so appear as objective pronouns. "Me" appears as an objective pronoun because it follows the preposition "to" in a list.

> **Tip:** The objective form of a pronoun appears after a preposition, despite an intervening list.

An increasingly common error is the use of a reflexive pronoun in the objective case.

Example   The coach gave the award to myself.

Corrected   The coach gave the award to me.

The reflexive form should be used to express an action done to oneself.

Example   He taught himself grammar.

The same form is also used as an *intensive* pronoun, simply to express emphasis.

Example   Although in favour of a clean-shaven look, the chief himself recognized that beards were not a sign of social rebellion.

The correct use of *who* or *whom* (forms of a relative pronoun) also causes confusion. The solution uses the same strategy as given above to decide between using *I* or *me*, *he* or *him*, *she* or *her*, *they* or *them*.

Example   She asked me to find out whom was coming to the reception.

Corrected   She asked me to find out who was coming to the reception.

Explanation   The pronoun stands in relation to the verb "was coming" as the subject of that verb. Therefore the subjective form *who* is correct.

Example   To who are you sending the invitations?

Corrected   To whom are you sending the invitations?

Explanation   The pronoun stands in relation to the preposition "to" as its object. The pronoun here is also the indirect object of the sentence (which stated another way is, *You* [subject of the sentence] *are sending the invitations to whom?*). Therefore, the objective form of the pronoun is required.

8. MISSING OR UNNECESSARY COMMA

Comma errors are common in first-year, undergraduate, graduate, and even professional writing. Often, bad advice circulates regarding the comma; this misinformation amounts to the claim that one should insert a comma wherever you would pause to draw breath if you were speaking. This bad advice, which is sometimes called "rhetorical punctuation," will mislead you. It whimsically bases itself on fluctuating vocal patterns. For example, since people from New Jersey have speech rhythms that differ from those of people from Saskatchewan, you need to rely on defined, logical, and mechanical rules to sort out the proper locations of commas rather than on inconsistent chit-chat from around the globe.

There are some distinct grammatical rules for use of the comma:

A) Comma after introductory phrase or clause

  Examples   Though she usually disagreed with Mike and Rebecca, Aimée finally conceded that Bryan Adams has an interesting voice.

  Although beautiful, the long Canadian winter depletes our bodies of vitamin D.

B) Two commas to set off a non-restrictive qualifier

  Examples   The loonie, our dollar, has gained strength against the US dollar.

  Tommy Hunter, a Canadian musician, is considered the quiet gentleman of country music.

C) Comma to separate initial independent clauses from subsequent dependent clauses

  Examples   Legal decisions at the Appeal Court are seldom unanimous, partly because judges represent opposing legal, social, and philosophical views.

  Mr. Simpson now likes golf and bingo, although he still enjoys the *New York Times* and some of the quieter musicals.

D) Comma before a qualifying phrase

  Examples   Vancouver residents receive the best health care, according to recent surveys.

  Tanya always liked to listen to the sounds of the New Brunswick night, especially ocean waves, crickets, freight trains, and wind in thick grass.

E) Comma before a coordinating conjunction

  Example   Tasha trekked 20 kilometres from the disaster site to the heights, but still she had the stamina to scale the bluff and to build a large signal fire.

F) No single comma between a subject and its verb

  Example   Gertrude O'Grady enjoys Toronto.

pro

Incorrect Example	Members of the control group representing the four territories involved in the study, were later interviewed individually.
Corrected #1	Members of the control group representing the four territories involved in the study were later interviewed individually.
Explanation	The writer reviewed the sentence and decided that surely a comma must be required after such a longish preamble. But the incorrect comma in this case creates a blockage, so to speak, between subject ("members") and verb ("were interviewed"). Remember that the basic English sentence structure is a direct movement from subject to verb. If anything of a parenthetical (nice-to-know but not essential) nature stands between the subject and verb, then a pause in flow is acknowledged by surrounding commas (e.g., *The members, who represented four regions, were later interviewed.*) In the example above, the words "of the control group representing the four territories" are all essential to defining the members in question. These words are therefore restrictive (see CE 15); that is, they must be there to clarify the subject. They may be thought of as a part of the subject (see the Handbook, Section 1, page 527 for discussion of a "complete subject," i.e., the main subject and its qualifying terms).
	From the point of view of style, note that the example above is in the passive voice (discussed under CE 14). Using the active voice and perhaps breaking the information into two sentences would help avoid the sense of extending the sentence for too long without a pause.
Corrected #2	Members of the control group represented the four territories involved in the study. Following the first stage of the experiment, a researcher individually interviewed each control group member.

Two rules of thumb for mastering commas are (1) if in doubt, leave it out, and (2) remove doubt by learning the advice offered here, in 8a–8f. Also see (B) under "2. Comma" in Section 2 of this Handbook, page 542.

9. MISUSED COLON OR SEMICOLON

These two pieces of punctuation are neither mystical nor inscrutable. The colon and semicolon are distinct units of punctuation and are governed by simple, definite rules.

The Colon

The colon allows several choices following it: that is to say, on the right side of the colon, you have options. However, the colon requires that an *independent clause* precede it: on its left side. The colon, sometimes called the full colon to distinguish it from the semicolon, can introduce a range of grammatical elements: a list, an independent or dependent clause, a phrase, or even a single word. Remember, however, that the colon must be preceded by an independent clause.

Incorrect use of colon	Some of the kind and interesting students from the SJHS Class of 1982 are: Tanya, Louise Mennier, Tzigane, Mike Moore, Peggy Grimmer, and Sue Logan.
Corrected #1	There are many kind and interesting students from the SJHS Class of 1982: Tanya, Louise Mennier, Tzigane, Mike Moore, Peggy Grimmer, and Sue Logan.
Corrected #2	Some kind and interesting students from the SJHS class of 1982 include the following: Tanya, Louise Mennier, Tzigane, Mike Moore, Peggy Grimmer, and Sue Logan.

Other uses of the colon include these options:

List	Many common household pets are quite small: poodles, cats, goldfish, and iguanas.
Phrase or dependent clause	Montreal has long been considered the Paris of North America: a city that offers francophone style and the second largest number of French speakers in the world.
Single word	Barbara teaches at one of Canada's best universities: Dalhousie.

The Semicolon

The semicolon joins independent clauses. The semicolon, however, is often misused as a comma (perhaps a comma with a hat). To use the semicolon correctly, you must be able to recognize an independent clause (a subject with conjugated verb).

Incorrect use of semicolon	Yellow golf pants are silly; especially for Mr. and Mrs. Almond.
Corrected	Yellow golf pants are silly; this is especially true for Mr. and Mrs. Almond.

10. TENSE PROBLEMS

Knowing when to use the various tenses in English can be a challenge; however, a number of tense errors occur simply because the writer is unfamiliar with the correct form of the verb called for in certain contexts.

Examples   Yesterday, he seen her skip class.

That evening she come back from the rock concert with a big poster and new T-shirt.

She was so tired today that she laid on the couch.

The correct form of the simple past of "see" is "saw," not "seen." "Seen" is a past participle, as in "She had seen the cougar in the ravine on several occasions before it was reported in the paper." In the second example, the correct word should be

tense

"came," the simple past of "come." The third example commits a common confusion between the verbs "to lie" and "to lay" (meaning to put down an object). The simple past of "lie" is "lay." The simple past of "lay" is "laid."

More detailed help with verb tenses is provided in the Handbook, Section 1, Appendix B, "Irregular Verbs," pages 535–40.

> **Tip**: When summarizing and analyzing an essay or other form of writing, use present tense (sometimes called "literary" or "historical" present), even if the reading itself uses past tense, and even if the work was written some time ago.

Example   In her essay "Canadians: What Do They Want," Margaret Atwood suggests that many Canadians resent the United States.

11. MIXED CONSTRUCTION

Because English has alternative syntactical ways to express the same idea, writers sometimes find themselves stuck between two approaches.

Example   By endorsing the candidate at today's meeting means having to support him next month as well.

The writer has become caught between two possible statements:

Corrected #1   Endorsing the candidate at today's meeting means having to support him next month.

Corrected #2   By endorsing the candidate at today's meeting, you [or possibly "we"] will have to support him next month.

Mixed constructions often involve clauses joined incorrectly by coordinating and subordinating conjunctions or conjunctive adverbs.

Example   *Because* you are such a good writer, *so* you should begin to outline a book.

Corrected #1   You are such a good writer that you should outline a book.

Corrected #2   Because you are such a good writer, you should outline a book.

Corrected #3   You are a remarkably good writer, so you should outline a book.

Be careful not to use subordinate adverbial clauses as subject complements.

Example   Another difficult situation in Scrabble *is when* your opponent has a blank and an "S."

Corrected   Another difficult situation arises when your opponent has a blank and an "S."

Be careful not to use subordinate clauses beginning with "where" to describe conditions.

Example   Envy *is where* you wish you had someone else's possessions.

Explanation	Envy, a quality or state of being, is not a place, so the modifying word "where" (normally used to refer to places) is inappropriate. Similarly, envy is not a until of time, so you should not use "where" in the above example.
Corrected	Envy involves wishing you had someone else's possessions or achievements.

12. PARALLEL STRUCTURE REQUIRED

Some sentence structures require a writer to complete—by making parallel—a grammatical structure that he or she has already begun earlier in the sentence. Parallelism requires this completion of a language pattern. This is really a matter of word order, which is also called syntax. Your sentence construction will be parallel if it expresses equivalent elements in equivalent syntactical divisions.

Be alert to the need for parallelism in sentence structures with the following:

A) lists
B) verbs
C) prepositions
D) a "not only . . . but also" construction
E) an "either . . . or" construction

A) Lists

Faulty parallelism	Canada has become famous for its defence of human rights, democratic health care, *for* the interspace Canadarm, and when SCTV produced all those good comedians.
Corrected	Canada has become famous *for its* human rights, health care, Canadarm, and SCTV comedians.

After "for its," the list now runs parallel to a series of nouns.

B) Verbs

Faulty parallelism	Recent biotechnology developments *have sparked* fierce health debates, consumer rights, outcries, and <u>have raised</u> general concern about "Frankenfoods" in everyone's grocery order.
Corrected	Recent biotechnological developments *have sparked* fierce health debates, consumer rights outcries, and general concern about "Frankenfoods" in everyone's grocery order.

By deleting "have raised" we make the sentence parallel as a list whose different items all hang on "have sparked" (have sparked a, b, and c).

C) Prepositions

Faulty parallelism	We asked for more popcorn, extra chocolates, and <u>for more</u> peanuts.
Corrected #1	We asked *for* more popcorn, chocolates, and peanuts.
Corrected #2	We asked *for* more popcorn, *for* extra chocolates, and *for* more peanuts.

p struc

Though both versions are grammatically parallel, #1 is more concise.

D) "Not only . . . but also" constructions

Faulty parallelism   John F. Kennedy cared not only for civil rights, but also cared about increased education.

Corrected #1   John F. Kennedy cared *not only* for civil rights *but also* for education.

Corrected #2   John F. Kennedy *not only* cared for civil rights *but also* advocated education.

Though both versions are parallel, #1 is more concise. In #1, "not only . . . but also . . ." are followed by nouns introduced by the same preposition. In #2, "not only . . . but also" are followed by the operative verbs.

E) "Either . . . or" constructions

Faulty parallelism   We either take the bus or a taxi.

Corrected #1   We *either* take the bus *or* call a taxi.

Corrected #2   We take *either* the bus *or* a taxi.

13. APOSTROPHE PROBLEMS

The apostrophe signals possession or contraction.

Possession

The possessive case signals that one noun possesses another. "The hat that belongs to Samantha" becomes "Samantha's hat." "The trouble in Denmark" is "Denmark's trouble."

There are two types of the possessive case: singular and plural. You can determine which one you require by asking yourself what number (how many) is or are *possessing*, not how many *are possessed*.

Singular possessive   The International Space Station's problems are serious.

Since there is only *one* space station here, you use the *singular* possessive case ('s).

Plural possessive   These various students' concerns are serious.

Since there is *more than one* student here ("various"), you would use the *plural* possessive case (s's or s').

> **Tip:** Watch out for collective nouns, which usually operate as singular nouns, though they refer to more than one person or thing.

Example   The committee's representatives asked for a meeting with the reporter.

Contraction

A contraction uses an apostrophe to note the omission of a character in a word. Do not confuse a contraction with the possessive case.

Example   The car wouldn't start this morning.

Do *not* use the apostrophe to express the plural of numbers or dates.

Example   Those who wish to get nine's, put up your hands.

Corrected   Those who wish to get nines, put up your hands.

Example   Neglect of grammar began with well-meaning ideas of the 1960's.

Corrected   Neglect of grammar began with well-meaning ideas of the 1960s.

14. OVERUSE OF PASSIVE VOICE

"Voice" is conveyed partly by the form of the verb and its helpers (the predicate); however, be careful to distinguish between the concepts of *tense* (when a thing is taking place) and *voice* (whether the subject of the action is stated as the grammatical subject of the sentence). Passive voice can operate in *any* tense.

Examples   That bridge will be crossed by me when it is gotten to by me.

That bridge is crossed by me when it is gotten to by me.

That bridge was crossed by me when it was gotten to by me.

Passive voice adds unnecessary words and often results in awkward indirectness. Note that the person doing the action in the examples above is relegated to serving as the complement of the verb "will be crossed." It is even possible to express a complete sentence in the passive voice without including the doer of the action at all.

Example   That bridge will be crossed when it is gotten to.

Grammatically, this sentence is considered complete, because "bridge" functions as the subject. As you can see, passive voice tends to be wordy, indirect, and vague. Someone will cross the bridge, but who? In certain cases, you and your reader do not need to be concerned with the identity of the doer of the action; sometimes the passive voice is preferred as a way to deflect accountability. (Example: "A problem was introduced during the processing stage." The writer may well be attempting to cover up for the culprit: who caused the problem?) Sometimes the doers of the action are less important to the idea and purpose than what they have done or said ("Smoking is prohibited," "*Basic Instinct* will be shown at midnight"). For most occasions, however, active voice is the better choice: it gives more complete information and communicates energy.

Some handbooks and instructors consider all forms of "being" or "to be" to constitute passive voice, since a state of being may be thought of as inert.

Example   She was doubtful of her chances.

pv

The same idea can be expressed more vigorously as "She doubted her chances." To constitute true passive voice as we are defining the concept, the above sentence would have to read, "Her chances were doubted [by her]." Regardless of the line between definitions, a good general rule is to make the *doer of the action* in any sentence you write the grammatical subject of your sentence—and when you can, try to add vigour by replacing verbs of being with more energetic alternatives.

15. CONFUSION OVER RESTRICTIVE AND NON-RESTRICTIVE QUALIFIERS

Some qualifiers require two commas to set them off from the rest of the sentence, while other qualifiers do not. Qualifiers that require commas are called non-essential or non-restrictive. They are not structurally necessary for the sentence in which they appear. Qualifiers that do not require commas are called restrictive and are essential for meaning in their sentences.

Restrictive	No commas, since qualifier is *essential* to meaning
Non-restrictive	Qualifier that is *not* essential to meaning
	Two commas if appearing within a sentence
	One comma if appearing at the beginning or end of a sentence

Example (non-restrictive) Violence in the Middle East, an ongoing problem, has disrupted the lives of all citizens in the region.

The qualifier "an ongoing problem" is extra, not essential to this sentence. Since the sentence's grammatical structure and meaning can work without this qualifier, it is non-restrictive: this qualifier does not restrict the meaning of what it qualifies. By placing two commas around the qualifier, you show that it is non-restrictive.

> **Tip:** Often, students will forget the second comma, therefore forgetting to close off the non-restrictive qualifier from the rest of the sentence. If you open the qualifier, remember to close it: "Our Irish friend, Ulton, likes funk music."

Example (restrictive) The Tragically Hip song "Cordelia" explores the attitude of a self-destructive man who takes the generous concern of others for granted.

Restrictive qualifiers are sometimes tricky. If you *cannot* "pop" the qualifier out of the sentence without changing or blocking the meaning of the sentence, then it is an essential or restrictive qualifier (and so requires no commas). In our example above, if you placed commas around "Cordelia," you would mistakenly turn it into a non-restrictive qualifier and just as mistakenly convey that it is optional, or non-essential, to the sentence's meaning. If "Cordelia" were not in the sentence as it is, what song would the sentence refer to? Since the Tragically Hip have several songs, the sentence's meaning would be unclear, so "Cordelia" is necessary, essential, and restrictive—and therefore appears without commas.

Example   People who live in glass houses should not throw rocks.

If you *can* "pop" the qualifier out of the sentence, then it is non-restrictive (or non-essential) and requires two framing commas. A non-restrictive qualifier provides extra, not essential information.

Example   Toronto and Vancouver, our largest cities, have high costs of living.

OTHER COMMON MISUSES FROM A–Z

If an instructor marks three short essays in one evening, chances are good that one of the following misused words or terms will appear at least once in the writing. For more common errors along these lines, see "50 Small But Generally Irritating Errors" on the Text Enrichment Site at <http://www.pearsoned.ca/brundage/>.

Incorrect	<u>Alot</u> of students say that grammar isn't important.
Correct but informal	<u>A lot</u> of students say that grammar isn't important.
Correct in scholarly writing	Many students say that grammar isn't important.
Explanation	*A lot* is two words, generally considered to express a colloquial tone.
Incorrect	She tested her ankle and said that it was <u>alright.</u>
Correct	She tested her ankle and said that is was <u>all right.</u>
Explanation	According to most sources, the only accepted spelling is *all right*.
Incorrect	The counsellor divided the 20 cookies <u>between</u> the 10 campers.
Correct	The counsellor divided the 20 cookies <u>among</u> the 10 campers.
Explanation	*Among* is used for three or more parties; *between* is used for two parties.
Exception	If an idea of reciprocity is involved, between is often used (*The problem was discussed between the three leaders.*).
Incorrect	The candidate shook hands with a large <u>amount</u> of citizens.
Correct	The candidate shook hands with a large <u>number</u> of citizens.
Explanation	*Amount* refers to quantity of mass (ink, food, etc.), while *number* refers to countable items.
Incorrect	Don't forget to <u>bring</u> your coat to the picnic.
Correct	Don't forget to <u>take</u> your coat to the picnic.
Explanation	*Bring* is used only for movement from a farther to a nearer location.

a–z

Incorrect	The instructor was cross because I had <u>sited</u> Wikipedia.
Correct	The instructor was cross because I had <u>cited</u> Wikipedia.
Explanation	*Site* is a noun meaning a particular place (*a camp site*).

Incorrect	As the crowd roared, the winger <u>come</u> out of nowhere and deflected the loose puck.
Correct	As the crowd roared, the winger <u>came</u> out of nowhere and deflected the loose puck.
Explanation	The verb form "come" is sometimes used in conversation as the simple past of "to come," but the standard simple past of the verb is "came."

Incorrect	He is the <u>craziest</u> of my two brothers.
Correct	He is the <u>crazier</u> of my two brothers.
Explanation	Adjectives may be changed to show degrees of quality or intensity. Three degrees occur (*big, bigger, biggest; interesting, more interesting, most interesting*). The first degree is called the positive form. Next is the comparative. The comparative (*crazier*) is used to compare *two* things, as in the case of two brothers. *Craziest,* the superlative form, is used to compare one of three or more things to the others.
	On a related note, in formal writing avoid using comparatives or superlatives in statements that do not explicitly provide the thing(s) being contrasted. [Not recommended: *By second term, I found English more helpful.* Better: *By second term, I found English more helpful than it had seemed at first,* or *By second term, I found English more helpful than my other courses.*] Completing your comparison explicitly ensures that the reader knows exactly what things are being contrasted. Sometimes the surrounding context of what you have just said or will say provides the needed clarity, but in formal writing, sentences containing comparatives usually need to state both sides of the comparison.

Incorrect	I'm tired of these <u>continuous</u> sales calls.
Correct	I'm tired of these <u>continual</u> sales calls.
Explanation	Unless the calls occur one immediately after the other, without a gap, the term should be *continual,* meaning *repeated. Continuous* means ongoing.

Incorrect	Despite the problems I have been having, I plan to <u>continue on</u> with my studies.
Correct	Despite the problems I have been having, I plan to <u>continue</u> with my studies.
Explanation	The preposition is redundant, since the meaning of *continue* includes the concept of something ongoing.

Incorrect	My textbook this year is extremely <u>different than</u> the one we used last year.
Correct	My textbook this year is extremely <u>different from</u> the one we used last year.
Explanation	*Different than* is used only colloquially, and only when the object of the preposition (the following words) is a clause. [Formal: *The house looked different from what he had remembered*. Informal: *The house looked different than he had remembered it*.]
Incorrect	I am <u>dis</u>interested in grammar.
Correct	I am <u>un</u>interested in grammar.
Explanation	Being *disinterested* means being without bias. The two words are increasingly used interchangeably, but any blurring of separate distinctions needs to be questioned, because it causes a loss of precision and choice.
Incorrect	My essay was returned unmarked <u>due to</u> my lack of in-text citations.
Correct	My essay was returned unmarked <u>because of</u> my lack of in-text citations.
Explanation	Many editors dislike this use of *due to* as a preposition to mean *as a result of*. It would be acceptable to use *due to* when introducing a subject complement (*My low mark was due to lack of citations*.)
Incorrect	The <u>affects</u> of stress seem to be hurting society more every year.
Correct	The <u>effects</u> of stress seem to be hurting society more every year.
Explanation	*Affects* is a verb meaning to influence or impact something: e.g., "This problem *affects* the whole community." *Effects* is usually a noun (meaning results), though it can sometimes be used as a verb to mean cause: e.g., "She hopes to *effect* a change in voter behaviour with her new campaign." Note that George Orwell would call "effect a change" a "verbal false limb," because to effect a change simply means to change. See "Politics and the English Language," page 471.
Incorrect	We hope to have <u>less</u> losses over the second half of the season.
Correct	We hope to have <u>fewer</u> losses over the second half of the season.
Explanation	*Less* refers to degrees, or values; *fewer* refers to numbers, to discrete items that can be counted.
Incorrect	The cat licked <u>it's</u> tail.
Correct	The cat licked <u>its</u> tail.
Explanation	*It's* is a contraction of "it is." The possessive pronoun for *it* is *its*.
Incorrect	These <u>kind</u> of errors should be corrected.
Correct	These <u>kinds</u> of errors should be corrected.

a–z

Explanation	Plural is preferred throughout the construction. If one error is referred to, then use singular throughout the construction (*This kind of error*).
Incorrect	<u>Hopefully</u>, we will lose less often in the second half of the season.
Correct	<u>We hope</u> to lose less often in the second half of the season.
Explanation	Used in the incorrect example, "hopefully" is meant to mean "we hope" or "it is hoped that." However, what it really says, grammatically, is "in a hopeful manner." This misuse may be considered akin to CE 5 and CE 6, because the modifier does not make the connection it is intended to. This error is also related to CE 1, in that the writer intends a fragment (one word) to express a complete thought. Many instructors and editors resist at this informal usage.
Not recommended	She told me my essay had some problems <u>in terms of wordiness.</u>
Recommended	She told me my essay <u>was wordy</u>.
Explanation	We use the categories *not recommended* and *recommended* in this case, because the concern is a matter of style rather than grammar. Expressions such as *in terms of*, *with respect to*, *in regards of,* and the like are almost always replaceable with more concise and more precise alternatives.
Incorrect	It was so hot yesterday that my dog <u>laid</u> on the floor all day.
Correct	It was so hot yesterday that my dog <u>lay</u> on the floor all day.
Explanation	*Lay* is the simple past form of "to lie." *Laid* is the simple past of "to lay," meaning to place (*She laid her books on the kitchen table.*). Consult your dictionary to clarify the correct verb forms between "to lie" and "to lay."
Incorrect	<u>Much</u> of these advances are the result of hard work.
Correct	<u>Many</u> of these advances are the result of hard work.
Explanation	The noun *advances* is countable, unlike a mass (like *sugar*, *ink*, or *honesty*), so the modifying term should be *many*. *Much* would be used for a noun that expresses a single amount rather than discrete units: e.g., "*Much* of this essay seems plagiarized." Note that words defined by *much* take the singular form of the verb, while those defined by *many* take the plural form of the verb.
Incorrect	No one can write a better essay <u>then</u> I.
Correct	No one can write a better essay <u>than</u> I.
Explanation	The writer has confused the adverb <u>*then*</u> with the preposition <u>*than*</u>. This likely happened because some of us pronounce the word *than* as if it were the word *then*. In formal English, using the subjective form of the pronoun (*I*) following the preposition is correct, because of the implied

or elliptical verb that follows the pronoun (*No one can write a better essay than I* [*can*].). Informal English would likely use the objective form of the pronoun (*No one can write a better essay* than me.).

Incorrect	She said she had <u>to</u> many assignments to get done this week.
Correct	She said she had <u>too</u> many assignments to get done this week.
Explanation	The adverb *too*, meaning *excessively*, is not spelled *to* (which is the preposition) or *two* (which is the number).
Incorrect	My friend has a <u>very unique</u> ability to drink water and snort it out his nose.
Correct	My friend has a <u>unique</u> ability to drink water and snort it out his nose.
Explanation	A number of adjectives, such as *unique, perfect*, *ideal*, *absolute*, and *straight*, refer to qualities that do not vary in degree. They are absolutes. They are what they are, and cannot be more than that.
Incorrect	I <u>would of</u> told you that the dog ate my essay, but I forgot.
Correct	I <u>would have</u> told you that the dog ate my essay, but I forgot.
Explanation	Substituting the preposition *of* for the auxiliary *have* is non-standard.
Incorrect	A <u>women</u> called to ask if I would donate to the university.
Correct	A <u>woman</u> called to ask if I would donate to the university.
Explanation	*Woman* is the singular word to designate one female person; *women* is the plural form to designate two or more female persons. Perhaps this error has become ubiquitous because people are starting to pronounce *–an* syllables as if they were *–en* syllables.

USING NUMBERS

Different professions and disciplines represent numbers differently. Scientific and technical writing almost always represents numbers as *numerals* (*There are 27.3 metres of electromagnetic activity stretching between our 5-metre observation post and the location of the reported outbreak of ectoplasm.*).

Non-technical writing, such as arts, humanities, and social sciences essays, usually represents numbers as *written words* (*The thirty-year-old police sketch artist produced four slightly differing portraits of the alleged offender.*).

Use *numerals* (1, 2, 3, 4 . . .) in the following instances:

- numbers that cannot be spelled out in only one or two words (*Carolyn has more than 1350 different pictures of Diana, Princess of Wales.*)
- dates (*Duran Duran slightly altered their musically significant hairstyles on May 5, 1985.*)

num

- page, act, scene, and line numbers (*In Jolene Armstrong's most recent play, Tear It Down in the Heatwave, a minor crisis on the work site occurs in Act 2, Scene 3 when the sledgehammer spontaneously combusts.*)
- decimals, fractions, ratios, and percentages (*There is a 90% probability that ³/₄ of all Jon Bon Jovi concerts have a 3:1 female-to-male ratio.*)
- amounts of money (*Press baron Conrad Black was sentenced to 6.5 years and fined $125,000 after being found guilty of mail fraud and obstruction in Chicago in 2007.*)
- addresses (*The Canadian prime minister lives at 24 Sussex Drive in Ottawa, while Dr. Lisa Schaefer-Ausman lives at 25 Arlington Road in Camden, England.*)
- temperatures (*While the Edmonton, Alberta, heat record is still 36 degrees Celsius, in the summer of 2007, temperatures hit 31 degrees Celsius, forcing some wine aficionados to switch to ice-cold beer.*)

Use *written words*, however, to express numbers in the following instances:

- numbers that can be spelled out in only one or two words (*At least seventy million music fans watched the 2007 Live Earth Concerts, simultaneously staged around the world on all five continents and closing with all three members of The Police performing four songs, including "Walking on the Moon" with surprise guests Kanye West and John Mayer.*)
- numbers that begin a sentence (*Two hundred and fifty-eight optimistic young people recently auditioned for Canadian Idol in Halifax, Nova Scotia.*)

  Note: It is less awkward to rearrange your sentences so that a large number does not appear at the beginning (*In Halifax, Nova Scotia, 258 people believe they can sing.*).

- Round dollar or cent amounts of one or two words are usually spelled out (*forty cents, five dollars*).

Other Helpful Notes

num

- If using more than one number to modify a noun, spell out the first number *or* the shorter of the two numbers to avoid confusion (*Jesse James, the famous outlaw, stood in the hot noon sun as the deputies pointed 100 six-shooters at him from various windows, doorways, and rooftops.*).
- With days as dates, use ordinal numbers expressed as numerals (*July 2nd, Dec. 7th*). For dates without the years, the ordinal numbers may also be expressed in words when the year does not follow (*April second*).
- When using "o'clock" to express time, spell the number (*two o'clock*).

Some Correct Examples of Usage (Non-technical Writing)

Although Leiann thought the sushi cost only $1.50 a piece, it was much more, almost four dollars. Nonetheless, we ordered sixteen pieces to eat while we watched some of the second season of *The Sopranos* at 7:30 p.m. Leiann's good friend Jenna, who will meet us at eleven o'clock in front of the Sudbury Regional Library, built in 1952, always enjoys dancing later in the evening. Jenna once toured through twenty cities with the musical *Grease* and danced before audiences of three hundred people or more. At 11:15 p.m., our taxi, which cost twelve dollars, took us to a club that featured 1970s funk music. We decided that for Leiann's upcoming birthday, Dec. 12th, we would call into the local radio show at 640 FM to request two full hours of jazz, so that even if it's -20 degrees Celsius outside, it will be hot where we are dancing.

APA Rules on Numbers

These rules come from the *Publication Manual of the American Psychological Association*, Fifth Edition.

General Rule

"The general rule governing APA style on the use of numbers is to use figures to express numbers 10 and above and words to express numbers below ten" (*APA Manual*, p. 122).

Numbers expressed as words are used "for numbers below 10 that do not express precise measurements" (*APA Manual*, p. 125).

There are exceptions and special usages. Sections 3.42 to 3.44 of the *APA Manual*, Fifth Edition, expand on this rule.

Sample Exceptions to the General Rule

- 3 of 21 analyses [mixture of numbers below and above 10]

- In the 2nd and 11th grades . . . the 2nd grade students

- 15 traits on each of four checklists [different categories of items that are not being compared]

- a 5-mg dose [immediately precedes a unit of measurement]

- multiplied by 5 [numbers that represent statistical or mathematical functions]

- in about 3 years [time]

- 1 hr 34 min [time]

- at 12:30 a.m. [time]

num

- January 10, 1952 [dates]

- the 2-year-old [ages]

- 7 participants and 7 subjects [but seven raters, six observers]

- scored 5 on a 7-point scale [scores and points on a scale]

- won $7 [sums of money]

- my essay was given a 6 [numerals as numerals]

- Chapter 5 [numbers that denote a specific place in a numbered series]

- Seventy-five percent of the sample was reviewed. [numbers that start sentences]

- one-fifth of the class [common fractions]

- the twelve Apostles [universally accepted usage]

- 2 two-way interactions [back-to-back modifiers]

- Step 1 [not Step I—use Arabic numbers for routine seriation]

- 1,000,000 [commas between groups of three digits in most cases of figures of 1,000 or more]

- sevens and eights [plural]

- 10s and 20s [plural]

- 1950s [plural]

MLA Rules on Numbers

The *MLA Handbook for Writers of Research Papers*, Sixth Edition, says the following:

> If you are writing about literature or another subject that involves infrequent use of numbers, you may spell out numbers written in one or two words and represent other numbers by numerals. . . . (98)

You would write *two thousand* but *2½*.

If, however, your paper calls for frequent use of numbers, then the guidelines are mostly the same as those for APA, but possibly with less use of abbreviations.

- Use numerals for all numbers that precede technical units of measure (*5 mL*).

- Use numerals for numbers that are presented together and that refer to similar things (*5 absences over 12 days in group 4; 6 absences over the same time in group 6*).

- Spell out numbers if they can be written in one or two words, if they do not precede units of measure, and if they are not presented with related figures. The following example comes from page 98 of the *MLA Handbook*: "In the ten years covered by the study, the number of participating institutions in the United States doubled, reaching 90, and membership in the six-state region rose from 4 to 15."

- Do not begin a sentence with a numeral.

- Use numerals with abbreviations and symbols (*6 lbs, 8 KB, 2"*).

- Use numerals in addresses (*4401 13th Avenue*).

- Use numerals in dates (*24 July 2007 or July 24, 2007*).

- Use numerals in decimal fractions (*4.6*).

- Use numerals in page references (*page 7*).

- Express related numbers in the same style (*7 of the 340 delegates*).

- For large numbers, you may use a combination of numerals and words (*7.3 million*).

A Final Word: Use a Guide and Be Consistent

As this section has suggested, different professions and publications may observe somewhat differing rules governing when to use words or numerals for numbers, as well as when and how to abbreviate for technical units. For comprehensive, reliable guidance, you should refer to the pertinent style guide, whether it be the *MLA Handbook*, the *APA Publication Manual*, the *Canadian Press Stylebook*, or some other reference produced by a publishing body (including in-house systems for internal readership). The rules and examples reproduced in *Acting on Words* will likely suffice for your first-year essays (especially for those in a non-numeric-based discipline). For advanced papers relying on statistics, however, you will need more guidelines than we can provide in this text.

The most important principle of all is this: be mindful of how you present numbers in various circumstances, and be consistent.

num

Literary Credits

Margaret Atwood, "Canadians: What Do They Want?" Reprinted with permission from *Mother Jones* (January 1982), © 1982 Foundation for National Progress.

Gisela Becker, "Scuba Diving." Reprinted by permission of the author.

Jenna Benko, "The Local Pub." Student essay 2007. Reprinted by permission of the author.

Wayne C. Booth, "The Rhetorical Stance." From *College Composition and Communication*, copyright © 1963 by the National Council of Teachers of English. Reprinted by permission.

Roch Carrier, "The Hockey Sweater." From *The Hockey Sweater and Other Stories* by Roch Carrier, translated by Sheila Fischman, copyright © 1979 House of Anansi Press. Reprinted by permission of the publisher.

Bryce Clayton, "Logic Will Betray Mankind Long Before the Robots Do." Reprinted by permission of the author.

Lorena Collins, "Timone." Reprinted by permission of the author.

Nancy Corscadden, "Sample Critique of 'Life in the Stopwatch Lane.'" Reprinted by permission of the author.

Douglas Coupland, "The Sun Is Your Enemy," from *Generation X* by Douglas Coupland. Copyright © 1991 by the author and reprinted by permission of St. Martin's Press, LLC.

Amy Willard Cross, "Life in the Stopwatch Lane." Originally published in the *Globe and Mail*, July 5, 1990. Reprinted by permission of the author.

Bernadette Cymbaluk, Excerpt from examination, 2006. Reprinted by permission of the author.

Robertson Davies, "The Pleasures of Love." Originally published in *Saturday Night* Magazine, December 23, 1961. Used by permission of the Estate of Robertson Davies.

Gail Deagle, "Euthanasia Reconsidered." Reprinted by permission of the author.

Pat Deiter-McArthur, "Saskatchewan's Indian People—Five Generations." From *Writing the Circle: Native Women of Western Canada*, edited by Jeanne Perreault and Sylvia Vance (Edmonton: NeWest Press, 1990). Reprinted by permission.

James Downey, "A Liberal Education Is Key to a Civil Society." From *Carleton University Magazine*, Spring 2000. Reprinted by permission of Carleton University Magazine.

Michael Downey, "Canada's 'Genocide': Thousands Taken from Their Homes Need Help." Reprinted with permission of the author.

"The World Is Flat" by W.L. Felker, *Countryside Magazine*, Vol. 187, No. 16 (Nov/Dec 2003), p. 91. First appeared in *Poor Will's Almanac* (2003). Reprinted with permission of the author.

Roger Fouts, "Brownie." From *Next of Kin* by Roger Fouts and Stephen Tukel Mills. Copyright © 1997 by Roger Fouts. Reprinted by permission of HarperCollins Publishers and William Morrow.

Carey Goldberg, "Subtraction by Addition: When More Adds Up to Less." *Edmonton Journal*, 19 February 2006. Originally published in the *Boston Globe*. Reprinted with permission of the *Boston Globe*.

Henderson, Brad. "Canadian Equals Canada." Student essay, 2007. Reprinted by permission of the author.

Danielle Hicks, "Polynesian Maple Leaf." Adapted from a longer student essay written in 2006. Reprinted by permission of the author.

Carl Jung, "On Synchronicity." Originally published in *The Structure and Dynamics of the Psyche,* Vol. 8 of the *Collected Works* (par. 969–97). © 1960 by Bollingen Foundation, New York, NY. Second edition © 1969 by Princeton University Press. Reprinted by permission of Princeton University Press.

Martin Luther King, Jr., "The Ways of Meeting Oppression," from Martin Luther King, Jr., *Stride Toward Freedom*. Copyright © 1958. Reprinted by arrangement with the Estate of Martin Luther King, Jr., c/o Writers House as agent for the proprietor, New York, NY.

Melanie Klingbeil, "Beyond the Answers." Reprinted by permission of the author.

Michael Lahey and Ari Sarantis, "Words and Bullets: A Rhetorical Analysis of E. A. Robinson's 'Richard Corey'." Reprinted by permission of the authors.

Evelyn Lau, "I Sing the Song of My Condo." Originally appeared in the *Globe and Mail*, 17 June 1995. Copyright © 1995 by Evelyn Lau. Reprinted by permission of the author. All rights reserved.

Colleen Leonard, "Introversion—The Dreaded Other," student essay, 2007, and "A Case for the Demotion of Beauty," student essay, 2006." Both reprinted by permission of the author.

John Markoff, "The Doomsday Machines." From *The New York Times*, March 19, 2000. Copyright © 2000 by The New York Times Co. Reprinted with permission.

Susan McClelland, "The Lure of the Body Image." From *Maclean's Magazine*, February 22, 1999. Reprinted by permission of Maclean's Magazine.

Sample Collage for "Thanks for the Ride" provided courtesy of Blaise McMullin, Athabasca University.

Miller, Joyce. "Beginning Riders: The Untold Story" and "Should Cats Be Allowed to Roam?" (a revised version of the original 2004 essay). Published by permission of the author.

Gustavo Miranda, "In the Words of Stompin' Tom Connors." Student essay, 2007. Reprinted by permission of the author.

Diane Mooney, "Newfoundlandese, If You Please." Reprinted by permission of the author.

Alice Munro, "Thanks for the Ride." From *Dance of the Happy Shades* by Alice Munro. Copyright © 1997 Alice Munro. Reprinted with permission of McGraw-Hill Ryerson Ltd.

George Orwell, "Politics and the English Language." (Copyright © George Orwell, 1946). By permission of Bill Hamilton as the Literary Executor of the Estate of the Late Sonia Brownell Orwell and Secker & Warburg Ltd.

Robert M. Penner, "Elementary Observations: The Special Skill of Sherlock Holmes." Reprinted by permission of the author.

Melissa Phung, "Building Blocks: Canada's Chinatowns." Student essay, 2006. Reprinted by permission of the author.

Kim Pittaway, "Crystal Balls." Originally published in *Chatelaine* Magazine, "herspective," January 2000. Reprinted by permission of the author.

Janice Procée, "The Case for Active Euthanasia." Reprinted by permission of the author.

Howard Richler, "The Seven Deadly Sins Are 'In' and Proud of It." From *A Bawdy Language: How a Second-Rate Language Slept Its Way to the Top* by Howard Richler (Toronto: Stoddart Press, 1999). Reprinted by permission of the author.

Leanna Rutherford, "An Anorexic's Recovery." First published in *Canadian Living* Magazine, October 1998 (vol. 23, no. 10). Reprinted with the permission of the author.

Habeeb Salloum, "The Other Canadians and Canada's Future." From *Contemporary Review*, March 1997. Copyright Contemporary Review Company. Reprinted with permission.

Sarah Schmidt, "From College Girl to Call Girl." From the *Globe and Mail*, April 29, 2000. Reprinted by permission of the author. Sarah Schmidt is a senior writer (education) for CanWest News Services.

Mark Simpson, "Betraying the Spirit of Punk? 'The Card Cheat.'" Reproduced by permission of the author.

David Suzuki, "The Right Stuff." From *Inventing the Future: Reflections on Science, Technology, and Nature* (Toronto: Stoddart, 1989). Reprinted by permission of David Suzuki, Professor Emeritus, University of British Columbia.

Pamela Swanigan, "I Am Half-Canadian." From *Saturday Night* Magazine, January 27, 2001. Reprinted by permission of the author.

Michel Tremblay, "The King and I." Reprinted from *Bambi and Me* by Michel Tremblay, translated by Sheila Fischman, © 1988 Talon Books Ltd. Reprinted with permission of the publisher.

Melisa-Maurice P. Janse van Rensburg. "Not Like the Movie." Student essay, 2007, reprinted by permission of the author.

Nina Varsava, "Read With Care—Non-fiction Isn't Fact." Reprinted with permission of the author.

Zawaski, Andrea. Excerpt from "'E Pluribus Unum': It's All in the Translation." Student essay, 2006. Reprinted with permission of the author.

Index